HERBS

RODALE

HERBS

The Essential Guide for a Modern World

Foreword by Rosie Atkins
Curator, The Chelsea Physic Garden

This edition first published in 2006 by
Rodale International Ltd
7–10 Chandos Street
London W1G 9AD
www.rodalebooks.co.uk

© 2006 Rodale Books International

Printed and bound by Star Standard Industries (PTE), Singapore,
using acid-free paper from sustainable sources.
1 3 5 7 9 8 6 4 2
A CIP record for this book is available from the British Library
ISBN-13: 978-1-4050-9554-9
ISBN-10: 1-4050-9554-7
This edition distributed to the book trade by Pan Macmillan Ltd

For Rodale Books International
Managing Editor: Miranda Smith
Senior Editor: Dawn Bates
Managing Designers: Jo Connor, Vivienne Brar
Production: Sara Granger, Emily Toogood

Produced for Rodale Books International by Hydra Packaging, 129 Main Street,
Irvington, N.Y. 10533, USA
Editorial Director: Lori Baird
Senior Designer: Shamona Stokes
Art Director: Edwin Kuo
Editors: Angda Goel, Nick Simonds, Wendy Hubbert, Lori Baird
Assistant Editor: Franchesca Ho Sang
Designers: Claire Legemah, Rachel Maloney, Tom Lawrence,
Brian MacMullen, Amy Henderson
Publisher: Sean Moore
Publishing Director: Karen Prince
Photographer: Dan Lipow
Contributors: Beth Baugh, Melinda Corey, Beth Hanson, Evelyn Leigh, Rob McCaleb,
Liz Mechem, Raquel Pelzel
Proofreaders: Franchesca Ho Sang, Tom Cavalieri
Production Director: Wayne Ellis
Production Manager: Sarah Reilly
Photo Researcher: Jeanne Leslie
Indexer: Nanette Bendyna Schuman

Commissioned photography by Philip James.
For other credits, see page 400.

This publication is intended as a reference volume only, not as a medical manual.
The information given here is designed to help you make informed decisions
about your health. It is not intended as a substitute for any treatment that may
have been prescribed by your doctor.

We inspire and enable people to improve their lives and the world around them

CONTENTS

PART I
All About Herbs

Through concise discussions of botanical nomenclature and plant classification, this chapter explains how herbs are defined and how they may be identified.

From North America to Australasia and Africa, this regional look at the history of herbs shows how they have played a significant role in human life in nearly every area of the globe.

From formal to informal gardens, and everything in between, this exploration of the typical elements and characteristics of herb gardens features images and descriptions of the world's most important and beautiful gardens. This chapter ends with a review of herb gardens open to the public all around the world.

PART II
Gallery of Herbs

PART III
Reference Guide

"THE AIR WAS FRAGRANT WITH
a thousand trodden aromatic herbs,
with fields of lavender, and with
the brightest roses blushing in tufts all
over the meadows. . ."

William Cullen Bryant
American Writer, 1794–1878

Camellia sinensis
(tea plant)

Foreword

It seems incredible that there is still so much about our planet we do not know including the total number of plant species that exist. However, everyone agrees on one basic fact – plants are essential to life. Plant-based traditional medicines are a crucial source of health care for 80 percent of the world's population and plants are still an essential ingredient in 25 percent of all pharmaceutical drugs. Over the millennia, plants, often called herbs, were collected because they had special uses. Accumulating knowledge about those uses has given people the power to kill and cure as well as to make vast fortunes. Today bio-prospecting is big business, but for the vast majority of the readers of this encyclopedic book of herbs, the appeal is in the wealth of stories associated with the wide range of plants as well as the pleasure of growing them.

The start of the new millennium has been an interesting time to be in charge of London's oldest botanic garden and the only botanic garden to keep the word physic in its name. The word "physic" originally meant "pertaining to nature" but grew into a description for a place dedicated to the study of the healing arts. The early physic gardens of Renaissance Europe were attached to hospitals and universities so that physicians and botanists could learn their hard-won craft often fuelled by wars, plagues and natural disasters. Many of these physic gardens went on to become the botanic gardens we know today.

When Chelsea Physic Garden was founded by the Worshipful Society of Apothecaries in 1673, London was recovering from economic ruin following the plague of 1665 and the Great Fire. The streets were deserted, infant mortality was high and the average life expectancy of a man was around thirty. Health care in both town and country took place in the home and was often the preserve of the women who collected wild herbs even if the household could afford a doctor.

Before 1624, the London apothecaries were members of the grocers' company which evolved out of the Guild of Pepperers originally formed in 1180. Apothecary comes from "apotheca" meaning a place where herbs, wines and spices were stored, but by the 13th century the word evolved into the name for a person who sold such goods. In 1624, the London apothecaries were formally given their own charter by King James I and acquired their own hall in Blackfriars. This was destroyed by the Great Fire but rebuilt on the same site in 1672 with the addition of an "Elaboratory" for the manufacture of drugs.

The next year the Apothecaries took a lease on a plot beside the River Thames in Chelsea where they could create a teaching garden for their apprentices. This four-acre garden was within easy reach of Blackfriars by boat, the river being the safest and quickest way to travel in those difficult days. Aspiring rather than wealthy, the Apothecaries also built boat-houses on their river frontage so they could house their gaily

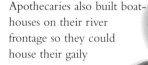

painted barge. This allowed them to take part in royal pageants and it also proved useful for carrying students on herborising expeditions. The Garden soon became a mecca for botanists and physicians who were keen to exchange knowledge and plants. The idea of a seed exchange between Chelsea and continental European botanic gardens was set up as early as 1683; today we exchange seed with 385 other botanic gardens and universities in 37 different countries around the world through our *Index Seminum* which is published annually.

These days we do not see many apothecaries at Chelsea Physic Garden, but the visiting public are fascinated to find plants growing there that they may have read on the box of a drug prescribed by their doctor, in a newly bought perfume or in a herbal tea. They are just as curious to see plants described in the book, *De Materia Medica*, written by the Greek army doctor Dioscorides (40-90 C.E.) which for 1,500 years was the standard reference of medicinal plants. The bed containing plants promoted by Paracelsus (1493–1541) under the Doctrine of Signatures always arouses interest. In the sixteenth century it was generally accepted that God had put a plant on the earth to cure every illness. The Swiss alchemist Paracelsus suggested the difference between a medicine and a poison was all about administering the correct dose. He believed that the appearance of a plant – "God's signature" – gave clues to its medicinal value. (The plant's name eventually came to reflect this use). For instance figwort, *Scrophularia nodosa*, which has nodules on its roots, was used to treat scrofula which causes the lymph glands to swell in the neck. And the spotted leaves of lungwort, *Pulmonaria officinalis*, were thought to resemble the lung, so the plant was used as an expectorant. Calamities would have resulted from these rather fanciful notions, but through trial and error, information was exchanged and valuable new discoveries made.

Plant knowledge spread with travel and the growth of the printing industry. Aloes, used as a purgative, originated in Asia and Africa and were introduced to Britain via the Americas following Columbus' expedition in 1492. Philip Miller, Curator for fifty years at Chelsea Physic Garden from 1722 to 1770 acquired a famous collection of aloes, some of which he kept in his heated glasshouses. Miller was also involved in hybridizing cotton to send out by boat to the newly formed American colony, Georgia. Everyone was competing to discover new lands and new plants.

Throughout the 18th century, Chelsea Physic Garden was a meeting-place for botanists such as Carl Linnaeus, keen to promote his new binomial system of classifying plants. Joseph Banks sent back seed to the Garden from his voyage to Australia and New Zealand. The Garden also attracted an illustrious roll-call of gardeners and curators including Philip Miller and William Curtis, and the Victorian plant hunter, Robert Fortune, who became famous for introducing tea from China to India. With the government reorganization of the Royal Botanic Gardens

Lonicera
(honeysuckle)

at Kew in 1841, Chelsea Physic Garden's fortunes began to wane. The Apothecaries had to give it up in 1899 and the City Parochial Foundation took over its management. The Garden continued to train botanists and pharmacists and conduct vital research on agricultural crops over the succeeding 70 years. In 1983, a new charity was formed and the Garden officially opened its doors to the public for the first time. Coincidentally, this was same year that the Herb Research Foundation, consultants for Rodale's *Herbs – The Essential 21st Century Guide*, was set up in Colorado.

In 1712, Sir Hans Sloane, the entrepreneurial physician and naturalist bought the manor of Chelsea, becoming the Apothecaries' landlord, because they could not afford the freehold. Ten years later he set up a deed of covenant which levied a rent of £5 a year rent in perpetuity as long as the Apothecaries agreed to certain conditions, including an agreement that the Garden should remain dedicated to the study of useful plants. Thanks to Sloane's foresight, the Garden has managed to survive the ravages of time. Now it seems that the world has once more become insatiable in its desire to know more about herbs; and at the same time people have started to question modern medicine and want to explore alternative therapies. In early 2006, a BBC television series on alternative medicine attracted 3.8 million viewers.

Chelsea Physic Garden grew out of the age of Enlightenment when doctors also had to train in botany using herbals as teaching aids. Roy Vickery, a botanist at the Natural History Museum has spent years collecting information about herbal remedies and plant lore. He suggests it was the educated élite who promoted myths regarding folk remedies in their treaties, while the illiterate poor had good practical knowledge about how to administer plant remedies which was passed down the generations. With urbanization and globalization, we are fast losing what local plant knowledge we have left, which is why it is so important to continue to collect data. Chelsea Physic Garden is working on a joint initiative called Ethnomedica, with Royal Botanic Gardens Kew, The Eden Project, Natural History Museum and the National Institute of Medical Herbalists, which aims to collect information about plant-based remedies in Britain before it is too late.

We live in uncertain and challenging times with the threat of global warming and the loss of biodiversity because of commercial pressures. We know there are still plant medicines to be discovered but it is a race against time. By the year 2050, about 60,000 species could become extinct, so conservation which preserves biological diversity is vital for the future. It is easy to see the irony in the fact that hoodia, a plant used to suppress the appetite of hunters in tribes living in the African desert, is of interest to drug companies to treat obesity in the affluent countries of the world. As humankind becomes even more removed from nature, it is comforting to see the renewed interest in growing your own vegetables and herbs. One way to keep a plant safe is by growing it.

It is estimated over 150 million people worldwide visit botanic gardens where they learn about the importance of plants in our everyday lives. At the Chelsea Physic Gadren, we welcome thousands of children each year from schools around London who are more familiar with a mobile phone than a mulberry bush. They are shocked when asked if they ate a plant for breakfast. In Britain, the National Institute of Medical Herbalists run a campaign called Herbal Medicine Awareness Week to heighten awareness of plant-based medicine. This is very important at a time when shops selling herbal remedies are springing up in every town, but with little control on these products the public never quite know what they are buying.

Chelsea Physic Garden is an island of continuity, charting the history of plant based medicines and economic botany. I am lucky to work with botanist, horticulturalists, physicians and practitioners of herbal medicine from all over the world who know it is just as important to be able to identify and demonstrate the uses of herbs today as it was three hundred years ago. I hope you enjoy finding out more about the herbs which do so much to enrich our lives.

Rosie Atkins, Curator, The Chelsea Physic Garden

"I ASKED THE BOY BENEATH THE PINES.

He said, 'The master's gone alone

Herb-picking somewhere on the mount,

Cloud-hidden, whereabouts unknown.' "

Chia Tao (777–841)

All About
HERBS

What *are* Herbs?

To a botanist, a herb is simply a herbaceous plant – that is, a nonwoody, seed-producing plant that usually dies back in the winter. The science of ecology specifically describes a herb as a plant that is less than 30.5 cm (12 in) tall and is made up of the type of forest vegetation known as the "herb layer". To a chef, the definition is completely different: a herb is any of a vast number of aromatic or savoury plants that are added dried or fresh during cooking to provide flavour and character to foods. To a gardener, a herb is a delightful, easy-to-grow addition to the perennial garden. And to anyone who uses plants medicinally, a herb is any plant or plant part that helps promote health and healing, either taken internally or applied to the skin.

Dried sage leaves, whole and pulverized.

Basics of Herbal Botany

The botanist's definition of a herb – any nonwoody plant – is so broad that it does not accurately describe many of the plants known today as medicinal herbs. Medicinal herbs come from all kinds of plants, including trees, shrubs, vines and grasses. And what about medicinal mushrooms, lichens, mosses and seaweeds? The term "herbs" is so all-encompassing, that many types of plants are included under this single umbrella term.

To further confuse the issue, many delicious culinary herbs do double duty as powerful medicinal plants. Such indispensable kitchen staples as garlic, ginger, cayenne and turmeric have been researched in modern clinical studies designed to investigate their health benefits.

Common cooking herbs such as rosemary, oregano, parsley and sage have been shown to provide potent antioxidant and antimicrobial properties. And these days, when the study of so-called functional foods is popular, everyday food ingredients such as soy, cranberries and green tea seem almost as likely to turn up in the dietary supplement aisle as on the grocery shelf.

In the garden, what blossoms are lovelier or more fragrant than those of the herbs lavender, rose and jasmine? What weeds are more potentially troublesome than the herbs dandelion and plantain? Some of the world's most delicate and beautiful wildflowers – including blue cohosh, trillium and gentian – have also served as

important botanical remedies. But from the perspective of a rancher trying to raise a healthy herd of cattle, the herb St John's wort is no time-honoured healing remedy, but instead a noxious weed that can cause photo sensitivity in light-coloured animals that graze on large quantities of the plant.

So just what is a herb – a nonwoody plant, a health-promoting remedy, a weed, a garden ornamental or a culinary staple?

The answer to the question appears to be "all of the above". *Merriam-Webster's Collegiate Dictionary* offers the following definition of a herb: "plant or plant part valued for its medicinal, savoury or aromatic qualities."

Sweet violet has several common names, such as common blue violet. But it has only one botanical name: Viola odorata.

Paeonia suffruticosa (*Japanese tree peony*).

Mentha requienii (*Corsican mint*).

UNDERSTANDING BOTANICAL NOMENCLATURE

In general, most well-known plants have at least two names: a common (or vernacular) name and a botanical (scientific or Latin) name.

The botanical name is the name scientists use to distinguish one particular plant species from all others in the world. This botanical name, or binomial, itself consists of two names: a genus name and a species name (see page 24 for a more detailed explanation of these terms). Using the plant *Ginkgo biloba* as an example, *Ginkgo* is the genus name and *biloba* is the species name.

A common name, as the term implies, is a name that is coined by nonscientists to identify a plant in their own locale – for example, sweet violet, catnip or dandelion. A plant may have many different common names, which are often colourfully descriptive and can provide valuable information about the plant's traditional uses, characteristics or growth habits. The name dandelion, for example, comes from the French *dente de lion*, which means "tooth of the lion" and describes the serrated edge of the leaf. Another common French name for dandelion, *pis en lit*, translates as "wet the bed", a reference to the powerful diuretic properties of the dandelion leaf.

Botanically speaking, sweet violet, catnip and dandelion are known as *Viola odorata, Nepeta cataria* and *Taraxacum officinale* respectively. Just like common names, botanical names offer fascinating clues about what plants look like, what they smell like, where they come from and even how they are used medicinally. Using the same three plants as examples, it is possible to infer from the species name *odorata* that this violet has a distinctive fragrance. The name *cataria* indicates that this member of the genus *Nepeta* is linked in some way to felines. And the name *officinale* (or *officinalis*), which translates as "once" in the official pharmacopoeia, is an indication that a plant was a widely accepted medicine at one time.

Although a plant may have several common names, it will have only one officially recognized botanical name. The advantage of using botanical names, or nomenclature, is that it allows anyone – no matter what their native tongue – to understand exactly which herb is being discussed. For example, the spiny shrub *Eleutherococcus senticosus* – commonly called Siberian ginseng or eleuthero in the United States, *ci-wu-jia* in China, and devil's shrub or thorny pepper bush in Russia – is understood to be *Eleutherococcus senticosus* whether one is European, American, Chinese or Russian. This is an important and basic standard, not only to botanists and other scientists, but also to herbalists, practitioners and members of the botanical trade, who need to be absolutely certain about the identity of the plants they use.

MODERN AND CONSERVED PLANT FAMILY NAMES

MODERN NAME	CONSERVED NAME	COMMON NAME
Apiaceae	Umbelliferae	carrot, parsley
Arecaceae	Palmae	palm
Asteraceae	Compositae	aster, sunflower
Brassicaceae	Cruciferae	cabbage, mustard
Fabaceae	Leguminosae	bean, pea
Hypericaceae	Guttiferae	St John's wort
Lamiaceae	Labiatae	mint
Poaceae	Graminae	grass

Similarly, in the United States, the native plant *Echinacea angustifolia* may be known by any of a long list of common names, which vary from region to region. Depending upon the speaker and the area in which he or she grew up, the same plant may be called purple cone-flower, black Sampson, red sunflower, Indian head or snakeroot. The common name snake-root, however, may also be applied to a host of other, completely unrelated plants, including *Polygala seneca*, *Centaurium minus*, *Eupatorium rugosum*, several members of the genus *Sanicula*, and even Indian's potent medicinal plant *Rauvolfia serpentina* – another compelling argument for understanding basic botanical nomenclature.

Many people feel more comfortable using common names for plants simply because they are more familiar and easier to pronounce. But those who are intimidated by the thought of having to learn botanical Latin may take comfort in knowing that many common plant names – iris, crocus, chrysanthemum and gladiolus, to name just a few – are in fact scientific names that have been so widely used that they have become household words.

PLANT CLASSIFICATION AND THE LINNAEAN SYSTEM

Plants, like all organisms, are categorized according to the Linnaean system of classification, an ingenious scheme devised by an 18th-century Swedish botanist Carolus Linnaeus, and refined by generations of scientists working to clarify relationships between organisms.

Linnaeus (1707–1778) introduced his classification system in 1753. His goal was to name and describe all known types of plants, animals and even minerals. He believed that in so doing, he would reveal the grand pattern of creation. Linnaeus introduced the world to the classification system that would eventually bear his name in a two-volume work called *Species Plantarum*, which means "the kinds of plants".

Scientists quickly adopted Linnaeus' system as a means of sorting out the vast numbers of new species being discovered at the time. Linnaeus originally utilized a polynomial (multiple-word) naming system to describe species, but this soon evolved into the binomial (two-word) naming system used today. The Linnaean system of classification is based on relationships among living organisms, from the most general (kingdom) to the most specific (species). A species, the smallest, most basic unit

Calendula officinalis is an angiosperm (producing seeds enclosed in an ovary) that belongs to the class called dicotyledons (plants with two seed leaves).

of organization in the system, is composed of individuals that resemble one another more closely than they resemble any other organisms and can breed to produce fertile off-spring. A number of different species that closely resemble one another are grouped together into a genus. Closely related genera (the plural of genus) are organized into families, and so on.

Far from static, these classifications change as new information alters scientists' understanding of the relationships among organisms. Originally, all organisms were classified into two kingdoms: animal and plant. Now, based on information that was unavailable when the Linnaean system was first introduced, scientists use a five-kingdom classification scheme that separates fungi and certain other kinds of creatures into kingdoms of their own.

The kingdom is the largest, most inclusive classification in the Linnaean system. Five kingdoms are now recognized: *Animalia* (animals), *Plantae* (plants), *Fungi* (fungal organisms, including mushrooms), *Protista* (simple organisms, such as protozoans and algae, whose cells have nuclei and organelles) and *Monera* (simple one-celled or colony-forming organisms, including bacteria, whose cells do not have nuclei or organelles).

Within the plant kingdom, organisms are first sorted into one of two large divisions: angiosperms (plants with seeds enclosed in an ovary) and gymnosperms ("naked-seed" plants). The next step is to subdivide the organism into one of two classes, monocotyledons (plants that produce one seed leaf) or dicotyledons (plants with two seed leaves), and then further categorize it into subclass, order, family, genus and then species.

Most of this technical information has little practical application for the nonscientist. The most important classifications to learn and understand are family, genus and species. The rest of the classifications are not essential to know, with the exception of class, which provides information that is helpful in plant identification. (See *Monocot or Dicot?*, on page 28.)

PLANT FAMILIES

Groups of related genera make up plant families. Some plant families are quite large – the orchid, aster and pea families are three of the biggest – while others, such as the ginkgo family, contain only one or two plants.

In an ongoing effort to standardize the classification and naming of plants, in recent decades botanists have modernized the naming of plant families. According to current rules, family names should end with the suffix "-aceae" and be taken from the name of a genus that is a good representative of the typical characteristics of that family. (Genus and species names are italicized in print, but family names are not. For example: *Salvia officinalis* [garden sage] is a member of the plant family Lamiaceae. In some cases, this resulted in only minimal change. For example, the original orchid family name, Orchidae, merely became Orchidaceae. But for other families, the changes were more sweeping and stirred resentment among those who felt the old family names were more descriptive and, therefore, easier to remember.

For example, the sunflower or aster family – formerly known as Compositae, because of the composite structure of the flower heads – was renamed Asteraceae, after the *Aster* genus. Similarly, the mustard family, once named Cruciferae after the four-petaled "cross" formed by the flower petals, is now Brassicaceae (for *Brassica*, the cabbage genus, which also contains mustard, kale, broccoli and brussels sprouts). The mint family – formerly Labiatae, meaning "two-lipped" in reference to the appearance of the flowers – became Lamiaceae, after the *Lamium* genus. And the carrot family, once known as Umbelliferae because of the umbrella-shaped flower clusters (umbels) typical of plants in this family, is now named Apiaceae, after *Apia*, the celery genus.

To mollify those who preferred the old family names, scientists have agreed to allow their use for a select group of eight plant families. For these eight plant families, two family names are now accepted: a modern, or uniform, name, and a conserved name (the old family name).

Some plant families are so large and so complex that they are further divided into subfamilies and what botanists call "tribes". The sunflower family (Asteraceae), one of the largest of all plant families, is subdivided into at least two subfamilies and thirteen different tribes. Such distinctions are not always clear-cut, and there is disagreement among botanists about how certain plants should be classified.

For example, some botanists consider aloe and amaryllis plants to be part of the lily family (Liliaceae); however, others would prefer to group aloe and amaryllis into

CLASSIFYING THE MINT FAMILY
❧ *LAMIACEAE* ❧

An aromatic plant with square stems, opposite leaves, and two-lipped, tubular flowers can almost certainly be identified as a member of the mint family. The mint family has very distinctive characteristics, and serves as a great example of the unique patterns displayed by different plant families.

The flowers of plants in the mint family have five petals that are fused into a kind of tube. This tube terminates in lobes that form the typical "lips" of mint family flowers. Inside the flower are four stamens, two long and two short. Another feature of mints is a square stem (although not all square-stemmed plants are in the mint family). The plants' simple leaves are arranged in pairs opposite one another, and flowers typically appear in the leaf axils (where the leaf joins the stem). Nearly all plants in the mint family are rich in volatile oils that give them strong aromas and flavours, making them valuable culinary, medicinal and fragrant herbs.

The chart below illustrates how *Mentha spicata* (spearmint) is classified beneath the mint family (Lamiaceae) in the Linnaean Classification System.

MENTHA SPICATA (SPEARMINT)

KINGDOM
Plantae (plant)

DIVISION
Magnoliophyta (angiosperms)

CLASS
Magnoliopsida (dicotyledon class)

SUBCLASS
Asteridae (aster subclass)

ORDER
Lamiales (mint order)

FAMILY
Lamiaceae (mint family)

GENUS
Mentha (mint genus)

SPECIES
Spicata (spearmint species)

Although these three plants are all from the Salvia genus, (left to right) *clary sage* (S. clarea)*, diviner's sage* (S. divinorum) *and garden sage* (S. officinalis)*, their leaves and flowers are all different.*

families of their own. Such botanical debates have given rise among botanists to the epithets "lumpers" and "splitters". Lumpers prefer larger, more inclusive classifications; splitters make finer distinctions.

Plant Genus

A genus consists of a group of species that are closely related to one another, determined primarily by the reproductive parts of their flowers. Some of the many genera in the mint family (Lamiaceae) are *Lavandula* (lavender), *Mentha* (mint), *Thymus* (thyme), *Salvia* (sage), *Rosmarinus* (rosemary), *Monarda* (bee balm), and Melissa (lemon balm). The rose family (Rosaceae) includes the genera *Rosa* (rose), *Prunus* (plum, almond and cherry), *Crataegus* (hawthorn), *Malus* (apple), *Rubus* (raspberry and blackberry), *Fragaria* (strawberry), and many others.

Plant Species

The species is the most basic of all classifications in the Linnaean system. Once the genus name has been established, it may be abbreviated thereafter. For example, *Salvia officinalis* and *S. sclarea* (clary sage) are both highly aromatic plants. Variety names are italicized; cultivar names are not. When a species or species name is unspecified, it may be indicated in print with the abbreviation "sp". For example, *Salvia* sp. indicates an unspecified species of sage. More than one species is indicated by the abbreviation "spp". These abbreviations are not italicized.

Botanical names are sometimes followed by a different kind of abbreviation, as in *Allium sativum* L. or *Citrus bergamia* Risso & Poit. These abbreviations give credit to the botanical authority (or authorities) responsible for identifying and classifying the species. For example, the abbreviation "L." stands for Linnaeus, who classified many plants. When a plant is reclassified based on new information, the name of the original author is included in parentheses and the new author added, as in *Alpina galangal* (L.) Willd. Such a designation indicates that the plant was first classified by Linnaeus and later reclassified by K. L. Willdenow. With this classification system credit is given to all authors involved in the classification.

Plant Subspecies and Varieties

A plant that differs genetically from most members of its species, but not enough to be classified as a species of its own, may be designated as a subspecies. Subspecies often result from interbreeding in geographically isolated populations. A subspecies is indicated by the abbreviation "ssp." or "subsp".

Plant subspecies can be further categorized into varieties. A variety, or variation in a species, is designated by the abbreviation "var." followed by an italicized variety name, as in the example: *Achillea millefolium* var. *rubrum*. This name indicates that the plant is a variety of common yarrow (*Achillea millefolium*) that has red (*rubrum*) flowers, rather than white ones.

Cultivars and Hybrids

Unlike subspecies and varieties, cultivars do not occur naturally, but have been developed and perpetuated by cultivation. The term "cultivar" was coined from the words "cultivated" and "variety." Cultivars may be hybrids created by breeding members of different species, or simply desirable selections made from one species. Cultivar names may be trademarked and can be registered with an International Cultivar Registration Authority according to certain nomenclatural rules. Names of cultivars appear in single quotation marks after species names. For example, *Rosmarinus officinalis* 'Tuscan Blue' is a dark blue-flowered cultivar of rosemary.

Hybrids, which may be natural or artificially created, occur when two different members of the same genus are bred. They are denoted with an "x" between the genus and species names, as in *Mentha x piperita* var. *piperita*.

HERB ANATOMY

Some people are content to discover the uses of herbs without learning how plants function or how to identify them. Others, however, find that learning to identify herbs and recognize them in their native habitat opens a new dimension of appreciation for plants and the natural world. It is not necessary to spend time collecting plants from the wild to benefit from the study of plant anatomy, and plant life cycles and survival mechanisms. But, many herbalists believe that developing a relationship with a healing plant – admiring its beauty, growing it in a garden, or learning to recognize it in the wild – is part of the medicine that that plant has to offer.

On a basic level, flowering plants are classified according to the number and arrangement of their flower parts, a fact that makes understanding flowers extremely important in plant identification. Biologically speaking, flower parts are the plant's reproductive organs, so they are essential to plant survival. The colours, fragrances and shapes that render flowers irresistible to humans are actually designed to lure pollinators to visit and pollinate the plant, thereby producing the seed that will bring forth the next generation of the species.

Leaves, too, are vital to plant survival. One of the main functions of leaves is photosynthesis, the process that causes plants to transform sunlight, water and carbon dioxide into food (sugars) and oxygen. Leaves also produce a vast variety of chemicals in highly specialized cells and glands. These chemicals serve functions vital for plant survival (not all of which are completely understood), and are also the compounds that give plants their characteristic tastes, colours, aromas and medicinal properties.

Identifying Plants

One of the best ways to learn to identify plants is to become familiar with the characteristics of whole plant families, not simply of individual plants. This is easier than it may sound, and it can streamline the entire process of plant identification.

The reason is simple: plant families display patterns that remain consistent from species to species. For example, flowers in the mustard family have four petals in a crosslike pattern and six stamens. Pea family flowers have five petals: two wing petals, one banner petal and two petals fused into what botanists call a keel. And lily family flowers are monocots with three petals, three sepals and six stamens.

Developing the ability to recognize family characteristics and identify plants takes a bit of practice and perseverance. Begin by looking closely at plants to become adept at recognizing subtle similarities and differences among them. How many petals does each flower have? Do the flowers grow singly or in clumps on the stem? Are the leaves shiny or fuzzy? Are they oval or pointed, round or heart-shaped? Are their edges smooth or serrated? How are the leaves arranged on the stem? Does the plant live in a shady habitat near water, or is it found growing only in dry, sunny locations?

Choose a particular plant and observe its life cycle as it grows throughout the seasons. Learn what it looks like as a seedling and when it is flowering. Watch as the flowers mature and produce fruits and seeds, and examine the seeds. Finally, see what happens as winter approaches and the plant dies back or enters dormancy. By becoming intimately acquainted with a plant in this manner, it will always be recognizable, like the familiar face of a friend in a crowd. The following ten plant families, each of which contains numerous herbs, are a good place to start:

Apiaceae (carrot and parsley family)
Asteraceae (aster and sunflower family)
Boraginaceae (borage family)
Brassicaceae (mustard family)
Fabaceae (pea family)
Lamiaceae (mint family)
Liliaceae (lily family)
Ranunculaceae (buttercup family)
Rosaceae (rose family)
Scrophulariaceae (snapdragon family)

While learning to identify herbs, a local field guide (a plant identification book) is a necessary and invaluable resource. Another good tool is a magnifying glass, helpful for examining small flower parts. The best kind of magnifying glass for plant identification is a jeweller's loupe with a magnification of at least 10x.

Nontechnical field guides are often organized according to flower colour, which can be helpful for beginners. Technical field guides, or floras, are more challenging for beginners because they utilize what is known as a dichotomous key. Such a key functions as a sort of flowchart that requires the reader to choose between two options at each point in the identification process. This necessitates at least a working knowledge of botanical terminology.

Botanists use a rich variety of highly specialized words to describe plant characteristics. Do not feel overwhelmed by the prospect of learning all of these terms. Become familiar with some of the most common, and look up unfamiliar words. Nearly all plant-identification books provide a glossary of essential terms.

Focus on Flowers

Biologically speaking, flower parts are all about reproduction. A flower's showy, colourful petals are designed to attract pollinators such as insects and birds. The grouping of petals together is called the corolla. Around the outside of the corolla are sepals, leaflike structures that enclose the flower before it opens. Sepals are often green, but may be so colourful they can be mis-

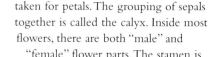

PARTS OF A FLOWER

Calyx

Corolla

Flower Head

Leaf

Stem

Root

taken for petals. The grouping of sepals together is called the calyx. Inside most flowers, there are both "male" and "female" flower parts. The stamen is the male flower part. Each stamen consists of a thin stalk called a filament, which is topped by an anther, the pollen-bearing structure of the flower. The pistil, or female flower part, is an upright structure in the centre of the flower that consists of one or more styles which are, tubelike stalks. The style supports the stigma, the part of the pistil that receives the pollen. Once pollen is deposited on the stigma, it travels down the style to the ovary at the bottom of the pistil. The ovary contains a number of ovules that, when fertilized by pollen, develop into seeds.

Although most flowers have both male and female parts, single-sex plants are not uncommon. These, technically known as dioecious plants, bear male and female flower parts on separate plants, which means both male and female plants must be present for pollination to occur. Dioecious herbs include ginkgo (*Ginkgo biloba*), corn (*Zea mays*) and nettle (*Urtica dioica*). Single-sex flowers are called imperfect flowers; flowers that have both male and female parts are called perfect flowers.

In terms of plant identification, flowers are the most important part of the plant. When identifying a plant, begin by determining

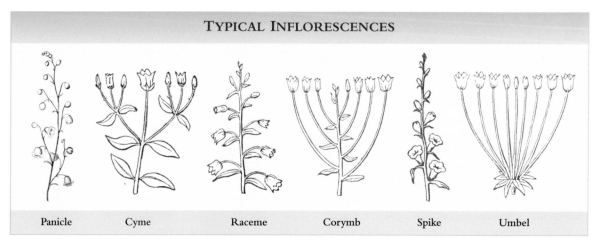

TYPICAL INFLORESCENCES

| Panicle | Cyme | Raceme | Corymb | Spike | Umbel |

A Composite Flower Head

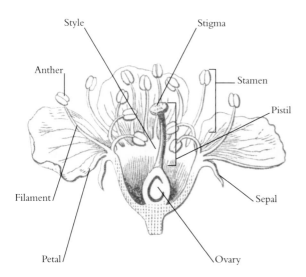

how many petals and sepals the flower has, and depending on the flower, this may be straightforward or tricky. Petals may be fused (joined together) or free. Flowers may be regular (symmetrical, with all petals the same size and shape, such as a mustard or rose family flower) or irregular (with some petals different from the others, as in a mint or pea flower). The colour of the flower may provide some help, but flower colour can be highly variable within a single species, making it an undependable characteristic for identification.

The aster family (Asteraceae) is the largest of all flowering plant families, and its flowers – called composite flowers – are unique in the plant world. Learning to recognize the basic characteristics of this kind of flower, makes it easy to quickly rule out other possibilities when trying to identify a plant.

The sunflower plant, which has a typical composite flower, is not a single big flower, but instead is made up of hundreds of tiny flowers that are arranged into a composite flower head. A typical composite flower head is composed of numerous ray and disk flowers. Ray flowers are longer, strap-shaped flowers that circle the edge of a flower head. Disk flowers are short, bristly flowers in the centre of a flower head.

Sunflower plants have both ray and disk flowers, as do feverfew and echinacea plants. Some composite flower heads, however, are composed solely of either ray or disk flowers. For example, dandelion and chicory flower heads are made up of ray flowers only. Pineapple weed (*Matricaria matricarioides)* a close relative of German chamomile, has only disk flowers. The way in which

❧ FLOWERS ❧

Flowers are designed for one purpose: reproduction. A flower's colour and fragrance attract pollinators, which play a vital part in a plant's reproductive process.

AXIS	An elongated, central, supporting structure.
BRACT	A modified leaf located close to the base of a flower.
CALYX	Collective term for the group of sepals (leaflike structures) that encloses a flower bud and encircles the petals when the flower is open.
COROLLA	Collective term for petals.
CORYMB	A short, broad, flat-topped flower cluster with individual flower stalks emerging at different points along an axis; the outermost flowers in a corymb open first.
CYME	A short, broad flower cluster that always has a flower on the tip of the axis; in a cyme, the central flowers open first.
INFLORESCENCE	The flowering part of a plant, usually used to denote a flower cluster.
PANICLE	An open flower cluster, sometimes pyramid-shaped, with no terminal flower on the tip of the axis that blooms from top to bottom; a branched raceme.
PEDICLE	A stalk of one flower in a multi-flowered inflorescence.
PEDUNCLE	A stalk of a solitary flower or inflorescence.
PERIANTH	The collective term for the corolla (petals) and calyx (sepals) together.
RACEME	A simple, elongated stem with flowers on short stalks; flowers on the lowest part of the stem bloom first.
SEPAL	Leaflike flower structure that encloses a flower bud and encircles the petals when a flower is open.
SPIKE	A simple, elongated stem with stalkless flowers or flower heads; lowest flowers bloom first.
UMBEL	Cluster of flowers with stalks of almost equal length attached to a common point; individual flowers form a flat or nearly flat top.

flowers are arranged on a plant's stem is called the inflorescence. This is another important identification feature. (See *Typical Inflorescences*, page 26, for illustrations of different types of inflorescences.)

Monocot or Dicot?

All flowering plants can be placed into one of two classes, either of which reveals a great deal about their structure. These classes, usually referred to as "monocot" (mono- means "one") and "dicot" (di- means "two") by botanists, refer to the type of seed leaf (cotyledon) a plant produces when it first sprouts. Monocotyledon plants, such as grass or corn, produce a single seed leaf when they sprout. Dicotyledon plants, such as peas or sunflowers, put forth two seed leaves.

The differences between the two classes become much more pronounced as plants mature, and serve as important distinctions in plant classification and identification. Although there are exceptions, there are generalizations one can make about each type of plant. For instance, the parts of dicot plants are generally arranged in multiples of four and five, and their leaves tend to have netted veins (veins that join together, resembling fish net). In addition, they usually have a taproot (a fleshy, central root). Dicot plants are far more numerous than monocots. Among the many dicot plant families that contain important herbs are the mint, rose, carrot, aster and pea families.

In monocot plants (which are less common than dicots), flower parts occur in multiples of three. Monocot leaves have parallel veins – veins that run parallel to the edges of the leaves – instead of the netted vein patterns seen in dicots. Monocots also have a fibrous, grasslike root system that spreads out just below the soil's surface: grasses are among the plants in the monocot class. Other good examples of monocots are lilies, irises and orchids.

Types of Leaves

Leaves, although not as important as flowers in terms of classification, nonetheless provide essential clues that can greatly help with identification.

When examining a plant, look at the way its leaves are arranged. The leaves may be opposite (arranged in pairs along the stem, as in plants of the mint family) or alternate (unpaired, occurring in an alternating pattern along the stem, as in plants of the borage family). Whorled leaves encircle a plant's stem, a pattern that can be seen in many plants of the lily family. The leaves of some plants, such as mullein and plantain, form what is called a basal rosette, a

---

❧ LEAVES ❧

Along with roots and stems, leaves are a basic organ of plants. The primary function of leaves is photosynthesis: the process by which a leaf combines energy from sunlight and carbon dioxide to make sugar and oxygen, which the plant uses as food. What follows is a basic glossary of leaf structure.

APEX	Tip.
BASAL	At the base (as in a basal rosette of leaves); arising at the base of a plant's stem.
BRACT	A modified leaf, often scalelike, that forms either on a flower stalk or as part of a flower head, as on a thistle.
CORDATE	Heart-shaped.
DISSECTED	Divided deeply into many thin segments.
ENTIRE	Leaf margins with no teeth or lobes.
LANCEOLATE	Lance-shaped, several times longer than wide; widest at the base and tapering toward the tip.
LINEAR	Narrow and flat with parallel sides, like a blade of grass.
LOBE	A segment of a leaf, especially when rounded.
NODE	The place on a stem from which leaves or branches originate.
PALMATE	With numerous leaf divisions running down to one point at the base.
PETIOLE	The stalk of a leaf blade or a compound leaf.
SERRATE	With sharp teeth, pointed forward.
SESSILE	Having no stalk.
STIPULE	A modified leaf part found at the base of the petiole in certain plant families, such as the rose family.
TRIFOLIATE	Leaves having three parts.

---

cluster of leaves arranged in a circular pattern on the ground at the base of the flower stalk. Leaf composition is another important element in identifying plants. Leaves can be simple (consisting of only one part) or compound (composed of multiple parts, or leaflets). In the rose family, for example, five rounded leaflets attached to a stalk make up a single compound leaf. Plants in the carrot and ginseng families have compound leaves. It is not always easy to determine whether a plant has compound leaves composed of multiple leaflets or simply many separate

ALTERNATE OR OPPOSITE?

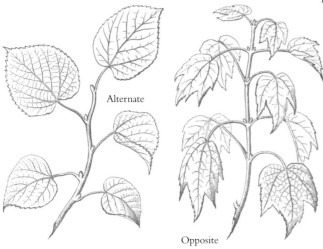

The terms opposite and alternate refer to how leaves attach to their stems.

leaves attached to a stem. When working with woody plants, look at the twig near the base of the leaf stalk. If it is a true leaf and not just a leaflet, next year's bud will have already formed there. For nonwoody plants, one trick is to examine the placement of the leaves (or leaflets) on the stem. The leaflets of a compound leaf will appear to be attached all on one plane, while real leaves are attached on several different planes.

Palmately compound leaves have leaflets attached all at one point to a plant's stem. A pinnately compound leaf is composed of leaflets arranged on two opposite sides of an elongated stem, or axis. Even pinnate leaves have an even number of leaflets, odd pinnate leaves have an odd number.

After determining whether a plant's leaves are compound or simple and how they are arranged on the plant's stem, take note of the shape and texture of the leaves. Leaves may be glaucous (smooth) or hirsute (hairy); the edges (or margins) may be serrate (toothed) or entire (smooth). And the shape of the leaves may be round, oval, heart-shaped, lance-like or any of many other shapes.

Fruits, Seeds, Stems and Roots

A fruit is the fertilized, ripened ovary of a flower. It contains the plant's seeds, fertilized ovules that holds the genetic material for a new plant. While some fruits are juicy, tasty structures such as apples, tomatoes and berries, others are merely hard, dry seedpods. Fruits and seeds provide important foods and medicines, and can also be vital for plant identification. To pinpoint some species in the carrot family, for example, botanists must examine their tiny seeds, making positive identification a highly technical process.

A plant's stem offers structural support and serves as a transport and storage system for nutrients and water. Along the stem, nodes or swellings indicate where leaves, buds or branches will arise. Stems can take many forms, both above and below the soil. A rhizome, for example, is often mistaken for a root, although it is actually an underground stem with roots attached. Roots are underground structures that anchor and support a plant, absorb nutrients and water, and store food for the plant.

LEAF SHAPE ARRANGEMENTS

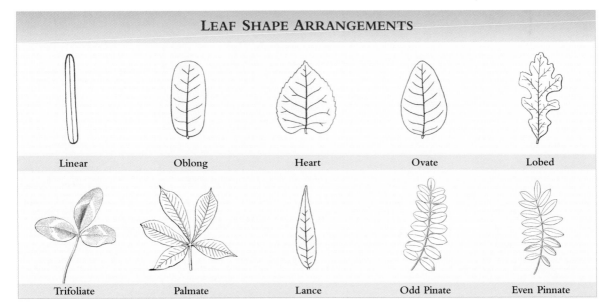

| Linear | Oblong | Heart | Ovate | Lobed |
| Trifoliate | Palmate | Lance | Odd Pinate | Even Pinnate |

ROOTS AND UNDERGROUND STEMS

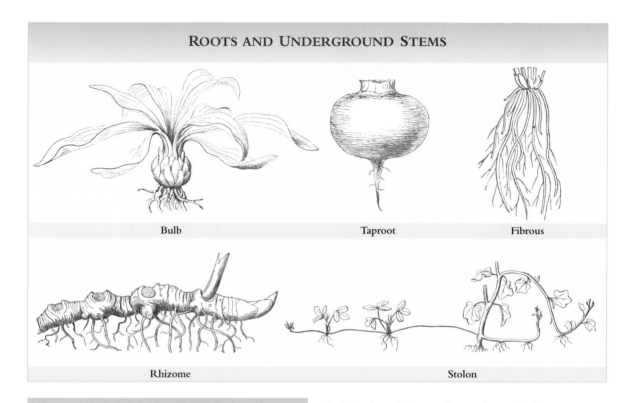

Bulb   Taproot   Fibrous

Rhizome   Stolon

FRUITS, SEEDS, STEMS ❧ AND ROOTS ❧

These various elements carry a plant's seeds, support its structure, anchor it in the soil, and absorb nutrients and moisture to nourish the plant.

POME	A fleshy fruit, such as an apple, with more than one ovary compartment.
PROSTRATE	A stem that lies flat on the ground.
RHIZOME	A prostrate, usually horizontal elongated underground stem that produces roots, such as that of iris or ginger.
RUNNER	A slender stolon.
SILICLE	A short fruit (seedpod) of the mustard family, generally not more than twice as long as it is wide.
SILIQUE	A long fruit (seedpod) of the mustard family, usually elongated.
STOLON	A specialized stem that trails on the ground and sends out roots at nodes.
TAPROOT	A thick tapering root that extends downward, such as that of a beetroot.
TUBER	A thickened underground stem (rhizome), usually with numerous buds (eyes), such as a potato.

Collecting Plants from the Wild

Strong plant identification skills are essential for those who wish to collect plants from the wild. First, it is a matter of safety. It is essential to be absolutely certain of the identity of the plants being gathered. Every herbalist has heard stories about people poisoning themselves and their families after mistaking foxglove – a deadly poisonous plant – for comfrey. Others have died after harvesting the wrong member of the carrot family, which includes extremely poisonous plants, such as poison hemlock, as well as wild medicinal herbs and edible varieties. Plants in the carrot family can be notoriously difficult to identify, even for experienced field botanists. While relatively few plants are as toxic as foxglove or water hemlock, the wisest policy is not to taste or sample unknown plants.

Another important issue to consider when harvesting plants from the wild is conservation. As habitats dwindle, wild plant communities increasingly face pressure from the encroachment of human activities, such as development, deforestation, recreation, and, in some regions, commercial harvesting. As people work on improving their health and well-being with herbal medicines, it is essential to make every effort to protect the well-being of the planet and its life-sustaining plants. Make a point of learning about which plants in a local area may be rare or endangered before collecting any plants.

In addition, it is vital to learn about sustainable wild-harvesting practices – ways of collecting plants that will help ensure the survival of the community from which they are being gathered. There are a few general rules to follow: first, never harvest rare herbs or plants of any kind. Even if the plant being collected is not rare, never harvest when there are only a few specimens growing in one place. A community of one or a few plants is probably not hearty enough to withstand the pressure of collection. Second, when a collector takes the root of a plant, the plant itself is destroyed, so do not harvest more plant material than is needed. Harvesting bark harms trees: removing a ring of bark around the trunk can be fatal to the tree.

Finally, be cautious about potential pollutants that can contaminate plants that are being gathered. Those collected near roadsides, for example, may contain unacceptably high levels of toxins. Plants gathered from streams may contain the same contaminants that the water does, including bacteria such as *E. coli*. In the end, the best course of action may be simply to grow medicinal plants or purchase herbs from a reputable supplier.

When gathering plants from the wild for any reason, it is essential to be aware of good wild-harvesting practices. Knowing how to harvest plants in ways that minimizes damage to their habitats ensures that the plant community will survive.

CHAPTER 2

A Global History

Herbs have played a key role in human life since before recorded history. Yarrow, groundsel and marsh mallow were found in the 60,000-year-old grave of a Neanderthal man unearthed in present-day Iraq. Ancient etchings on cave walls depict men gathering roots, rubbing leaves on their bodies and arranging plants in ceremonial patterns. Ancestral languages such as proto-Austronesian had words for herbs including one for ginger, a herb that may have been carried and traded during the earliest human migrations across Asia.

Five thousand years ago, ancient Sumerian healers wrote prescriptions on tablets of clay for treatments that used caraway and thyme. As far back as 2700 B.C.E., Chinese healers produced written records of dozens of plants used to treat the sick. Ancient Egyptian paintings depict some of the earliest herb gardens, including one from 1400 B.C.E. that clearly shows pomegranate trees and grapevines surrounding a fishpond.

The march of progress and the passing of time have not slowed humanity's interest in herbs. The discovery of new herb uses continues today, from the microbiology laboratories of scientists to the bio-diverse rainforests of the Amazon.

Herbs played a vital role in the daily life of ancient Egyptians. This sculpture, from around 1335 B.C.E., depicts Queen Meritaten holding mandrake roots, which were used as an aphrodisiac, and papyrus plants, which were turned into writing paper.

Exploring the World of Herbs

For millennia, people on every continent have incorporated beneficial herbs into their daily lives. Whether used medicinally, in cooking, to enhance beauty, or in gardening and handicrafts, herbs and their lore have been seamlessly woven into the economic, scientific and social structure of every culture around the world.

The first organized systems of medicine in China and Sumeria centred around herbal treatments. Some of the oldest religions in India and Egypt viewed many herbs as sacred gifts from the gods. For centuries, flavour-enhancing herbs, such as pepper and cinnamon from the Far East have been coveted by Western cooks. During eras when regular bathing was rare, perfumes extracted from fragrant herbs made social life in Europe and Africa a little more pleasant. Around the world, herbs have long been grown in gardens for their beauty and for their many uses.

Modern medicine can trace its roots back to ancient herbalism. Chinese Taoists used a tonic of ginseng as a stimulant for the body's vital essence or "qi" as long ago as 3000 B.C.E. Records show that, throughout Egypt in 1500 B.C.E., aloe was used as a salve to heal the wounds of soldiers. In the Americas, native shamans and folk healers treated patients for conditions ranging from rashes to depression to infections using local plants such as sassafrass, coca and cashews.

Much of the knowledge held by early healers was passed down orally from generation to generation, often in sacred rituals. In this way, many medicinal herbs took on an additional spiritual significance. In traditional Persian weddings for example, incense made from rue seeds was burned and bunches of herbs such as mint, parsley and nigella, were spread before the bride and groom to protect them from evil spirits.

Historically, one particular ritual, the taking of tea and coffee has been a part of almost every culture on Earth. It is said that the tea plant originated when Buddha, in an effort to stay awake while meditating, cut off his eyelids and hurled them to the ground, producing a herb with the power to keep him alert. In England, Japan and China, the taking of tea evolved into elaborate, carefully orchestrated processes that required years of education and practice to perfect. Coffee was first used as a stimulant more than 1,000 years ago in Ethiopia, where tribesmen mixed crushed arabica berries with animal fat into balls that were eaten as food. By the 1600s, Italian traders had introduced coffee from Arabia to Europe and it was well on its way to becoming a popular drink.

Over the centuries, people across the world have cooked, steamed, ground, sprinkled and infused herbs into every conceivable dish. As early as 3000 B.C.E., ancient Babylonians included garlic in meals, while in 400 B.C.E., the Romans created a condiment from mustard by mixing ground seeds with grape juice. Long before their names graced a famous folk song, parsley, sage, rosemary and thyme were all used widely throughout Europe to turn cooked meats into palatable meals. Hundreds of years ago, a traveller to East Asia would be treated to meals saturated in sesame seeds and ginger. Dinner on a Caribbean island would have contained plenty of jerk seasoning, made from dried chillies, pepper

Javanese tea leaf pickers on a tea plantation in Java, Indonesia. Tea is an important crop throughout Asia.

and allspice. And a welcome feast for visitors to the Hawaiian Islands would certainly have included several of the one thousand varieties of taro poi.

While countless herbs have been used to improve the flavour of food, many others have been used to beautify human appearance. The Egyptians invented cosmetics made from the oils of herbs such as olives, almonds, cucumbers, figs, limes, lilies and generous doses of frankincense and myrrh. Early Arab scientists distilled the fragrant oil of the rose, which was used to make soaps, bath oils and aromatic rose water. In medieval France, both men and women used pomanders – small balls of ambergris with herbs and perfumes added – to mask the stench of unsanitary surroundings.

The world's earliest civilizations built herb gardens to beautify the land. The legendary Hanging Gardens of Babylon did not actually hang but rather grew on terraced rooftops built to resemble a mountain. In China, scholar gardens were created to allow retired officials from the Emperor's court to spend days of leisure wandering among shapely pine, bamboo and plum trees. The pleasure gardens of Persia, dating from 500 B.C.E., introduced the concept of arranging plants in regular, straight rows. The villa gardens of the Roman Empire contained geometrically precise raised beds of coriander, dill and fennel. The physic gardens of medieval Europe produced a variety of culinary and medicinal botanicals.

Culturally and geographically, there are no limits to the uses humans have found for herbs. From the ancient Abyssinians, who stuffed their pillows with fresh celery leaves, to Native American tribes who used pennyroyal as an insect repellent, people have always made herbs an essential part of their lives. Today, herbs of all kinds are found in cosmetics and clothing dye, growing beside houses and spicing up dinner plates, and in the pages of medical texts and history books. There is no part of human culture that herbs have not transformed.

ASIA

Much of the world's herb lore, and many of its most highly regarded herbs, can be traced in origin to Asia. The world's largest continent is home to a wide range of plant habitats, from the barren wilderness of Arctic tundra and deserts to lush forests of every type: coniferous, oak, tropical rainforest and bamboo. With a very high concentration of people and plants, it is not surprising that Asia has produced some of the oldest known herbal rituals, recipes, gardens and systems of medicine. The most influential cultures in the region are two of the most populous countries: China and India. Over the millennia, their ancient herbal beliefs and practices spread throughout Asia, adapting to reflect the local flavour of countries such as Korea, Japan, Thailand and Tibet. Today, the influence of the Far East extends to much of the world.

CHINA

According to legend, the first emperor of China, a sage named Fu His (ca. 4000 B.C.E.), single-handedly changed his people from hunter-gatherers to agriculturalists. The plants they grew became integral to the spiritual beliefs of their early society, which included the I Ching, a system of divination. The stalk of the yarrow plant (*Achillea millifolium*) was particularly significant in the I Ching: Fu Hsi instructed wise men to cast sticks of yarrow on the ground and interpret their arrangement in relation to each other in order to predict future events.

Chinese herbs and philosophy have always gone hand in hand, and they mix particularly well in the history of Chinese cooking. The great philosopher Confucius (552–479 B.C.E.) believed that a good cook must be a skilled herbal matchmaker: condiments and spices in food must blend harmoniously or there would be no flavour. He would eat no meal that did not contain a little ginger.

Ancient practitioners of Taoism, another dominant Chinese philosophy, saw cooking less as the pursuit of

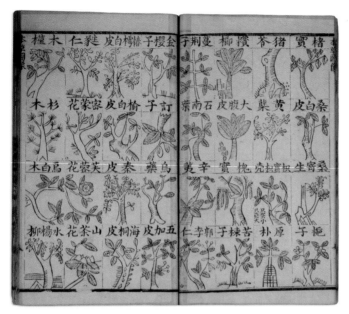

These pages from the first volume of the 1740 book Hu, Tsung-wen Shen-nung pen ts'ao pei yao i fang ho pien, *or Herbal and Prescriptions, is a classic text of Traditional Chinese Medicine.*

beauty and more as the pursuit of health. Plant leaves, roots, stems, flowers, seeds, bark and funghi were all prepared, tested and consumed for their health effects. As a result, most varieties of Chinese cuisine contained plenty of vegetables, grains and herbs, all cooked in ways that ensured their medicinal value would not be lost.

Herbal tea has a long history of use in China, dating back more than 4,000 years. According to legend, one of the first Chinese emperors, Yan Di (2852–2737 B.C.E.), discovered the medicinal powers of tea by accident while he was testing the effects of other herbs on himself. After eating a poisonous plant, he fell to the ground on the verge of death. When a drop of water from the leaf of a tea tree fell into his open mouth, he was cured. During the early Zhou Dynasty (1000–250 B.C.E.), Chinese people used tea as a religious offering, and ate fresh tea leaves as vegetables in the spring and autumn. Later, during the Tang Dynasty (618–907 C.E.), the taking of tea became a cultural event. Tea shops opened throughout China, and a seminal book, *Tea Classics* by Lu Yu, outlined the rules of growing and processing tea as well as the etiquette of tea tasting. Tea ceremonies grew successively more refined, elaborate and lengthy.

The first Chinese gardens were cultivated during the Zhou dynasty. Members of the aristocracy sectioned off particularly beautiful parts of the natural world to use for hunting and strolling. During the Han Dynasty

(207 B.C.E.–202 C.E.), wealthy Chinese people developed an interest in constructing more personal gardens where they could collect and display rare plants. By the fourth century C.E., the literati of China became associated with scholar gardens, which were small, enclosed areas containing unusual rocks, water features and interesting plants that reflected the personalities and knowledge of their owners. Chinese gardens across all eras were meant to be reflections of the larger natural world, with random placement of plants favoured over geometric shapes and lines, and woody trees and green herbs favoured over cultivated blossoms and flowerbeds. Chinese gardens, much like Chinese herbal medicines, were designed to create the perfect balance between the two opposing Taoist life energies, yin and yang.

Chinese Herbal Healing

Traditional Chinese Medicine has very deep historical roots. Sometime between 3700 and 2600 B.C.E., the emperor Shen-nung reputedly created the first Chinese written pharmacopoeia, called the *Pen-ts'ao* (*Herbal*). It contains 365 medical preparations, all but 51 of which are herbal. It was followed by the *Huang-ti Nei ching* (*The Yellow Emperor's Classic of Internal Medicine*), allegedly written by emperor Huang Ti (2674–2575 B.C.E.). During the Han dynasty, a physician named Chang Chung-ching wrote the *Shang han lun* (or *Treatise on Colds and Fevers*), which eventually became the theoretical framework for all herbal prescriptions in Traditional Chinese Medicine. It contained more than 100 formulas, many of which are still in use today.

In 1590 C.E., a herbalist named Li Shih-chen (1518–1593) published the *Compendium of Materia Medica*. It contained 12,000 prescriptions and formulas, analysed 1,074 plant substances, filled 52 volumes and took nearly 27 years to write. It became the first major Chinese work to be translated into Western languages, and its publication coincided with a dramatic rise in Chinese global exportation of herbs and spices.

In the early 20th century, the rise of the Communist Kuomintang party in China brought with it a disdain for all things associated with traditional Chinese culture, including herbal medicine. China's scientists were instructed to examine native plants using Western scientific methods. Many important discoveries resulted, such as the isolation of the drug ephedrine from the *Ephedra sinica* plant. Ephedrine quickly became one of the world's most effective decongestants and asthma treatments, and China its principal supplier. Modern hospitals and clinics were constructed, and advanced instruments and synthetic drugs were brought into heavy use.

In 1949, however, when the People's Republic of China was established, China's leaders recognized that the most effective healthcare system for a nation of more than one billion people was a combination of Western and traditional herbal methods. Colleges were established to train doctors in both disciplines. An army of "barefoot doctors" was created to serve the rural population. The immediate effect was an increased demand for herbs, which the Chinese government answered by establishing a programme of medicinal plant cultivation. Nearly 323,748 ha (800,000 acres) of land were set aside and devoted solely to the production of medicinal herbs. Today, of the 35,000 species of plants growing in China's various habitats, some 5,000 are used in Traditional Chinese Medicine, which provides 40 percent of all China's pharmaceuticals.

TIBET

While Tibetan medicine is currently practised in many countries around the world, its central sphere of influence is where it was developed centuries ago – Tibet, several neighbouring provinces of China, and the kingdoms of Bhutan, Nepal, Ladakh and Sikkim. The popularity of traditional Tibetan medicine may be attributed to its rich history of success, a history that can be traced back to 300 B.C.E. with local folk traditions known as *bon*.

According to ancient legend, Tara, the Buddhist god of compassion, commanded two Indian physicians to go to Tibet to teach the ways of Buddhism, including the secrets of herbal healing. For their efforts, the doctors were granted immortality. Current folklore says that they live on today in the sandalwood jungles of the region.

The doctors' most famous relative was Yuthog Yonten Gonpo, who reportedly lived to the ripe old age of 125 in the ninth century C.E. Yuthog established the first Tibetan medical school, and wrote no fewer than thirty seminal herbal books, each incorporating many aspects of Traditional Chinese Medicine and Indian Ayurveda. His research led him to reorganize and compile the Four Medical Tantras, the basis of Tibetan medicine. The first three tantras focus mainly on the study of behaviour, diet, and the causes of diseases. The fourth tantra is completely devoted to the use of herbs in medical treatment, through pills, tonics, ointments and moxibustion, which utilizes a substance called moxa, made from the herb mugwort (*Artemisia vulgaris*). Heat from burning moxa is applied to specific external points on the body, activating the internal organs, increasing blood circulation, and improving the flow of ki, or lifeforce (similar to the Chinese qi.).

Though many of the medicinal herbs used in Tibet came from India and China, about one-third were unique to the region. The herbs were occasionally used to make powders or tonics, but by far the most common form of Tibetan treatment was in the form of a pill, which was made up of as many as 25 herbal ingredients.

Engraving of a Chinese tea trader. Tea trade has existed among the areas of Sichuan, Yunnan and Tibet for over 1,000 years.
Europeans became aware of the Chinese herb when Portuguese missionary Jasper de Cruz first tasted and wrote about it in 1560.

❧ OPIUM AND THE EAST ❧

Science has never created a painkiller as effective as opium, a highly addictive, natural derivative of the opium poppy. In the early 1800s, most opium poppies came from India, distributed to the world by the British East India Company. The Chinese port of Canton was a key trading hub, where tonnes of opium were exchanged for manufactured goods and tea. As a result, millions of Chinese people became helpless opium addicts, spending what money they had in squalid urban opium parlours while their families suffered in poverty.

In the late 1830s, the Chinese government made a concerted effort to address the problem. They destroyed opium stocks, prosecuted British traders, and attempted to close the country's borders to opium trade. The British declared war on China, prevailing against them in a series of lopsided battles. In 1842, the Chinese were forced to agree to the Treaty of Nanking, a humiliating agreement that opened new trade ports to the British, exempted British nationals from Chinese law and more than doubled the trade of opium to China.

The utter defeat of the Chinese in the Opium Wars, however, spurred a modernization of every aspect of Chinese culture. Investing heavily in scientific and technological research, in less than a century China transformed itself from an undeveloped agricultural society to a world superpower. Ironically, the country's newly trained scientists applied their skills to the study of opium, yielding derivative drugs such as morphine, methadone and codeine. These substances are impossible to "synthesize", or manufacture chemically in a laboratory, which means that today, the growing and processing of opium poppies for the pharmaceutical industry is an increasingly important part of world trade.

In an area as difficult to navigate as mountainous Tibet, pills were the easiest form of medication to transport and administer to patients. They could be prepared in advance at a medical facility with wide access to a variety of herbs, then preserved by rolling them back and forth in cloth to reduce the air inside and prevent the growth of bacteria. Local doctors kept as many as 200 different varieties in stock to treat their patients.

EAST AND SOUTHEAST ASIA

Historically, many of China's neighbours borrowed heavily from China's herbal traditions in creating their medicinal systems. Over the years, however, Japan, Korea and Vietnam also developed unique herb uses of their own. In Japan, the herbal medicine system of kampo traces its roots to the seventh century C.E., when the empress Suiko sent emissaries to China to study and bring back theories of herbalism. Kampo takes its name from *kan*, meaning "ancient China", and *po*, meaning "medicine". At first, the main practitioners of kampo were Buddhist monks who adhered to a strict vegetarian diet and so rejected all Chinese remedies that contained animal products. This, along with the Buddhist ideals of simplicity, safety and prevention, led the monks to reduce the tens of thousands of Chinese remedies to 365 essential herbal treatments used in kampo. In 20th-century Japan, as in China, the use of traditional medicinal methods declined in favour of Western medicine, only to return in recent decades as an integral part of the national health plan. Today 75 percent of Japanese physicians use a combination of Western and kampo medicine to treat patients.

Zen Buddhists in the 9th century C.E. also carried Chinese tea into Japan, beginning with traditional black tea (*Camellia* spp.), and evolving into *matcha*, derived from the same plant but used unfermented and in powdered form. By the 13th century, Japanese samurai warriors had laid the foundations of the formal Japanese tea ceremony, characterized by *wabi*, or quiet, sober refinement.

In Korea and Vietnam, the most important contributions to herbal history were medicinal. Korean healers adapted many of the tenets of Chinese medicine for their own use. They wrote the *Hyangyakjibsongbang*, published in 1433 C.E., which presents over 10,000 uniquely Korean prescriptions and describes the collection and preparation methods for 700 Korean herbs. A decade later, a 365-volume medical encyclopedia, the *Uibangryuchi*, outlined methods of preventing 95 diseases.

In Vietnam, the earliest pharmacopoeiea was the 14th-century *Thuoc nam*, which described 650 indigenous herbs and their uses for treating dozens of diseases. The practices described continued even as Western medicinal techniques and pharmaceuticals were adopted. During World War II, when supplies of anti-malarial quinine were cut off, Vietnamese malaria patients were treated using extracts of *Dichroa febriguga*, a local shrub.

INDIA

Very early in its history, India became a coveted destination for traders who were eager to profit from the region's bounty of native herbs and spices. In the early Middle Ages, the people of Europe and Mediterranean Africa developed a voracious appetite for the exotic spices of India and the Far East, including cinnamon, cloves, pepper, cardamom, nutmeg and mace. Arabs, who occupied the middle ground between the two regions, became experts in spice trading, establishing overland east-to-west trade routes. Later, sea routes were added.

By the early 1600s, the Dutch East India Company had established a near-monopoly on the spice trade. The British, seeking a piece of this lucrative market, founded the British East India Company. Soon, British-built factories in India were profitably cultivating herbs such as tea and indigo by the tonne. Seeking a permanent foothold in the region, the British negotiated a treaty with India that gave the East India Company exclusive rights to build factories in certain major ports. By 1647, the company had 23 factories in India, far outnumbering the outposts of its Portuguese and Dutch competitors.

By 1690, the British East India Company had become almost a sub-country within India. It minted its own money, acquired its own territories, held criminal jurisdiction and commanded its own substantial army. In 1773, lobbyists working on behalf of the East India Company convinced the British Parliament to ratify the Tea Act, which gave the company the right to trade tea, tax-free, to the American colonies. Outraged because they could not compete with the tax-free prices offered by the East India Company, American merchants stormed one of the company's ships and dumped its entire tea cargo into Boston Harbor. The event, which became known as the Boston Tea Party, was one of the catalysts of the American War of Independence (1775–1783).

Opium poppy (papaver soniferum), *from which morphine, methadone and codeine are derived, was first cultivated in lower Mesopotamia around 3400 B.C.E.*

Indian Herbal Medicine

The bounty of herbs native to India gave rise to a system of medicinal and spiritual healing known as Ayurveda, meaning "science of life". According to folklore, Ayurvedic herbal remedies were given to the people of India by the gods as early as 10,000 B.C.E. They were then incorporated into texts called *vedas*, upon which the Hindu religion is based. The *Rig Veda*, dating to at least 2000 B.C.E., lists over 1,000 medicinal herbs and tells tales of gifted sages who unlocked the secrets of plants. These proto-doctors were said to be advanced in their methods: they performed surgery with instruments, cauterized wounds, constructed artificial limbs and may have pioneered the use of an anaesthetic made from mushrooms.

In the first century C.E., the *Charaka Samhita* appeared. This Ayurvedic text listed 500 herb- and vegetable-based drugs classified into 50 groups on the basis of their action on the body. One important drug came from gotu kola (*Centella asiatica*), a key ingredient in a "miracle elixir" that was purported to extend life and to cure leprosy.

The influence of Ayurvedic medicine continued to spread throughout India's history, from the expansion of the Roman Empire into the region, to the Islamic invasions of the 16th century, to the period of British control in the 19th century. The Greek physician and botanist Dioscorides (40–90 C.E.) made many references to Indian herbalism in his *De Materia Medica* (*The Materials of Medicine*). *The Book of Simple Drugs,* by 12th-century Arabic pharmacologist al-Ghafiqi codified Ayurvedic healing prescriptions for the Islamic world. Today, Ayurvedic medicine remains pervasive worldwide. It is estimated that 90 percent of medicinal herbs used in India are still harvested from the wild, and the herbal remedies are used in both hemispheres, much as they were centuries ago.

Other Herbal Uses

India has a long history of vegetarianism, driven mainly by the Buddhist and Hindu religions, which hold many animals as sacred. As early as 800 B.C.E., there is evidence that Indian people were eating less meat and more cultivated vegetables, fruits and cereals. The Muslim invasions of India in the 16th century brought new herbal influences to India's cuisine. The result: an Arabic-influenced Indian cuisine called Mughlai saw spices such as dhal curry (a powder derived from *Murraya koenigii*) being added to traditional Indian cream, butter and rice. Meat dishes came back into vogue, garnished with pistachios, raisins, almonds and cashews. Muslims also introduced the idea of ending a meal with dessert, usually a rice cake or wheat bread flavoured with sugar, coconut or rose water.

The cosmetic use of herbs in India coincides with the rise of the Buddhist and Hindu religions. Paintings found in caves in Ajanta and Ellora, India, dating from the second and first centuries B.C.E., depict Buddhist men and women applying makeup and perfumes in religious ceremonies. Texts of the period suggest that these cosmetics were made from herbs such as turmeric, saffron, indigo and nettles. Henna (*Lawsonia inermis),* or mehendi, was widely used as a reddish hair dye and conditioner. Early Hindus used herbal cosmetics as symbols of social class and religious adherence. Applied to the forehead as a sign

of auspiciousness, the *tilak* is a dot of red turmeric powder or sandalwood paste. Perfumes made from agaru (*Auilaria malaccensis*) were worn to honour the gods, and incense from the tree was burned in Hindu ceremonies.

Although no archeological evidence remains of the earliest Indian gardens, 3,000-year-old *vedas* give accounts of palaces surrounded by gardens of fruit trees and town houses with enclosed outdoor gardens. These cultivated areas were venerated by early Hindus, who saw the trees within gardens as the embodiment of the god Brahma, his roots firmly connected to the primal being of earth.

WESTERN ASIA

The civilizations of Mesopotamia, today's Iraq and Syria, were the first to develop irrigated agriculture. Sometime between 4,500 and 3,000 B.C.E., the Sumerians who settled in this fertile area began harvesting crops of barley, growing orchards, and inscribing on stone or clay tablets the medicinal use of herbs. Their herbal healers, the *asu*, were experts at mixing plant resins and animal fat to apply to wounds. In this same region, from 3000 to 400 B.C.E., the ancient Babylonians and Assyrians established cities that included wondrous gardens, the most famous of which was the Hanging Gardens of Babylon, said to have been built around 600 B.C.E. by Nebuchadnezzar II as a gift to his favourite wife, Amyitis. He built a mountain of massive stone buildings with terraces so that trees, flowering plants and herbs could be grown on the rooftops. Written descriptions of other gardens of the time show the Babylonians may have planted herbs such as saffron, mandrake, help, anise and thyme. One tablet from an Assyrian library, dated ca. 660 B.C.E., identifies more than 250 vegetable-based drugs, such as turpentine made from opium, myrrh, crocus, cannabis and hellebore.

In 333 B.C.E., Alexander the Great (356–323 B.C.E.) conquered most of the lands between his home, Greece, and Persia. Through his doctrine of cultural integration, both Greek herbal medicine and the gardening styles of Mesopotamia spread throughout the known world. By biblical times (300 B.C.E.–500 C.E.), many herbs were being cultivated in the area, including anise, cumin, bay, garlic, hyssop, mustard, cherbil and mallow. The bible itself contains descriptions of herbal treatments, including boiling rosemary twigs to treat a fever, crushing comfrey leaves into an ointment to soothe sprained limbs, and steeping mullein flowers in olive oil to relieve earache.

Woman working among red peppers in a marketplace in Rajasthan, India. India is the largest consumer, producer, and exporter of chilli peppers in the world today. The potency of the peppers is traditionally believed to have supernatural origins.

❧ MAJOR HERBS OF ASIA ❧

NAME OF HERB	USE
Camphor (*Cinnamomum camphora*)	Soothes muscle and joint pain
Cardamom (*Elettaria cardamomum*)	Used as a flavouring for baked goods and curries
Cinnamon (*Cinnamomum zeylanicum*)	Used as a digestive aid
Ephedra (*Ephedra sinica*)	Relieves bronchial congestion
Forsythia (*Forsythia suspensa*)	Treats acute infection
Ginkgo (*Ginkgo biloba*)	Improves circulation of blood to the brain
Ginseng (*Panax ginseng*)	Provides the basis of many Chinese foods and medicines
Gotu kola (*Centella asiatica*)	Improves circulation
Guggul (*Commiphora wightii*)	Reduces cholesterol
Japanese peppermint (*Mentha arvensis*)	Flavours tea, prevents milk from curdling
Jasmine (*Jasminum sambac*)	Used in perfumery and tea flavouring
Liquorice (*Glycyrrhiza uralensis*)	Gives sweets a delicious flavouring
Myrobalan (*Terminalia spp.*)	Believed to be an Ayurvedic cure-all
Peony (*Paeonia lactiflora*)	Improves circulation
Pepper (*Piper nigrum*)	Adds spice to foods
Qing Hao (*Artemisia annua*)	An antimalarial
Rhubarb (*Rheum spp.*)	Acts as a purgative
Sacred lotus (*Nelumbo nucifera*)	Stimulates vitality and energy
Sandalwood (*Santalum album*)	Applied as an astringent, also used in aromatherapy
Serpentwood (*Rauvolfia serpentina*)	Soothes the mind

ARABIC HERBALISM

At the height of the Roman Empire, Arabic people from present-day Saudi Arabia supplied Roman dinner tables with pepper, cinnamon and cloves in return for gold. As the power of the empire began to wane, the Arabs began to incorporate the teachings of the great Greek and Roman physicians and herbalists into their culture. From the founding of Islam in the 6th century C.E., the Arabic

Hippocrates (470–410 B.C.E.) believed that illness had a physical and a rational explanation and that the body must be treated as a whole and not just a series of parts. He was also the first physician to speculate that feelings and thoughts originated in the brain, and not the heart.

purify mosques, infuse prayer beads with fragrance, sprinkle guests as they entered houses and flavour everything from sherbet to sweets. They isolated the essential oils of other herbs as well, and through this work, aromatherapy developed as a popular medicinal treatment. During the Middle Ages, much of the Arab world used aromatic baths, powder and salves to cure a variety of ills and Arabic science and herbal medicine remained highly influential throughout the Western world for hundreds of years.

EUROPE

The history of herbs in Europe is a grand collage of plants and traditions from all over the world. Europeans have always imported ideas about herbal medicine, cosmetics, gardening, cooking and the herbs themselves from Asia, Africa, the islands of the Pacific and the shores of the New World. This global eclecticism is so entrenched throughout Europe that travellers there are as likely to stumble on an Ayurvedic bookstore or Japanese garden as they are a French perfumery or Italian spice shop.

Europe is also home to some of the world's most famous and sought-after indigenous herbs. No kitchen in the world is complete without the flavours and scents of lavender, olive, oregano, rosemary or bay.

world became the centre of scientific and medical knowledge. By the 9th century, surgical hospitals had been built in Baghdad, as well as pharmacies that dispensed herbal medicines. Arabs had used hollow needles to deliver medicines, and administered herbal narcotics as anaesthetics. The most important Arabic herbalist and physician was Ibn Sina (980–1037) known to the Western world as Avicenna. His *Canon* became the definitive tome on herbal medicine in the Arab world, and its influence spread through Europe as Crusaders carried it back to their home countries from the Middle East.

As early as the 7th century, Arab alchemists had developed a process for distilling rose oil, which was used to

GREECE AND ROME

The long culture of herb use in Europe begins with the ancient Greeks and Romans. Greek mythology offers dozens of elaborate stories to explain the origins of important plants and herbs. For instance, as Hera, the queen of the gods, nursed her son Hercules, a few drops of milk are said to have fallen to the ground, where the first white lily grew. And Aphrodite, the goddess of love, pricked her foot on the thorn of a white rose on the way to meet her lover, Adonis. Her blood turned the rose red, making it the ultimate symbol of love. One of Greece's most enduring herbal legacies comes from the myth of

Apollo and Daphne. Apollo berated the young Cupid one day, saying that a god of love should not play with bows and arrows. In revenge, Cupid fired an arrow into Apollo to ignite love, and another into the beautiful maiden, Daphne, to repel love. From then on, Apollo pursued Daphne relentlessly until, finally, Daphne begged the river god, Peneus, to help her escape, and was transformed into a laurel tree. Upon seeing her new form, Apollo declared the laurel (*Laurus nobilis*) sacred, and wore a wreath of laurel around his head as a sign of his undying love and honour. This is why athletes in the first Greek Olympic games were crowned with laurel, and it is the origin of many terms depicting high honours.

Several other herbs gained special, and sometimes superstitious, significance in ancient Greece and Rome.

Cover of 1621 medical textbook The Anatomy of Melancholy. *Author Richard Burton's text expanded upon the medicinal uses of herbs detailed in Galen's writings on the four humours. The bottom of the cover features the herbs borago and helleborus.*

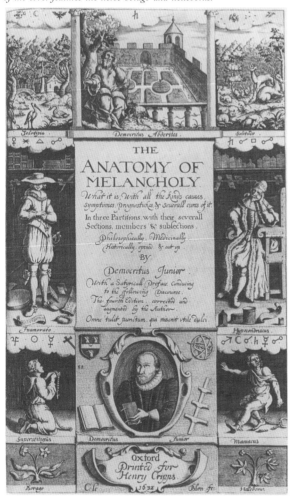

Many Greeks avoided basil (*Ocimum minimum*) because they believed that scorpions would breed under pots of it, while the Roman name for basil was *basilescus* because Romans believed that ingesting it protected warriors from the deadly gaze of the basilisk, a mythical serpent. Marjoram (*Origanum dictamnus*) was a symbol of love and peace. The Greeks believed that by anointing themselves with marjoram before bed they would dream of their future spouses. They also planted marjoram on graves to comfort the dead and provide eternal peace.

Greek students wore braids of rosemary (*Rosemarinus officinalis*) around their necks or in their hair because they believed it would improve their memory when taking written tests. Romans who were overly fond of food would chew stalks of fennel (*Foeniculum vulgare*) because they believed it would control obesity. Both the Greeks and Romans used thyme (*Thymus* spp.) in massage oils, bath oils, perfumes and incense and Roman soldiers would bathe in water scented with thyme for good luck and honour before they went into battle.

According to written records, the Romans ate vegetables and herbs with almost every meal. A light lunch, or *prandium*, often included olives, nuts and figs. Dinner, or *cena*, was a more elaborate affair, especially for wealthy Romans. The main course was inevitably meat, but it was accompanied by vegetables such as carrots, parsnips, celery and peas, and seasoned with dill, coriander, chervil and even opium. Wild fruits such as blackberries, strawberries and crabapples were served alongside cultivated fruits such as plums, grapes, medlars and mulberries.

The Romans grew many of their herbs using gardening techniques developed by the Greeks, Persians, Egyptians and Mesopotamians, but the enclosed courtyard villa gardens they designed were uniquely Roman. In these villa courtyards, raised flower beds were arranged symmetrically alongside herb beds of dill, fennel, bay, rosemary, myrtle and parsley, all interspersed with topiaries, trees, canals, fountains and statues collected from Greece. Even in the cities, Roman houses were designed with garden rooms that were open to the sky. Their orderly rows of herbs and flowers extended to the walls, which were painted with complementary scenes of plant rows extending into the distance to give the impression of a larger villa garden.

Greek and Roman Medicine

Herbs played a prominent role in ancient Greek and Roman medicine. Hippocrates (470–410 B.C.E.), author of the Hippocratic Oath and described by many as the father of modern medicine, was among the first in

Monk gardening at the Great Meteoron monastery in Thessaly, Greece. It was founded around 1340 by the scholar monk of Mount Athos, Saint Athanasios Meteorites.

the Western world to reject the idea that diseases were caused by magic, hexes or the gods. He offered rational explanations, and believed the body should be treated as a whole, considering all aspects of life as potential contributors to both sickness and health. Hippocrates assigned health effects to the different herbs used in food, categorizing them as hot, cold, dry or damp. His natural healing process included a balance of these herb types, along with exercise and fresh air. He did not prescribe, however, as he believed that the body would always re-balance itself over time.

Like most Europeans throughout history, the Greeks and Romans drew much of their herbal knowledge from other civilizations, such as Egypt, Assyria, Persia and India. The first of the Greek philosophers and doctors to compile this collected learning was Theophrastus (372–287 B.C.E.). As inheritor of the library of Aristotle and an avid student of the many regions conquered by Alexander the Great, Theophrastus may have known more about the world's botany than any man before him. His two surviving works, *Historia Plantarum* (*The History of Plants*) and *De Causis Planatarum* (*The Growth of Plants*), described the structure, growth, habitat, cultivation and medicinal uses of hundreds of herbs, and became the basis of all botanical understanding for centuries to come.

In 77 C.E., the Roman natural historian, Pliny the Elder (23–79 C.E.), expanded on Theophrastus' work in his thirty-seven volume *Naturalis Historiae* (*Natural History*). Nearly half the volumes describe the many uses of plants, from olive oil production to spinning flax, and several explain in detail the herbal treatment of diseases and various drugs obtained from herbs. Pliny was the first to categorize herbal drugs according to the type of plant from which they were derived. For example, one volume covered drugs derived from garden plants such as garlic and cabbage, another wild plants such as aconite and wormwood, and another forest trees such as cork and juniper.

In the first century C.E., Greek writer Dioscorides (ca. 40–90 C.E.) joined the pantheon of iconic European herbalists. Dioscorides travelled extensively around the Mediterranean with the Roman legions studying local herbs and their uses between battles. The result of his research was the first true herbal, *De Materia Medica*, which described nearly 600 medicinal plants and prescribed close to 5,000 cures, including the use of parsley as a diuretic, fennel to promote the flow of mother's milk, and white horehound with honey, used as an expectorant. The *De Materia Medica* became the chief reference (in most cases, the only reference) of herbalists from Italy to Scandanavia, and from Britain to Russia.

Less than a century later, the great Greek physician Galen (130–200 C.E.) promoted the idea of a system of four humours – blood, phlegm, black bile and yellow bile – similar to the Ayurvedic system in India. A higher or lower level of any one of these humours not only affected a person's health, but his personality and mood as well. Galen wrote more than 500 treatises on medicine, only one of which has survived to this day – a recipe book of 130 herbal antidotes and medicines, each designed to bring one or more of the humours back into balance. Like the writings of Dioscorides, Galen's theories of humours and herbal healing were followed by practitioners throughout Europe for the following 1,600 years.

THE MIDDLE AGES

In Europe, the Middle Ages were a time of few advancements and many superstitions in herb lore. In an era that witnessed Druid rituals and the practice of witchcraft, herbs played a major role in daily life, even if their uses were often informed by fantasy and imagination rather than scientific experimentation. Nearly every tree, bush or root in the forest was believed to have some sort of magical power. For instance, the elder tree (*Sambucus nigra*) was considered sacred in Germany and Denmark, particularly among gypsies who believed that if a cradle was made from its wood, the Hylde Moer, or Elder Mother, would strangle the baby in revenge. Pagan fertility rituals in Britain coincided with the annual first bloom of hawthorn, or may (*Crataegus laevigata*). On May Day, celebrants would go a-maying, which is to say they would crown a May Queen with wreaths of hawthorn in the hope that a bountiful harvest would follow.

The folklore surrounding mistletoe (*Viscum album*) was particularly colourful. Druids in Britain and Gaul (France) carried branches of mistletoe to celebrate the new year, and since mistletoe could be cut only during a certain phase of the moon and with a sacred golden knife, these branches were known as golden boughs. Germans thought that mistletoe gave people the power to see ghosts. The Norse believed the plant was banished to the treetops because a Norse god had been killed by a mistletoe dart. People meeting under a mistletoe branch would be required to kiss in order to compensate for the death of the god.

The powers of mandrake (*Mandragora officinarum*) were thought to be even more fantastic. European practitioners of witchcraft believed that mandrake would allow them to fly; in fact, when the plant is rubbed against the skin, or crushed and inhaled, it does have an intoxicating effect that may evoke a feeling of flying. The mandrake root resembles a human figure, so many believed it would make a shrieking sound when pulled out of the ground. They feared that anyone who heard the shriek would die instantly, so they often harvested the plant by tying a dog to it, then calling to the dog from a safe distance.

For centuries throughout Europe, the prevailing belief that herbs had magical powers caused people to wear them around their necks as amulets to ward off evil spells (the four-leaf clover, for instance), to mix them into ointments that provided protection against baldness and sunburn, to hang them from doorways as charms to protect cattle or cure madness, and to combine them with ale, milk, vinegar or honey, creating powerful potions.

Medieval Europeans also used herbs liberally in their daily diets, as the ancient Greeks and Romans had before them. The use of spices was more than a matter of livening up dull food. In the Middle Ages, Europeans had very little access to fresh vegetables, no sugar, coffee or chocolate for flavouring, and no refrigeration for preserving weeks-old meat; so spices were needed to make such fare palatable, to mask repulsive odours and flavours, and even to prevent the diner from getting sick.

Local people usually gathered herbs such as horseradish, parsley and fennel from nearby fields and forests, but those with more social status and larger incomes relied on intrepid explorers to import exotic spices from the Far East. The kings and gentry of Europe often ate meals and drank wines seasoned with cinnamon, pepper and ginger grown continents away.

Medieval Europeans also grew spectacular gardens of their own. While herbal medicine and scientific knowledge advanced very little over the course of 1,000 years, the art of gardening went through several phases. After the fall of the Roman Empire, most of the gardening in Europe took place within the walls of monasteries. In fact, gardening was considered a devout duty for monks; so much so that, by the time the Benedictine order was founded in Italy in 540 C.E., gardening had become second in importance, behind only prayer, in the monastic hierarchy. For the European fiefdoms, monasteries acted as cottage industries, growing fruits and herbs for food and flavouring, for medicine and incense, for dyeing clothes, and for blending with ale and wine.

The first person to record the monastic theories of gardening was Walahfrid Strabo (870–840 C.E.), the abbot of Reichenau in Switzerland. His poem "Hortulus" ("The Little Garden") was an ode to his love of the labour of gardening, as well as an elaborate instruction manual.

St John's Wort (Hypericum perforatum) *has been used for centuries as a sedative and a balm for wounds, burns, and insect bites as well as a treatment for mental disorders, nerve pain and malaria.*

He explained how to grow plants in raised beds just as the Romans had 1,000 years earlier, and offered planting directions for dozens of plants, such as sage, melon, fennel, mint and wormwood.

Saint Hildegard (1098–1179 C.E.), the Abbess of Bingen, followed suit with four treatises on medicinal herbs. She wrote of fragrant herbs grown in the abbey's garden, which were turned into perfumes and medicinal concoctions such as lavender water, aqua mirabilis (miracle water), Benedictine liqueur and the highly prized Carmelite water. By the 13th century, products such as Carmelite water, a fragrance and complexion aid made from lemon balm, melissa, nutmeg, coriander and angelica root, had prompted many wealthy European houses to seek instruction from monks and nuns on how to grow gardens of their own. These ranged from simple household gardens stocked with herbs for the kitchen and flowers for the table to elaborate pleasure gardens with a centre lawn

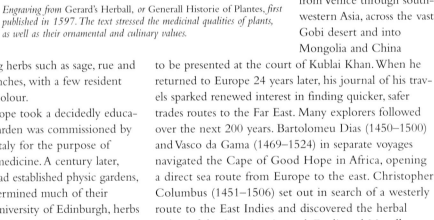

Engraving from Gerard's Herball, *or* Generall Historie of Plantes, *first published in 1597. The text stressed the medicinal qualities of plants, as well as their ornamental and culinary values.*

surrounded by sweet smelling herbs such as sage, rue and basil, plus shade trees and benches, with a few resident peacocks adding a splash of colour.

In 1545, gardening in Europe took a decidedly educational turn: the first physic garden was commissioned by the University of Padua in Italy for the purpose of teaching botany and herbal medicine. A century later, universities all over Europe had established physic gardens, and how they were used determined much of their design; for example, at the University of Edinburgh, herbs were arranged by rows in alphabetical order. The educational value of physic gardens grew as explorers carried new plant species back to Europe from all over the world, and as scientists grew ever hungrier for more knowledge about how herbs could be used.

The Global Spice Race

Throughout history, Europeans have travelled the world searching for new trade goods and establishing better trade routes. For centuries, herbs and spices have been among the most valuable commodities, and the ancient Greeks and Romans were the first Europeans to seek them out. Since the seas were considered treacherous and unpredictable, the majority of trade with the Far East took place over land, until in 40 C.E., a Greek merchant named Hippalus made a discovery about the monsoon patterns over the Indian Ocean. Hippalus realized that a ship leaving Egypt could reach India or the Indonesian Spice Islands faster with the prevailing southwesterly winds that blow in the summer months, and return more easily on the northeastly winds of the winter. Using this knowledge, a major expedition could be completed in just one year. The Romans took particular advantage of this insight, importing tonnes of pepper, cinnamon, cloves and nutmeg and decreasing their reliance on the overland trade routes through Persia.

Few new trade routes were discovered until the 13th century, when Marco Polo (1254–1324) travelled from Venice through southwestern Asia, across the vast Gobi desert and into Mongolia and China to be presented at the court of Kublai Khan. When he returned to Europe 24 years later, his journal of his travels sparked renewed interest in finding quicker, safer trades routes to the Far East. Many explorers followed over the next 200 years. Bartolomeu Dias (1450–1500) and Vasco da Gama (1469–1524) in separate voyages navigated the Cape of Good Hope in Africa, opening a direct sea route from Europe to the east. Christopher Columbus (1451–1506) set out in search of a westerly route to the East Indies and discovered the herbal riches of the Americas instead. Ferdinand Magellan (1480–1521) circumnavigated the globe and discovered the Philippine Islands, a discovery that led to the establishment of Manilla as one of the world's great spice trading capitals.

Age of Herbals

The advances in gardening in 16th-century Europe reflected a quantum leap in herbal knowledge, and led to the publication of several new and interesting European herbals. In previous centuries, herbals for the common people were typically copied by hand from ancient Greek or Roman works, and repeated translations over the years led to a multitude of errors. However, after the invention of printing in 1440, authors could make more accurate descriptions and detailed illustrations of herbs available to the public. This brought renewed interest in the study of botany and the uses of herbs.

The power of accurately printed botanical illustrations was demonstrated by Leonhard Fuchs (1501–1566) of Germany in his works, *Neue Krueterbuch* (1543) and *De Historia Stirpium* (1545). A first in herbal publishing, these contained more than 500 large, clear, woodcut prints of plant specimens with little or no text. These illustrations became extremely popular and were widely copied throughout Europe. As a doctor and professor of medicine, Fuchs felt compelled to create accurate depictions of medicinal herbs in large part because he witnessed a great deal of ignorance among the general public, and even among his fellow physicians. His writing, however, brought little new information to light, as, like most European authors before him, he simply rehashed the herbal remedies of Theophrastus and Dioscorides.

While Fuchs borrowed from the works of the ancient Romans, a charismatic Swiss physician and alchemist who called himself Philippus Aureolus Paracelsus (1493–1541) built on them. He travelled throughout Europe, Egypt and the Middle East researching folk remedies, and considered himself a practical man who spoke for the common people. He rejected Latin and wrote most of his books in German. He also rejected Galen's theory of four humours, which had been practised and mandated by the medical establishment for nearly 1,500 years. Paracelsus was the first European to promote the idea of evidence-based medicine. He believed that one could identify the active ingredient in each substance, be it animal, vegetable or mineral, then extract it, purify it and prescribe in the correct dose to heal the sick. This approach lead to the development of new herbal treatments – he dissolved opium in alcohol to produce laudanum, a highly effective painkiller – and the debunking of current one – he demonstrated that guaiac, *Guaicum officinale*, imported from the West Indies was not an effective treatment for syphilis, as most Europeans believed, but that instead small doses of toxic mercury were very effective.

Paracelsus also believed that each and every plant was marked by God with a distinctive sign. This sign was both the key to unlocking the active ingredient inside and a clear indicator of God's purpose for the plant. This theory was not entirely new, but it did take on a new prominence in the world of herbalists when Jacob Boehme (1575–1624) codified it in *Signatura Rerum* (*The Signature of All Things*). This Doctrine of Signatures was extremely popular with the public because it made herbal remedies more identifiable and accessible to everyone. The spotted leaves of lung wort (*Mertensia* spp.), for example, were shaped vaguely like lungs, so clearly, the plant could be used to treat lung ailments. Goldenrod (*Solidago* spp.) was yellow, so it must be an effective treatment for jaundice. Unfortunately, these simplistic "signatures" rarely corresponded with the actual medicinal value of their plants, and hundreds of new herbal myths grew without thorough scientific testing.

In the later part of the 16th century, English herbalists began to make their mark with books that added to both the fact and fiction of herbal knowledge. John Gerard (1564–1637) published his *Generall Historie of Plantes* in 1597, but it was really a cribbed translation of an earlier Belgian herbalist's work. It was supplemented by Gerard's personal observations, some quite accurate and others based more on popular beliefs of the time. Gerard's book painstakingly described the proper care and use for thousands of herbs, including many exotics given to him by travelling friends. In addition to advocating aromatherapy and the absorption of herbal oils through the skin, he believed in the power of herbal tonics to soothe the mind and spirit. Among his recommended herbal treatments were peony seeds in wine, taken to ward off nightmares, and concoctions made from rosemary to comfort the brain.

In 1640, another English herbalist,

Foxglove (Digitalis purpurea). *Though also known as Witches' Glove and Dead Man's Bells, it is a source of digitalis, which is prescribed to strengthen and regulate the heart.*

❧ MAJOR HERBS OF EUROPE ❧

NAME OF HERB	USE
Dandelion (*Taracum offinale*)	Strong diuretic
Deadly nightshade (*Atropa belladonna*)	Poison and sedative
Hops (*Humulus lupulus*)	Key flavouring ingredient in beer
Horse chestnut (*Aesculus hippocastanum*)	Shampoo ingredient
Lavender (*Lavendula spp.*)	Perfumes and aromatherapy
Marigold (*Calendula officinalis*)	Beautiful garden flower, flowers and seeds are edible
Oregano (*Origanum spp.*)	Flavour in Italian and Greek cuisine
Saffron (*Crocus sativus*)	Expensive culinary herb
Sage (*Salvia officinalus*)	Popular culinary herb, aids digestion
Yellow gentian (*Gentiana lutea*)	Soothes gastrointestinal disorders

John Parkinson (1567–1650) published a far more ambitious work. The *Theatrum Botanicum* consisted of 1,800 pages covering more than 3,800 plants drawn from the four corners of the earth. Unlike his predecessors, Parkinson combined horticulture, botany, pharmacy and history in one volume. He made the first serious attempt to classify plants into similar groups, which he called "tribes". Among his fascinating tribe descriptions are "hot and sharpe biting plants", "strange and outlandish plants", and "venomous sleepy and hurtfull plants and their counter poisons".

The most successful English herbalist was Nicholas Culpeper (1616–1654). First, he translated the *London Pharmacopoeia* from Latin to English and published it for the masses as the *Physicall Directory*. In effect, this put the herbal medical knowledge, previously accessible only to doctors, into the hands of the apothecaries who, at the time, did most of the prescribing. This made Culpeper popular with members of the general public, but decidedly less so with the medical establishment.

In another book, *The English Physician* (also called *The Complete Herbal*), published in 1651, Culpeper, a devoted astrologer, ascribed a celestial cause to every illness, with a corresponding treatment based on the planetary aspect of every plant. He believed that the planet Venus, for example, governed the sexual organs, and that emollients made from heavily scented Venusian plants such as the

Damascus rose or apple blossom could be used to create a desired sexual effect. Jupiter, decreed Culpeper, ruled the liver, spleen and kidney, so plants that astrologers associated with Jupiter, such as chestnut and apricot, could be used to treat problems with these organs.

Culpeper's books and theories were soon eclipsed by the more rigorous science of his contemporaries. In 1646, Sir Thomas Browne fired the first shot across the bow of sensationalist herbals with a book called *Vulgar Error*, and the second in 1658 with *Pseudodoxia Epidemica*. As explorers brought home new plants from newly discovered continents, and physic gardens appeared in more and more universities, European physicians, scientists and pharmacologists made concentrated efforts to unlock the true medicinal value of all herbs, familiar and new.

SCIENCE AND CROSS-POLLENIZATION

In the 18th century, colonists travelling to the New World carried with them European plants, herbal books and gardening styles. In return, traders carried back New World herbs such as tobacco, tomatoes and corn. The European public quickly found domestic uses for these plants, while the scientific community explored the medicinal possibilities of herbs such as Jesuits' bark (*Cinchona pubescens*), the source of anti-malarial quinine and sassafras (*Sassafras albidum*), which was believed at the time to cure venereal diseases.

In Europe, as the Age of Reason led to the Industrial Revolution, scientists were becoming ever more disciplined in their approach to herbal medicine. They learned how to distill the active ingredients in plants and, eventually, they were able to chemically synthesize beneficial molecules and oils. The science of botany continued to develop, with writers and artists creating highly accurate textbooks on the plant world that supplanted the sometimes highly subjective herbals.

In gardening, the formal gardens of the French chateaux gave way to a deliberately informal approach. Symmetry was discarded in favour of the creation of natural landscapes. Yet, simple cottage and kitchen gardens never went out of style. In urban centres, the limitations of space led to the invention of the window-box, and more and more people moved their plants indoors to live in pots. Even as scientific advances removed the people of Europe further from nature, they still found ways to connect with the feel, smell and taste of their favourite herbs.

This artistic rendering shows the interior view of an Arabic apothecary shop and also features miniatures depicting heliotherapy and balneology, a cupping procedure, bloodletting and surgery on a patient's chest.

African market selling tomatoes and onions. Tomatoes and other plants related to nightshade (Atropa belladonna LINN.) contain solanine, a compound once used to treat epilepsy.

AFRICA

Africa hosts as many herb varieties as it has climates: from the culinary herbs of the fertile Mediterranean coast, to the cosmetic herbs of the northeastern regions, to the medicinal plants found in the desert oases, dry savannas, mountainous woodlands and lush rainforests of central and southern parts of the continent.

ANCIENT EGYPT

The history of herb use in Africa begins in ancient Egypt, where pharaohs and commoners alike used herbal medicines extensively. Some of the world's earliest known herb gardens were planted nearly 4,000 years ago in Egypt, often near temples where certain herbs and flowers were needed on a daily basis for worship. One such flower, the water lily or lotus (*Nymphaea lotus*), was considered sacred, and every part of the lotus plant was used in Egyptian art, food and medicine. Another very important herb, garlic (*Allium sativum*), was found in the tomb of Tutankhamun (1370–1352 B.C.E.), and was thought to possess magical powers. If Egyptians took a solemn oath, they swore on clove of garlic, and garlic was eaten by slaves as they built the great pyramids at Giza because it was believed that it would endow the workers with strength and endurance. Frankincense (*Boswellia sacra*) and myrrh (*Commiphora myrrha*) were important in Egyptian rituals. Reliefs in the tomb of Queen Hatshepsut (1512–1482 B.C.E.) in Luxor show frankincense trees growing in pots. Myrrh was believed to cure cancer, leprosy and syphilis, and was used in embalming.

Believing that they could keep alive the soul of the dead by preserving the bodies of their dead, the Egyptians evolved the process of embalming and mummification. They first removed the brain and all internal organs except for the heart, which was believed to be essential to the survival of the soul. The body cavities were then cleansed with frankincense, myrrh and palm wine. Moisture was removed with natron salt, and the cavities packed with linens, salt, muslin packets of wood shavings and spices such as cinnamon, chamomile, cassia, anise, marjoram and cumin. The eyes were replaced with glass or gems, the skin was painted to give it a lifelike hue, and the body was rubbed with a mixture of five oils: frankincense, myrrh, lotus, palm and cedar. Finally, the body was wrapped in linen and sealed with natural resin. The process took about seventy days.

The earliest surviving scrolls are dated to 2000 B.C.E., but the Egyptians were administering herbal treatments long before that. The most valuable source of herbal information is a remarkable papyrus dated to 1550 B.C.E. and looted from a tomb of the 18th dynasty. Bought by the German Egyptologist Georg Ebers (1837–1898 C.E.), the Ebers papyrus is a complete, undamaged scroll about 65 ft (20 m) long containing 3,000 lines of Hieratic text. It compiles treatments, diagnoses, prescriptions and even surgical techniques dating back to the first Egyptian dynasty, or around 3400 B.C.E. It lists 811 medicinal drugs and their presumed effects, including poppies to induce sleep, aloe to treat excess mucus and crocus as a diuretic. It also describes the healing effects of anise, mustard, linseed, peppermint, watermelon, fenugreek, caraway, wormwood, elderberry, fig, nasturtium, flax, and of course, garlic. These herbs are prescribed in complex and carefully measured recipes, and recommended for administration as ointments, infusions, pills, gargles, snuffs, poultices, suppositories and enemas.

Perfumes and Cosmetics in Ancient Egypt

Wall paintings show that most Egyptians wore a heavy black makeup called kohl from childhood. Kohl was a fairly toxic mixture of galena (lead sulphate), powdered malachite, frankincense, gum and goosefat. It was placed in cow dung and burned, then pounded in a mortar with milk and rainwater, decanted, and finally dried and formed into tablets or eye pencils. These valuable beauty products were kept in ceremonial jars, many of which have been found buried in tombs with the kohl still inside.

The Egyptians used the dried powdered leaves of henna (*Lawsonia inermis*) to dye their nails, palms, soles, fingertips and moustaches a rich orange-red colour. Mixed with indigo, henna was used as early as 3200 B.C.E. to dye hair, as well as the manes and tails of horses. Henna tattoos were applied to the chests, shoulders, arms and thighs of exotic dancers, musicians and servants.

Beauty creams were commonly used by ancient Egyptians. These included depilatories made of gum, cucumber and fig juice; cleansing lotions of oil and lime, and hair tonics of lettuce, fir oil and juniper berries. Daily applications of wrinkle creams were made from frankincense gum, the oil of the moringa tree and fermented cyperus grass. Papyrus scrolls dating from 2700 B.C.E. describe fragrant herbs, oils, perfumes and incense being used in ceremonies and as protective skin salves.

Perfumes were commonly made from frankincense and myrrh, combined with animal fats and oils, mixed into gum resins, and burned as incense or applied liberally as ointments. Other popular scents included almond, sesame, olive, balanos oil and lily oil made from the petals of 2,000 lilies mixed with cardamom, cinnamon and sweet flag. One powerful fragrance, called kyphi, was made from pistachio resin, cinnamon, frankincense, myrrh, spikenard, henna and calamus. Kyphi was burned at sunset to honour the sun god Ra, and used as an aromatic oil to eliminate sorrow and anxiety and increase the vividness of dreams. Ancient Egyptians rubbed fragrant gums and creams under their arms and between their legs, and some made pomades of spikenard into "bitcones," and wore them on their heads, where they gradually melted down over their hair and bodies as the day progressed.

NORTH AFRICA

The history of North Africa is one of conquest, survival and lucrative trade. The indigenous people of the areas now called Libya, Tunisia, Algeria and Morocco were the Berbers. The first of the invaders of this region were the Phoenicians, who established the city of Carthage in present-day Tunisia. Though the Berbers eventually gained control of Carthage, it finally succumbed to Roman rule in 24 C.E. The Berbers then moved southwards and

westwards, establishing important trading posts throughout most of North Africa, particularly in today's Morocco, which became an important stop for spice trading ships travelling to and from Europe.

Many of the foods and spices now associated with Moroccan food came from the influence of Islamic Arabs, who conquered the region in the 7th century. In the centuries that followed, most of the countries of Europe battled for control of Morocco, a fight finally won by France in 1912. Morocco gained its independence in 1956, inheriting a population that was 80 percent Berber, with heavy Arabic, Spanish and French influences.

Some of the crops grown in Morocco over the last thousand years were almonds, dates, walnuts, chestnuts, prickly pear, cherries, oranges, lemons, apricots, olives and mint. Spices imported and incorporated into the region's food include paprika, black pepper, nutmeg, turmeric, ginger, cinnamon, cumin, cloves and saffron. Proprietors of spice shops developed secret mixtures known as *ras el hanout* ("head of the shop"), which contained as many as 100 carefully blended spices. While there are subtle variations in cuisine across North Africa today – Tunisian foods contain more fiery spices than those of Morocco – the blended influence of indigenous, Middle Eastern and European peoples have created a cohesive herbal tradition that stands on its own.

WEST, CENTRAL AND EAST AFRICA

In many areas of Africa, local systems of herbal medicine began as religious rituals, such as holy men drinking herbal tonics to better commune with a god or gods. Over time, religious leaders transformed themselves into tribal healers, harvesting herbs, tree bark, roots and berries to cure a variety of common ills and combat diseases such as malaria and yellow fever.

Almond
Prunus dulcis

In the Yoruba religion, which dates back 4,000 years, medicinal plants and herbs, called *ewe*, were believed to possess strong spiritual powers. Cemeteries, for example, were the territory of Oya Orisha, the goddess of change, so ewe harvested there was thought to possess her ability to bring about violent but necessary transformations. Most of the herbs used in Yorubic medicine, including skullcap, kola nut, burdock, squawvine, motherwort, chickweed, saw palmetto and hibiscus, were steeped and prepared as teas,

❧ MAJOR HERBS OF AFRICA ❧

NAME OF HERB	USE
Aloe (*Aloe vera*)	Skin protection and healing agent
Buchu (*Agathosma spp.*)	Herbal tea and insect repellent
Castor bean (*Ricinus communis*)	Used to make both paint and paper
Devil's claw (*Harpagophytum procumbens*)	Arthritis treatment
Iboza (*Tetradenia riparia*)	Fever reduction
Johimbe (*Pausinystalia johimbe*)	Aphrodisiac
Lotus (*Nymphaea lotus*)	Sacred flower
Milk bush (*Euphorbia tirucallii*)	Wart remover
Rooibos (*Aspalathus linearis*)	Caffeine-free tea substitute
Wormwood (*Artemisia afra*)	Bronchitis remedy

and some administered as enemas. A recipe for medicinal soup, or *ose*, is a mixture of water, oil, salt, pepper and cooked melon and locust seeds.

In much of Central Africa, the history of herb use varied depending on the local flora and the traditions of individual tribes. Natives of Cameroon, Gabon and the Congo have long believed that the bark of the tall evergreen yohimbe (*Pausinystalia yohimbe*) could cure coughs, fevers and leprosy. The long-standing trade of kola nuts (*Kola vera*) has its genesis in the belief that chewing kola before each meal aids digestion and sustains strength. In Ethiopia and Somalia, traditional herbal medicine has been practised for nearly 2,000 years, with recipes being passed down from healer to healer by word of mouth because of the belief that a herb would lose its medicinal power if a patient knew its name. For centuries, Ethiopian healers have prescribed ground twigs and buds of African pencil cedar (*Juniperus procera*) to treat stomach worms; flax seed (*Linum usitatissimum*) as a laxative and to speed the healing of deep wounds; and bosoke (*Kalanchoe* spp.) to treat boils, malignant wounds and gonorrhoea.

Other tribes had traditional uses for herbs. Slukari hunters in the Congo rubbed the gel of aloe over their bodies to mask their scent from prey. The algum tree of Somalia, probably a type of sandalwood, was prized for its ability to produce fragrant incense. The Masai people of eastern Africa have always supplemented their staple foods of beef, milk and yogurt with wild weeds, tree bark and tree gums that may help counterbalance their cholesterol-rich diet. Traditionally, cassava tubers (*Manihot esculenta*) have been the primary food of millions of people in Uganda. In times of famine when grain crops failed, Ethiopians routinely gathered and ate the wild weed *Ensete ventricosum* in order to survive.

SOUTH AFRICA

In 1652, an outpost of the Dutch East India Company was established at the Cape of Good Hope. Initially, the purpose was to re-supply company ships travelling between Europe and the East Asian Spice ports, but soon, a full Dutch colony was established there. As colonists planted kitchen gardens for their own use in the early 1700s, they began to learn more about the local herbs. Probably by observing local tribes such as the KhoiSan, the Dutch discovered that honeybush (*Cyclopia* spp.) was a passable substitute for tea. Honeybush tea also proved to be an effective treatment for coughs and other respiratory conditions, so before long it became another profitable export for the Dutch East India Company. The popular herb rooibos (*Aspalathus linearis*), long used by tribes as a mild sedative and to relieve colic in babies, gained worldwide acceptance as another tea substitute. Blended with cinammon, cardamom and nutmeg, rooibos creates a full-bodied, caffeine-free red tea filled with antioxidants.

Through the centuries, practitioners have gone by a variety of names: *inyanga* or herbalist; *sangoma* or diviner; and, after the arrival of the Dutch, *bossiedokter*. These healers all collected herbs from the wild, or "bush". Some of the more popular herbs in traditional South African medicine were devil's claw (*Harpagophytum procumbens*), used for arthritis and gastrointestinal disorders; pepper-bark (*Warburgia Salutaris*), used for sinusitis and disorders of the lungs; African wormwood (*Artimesia afra*), used for measles and malaria; and wild willow (*Salix mucronata*), used for rheumatism and fevers.

Some 70 percent of native South Africans still regularly consult herbal healers, and large quantities of herbs collected from the wild are still prescribed and sold. Even newly introduced diseases have generated a herbal treatment. Today, the South African healthcare community uses the African potato (*Hypoxis hemerocallidea*) as an immunostimulant for HIV/AIDS patients. It is not its

At the "pharmacy" with an inyanga, or South African herbalist. Devil's claw (Harpagophytum procumbens), *an analgesic and anti-inflammatory, is among the most common remedies he provides.*

first medical role – for centuries, Zulu healers have used it to treat such varied conditions as urinary tract infections, cardiac disorders, tumours and nervous disorders.

THE AMERICAS

Isolated from the rest of the world's landmass for millions of years, the Americas developed a fascinating flora and fauna all of their own. People probably first took advantage of these new plants and herbs about 12,000 years ago when they migrated to the western hemisphere over the Bering land bridge. In the millennia that followed, they learned the many uses of plants that grew around them. The Navajo Indians, for example, used the desert plants of present-day Arizona in religious ceremonies. Mayan Indians incorporated the richness of the Mexican rainforest into daily spiritual ritual. Incas created medicines from the high-altitude herbs of the Peruvian mountains, and each culture created its own herb lore.

NORTH AMERICA

Many of the first North American inhabitants became expert botanists and developed sophisticated philosophies of herbal medicine, represented most clearly by the medicine wheel. On the wheel, the four cardinal directions, north, south, east and west, represent the proper balance of bodily energies, an idea that is remarkably similar to Chinese, Indian and Greek herbalism. In a Native American herb wheel, the directions are represented by different animal totems, personality types, colours, and herbal medicines. Shamans used these symbols to travel spiritually through the cosmos searching for the souls of the sick and seeking spirit guides to assist in their healing.

To become a shaman, individuals were required to learn plant identification, preparation and medicinal use, patient diagnosis, and tribal rituals and songs. Sometimes they underwent a spiritual awakening, called a vision quest, which required them to spend a period of time alone in the wilderness. Initiated shamans were expert healers who were well-versed in the medicinal power of their region's native herbs. Navajo shamans used a tea prepared from Fendler's bladderpod (*Lesquerella fendleri*). The Meskwaki tribe of Minnesota ground the flowers of goldenrod (*Solidago rigida*) into a lotion and applied it to bee stings. Plains Indian tribes applied purple coneflower (*Echinacea purpurea*) to any insect or animal bites. Cherokees covered their bodies with an insect-repellent made of a mixture of pounded goldenseal roots (*Hydrastis canadensis*) and bear fat. Many tribes had natural treatments for more serious ailments as well. The Winnebago and Dakota peoples ate or smoked the roots of skunk cabbage (*Simplocarpus foetidus*) to remove excess phlegm produced by asthma, whooping cough, bronchitis and hay fever. Many Native American Indians used dandelion (*Taraxum officinale*) as a tonic for problems ranging from liver spots and kidney pain to sore throats and indigestion. The tubers of wild yam (*Dioscorea villosa*) were a food staple for many tribes. The root of the yam was also used by shamans to restore lost libido and relieve pain specific to women.

The process of childbirth was aided by many natural remedies. Partridgeberry tea (*Mitchella repens*) was used by Cherokee women to speeds labour. Other tribes used warm infusions of blue cohosh (*Caulophyllum thalictroides*) to produce the same effect. The broom snakeweed plant (*Gutierrezia sarothrae*) was used by Navajos to make a tea to promote the expulsion of the placenta. Smooth upland sumac (*Rhus glabra*) was boiled and applied as an external wash by the Omahas to stop excess bleeding after birth. The Alabama and Koasati tribes made a tea of cotton roots (*Gossypium herbaceum*) to alleviate the pain of labour.

There were also natural methods for preventing pregnancy. Teas made of ragged leaf bahia (*Bahia dissecta*) or dogbane (*Apocynum cannabinum*) were consumed as a form of contraception by many tribes. Hopi women drank a tea of Indian paintbrush (*Castilleja mutis*) to dry up their menstrual flow. Mendocino tribes drank an American mistletoe tea (*Phoradendron flavescens*) to induce abortion, and in the Shoshoni tribe of Nevada, women drank cold water infusions of stoneseed roots (*Lithospermum ruderale*) in a quest for permanent sterility.

Herbs were used by Native Americans in spiritual ceremonies. One of the most common was that carried out in sweat lodges which were special huts or teepees. The ceremony allowed tribesmen and women to heighten their spiritual consciousness, mentally prepare for important events like war or a hunt, and physically "sweat out" toxins or illness. To create a sauna-like atmosphere inside, rocks were heated on fires, then placed in a depression in the middle of the lodge floor. Water was poured onto the rocks, often mixed with healing herbs such as cedar (*Thuja plicata*), sage (*Salvia officinalis*) and sweetgrass (*Muhlenbergia filipes*), to create steam. Participants would sit inside for hours on freshly cut flat cedar bows, smoking a ceremonial pipe filled with exactly four pinches of tobacco.

Another herb-based ritual was the peyote ceremony, first documented in 1560 but practised by Plains Indians such as the Osage, Ute, Navajo and Mescalero Apache tribes for centuries before that. The ceremony centred around the consumption of dried brown pieces of the hallucinatory peyote cactus (*Lophophora williamsii*), or

Native American Lakota shamansk, or healers, carried their ritual herbs and pipes in a wolf skin medicine bundle.

wysoccan, which was given to adolescent boys transitioning into manhood. It was meant to induce memory loss so that they would not cling to childish thoughts.

Tribes who settled in the far northern regions of present-day Canada and Alaska used herbal teas to provide essential vitamins during long winters when no crops could be grown. The Anishnaabeg people of Ontario drank tea made from dried leaves, flowers and twigs of chokeberry, wintergreen, pine, slippery elm, mint, clover and goldenrod. Many natives of the north drank swamp tea, also known as Labrador tea (*Ledum glandulosum*). This plant grew year-round, even in cold wet conditions. Rich in caffeine and tannins, it provided them with a coffee-like drink to help ward off the cold.

The Arrival of Europeans

When the first Europeans set foot in North America in the early 1500s, they began to exchange herbs and knowledge of their uses with Native Americans. They introduced natives to thyme, caraway, basil, rosemary, chamomile, liquorice and plantain, also known as "white man's foot" by the natives because it seemed to appear wherever the settlers lived. In return, the Indians offered crop plants such as potatoes, tomatoes and tobacco, as well as medicinal plants such as American ginseng, goldenseal, sassafras, purple coneflower, pleurisy root and witch hazel. Early French explorers noted the prominence of tribal shamans, and called them "medicine men". The medicine men taught colonists how to heal wounds and diseases, and were often better educated in safe childbirth practices, surgical procedures and the herbal treatment of infections.

mescal buttons. Several participants sat around a fire and an altar inside a teepee smoking pipes, then everyone was invited to speak about an illness or problem. Next, sprigs of sagebrush were rubbed between the hands and over the limbs and chest to purify the body. Finally, each person chewed four buttons of peyote, then sat silently in prayer as plant-induced visions overtook them.

Mind-altering plants played a role in many ceremonies. Thorn apple seeds (*Datura stramonium*) were a powerful narcotic used in divination and prophecy. The Algonquins used the seeds to create a mixture called

The ceremonies that occured in native American sweat lodges were often meant to allow tribesmen and women to "sweat out" illness. Water to which herbs were added were poured over hot rocks, which in turn created a healing steam.

Soon, the bounty of botanicals led to the publication of New World herbal texts. In 1565, a Spanish doctor, Nicolas Monardes (1493–1588), published the first-ever illustrations of tobacco, coca, sunflowers and sarsparilla in a herbal translated as *Joyfull Newes Out of the Newe Found Worlde*. More than a century later, Englishman John Josselyn (1610–1675) published *New-England's Rarities Discovered in 1672*. Following Josselyn's guidelines, the colonists were able to grow a wide variety of herbs for preparing sallets (salads of greens sometimes mixed with bacon fat) and potages (hearty stews made of meat, poultry, game and fruit), such as sorrel, burnet, and purslane; herbs for general flavouring, such as chervil, mint, fennel, dill and savory; and herbs for dyeing clothes, such as saffron, woad, alkanet and calendula.

Exploration and Industrialization

In the early 1700s, cash crops of tobacco, cotton, sassafras and ginseng were grown on the abundant farmlands of North America and Canada, then exported to Europe. A Pennsylvania Quaker farmer, John Bartram (1699–1777), sent hundreds of drawings, seeds and specimens to England for cultivation and study. Swedish scientist Carl Linnaeus (see page 22) described Bartram as the greatest natural botanist in the world, and relied heavily on the specimens for his classifications of American plants. In 1728, Bartram founded North America's first botanical garden near Philadelphia. He also treated the sick with herbal medicines called simples, made from liquorice, green figs, spearmint, pennyroyal or marsh mallow.

Samuel Thomson (1769–1843) transformed Native American herbalism and simple colonial remedies into a national movement known as physiomedicalism. He used natural healing practices such as herbal treatments, mineral bathing and body heating, creating "Thomson's Improved System of Botanic Practice of Medicine," a kit that contained basic medicines and handbooks for self-diagnosis and treatment. He classified herbs as stimulating or sedating, relaxing or astringent, and prescribed a balanced regimen of these four types for each illness. Many of the herbs he promoted, such as black root, black and blue cohosh, agrimony, cayenne and true unicorn root, were already familiar to Native Americans. By the mid 1830s, three million Americans owned one of his kits.

Around the same time, the Shakers, an offshoot of the Quaker religious sect, created large "physick" gardens stocked with as many as 200 herbs such as bayberry,

Plains Indians used Echinacea (Echinacea angustifolio) to treat insect and snake bites, toothache, sore throat, mumps, smallpox and measles.

feverfew, sage, calendula and rue. They harvested the herbs and either pressed the dried, chopped plant materials into bricks or mixed them into tonics, which they labelled and sold. The Shakers even established a mail-order business to ship their herbal products far and wide. For more than a century, the Shaker label was synonymous with high-quality, reliable, herbal medicines.

By the 1840s, there emerged a more scientific approach to herbal healing, called eclecticism. The Eclectics established a medical school in Cincinnati, Ohio, where they analyzed the chemical compositions of herbs. They were able to isolate many active ingredients, create liquid extractions for medical use. Though the American pharmaceutical industry can trace its roots directly back to the Eclectic movement, the influence waned early in the 1900s, as philanthropists such as John D. Rockefeller and Andrew Carnegie began to give financial support to "orthodox" medical schools.

In the first half of the 20th century, America's reliance on scientific medicine and synthesized drugs grew, and popular interest in herbs declined almost to nothing, except among the unwitting victims of travelling "snake oil" salesmen. It remained this way until the hippie

MAJOR HERBS OF NORTH AMERICA

NAME OF HERB	USE
American ginseng (*Panax quinque folius*)	All-purpose medicine and tea
Bloodroot (*Sanguinaria canadensis*)	Dental plaque inhibitor
Jojoba (*Simmondsia chinesis*)	Lubricant and cosmetic oil
Mayapple (*Podophyllum peltatum*)	Anti-cancer drug ingredient
Pokeberry (*Phytolacca Americana*)	Antiviral and pesticide
Rooibus (*Aspalathus linearis*)	Caffeine-free tea substitute
Sarsaparilla (*Smilax glauca*)	Tonic and soft drink flavouring
Sassafras (*Sassafras albidum*)	Tea and cure-all
Saw palmetto (*Serenoa repens*)	Prostate treatment
Unicorn root (*Aletris farinosa*)	Digestive tonic
Witch hazel (*Hamamelis virginiana*)	Astringent

movement of the 1960s, when many Americans began to distrust clinical medicine and turned once again to herbal cures. The herbal vitamin and supplement industry flourished as people sought out better personal fitness and healthier lifestyles. This trend led to a renewed interest in herbal cuisine and organic foods, which today has driven unprecedented growth in the demand for a wide variety of herbs all over North America.

CENTRAL AND SOUTH AMERICA

Centuries ago, the warm, tropical climate of Central America and most of South America promoted both human settlement and the development of a diverse ecosystem of plant life. People began to migrate southward and settle in Mexico, the Caribbean and South America around 10,000 B.C.E. In the years that followed, several major civilizations arose, each developing a multitude of uses for the herbs that grew around them.

CENTRAL AMERICA AND THE CARIBBEAN

The first of Central America's ancient civilizations were the Olmecs who, from 1200 B.C.E., grew to prominence in present-day Veracruz. Little is known of how they used the richness of the Mexican rainforest in their daily lives, but it is clear that cacao, or chocolate (*Theobromac cacao*), was valued as a food, a flavouring and a diuretic, as well as for use as a skin balm.

The Maya people established a civilization that spanned most of Central America by 250 C.E. They built underground reservoirs to store rainwater for irrigation, and cleared large sections of rainforest to grow corn,

Mexican marigold (Tagetes lucida). *Also known as Sweet Marigold and Winter Tarragon.*

manioc, sunflowers, cacao, chilli peppers and squash, sometimes in raised gardens or on terraced mountainsides. They also gathered wild avocado, coconut, mamey and breadnut. They had highly trained spiritual healers, both men and women, and some of their remedies were innovative, such as the practice of blistering the leaves of hierba santa (*Piper umbellatum*) over an open flame, before wrapping them around a wrist or ankle to reduce inflammation. Yucca (*Yucca spp.*) was given to patients who suffered from joint pain. The boiled stems of cliffrose (*Purshia mexicana*) were used to cleanse wounds and suppress coughs. The Mayans also developed a variety of aromatic facial astringents and anti-bacterial topical tonics that incorporated local herbs such as creosote bush, sagebrush and catclaw acacia.

By the 12th and 13th centuries, the Aztec civilization had become established in the area now known as the valley of Mexico. The Aztecs instituted a remarkable system of landfilling the swampy area. They covered floating log rafts with mud, and planting seeds from the jungle on top to create root systems and soil. Before long, a network of artificial islands, or *chinampas*, had been formed on which they cultivated food crops: beans, squash, cacao, chillis, vanilla, a wide variety of corn (maize), amaranth for its protein-rich seeds, and maguey or century plant (*Agave americana*). They developed a unique system of traditional medicine using nearly 3,000 herbs gathered from the wild and grown on extensive medicinal *chinampas*. The rest of the world knew nothing of their herbal cures until the mid-16th century, when Spanish scholars and priests began to translate written Aztec works.

Invasion and Slavery

The tribe dominating the islands of the Caribbean when Christopher Columbus arrived in 1492 was the Arawak, also known as the Tainos. Arawak herbal healers, known as *butuous*, gathered herbs from the lush island jungles and grew healing plants and fruits in raised-bed gardens, known as *conucos*. These healers prescribed treatments for a variety of illnesses, from teas made from large-leaf thoroughwort (*Hebeclinium macrophyllum*) and aloe vera for the common chest cold, to sucking on the bark of the yarayara tree (*Unonopsis glaucopetala*) for snakebites, to burning the foul-smelling leaves of huamansamana (*Jacaranda copaia*) under the hammock of a person with an "illness caused by spirit attack".

With the arrival of Christopher Columbus on the islands of the Bahamas, Cuba, Hispaniola and Dominica in search of a new trade route to the Far East, the era of two-way commerce between the eastern and western

Bags of herbs for sale in a traditional open air market or mercado in San Miguel de Allende, Mexico. Curanderos, natural healers and yerberos, herb salesmen, keep ancient traditions alive.

hemispheres had begun. The Spanish established a system of agriculture in the New World called *encomienda*, which subjected natives to the production of cotton, sugar and tobacco for export. Within 30 years, the Arawaks had nearly been wiped out because of slave labour, malnutrition and introduced diseases that included smallpox.

One popular New World plant that was quickly exported to Europe was the chilli pepper (*Capsicum* spp.). And with the establishment of sugarcane planatations and the importing of slaves, molasses syrup was produced, fermented and distilled, then mixed with cinnamon, rosemary or caramel to make rum. Slavery was finally abolished in the 19th century, but in the slave populations, the religious beliefs of santeria (a New World hybrid of Yoruba and Christianity) and voodoo had become established itself in many islands, as well as in parts of the Central America and the United States. Practitioners used literally hundreds of different plants and flowers in magic rituals in order to obtain the power, or "ashe", of the saints for the strength to live their arduous lives. Even today, it is not uncommon for practitioners to use basil to drive away the evil eye,

marigold to produce lucky number dreams, juniper berries to increase virility in men and oregano to keep away annoying in-laws.

SOUTH AMERICA

This jungle-covered continent is home to what may be the world's most diverse supply of plant life. But the herbal habits of tribes in the vast, forbidding Amazon region remained largely undiscovered until recent centuries, when anthropological studies and oral histories began to reveal how herbs were used by ancient peoples. The Yanomamo people of Brazil and Venezuela, for example, are believed to have moved to the region nearly 8,000 years ago. They have lived very much the same way ever since, the Amazon jungle providing them and many other tribes with berries of onoto (*Bixa orellana*) for red dye to decorate their bodies and loin cloths; fibres of the kapok tree (*Ceiba pentandra*) to weave baskets; and materials to make deadly hunting blowguns and darts. In the Siona tribe of Colombia, there were *brujos*, or stem collectors, who mixed herbs such as yage (*Banisteriopsis caapi*) and chagropanga (*Diploterys cabrerana*) into a ritual drink that

An 18th-century hand-coloured engraving, Doctor-priest of Tierra del Fuego. *Traditional South American healers still treat the sick with herbs and rituals that date to pre-Incan times.*

of the drug cocaine, which was done to stimulate and stave off the fatigue and hunger associated with living in the rugged mountains or dangerous jungle. Coca's importance in rituals gave it a high value in early societies.

In around 1450 B.C.E., the Incas rose to power in the Andean mountain region, and in less than a century, developed a civilization nearly as sophisticated as that of the ancient Romans. The Incas built reliable irrigation systems by diverting rivers, building aqueducts and digging canals along terraces, on which they produced maize, cotton, quinoa, peanuts, coca, potatoes and tomatoes, as well as medicinal herbs such as vilcacora or cat's claw (*Uncaria tomentosa*), an anti-inflammatory; manayupa (*Desmodium adscendens*), a detoxicant and blood purifier; and sangro de drago or dragon's blood (*Croton lechleri*), a treatment for malaria and fevers.

From the time of the Spanish conquest to the present day, thousands of important herbal medicines have been discovered in South America. In 1638, a European doctor visiting Peru allegedly observed a puma with a fever chewing the limbs of a Peruvian bark tree (*Chinchona* spp.). The bark was later found to contain the alkaloid quinine, a drug that reduced fevers and helped prevent malaria. Quinine remained the world's most effective anti-malarial agent until the invention of a synthetic equivalent several hundred years later. Curare, from *Strychnos toxifera*, and strychnine, from the seeds of *Strychnos nux-vomica*, were deadly poisons. Curare later became useful as a surgical anaesthesic and as a treatment for chronic muscle spasms.

Today, South America remains unparalleled in the world for the richness of its flora. There are 55,000 species of flowering plants in Brazil alone. Scientists and pharmaceutical companies continue to scour the Amazon rainforest for plants that may be the source of valuable new drugs to combat such deadly diseases as cancer, AIDS and Alzheimer's disease.

produced hallucinatory visions of the spirit world. In the western Amazon region, shamans made a medicine by combining the ayahuasca vine (*Banisteriopsis caapi*), "vine of the soul", with the leaves of chacruna (*Psychotria viridis*), to cure a wide range of physical, psychological and spiritual illnesses.

Two of the earliest plants established in the Andean highlands of Peru were maca root (*Lepidium meyenii*) and potato (*Solanum tuberosum*). Maca is said to enhance physical strength and endurance as well as sexual prowess. One tradition practised among Andean and Amazon civilizations as early as 2000 B.C.E. was the chewing of the leaves of coca (*Erythroxylum coca*), the source plant

AUSTRALASIA AND THE SOUTH PACIFIC ISLANDS

In Australia and the islands of the South Pacific, herb use originated with indigenous peoples whose cultures date back thousands of years. Antiseptic tea-tree oil, for example, was first prepared by Aboriginals from the leaves of the Melaleuca tree (*Melaleuca* spp.). Australian rainforests also hold the promise of new medicines, such as the black bean, (*Castanospermum australe*), which may be an effective treatment for AIDS.

Indonesia's dense tropical rainforests have been home to some of the world's most important spice plants, such as nutmeg, cloves and mace, as well as a number of important plant families, such as Apocynaceae, a source of cardiac and tranquilizing alkaloids. From the South Pacific islands comes the immunostimulant noni (*Morinda citrifolia*) and the starchy taro (*Colocasia esculenta*), used to treat everything from boils to heart complaints.

AUSTRALIA

Northern Australia has a tropical climate, while the southern coast is relatively cool and moist. A vast, arid desert covers the interior. Much of the continent is subject to brushfires, and many native plants, such as the eucalyptus (*Eucalyptus* spp.) have oils and resins in their aerial parts that encourage a rapid burning that leaves woody tissues and underground parts unharmed.

The early aboriginal people of Australia were hunters and gatherers who travelled vast distances on foot. They had more than 150 different herb species for the treatment of inflamed wounds and eyes. To alleviate the hunger and fatigue they experienced on long journeys, they commonly chewed pituri, a substance made from nicotine-containing plants of the nightshade family (*Solanaceae* spp.). Eucalypt gum or kino, was widely used to control infections, bleeding and diarrhoea. They also mixed herbal medicines to treat burns, headaches, digestive upsets, jellyfish and insect stings, and snakebites.

The Aboriginals believed that most ailments and accidents were caused by spirits. Spiritual doctors, both men and women, performed sacred rites to counteract the sorcery. The healers would administer herbal treatments in different ways. Patients could inhale the steam from leaves placed over a fire. Aromatic herbs could be crushed and

Eucalyptus
Eucalyptus globulus

inhaled, inserted into the nose or prepared into a sleeping pillow. Crushed leaves and bark could be soaked in water as an infusion, to be ingested. Many remedies were applied topically: a patient could be rubbed with crushed seed paste, fruit pulp or sap. Newborn babies and new mothers were exposed to steam or rubbed with oils to give them strength.

Bush medicine focused on commonly found plants, such as the fuchsia bush (*Eremophila spp.*), the bloodwood tree (*Eucalyptus terminalis*), lemongrass (*Cymbopogon spp.*), and jirrpirinypa (*Stemodia viscosa*). Some medicines varied in strength with the seasons – wet season growth of green plum leaves (*Buchanania obovata*) was considered stronger than dry season as a toothache remedy.

In 1770, Captain James Cook (1728–1779) arrived and claimed Australia for the British crown. The land was established as a British penal colony, and for the next eighty years, nearly 160,000 men and women were transported from England to Australia as convicts.

The new arrivals brought with them a host of non-native crops, from cereal grains to potatoes, onions, sugar cane, tobacco and grapevines. The Europeans

MAJOR HERBS OF CENTRAL AND SOUTH AMERICA

NAME OF HERB	USE
Allspice (*Pimenta dioica*)	Clovelike spice
Cashew (*Anacardium occidentale*)	Important food crop
Epazote (*Chenopodium ambrosioides*)	Mexican cooking herb
Ipecac (*Cephaelis ipecacuanha*)	Potent emetic and expectorant
Lignum vitae (*Guaiacum officinale*)	Fine lumber tree
Lipstick tree (*Bixa orellana*)	Cosmetic colourant
Mexican yam (*Dioscorea macrostachya*)	Oral contraceptive
Papaya (*Carica papaya*)	Sweet fruit and digestive aid
Vanilla (*Vanilla planifolia*)	Popular flavouring and perfume
Yerba mate (*Ilex paraguariensis*)	Stimulating and popular tea

MAJOR HERBS OF AUSTRALASIA AND THE SOUTH PACIFIC

NAME OF HERB	USE
Corkwood (*Duboisia spp.*)	Narcotic stimulant
Gum tree (*Eucalyptus spp.*)	Astringent and cough medicine
Jequirity (*Abrus precatorius*)	Aboriginal body ornament
Mint bush (*Prostanthera spp.*)	Antibiotic and fungicide
Mountain pepperberry (*Tasmannia lanceolata*)	Hot, pepper-like spice
Myrtle (*Backhousia spp.*)	Scented leaves
Native caper (*Capparis canescens*)	Mustard substitute
Old man saltbush (*Atriplex nummurlaria*)	Source of vitamin C, scurvy cure
Sticky hop bush (*Dodonaea viscosa*)	Toothache and insect sting remedy
Taro (*Colocasia esculenta*)	Staple food and all-purpose medicine nt preparation

also named native plants after species the plants resembled in their homeland. Today, native, or "bush", potatoes, bananas, cherries, pears and plums unrelated to their European namesakes are found throughout Australia. These plants were intertwined with exotic imports, edible and medicinal plants cultivated by settlers and spread into the wild.

In all, at least 2,700 new plants were introduced in Australia, where they have now established populations. Some, such as arum lily (*Zantedeschia aethiopica*), fleabane (*Conyza spp.*), and the ubiquitous lantana (*Lantana* spp.), have become invasive weeds, spreading throughout the country and edging out indigenous species. Others, such as tobacco (*Nicotiana glauca*), were simply integrated by aboriginal people into the traditional medicine.

NEW ZEALAND

The plant life of northern New Zealand resembles that of tropical southeastern Asia, while the country's central regions have a temperate climate and the southern zone is cool and wet. New Zealand's first inhabitants were the Maori people, who arrived, almost certainly from southeastern Asia, around 1000 C.E. They had an intricate healing system, centred around the Tohunga, who was both doctor and spiritual leader. The Tohunga administered herbal remedies as well as spiritual rituals and vapour

baths. Native species such as New Zealand flax (*Phormium tenax*) and manuka (*Leptospermum scoparium*), now familiar worldwide as ornamental plants, were used to treat a wide range of ailments, including topical wounds.

THE SOUTH PACIFIC ISLANDS

The islands in the South Pacific provide homes for hundreds of interesting herbs: Fiji has 2000 native plant species; Papua New Guinea has 15,000 and Samoa has 550. The further out into the Pacific the islands are, the fewer plant species they produce and the less likely the plants are to contain chemical substances that give herbs their active medicinal or aromatic properties.

Much of the collective history of the Pacific Islands lies in the stories of how people there used the individual plants. Many of the islands are home to the world's supply of kava and noni. The islands also produce small quantities of wild ginger, coconut, gardenia, red algae and hibiscus. Kava (*Piper methysticum*) contains high levels of kavalactones, which have analgesic, anaesthetic and tranquillizing effects. The herb has gained worldwide popularity as a stress-reliever and mild antidepressant.

Noni, or Indian mulberry, is the fruit of the shrubby, evergreen *Morinda citrifolia* tree. Fermented noni juice is consumed daily throughout the Pacific as a traditional prophylactic, and traditionally, the fruit is believed to cure sore throats and the sting of the poisonous stonefish. Noni fruit and juice contain compounds that may help in the treatment of a variety of ailments, including Alzheimer's, high blood pressure, arthritis and cancer. Vanilla is also a key herbal export of the islands. A climbing vine of the orchid family, vanilla produces beans that are used for manufacturing extracts, oleoresins and alcoholic tinctures, and flavourings for ice cream, baked goods, chocolate, alcohol, soft drinks, tobacco and perfumes.

The screwpine, or pandanus, (*Pandanus tectorius*), has always been one of the South Pacific's most useful plants. In Samoa, fragrant pandanus flowers are used to make wreaths called lei, worn by chiefs. In Tahiti, juice from pandanus root tips is used to treat skin inflammation. In Tonga, the juice is mixed with turmeric (*Curcuma longa*) and grated coconut, and applied to topical sores. The skin of ripe pandanus fruit is used to treat urinary tract problems, and in Fiji, a tea made from pandanus leaves is drunk as a remedy for diarrhoea. Numerous other medicinal uses for the herb include the treatment of asthma, back pain, heart conditions and internal fractures.

Fijian man preparing kava (Piper methysticum) *with a stone mortar and pestle to make a slightly intoxicating ceremonial beverage.*

Herb Gardens

From the earliest documented gardens of ancient Mesopotamia to the eclectic landscapes of the 21st century, people all over the world have grown gardens to beautify their surroundings and to provide useful plants for food and medicine. Defined as "plant-filled spaces created and tended by humans", gardens have constantly evolved over time in style and form.

Today, herb gardens serve many functions. In some regions, the herb garden is a pleasant spot to enjoy the scents of flowers and aromatic foliage, or perhaps to study their cultivation and history. Elsewhere, the herb garden is a necessity, yielding crops essential to life. As travel between countries and continents increases, gardens around the world contain ever wider selections of plants, enriching the world of herbs for all.

The Garden of World Medicine at London's Chelsea Physic Garden features plants used medicinally by people all over the world.

Garden Styles & Their Evolution

Gardens likely began as basic agricultural fields where staple foods such as grains and legumes were cultivated. Evidence of plant domestication dates back 10,000 years, when gardening was simply a way to ensure that edible plants would be available near the home. Later, people began to grow gardens for their aesthetic appeal, as well.

Egyptian tomb paintings dating to 3000 B.C.E., depict early domestic gardens that appear remarkably similar to modern domestic gardens. These walled spaces contained plants that were edible as well as beautiful, and included such features as fruit trees, fishponds, potted plants, climbing vines and pools of water. The earliest surviving detailed garden plan is Egyptian. Dating to about 1400 B.C.E., it shows tree-lined avenues, pavilions and rectangular ponds.

The gardens of ancient Assyria, Babylon and Persia were primarily of three kinds: large, enclosed game reserves such as the Old Testament's garden of Eden; pleasure gardens, offering shade and cool water; and sacred enclosures such as the Hanging Garden of Babylon (dating to 540 B.C.E.), where trees and shrubs were planted in terraces to form an artificial hill. In China, opulent and extensive gardens, which usually harmonized with the natural landscape and featured decorative rocks gathered from great distances, were typified by the palace grounds of the emperor Ch'in Shih Huang-ti (207 B.C.E.).

Gardens were cultivated in ancient Greece long before the rule of Alexander the Great (356–323 B.C.E.). Typically situated in open-air courtyards within houses, they featured potted plants surrounding a water supply. Ancient Roman gardens introduced the concept of arranging plants in regular, straight rows. The classic Roman courtyard, or villa garden, featured geometrically precise plantings, elaborate topiaries (boxwood sculpted

into desired shapes), colonnades and statuary, water canals and fountains, and raised beds of flowers and herbs such as coriander, dill, parsley, fennel and rosemary.

Gardens grew in importance in Europe with the establishment of Christian monasteries beginning in the 1st century C.E. Modelled after the peristyle gardens of Roman villas, in which the garden space was enclosed by a colonnade, monastery gardens were designed with plantings in shapes resembling knots or wheels, or simple, raised, rectangular beds separated by walkways. Placing an emphasis on the growing of herbs to heal the sick, these gardens supplied local healers with herbs, sometimes for hundreds of years. The monks at the Bury St Edmonds abbey in England, for example, supplied their neighbours with medicinal plants for more than 1,200 years – from the 7th century until 1950.

As Europe transitioned from Roman rule to the medieval period, the Persian pleasure garden again became popular as small, enclosed spaces containing water features, aromatic herbs including rosemary and lavender, free-roaming ornamental fowl, and seats built against walls or under trees were created. European monastery gardens during the medieval period were often divided into three sections: a vineyard, an orchard and a herbarium. The herbarium was further divided into separate areas for kitchen plants and medicinal plants. In the Middle Ages, the term "pot herbs"

Circular gardens, such as this one, are a favourite formal garden design.

Cottage gardens are much less formal and impart a spontaneous feel.

referred to vegetables as well as scented herbs that were strewn on floors to mask unpleasant odours, and culinary herbs that were used to flavour food.

Herb gardening increased in popularity during the 13th century. During that time, most large households grew a wide variety of herbs for daily use, while more humble properties were surrounded by a mixture of orchard, grass and kitchen garden in which vegetables, herbs and flowers grew. In the 16th century, herb, or "physic" gardens were planted by universities to support the teaching of botany and medicine. By the end of the 17th century, physic gardens were common at universities throughout Europe. The plants in these gardens were often arranged alphabetically by scientific family name.

During the European Renaissance (c.1400–1600), formal garden design on a grand scale again became popular. In France and Italy, elaborate châteaux gardens called *parterres* became fashionable among the nobility. These majestic spaces featured ancient Roman-inspired geometric plantings with fountains and statuary. The elaborate style became widespread – even kitchen gardens were for many years planted in formal, geometric patterns.

But in the 18th century, particularly in France and England, gardeners began to discard the notion of unnatural symmetry in favor of allowing plants to grow in "natural", pleasingly haphazard patterns. Peasants, who commonly lived in small cottages, had only small plots of land on which to plant and supply their family's food needs. They packed their gardens with practical and productive plants, often using fences and hedges to keep out the livestock and other animals.

CONTEMPORARY HERB GARDENS

Herb gardens today are created for various reasons: to harvest medicinal plants as needed, to have easy access to fresh culinary herbs, to revel in fragrant plantings, or to simply enjoy the subtle beauty of many of these plants.

Stylistically, the best gardens are unified compositions that take inspiration from history and nature itself to present pleasing and interesting environments that remain inviting even as the plantings change over time.

Formal, Informal, Combination

Contemporary garden design has evolved from two primary traditions: the formal, geometric, stately, and sculptured gardens of ancient Rome and Renaissance Europe, and the informal gardens grown in less grand circumstances, particularly in the cottage gardens of rural English and French homes.

The formal garden presents plants in orderly, geometric patterns, usually subdivided by paths or dwarf hedges into symmetrical compartments. They may be square, rectangular, circular, star-shaped or triangular in outline, or may combine different shapes. Topiaries, borders, raised beds, fountains and statuary are characteristic elements of a formal garden.

In the informal cottage garden tradition, plantings look unplanned and spontaneous, with herbs tucked here, there and everywhere. In some gardens this may actually be the case. However, even cottage garden design is usually thoughtful and artistic, creating a feeling that is at once spontaneous and exuberant, balanced and harmonious. An informal garden generally features small areas of plantings with specific purposes: a grouping of culinary herbs, for example, or a concentration of medicinal or fragrance herbs. Informal gardens may begin with a formal, geometric outline, but will not have the planned symmetry of the formal garden.

The design of many contemporary gardens reflects a comfortable middle ground between these two contrasting styles. A cottage garden abundance of plants may be presented against a well-defined context of linear walls and paths, or a classic Roman statue may be enveloped by an unconstrained climbing vine.

Themed Herb Gardens

In addition to following a formal or informal style or a combination of the two, the modern herb garden may be planted in ways that celebrate the astounding variety of the herb universe. A garden could be composed entirely of varieties of sages, for example, incorporating tricolour sage, golden sage, purple sage, clary sage and pineapple sage, among the dozens of other Salvia species (see pages 294–295).

Alternatively, a particular colour palette could dictate the design of an herb garden. A garden with a grey-green colour theme, for example, could include herbs with silvery, downy foliage – lamb's ear, lavender, common sage, artemesia and wormwood.

Tea drinkers might concentrate on a garden composed of chamomile, lemon balm, mints, basils, rosemary and the natural sweetener stevia from which to make their own infusions. A collection of lemony herbs might include some of the vast number of herbs bred for their citrus scent: lemon verbena, lemon balm and lemon thyme are just a few. Pelargoniums, the scented geraniums, have hundreds of varieties – there are more than fifty types of rose-scented geraniums alone.

Tricolour sage (Salvia officinalis 'Tricolour') makes a wonderful addition to both fragrance and colour-oriented herb gardens.

The Medicinal Garden

With a history dating back to medieval monastery gardens and the 17th-century university physic garden, contemporary medicinal gardens reflect many traditions and styles of garden design. Some herbalists grow herbs in formal or cottage garden settings, according to their aesthetic preference. Others follow the philosophy of the 17th-century physician–astrologer Nicholas Culpeper (1616–1654), organizing herbs according to the astrological sign with which Culpeper believed them to be associated.

Herbs may also be grouped in gardens by plant family. Strongly scented antiseptic mints may appear in one bed, for example, while hairy-leaved, soothing borages may be planted in another. Yet another useful system for planting medicinal herbs is to arrange them in groups according to the ailment, symptom, or part of the body they are used to treat.

The Queen's Garden is a 17th-century-style garden located behind Kew Palace in London. Enclosed within low hedges of boxwood (Buxus sempervirens 'Suffruticosa'), *are plantings that include lavender* (Lavandula angustifolia 'Hidcote'), *sage* (Salvia officinalis), *and rosemary* (Rosemarinus officinalis).

The Fragrance Garden

Fragrance gardens are designed for lingering. They often feature comfortable seating arrangements that encourage visitors to enjoy the garden's interplay of scents. These seating areas may themselves be scented: for example, gardeners have devised planter benches with seats and arms that can be filled with fragrant plants.

Fragrance gardens are generally enclosed by a fence, trellis or scented hedge along one or more sides, allowing air to circulate the aroma of the plants around the garden. Vertical elements are included to support aromatic climbers, such as roses, jasmine, honeysuckle and passionflower.

Herbs are by definition aromatic. Laden with fragrant essential oils, they are excellent selections for this type of garden. Gardeners sometimes plant small lawns of herbs such as thyme and chamomile; their aromas are released when walked on. Scented herbs may be planted in raised beds or containers, where they are closer to the nose.

MEDICINAL GARDEN HERB GROUPINGS

HERBS FOR ALLERGIES

Allium sativum	Garlic
Anthemis nobilis	Chamomile
Chrysanthemum parthenium	Feverfew
Cochlearia armoracia	Horseradish
Ginkgo biloba	Gingko
Urtica dioica	Stinging nettle

HERBS FOR RESPIRATORY AILMENTS

Althaea officinalis	Marshmallow
Angelica archangelica	Angelica
Hyssopus officinalis	Hyssop
Inula helenium	Elecampane
Thymus vulgaris	Thyme
Tussilago farfara	Coltsfoot
Verbascum thapsus	Mullein

HERBS FOR HEADACHE

Chrysanthemum parthenium	Feverfew
Lavandula spp.	Lavender
Mentha piperita	Peppermint
Rosmarinus officinalis	Rosemary
Scutellaria laterifolia	Skullcap
Spiraea ulmaria	Meadowsweet
Stachys betonica	Wood betony

❧ FRAGRANCE GARDEN HERBS ❧

Aloysia triphylla	Lemon verbena
Angelica archangelica	Angelica
Artemisia abrotanum	Southernwood
Artemisia arborescens x absinthium	Artemesia 'Powis castle'
Balsamita vulgaris tanacetoides	Costmary
Chamaemelum nobile	Roman chamomile
Citrus spp.	Lemon, lime, orange
Foeniculum vulgare	Fennel
Helichrysum angustifolium	Curry plant
Jasminum grandiflorum	Jasmine
Lavandula spp.	Lavender
Levisticum officinale	Lovage
Lonicera spp.	Honeysuckle
Melissa officinalis	Lemon balm
Mentha spp.	Mint
Monarda didyma	Bergamot
Myrtus communis tarentina	Myrtle
Passiflora incarnata	Passionflower
Pelargonium spp.	Scented geranium
Pogstemon cablin	Patchouli
Rosmarinus officinalis	Rosemary
Salvia officinalis	Sage
Santolina neapolitana	Lavender cotton
Satureja hortensis	Summer savory
Tanacetum vulgare	Tansy
Thynus x citriodora 'Aureus'	Golden thyme
Valeriana officinalis	Valerian
Viola odorata	Sweet violet

Lavender (Lavandula *spp.*) *is just one of the dozens of herbs that can be grown in a fragrance garden. By combining different scents with different colours, a gardener can create an oasis at home.*

There are hundreds of highly scented herb species and cultivars, easily identifiable by their common names. Grape-scented sage, tangerine-scented marigold, liquorice mint, and chocolate-scented daisy are just a few examples.

The Potager Garden

Potager gardens developed from Medieval European monastic gardens. *Potager,* the French word for soup, is also the term for a garden that includes a mixture of practical and ornamental herbs, fruits, vegetables, perennials, vines and trees – all grown together in an interesting mélange that may be either orderly or chaotic.

One of the most well-known potagers is the magnificent kitchen garden at the Château de Villandry in France's Loire Valley. A 20th-century adaptation of a 16th-century design, this enormous garden is arranged in a formal geometric pattern comprised of nine huge squares. Each square is patterned differently from a number of smaller rectilinear beds, each filled with one or two types of plants – for example cabbages, aubergines or carrots –

bordered by tightly clipped, low hedges of boxwood. Gardeners rotate the more than forty types of vegetables, orchestrating the interplay of colour and form.

A potager may be formal and geometric, perhaps featuring a mosaic pattern made of lettuces and salad leaves and plant beds divided by borders of low-growing herbs such as parsley, dwarf basil, alpine strawberries or hyssop. A few rectilinear beds may brim with cabbages, while others contain aubergine. In such a formal layout, the decorative beauty of many vegetable plants will provide a visual surprise.

At the other end of the spectrum, the potager garden may be completely informal, without a straight line in sight. Annuals and perennials may be left to spread freely, sprouting in undisciplined profusion. Chives and marjoram may mingle with nasturtium, calendula, red cabbage, coriander, chilli peppers and salad burnet.

Both the formal and the informal potager gardens may include climbing plants such as beans, nasturtiums, passion flower and hops on climbing structures planted

The Château de Villandry in France's Loire Valley is home to what may be the world's best-known potager garden. Each of the nine separate gardens is comprised of just one or two types of plants, such as carrots or aubergine, and bordered by boxwood, a traditional garden hedge.

close together. In a formal garden, this density will help create a sense of order. In an informal garden, it will convey a sense of abundance.

The Container or Potted Garden

Many herbs thrive in containers, which can be placed either indoors or outdoors, and in window boxes, which add colour and fragrance to a windowsill.

Gardening in pots and containers offers many advantages. A container allows the gardener to experiment with plant combinations. Most containers are portable, and can be moved to follow the sun or to fill gaps in a border. In addition, containers can range in size from tiny, single-plant pots to constructed boxes large enough to hold a small tree or even an entire garden.

Multiple plants can be grown together in one large container or, individual plants can be grown in a series of separate pots. Container gardens may exist entirely indoors, or – on a patio or terrace – entirely outdoors. Potted plants may be transplanted into a container that is then sunk into the ground to limit the growth of invasive herbs such as catnip and mint.

Many culinary herbs – such as those native to the Mediterranean region or the tropics – are not able to survive outdoors during cold months. However, an indoor spot on a sunny kitchen windowsill is a perfect location for them. On the other end of the scale, trees and shrubs, such as citrus trees and olive trees, may also be grown in containers, so that they may be transferred indoors when temperatures drop outdoors.

The Culinary Garden

Culinary herbs have been grown in so many places and in so many ways that there are a tremendous number of traditions from which to choose. Throughout history, people all over the world have traditionally grown mixed herbs in convenient beds just outside the doors of their kitchens or in boxes suspended from their windows. These gardens supplied households with easily accessible food, flavouring, medicine, clothing dye and insect repellent.

Most culinary herbs are native to the hot, arid regions around the Mediterranean Sea and require at least six hours of sunlight each day. Many of those herbs, which include sage, thyme, rosemary, oregano, verbena and hyssop, display a great variety of foliage size, colour and texture. They will flourish whether planted in a formal garden or in an informal bed or border.

DESIGNING A GARDEN

When choosing a garden design, it is important to take into account a number of practical considerations, beginning with the experience and time limitations of the

HERBS FOR EDGING AND DIVIDING ❧ POTAGER BEDS ❧

Fragaria spp.	Strawberry
Lactuca spp.	Lettuce
Lavandula spp.	Dwarf lavender
Nepeta racemosa	Catnip (low-growing)
Ocinum basilicum	Dwarf basil
Petroselinum crispum	Parsley, curly
Santolina spp.	Santolina
Stachys lanata	Lamb's ear
Tagetes spp.	Dwarf marigold
Teucrium chamaedrys	Germander
Thymus spp.	Thyme, bush
Tropaeolum majus	Nasturtium, dwarf
Viola spp.	Violet

gardener. A novice gardener for example, would be wise to begin with a small herb garden – one whose design is simple and will be easy to plant and to maintain. A surprising number of herbs may be grown in a 2 to 2.5 m (6 to 8 ft) square or circular garden, or even a small border or windowbox. As the gardener gains in experience and confidence, the garden's shape and design can be evolve and become more complex, allowing for new features and more ambitious plantings.

Creating a formal garden can expensive and time-consuming, requiring the gardener to first create a "blank slate" in the garden space before installation can take place. However, formal gardens are relatively easy to maintain, and they achieve a desired appearance as soon as they are completed. The informal garden is a more flexible arrangement that allows the gardener to utilize plants and features are already in the chosen space. But the aesthetic effect of an informal garden depends on

The Ballymaloe Cookery School in Shanagarry, Ireland, is home to an extensive culinary herb garden, including a formal parterre herb garden (below) and a potager-style kitchen garden.

❧ CULINARY GARDEN HERBS ❧

Allium sativum	Garlic
Allium schoenoprasum	Chives
Anethum graveolens	Dill
Anthriscus cerefolium	Chervil
Artemesia dracunculus var. *sativa*	Tarragon
Coriandrum sativum	Coriander
Foeniculum vulgare	Fennel
Laurus nobilis	Bay
Levisticum officinale	Lovage
Melissa officinalis	Lemon balm
Mentha spicata	Spearmint
Ocimum basilicum	Sweet basil
Origanum majorana	Marjoram
Origanum vulgare hirtum	Greek oregano
Petroselinium crispum	Parsley
Rosmarinus officinalis	Rosemary
Salvia officinalis	Sage
Satureja hortensis	Summer savory
Satureja montana	Winter savory
Thymus vulgaris	Thyme

the interplay of plant growth in groups and combinations, which, compared to the formal garden, takes time. A combination of styles can be designed to suit almost any location and level of experience.

Creating a Garden Plan

Before beginning, it is wise to draw a diagram of the available garden space. A garden plan should be based on accurate measurements of the area's boundaries and structures. Existing plantings should be marked, especially trees and shrubs that may shade the space at certain times of day. It is also important to note the location and size of any features to be concealed by plantings – such as an unsightly wall – as well as focal-points to be highlighted: doorways, impressive trees or windows.

The new garden may then be planned on paper. By working out the details of the garden in this way, the chance of having to undo work later is minimized. The placement of beds and the type and number of plants should be noted, along with basic elements of garden design such as borders, paths, focal-points such as statuary, and special arrangements of beds such as knots and wheels.

Borders

Garden beds that have one or more sides along a boundary such as a wall, walkway, hedge or fence are called borders. These types of structures help define the garden bed, and serve as a contrasting or complementary backdrop for the plantings. They may provide a surface on which climbing plants can clamber. Borders can be planted in a tightly controlled, geometric design, but are more often grown in a cottage garden style.

A border should either be narrow enough so that the back can be reached without stepping onto the soil, or it should have a narrow work area along the back so that plants may be reached from both sides. Most perennials and herbs look best when planted in drifts made up of several similar-looking plants that blend gradually and naturally into each other. Landscape designers usually recommend planting uneven numbered groups – threes, fives or more of each plant.

The edge of the border should be well-defined, with a material such as brick or stone, both for visual definition and to make mowing and other chores such as weeding easier. Tight, compact-growing plants can also work as edgings or border plantings, as well as herbs with shrubby, upright growing habits, such as lavender cotton, lavender, sage, basil and wormwood.

Paths

Garden paths serve two purposes: they make the movement of visitors and gardening equipment possible and provide an important visual element that defines a garden and leads the eye through it. Paths may be constructed of brick, stone or pavers made from composite materials,

IN-GROUND AND CONTAINER ❧ GARDENS ❧

IN-GROUND GARDENS...
• Generally require soil preparation
• May be very large
• Are subject to environmental fluctuations
• Offer no size limitations for plants with long tap roots
• Make it difficult to isolate plants affected by disease or insect infestation

CONTAINER GARDENS...
• Are dependent on gardener for watering and feeding
• Are usually smaller than in-ground gardens
• Make it possible to move plants to the most appropriate environment
• Are limited in terms of types of plants grown
• Make it easy to treat disease and insect problems

giving a garden a formal feel. Gravel- and wood chip-covered paths are more casual. Materials may also be used in combination; brick mixed with slate or stone set in grass, for example, or cross-sections of a tree trunk set in gravel are all options.

Grass and low-growing herbs may also be used to make a path that blends in color with surrounding plantings but contrasts in texture. Low-growing or creeping herbs, including thyme, oregano, chamomile, sweet woodruff, Irish or Scotch moss, and pennyroyal can be used to soften stepping-stones and walkways.

Fences and Walls

Garden enclosures – walls, fences, and hedges – serve many purposes. They can capture and hold the scents of plants, keep out large garden predators such as deer, create a private sanctuary within the garden area and separate a planting area from its surroundings. These enclosures also serve as a background for a garden, framing it and drawing attention to the plantings. They furnish support for taller plants and vines, and impose a sense of order, defining a garden both visually and physically. Such a boundary does not have to completely surround a garden; a fence, wall or hedge can border just one or two sides.

❧ HERBS FOR HEDGES ❧

Many herbs can be planted to make small or large hedges, or to line formal borders or beds in a knot garden. Small hedging plants include box, lavender, cotton lavender, hyssop and germander. Large hedging plants include yew, barberry, hawthorn, cedar, holly, common beech and privet.

EVERGREEN

Buxus sempervirens 'Suffruticosa'	Box
Ilex aquifolium	Holly
Lavendula angustifolia	Lavender
Ligustrum lucidum)	Privet
Santolina chamaecyparissus	Lavender cotton
Taxus baccata	Yew
Teucrium fruticans	Germander
Thuja plicata	Cedar

DECIDUOUS

Berberis thunbergii	Barberry
Crataegus monogyna	Hawthorn
Fagus sylvatica	Common beech
Hyssopus officinalis	Hyssop

Focal-points

Gardens can feature one or more focal-points – elements such as birdbaths, sundials, fountains, statuary, topiaries and container-grown plants that help focus or direct the viewer's eye. In a formal garden with straight lines and views, a focal point is often sited where paths converge. Water sources such as bird baths do double duty. Not only do they work as a focal-point, but they also attract birds and butterflies while releasing moisture into the air that intensifies the scent of fragrant plantings.

Wheels

Circular herb gardens whose beds radiate outward from a central point have a longstanding tradition in garden design. Wheel-shaped gardens are divided into wedge-shaped, planted beds. The beds can be organized by the colour of foliage or flowers of the plants contained within, creating a feature called a colour wheel. They can also be planted with medicinal herbs, creating a medicine wheel.

In a large garden, herb wheels can be scaled-up, with walkways and paths forming the spokes and the beds densely planted with herbs. A large-scale wheel garden can have a focal-point – a bird bath, sundial, statue, or seating – at the centre.

Knots

A knot is a geometric design, made by planting ribbon-like beds of different coloured plants that cross over and under each other and interlock in intricate patterns. The beauty and intricacy of a knot is best appreciated from above, so if possible it is best to site a knot garden where it can be seen from an overhead vantage-point.

Herbs traditionally used to create knot gardens are compact-growers such as lavender cotton, germander, thyme, juniper, boxwood, barberry, savory, curly parsley or hyssop. Plants intended for use in a knot should contrast with each other in colour and/or texture, but be similar in growth habits so that one does not overwhelm another.

The areas between planted ribbons should be filled with gravel, mulch, ground-hugging herbs, or bulbs and annuals that contrast with the colours of the herb ribbons. "Open" knot gardens have paths weaving through them as part of the design. "Closed" knot gardens are solid with plantings. Knot patterns to consider include interlocking circles, diamonds, squares, and Celtic knots or other traditional symbols.

Knot gardens, such as this one at the Wellsweep Herb Farm in the United States, can be simple or complex, depending on the gardener's level of experience and the time available to tend the design.

International
Gardens

Herb gardens are universal. In nearly every country on nearly every continent, botanical gardens, arboretums and heritage gardens keep alive centuries-old traditions of planting. From the formally geometric designs of palace grounds, to the studied disarray of cottage gardens, to the ordered display of medicinal plants, the world abounds in herb gardens that inspire, educate and delight the senses.

Many of the herb gardens listed here contain native species not found in any other part of the world. Others have a wider scope, representing plants from many continents brought together in one place for study and comparison. Greenhouses enable gardeners to replicate humid, tropical climates even in cold or arid regions, and vice versa, so that visitors can enjoy a botanical world tour without ever leaving the garden.

Some of these gardens have historical interest, either as faithful reproductions of famous gardens of the past, or as wonderfully preserved examples of historically important garden styles. The formal plots in the gardens of the Château de Villandry in France, for example, are said to have influenced garden design the world over. Still other gardens focus on herbs and plants grown for their usefulness, and are laid out according to the purpose for which plants are grown: medicinal, culinary or fragrance plants, for example. Of particular interest are those gardens displaying indigenous or threatened species.

From a small, jewel-like grouping of ornamental herbs, to a sprawling public garden, a herb garden can take many forms. This listing is by no means exhaustive, but merely serves as a starting-point for those curious about herb gardens all over the world. All the gardens listed here are open to the public.

NORTH AMERICA

CANADA

Devonian Botanic Garden, University of Alberta • *Edmonton, Alberta*
This extensive herb garden includes beds featuring culinary plants, poisonous plants, medicinal plants, Chinese herbs, woodland herbs, and climbing plants such as hops. The beds are bordered by a low-growing hedge of pygmy caragana. Some of the more exotic herbs grown here include *Artemesia sinthium* (wormwood, absinthe) and *Papaver somniferum* (opium poppy).
www.devonian.ualberta.ca

Governor's Garden, Château Ramezay Museum • *Montreal, Quebec*
The newly recreated garden at this 300-year-old château is modeled after formal gardens of "New France". It is divided into several sections: a kitchen garden, an orchard and a pleasure garden. Surrounding these sections is a fourth section consisting of herbs and medicinal plants informally distributed.
www.chateauramezay.qc.ca/index2.htm

The Devonian Botanic Garden at the University of Alberta, Canada, features the low-growing hedge Pygmy Caragana (Caragana pygmea).

Harriet Irving Botanical Gardens, Acadia University • *Wolfville, Nova Scotia*

The Medicinal Garden here is divided into three separate sections. The Native Bed contains plants used by indigenous peoples for medicinal, culinary and ceremonial purposes. The Scented Garden includes both native and introduced species, more closely resembling a modern herb garden. The Acadian Garden is a potager similar to those planted by early French settlers, with vegetables, flowers and aromatic herbs. A conservatory allows visitors to see a plant species from each habitat year-round.
www.botanicalgardens.acadiau.ca

University of British Columbia Botanical Garden • *Vancouver, British Columbia*

The formal design of the Physic Garden showcases medicinal herbs, many of which were used as long ago as 50,000 B.C.E. Interpretive panels match plants with the maladies they have been used to treat, or from which modern medicines are derived. Particular focus is given to plants that were in use in England's medieval, Tudor and Elizabethan periods.
www.ubcbotanicalgarden.org

Van Dusen Botanical Garden • *Vancouver, British Columbia*

Herbs can be found in numerous areas of this extensive botanical garden, including in the Mediterranean Garden and the Canadian Heritage Garden, which includes a section of medicinal plants native to British Columbia. The garden, which covers an area of 22 ha (55 acres), also features a small, formal herb garden, which uses the heat-retaining properties of brick paving for the benefit of herbs native to the Mediterranean. In total, the Van Dusen houses 11,000 plants from five continents.
www.city.vancouver.bc.ca/parks/parks/vandusen/website/index.htm

UNITED STATES

Brooklyn Botanic Garden • *Brooklyn, N.Y.*

Over 300 varieties can be found in the herb garden, organized into several theme beds: fibres, dyes and oils; smoking, drinking and chewing; fragrance and botanicals for the skin; poisons and curiosities; medicinal plants; and two culinary beds. Unusual tropical plants and perennials share space with annuals grown yearly from seed.
www.bbg.org

Cleveland Botanical Garden • *Cleveland, Ohio*

The herb garden at this large botanical garden is sponsored by the Western Reserve Herb Society. It has been called one of the finest public herb gardens of the world. Designed to educate visitors about how herbs have been used throughout history, the garden is home to more than 4,000 plants.
www.cbgarden.org

Cornell Plantations, Cornell University • *Ithaca, N.Y.*

Cornell's Robison York State Herb Garden was recently called one of the best herb gardens in America. Its seventeen themed beds include plants used by Native Americans, culinary and medicinal plants from all over the world, and many speciality collections, including scented geraniums, bee herbs, herbs found in literature, sacred herbs and dye herbs.
www.plantations.cornell.edu

Kanapaha Botanical Garden • *Gainesville, Fla.*

The herb garden here is the largest in the southeastern United States. The primary section contains medicinal herbs, while a second garden area features aromatic

Corn poppy (Papaver rhoeas), *which blooms in late spring/early summer is just one of the many herbs on display at the Brooklyn Botanical Garden in New York City in the United States.*

species, including culinary and fragrance herbs, in raised beds built of reclaimed brick.
www.kanapaha.org

Matthaei Botanical Gardens and Nichols Arboretum, University of Michigan • *Ann Arbor, Mich.*

The Alexandra Hicks Herb Knot Garden is a modern interpretation of a Tudor medicinal garden. Its design incorporates symbolic elements from 16th-century England, such as four-way symmetry, hedges and a central knot. Lavender, creeping thyme, and winter savory are incorporated into the Tudor knot. Outer beds feature cooking, medicinal, fragrance and everlasting herbs.
http://sitemaker.umich.edu/mbgna

The National Herb Garden • *Washington, D.C.*

This garden, the largest designed herb garden in the United States that includes annual, perennial and woody herbal plants, centres around ten themed gardens. Among them are a dye garden, medicinal and culinary gardens, a fragrance garden, an industrial garden and a beverage garden. A wider cultural and historical scope is evident

in the Native American, Colonial and Asian gardens, while the Dioscorides Garden pays homage to the ancient Greek physician and botanist of the same name.
http://www.usna.usda.gov/Gardens/collections/herb.html

Tucson Botanical Gardens • *Tucson, Ariz.*

The formal herb garden displays a wide variety of culinary, medicinal and fragrance herbs that grow in the Tucson area. Other features of the wider botanical garden also include herbs, such as those in the Native American Crops section, and the garden including plants that are important to the native Tohono O'odham people who once lived in Arizona's Sonoran Desert.
http://www.tucsonbotanical.org/

University of Washington Medicinal Herb Garden • *Seattle, Wash.*

This garden, one of the largest medicinal herb gardens in the country, features beds that are arranged into outdoor "rooms", which together display more than 600 varieties of medicinal herbs, trees and plants.
http://nnlm.gov/pnr/uwmhg/

CENTRAL AMERICA

BELIZE

Belize Botanic Garden • *San Ignacio, Cayo*

A display garden here called Plants of the Maya features medicinal and culinary herbs used by the indigenous Maya. More than 100 species of orchids can be found in the Native Orchid House, while the Habitat zones of the garden display plants from the varied ecosystems of Belize.
http://www.belizebotanic.org

COSTA RICA

INBioparque
National Biodiversity Institute (INBio) of Costa Rica • *Santo Domingo de Heredia*

This park features a butterfly garden, lagoon, aquarium and a farm. Here, medicinal plants, aromatic herbs and spices, vegetables, flowers, and fruit and foliage trees are collected into twelve plots. The institute offers extensive educational programmes for children and adults.
http://www.inbio.ac.cr/es/default2.html

MEXICO

UNAM Botanical Garden • *Mexico City*

A large section of this well-kept botanical garden is devoted to ornamental and medicinal plants, as well as culinary herbs integral to traditional Mexican cuisine. Some notable plants include hoja santa, used to treat digestive complaints; native borage, a widely-used medicinal plant; and carob, used for cough treatments.
http://www.planeta.com/ecotravel/mexico/gardens/unam.html

Jardín Etnobotánico y Museo de Medicina Tradicional • *Cuernavaca, Morelos*

Built on the palace grounds of former Emperor Maximilian (1832–1867), this garden displays a wide variety of herbs used for medicine, cookery, dyes and colourants, insecticide and ceremonial rituals. Both native and introduced plants are represented, with emphasis placed on traditional methods of herbal medicine.
http://www.inah.gob.mx/jardin_etnobotanico/Arch/dos_infgral.htm

SOUTH AMERICA

ARGENTINA

Arturo E. Ragonese Botanic Garden • *Castelar, Buenos Aires*

This garden is one of thirty-five members of the Argentine Botanic Garden Network. Located in a semiarid pampas region of the country, the garden displays native grasses and ornamental and medicinal herbs, with a focus on threatened and endangered species.
http://www.bgci.org.uk/argentina_en/JBAER/

The leaves of yerba maté (Ilex paraguayensis) are brewed to make a tea popular in many South American countries.

Jardín Botánico Dr. Miguel J. Culaciati Huerta Grande • *Córdoba, Argentina*

Over 100 species of aromatic and medicinal herbs grow wild in the Sierras de Córdoba region and play an integral role in the local economy. The plant collection is comprised primarily of these herbs, along with exotic ornamentals. The garden educates the community about conservation, ecology, and organic growing practices, with the aim of preventing over-harvesting.
http://www.uga.edu/ethnobot/SisArgentina.html

BRAZIL

Jardin Botanico do Rio de Janeiro • *Rio de Janeiro*

The Rio de Janeiro Botanic Garden is the oldest botanic garden in Brazil. The Sensorial Garden, designed for the disabled, contains herb and spice plants chosen for their aromatic and tactile properties. A separate garden of medicinal plants contains more than 90 species.
http://www.jbrj.gov.br/ingles/arboreto/sens_gd.htm

CHILE

Jardin Botanico Nacional • *Vina del Mar*

Formal plantings in 19th-century French style are laid out alongside more naturalistic beds, which focus on native plants. A collection of medicinal, culinary and aromatic herbs will soon join a cactus collection and a garden of the Chilean Ocean Islands.
http://www.jardin-botanico.cl/

COLOMBIA

Jardin Botanico de Plantas Medicinales • *Mocoa, Putumayo*

At just over 3 ha (7 acres), this garden features 634 species of medicinal and aromatic plants. Demonstration areas serve to educate about the uses of medicinal plants, both native and introduced.
http://www.corpoamazonia.gov.co/ce_jarbot.htm

VENEZUELA

Botanical Garden of Caracas • *Caracas*

Created in 1944, this urban botanical garden includes some 60 ha (148 acres) of old-growth forest. The remaining area includes medicinal herbs, bromeliads, orchids, palms, succulents, and tropicals such as banana and ginger.
http://www.ucv.ve/Fundacion2001/Jardin/

The National Botanical Garden of Belgium is one of the largest botanical gardens in the world, featuring plants from every continent as well as those native to Belgium.

EUROPE

AUSTRIA

The Botanical Garden of the University of Vienna • *Vienna*

Founded in 1754, this botanical garden now includes 9,000 species of plants. The layout includes a typical 19th-century landscape garden, a systematic display of plants, and smaller collections of useful plants, including several varieties of herbs, succulents, alpine flora, and native Austrian species.
http://www.botanik.univie.ac.at/hbv

BELGIUM

National Botanic Garden of Belgium • *Meise, Brussels*

This is one of the largest botanical gardens in the world. In addition to representative plants from every continent, many housed in the extensive greenhouses, there are wild areas dedicated to the indigenous plants of Belgium.
http://www. br. fgov.be

DENMARK

Botanic Garden, University of Copenhagen • *Copenhagen*

Orchid and bromeliad houses are a central feature of this garden, along with greenhouses for tropical species and succulents, and extensive outdoor plantings, which include many species of herbs and spices.
http://www.botanic-garden.ku.dk

FRANCE

Villandry Castle Gardens • *Villandry*

The extensive herb garden at this famous Renaissance castle is laid out in a formal plan, and contains aromatic, medicinal, and culinary herbs. The vegetable garden, with its highly stylized design, is also of interest.
http://www.chateauvillandry.com

Le Potager du Roi • *Versailles*

Designed in 1670 as the kitchen gardens for Louis XIV (1638–1715), the herb garden here contains 40 herbs, and includes more than 100 varieties of espaliered apple.
http://www.potager-du-roi.fr/

The Nine Gardens of La Chatonnière • *Azay-le-Rideau, Loire*

These Renaissance castle gardens include the Garden of the Senses, planted with aromatic herbs and roses. The Garden of Prosperity contains vegetables and culinary herbs, while the Crescent of Wonder combines roses with California poppies.
http://www.lachatonniere.com/

Fondation Claude Monet • *Giverny*

A profusion of perennial and annual flowers and herbs can be found in the famous garden of the painter Claude Monet. There is also an orchard and a water garden. Three hothouses contain begonias, ferns and orchids.
www.fondation-monet.com

GERMANY

Berlin-Dahlem Botanical Garden • *Berlin*

The medicinal plant bed is laid out in the shape of a human body, and planted with herbs corresponding to particular ailments. There is also a fragrance and touch garden for the disabled, a useful plants section and plant geography areas representing each continent.
http://www.bgbm.org

Bonn University Botanic Garden • *Bonn*

About 3,000 species are grown in this 6 ha (15-acre) garden and arboretum. Three sections separate sections of interest are the Systematic section, the Flower and Fruit Biology section, and the Medicinal Plant section.
http://botgart.uni-bonn.de/

Botanical Garden of Munich • *Munich*

Extensive greenhouses display plants from tropical, temperate, and arid regions. The Economic and Medicinal Plant area combines vegetables with herbs, and a separate area shows native Bavarian plants.
http://www.botanik.biologie.unimuenchen.de/botgart/e/default.html

IRELAND

Ardgillan Demesne Regional Park • *Fingal, Dublin*

The walled herb garden contains herbs suitable for culinary, medicinal, dyeing, and aromatic purposes. The Irish and Four Seasons gardens are also of interest.
http://www.fingalcoco.ie/LeisureandTourism/ParksHeritageProperties

Ballymaloe Cookery School Herb Garden • *County Cork*

The formal herb garden of this renowned cooking school grows in a microclimate created by ancient, 2 m (6 ft) high beech hedges. Herbs and edible flowers grow in patterns of contrasting colour.
http://www.cookingisfun.ie/index.html

ITALY

Botanic Garden of Padua • *Padua*

Believed to be the world's first botanic garden, the Orto Botanico was created in 1545 for the cultivation of medicinal herbs. The garden still retains its original circular layout, and now houses many rare trees, extensive collections of native, introduced and endangered species, and a garden for the blind.
http://www.ortobotanico.unipd.it/

Hanbury Botanic Gardens, University of Genoa • *La Mortola*

Founded in 1867 by the English merchant Sir Thomas Hanbury. Exotic and Mediterranean plants are grouped into special zones, including an Australian Forest, a Japanese Garden, and a Garden of Perfumes.

Botanical Garden of Rome, University of Rome • *Villa Corsini, Rome*

Over 3,500 species of plants grow at this historic botanical garden on the grounds of the Villa Corsini. There is a scent and touch garden of aromatic herbs and spices, for the blind, and many rare and unusual plants.
http://www.mediterraneangardensociety.org/gardens/Hanbury.Botanic.html

Giardino dei Semplici • *Florence, Tuscany*

This garden originated as a study centre for medicinal herbs. It is the third botanic garden established in Italy, and has been continually updated to include plants of temperate climates and hothouses, while retaining the long avenues, fountains and statuary of the original plan.
http://www.horti.unimore.it/CD/Firenze/obfi_home.html

LITHUANIA

Vilnius University Botanical Garden • *Vilnius*

The botanical garden at one of Europe's oldest universities has large showings of flowers and herbaceous perennials, bulbs and tubers, and a department of pomology, which selects and introduces berry plants.
http://www.botanikos-sodas.vu.lt/

NETHERLANDS

Hortus Botanicus • *Amsterdam*

One of the oldest botanical gardens in the world, dating from 1638, the Hortus Botanicus was originally designed as a medicinal herb garden. Today the garden houses a formal herb garden, along with seven greenhouses, each representing a different climate.
http://www.hortus-botanicus.nl/

Stekkenplek Zwingelspaan • *Zwingelspaan*

This charming family-run garden is designed in the English cottage-garden style, displaying a wealth of annuals, perennials, herbs, bulbs, roses and fruit trees.

POLAND

Warsaw University Botanic Garden • *Warsaw*

Established in 1818, this botanic garden is home to an extensive collection of perennial beds as well as a systematic section, which houses thousands of species from different geographic regions of the world. The garden also includes a section devoted to native Polish lowland flora. Plant species used in everyday life are grown in and exhibited in sections of medicinal and useful plants. *http://www.ihar.edu.pl/gene_bank/Gardens/Warszawa/ptob_e.html*

PORTUGAL

Madeira Botanical Garden • *Madeira*
Established in 1960 in the grounds of a historic estate, this garden includes many indigenous plants that thrive in this temperate island climate. There is a good collection of aromatic herbs, and an extensive collection of spices and culinary plants, including citrus and other fruit trees. Orchids, succulents, palms and cycads are all displayed here as well.
http://www.sra.pt/jarbot/

SPAIN

Royal Botanical Garden • *Madrid*
Occupying its present location since 1755, the Royal Botanic Garden garden houses extensive plant species, including many medicinal, aromatic and ornamental herbs in the *terrazza de los cuadros*.
http://www.rjb.csic.es/

The medieval garden at the Botanic Garden Berlin-Dahlem, Germany, features plants such as chicory (Cichorium intybus), *English lavender* (Lavandula angustifolia) *and oleander* (Nerium oleander).

London's Kew Garden displays herbs such as lavender in several areas, including the extensive Order Beds.

Marimurtra Botanical Garden • *Blanes, Costa Brava*
Built in the 1920's by German gardener Karl Faust, the name of the garden means "Sea and Myrtles". It contains 17 ha (41 acres) of Mediterranean plants, and conducts research on endangered native species.
http://www.jbotanicmarimurtra.org/eng/historia.htm

UNITED KINGDOM

Chelsea Physic Garden • *London, England*
Founded in 1673, as an Apothecaries' Garden, the Chelsea Physic Garden still maintains educational programmes. Speciality areas include the Garden of World Medicine, the Pharmaceutical Garden, the Perfumery and Aromatherapy Borders, the Glasshouse and a vegetable plot.
http://www.chelseaphysicgarden.co.uk/

The Herb Garden • *Pilsley, Chesterfield, Derbyshire, England*
The mixed herb garden comprises the bulk of the collection; three additional display gardens, a physic garden, a scented garden and a lavender garden are of interest.
http://www.peakdistrictonline.co.uk/content.php?categoryId=1785

Royal Botanic Gardens, Kew • *Richmond, Surrey, England*
One of the world's foremost botanical gardens, Kew covers 121 ha (300 acres), and houses several speciality collections. The garden includes extensive Order Beds, the famous Victorian glass Temperate House, a pagoda and a Japanese garden.
http://www.rbgkew.org.uk/

The Royal Botanic Garden • *Edinburgh, Scotland*

Founded in the 17th century for the study of medicinal plants, the RBGE now occupies four sites and houses some of the richest botanical collections in the world. Herbs and spices from around the world can be found in glasshouses, the rock garden, and numerous garden environments in each location.
http://www.rbge.org.uk

National Botanic Garden of Wales • *Llanarthne, Carmarthenshire, Wales*

A large, well-organized botanic garden, the Apothecaries' Garden features medicinal and aromatic herbs from around the world, while the Great Glasshouse contains thousands of plants from varied climates.
http://www.gardenofwales.org.uk/

ASIA

CHINA

Guangxi Medicinal herb Garden • *Nanning, Guangxi Province*

One of the largest medicinal herb gardens in China, with over 2,000 kinds of plants, the garden also houses research and teaching facilities. Seven different zones include native regional plants, woody plants, and a herb section.

Lavender Garden • *Hong Kong*

Designed as a family desti-nation, this garden grows many varieties of lavender, as well as sage, lemon balm and other herbs. A nursery sells plants and products made from lavender.
http://www.lavendergarden.com.hk/Introduction.asp

Gotu Kola (Centenella Asiatica)

Nanjing Botanical Garden • *Jiangsu Province*

Established in 1929, Nanjing was China's first national botanic garden, and today features extensive research facilities. It has numerous speciality display areas, including medicinal plants, a greenhouse, a garden for the visually handicapped, and a herbarium with 700,000 specimens.
http://www.cnbg.net/default_en.asp

BHUTAN

The Royal Botanical Garden • *Serbithang*

This conservation garden in the Himalayan Mountains displays specimens from the varied climactic zones of the nation. These include over 800 species of native orchid, medicinal and economic plants, plants for fruit and fodder and a Japanese garden.
http://www.geocities.com/royalbotanicgarden_bhutan/Welcome.htm

INDIA

Mughal Garden • *Rashtrapati Bhavan, New Delhi*

The official residence of the President of India. The gardens here, designed by Sir Edward Lutyens in 1929, combine elements of traditional Mughal and English gardens. The small herb garden grows essential Indian herbs, mixed with European species.
http://presidentofindia.nic.in/mughalGarden.html

ISRAEL

Jerusalem Botanical Gardens • *Jerusalem*

The various sections of this garden include more than 6,000 species, representing every continent. Most of the herbs can be found in the Mediterranean section. The greenhouse displays orchids, spice plants and many tropical species.
http://www.botanic.co.il/english/index.htm

Tel Aviv University Botanic Gardens •*Tel Aviv*

The five phyto-geographic regions of Israel are repre-sented in the ecological section of this garden. There is a tropical greenhouse, a centre for medicinal and economic plants, and a carefully planned Garden for the Blind.

JAPAN

Koishikawa Botanical Garden • University of Tokyo, *Tokyo*

The oldest in Japan, this botanical garden was originally established in 1684 as a medicinal herb garden. Some of the historic plants remain, but the living plant collection

is largely comprised of indigenous east Asian species. The garden is also a favoured spot for viewing cherry blossoms.
http://www.bg.s.utokyo.ac.jp/koishikawa/eigo/e.html

Nunobiki Gardens • *Kobe*
Over 200 kinds of herbs can be found in this garden, including many varieties of salvia and lavender.
http://www.kobe-park.or.jp/

SOUTH KOREA

Korea National Arboretum • *Guangneung Forest*
This large botanical garden includes fifteen specialized gardens, a forest museum and a herbarium. Herbs can be found in the edible plant, aroma and touch, and medicine gardens – the medicinal collection numbers 240 species of 79 families.
http://www.koreaplants.go.kr:9300/KnaServlet?cmd=E000

RUSSIA

Botanical Garden of the Irkutsk State University • *Siberia*
Display collections at this garden, which covers an area of over 27 ha (67 acres), include outdoor displays of more than 600 species of ornamental and tropical plants, including medicinal herbs, and rare and endangered plants of Central Siberia.
http://bogard.isu.ru/indexe.htm

Komarov Botanical Institute, Russian Academy of Sciences • *St. Petersburg*
Established as a pharmaceutical garden in 1714 by Tsar Peter I (1672–1725), this is now the leading botanical institution in Russia. The study of wild useful plants of Russia is new area of research here, and many of these species are on display.
http://spbrc.nw.ru/!english/org/bin.htm

SRI LANKA

Royal Botanical Gardens • *Peradeniya, Sri Lanka*
This history of the Royal Botanical Garden dates to 1371; its herb garden displays plants used in Ayurvedic medicine; in addition there is a spice garden, an orchid house, a bamboo grove, and many rare and unusual native plant species.
http://www.agridept.gov.lk/NBG/RBGindex.htm

VIETNAM

Tam Dao Botanic Garden • *Tam Dao*
This newly established garden is dedicated to the preservation of endangered wild plant species, used for medicine, food and economic purposes.

AFRICA

ALGERIA

Botanical Garden of Hamma • *Hamma*
Trees from all over the world are collected here; there is also an English garden, a French garden, and collections of useful and medicinal plants.

GHANA

Aburi Botanic Garden • *Aburi*
A garden and botanical reserve, the focus here is on conservation of native species, in particular the sustainable use of medicinal plants.
http://www.unep-wcmc.org/species/plants/ghana/aburi.htm

University Botanical Gardens, University of Ghana • *Legon, Accra*
Tropical plant conservation is the focus at this 50 ha (123 acre) garden. Many medicinal herbs have been planted, as the university researches useful applications for native plants.
http://www.ubglegon.org/garden_guide_home.html

KENYA

Nairobi Arboretum • *Nairobi*
This green oasis in the middle of Nairobi features trees, shrubs and herbaceous plants. The focus here is on education, biodiversity, and conservation. A small number of medicinal plants are on display.
http://www.naturekenya.org/FONArboretum.htm

MAURITIUS

Sir Seewoosagur Ramgoolam Botanical Garden • *Port Louis*
In the 19th century, horticulturalist Pierre Poivre introduced plant species from around the world, interspersed with indigenous species. Palms, spice and fruit trees grow here, and there is a medicinal herbs corner as well.
ncb.intnet.mu/moa/ssrbg/index.htm

Eucalyptus (Eucalyptus globulus) *is indigenous to Australia and Tasmania. The genus contains approximately 300 species and is one of the most characteristic plants of Australia.*

National Botanical Gardens • *Bloemfontein, Free State*

A demonstration garden here is devoted to native medicinal plants of South Africa and the Free State.
http://www.nbi.ac.za/freestate/main-page.htm

AUSTRALASIA

AUSTRALIA

Alice Springs Desert Park • *Northern Territory*

A newly opened park dedicated to the preservation and promotion of Australia's desert flora and fauna. Exhibits interpret traditional Aboriginal uses for the many plants native to this arid region.
http://www.alicespringsdesertpark.com.au/

MOROCCO

The Botanic Garden, Institut Agronomique et Vétérinaire Hassan II • *Rabat*

Primarily concerned with the conservation of Morocco's economic plants, the garden has collections of native and introduced plants used in agriculture and medicine.

SOUTH AFRICA

Johannesburg Botanical Garden • *Johannesburg*

The large formal herb garden includes African medicinal herbs and international medicinal, culinary, dye and oil-producing herbs. The Shakespeare Garden also contains many herbs, each labelled with reference to the plays.
http://www.jobot.co.za/

Kirstenbosch National Botanical Garden • *Cape Town*

Only native South African plants are grown in this garden, which includes a section for medicinal and useful plants. The herb rooibos is a notable species here. There is also a fragrance garden, designed for easy access for the blind.
http://www.nbi.ac.za/frames/kirstfram.htm

Australian National Botanic Gardens • *Canberra*

The native plants of Australia are the focus of this botanical garden. Plants represented here include the wattle (Acacia), eucalyptus and protea. A separate section, called the Aboriginal Trail, displays plants used by Australia's indigenous people, including those used for medicinal and culinary purposes.
http://www.anbg.gov.au/anbg/

Royal Botanic Gardens • *Sydney*

The formal herb garden displays culinary, medicinal and aromatic herbs. Exotic and tropical flowers such as orchids and carnivorous plants are on display in the Sydney Tropical Centre. Also of interest are the Rare and Threatened Plant Garden and the Native Rockery, which displays Australian native plants.
http://www.rbgsyd.nsw.gov.au/royal_botanic_gardens

NEW ZEALAND

Christchurch Botanic Gardens

A large botanical garden that includes a formal herb garden. The plants are grouped into displays according to their purpose: culinary, dyeing and medicinal.
http://www.ccc.govt.nz/Parks/BotanicGardens/

How Herbs Work

Modern research has shed much light on how herbs work. Sometimes — especially for herbs that are very powerful — scientists have been able to identify one constituent that stands out as the herb's "active ingredient". This is certainly the case with herbs such as purging buckthorn *(Rhamnus cathartica)*, whose strong laxative effect can be clearly attributed to the anthraquinone compounds it contains. Scientists have also identified many of the compounds that give culinary and aromatic herbs their familiar flavours and scents. When it comes to other herbs, especially those used primarily as medicinal remedies, explanations can be far less clear-cut. Scientists try to isolate active ingredients to better understand how herbs work. But some herbalists contend that the effects of entire plants — the combination of constituents working together — are key to the medicinal properties of most herbs. The primary medicinal effect of a plant can rarely be linked to a single chemical compound, they believe. More often, a plant's effects are caused by compounds acting together.

A magnified leaf reveals the complex maze of a plant's internal structure. In many herbs, fragrance, flavour and medicinal compounds are contained within the plant's leaves.

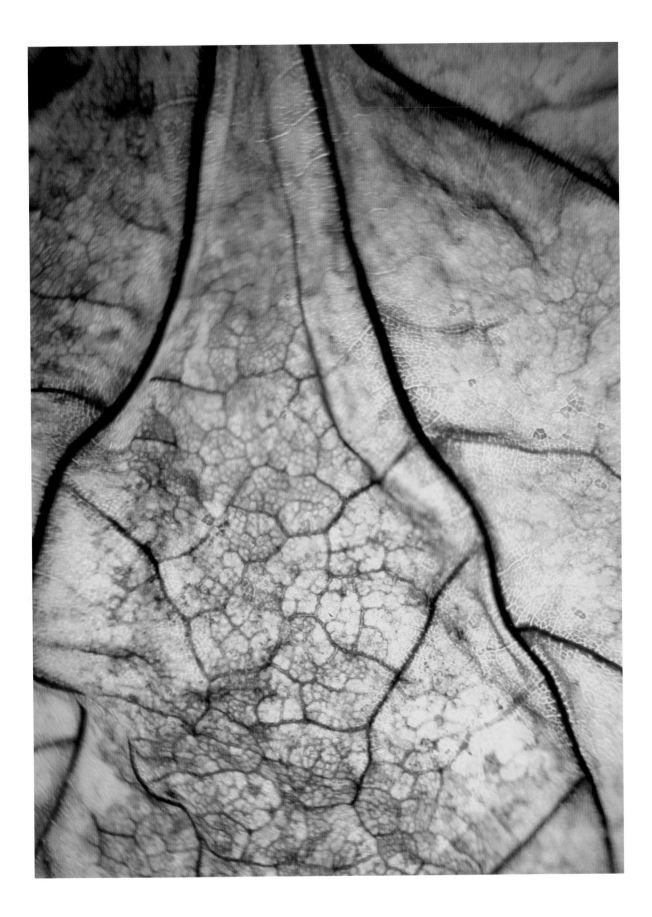

Plant Chemistry
An Introduction

Plant chemistry, also known as phytochemistry, is the study of the chemical compounds in plants. All living things on Earth are made up of chemicals. In fact, the chemical composition of plants and people are very similar. Both consist of common elements, including carbon, hydrogen, oxygen and nitrogen. Chlorophyll – the green pigment essential to photosynthesis, the process in plants that transforms water and sunlight into food – has been called "green blood" because it is so similar in chemical makeup to the haemoglobin in human blood. A molecule of chlorophyll and a molecule of haemoglobin each consist of carbon, nitrogen and oxygen atoms, but in different proportions. There are other important chemical differences between haemoglobin and chlorophyll, but the basic similarities are striking.

PLANT METABOLITES

Plants produce a variety of chemical compounds, called metabolites, as part of their normal life processes. Some of these compounds allow plants to store energy in the form of sugar, for example, while others help plants defend themselves against disease or predators.

There are two varieties of plant metabolites: primary and secondary metabolites. Primary plant metabolites, which include carbohydrates and lipids, are compounds that are essential to the life of the plant. In addition, they are essential to human health and nutrition.

Plants produce secondary metabolites using primary metabolites as building blocks. Secondary metabolites (among them terpenes, polyphenols, alkaloids and some glycodsides) are largely responsible for the characteristic aromas, flavours, colours and medicinal actions of the herbs and spices we use as foods, medicines, dyes, perfumes and other products from disinfectants to poisons. These properties also serve a vital purpose for plant life. For example, secondary metabolites are responsible for the fragrance and colour of a flower. Fragrance and colour attract the pollinators a plant needs to set seed and produce the next generation of the species. The dividing line between primary and secondary metabolites is not always clear, and the two are integrally linked.

Among all plant chemicals, terpenes, polyphenols, alkaloids and some glycosides, are important in the study of herbs. Each of these groups contain numerous compounds that are vital to the flavour, aroma, nutritional value and medicinal properties of plants.

Allium sativum (garlic) *contains compounds that can inhibit gastric ulcers.*

The seeds of flax (Linum usitatissimum) *contain omega-3 fatty acids.*

Primary Metabolites: Carbohydrates

Carbohydrates are essential to life and are part of the makeup of all living creatures. In addition to providing humans and animals with energy and fibre, carbohydrates are the basic building blocks for all other plant chemicals.

Carbohydrates are composed primarily of sugars (saccharides) whose molecules are arranged in particular ways. Monosaccharides, for example, contain one sugar unit (*mono-* means "one"), while polysaccharides contain ten or more sugar units linked together. Oligosaccharides contain between two and ten sugar units. Glucose and fructose are two of the most common monosaccharides found in plants. Sucrose, found in sugarcane, is a disaccharide (*di-* means "two") formed by a link between the sugars glucose and fructose.

Cellulose, the main component of plant cell walls and the most abundant organic compound on Earth, is a homopolysaccharide, a compound made up of chains of a single type of monosaccharide. Other important homopolysaccharides include starch, fructans and inulins. These important dietary substances are commonly called complex carbohydrates.

Many other categories and subcategories of carbohydrates are found in plants and fungi. For example, mycopolysaccharides form the cell walls of mushrooms, and are rich in fibrous carbohydrate substances called ß-D-glucans (pronounced beta-D-glucans), which have been studied for their immune-stimulating effects. Other ß-glucans are found in grains, including oats. They are an important source of soluble fibre.

Gums and mucilages – two other varieties of carbohydrates with various uses as food and herbal medicines – are also made up largely of monosaccharides. The term

When garlic is crushed, the chemical allicin is released, giving off its recognizable odour. Allicin has also been found to inhibit the bacteria responsible for gastric ulcers.

"gum" is generally understood to mean a sticky plant substance, such as gum arabic, made from *Acacia catechu*. Mucilages are slippery substances used in herbal medicine to coat and soothe irritated or inflamed tissues (such as a sore throat). Marsh mallow (*Althaea officinalis*), psyllium (*Plantago ovata*) and comfrey (*Symphytum officinale*) are all rich in slippery mucilage. Another important mucilage is carrageenan, which comes from the seaweed Irish moss (*Chondrus crispus*). Carrageenan is commonly used as a thickening agent in commercial food products.

Primary Metabolites: Lipids

Lipids – more commonly known as fats – are a major component of membranes in both plants and animals. They serve as reservoirs of energy to fuel essential cell functions. They are important components of certain vitamins (such as vitamins E and A) and various hormones. Like carbohydrates, lipids also serve as building blocks for a range of secondary plant metabolites.

Among the most important plant lipids for human health and nutrition are fatty acids. Unlike the fats found in animal products, plant fats are rich in unsaturated fatty acids, which research shows are critical for heart health. The human body is capable of producing almost all fatty-acid structures; however, some fatty acids cannot be manufactured by the body and therefore must be supplied through the diet. These fatty acids are of critical importance to human health, and are termed essential fatty acids.

Two essential fatty acids that have been most closely linked to human health are omega-3 and omega-6. Although fish oils from tuna, mackerel, herring and sardines may be the best source of omega-3s, flaxseed

❧ ANTIOXIDANTS ❧

These compounds defend the body against the effects of harmful chemicals called free radicals or reactive oxygen species. Free radicals are unstable compounds that are products of oxidation in the body.

The human body produces free radicals in response to a variety of factors, including exposure to airborne pollutants, cigarette smoke, and pharmaceutical and recreational drugs. Free radicals can wreak havoc in the body, damaging cells and contributing to accelerated ageing and a host of health problems, including cancer and heart disease. Oxidation of blood fats, for example, plays a role in the development of atherosclerosis (hardening of the arteries), which can lead to serious circulatory problems including heart attacks and strokes. Antioxidants "scavenge" or "quench" free radicals to protect the human body against these harmful effects, which is why they are considered to have "anti-ageing" properties.

Antioxidants are found widely in plants, and are plentiful in fruits, vegetables and herbs. Some herbs have particularly potent antioxidant actions; some of those include green tea *(Camellia sinensis)*, milk thistle *(Silybum marianum)*, turmeric *(Curcuma longa)*, ginkgo *(Ginkgo biloba)*, ginger *(Zingiber officinale)*, artichoke leaf *(Cynara scolymus)*, garlic *(Allium sativum)* and horse chestnut *(Aesculus hippocastanum)*.

Both black and green teas are a good source of antioxidants, which protect the body's cells against age-related damage.

(Linum usitatissimum) and the seeds of hemp *(Cannabis sativa)* contain omega-3 alpha-linolenic acid, providing valuable nonanimal sources of essential fatty acids.

Secondary Metabolites: Terpenes

Terpenes make up the largest group of secondary plant metabolites. Thousands of different terpene compounds are found in a wide variety of plant species, and many appear to have important functions for the plants that produce them. For example, some give off aromas that lure pollinators or deter predators.

Terpene-rich volatile (essential) oils have great importance in herbal medicine and cooking. These aromatic compounds are responsible for the fragrances and flavours of kitchen favourites such as thyme *(Thymus* spp.), ginger *(Zingiber officinale)*, peppermint *(Mentha x piperita)* and citrus peel. These plants are not only tasty and aromatic, but also have valuable antispasmodic, antimicrobial and carminative effects (carminative herbs enhance digestive function and relieve gas and indigestion).

Terpenes give us many other valuable medicinal compounds as well, including bitters, anti-inflammatory agents, expectorants and sedatives. Limonene, a monoterpene found in citrus peel as well as mint, dill and caraway, has been studied for potential cancer-preventive effects. Another important group of terpenes are the carotenoids – orange plant pigments in oranges, peppers and carrots – that the body converts into vitamin A.

Secondary Metabolites: Polyphenols

This group of plant chemicals contains thousands of different compounds that share common chemical characteristics. At least half of all polyphenols are part of a large subgroup called flavonoids. Flavonoids contain many important antioxidant compounds, which help eliminate harmful substances, called free radicals, from the body. The flavonoid category itself can be divided into numerous smaller subgroups of flavonoid compounds, including isoflavonoids, flavones, flavonols, flavolignans, anthocyanins and proanthocyanidins.

Green tea *(Camellia sinensis)* is one of many polyphenol-rich plants with valuable health properties. It contains antioxidant polyphenols called catechins. These compounds have been the subject of hundreds of studies that suggest they may help prevent cancer and heart disease. Many plants in the pea family (legumes) contain isoflavonoids, which have also demonstrated impressive cancer-fighting and hormone-balancing effects in modern studies. Plants rich in isoflavonoids include soy *(Glycine max)* and red clover *(Trifolium pratense)*.

of milk thistle (*Silybum marianum*). Modern studies have shown that milk thistle may protect the liver from the effects of toxins, including pharmaceutical drugs, and may help the liver regenerate damaged cells.

Secondary Metabolites: Alkaloids

This group of plant chemicals contains a large number of constituents that are highly active, meaning they can have powerful effects in the human body. Although not all alkaloids have profound effects, this group includes numerous potent medicinal constituents as well as various addictive and toxic chemicals.

Caffeine, a naturally occurring stimulant and diuretic in coffee (*Coffea arabica*), green tea (*Camellia sinensis*), among other foods, is an alkaloid with which nearly everyone is familiar. Other potent alkaloids include ephedrine (a decongestant taken from *Ephedra sinica*), theophylline (a bronchial smooth-muscle relaxant present in small quantities in tea), reserpine (a tranquilizer and antihypertensive made from the Indian plant *Rauvolfia serpentina*), and vincristine and vinblastine (cancer-fighting compounds made from Madagascar periwinkle (*Catharanthus roseus*). Many of these compounds are toxic in high doses.

A number of alkaloids have hallucinogenic effects, including mescaline, which is extracted from the peyote cactus, (*Lophophora williamsii*) and psilocybin, which is found in mushrooms in the genus *Psilocybe*. Other alkaloids have been found to be highly addictive. They include cocaine, a stimulant and anaesthetic taken from the leaves of the South American plant *Erythroxylum coca*, nicotine, taken from the leaves of the tobacco plant (*Nicotiana tabacum*), and morphine, a pain-reliever extracted from the opium poppy (*Papaver somniferum*).

Certain pyrrolizidine alkaloids, such as those found in plants of the borage family including comfrey (*Symphytum officinale*), can cause liver damage. Other poisonous alkaloids include strychnine (found in *Strychnos nux-vomica*), atropine (found in *Atropa belladonna* and *Datura stramonium*) and coniine (a deadly toxin made from poison hemlock, *Conium maculatum*).

Green teas are rich in antioxidant polyphenols (see Antioxidants, *left), powerful plant chemical compounds that may protect the body against health problems including cancer and heart disease.*

Many of the pigments that give plants their colouring are polyphenols. Antioxidant polyphenols called anthocyanins provide the blue and red colours of berries such as blueberries and cranberries. Red grapes (*Vitis vinifera*) and red wine contain anthocyanin pigments as well as resveratrol, another polyphenol. As has been found with green tea, studies have shown that berries and red wine may have healthful antioxidant effects.

Tannins are highly astringent polyphenols that have uses not only as tanning agents for the leather industry, but also as medicines. Astringents tone and tighten tissues throughout the body, including mucous membranes and skin; they are responsible for the puckering sensation caused in the mouth from a strong cup of black tea. In addition to black tea, some tannin-rich herbs are oak bark (*Quercus* spp.), witch hazel (*Hamamelis virginiana*) and agrimony (*Agrimonia eupatorium*).

Other important polyphenols include curcumin (found in turmeric, *Curcuma longa*), a powerful antioxidant that has anti-inflammatory and cancer-preventive properties, and silymarin, a mixture of flavolignan compounds that is largely responsible for the health benefits

(Continued on page 96)

Plant Metabolites

The following charts list specific plant metabolites – the primary metabolites carbohydrates and lipids and secondary metabolites terpenes, polyphenols, alkaloids and glycosides. Also included are examples of each metabolite, a description of their actions, (for more information, see Understanding Herbal Actions, pages 96 to 100), and specific herbs in which the metabolite can be found. While not exhaustive, these charts provide a starting point for those who wish to better understand the basics of plant chemistry.

CARBOHYDRATES

CATEGORY	EXAMPLE	ACTION	SOURCE
Mucopolysaccharide	Mucilage	Demulcent, emollient	Irish moss (*Chondrus crispus*), comfrey (*Symphytum officinale*), marsh mallow (*Althaea officinalis*), psyllium (*Plantago ovata*)
Oligosaccharide	Inulin	Prebiotic	Chicory (*Chicorium intybus*), beans, dandelion (*Taraxacum officinale*), echinacea (*Echinacea* spp.), elecampane (*Inula helenium*), onion (*Allium cepa*)
ß-D-glucan (polysaccharide)	Lentinan	Immunomodulator	Shiitake mushroom (*Lentinus edodes*)
Polysaccharide	Arabinogalactans	Immune stimulant	Echinacea (*Echinacea*), larch (*Larix occidentalis*), reishi mushroom (*Ganoderma lucidum*)

LIPIDS

CATEGORY	EXAMPLE	ACTION	SOURCE
Polyunsaturated fatty acid	Alpha-linolenic acid (omega-3)	Anti-inflammatory, supports cardiovascular health	Flaxseed (*Linum usitatissimum*), hemp seed (*Cannabis sativa*)
Polyunsaturated fatty acid	Gamma-linolenic acid (omega-6)	Prostaglandin precursor	Seed oils of blackcurrant (*Ribes nigrum*), borage (*Borago officinalis*), and evening primrose (*Oenothera biennis*)
Hydrocarbon sulfide	Allicin	Antimicrobial; inhibits clumping of blood platelets; lowers cholesterol and blood pressure	Garlic (*Allium sativum*)

TERPENES

CATEGORY	EXAMPLE	ACTION	SOURCE
Monoterpene (hydrocarbon)	Limonene	Aromatic, expectorant, sedative	Citrus fruits, dill (*Anethum graveolens*), fir (*Abies* spp.), mint (*Mentha* spp.)
Monoterpene (alcohol)	Geraniol	Antiseptic, aromatic	Lemongrass (*Cymbopogon citratus*), palmarosa (*Cymbopogon. martinii* var. *martinii*), rose (*Rosa* spp.), rose geranium (*Pelargonium graveolens*)
Monoterpene (alcohol)	Linalool	Antifungal, antiseptic, aromatic, sedative	Bergamot (*Citrus bergamia*), coriander (*Coriandrum sativum*), lavender (*Lavandula* spp.)
Monoterpene (alcohol)	Menthol	Carminative, decongestant	Peppermint and other mints (*Mentha* spp.)

TERPENES *(continued)*

CATEGORY	EXAMPLE	ACTION	SOURCE
Monoterpene (aldehyde)	Citronellal	Aromatic, antiseptic, insect repellant, sedative	Citronella (*Cymbopogon nardus*). eucalyptus (*Eucalyptus* spp.), lemon balm (*Melissa officialis*)
Monoterpene (ketone)	Camphor	Aromatic, moth repellant, rubefacient	Camphor tree (*Cinnamonum camphora*), Spanish sage (*Salvia lavandulifolia*), tansy (*Tanacetum vulgare*)
Monoterpene (phenol)	Carvone	Aromatic, antiseptic, carminative	Caraway (*Carum carvi*), dill (*Anethum graveolens*), spearmint (*Mentha spicata*)
Monoterpene (phenol)	Carvacrol	Aromatic, antiseptic, antifungal	Oregano (*Origanum vulgare*), summer savory (*Satureja hortensis*), thyme (*Thymus spp.*), winter savory (*S. montana*)
Monoterpene (phenol)	1,9-cineole	Antiseptic, expectorant	Cajeput (*Melaleuca quinquenervia*), eucalyptus (*Eucalyptus* spp.)
Monoterpene (phenol)	Thujone	Anthelmintic (toxic)	Sage (*Salvia officinalis*), tansy (*Tanacetum vulgare*), thuja (*Thuja occidentalis*), wormwood (*Artemisia absinthium*)
Monoterpene (phenol)	Thymol	Antiseptic, antifungal, aromatic	Oregano (*Origanum vulgare*), thyme (*Thymus* spp.)
Monoterpene (iridoid)	Harpagoside	Analgesic	Devil's claw (*Harpagophytum procumbens*)
Monoterpene (iridoid)	Valerenic acid	Antispasmodic	Valerian (*Valeriana officinalis*)
Monoterpene (iridoid)	Gentiopicrin	Bitter	Gentian (*Gentiana lutea*)
Sesquiterpene	Bisabolol	Anti-inflammatory, antispasmodic	German chamomile (*Matricaria recutita*)
Sesquiterpene	Chamazulene	Anti-inflammatory, antispasmodic	German chamomile (*Matricaria recutita*)
Sesquiterpene lactone	Absinthin	Bitter principle	Wormwood (*Artemisia absinthium*)
Sesquiterpene lactone	Artemisinin	Anticancer, antimalarial	Sweet Annie (*Artemisia annua*)
Sesquiterpene lactone	Parthenolide	Antibacterial, antifungal, antitumor	Feverfew (*Tanacetum parthenium*)
Diterpene	Coleonol	Lowers blood pressure	Coleus (*Coleus forskohlii*)
Diterpene	Ginkgolide A	Bronchodilator, bitter	Gingko (*Ginkgo biloba*)
Diterpene	Stevioside	Sweetener	Stevia (*Stevia rebaudiana*)
Triterpene saponin	Aescin	Anti-inflammatory	Horse chestnut (*Aesculus hippocastanum*)
Triterpene saponin	Glycyrrhetic acid	Antiulcer, anti-inflammatory, raises blood pressure	Licorice root (*Glycyrrhiza glabra*)
Triterpene saponin	Glycyrrhizin	Antiulcer, expectorant	Licorice root (*Glycyrrhiza glabra*)
Steroid saponin	Ginsenoside Re	Analgesic	Ginseng (*Panax* spp.)
Phytosterol	Cholesterol	Component of membranes	Date palm (*Phoenix dactylifera*)
Phytosterol	Guggulsterone (a mixture of steroid compounds)	Lowers cholesterol	Guggul resin (*Commiphora mukul*)
Carotenoid	ß–Carotene	Vitamin A precursor	Orange and yellow roots and flowers (e.g., carrots, sweet potatoes); green leaves
Carotenoid	Lycopene	Anticancer, antioxidant, protects heart health	Tomato (*Lycopersicon esculentum*)

POLYPHENOLS

CATEGORY	EXAMPLE	ACTION	SOURCE
Simple phenol	9-tetrahydrocannabinol	Antiemetic, anti-inflammatory	Cannabis (*Cannabis sativa*)
Curcuminoid	Curcumin	Anti-inflammatory, antimutagenic, antioxidant	Turmeric (*Curcuma longa*)
Coumarin	Coumarin	Anticoagulant	Sweet clover (*Melilotus* spp.), sweet woodruff (*Galium odoratum*), tonka bean (*Dipteryx odorata*)
Coumarin	Khellin	Antiasthmatic, antispasmodic	Khella (*Ammi visnaga*)
Anthraquinone	Aloe-emodin	Laxative, purgative	Aloe (*Aloe vera*), senna (*Senna alexandrina*)
Anthraquinone	Emodin	Laxative, purgative	Buckthorn (*Rhamnus cathartica*), Chinese rhubarb (*Rheum officinale, R. palmatum*)
Anthraquinone	Rhein	Laxative, purgative	Aloe (*Aloe vera*), buckthorn (*Rhamnus cathartica*), Chinese rhubarb (*Rheum officinale, R. palmatum*)
Stilbenoid	Resveratrol	Antioxidant, antithrombotic	Red grape (*Vitis vinifera*), red wine
Flavonoid (anthocyanidin)	Cyanidin	Antioxidant, pigment	Bilberry (*Vaccinium myrtillus*), blueberry (*V. angustifolium*), cranberry (*V. macrocarpon*), red grape (*Vitis vinifera*)
Flavonoid catechin)	Epigallocatechin gallate	Antioxidant	Green tea (*Camellia sinensis*)
Flavonoid (isoflavone)	Genistein	Antioxidant, phytoestrogen	Soy (*Glycine max*), red clover (*Trifolium pratense*), many other legumes
Flavonoid (flavonol)	Quercetin	Anti-inflammatory, antioxidant	Tea (*Camellia sinensis*); very common in higher plants
Flavonoid (flavonol)	Apigenin	Anti-inflammatory, sedative	German chamomile (*Matricaria recutita*), rosemary (*Rosmarinus officinalis*), thyme (*Thymus* spp.)
Condensed tannin (proanthocyanidin)	Epicatechin	Antioxidant, astringent	Grape seed, green tea (*Camellia sinensis*), red grape (*Vitis vinifera*)
Lignan	Silymarin (a complex of flavolignans)	Antioxidant, liver protectant	Milk thistle (*Silybum marianum*)
Lignan	secoisolariciresinol diglucoside	Anticarcinogenic, phytoestrogen	Flaxseed (*Linum usitatissimum*)

ALKALOIDS

CATEGORY	EXAMPLE	ACTION	SOURCE
Tropane	Atropine	Anticholinergic (inhibit transmission of parasympathetic nerve impulses); highly toxic	Belladonna (*Atropa belladonna*), jimsonweed (*Datura* spp.)
Tropane	Cocaine	Anesthetic, central nervous system (CNS) stimulant	Coca (*Erythroxylum coca*)
Pyrrolizidine	Symphytine	Liver toxin	Comfrey (*Symphytum officinale*)
Purine (methylxanthine)	Caffeine	CNS stimulant	Coffee (*Coffea arabica*), chocolate (*Theobroma cacao*), green tea (*Camellia sinensis*), guarana (*Paullinia cupana*), maté (*Ilex paraguarensis*)
Purine (methylxanthine)	Theobromine	Bronchial relaxant, CNS stimulant, diuretic	Tea (*Camellia sinensis*), chocolate (*Theobroma cacao*)

ALKALOIDS (continued)

CATEGORY	EXAMPLE	ACTION	SOURCE
Purine (methylxanthine)	Theophylline	Cardiac stimulant, diuretic, slight CNS stimulant	Tea (*Camellia sinensis*)
Isoquinolone	Berberine	Antimicrobial, liver protectant	Barberry (*Berberis vulgaris*), Oregon grape (*Mahonia aquifolium*), goldenseal (*Hydrastis canadensis*), bloodroot (*Sanguinaria canadensis*)
Isoquinolone	Codeine	Analgesic, antitussive	Opium poppy (*Papaver somniferum*)
Isoquinolone	Morphine	Analgesic, hypnotic	Opium poppy (*Papaver somniferum*)
Indole	L-ephedrine	Bronchodilator, CNS stimulant, decongestant	Ephedra (*Ephedra sinica*)
ß-carboline	Mescaline	Hallucinogenic	Peyote (*Lophophora williamsii*)
ß-carboline	Reserpine	Antihypertensive, sedative	Rauvolfia root (*Rauvolfia serpentina*)
ß-carboline	Vinblastine	Antitumour	Madagascar periwinkle (*Catharanthus roseus*)
Quinoline	Quinine	Antimalarial, bitter	Cinchona (*Cinchona* spp.)

GLYCOSIDES

CATEGORY	EXAMPLE	ACTION	SOURCE
Cyanogenic glycoside	Cyanide	Poison	Bitter almond (*Prunus dulcis* var. *amara*)
Cyanogenic glycoside	Prunasin	Expectorant, sedative	Wild cherry bark (*Prunus serotina*)
Cardiac glycoside	Convallatoxin	Cardioactive (toxic)	Lily of the valley (*Convallaria majalis*)
Cardiac glycoside	Digoxin	Cardioactive (toxic)	Foxglove (*Digitalis* spp.)
Phenolic glycoside	Salicin, salicylic acid	Analgesic, anti-inflammatory	Meadowsweet (*Filipendula ulmaria*), poplar (*Populus* spp.), willow (*Salix* spp.)
Phenolic glycoside	Arbutin	Antitussive, diuretic, urinary antiseptic	Bearberry (*Arctostaphylos uva-ursi*), bilberry (*Vaccinium myrtillus*)
Glucosinolate	Sinigrin	Pungent principle	Horseradish (*Armoracia rusticana*), black mustard (*Brassica nigra*)
Glucosinolate	Indole-3-carbinol	Anticarcinogenic	Broccoli, cabbage (*Brassica* spp.), kale

(Continued from page 91)

GLYCOSIDES

Another type of plant chemical, glycosides are particularly important in the study of herbal medicine. These carbohydrate-based compounds contain a sugar unit attached to a noncarbohydrate molecule, called the aglycone. This category of chemical contains many compounds that have important medicinal actions, as well as some dangerous toxins. For instance, cyanogenic glycosides, found in bitter almond and apple seeds, produce the deadly poison cyanide. Other cyanogenic glycosides have medicinal effects when taken in small quantities, such as prunasin, an expectorant component that is found in wild cherry bark (*Prunus serotina*). Cardiac glycosides, such as those in lily of the valley (*Convallaria majalis*) and foxglove (*Digitalis* spp.) are extremely potent chemicals that should never be taken for self-treatment. Cardiac glycosides improve the heart's efficiency without increasing its need for oxygen. Plants containing these compounds were once the only available treatments for serious heart conditions, such as congestive heart failure (a disease in which the heart loses its ability to efficiently pump blood). However, because cardiac glycosides are eliminated from the body slowly, dangerous levels may accumulate in the blood. Today, it is safer to take modern pharmaceuticals that have been developed to treat congestive heart failure. It is easier for doctors to monitor and control the dosages of these drugs. An important drug in this category is digoxin, a compound first isolated from *Digitalis lanata*.

Catnip (Nepeta cataria)*, a member of the mint family, is known for its effect on cats, but its leaves also make a popular tea.*

Another group of glycosides are the glucosinolates found primarily in cruciferous vegetables (members of the mustard family, Brassicaceae), such as mustard, horseradish, cabbage, broccoli, kale and radish. When the plant is crushed, its glucosinolates undergo a chemical reaction that creates the volatile oil compounds we know as mustard oils. When applied to the skin, mustard oils have a warming, stimulating effect, which is why mustard poultices have traditionally been used to relieve chest congestion. Research has shown that indole-3-carbinol may help prevent certain cancers, including colon and breast cancers. Indole-3-carbinol is produced in the body as it breaks down a glucosinolate found in cruciferous vegetables.

UNDERSTANDING HERBAL ACTIONS

Scientific research has contributed a great deal to our understanding of how herbs work. But the actions of most herbs were discovered by traditional healers through a process of trial and error, intuition and observation. Herbs have been used empirically for thousands of years – meaning that their applications were learned, verified and passed along through a process of experimentation and documentation. The hands-on healers who made these discoveries – folk doctors and village healers, shamans, monks and nuns, quietly serving their communities – are the ones to thank for many so-called scientific discoveries about herbs. For example, if folk healers had not discovered that black cohosh (*Cimicifuga racemosa*) was effective in easing women's transition through menopause, it is unlikely that any scientific research would have been conducted to confirm this use. And although laboratory research shows that garlic (*Allium sativum*) has antimicrobial activity, traditional healers knew this through experience and have long used the herb to treat all kinds of infections, from colds and flu to infected skin wounds.

One way to learn to use medicinal herbs is to gain an understanding of the various effects, or actions, that herbs may have on the human body. Many of these are similar to the effects of modern pharmaceuticals, including antispasmodic (muscle-relaxing) effects, analgesic (pain-relieving) effects and anti-inflammatory effects. Others are described according to terminology unique to herbal medicine, such as adaptogens (herbs that help the body defend against physical stress), alteratives (herbs that slowly restore efficient body function), and carminatives (herbs that enhance digestion).

Herbs appear to have what herb researchers call "affinities", to particular body systems; in other words, the effects of the herbs are more pronounced in some parts of the body than others. Among demulcent herbs, those that provide protective coatings for inflamed or irritated tissues, corn silk (*Zea mays*) is one example that provides comfort for the urinary tract, while marsh mallow root (*Althaea officinalis*) soothes the digestive tract.

Kava (*Piper methysticum*) is an antispasmodic that relaxes muscles all over the body, while wild cherry bark (*Prunus serotina*) acts primarily to relax respiratory muscles. Hawthorn (*Crataegus laevigata*) strengthens the heart and blood vessels, while raspberry leaf (*Rubus idaeus*) tones the tissue of the uterus.

Turmeric (Curcuma longa), *shown at left in its dried form and at right as a fresh root, contains anti-inflammatory compounds that can reduce the swelling and redness associated with inflammation.*

In addition, even though a herb may be especially well known for a certain effect (and so is termed a "specific" for a particular condition) most herbs provide a combination of actions. Chamomile (*Matricaria recutita*), for example, is known as a specific for the treatment of stomach ulcers because it has an anti-inflammatory effect on the digestive tract. It also soothes frazzled nerves, relaxes tense muscles, alleviates indigestion and is a valuable anti-inflammatory remedy for skin irritations. Feverfew (*Tanacetum parthenium*) is best known for helping prevent migraine headaches, but it has also been used to treat arthritis, dizziness, tinnitus and painful menstruation or sluggish menstrual flow.

In other words, herbs have both primary and secondary actions. Herbalists base their treatments not only on alleviating symptoms, but also finding the underlying cause of those symptoms and correcting weaknesses in order to prevent further disease. By taking into account a herb's primary and secondary actions as well as its body-system affinity, it is possible to choose a herb (or a combination of herbs) appropriate for not only relieving an acute problem, but also improving chronic conditions or heading off future problems.

To use a simple example, catnip (*Nepeta cataria*) is an antispasmodic herb that also relieves indigestion and acts as a mild sedative. It is therefore an excellent choice for someone who suffers from stress-related indigestion. In a slightly more complicated scenario, someone who has bronchitis but also has a family history of heart disease would benefit from taking garlic, which will provide relief for chest infections while also improving the health of the circulatory system.

Tonics and Effectors

Medicinal herbs can be grouped roughly into two very broad categories, according to the intensity of their activity: tonics and effectors. Tonics are mild herbs that can be taken long-term as preventive medicines or to gently correct and balance body functions.

Feverfew (Tanacetum parthenium) *is best known for helping prevent migraine headaches, but has also been used to treat arthritis, dizziness, tinnitus and painful menstruation.*

These herbs are more like foods than medicines and are among the safest of plant remedies. Some examples of general tonics are nettle (*Urtica dioica*) and cleavers (*Galium aparine*). Like all herbs, tonics display affinities for particular body systems. For example, hawthorn (*Crataegus laevigata*) and garlic (*Allium sativum*) are excellent tonics for the cardiovascular system, while bitter herbs, such as mugwort (*Artemisia vulgaris*), are effective for the digestive system.

Effectors, on the other hand, are herbs that have a more immediately noticeable effect upon the body. Herbalists call on these herbs to treat acute illnesses (such as infections), and relieve specific symptoms (such as a cough or sore throat). While many effectors are mild and can even be used as tonics, others contain powerful chemical constituents and must be used with caution. Some may even be toxic in high doses.

Mild effector herbs include feverfew (*Tanacetum parthenium*), saw palmetto (*Serenoa repens*) and turmeric (*Curcuma longa*). Strong effectors include stimulant laxatives such as senna (*Senna alexandrina*) and buckthorn (*Rhamnus cathartica*), as well as powerful, potentially toxic herbs, such as lobelia (*Lobelia inflata*), used in small doses to relax muscles in cases of asthma and bronchitis, and pokeweed (*Phytolacca americana*), used in small doses to treat infection and promote lymphatic drainage.

A Glossary of Herbal Actions

Many terms, "alterative" among them, are specific to the practice of herbal medicine. Others – "antioxidant", for example – were unknown to traditional healers of yesterday but are important concepts in our current understanding of how herbs work.

The terms on the following pages are not a comprehensive list of herbal actions, but are meant to serve as a starting-point for those who are interested in studying herbs. Note also that these terms and definitions are more relevant to Western herbalism than to systems such as Traditional Chinese Medicine and Ayurveda, which are based on completely different concepts and have a terminology all their own (see pages 120 to 127 for more on these healing systems).

Adaptogens are compounds found in herbs that can help the body adapt to and defend against the effects of physical stress, such as extreme cold or sleep deprivation. Scientists do not yet understand exactly how adaptogens work. Some theories suggest that they may help control the release and effects of stress hormones and modulate blood glucose levels, which in turn counteracts the damaging effects of stress on the body. Among the more common adaptogenic herbs are ginseng (*Panax* spp.), eleuthero or Siberian ginseng (*Eleutherococcus senticosus*), and reishi mushroom (*Ganoderma lucidum*).

Alteratives are herbs used to gradually bring about fundamental changes in health. They work over time to restore body function, and are often used as part of herbal treatment for skin conditions, such as eczema. It is difficult to explain how they do this. In older herbal books, alteratives are often described as having "blood cleansing" abilities. Researchers are as yet unsure of how exactly they work, but scientific studies offer a number of possibilities. Some alteratives, such as burdock (*Arctium lappa*), nettle (*Urtica dioica*) and yellow dock (*Rumex crispus*), seem to improve the efficiency of basic body functions, such as digestion, assimilation of nutrients and elimination of wastes. Others, such as echinacea (*Echinacea* spp.) and cleavers (*Galium aparine*) have beneficial effects on immune system function. As with many herbs, it is likely that alteratives work via a combination of effects.

Analgesics and anodynes are pain relievers. Herbal examples include willow bark (*Salix* spp.), poplar (*Populus* spp.) and devil's claw (*Harpagophytum procumbens*).

Anticatarrhal herbs help the body eliminate excess mucus. Many of these herbs contain astringent tannins; others are rich in volatile oils. Examples include echinacea (*Echinacea* spp.), elecampane (*Inula helenium*), hyssop (*Hyssopus officinalis*) and thyme (*Thymus* spp.).

Anticholesterolemic herbs lower cholesterol levels by either inhibiting the body's production or absorption of cholesterol or by enhancing its excretion. Some examples are garlic (*Allium sativum*), artichoke leaf (*Cynara scolymus*), green tea (*Camellia sinensis*) and soy (*Glycine max*).

Anti-inflammatory agents reduce swelling and redness associated with inflammation. Some examples of anti-inflammatory herbs for internal use include turmeric (*Curcuma longa*), meadowsweet (*Filipendula ulmaria*), wild yam (*Dioscorea villosa*), devil's claw (*Harpagophytum procumbens*) and *Boswellia serrata*. Some anti-inflammatory herbs for external use are St John's wort (*Hypericum perforatum*) and arnica (*Arnica montana*).

Antimicrobial herbs contain compounds that kill pathogens, which are disease-causing organisms. Herbs with antibacterial, antifungal and antiviral actions are all considered antimicrobial. Some antimicrobials, such as echinacea (*Echinacea* spp.), also stimulate the activity of the immune system. Cranberry (*Vaccinium macrocarpon*) and related plants, such as blueberry (*v. angustifolium*) are unique among antimicrobial plants; research has shown that they are effective in preventing urinary tract infections because they discourage the attachment of bacteria to the walls of the urinary tract.

Antioxidants protect the body from the damaging effects of free radicals and may help protect against various degenerative diseases. (See Antioxidants, page 90).

Antirheumatic is a somewhat vague term applied to herbs that are helpful in the treatment of arthritis and other rheumatic conditions. Some of the herbs in this category include devil's claw (*Harpagophytum procumbens*), turmeric (*Curcuma longa*), nettle (*Urtica dioica*), boswellia (*Boswellia serrata*), bogbean (*Menyanthes trifoliata*) and feverfew (*Tanacetum parthenium*).

Antispasmodic herbs relax muscles and ease muscle spasms and cramps. Some may alleviate muscle tension throughout the body; others are specific to certain types of muscle tissue or organ systems. Many are also relaxing nervines, easing psychological tension as well. For example, chamomile (*Matricaria recutita*) and valerian (*Valeriana officinalis*) relax spasms in the digestive tract and also calm nervous tension. Wild cherry bark (*Prunus serotina*) and gumweed (*Grindelia squarrosa*) relieve spasms in the respiratory tract. Cramp bark (*Viburnum opulus*), black haw (*V. prunifolium*) and valerian help ease muscle tension throughout the body.

Astringent tighten and tone tissues, especially mucous membranes, usually due to their tannin content. They also help dry excess secretions. They may be taken internally to treat conditions such as diarrhoea, or externally, as styptics, to stop bleeding. Examples include yarrow (*Achillea millefolium*), witch hazel (*Hamamelis virginiana*), oak bark (*Quercus* spp.), and cranesbill (*Geranium maculatum*).

Bitter herbs stimulate digestion, enhancing the flow of digestive juices and the muscle action that moves food through the digestive tract, or peristalsis. Some

bitter salad greens are commonly eaten before a meal to aid digestion. Gentian (*Gentiana lutea*), mugwort (*Artemisia vulgaris*), wormwood (*A. absinthium*), dandelion leaf (*Taraxacum officinale*), and agrimony (*Agrimonia eupatoria*) are all examples of bitter herbs.

Carminative herbs relieve gastrointestinal stress. They also enhance peristalsis, the action that moves food and gas through the digestive tract. Many plants that have carminative actions are also popular culinary herbs and spices; those include thyme (*Thymus* spp.), dill (*Anethum graveolens*), caraway (*Carum carvi*) and ginger (*Zingiber officinale*).

Cholagogue herbs act by stimulating the flow of the digestive enzyme bile, which aids the digestive process. Some examples include barberry (*Berberis vulgaris*), dandelion root (*Taraxacum officinale*) and artichoke leaf (*Cynara scolymus*).

Demulcent herbs soothe and protect irritated or inflamed tissue, and are often specific to one or more body system. For instance, corn silk (*Zea mays*) and marsh mallow leaf (*Althaea officinalis*) are both urinary tract demulcents; marsh mallow root and liquorice (*Glycyrrhiza glabra*) are digestive system demulcents. Respiratory tract demulcents include mullein (*Verbascum thapsus*), liquorice and marsh mallow root.

Ginkgo biloba (Ginkgo biloba) dilates blood vessels, which helps cardiovascular conditions such as high blood pressure.

Diaphoretic herbs induce perspiration, helping to "break" a fever and improve circulation, and they have long been used to treat colds and the flu. Examples include yarrow (*Achillea millefolium*), boneset (*Eupatorium perfoliatum*) and ginger (*Zingiber officinale*).

Diuretic herbs stimulate the flow of urine and help the body eliminate excess fluid. Some also have antiseptic actions in the urinary tract, making them useful for urinary tract infections. These may, however, be too irritating for people with kidney problems. Examples of diuretics include dandelion leaf (*Taraxacum officinale*), parsley (*Petroselinium crispum*), corn silk (*Zea mays*) and saw palmetto (*Serenoa repens*). Diuretics with strong antiseptic properties include the plants juniper (*Juniperus communis*) and buchu (*Agathosma betulina*).

Emmenagogue is a term that once referred to herbs that induced menstrual flow, but has come to be used more loosely to describe herbs that benefit female reproductive health. Examples of herbs thought to stimulate sluggish menstrual flow include yarrow (*Achillea millefolium*), feverfew (*Tanacetum parthenium*), mugwort (*Artemisia vulgaris*) and partridgeberry (*Mitchella repens*). Other emmenagogues include black cohosh (*Cimicifuga racemosa*) and vitex (*Vitex agnus-castus*), which help normalize the function of the female reproductive system. Raspberry leaf (*Rubus idaeus*) is an important uterine tonic.

Expectorant herbs promote the elimination of mucus from the lungs. The term is also used more generally to describe herbs that have beneficial or tonic effects in the respiratory system. Relaxing expectorants soothe bronchial spasms and dry coughs. These herbs often work through demulcent or antispasmodic actions. Two examples are liquorice ((*Glycyrrhiza glabra*) and marsh mallow root (*Althaea officinalis*). Stimulating expectorants, which commonly contain volatile oils, saponins or alkaloids, help the lungs expel mucus. This group includes horehound (*Marrubium vulgare*) and elecampane (*Inula helenium*). Herbs with a broader expectorant action include mullein (*Verbascum thapsus*) and garlic (*Allium sativum*).

Galactogogue herbs help stimulate the flow of milk in breastfeeding mothers. Galactogogues include dill (*Anethum graveolens*) and fennel (*Foeniculum vulgare*). Both of these herbs are also classic remedies for infant colic.

Hepatic and hepatoprotective herbs have been found to be helpful in improving liver function. Examples include milk thistle (*Silybum marianum*), barberry (*Berberis vulgaris*) and liquorice ((*Glycyrrhiza glabra*).

Hypnotic herbs induce sleep and can be taken to treat insomnia. Examples include hops (*Humulus lupulus*), valerian (*Valeriana officinalis*), passionflower (*Passiflora incarnata*) and California poppy (*Eschscholzia californica*).

Hypotensive herbs help lower blood pressure. These include linden (*Tilia platyphylos*), garlic (*Allium sativum*) and hawthorn (*Crataegus laevigata*).

Immunomodulator herbs affect immune function. Some, such as echinacea (*Echinacea* spp.), stimulate immune cells such as phagocytes, which fight infection by destroying invading pathogens. Others are the subject of ongoing clinical research to determine and clarify their activity.

Among these herbs are astragalus (*Astragalus membranaceus*), shiitake mushroom (*Lentinus edodes*) and reishi mushroom (*Ganoderma lucidum*).

Laxative herbs stimulate the action of the bowels. Bulk-forming laxatives are high in fibre. Stimulant laxatives chemically induce peristalsis, the muscle activity that moves food through the digestive system. In high doses, stimulant laxatives act as cathartics or purgatives, but are not recommended for long-term use. Bulk-forming laxatives include psyllium (*Plantago ovata*) and flaxseed (*Linum usitatissimum*). Stimulant laxatives include senna (*Senna alexandrina*), cascara sagrada (*Rhamnus purshiana*) and buckthorn (*R. cathartica*). Mild laxatives that work through other actions (by stimulating bile flow, for example) include dandelion root (*Taraxacum officinale*) and yellow dock (*Rumex crispus*).

Nervine herbs affect the function of the nervous system. Nervines may be relaxing, tonic or stimulating. Relaxing nervines include valerian (*Valeriana officinalis*), passionflower (*Passiflora incarnata*) and chamomile (*Matricaria recutita*). Relaxing nervine tonics include oats (*Avena sativa*), skullcap (*Scutellaria lateriflora*) and St. John's wort (*Hypericum perforatum*). Herbs that stimulate the activity of the nervous system include caffeine-containing plants such as tea (*Camellia sinensis*) and guarana (*Paullinia cupana*), as well as volatile-oil rich plants such as rosemary (*Rosmarinus officinalis*) and peppermint (*Mentha x piperita*).

Rubefacients are herbs that, when applied externally, draw blood to an area for a localized warming effect. Some examples include ginger (*Zingiber officinale*), black mustard (*Brassica nigra*) and cayenne (*Capsicum annuum*).

Vasodilator herbs cause dilation of blood vessels, which is useful in the treatment of cardiovascular conditions such as high blood pressure. Examples include ginkgo biloba (*Ginkgo biloba*), ephedra (*Ephedra sinensis*) and feverfew (*Tanacetum parthenium*).

Vulnerary herbs speed the healing of wounds. Examples include aloe (*Aloe vera*), comfrey (*Symphytum officinale*), calendula (*Calendula officinalis*), St. John's wort (*Hypericum perforatum*) and echinacea (*Echinacea* spp.). Vulnerary herbs may also be used internally.

Chamomile (Matricaria recutita) is a vulnerary herb, which means that it helps speed wound healing. Chamomile has traditionally been used to treat stomach ulcers.

CHAPTER 5

Beauty *with* Herbs

Since the earliest days of recorded history, humans have used herbs and other plant ingredients to beautify their skin, hair and nails. Ancient records reveal recipes for fragrant hair treatments, healing herb-infused oils, and tonics for longevity and youthful appearance. Botanical cosmetics have been discovered in the tombs of ancient Egyptians, and legendary beauties Cleopatra and Nefertiti are reputed to have claimed aloe as one of their anti-ageing secrets. For centuries, Indian women have decorated their hair and skin with henna and anointed their bodies with fragrant botanical oils. Hippocrates, the ancient Greek physician, studied the link between health and beauty and is credited with developing the science of dermatology.

Herbs are no less popular today as cosmetic ingredients. Herbs and other botanical ingredients from gentle, emollient vegetable oils to fruits rich in skin-softening plant compounds offer an alternative to the harsh chemicals found in many commercial beauty products. Equally important, they provide exquisite natural fragrances that uplift the spirit and add to personal allure.

Take a milk bath with rose petals – the lactic acid in milk makes it a good skin cleanser; rose is an aromatherapy remedy for tension.

Skin Health

Beautiful skin is healthy skin. Used on the outside of the body, herbs and other botanical ingredients can help keep skin looking fresh and youthful by exfoliating dead skin cells, improving skin tone and blood circulation, and keeping skin supple and hydrated. They can also soothe irritated skin, combat inflammation, fight skin infections and help to heal wounds and burns. Taken internally, many herbs have a long history of traditional use for helping to treat skin problems from the inside out – for example, burdock, nettle and red clover. The botanical world is also rich in alpha hydroxy acids (AHAs). These acidic plant compounds help exfoliate and soften the skin and are used in many of today's anti-ageing skin products.

However, radiant, healthy skin does not depend only on what we put on the skin that covers our bodies, but also on what we put into those bodies. Drinking plenty of water is essential to keep skin hydrated and looking its best. Skin, hair and nail health all require, and benefit from, a balanced diet that includes plenty of nutrient-rich fruits, vegetables, legumes, whole grains and healthful oils, especially those foodstuffs that are rich in antioxidants and essential fatty acids. Regular exercise promotes blood flow to the skin and affords a healthy glow that keeps skin looking fresh and youthful. And never underestimate the cosmetic value of adequate sleep – called "beauty rest" for good reason.

Other lifestyle choices are just as important to healthy skin as proper diet and exercise. Exposure to the sun's rays and cigarette smoking are recognized as two of the leading causes of skin wrinkling and other signs of

premature ageing. Experts advise that people should wear adequate sun protection, such as sunscreen and a wide-brimmed hat, whenever they expose themselves to the damaging rays of the sun.

BEAUTY THROUGH THE AGES

From the earliest times, herbs have been used to make people feel and look better, and all over the world much time and energy – and in today's world, money – have been spent in developing herbal products for cosmetic and medicinal use.

At a time when other civilizations were still in their infancy, Chinese herbalists were experimenting with the possible uses of plants, seeking to find the combination of herbs that would do most to nourish and cure. The Ancient Egyptians used eye pencils, depilatories, deodorants, hair tonics and cleansing creams, all made from

Dried herbs and flowers can be added to homemade facial steams.

Teas made from fresh herbs and herb flowers can be used as a hair rinse.

herbs such as limes, lilies, frankincense and myrrh. In India, makeup and perfumes were being used for religious ceremonies as early as the second and first centuries B.C.E., with both men and women adorning themselves with jewellery, scents and cosmetics. The word lavender comes from the Latin *lavare,* meaning "to wash", and this herb was used by ancient Romans to scent bathwater and linen, and soothe wounds. In Biblical times in the Middle East, perfumes and bath oils were made from saffron, cassia, cinnamon and camphire (henna). By the ninth century C.E., Arab scientists had perfected the process for extracting a herb's essential oil. Over the centuries that followed, much of the Arab world was using aromatic baths, powders and salves to cure a variety of ills. Through their work, aromatherapy developed as a popular medicinal treatment.

Certain plants have had a special significance for hundreds of years. One that was introduced to Europe from the Middle East during the Crusades was the damask rose (*Rose damascena*). Roses and the fragrant oils they produce have held a place of supreme importance in the Muslim world since Mohammed's lifetime (570–632 C.E.), and as early as the 7th century, Arab alchemists distilled rose oil, which they used to purify mosques, infuse prayer beads with fragrance, sprinkle guests as they entered houses and flavour foods ranging from sherbet to candy. In fact, one of the books by the Arabic herbalist Avicenna (980–1037) was devoted entirely to roses. Today, rose oil is still an important ingredient in aromatherapy and other beauty products.

HERBAL BEAUTY PRODUCTS

A walk down the cosmetics aisle of a grocery or health food shop is likely to reveal a bewildering array of products that promote the benefits of the herbs and other botanical ingredients that they contain, from shampoos and conditioners to soaps, cleansers and anti-ageing face creams. Many commercial skin and hair care products touted as "natural" contain synthetic ingredients, including preservatives. If herbal beauty products are being bought from a shop, it is a good idea to become educated about the ingredients they contain, and labels should be read carefully to ensure that the products will deliver the benefits they promise.

An easy, economical alternative is to make herbal skin and hair care products in one's own kitchen. Herbs may be incorporated into beauty products in many ways. Dried herbs can be added whole to facial steams or ground to a powder to make facial scrubs. Herbal infusions or decoctions (teas) can be used as rinses to add shine to hair or to bring therapeutic benefits to a bath or foot soak. Infused in oil (such as sweet almond oil), herbs may be applied directly to the skin or incorporated into creams, lotions and salves with soothing and emollient properties. All kinds of botanicals and kitchen ingredients, including fruits and milk products, can be used to make rejuvenating facial masks. By choosing herbs and other ingredients recommended for specific skin types or problems, it is simple to customize herbal beauty products that will not only enhance one's appearance, but also improve skin health.

Calendula (Calendula officinalis) *is a common ingredient in creams that soothe skin irritations.*

Oatmeal, lavender and cornmeal make an invigorating homemade facial scrub.

It is easy to personalize homemade beauty products by scenting them with aromatic herbs or essential oils, which are a great deal more concentrated than herbs. (See page 133 for more information and cautions about using essential oils.) Floral scents, such as rose, jasmine, lavender and orange blossom, are generally more popular with women than with men. To give homemade herbal beauty products a masculine flair, focus on plants with woodsy, spicy or "green" scents, such as fir, bay, peppermint or rosemary. By choosing herbs with clean, light or neutral aromas, such as calendula, lavender or citrus, it is easy to make natural skin care products that will appeal to both men and women.

Homemade herbal beauty products do not contain chemical preservatives, so they will have a shorter shelf life than their commercial counterparts. To reduce the risk of spoilage, make sure that all the equipment used to make herbal cosmetics is scrupulously clean. Avoid dipping fingers directly into these mixtures; instead, use a spatula or other clean utensil. It is best to make herbal beauty products in small batches, and then store them in the refrigerator to keep them fresh as long as possible.

Be sure to test any new herbal product on the inside of the arm before applying it to the face, to be sure it will not cause an allergic reaction. It is essential to avoid getting any facial products in the eyes.

Herbal Steams

A herbal steam opens the pores and stimulates circulation of blood to the facial skin. However, for those people who have extremely sensitive or dry skin, suffer from a skin complaint or are prone to developing tiny broken veins or capillaries (couperose skin), it may be best to avoid herbal steams unless recommended by a doctor or other healthcare provider, as they may be too irritating for delicate or damaged skin.

To make a homemade facial steam, add about 36 g (1¼ oz) of dried herbs to a pot of steaming water. (It depends on skin type, but some appropriate herb choices for facial steams include calendula, German or Roman chamomile, lavender flowers, rose petals, orange or other citrus peel and peppermint.) Position the face about 30 cm (12 in) over the bowl containing the steaming water, drape a towel over the head, and allow the steam to bathe the skin of the face for a moment or two. Then remove the towel, raise the head and take a few breaths of fresh air. Repeat the process for a maximum of five to ten minutes.

As the herbs steep, the rising steam will open the pores and carry the aromatic volatile oil components of the herbs to the facial skin. Finish the process by cleansing thoroughly and splashing with cool (not cold) water or toner to close the pores again.

A HERBAL FACIAL ❧ STEP-BY-STEP ❧

A homemade herbal facial is a gentle and wonderful way to cleanse, exfoliate and enhance blood circulation to the skin of the face. Performed once a week, it can keep the skin looking vibrant and feeling supple by customizing the facial treatment to meet the needs of a particular skin type.

The first step to a home facial is to cleanse the skin with a mild cleanser. Next, steam the pores open with a herbal steam (or, if dealing with very sensitive skin, with a warm washcloth). Next, gently exfoliate with a herbal scrub, being careful not to rub too hard and to avoid the delicate skin around the eyes. Rinse and apply a mask of appropriate for the skin type (a clay-based mask for oily skin, for example, or a cream and avocado mask for dry skin). After carefully removing the mask from the face with cleanser and warm water, finish by splashing with toner, blot dry and apply moisturizer.

Scrubs, Cleansers and Toners

The mild exfoliating action of a herbal scrub sloughs off dead skin cells and stimulates circulation to the skin, leaving the face glowing and feeling baby-soft. Be aware that scrubbing too vigorously can leave unsightly blotches on the skin, although these will fade with time. Those who have sensitive skin should remember to be extra gentle, and to avoid scrubbing with these herbal cleansers more than once a week.

To make a basic herbal facial scrub, place 156 g (5½ oz) oatmeal, 69 g (2½ oz) cornmeal, and 24 g (1 oz) of dried herbs (for example, lavender, calendula, peppermint, rose petals or a mixture of herbs) into a clean coffee grinder, or use a pestle and mortar. Grind the mixture to a fine powder, and then store in a tightly sealed container. To use, place some of the mixture in the palm of the hand and add enough water to make a paste. Apply this mixture evenly all over the face, taking care to avoid the eyes. Massage the scrub gently into the skin, using circular motions and avoiding the delicate skin around the eyes. Then rinse it off thoroughly. Other good scrub ingredients include ground almonds, clay and sugar.

To create a mild skin cleanser, combine powdered milk with a herbal infusion. Make an infusion with a herb that is appropriate for your skin type, allow it to cool to a comfortable temperature, and then mix in one tablespoon (5 g/¼ oz) powdered milk per cup of infusion. This mixture will not keep well, so make only as much as you plan to use within a day or two and immediately refrigerate any unused portion.

Applying a toner after cleansing the skin helps restore its acid balance (pH) and provides an astringent action that tightens pores. A simple toner may be made by combining about one tablespoon (15 ml/½ fl.oz) of apple cider vinegar or lemon juice with 238 ml (8 fl. oz) water. Splash or spray the face with the toner, again being careful to avoid the eyes. Hydrosols (flower waters that are created as a distillation by-product during the manufacture of essential oils) make soothing, aromatic toners. Witch hazel is an excellent toner for oily skin.

Chamomile (Chamaemelum nobile) added to a facial steam can soothe itchy, irritated skin.

❧ QUEEN OF HUNGARY'S WATER ❧

Handed down through the generations, Queen of Hungary's water is a classic vinegar-based skin toner that tightens pores, balances pH and improves skin tone.

Herb-infused vinegars provide myriad cosmetic benefits and are remarkably easy to make. Although some modern women may shy away from using vinegar as a skin-care ingredient, herb-infused vinegars have been treasured cosmetics for centuries, and in fact, few ingredients are as effective for balancing the skin's pH. The aroma of the vinegar dissipates quickly and does not linger on the skin.

The ingredients and proportions used in Queen of Hungary's water can vary according to what is on hand, but the basic ingredients are dried lemon balm (melissa), chamomile, rosemary, calendula, rose petals, lemon peel, sage, comfrey and elder flower. Place the herbs in a jar, cover completely with apple cider vinegar, and soak (macerate) in the vinegar for at least two weeks. Strain. To each 238 ml (8 fl.oz) of herb-infused vinegar, add 119 ml (4 fl.oz) of rosewater.

Masks

Depending on skin type, a botanical mask may be designed as a hydrating, emollient, deep moisturizing treatment, or an astringent, skin-tightening treatment.

Many fruits are rich in skin-softening alpha hydroxy acids (AHA), which make them an excellent addition to facial masks. Among many others, AHA-rich botanicals include apples, citrus fruits, sugar, grapes and strawberries. In addition to herbs and botanicals, other good ingredients for facial masks are milk products (yogurt, cream or powdered milk, which are all rich in AHA), clay (an especially helpful ingredient for those with oily skin), avocado, honey, egg yolks (each of which provides emollient and moisturizing benefits) and egg whites (which provide astringent and toning action).

For a mask, mix the chosen ingredients in a bowl and mash into a paste. Apply the mask to facial skin and leave on for twenty minutes, or as long as is comfortable. Cleanse the skin thoroughly. Because these ingredients do not keep well, make only enough of the mask as is needed for one application.

Combine one mashed avocado with one tablespoon (15 ml/¹/₂ fl.oz) olive oil and then spread on the face for a moisturizing facial mask.

Avocado (Persea americana) *is a popular ingredient in many skin moisturizing products.*

Herb-Infused Oils

Infused oils – vegetable oils in which herbs have been steeped to extract their healing compounds – have cosmetic applications as well as many therapeutic benefits for the skin.

To make a herb-infused oil, fill a jar about three-quarters full of powdered, dried herb (calendula flowers, for example) and then pour a vegetable oil of your choice over the herb. Be sure the herb is completely submerged in the oil, because any plant material exposed to air can generate spoilage. Allow the herb to soak (macerate) in the oil for at least two weeks and then strain carefully. Store in the refrigerator until needed.

Herb-infused oils may be applied directly to the skin of the face or body for moisturizing and other cosmetic effects. Good choices of oils for cosmetic use include kukui nut, sweet almond and grapeseed oils – these all tend to be lighter and feel less greasy than many other vegetable oils. Olive oil is often used to make infused oils intended for therapeutic application. For example, olive oil infused with the flowers of St John's wort makes an effective massage oil for treating sciatic nerve pain.

Infused oils are important ingredients in other herbal cosmetics and skin care products, such as moisturizing face creams, body lotions and healing salves.

HERBAL BATHS

Adding herbs to the bath for a good, long soak is an excellent means of bringing botanical benefits to the skin of the entire body. An aromatic herbal bath is also an unbeatable way to relax properly and ease away the tensions of a stressful day at work.

The skin is the largest organ of the body. Because the body is able to absorb some medicinal compounds through the skin, herbal baths have as many therapeutic uses as they do cosmetic benefits. Hydrotherapy and balneotherapy are two terms regularly used to describe the use of baths to treat physical ailments, which in turn often brings benefits to tired or damaged skin. Among many other applications, therapeutic herbal baths can help ease sore muscles, treat stress and insomnia, reduce fevers, and heal problems in the anal and genital regions, not to mention the fact that they can soothe itchy skin and other skin complaints.

Frequent hot baths can be drying to the skin, so those with dry skin may wish to include colloidal oatmeal or other emollient herbs (such as seaweed), or add herb-infused vegetable oils directly to the bathwater. If adding oil, be extra careful not to slip on the oily surface when getting in and out of the tub.

Because herbal constituents are also easily absorbed through the soles of the feet, foot soaks can confer therapeutic benefits as well. Simply add a herbal infusion of your choice to a large bowl of warm water and soak.

Essential oils, which are highly concentrated and must be used with care, represent another excellent way to bring the pleasures of herbs into the bath. To make fragrant bath salts, add approximately 50 drops (½ tea-spoon/2.5 ml) of essential oil per 290 g (10 oz) of bath salts – Epsom salts, for example. Combine well and store in an airtight jar. Use 75 to 145 g (2½ to 5 oz) of the mixture per bath. Before experimenting with essential oils, consult a book by an aromatherapy expert. Essential oils should always be treated with care. (See page 133 for more information about essential oils.)

HERBAL HAIR CARE

Herbs have long been held in high esteem for natural hair care. Throughout history, herbs and other botanicals have been used in all kinds of hair care products, from hair rinses and deep-conditioning treatments to remedies for dandruff, hair loss and other scalp problems.

Herbs recommended for oily hair include sage, burdock and lemon peel. Herbs with a traditional repu-tation for treating dry hair include calendula, comfrey leaf and root, and marsh mallow root. Herbs appropriate for all hair types include nettle, lavender, chamomile, rosemary and rose. Scalp irritations may be soothed with calendula, German chamomile and comfrey. Herbs used to help with dandruff include burdock, ginger, nettle, rosemary, garden sage and willow bark.

Herbs are also used to enhance hair colour. The most important herbal hair dye comes from henna (*Lawsonia inermis*), used in Egypt, India and the Middle East for at least 8,000 years to provide hair with shine and strik-ing red highlights. Other herbs such as turmeric and saffron (yellow), and the nettle (green) were also used. Commercial henna hair dyes come in a variety of col-ours, but only true, unadulterated henna creates the red colour. Black henna, for example, contains a synthetic black hair dye. Henna is also used to create temporary tattoos that are an important part of traditional Indian wedding ceremonies. The longer the henna remains on the skin, the darker and longer-lasting the tattoo will be. The henna dye soaks into the outermost layer of skin and coats the hair shaft, but does not permanently stain skin or hair.

Various other herbs can be used to enhance the beauty of one's natural hair colour, even though they are not true dyes. For example, German and Roman chamomile are used to add shine and bring out high-lights in blond hair. Rosemary and sage are believed to help enhance the natural beauty of brunette hair.

Herbal Hair Rinses and Conditioners

Rinses and conditioners are the best ways to bring the benefits of herbs to the hair. Many commercial shampoos also tout the benefits of the herbs they contain. How-ever, because shampoo remains in the hair for only a short time before it is rinsed out, a herbal shampoo can do little to truly affect hair health. Shampoos that contain aromatic herbs or essential oils smell wonderful, however, and can provide benefit simply by uplifting one's mood.

HOW TO MAKE A HERBAL BATH

There are two primary methods for incorporating herbs into bathwater. One way is to make a strong herbal infusion (tea) by steeping dried herbs in boiling water. Because the herbal infusion will be further diluted once it is added to the bathwater, it is important to use a higher ratio of herbs to water than if making an infusion for drinking. Once it's prepared, add about 449 ml (1 pint) of the herbal infusion to the bathwater.

Another easy way to make a herbal bath is to place a mixture of herbs into a cloth bag (muslin and cooking cheesecloth both work well) and suspend this from the bath tap so that the hot water flows through and soaks the herbs as the bath fills.

To take advantage of one of the best-kept beauty secrets of the ancients, try also adding about 130 g (5 oz) of powdered milk to the bathwater. Milk products, rich in AHA, exfoliate, tone and leave the skin feeling exceptionally soft and supple.

Luxurious and inviting, milk baths have a long history of use in the ancient world. Not only is a warm milk bath good for the skin, scenting it with flower petals can help reduce stress, as well.

For more lasting benefits for the hair, select herbal rinses and deep conditioners, which are left in the hair for a longer period of time and therefore are better able to coat and penetrate the hair shaft.

Create a simple herbal hair rinses in the home by making an infusion (a tea) and pouring it through the hair. A good choice of herb for a rinse is nettle, which is considered appropriate for all hair types. To make a herbal hair rinse, pour boiling water over the dried herb of your choice, using a ratio of about one teaspoon dried herb to 240 ml (8 fl.oz) of water. Steep, covered, for ten to fifteen minutes. Strain, cool to a comfortable temperature and pour through hair. To restore the hair's natural pH (the measure of acidity or alkinity), add about a table-spoon (15 ml/½ fl.oz) of apple cider vinegar or lem-on juice to 240 ml (8 fl.oz) of infusion before use. The vine-gar scent dissipates quickly; it will not remain in the hair.

Dry hair benefits from deep-conditioning treatments that are left in the hair for an extended period before washing out. Oil- and protein-rich ingredients are espe-cially helpful. Make a simple deep conditioning treatment by combining avocado, yogurt or powdered milk, and an egg yolk with water and oil (such as olive oil, shea butter, or coconut oil). Work mixture thoroughly through the hair (paying special attention to the ends), cover the head with a shower cap or plastic bag and relax for ten to twenty minutes. Rinse and then wash the hair thoroughly through with a pH balanced shampoo.

True henna (Lawsonia inermis) is used to create temporary tattoos that are an important part of traditional Indian wedding ceremonies.

Folk Remedies for Hair Loss

Hair loss (alopecia) can be a distressing problem for both men and women, although the condition is much more common in men. Herbal folk remedies that are reputed to help with hair loss abound, but there is little scientific evidence that any of them works. Once a hair follicle actually stops producing hair, it is difficult – if not impossible – to reverse the process.

Herbs that have garnered a traditional reputation for stimulating hair growth (or at least slowing hair loss) include rosemary, nettle, sage and peppermint. Aloe, burdock, chamomile and liquorice have also been used, and in Chinese herbal treatments, mulberries. Saw palmetto's active compounds – free fatty acids and phy-tosterols – are thought to help reverse genetic hair loss, including male-pattern baldness. One traditional remedy for treating hair loss recommends massaging the scalp daily with an oil (such as olive oil) that has been infused with rosemary. However, the most bene-ficial portion of the treatment may be the massage itself, which stimulates circu-lation to the scalp and hair follicles.

Bath salts, grapefruit oil and rose water are all popular ingredients in skin care products.

HERBS FOR DIFFERENT SKIN TYPES

NORMAL SKIN
Calendula *(Calendula officinalis)*
German chamomile *(Matricaria recutita)*
Lavender *(Lavandula angustifolia)*
Rose *(Rosa* spp.*)*

DRY SKIN
Calendula *(Calendula officinalis)*
Comfrey *(Symphytum officinale)*
Elder flower *(Sambucus* spp.*)*
Fennel *(Foeniculum vulgare)*
German chamomile *(Matricaria recutita)*

Jasmine *(Jasminus officinalis)*
Kelp *(Laminaria* spp.*)*
Oats *(Avena sativa)*
Rose *(Rosa* spp.*)*

OILY SKIN
Atlas Cedar *(Cedrus atlantica)*
Burdock *(Arctium lappa)*
Cedarwood *(Juniperus virginiana)*
Citrus *(Citrus* spp.*)*
Elder flower *(Sambucus* spp.*)*
Peppermint *(Mentha x piperita)*

Sage *(Salvia officinalis)*
Rosemary *(Rosmarinus officinalis)*
Witch hazel *(Hamamelis virginiana)*
Yarrow *(Achillea millefolium)*

SENSITIVE SKIN
Calendula *(Calendula officinalis)*
German chamomile *(Matricaria recutita)*
Lavender *(Lavandula angustifolia)*
Marshmallow root *(Althaea officinalis)*
Oats *(Avena sativa)*
Rose *(Rosa* spp.*)*

HERBS FOR SKIN CARE AND BEAUTY

HERB	EFFECT	HERB	EFFECT
Aloe *(Aloe vera)*	Antifungal, anti-inflammatory, emollient; helps heal wounds and burns	Neem *(Azadirachta indica)*	Antifungal, anti-inflammatory, helpful against dandruff
Burdock *(Arctium lappa)*	Antifungal, anti-inflammatory, emollient; used externally and internally for acne, eczema, psoriasis	Nettle *(Urtica dioica)*	Astringent, helpful against dandruff, nutritive
Calendula *(Calendula officinalis)*	Antifungal, antiseptic, anti-inflammatory, astringent, styptic; helps heal wounds, burns, sunburns relieves	Oats, oatstraw *(Avena sativa)*	Emollient, nutritional
Chickweed *(Stellaria media)*	Helps relieve itching	Peppermint *(Mentha x piperita)*	Antiseptic, astringent, cooling, stimulating
Comfrey *(Symphytum officinale)*	Emollient, stimulates cell growth, helps in wound healing	Plantain *(Plantago major)*	Antiseptic, anti-inflammatory, astringent, emollient; helps with wound healing
Echinacea *(Echinacea* spp.*)*	Fights infection, helps in wound healing	Red clover *(Trifolium pratense)*	Anti-inflammatory; used externally and internally for acne, eczema, psoriasis
Elder flower *(Sambucus* spp.*)*	Anti-inflammatory, astringent, emollient	Rose *(Rosa* spp.*)*	Antiseptic, aromatic, astringent, emollient
Fennel *(Foeniculum vulgare)*	Anti-inflammatory, aromatic	Rosemary *(Rosmarinus officinalis)*	Antiseptic, aromatic, astringent, stimulating
German chamomile *(Matricaria recutita)*	Anti-inflammatory, helps in wound healing	Sage *(Salvia officinalis)*	Antiseptic, aromatic; used to treat acne
Gotu kola *(Centella asiatica)*	Helps promote wound and scar healing; encourages production of collagen	St John's wort *(Hypericum perforatum)*	Anti-inflammatory; helps heal wounds and burns (avoid sun exposure after applying to skin)
Kelp *(Laminaria* spp.*)*	Emollient, nutritional	Tea tree *(Melaleuca alternifolia)*	Antibacterial, antifungal, antiseptic; used to treat fungal infections, acne, dandruff, eczema
Lavender *(Lavandula* spp.*)*	Antiseptic, anti-inflammatory, aromatic	Nettle *(Urtica dioica)*	Astringent; used in hair rinses for all hair types
Lemon balm *(Melissa officinalis)*	Antiseptic, aromatic	Witch hazel *(Hamamelis virginiana)*	Anti-inflammatory, antiseptic, astringent, styptic; helps relieve itching
Marsh mallow *(Althaea officinalis)*	Anti-inflammatory, emollient	Yarrow *(Achillea millefolium)*	Anti-inflammatory, antiseptic, astringent, styptic (stops bleeding)

CHAPTER 6

Health *and* Healing

Herbs were humanity's first medicine. One of the earliest known records of them being used for health was in ancient Sumeria. In about 2000 B.C.E., King Assurbanipal ordered the compilation of the first known materia medica – an official listing of medicines – which contained an impressive 250 herbal drugs.

Even today, despite the widespread availability of modern pharmaceutical medicines, plants continue to play a vital role in their everyday healthcare for millions around the world.

For more than 80 percent of the modern world's population, herbs serve as a primary tool of healthcare – not only in developing nations, but also in industrialized countries such as the United Kingdom, France, Germany, China and Japan. Even in these nations, however, interest in herbs as preventative medicines, self-care for minor health conditions, and low-cost, nontoxic alternatives to standard treatments for common health problems continues to grow.

Dried herbs such as chamomile and star anise
are used in herbal medicine to aid digestion.

Herbs as Medicine

Herbal medicines are used today in myriad ways, recommended as treatments by practitioners operating within a number of different traditional healthcare systems. Traditional healthcare systems that rely on whole plant medicines – herbal remedies in their most natural form – include Traditional Chinese Medicine (TCM), Ayurvedic medicine, Tibetan medicine and the traditional medicines of Africa, South and Central America, and Australia. Whole plant medicines are also used in Western herbalism, a system of herbal therapeutics that evolved in Europe and North America. Traditional healers often rely on combinations of herbs called formulas that can be tailored to the specific needs of each patient. Some of these traditional healing systems have been in continuous use for centuries.

HERBS IN MODERN HEALTHCARE

The use of herbal medicine is finding its way into what is known as "Western medicine" – in other words, conventional medicine as practised by medical physicians in industrialized nations. In some developed nations, such as China, traditional herbal medicine exists side by side with Western medicine, and some physicians are trained to practise both traditional and conventional medicine. In the United States and Canada, on the other hand, most conventional physicians receive little or no training in the use of herbal medicines and are often sceptical about their use.

Most European countries fall in the middle of the industrialized-nation spectrum. In most European nations, hundreds of herbs have been approved as official medicines by health agencies. Conventional physicians often prescribe certain herbal medicines as low-cost, nontoxic alternatives to standard pharmaceutical treatment for common ailments. Saw palmetto (*Serenoa repens*) is now a preferred treatment in Europe for benign prostatic hyperplasia (enlarged prostate), a common health problem for men older than fifty. Black cohosh (*Cimicifuga racemosa*) is a popular remedy for treating symptoms of menopause, such as hot flushes.

"Complementary medicine" is a term increasingly used to describe the practice of administering alternative therapies, such as plant medicines, in combination with conventional treatment. Global commerce has helped encourage the adoption of complementary herb use into mainstream medical practice. Today, practitioners and

Ginger in its fresh, dried, ground and capsule forms.

Chinese apothecaries store herbs used in many holistic treatments.

consumers of conventional (Western) healthcare have access to herbs from around the world. For example, in Europe, the Polynesian herb kava (*Piper methysticum*) is a popular treatment for anxiety. Turmeric (*Curcuma longa*), native to India, is approved in Germany for the treatment of indigestion. The Chinese herbs astragalus (*Astragalus membranaceus*) and shiitake mushroom (*Lentinus edodes*) have found a place in China and the United States as supportive therapy for people undergoing chemotherapy for the treatment of cancer.

In addition to being recommended by healthcare practitioners, herbal medicines are also widely self-administered by people in all cultures. This practice is called folk medicine – the everyday medicine of the people. All over the world, people use herbs to treat themselves for minor illnesses and injuries.

For people living in rural areas, herbal medicines are affordable and can be gathered locally and prepared at home. Even in big cities, anyone who applies aloe vera from a potted houseplant to soothe a burned finger or calms an upset stomach by drinking ginger ale is practising herbal folk medicine. Simple herbal medicines such as chamomile tea (*Matricaria recutita*) are widely accepted as safe, effective self-treatment for common ailments such as stomach upset and insomnia.

Understanding Holistic Medicine

Holistic medicine is medicine that is used to treat the entire person – body, mind and spirit – not just the symptoms of disease. According to this definition, most (if not all) systems of traditional medicine are considered holistic, or "whole body" healing systems. Traditional Chinese Medicine, Ayurveda and Western herbalism all fall under the umbrella term "holistic therapies".

All "whole body" systems of healing encompass diet, lifestyle, emotional health, spiritual considerations and physical activity, in addition to the use of herbs or other

medicines. Holistic healers believe that health and disease are products of a complex interplay among a person's mind, body and spirit. Each patient is considered a unique individual with specific issues and healthcare needs. In holistic healing, the patient is a partner in the treatment process, not a passive bystander. A holistic herbalist expects patients to play an active role by making lifestyle choices that foster health.

Holistic healers seek to stimulate the body's own self-healing mechanism or "vital force". When presented with an illness by a patient or client, holistic herbalists are likely, when dispensing pharmaceutical prescriptions, to recommend tonic herbs that nourish specific body systems and gently correct long-standing imbalances that they believe are the root cause of a disorder or disease. Holistic healers recommend plant remedies not because they provide rapid relief of symptoms, but rather because these nourishing tonics support the body's own efforts to heal itself. In contrast, conventional (Western) medicine adheres to what is known as the biomedical model, which asserts that all diseases have physical causes and should be treated accordingly with specific pharmaceuticals or surgical procedures.

Another hallmark of holistic herbal medicine is its focus on practices and behaviour that are intended to support health and prevent disease, rather than simply treating disease when it occurs. For example, treatment suggested by a holistic herbalist will almost certainly include advice about how lifestyle can affect overall health, encompassing not just herbs but also dietary modifications, bodywork (such as massage or chiropractic), psychological counselling (to manage emotional issues and stress), and exercise (yoga, dance, t'ai chi, walking or some other appropriate physical activity).

Even conventional medicine can be part of holistic treatment – as long as the treatment takes into account the whole person: body, mind and spirit.

Many medicines in common use today, such as the pain reliever codeine and the cancer treatment drugs vinblastine and pacliaxel were derived from extracts taken from plants.

Whole Plant Herbal Remedies and Phytomedicines

In the past, herbs were used only in their most naturally occurring form – as fresh or dried plants. They might be consumed whole or made into any of a variety of whole plant remedies – medicinal teas, tinctures (a medicinal substance in an alcoholic solution), poultices and many other traditional applications. Herbs are still used in this manner in most traditional healing systems, such as Traditional Chinese Medicine (TCM) and Ayurveda, as well as in folk medicine.

Holistic herbalists maintain that it is impossible to understand the uses of parts separated from the whole, and that plants are best able to confer their benefits when taken in whole form, the way nature created them. In fact, this is part of the meaning of the word

"holistic". On the other hand, whole plants contain hundreds of different chemical compounds. Plants grown in different places or under different conditions may contain varying concentrations of key chemical compounds. This means that it can be difficult, if not impossible, to make accurate generalizations about how a mixture made from a whole herb will act in the body.

To solve this dilemma, researchers try to determine precisely which compound or compounds are the source of a plant's medicinal effects, or actions. To do this, they must isolate and concentrate the specific plant chemical they believe is responsible for the plant's effects: its so-called "active ingredient". Researchers may then create a type of phytomedicine, a highly processed herbal medicine also called a standardized extract, that contains a specified amount of only one or two chemicals, called "marker compounds". The goal is to end up with a compound of only the desired plant chemicals. But isolating specific compounds can have unintended consequences. In separating out one specific ingredient, scientists leave behind dozens or even hundreds of other constituents that contribute to the whole plant's activity, and that temper the sometimes very potent effects of its compounds. With such buffering substances removed, isolated constituents may be more likely to cause side-effects that do not occur when the whole plant is used.

Plant Materials in Pharmaceutical Drugs

Although this is not a part of herbal medicine, plant materials are also used in the manufacture of certain conventional pharmaceutical drugs. Many modern pharmaceuticals used in conventional (Western) medicine have been developed as a direct result of the study of active plant ingredients. In fact, at least 25 percent of contemporary prescription medicines are extracted directly from plants or are synthetic copies of plant chemicals. Many other drugs require plant chemicals as building blocks for manufacturing. Paclitaxel, for example, a breakthrough anti-tumour compound used to treat breast and ovarian cancer, cannot yet be completely synthesized (produced in a laboratory using manufactured chemicals). Paclitaxel is still made using compounds taken directly from the yew tree (*Taxus* spp.).

Modern Research on Herbs

It is a common misconception that there is little or no scientific evidence to support the health benefits and safety of herbs. The truth is that thousands of scientific studies have been conducted on hundreds of herbs – from basic laboratory studies in test tubes to long-term clinical studies. Much of this research has been conducted in Europe, particularly in Germany, and in Asia, especially in India, China and Japan. While the quality of some research has been criticized, studies have at least begun to validate important traditional uses of herbs.

Mannose, a compund found in cranberries and cranberry juice, has been found to fight urinary tract infections.

Scientific research has not verified every potential use of every common herb, nor have researchers confirmed the safety and traditional applications of all medicinal plants. But it is important to remember that a lack of research into a plant does not indicate that the plant is ineffective or unsafe, or that its traditional uses are questionable. More likely, it suggests that funding for research has been lacking.

In scientific research the best method is the double-blind test – meaning that neither the study participants nor the researchers know which group is getting which substance, a practice intended to eliminate bias. Double-blind, placebo-controlled clinical studies are considered very reliable for testing the medicinal uses of herbs. These studies compare the effects of herbal medicine on two groups of human volunteers, one of which takes the herb while the other takes a placebo (an inactive substance that resembles the test medicine). The following ten herbs provide examples of remedies that have undergone a significant amount of clinical testing. Many of them are recommended by doctors all over the world.

Black cohosh (*Cimicifuga racemosa*) The roots and underground stems (rhizomes) of this plant are widely used to treat the symptoms of menopause. According to several studies, among them one published in the November 2005 issue of the journal *Obstetrics & Gynecology,* black cohosh effectively relieves both physical and psychological symptoms, including hot flushes, night sweats, heart palpitations, insomnia, depression and irritability.

Cranberry (*Vaccinium macrocarpon*) This juice provides a good example of a folk medicine remedy that is now supported by scientific evidence. Cranberry juice also helps prevent and treat urinary tract infections by interfering with the attachment of bacteria to the walls of the urinary tract.

Echinacea (*Echinacea* spp.) Dozens of clinical studies conducted in Germany and the United States in the 1980s and 1990s have shown that when taken at the first sign of infection, echinacea can shorten the duration of colds and the flu. In many European countries, echinacea is approved to treat a variety of infections.

Feverfew *(Tanacetum parthenium)* Feverfew is widely accepted and prescribed by doctors in many European countries to prevent migraine headaches. Clinical studies, such as one published in the medical journal *Lancet* in 1988, have shown that this herb is effective for many people in reducing the frequency, duration and intensity of migraine headaches.

Garlic *(Allium sativum)* One of the most extensively researched medicinal herbs, garlic has been the subject of hundreds of clinical, laboratory and population studies investigating its properties: in addition to its antimicrobial and antioxidant

Ginkgo biloba has been used to treat Alzheimers, depression and improve brain functioning.

properties, garlic has been found to lower cholesterol. In addition, studies have shown that regular consumption of garlic helps keep the heart and circulatory system healthy and may protect against a variety of common cancers, especially cancers of the gastrointestinal tract.

Ginger *(Zingiber officinale)* Several clinical studies – including one published in the journal *Acta Oto-Laryngologica* (1988) and another published the medical journal *ORL* (1986) – show that ginger may be as effective as conventional drugs in preventing motion sickness.

Ginkgo *(Ginkgo biloba)* This herb, widely used to help slow the progression of Alzheimer's disease, improve memory and concentration, and promote healthy blood circulation,

Garlic has been proven to be beneficial in treating medical ailments, including high cholesterol and high blood pressure.

has been the subject of numerous clinical and laboratory studies. Ginkgo improves microcirculation (the flow of blood through tiny vessels), helping protect cardio-vascular health and brain function.

Milk thistle *(Silybum marianum)*
This herb has the ability to reverse liver damage as well as protect the liver against toxins, and has been researched in clinical and laboratory studies. The plant first came to the attention of doctors in Germany when they discovered people using it to try to block the effects of deadly toxins after consuming the deathcap mushroom *(Amanita phalloides)*.

St John's wort *(Hypericum perforatum)* Clinical studies have confirmed that standardized St John's wort extract is an effective treatment for mild to moderate depression. In some studies, the herb was shown to be as effective as fluoxetine hydrochloride, a popular synthetic antidepressant of the type known as selective serotonin reuptake inhibitors (SSRI).

Saw palmetto *(Serenoa repens)* Strong clinical evidence shows that standardized saw palmetto can be as effective as a standard drug treatment, but with fewer side effects, for enlarged prostates (benign prostatic hyperplasia, or BPH). The herb is widely recommended by doctors in Europe as a low-risk, inexpensive treatment for this common condition.

HEALING THERAPIES

Herbs in their many forms play a role in the folk medicine of all nations, as well as all of the world's traditional health-care systems, from Traditional Chinese Medicine to Indian Ayurveda, and other common healing therapies, such as aro-matherapy and homeopathy.

With homeopathic remedies gaining popularity, medical providers are learning to incorporate herbal treatments into their practice. Many are advising the use of herbal extracts that have been clinically proven to be safe, such as saw palmetto or St John's wort.

Herbal teas, such as echinachea, are often praised for their medicinal benefits. Some have been proven to help relieve pain and boost the immune system.

Therapies practised all over the world incorporate herbs in one form or another. The following is an overview of major healing therapies that rely upon medicinal plants.

WESTERN HERBALISM

The term "Western herbalism" is used to refer to the way herbalism is practised by North American and European herbal healers. Today's practice of Western herbalism has roots not only in the works of the classical Greek and Arab physicians, but also in the folk healing systems of Europe and North America. For example, European settlers to the North American continent carried with them to the New World their favourite medicinal plants. They were also eager to learn the uses of North American plants from Native American healers. European physicians readily adopted native North American plants, including echinacea *(Echinacea purpurea)*, saw palmetto *(Serenoa repens)* and black cohosh *(Cimicifuga racemosa)*.

Medicinal Marijuana

Although cannabis *(Cannabis sativa)* is an illegal recreational drug in many countries, it has been used as a medicine for thousands of years in Europe, the Middle East and Asia. The earliest written accounts of its use were discovered in Assyrian tablets from the seventh century B.C.E. The ancient Chinese pharmacopoeia *Shen-nung Pen-tshao Ching*, written more than 2,000 years ago, cites the use of liquid and food preparations of cannabis to treat joint inflammation and digestive disorders. In 60 C.E., the Greek physician Dioscorides wrote about the use of marijuana to treat conditions including earache and jaundice, marking the first mention of the herb in a Western medical treatise. Today's resurgence of interest in marijuana as a medicine is in keeping with a growing public interest in plant medicines as nontoxic alternatives to synthetic pharmaceutical drugs. Compounds called cannabinoids in marijuana are believed to give it analgesic, muscle-relaxing, appetite-stimulating and anti-nausea effects. Although the herb's medicinal use remains controversial in many Western nations, patients with a variety of chronic illnesses such as multiple sclerosis, cancer, glaucoma and AIDS continue to depend on it to manage their symptoms and the side effects of conventional drug treatment.

TRADITIONAL CHINESE MEDICINE

Traditional Chinese Medicine (TCM) is an ancient healing system that originated in China but is used today to treat millions of people all around the world. TCM applies treatments including acupuncture and herbs according to a highly developed, holistic philosophy of health and disease. Treatment is based on balancing and regulating the flow of qi (pronounced "chee," and also sometimes spelled chi) – the body's life energy or vital force. Japan, Korea and Vietnam have all developed traditional medicine systems of their own based on concepts and practices that started in China at least 3,000 years ago, which is why traditional Chinese medicine is sometimes simply called Oriental medicine.

Principles of TCM

The principles of Traditional Chinese Medicine are deeply rooted in the Chinese philosophy and way of seeing the universe. It can be difficult for some people to fully understand the concepts of Traditional Chinese Medicine, which do not accord with conventional (Western) ideas about science and medicine. Traditional Chinese healers believe that human beings are subject to the same laws that govern nature, and that disease results from imbalances or lack of harmony in forces that influence the workings of the body.

The "complementary opposites" known as yin and yang lie at the heart of Chinese philosophy and TCM. In extremely simplified terms, yin and yang are idealised polarities: yin represents dark and yang represents light, yin represents the female and yang the male, and so on. In the Chinese worldview, however, the concept is much more complex than this. Yin and yang are not at odds or in conflict with one another, but represent a constant flow and exchange of energy from one to the other. They exist only in relation to one another, but at the same time, they are constantly blending with and

One of traditional Chinese medicine therapy is moxibustion, which is the practice of burning moxa sticks over acupuncture points on the body. Acupuncturists use this method to stimulate the blood flow and the energy in various areas of the body.

becoming one another. In an idealized state, yin is the absence of yang, but in reality, there is always some yang in yin and vice versa.

An example may help clarify the concept. The original Chinese character for yang shows a picture of the sun and a mountain and means "the light side of the mountain". The original character for yin depicts a cloud and a mountain and means "the dark side of the mountain". They are opposites, but each has the mountain in common. Each is incomplete without the other, and together, they represent the whole known in Chinese as the tao.

In Traditional Chinese Medicine, the body is divided into yin parts and yang parts. Herbs, foods and even activities are classified along a spectrum of most yin to most yang. The attraction and tension between yin and yang creates qi, the body's life force.

Yin elements are: Earth, moon, dark, female, expansive, passive, cold, night, slow, moist and winter. The associated yang elements are the heavens, sun, light, male, contractive, aggressive, hot, day, fast, dry and summer.

The Chinese Five Elements (Wu Xing), also known as Five Element Theory, is another governing concept in TCM. The Five Elements – wood, fire, earth, metal and water – represent fundamental relationships among forces and cycles of nature and the effects they have upon the human body. Each element is associated with specific body functions, organs and senses as well as emotions, activities, foods, flavours and temperatures.

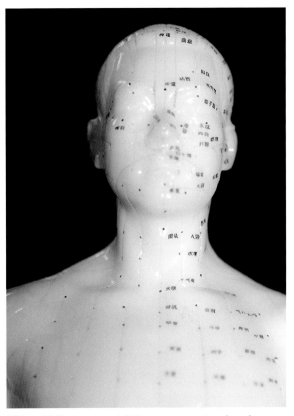

This model illustrates over 1,000 acupuncture points along the 12 meridian lines on the human body. A TCM practitioner will stimulate any one of these points to balance the flow of qi.

The Practice of TCM

A TCM practitioner's first step is to pinpoint imbalances that have resulted in a patient's physical problems. In TCM, all disease is seen as the result of energetic imbalances (excess or deficiency) caused by the patient's way of life and relationship with the universe. There are six external causes of disease (wind, cold, heat, dampness, dryness and summer heat) plus seven internal causes or emotions (joy, anger, sadness, pensiveness, grief, fear and fright) that contribute to physical manifestations of disharmony. A practitioner may arrive at the conclusion that a patient's disease is caused by excessive "wind" in the body, too much "heat" in a specific organ, or by "qi deficiency" or "deficient spleen yang".

THE FIVE ELEMENTS AND ASSOCIATIONS

ELEMENT	SEASON	TASTE	EMOTION	BODY PARTS
Wood	Spring	Sour	Anger	Liver, gallbladder, eyes, tendons
Fire	Summer	Bitter	Joy	Heart, small intestine, tongue, blood vessels
Earth	Indian summer	Sweet	Worry	Spleen, stomach, mouth, muscles
Metal	Autumn	Pungent	Grief	Lungs, large intestine, nose, skin
Water	Winter	Salty	Fear	Kidneys, bladder, ears, bones

❧ IMPORTANT HERBS IN TRADITIONAL CHINESE MEDICINE ❧

ASTRAGALUS (*ASTRAGALUS MEMBRANACEUS*)

Astragalus root, called huang qi in Chinese, is an important qi tonic that is considered slightly warming and sweet. It is used to treat conditions characterized by deficient qi. These include frequent colds, general weakness and fatigue, weak digestion and lack of appetite, and chronic weakness of the lungs with shortness of breath. For use as a daily tonic, pieces of astragalus root may be cooked into soups or other foods. A combination of astragalus and ginseng (*bu zhong yi qi tang*) is prescribed for cases of debility and fatigue.

DONG QUAI (*ANGELICA SINENSIS*)

Dong quai root (also called dang gui or Chinese angelica) is considered warm, sweet, acrid and bitter. Perhaps the most important "blood tonic" in traditional Chinese medicine, it is employed in to invigorate the blood and relieve blood stagnation. Because women's health is closely tied to blood in Traditional Chinese Medicine, dong quai is often called the female ginseng and is also widely used in combination with other herbs to treat women's

health conditions, such as irregular menstruation, menopausal symptoms and post-partum debility (weakness after giving birth). Four Things Soup, a classical Chinese formula, is a women's tonic widely prescribed throughout China. This formula contains dong quai, Chinese peony (*Paeonia lactiflora*), rehmannia (*Rehmannia glutinosa*) and ligusticum (*Ligusticum sinense*) in equal parts and is prepared by simmering the herbs.

GINSENG (*PANAX GINSENG*)

Ginseng root, known as ren shen in Chinese, is classified in TCM as a "superior" herb, or one of the most useful and safe remedies available. An important qi tonic, it is considered warming, sweet and slightly bitter, and is used to treat loss of qi that is caused by any of a number of factors. Ginseng has been used traditionally to treat extreme fatigue, debility caused by illness or old age, and heart and blood pressure problems. It is generally prescribed only for people over the age of forty-five or fifty, and is considered inappropriate for young people unless they have severe qi deficiency.

A traditional Chinese physician utilizes a unique array of diagnostic techniques. In addition to carefully questioning patients about their health, lifestyle and behaviour, the doctor examines patients' tongues for signs of illness, observes all aspects of their appearance, palpates their abdomen and analyzes their pulse. Chinese pulse diagnosis is a highly refined art that takes many years to master.

Acupuncture and herbs, often used in combination, are the two most important components in the practice of TCM. Other treatments may include nutritional therapies, restorative physical exercises such as qigong or taiji (t'ai chi), meditation and massage.

Acupuncture, which originated in China at least 2,000 years ago, remains one of the most commonly used medical procedures in the world. Acupuncture involves the insertion of tiny needles in specific places along the body's meridians – pathways that serve as channels for the flow of qi. There are twelve major meridians and thousands of acupuncture points along the meridians.

Chinese herb grinders, such as this one, are very often used to make powders from hard roots.

Through the precise placement of needles on these points, the skilled acupuncturist manipulates the flow of qi to reduce excess, counteract deficiency, or otherwise correct underlying energetic imbalances to treat disease. Modern clinical studies conducted in China and in the West indicate that acupuncture may be an effective treatment or supportive therapy for health problems including osteoarthritis pain, postoperative dental pain, low-back pain, menstrual cramps, headache, carpal tunnel syndrome, asthma, fibromyalgia, stroke rehabilitation, addictions, and postoperative and chemotherapy-related nausea and vomiting.

Chinese Herbal Formulary

Herbs in China are classified according to four energies (cold, cool, warm and hot) and five flavours (spicy, sweet, sour, bitter and salty). Cooling herbs may be prescribed to relieve conditions caused by excess heat in the body,

Herbal teas such as green tea have been long praised for their health benefits. Green tea is said to lower cholesterol and blood sugar. It may also have anti-cancer effects and the ability to boost metabolism.

for example, or sweet herbs used to tonify qi and nourish the blood. Herbs are rarely used singly in TCM, but instead are compounded into formulas. A single herb may have a number of different effects, and is thus carefully chosen by a practitioner and combined with other herbs in a prescription designed to address myriad health issues at the same time.

A Chinese herbal formula is a mixture that can contain up to twenty or more herbs. In creating an herbal formula, traditional Chinese practitioners can choose from nearly six thousand herbs. The traditional Chinese pharmacopoeia lists hundreds of different formulas for specific patterns of disharmony. The practitioner adjusts these formulas, which usually contain at least ten to fifteen different herbs, to take into account the unique characteristics and needs of his patient.

Chinese herbs are often prescribed as decoctions (teas made by simmering dried herbs) to be brewed and drunk several times a day. They may also be taken as powders or pills, made into alcohol-based tinctures, or incorporated into soups, porridges or other foods. Some classic Chinese formulas are available as ready-to-use "patent remedies" that are made according to a specific formula and mass-produced. These are usually sold in pill form.

An external herbal treatment called moxibustion is often used in combination with acupuncture. To perform moxibustion, the practitioner applies heat to acupuncture points by burning moxa (a dried herb, usually *Artemesia vulgaris*, or mugwort) near or on the skin. The heat is believed to penetrate into the meridians to influence qi and blood flow. Moxa is available in a variety of forms for different applications, including loose powder, cones and sticks. Moxa cones may be burned directly on the skin, but moxa is also often applied indirectly, for example, by wrapping a ball of the herb around the end of an acupuncture needle before lighting it.

AYURVEDA

One of the ancient healing system of India, ayurveda, combines diet, herbs, physical activity and spiritual practice to preserve health and promote longevity. Ayurvedic medicine stretches back at least 5,000 years. Today, this holistic system is becoming increasingly popular outside

Ayurvedic massage is often used to rid the body of toxins through the stimulation of pressure points on the body. It is also used to alleviate pain associated with arthritis.

THE THREE DOSHAS			
	VATA	**PITTA**	**KAPHA**
Element	Air/space	Fire/water	Water/earth
Body type	Thin build; narrow shoulders; may be very tall or short	Well-proportioned, muscular, fair or ruddy colouring; average height	Thickset, strong, graceful, slow-moving; may be prone to weight gain
Personality	Creative, enthusiastic, vivacious, imaginative, anxious; quick, nervous movements; tendency to waste	Sharp-witted, intense, driven, confident, quick to anger, impatient, ambitious; can be aggressive and competitive	Stable, patient, tranquil, affectionate, complacent; can be possessive
Basic body function	Movement	Metabolism	Structure
Seat	Colon	Small intestine	Lungs
Season	Autumn/early winter	Summer	Middle of winter
Time of day	Dawn	Midday	Evening
Tastes/foods that aggravate	Pungent, bitter, astringent; raw foods	Sour, salty, pungent; red meat	Sweet, sour, salty; dairy products
Tastes/foods that pacify	Sweet, sour, salty; moist, warming foods; cooked root vegetables	Sweet, astringent, bitter; cooling foods, such as salads; mushrooms, fish, chicken, tofu	Pungent, bitter, astringent, hot and spicy foods; leafy vegetables, legumes, apples and pears

of India among people attracted to its emphasis on balancing body, mind and spirit for optimal health and well-being. The word Ayurveda comes from the Sanskrit *ayur* (meaning "life" or "longevity") and *veda* (meaning "knowledge" or "wisdom"). The practice of ayurveda is based upon the Atharva Veda, the fourth in the series of Hindu books of knowledge called Vedas. The Atharva Veda contains ancient wisdom about healing and sickness. Modern ayurvedic healers continue to practice in accordance with its traditional philosophies and techniques.

The "Science of Life"

Ayurveda, often called "the science of life", aims not to address particular symptoms or diseases, but instead to treat the whole person – body, mind and spirit – to ensure optimal health. The emphasis is on maintaining good health (swasthavrtta) through daily and seasonal lifestyle regimens. These regimens, which incorporate diet, herbs, exercise, hygiene, and spiritual and mental health, are designed to balance vital forces to maintain physical well-being as well as a harmonious relationship between the body and the mind. Ayurveda addresses all aspects of everyday life with a goal of improving and preserving the health of the whole person.

Ayurveda is based on a belief that the body has a vital energy, called prana, which activates the body and mind. Breath is believed to be the bodily manifestation of prana. Seven energy centres called chakras keep prana flowing smoothly though the body. According to Ayurveda, the human body and the whole universe are composed of five basic substances that occur in various combinations and proportions. These five great elements (panchamahabjutas) are space (akasha), air (vayu), fire (agni), water (jala) and earth (prthvi). The five elements symbolize the physical substances that give the human body form. Each is associated with different physical properties, actions and sensory functions.

The Three Doshas

Ayurveda recognizes three primary life forces or energies, called doshas: vata, pitta and kapha. Each dosha is composed of a combination of two of the five great elements. These constantly fluctuating energies are essential components of the body and are responsible for a person's health. Each person displays a unique combination of doshas that determines his main physical strengths and weaknesses, personality and intellectual function. One or two doshas tend to dominate for each individual; a person may be primarily vata, for example, or a combination of vata–pitta. This proportion of doshas determines a person's basic nature from birth (called prakriti) and affects the way prana flows through the body. Optimal health can be achieved only by harmonizing the doshas with one's basic nature.

Ayurvedic practitioners believe that the levels of the doshas in individuals fluctuate daily according to numerous influences, including foods eaten, time of day, season,

IMPORTANT HERBS IN ❧ AYURVEDA ❧

ASHWAGANDA (WITHANIA SOMIFERA)

Ashwaganda is used in ayurveda to treat debility and weakness in the elderly, people with chronic illnesses, and those exhausted by overwork or lack of sleep, in a fashion that is very similar to the way ginseng is used in Traditional Chinese Medicine. Ashwaganda is also considered the best rejuvenative herb for the vata constitution. It is often prepared as a milk decoction to which may be added sweetener and rice. Ashwaganda is bitter and astringent. It is considered calming and clarifying to the mind, and may be used to help promote restful sleep.

FRANKINCENSE (BOSWELLIA SERRATA)

Recent studies have shown frankincense to limit the production of leukotrienes, which cause inflammation. Frankincense is acquired from the tree *boswellia serrata* that produces resin which hardens into gum when its bark is peeled away. When the resins and gums are put together they are known as guggals. Guggals were traditionally used to treat arthritis, digestive disorders, pulmonary and ringworm.

GINGER (ZINGIBER OFFICINALE)

Pungent, sweet, warming ginger pacifies kapha and vata, increases pitta, and has been called "the universal medicine" (vishwabhesaj) by ayurvedic practitioners. Dried ginger is considered hotter and better for relieving kapha, while fresh ginger is a more effective diaphoretic (fever-reducer) and better for relieving vata. Ginger is used extensively in ayurveda to treat digestive and respiratory conditions, including colds, flus, indigestion and wind. It is valued for relieving menstrual and abdominal cramps. The herb is also an important Ayurvedic remedy for arthritis and a heart tonic.

GOTU KOLA (CENTELLA ASIATICA)

Considered perhaps the most important rejuvenative herb in Ayurveda, gotu kola is used to revitalize the nervous system, brain and immune system, in addition to strengthening the adrenal glands. Called brahmi in Sanskrit, gotu kola is thought to clarify the mind, improve memory and concentration, and promote overall intelligence and longevity. Himalayan yogis consume gotu kola as food or brewed into a tea to enhance their meditation practice. Bitter and cooling, gotu kola is a rejuvenating tonic for pitta people, but it also reduces excessive kapha and calms vata. It is a helpful for skin conditions such as eczema and psoriasis.

stress level and emotions. Each dosha has a "seat" in the body that helps keep imbalances in check. Chronic imbalances in the doshas, however, disrupt the flow of prana and can result in disease. For best health, one must take responsibility for managing imbalances and fluctuations by "pacifying" excesses in the doshas with foods, herbs, exercise and various stress-reducing techniques.

Diet, Herbs, and Lifestyle

Before prescribing treatment, the ayurvedic practitioner determines a patient's tridosha (doshic constitution) and diagnoses any imbalances. Diagnosis begins with a detailed history that takes into account lifestyle factors as well as physical symptoms. As in Traditional Chinese Medicine, the Ayurvedic practitioner examines the patient's pulse and tongue, and may also look at the eyes, listen to the organs, and palpate the abdomen to pinpoint doshic imbalances.

The Ayurvedic practitioner then takes all physical and lifestyle factors into account to custom-design an individualized daily regimen – called a rasayana – to balance the patient's doshas for optimal health and well-being. The practitioner may instruct the patient to change various lifestyle practices – for example, how much sleep to get or how and when to eat. A practitioner may recommend yoga, meditation, massage or breathing exercises to help reduce the effects of stress and further pacify the doshas.

Herbal rasayanas incorporate herb, food and mineral mixtures. As in TCM, Ayurveda uses herbs and foods according to what is known as a system of "energetics", properties of foods and healing substances. This system takes into account flavour (rasa) and energy (virya, defined as heating and cooling properties). Ayurveda classifies foods according to six primary tastes: sweet, sour, salty, pungent, bitter and astringent. Each of these tastes has specific effects on the doshas. Ayurvedic remedies can contain as many as twenty different herbs, foods and minerals.

In Ayurveda, herbs are usually prepared in one of five different ways: as part of a fresh juice, a crushed pulp or paste, a decoction (made by boiling herbs in liquid), a hot infusion (made by steeping herbs in hot liquid), or a cold infusion (made by steeping herbs in cold liquid). Other common vehicles for herbs include powders, milk decoctions and medicated wines, jellies, jams, ghee (clarified butter) and sweets. Medicated oils, usually made by heating herbs in sesame oil, are employed in massage or as ointments, douches or internal remedies.

Many Ayurvedic practitioners also advise patients to undergo purification practices such as panchakarma (five actions). This is a rigorous multi-step detoxification process that aims to help the body eliminate impurities

Tai chi, a form of soft martial arts which focuses on soft fluid movements, is often considered to be moving meditation. Long-term practice increases flexibility and may reduce stress and anxiety.

(ama) to further balance the doshas. It includes specialized treatments such as oil therapy, sweating, purging, enemas, bloodletting and nasal drops.

HOMEOPATHY

The medicinal practice of homeopathy is very different from herbal medicine. It is often included in discussions of herbs, however, because many homeopathic remedies contain tiny dilutions of plant substances.

Homeopathic remedies are preparations of highly diluted natural substances that are used to stimulate the body's own healing responses. In herbal medicine, relatively large doses of plants are used to achieve therapeutic effects. In homeopathy, on the other hand, extremely diluted preparations of plants or other natural substances are used.

The homeopathic system was developed in the early 19th century by a German physician and chemist, Samuel Christian Hahnemann (1755–1843). Discouraged by the practice of conventional medicine – which at the time relied in large part on the prescription of highly toxic drugs, purging and bloodletting – Hahnemann embarked on a series of experiments with plant medicines that led to the development of the first homeopathic remedies.

In the first of these experiments, which came to be known as "provings", Hahnemann dosed himself with cinchona bark, a plant medicine used to treat malaria. Hahnemann was surprised to find that after taking cinchona bark, he developed symptoms similar to those of malaria. He eventually developed the Law of Similars, a guiding principle of homeopathy (see page 28). In his lifetime, Hahnemann proved the effectiveness of about 100 remedies; today, more than 3,000 remedies are available.

Homeopathy is most widely practised in Europe and North America. In Europe, the practice is supported by legislation passed in 1997 by the European parliament. Both conventional physicians and professional homeopaths (those trained primarily in homeopathy) are legally permitted to practise in most European countries. No official training standards for homeopaths exist, but many professionals undergo three to six years of training.

In the United States, homeopathy is usually practised along with a licenced medical discipline, such as conventional medicine, naturopathy, chiropractic or veterinary medicine. Homeopathy is a regular part of training for naturopathic doctors; other health practitioners receive training through diploma and certificate programmes and correspondence courses. Since 1938, homeopathic remedies have been regulated as over-the-counter (nonprescription) drugs in the United States, unlike herbs, which are currently regulated as dietary supplements.

More than 100 modern studies have investigated the clinical use of homeopathy, and positive results have been demonstrated in studies on influenza, hay fever, allergic asthma, acute childhood diarrhea, vertigo and osteoarthritis pain. Other clinical studies have had conflicting results, and some of the research has been criticized as being of poor quality. Although many theories have been proposed, researchers have not yet been able to find any conclusive scientific explanation for how homeopathic remedies work. This is a subject of ongoing controversy and debate in the scientific community. Sceptics claim the benefits of homeopathy can be attributed to the placebo effect – an improvement due only to the expectations of the patient.

However, growing numbers of researchers believe that homeopathy's effects can be explained by quantum physics, an area of science that is still evolving. Whatever the most accurate explanation may be, millions of people around the world rely on homeopathy to treat a variety of conditions.

❧ HYDROSOLS ❧

Hydrosols – true "flower waters" – are a by-product of the steam distillation of essential oils. Hydrosols are the water component that is left behind when a plant's essential oil is separated out in the distillation process. Hydrosols contain water-soluble compounds that make them fragrant and soothing to the skin.

Two of the best known and most popular hydrosols are orange flower water and rose water, both of which have traditionally been used as cosmetics and for culinary flavourings. Hydrosols also make refreshing, aromatic body mists and skin toners – and are generally sold for this purpose in spray bottles. Some commercially available hydrosols include lavender, geranium, chamomile, rose, neroli (or orange blossom) and rosemary. When purchasing a hydrosol, look carefully at the label to be sure it is a true hydrosol and not an aromatic water, which is a blend of water and essential oils.

Principles of Homeopathy

Homeopaths believe that every person has a "vital force" or self-healing ability that can be called upon to treat or prevent disease. Homeopathic medicine aims to stimulate the body's own self-healing response through the use of carefully chosen homeopathic remedies.

Homeopaths base diagnosis and treatment upon an in-depth case history that provides a complete picture of an individual's current and past physical symptoms as well as many other factors, including outlook on life, emotional temperament, food preferences and reactions to stress. Treatment is based upon the Law of Similars, or "like cures like". (The word homeopathy comes from the Greek *homeo*, meaning similar, and *pathos*, which means disease or suffering.)

A simple explanation of this principle is that a substance that causes a certain symptom when given in a large dose can be used in minute amounts to treat that same symptom. For example, the pungent compounds in onions are known to cause watery eyes and nose, throat irritation, coughing and sneezing. Homeopathy, a diluted preparation of onion is used to treat colds or allergies in which the patient experiences symptoms similar to those just described.

Practitioners of homeopathy believe that self-treatment with homeopathic remedies is appropriate for minor acute problems and injuries, but that a qualified homeopath should be consulted for more serious problems.

Homeopathic Remedies

Preparations of highly diluted natural substances that may come from plants, minerals or animals is called homeopathic remedies. Even bacteria and very poisonous substances, such as arsenic and cadmium, are used. In most highly diluted remedies, however, not even a molecule of the original substance can be detected in the finished product. For this reason, homeopathic remedies are generally considered safe and nontoxic.

A homeopathic remedy is created through a multi-step process. First, the plant, mineral or animal material being used to make the remedy is extracted in alcohol to create what is called a "mother tincture". Next, one drop of this mother tincture is added to ninety-nine drops of an alcohol-water solution and "succussed" (shaken vigorously). This process of dilution and succussion is repeated until the desired dilution has been attained.

Homeopathic remedies are sold in liquid, tablet, pellet, powder, and ointment forms. The strength of the remedy, known in homeopathy as potency, is indicated on the

❧ FLOWER REMEDIES ❧

Flower remedies are a type of homeopathic remedy intended to work not on physical problems, but rather on psychological and emotional disturbances. (Flower remedies are called flower essences in the United States to comply with regulatory requirements.)

The Bach Flower Remedies constitute the original flower remedy system, introduced in the early twentieth century by a British physician, pathologist and immunologist named Edward Bach (1886–1936). Bach's system of thirty-eight flower remedies is still in wide use today. In addition, a combination called Rescue Remedy has become one of the most popular of all the Bach flower remedies. It is a formula of five flower remedies that is widely used for treating emotional shock and trauma in both humans and animals. Composed of flower essences of impatiens, clematis, rock rose, cherry plum and star of Bethlehem, Rescue Remedy is available in liquid and cream formulations. Other flower essences are available primarily as liquids.

Bach devoted his life to discovering and teaching the uses of his flower remedies. The Dr Edward Bach Centre in Mount Vernon, England, continues his work to this day. Practitioners of the Bach system can be found all over the world, particularly in the United Kingdom, Germany and the United States. Numerous other flower remedies systems have been developed in more recent years, using flowers indigenous to different regions of the world. No clinical studies have been conducted to test the effects of flower remedies, so reports of their effectiveness are all anecdotal.

To make a flower remedy, an "essence" of the plant is first prepared, either by floating blossoms for several hours in pure water in a clear glass bowl set in the sun, or by boiling the plant material. The essence is then preserved in brandy to create a stock from which individual medicines are made. An individual medicine consists of 2 drops of the stock medicine mixed with 30 ml (1 oz) of pure water in a dropper bottle. According to Bach, a patient should take four drops of a remedy four times a day.

Bach flower remedies have been known to ease fear, anxiety and stress. They have also been helpful in the treatment of shock and trauma.

label on a scale from highest potency (3c or 3x) to lowest potency (30c or 30x). The higher the number, the lower the potency. Potency is usually determined by the amount of times the solution is shaken and diluted during preparation. The lower the potency (in other words, the more dilute the remedy), the more effective the remedy is believed to be.

AROMATHERAPY

The use of highly concentrated, aromatic plant essential oils to bring about healing effects, is often called aromatherapy. While the term aromatherapy may be relatively new, the use of fragrant plant oils as medicines, perfumes, and cosmetics is ancient. Distillation methods to extract essential oils from plants were invented as early as 1000 B.C.E. in the Middle East. By the Middle Ages, essential oils were popularly used in Europe as perfumes and medicines.

Essential oils, also called volatile oils, are produced by plants in specialized oil glands located in their leaves, flowers, rinds, seeds, bark and roots. These oils have long been important in commercial perfumery and are still used today to create exquisite and expensive perfumes. Essential oils are also widely employed as flavourings for commercially produced foods and beverages. Many are antiseptic and are incorporated into products designed to kill germs. Essential oil of thyme, for example, is one of the main ingredients in some mouthwashes. Pure plant essential oils are popular in the manufacture of natural cosmetics because they have properties, including anti-inflammatory and antiseptic abilities, which help soothe and rejuvenate the skin.

One of today's most popular uses of aromatherapy is to affect one's mood or state of mind. Some plant oils have uplifting and invigorating effects, helping refresh and clear the mind. Others are calming, and can help induce relaxation or even sleep. The fact that aromas can have profound effects on human emotions has been well documented scientifically, and essential oils have found use among consumers and holistic healers as supportive treatments for disorders such as depression and anxiety. The clinical use of aromatherapy (sometimes called medical aromatherapy or aromacology) has

Essential oils are often applied directly on the skin, after dilution, to avoid irritation of the skin. Oils may also be added to creams, bath water and lotions for everyday use.

increased in popularity in Europe, particularly in the United Kingdom and France. A growing body of research supports the clinical use of aromatherapy. One small clinical study, for example, showed that, in a hospital intensive care unit, massage with lavender essential oil reduced the anxiety experienced by patients. Other clinical studies have confirmed the traditional use of lavender essential oil to treat insomnia. Thousands of laboratory studies have documented the antiseptic and anti-inflammatory, as well as the immune-stimulating properties of other essential oils.

How Aromatherapy Works

Essential oils are composed of molecules of aromatic compounds. One essential oil may contain hundreds of these aromatic compounds, which contribute to the oil's unique aroma and physiological actions. Chemists call these volatile compounds because their molecules easily evaporate, or volatize, into the air.

Essential oils can enter the body via absorption through the skin. In addition, the aromatic molecules floating around in the air enter the nose and are picked up by olfactory receptors. These transport information to the olfactory bulb located at the top of the nasal passage at the base of the brain. From there, scent information is passed on to the limbic system, a primitive part of the brain responsible for very basic body functions. The limbic system communicates with the hypothalamus and pituitary, master glands that affect and regulate fundamental body processes including the secretion of hormones and the regulation of moods, digestion, appetite, sexual arousal and heartbeat. Aromas also stimulate the parts of the brain that control memory.

Important Cautions

Essential oils are extremely concentrated and must be treated with respect. A good rule of thumb is that more is not better! Undiluted essential oils is not recommended for use directly on the skin and they should never be taken internally. Essential oils should also be kept away from the eyes. It is important to use only high-grade, pure plant essential oils (not synthetic fragrance oils) and become educated on the use of essential oils by reading a reputable book devoted to the subject or consulting a trained aromatherapist.

Essential oils are estimated to be about fifty times stronger than the whole herbs from which they are made. Essential oils made from flowers (such as rose or orange blossom) are the safest and mildest essential oils. But some herbs that are perfectly safe to eat or to drink as a tea contain very strong, potentially toxic essential oils that must be used with caution. Examples include cinnamon bark (*Cinnamomum verum*), clove (*Syzygium aromaticum*), oregano (*Origanum vulgare*), savory (*Satureja* spp.) and thyme (*Thymus vulgaris*). Other essential oils, such as arnica and tansy, are so toxic they should not be used at all in aromatherapy.

Using Essential Oils

Two of the most popular ways to use essential oils are inhalation (smelling them) and application to the skin (in a massage oil or facial oil). Other ways to incorporate aromatherapy into daily life include adding essential oils to bathwater, skin creams, and lotions. Essential oils may also be used to scent bedding, clothing, and laundry, and can easily be incorporated into homemade air-fresheners. A diffuser (a device specially designed to disperse essential oils into the air) can be used to fill an entire room with fragrance.

To make an inhalation, add a few drops of essential oil to a piece of cloth or a cotton ball. To make a steam inhalation, add three to five drops of essential oil to a pot of steaming water. Steam provides a vehicle not only for inhaling essential oils, but also for carrying essential oils to the skin. Position the face about 31 cm (12 ins) over the steaming water, drape a towel over the head and breathe the steam for a moment or two. Remove the towel and take a few breaths of fresh air. Repeat the process for a maximum of five to ten minutes total.

Proper dilution of essential oils is a must for application to the skin. To protect the skin from irritation, essential oils are added to a carrier oil (a vegetable or fruit oil) before applying to the skin. A wide variety of different oils may be used as carrier oils, including sweet almond, grapeseed, sunflower, olive, jojoba, apricot kernel, kukui nut, hazelnut and sesame oils. Almond oil is a good all-around choice for massage oils and skin care because it is affordable and has only a light fragrance.

Aromatic waters are another easy and pleasant way to bring essential oils into everyday life. Aromatic waters are made by adding 10 drops of essential oil to 30 ml (1 oz) of water in a spray bottle. After being thoroughly shaken, the mixture can be used to mist the body and face. Be sure eyes are closed before spraying aromatic waters near the face.

How Essential Oils are Produced

All plant aromas can be attributed to the presence of essential oils, which perform vital functions in the life cycles of plants. The aromas of some essential oils serve

In a diffuser, a small candle heats a mixture of water and a herb's essential oil. The heat disperses the scent molecules into the air.

to attract pollinators. Some aromas repel pests or discourage grazing animals from eating the plant. Others protect plants against infection by bacteria, viruses and fungi.

For commercial use, huge amounts of plant material are needed to produce relatively small quantities of essential oils, which explains why some essential oils are so costly to buy. Depending on the plant, any of a number of different commercial extraction techniques may be used.

DILUTIONS FOR COMMON USES OF ESSENTIAL OILS

USE	DILUTION
Bath	three to six drops per tub
Body or facial oil	six to eight drops to 30 ml (1 oz) of carrier oil
Body mist (aromatic water)	ten drops to 30 ml (one oz) of water
Foot bath	five drops to one basin of water
Massage oil	six to eight drops to 30 ml (1 oz) of carrier oil
Room spray	fifteen to twenty drops to 30 ml (1 oz) of water
Skin cream or lotion	six to eight drops to 30 ml (1 oz) of lotion or cream
Steam inhalation	three to five drops of essential oil to 1 litre (1 quart) of steaming water

❧ NATURAL PERFUMES ❧

Using essential oils to create original fragrance blends for homemade cosmetics, air fresheners or perfumes is fun and easy. Begin by choosing one essential oil to serve as the backbone of the fragrance and then add small amounts of other oils, sniffing to judge the effect after each addition. You may also wish to use a fixative, which helps to reduce the evaporation rate of essential oils. Phtalates and glycerin are the most commonly used ones, but you should test a small are of skin before using them in any fragrance as they may cause allergic reactions.

Pay attention to the intensity of each oil, and use extremely strong-smelling oils sparingly so their presence does not overwhelm the others. A good rule of thumb is to use only one drop of very strong-smelling oil – rosemary, ylang ylang, jasmine or patchouli, for example – to five to ten drops of milder-smelling oil, such as citrus, cedarwood or lavender.

Make small batches of fragrance until the process becomes comfortable. Take notes, so a successful fragrance can be duplicated later on. To make a perfume, add about twelve drops of a blend to 30 ml (1 fl.oz) of carrier oil. Jojoba oil makes a good perfume base.

The citrusy scent of lime is often added to fragrance oils which are used in air refresheners, perfumes and candles.

Distillation is the most common way to extract essential oils. Approximately 80 percent of plant essential oils are produced through one of the most common distillation methods, which employ steam, heat, and condensation to separate essential oils from the solid and water components of the plant. No solvents are used, so this technology results in a very pure product. Essential oils produced through steam distillation include lavender, rosemary, peppermint and eucalyptus.

For very delicate plants that are easily damaged by heat, various other extraction techniques are available. Solvent extraction utilizes liquid solvents to dissolve and extract essential oils from the plant; the solvent is then evaporated under pressure. The initial product, called a concrete, is a sticky substance that contains plant waxes and pigments in addition to essential oils. The concrete may be sold as is or further refined to create a product called an absolute. This process is expensive, so it is generally used only to extract desirable and costly fragrances, including jasmine, rose and vanilla, that cannot be produced through distillation. Because solvent-extracted concretes and absolutes may contain traces of the solvents used to make them, they are not appropriate for therapeutic use, but are fine to use as perfumes or room sprays.

Supercritical carbon dioxide (CO_2) extraction is a newer technology used to extract essential oils using carbon dioxide gas under low heat conditions. Because less heat is used, the aroma of an essential oil produced through CO_2 extraction is very close to that of the original plant. In addition, because only carbon dioxide gas is used, the final product is free of solvent residues and is considered to be very pure. However, the equipment needed for CO_2 extraction is expensive, as are the oils produced in this way.

Two types of essential oils are produced through CO_2 extraction, using slightly different technologies. The first type, a liquid product composed primarily of volatile compounds, is called a selective extract. Oils produced in this way include frankincense and myrrh. The second type of CO_2 extract is called a total extract and contains not only volatile components, but also fats, waxes and pigments with medicinal properties. This technology, which is also used to manufacture high-quality herbal extracts, is used to produce essential oil extracts including carrot seed, calendula, chamomile and vanilla.

The essential oils of citrus fruits such as lemon, grapefruit, orange and lime are contained in special oil glands in the rind. These oils are often extracted through a process called cold expression, which involves crushing the rinds to press out the oil in a process similar to that used to manufacture olive oil. Citrus oils may also be produced through distillation.

The oldest method for producing essential oils, rarely used today, is called enfleurage. The procedure involves placing fragrant blossom on solid sheets of animal or vegetable fat and allowing the scent of the flowers to permeate the oil. When the blossoms are exhausted, they are removed and replaced with fresh flowers. This process is repeated until the fat is saturated with volatile oils. Before the advent of solvent extraction, enfleurage was the only method available for extracting essential oils from delicate flowers such as rose, jasmine and tuberose.

USING HERBS AS MEDICINE

The most basic way to get the benefits of herbs is to put plant material in one's mouth and chew it, but this is rarely the most convenient or pleasant way to take an herbal remedy. Before using an herb for its medicinal benefits, it is usually necessary to first extract or otherwise package the desirable compounds into a form that is easy to take. Some types of herbal preparations – those that contain alcohol, for example – also serve to preserve the herbs against spoilage.

Extracting medicinal compounds from a plant generally requires the action of a solvent, a substance capable of separating out the desired constituents and leaving the rest behind. When someone makes an herbal infusion or decoction (tea), for example, the boiling water functions as the solvent. Not all plant compounds, however, are soluble in water. Some require alcohol or even oil for effective extraction. Oil-soluble compounds are usually also soluble in alcohol. Other solvents include vegetable glycerin and vinegar.

Types of Herbal Preparations

Medicinal herbal preparations run the gamut from low-tech "kitchen medicines" made from fresh, whole plants, to high-tech standardized extracts produced in modern manufacturing facilities. While knowledge of how to prepare herbal remedies at home was once commonplace, today many people enjoy the convenience of purchasing herbal remedies that are ready to use.

Many herbs and herb extracts are now available in tablet form. These are made by eliminating the water from a plant or extract, powdering it and pressing it into the form of a tablet, sometimes with the help of fillers or excipients (inert substances included to help the tablet hold its shape). Herbs may also be found in the form of

ESSENTIAL OILS AND PROPERTIES

ESSENTIAL OIL	EFFECTS
Carrot seed (Daucus carota)	Stimulates and regenerates skin cells; good for dry and mature skin
Chamomile, German (Matricaria recutita)	Anti-inflammatory; calms upset stomach; soothes sensitive skin and sore muscles; relaxing, uplifting aroma; may help ease depression and insomnia
Clary sage (Salvia sclarea)	Eases muscle tension and menstrual cramps; helpful for oily skin; relaxing, euphoric aroma; may help ease depression and anxiety
Eucalyptus (Eucalyptus globulus)	Antibacterial, decongestant; clears sinuses and bronchial tubes; stimulating aroma
Geranium (Pelargonium graveolens)	Anti-inflammatory, antibacterial, antifungal; stimulates and regenerates skin cells; helpful for mature skin; relaxing aroma; soothes stress, may help ease depression
Lavender (Lavandula angustifolia)	Anti-inflammatory, antibacterial, antifungal; general first aid; stimulates and regenerates skin cells; helpful for sensitive and mature skin; calming and relaxing, may help ease depression, anxiety and insomnia
Lemon (Citrus limon)	Antibacterial, antifungal; helpful for oily skin; uplifting, may help ease stress, insomnia and depression
Peppermint (Mentha x piperita)	Antibacterial; soothes gastrointestinal spasms, stomach upset and nausea; uplifting, stimulating aroma
Rose (Rosa x centifolia or R. x damascena)	Antiseptic, anti-inflammatory; stimulates and regenerates skin cells; helpful for sensitive and mature skin; soothes stress and depression
Rosemary (Rosmarinus officinalis)	Calms upset stomach, soothes muscle aches, stimulates circulation; helpful for mature skin; stimulating aroma
Tea tree (Melaleuca alternifolia)	Antibacterial, antifungal, anti-inflammatory

cough syrups, ointments, creams suppositories and lotions. Herb infusions (water-based teas) may be added to baths, as the body can absorb some medicinal components through the skin, and can also be used as compresses, douches, enemas, gargles and mouthwashes.

Making Herbal Infusions and Decoctions

Herbal infusions and decoctions, commonly called "herbal teas", represent one of the simplest and most effective ways to take herbs that have water-soluble constituents. The infusion method is gentler than decoction. It is best suited to leaves and flowers, which are delicate and can be destroyed by excessive heat. Decoction is used to extract water-soluble compounds from harder plant materials such as roots, seeds and bark. However, roots with a particularly high content of volatile oils, such as valerian, should not be decocted, but instead ground into a fine powder and steeped as an infusion to prevent the loss of volatile oils.

Tinctures, salves, ointments and tea can be made at home or store bought.

To make an infusion, pour boiling water over dried or fresh leaves or flowers, and cover tightly to prevent the escape of volatile oils. Let steep for ten to fifteen minutes, strain, and drink. The exact proportion of plant material to water will vary with the herb that is being used, but a general rule of thumb is to use 225 ml (8 fl.oz) of water to 1 tsp (1.5 g/0.05 oz) of dried herbs. Fresh herbs have a high water content, so you will need to use about three times as much fresh herb for a similar concentration.

To make a decoction, place herbs (roots, bark or seeds) with water in a pot. Cover, bring to a boil, lower heat, and simmer for about twenty minutes. Strain and drink. General proportions for decoctions are 225 ml (8 fl.oz) of water to 28 g (1 oz) of dried herbs.

Making Tinctures

Tincturing is a method for extracting and preserving the medicinal constituents of herbs in a solution of alcohol and water. Properly made and stored, tinctures can last for ten years or more. For the home medicine-maker, vodka is an excellent solvent for most herbs, because it has a mild flavour and contains enough alcohol (40 percent) to serve as a good preservative.

However, any alcohol can be used, and some people like the taste that brandy imparts to their home remedies. To make a tincture at home, fill a 1 litre (1 quart) jar about two-thirds full of dried herb, such as nettle leaf. The herb will expand when the liquid is added, so the jar should not be too full. The herb should be powdered or cut as finely as possible. Add vodka to the rim of the jar, which should be capped tightly. Allow the herb to soak in the alcohol for at least two weeks, shaking the jar daily to extract the medicinal compounds from the plant material. Drain the resulting mixture through a coffee filter or a strainer lined with muslin or cheesecloth, pressing as much liquid as possible out of the herb. Store the tincture in a dark-coloured glass bottle.

Understanding Standardized Extracts

To make a standardized extract, or commercial herbal preparation, it must be made in a way that guarantees content of a specified amount of one or more chemical constituents. These chemical constituents, often called marker compounds, represent scientists' best guess as to the "active ingredients" of the herb. Chemists test for marker compounds using sophisticated laboratory technologies. High-pressure liquid chromatography (HPLC), for example, provides a chemical profile that shows exactly what compounds an extract contains, and in what proportions.

Standardized extracts are usually sold as capsules or tables. They are labelled to indicate the percentage of marker compounds the product contains. Milk thistle (*Silybum marianum*), for example, is standardized to contain 70 to 80 percent silymarin. Saw palmetto (*Serenoa repens*) is standardized to 85 to 95 percent fatty acids and sterols. Some herb extracts are not only standardized, but are also concentrated to increase the level of certain constituents. For example, standardized ginkgo biloba extract is a fifty-to-one concentrated extract standardized to contain 24 percent ginkgo flavone glycosides and 6 percent terpene lactones.

Standardized extracts have both advantages and drawbacks. One of the main advantages is that they enable herbal product manufacturers to ensure that a herb extract contains the same quantity of marker compounds each and every time it is made. In nature, the amount of chemicals produced by a given plant can vary according to a wide range of natural factors, including weather, altitude and soil composition. The technologies used for producing standardized extracts allow manufacturers to compensate for this natural variability by testing for and adjusting the level of desired chemical compounds in the finished product. Doctors and clinical researchers appreciate standardized extracts, because they allow the same dosage to be administered to a patient time and time again, ensuring consistency of results.

One of the main drawbacks to standardized extracts, however, is that it is not always possible to tell which of an herb's many chemical compounds is the active ingredient. The effects of many herbs appear to be due to a number of constituents working together, making the selection of an appropriate marker compound challenging. In addition, standardized extracts are usually more expensive than simpler, more traditional herbal preparations, and cannot be made at home. Some herbalists and consumers are uncomfortable using standardized extracts because they seem more like high-tech pharmaceuticals than natural plant remedies.

Plant Parts as Medicine and Food

More than 10,000 plants are used medicinally around the world, and virtually all plant parts have been employed in various ways as medicines, foods or spices. The most commonly used plant parts are leaves, flowers, roots, seeds, fruits and bark. Root bark, stems, resin and even specific flower parts such as stamens or calyces, may also be used. Sometimes the whole plant is used, or just the aerial parts, meaning all of the plant's above-ground parts.

A good herbal reference book will always describe the part of the plant to be used and how it should be taken. To know that milk thistle (*Silybum marianum*) helps improve liver health does no good unless one also knows that it is the milk thistle seed – not the leaf or the root – that confers the herb's health benefits. In some cases, a combination of plant parts may be

---

❧ GLOSSARY OF HERBAL REMEDIES ❧

CAPSULE
A two-part shell (made of gelatin, starch or cellulose) filled with powdered herb.

DECOCTION
A water-based herbal preparation made by simmering roots, bark, seeds or other tough, hard plant material with water.

ELIXIR
A flavoured liquid herbal preparation usually containing alcohol and a sweetener.

INFUSION
A water-based preparation made by steeping dried or fresh leaves or flowers (and roots or seeds with volatile compounds) in boiling water.

LINIMENT
A preparation for external use (to be rubbed into the skin) usually made by macerating (soaking) herbs in rubbing alcohol.

LIQUID EXTRACT OR FLUIDEXTRACT
A liquid herbal preparation prepared by percolating alcohol or other solvent through plant material; fluid extracts are more concentrated than tinctures.

OIL INFUSION
A "herbal oil" preparation for external use made by macerating (soaking) herbs in oil, such as olive oil, to extract their medicinal compounds.

POULTICE
A paste prepared from moistened herbs and applied directly to the skin to treat inflamation or bruises. Poultices may be applied cold or hot; the technical name for a hot poultice is a fomentation.

SALVE
A semi-solid preparation for external use made of a combination of herbs with oil or beeswax.

STANDARDIZED EXTRACT
A herb extract that contains a guaranteed quantity of a specified chemical constituent or constituents.

SUCCUS
A fresh plant juice.

TINCTURE (OR HYDROALCOHOLIC EXTRACT)
A liquid preparation that utilizes a combination of alcohol and water (and sometimes glycerin) to extract desired constituents from an herb; alcohol helps preserve the solution, causing it to break down less quickly.

recommended: hawthorn leaf, flower and fruit, for example, or echinacea root, leaf and flower. Different parts of the same plant may have very different medicinal effects. Dandelion leaf, for example, is a potent diuretic, while the root gently stimulates the liver and acts as a mild laxative. Nettle leaf has traditionally been employed as a tonic, and modern research suggests that it may be helpful in the treatment of arthritis. Nettle root, on the other hand, is incorporated into men's formulas designed to improve prostate health.

Using Herbs Safely

Herbs are best used in moderation, with a goal of gently supporting and maintaining health and protecting the body against the development of disease. Used sensibly, most herbs have an excellent safety record based on centuries of human use as medicine and food.

On the other hand, every substance a person ingests carries some degree of risk. As with any substance, including foods, it is possible for one person to have an allergic or otherwise unusual reaction to an herb that most people can use without problems. Documented herb allergies are very rare. For example, people who are allergic to ragweed and other plants in the Asteraceae family are cautioned to avoid chamomile, but only a few cases of chamomile allergy have actually been reported.

The fact remains that the vast majority of herbs are safe and nontoxic when used as directed. But herbs should never be used as a substitute for proper diagnosis and treatment by a healthcare professional. Certain individuals, including pregnant women, children, people with serious health conditions (such as high blood pressure, liver problems or kidney disease), and those who are taking pharmaceutical drugs, should always consult a doctor before using herbs.

Many of the problems reported with herbs in recent years can be attributed to what amounts to "herb abuse" – for example, employing ephedra (*Ephedra sinica*) for weight loss or energy enhancement. Using herbs in high doses to enhance weight loss or sports performance is not a wise use of plant remedies, nor is it in keeping with traditional herb applications.

With some herbal remedies, the same chemical compounds that confer medicinal effects in small doses may cause side effects in overdose. Stimulant laxatives –

Good judgement should always be exercised when using any herbal remedy. Be careful not to overuse or misuse any herb, as some plants like this bloodroot may be toxic.

those that induce bowel activity through chemical irritation – are one category of herb that should be used in moderation. Occasional short-term use is fine, but long-term use of stimulant laxatives can lead to the bowels can losing their ability to function without help. Chronic use can also lead to dangerous fluid depletion, electrolyte imbalances and other problems. Herbal stimulant laxatives include casacara sagrada (*Rhamnus purshiana*), senna (*Senna alexandrina*), purging buckthorn (*R. cathartica*), alder buckthorn (*R. frangula*), Chinese rhubarb (*Rheum officinale*, *R. palmatum*) and the dried latex from the leaves (not the gel) of the aloe plant (*Aloe vera*).

Some herbs are toxic if used in large doses, and certain herbs are so potent that they should simply not be used as remedies under any circumstances. It is important to become as educated as possible about an herb before taking it. If in doubt about the safety of any herb or herbal remedy, be sure to consult a qualified herbalist or reputable herbal guidebook.

Herb-drug Interactions

Just as some pharmaceutical drugs can produce dangerous interactions if taken in combination, certain herbs may have the potential to interfere with the activity of pharmaceuticals. In fact, even foods can interact with medications. As recently as 1991, a study published in the British medical journal *Lancet* showed that consumption of grapefruit juice may inhibit the activity of liver enzymes that are important in drug metabolism (the way the body processes drugs), thus elevating blood levels of certain pharmaceuticals.

St John's wort (*Hypericum perforatum*) is metabolized by the same liver enzyme system, and in 2000, clinical researchers conducting a study in the United States observed that in healthy volunteers, the herb lowered blood levels of a number of drugs, including indinivir (a drug used to treat HIV infection), cyclosporine (used to prevent organ transplant rejection), digoxin (a treatment for congestive heart failure) and theophylline (an asthma treatment). Since then, some small studies conducted in the United States have suggested that kava (*Piper methysticum*) may have the potential to cause similar interactions. However, much more research is necessary before conclusions can be drawn about the potential of herbs to cause this kind of interaction with pharmaceuticals.

Combining two substances with similar effects can cause what is known as an additive effect. For example, combining alcohol and valerian (a sedative herb), could theoretically compound the sedative effects of both substances. The same might be true for other herbs that have sedative effects – kava (*Piper methysticum*) or hops (*Humulus lupulus*), for instance. It is wise not to combine such herbs with alcohol or pharmaceuticals that have sedative effects, such as benzodiazepines (diazepam-type drugs).

Blood-thinning herbs are another category in which additive effects may occur. People who take anticoagulant (blood-thinning) medications, such as warfarin, should not take high doses of herbs that have blood-thinning effects. These include garlic (*Allium sativum*), ginkgo (*Ginkgo biloba*) and ginger (*Zingiber officinale*). In addition, although few if any actual adverse reactions have been documented in this area, the use of blood-thinning herbs should be discontinued before surgery in order to reduce the risk of bleeding complications.

PLANTS PARTS USED AS MEDICINE AND FOOD

PLANT PART	EXAMPLES
Bark	Cinnamon (*Cinnamomum verum*), oak (*Quercus spp.*), slippery elm (*Ulmus rubra*), wild cherry (*Prunus serotina*), willow (*Salix alba*), yohimbe (*Pausinystalia yohimbe*)
Calyx	Hibiscus (*Hibiscus sabdariffa*)
Flower	Arnica (*Arnica montana*), calendula (*Calendula officinalis*), chamomile (*Matricaria recutita*), feverfew (*Tanacetum parthenium*), lavender (*Lavandula angustifolia*)
Fruit	Cayenne (*Capsicum annuum*), cranberry (*Vaccinium macrocarpon*), medicinal mushrooms (*Lentinus edodes, Ganoderma lucidum, others*), saw palmetto (*Serenoa repens*)
Leaf	Artichoke (*Cynara scolymus*), ginkgo (*Ginkgo biloba*), oregano (*Origanum vulgare*), rosemary (*Rosmarinus officinalis*), thyme (*Thymus vulgaris*)
Resin	Boswellia (*Boswellia serrata*), frankincense (*Boswellia carteri*), guggul (*Commiphora mukul*), myrrh (*Commiphora molmol*)
Rhizome	Ginger (*Zingiber officinale*), turmeric (*Curcuma longa*)
Root	Black cohosh (*Cimicifuga racemosa*), dong quai (*Angelica sinensis*), ginseng (*Panax spp.*), goldenseal (*Hydrastis canadensis*), kava (*Piper methysticum*)
Root bark	Cat's claw (*Uncaria tomentosa*), eleuthero (*Eleutherococcus senticosus*)
Seed	Dill (*Anethum graveolens*), evening primrose (*Oenothera biennis*), fennel (*Foeniculum vulgare*), horse chestnut (*Aesculus hippocastanum*), nutmeg (*Myristica fragrans*), soy (*Glycine max*)
Seed coat	Mace (*Myristica fragrans*)
Seed kernel	Cola (*Cola acuminata*)
Stamen	Corn silk (*Zea mays*), saffron (*Crocus sativus*)
Stem, branches	Ephedra (*Ephedra sinensis*), horsetail (*Equisetum arvense*)

CHAPTER 7

Herbs *in* Cooking

For thousands of years, people all over the world have been cooking with herbs and spices. Whether used as preservatives for food, to mask the bad taste of spoiled meats before the days of refrigeration, or simply to enhance the flavour of a dish, herbs and spices have always played an important role in cuisine. Although spices are technically herbs, the two terms in cooking are applied separately according to their usage. In culinary terms, a herb is generally the leaf of a plant, and it is often used fresh. Spices, on the other hand – the seeds, roots, bark, buds or fruits of a plant – are usually used in their dried forms.

In the Middle Ages, early explorers such as Marco Polo brought exotic spices such as peppercorns, cloves and cardamom from the Far East to Europe and South America. Spices were so valued in medieval times that they were used as currency. In fact, the search for a shorter trade route to Asia for spices took Christopher Columbus and others across the Atlantic and led to the discovery of the New World. Today, it is nearly impossible to imagine certain dishes without the flavour of the herbs and spices introduced so many years ago.

Fresh and dried herbs and spices are the key to delicious cookery.

Herbs and Spices
In the Culinary World

Over the course of human history, many world cultures have incorporated herbs and spices into a unique culinary signature. In Japan, for example, a seven-spice powder, which includes sesame seeds, poppy seeds, and dried chillies, is sprinkled over udon noodles and grilled chicken yakitori. In India, *garam masala*, an intricate blend of up to twelve spices, adds nuance to grilled meats. In Italy, basil and garlic mingle with olive oil, pine nuts and Parmesan or pecorino cheese to make a delicious pesto sauce.

HERBS AND SPICES
AROUND THE WORLD

A trip to the Caribbean is incomplete without experiencing the sultry spice of jerk seasoning, made with dried chillies, thyme, garlic, pepper and allspice. A journey to Mexico should include a sampling of one of the country's magical *mole* sauces, which commonly includes peppercorns, seeds, chillies, cinnamon and chocolate. In northern Europe, fresh herbs such as dill and juniper berry are key additions to Scandinavia's ubiquitous pickled herring.

On the following pages are just a few examples of how herbs and spices have come to be identified with, and how they have influenced, the food customs of various areas of the world.

North America
and the Caribbean Islands

The culinary traditions of North America and the islands of the Caribbean are largely shaped by the influences of European colonialism, which imported the spices of Asia. As a result of this juxtaposition of cultures and cuisines, the unique cooking of North America and the Caribbean region cobbles together the flavours of the world. In the United States, a melting pot of flavours includes the spices cinnamon and paprika, and herbs such as basil, oregano and parsley. In Cuban cuisine, the salsalike *mojo* is made with garlic, orange juice, dried oregano, cumin and coriander. In the Caribbean Islands, the spices nutmeg, allspice, and ginger are used to flavour dishes including stews and grilled meats.

Central and South America

The cuisines of Central and South America are greatly influenced by European explorers of the 16th century. In Mexico, Chile and Argentina, herbs and spices introduced by Spanish conquistadores were integrated with native dishes based on corn, beans and cassava. In Mexico, *recado* spice pastes are made with clove, cumin, coriander and oregano. In Chile, *pebre* sauce, used to flavour casseroles, is a combination of garlic, chillies and coriander. In Argentina, *chimichurri* sauce, made with oregano, parsley, garlic and paprika, adds a flavourful edge to soups, vegetables and grilled meats. Portuguese colonialists and African slaves contributed much to the

Nutmeg's outer shell appears dry and tough; however, once grated, its beautiful, fragrant interior is exposed.

cuisine of Brazil: the Portuguese influence is evident in the use of herbs such as garlic and parsley along with ingredients such as dried and salted cod, olives, wine, garlic and onions; the African influence is evident in the extensive use of coconut, plantain and palm oil.

Northern and Eastern Europe

Eastern Europe's generally chilly climate has exerted a strong influence on its cuisine. Warming herbs and spices with strong flavours, such as nutmeg, mustard seed and clove are frequently added to hearty soups and casseroles, stews, meat pies, pickled and cured fish and dumplings. In warmer months, fresh herbs such as dill, stinging nettle and tarragon are used to lighten the flavour of heavy fare. In Russia, foods such as the rich beet soup borscht are flavoured with dill. In Scandinavia, caraway is used in breads. In Germany, juniper berry is used to season meat, and in Poland, bay leaf is used to flavour *bigos*, a traditional hunter's stew.

The Mediterranean Region

Mediterranean cooking is best known for its use of fresh herbs, such as sage and tarragon. In Greece, dried oregano and thyme find their way into dishes ranging from fish and stuffed vegetables to the lasagne-like *moussaka,* while in Spain, saffron elevates paella from a humble rice and seafood dish to a culinary tour de force. The cuisines of southern Italy and France draw heavily upon fresh basil, oregano and rosemary, as does that of Portugal, with its use of garlic, coriander and parsley.

The Middle East,
North Africa, East Africa

Middle Eastern and northern African cuisine tends to draw upon spices that passed through the region while being transported to Europe and the West from the Far East. Iranian dishes often call for the addition of luxurious aromatics, such as rose and saffron. Cinnamon is a key ingredient in Moroccan couscous dishes. Ethopia's curry-like stews bear similarity to foods of the Middle East and India, and often feature a mix called *berbere*, a combination of spices including cinnamon, allspice and cloves.

East and Southeast Asia

The cuisines of China, Japan and Korea have three spices in common: garlic, ginger and sesame seed. But there are as many differences as similarities. The spiciest, Korean cuisine, is characterized by the use of chillies, garlic and ginger to make *kimchi*, a pickled cabbage used as a condiment. China's cuisine varies in flavour according to region, from the intense pungency of Sichuan preparations (which typically use dried chillies and garlic) to the subtle flavours of the lower Yangtse plains (incorporating ginger). The cooking of Japan is the most austere, with sesame seed, ginger or wasabi root used to add dimension and decoration to pristine presentations of singular items such as raw fish or grilled beef.

India and South Asia

This region is home to many of the world's most beloved spices, such as peppercorn, star anise, garlic and ginger. In northern India, two spice blends are quite common: *garam masala* and *chaat masala,* which include cumin, fennel seed and cardamom. In southern India, one common spice blend is made of up to 20 ingredients, including coconut, tamarind and curry powder. Indonesian cuisine draws heavily from curry leaves, galangal and lemongrass. The foods of Malaysia are often flavoured by *sambal bajak*, a condiment that is comprised of chillies, tamarind, galangal, garlic and wild lime leaves. Vietnamese *pho*, a traditional noodle dish, is flavoured with coriander, basil, lemon or lime and chillies. In Thailand, the most important flavoring agents include coriander, basil, garlic and ginger.

Richly flavoured spices such as (from bottom left) cinnamon, star anise, allspice, dried cloves and fennel seed (centre), are at the heart of many Asian cuisines.

cook to travel around the globe by simply opening a kitchen cupboard or stepping into a garden.

As with any culinary ingredient, a certain amount of know-how should accompany the usage of herbs and spices, beginning with how to select, store and preserve them.

Selecting and Storing Herbs and Spices

Herbs and spices get their aroma and flavour from essential oils and oleoresins, present in their fresh and dried states. These oils are fragile and dissipate over time, making it critical to purchase the freshest herbs and spices available from grocers whose herbs and spices sell quickly and are replaced often.

When purchasing fresh herbs, look for healthy, unblemished leaves that are vibrant in colour and not bruised, yellowed or browning. They should be fragrant, especially when rubbed between the fingers. If purchasing dried herbs from a bulk bin, evaluate for both colour and aroma prior to buying. Their perfume should be deep and heady, not musty.

When purchasing dried spices, check for an aroma that is vivid and rich. To test whole spices, break off a piece of the stick or scrape off some of the nut and examine its colour and fragrance. For ground spices, check the packaging date on the bottle or jar. It is generally best to buy dried herbs and spices in tightly sealed bottles. Self-serve bulk bins or packaging of cardboard and cellophane allow oxygen to reach the herb, causing the deterioration of its fragrance and flavourful essential oils.

Once herbs have been selected for use, it is important to store them properly. Fresh herbs have a limited shelf life, with some lasting only a couple of days before wilting and losing their potency. If the plan is to use them within a few hours, leafy, delicate herbs may be inserted into a glass of water at room temperature, like a bouquet of flowers. To store fresh herbs for later use, place them in a plastic bag and put it into the crisper section of the refrigerator. Tender herbs such as basil and chervil may

Australia and the South Pacific

In Australia and New Zealand, influences from British colonists and Southeast Asian immigrants combine with the popularity of trendy Mediterranean flavours to form a cuisine that is still in the process of forming a consistent national flavour. Ingredients traditionally used by native Aborigines, including Tasmanian pepper leaf, hibiscus flowers and purslane, are also beginning to find their way onto restaurant menus. In the South Pacific, the cuisine of the islands of French Polynesia has been influenced by the flavours of nearby neighbours Asia and North and South America, as well as by colonial Europe. Popular dishes range from French-inspired foie gras with vanilla bean to ginger-laden chow mein to fish salad with coriander.

HERBS AND SPICES IN THE KITCHEN

Herbs and spices were once too expensive and precious for daily use by people of modest economic means. Today, they are affordable and are an integral element of contemporary cooking. Incorporating these flavours into marinades, stir-fries and even desserts allows the

When air-drying herbs such as (from left) sage, thyme or oregano, choose a well-ventilated and shady spot so they will dry thoroughly.

be wrapped in a damp paper towel that is then placed in a plastic bag to prevent wilting. Keep them in a moderately cool area of the refrigerator, such as in the door shelf or on a top shelf.

Rather than storing dried herbs in a kitchen spice rack, where they may be exposed to the effects of heat or the sun, keep them in a cool, dark, dry place such as a pantry or cupboard. Check dried herbs and spices every six months, and discard any that are dull in colour and fragrance, or that do not release essential oils when crushed between fingers, grated or broken in half.

Preserving Herbs and Spices: Drying Herbs

This is by far one of the easiest ways to preserve them for future use. A number of techniques can be used to remove moisture that would otherwise lead to decay.

Air-Drying For centuries, people have dried herbs by tying them in bunches to hang upside down. Over the course of days or weeks, the herbs gradually lose their moisture and become brittle. They remain flavourful, however, because gravity forces the plant's essential oils down into the leaves. The best herbs to air-dry are sturdy, low-moisture plants, such as bay, lavender, lemon verbena, mint, oregano, rosemary, sage, thyme and winter savory. Always work with newly harvested plants. After cleaning

the stems and leaves, use a rubber band, string or twine to tightly fasten together several stems at their ends. (As stems shrink during drying, rubber bands will tighten around them, while string may need to be retied periodically.) Hang the bunches upside down in a dark, dry place where air can flow freely around them: from a rafter, ceiling hook or on a rack. Do not hang them near a stove or furnace, as heat will speed the breakdown of the herbs' essential oils, affecting their flavour.

Light can also break down essential oils, and dust will collect on the leaves if they are left in the open; protect herb bunches by tying paper bags, punctured with small slits for circulation, over them. Do not tightly bundle large-leaved, tender herbs, such as basil, as they may rot. Tender herbs will dry more quickly and retain their colour better if they are tied in loose bunches.

Herbs can also be air-dried on trays. This approach works especially well for tender herbs. Spread short-stemmed herbs or individual leaves in a single layer on racks or screens. An old window screen can be used, or make a tray by stretching steel screening or cheesecloth over a wooden framework. (Do not use galvanized-metal screens; some plant acids can react with them to form toxic compounds.) Trays can be stacked by placing a wooden block or other spacer at each corner to allow air to circulate between them. Keep trays in a warm, dry place until leaves become brittle.

When drying herbs such as mint in the oven, check after two hours. If they are not completely dried, return to the oven.

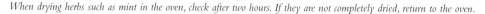

Trays can be used to dry the roots, bark and sturdy stems of plants such as ginger, ginseng, horseradish, liquorice, and marsh mallow. Clean the plant parts; do not peel roots. Chop, slice or shred the roots and stems into small pieces; they can become extremely hard once dried, making them difficult to cut or grind later. Lay plant parts on racks and turn them periodically until they are dry; this can take two to three weeks. When thoroughly dried, roots and stems become light and brittle. Store them in airtight tins or in dark-glass jars.

To dry herb seeds (fennel, caraway, coriander, dill, for example) put the almost-ripe seed heads into paper bags, keeping different varieties in separate bags. Handle the heads carefully, as seeds drop easily when ripe. Hang the open bags in a well-ventilated spot for two or three weeks to finish drying, then spread the seed heads on paper or a tray with very fine mesh. When they are dry and papery, rub or shake the seed heads, separating the seeds from the chaff by blowing or sieving the chaff away. Label and store the seeds in airtight jars.

Oven Drying An effective way to accelerate the herb-drying process is by adding heat. Proceed carefully, as heating the herbs too much or too quickly can result in the loss of essential oils and aromatic compounds, which will negatively affect flavour. To speed dry using an oven, first remove the leaves from cleaned herbs and spread them on a baking sheet or drying rack. Place in the oven on low heat (32°C/90°F) for several hours. It may not be possible to set older gas ovens to a low enough temperature, so try drying herbs in these ovens with the heat from the pilot light. Roots and tough stems can be dried at 49°C (120°F). Check the herbs regularly to make sure they do not blacken and shrivel.

Microwave Oven Drying Another way to speed dry herbs is by putting them in a microwave oven. Begin by washing the herbs, then remove leaves from the stems. Spread the leaves in a single layer on top of a thick pad of paper towels, and then transfer to a microwave oven. Run on high heat for one minute, and then check the leaves. If they are still fairly moist, microwave again for one minute. If necessary, continue heating the leaves in 20-second intervals until they are crisp but not burnt. It may take a few trials to get this process right. Cool leaves on a baking rack, then store in airtight containers.

Dehydrators Dehydrators are appliances that blow warm air over foods, removing their moisture. Lay herbs in a single layer on the trays of the dehydrator, and set

Arrange fresh herb leaves on a paper towel covered plate so that they are not touching before drying in a microwave oven.

the device on 90°F to 100°F (32°C to 38°C). Do not set the temperature higher, as the oils in the herbs may dissipate. The herbs will dry in several hours.

Dessicants Dessicants are moisture-absorbing materials such as sand, borax and cornmeal. Herbs dried with dessicants retain much of their original shape and colour. They are generally not edible. This method is commonly used to dry herbs that will be used to make handcrafts, such as wreaths, potpourris, garlands and table decorations. To dry herbs and flowers in a traditional dessicant, lay them in any type of container (from cardboard shoebox to ceramic baking dish to plastic storage container) and cover them with clean, dry sand or a mixture of one part borax to three parts cornmeal. Leave the container open to allow for evaporation. The herbs should be completely dry in three to five days.

❧ ARE THEY DRY ENOUGH? ❧

To test the dryness of herbs, bend a leaf in half. If it cracks and crumbles, it is completely dry. If it bends, folds or has a leathery feel, it still contains moisture and should be dried further.

Herbs can also be tested for moisture by sealing a small quantity of dried herbs in an airtight jar. After a day or two, check the contents. If condensation has formed inside the jar, the herbs are still moist and need to be dried for a longer period. It is important to dry herbs completely because those stored with even a small amount of moisture will develop mould. If mould is visible at any point, discard the entire batch of herbs.

Add frozen herb cubes, made with fresh herbs such as parsley (above), chives or basil, to sauces and soups to add flavour.

Another dessicant is silica gel, a chemical compound that resembles sea salt. It is widely available in craft stores, and is reusable. Its light granules are less likely than sand, borax or cornmeal to damage the delicate leaves and petals of the herb or flower.

To use the gel, spread a 1 in (2.5 cm) thick layer on the bottom of a shallow, airtight glass or plastic container. Lay flowers and leaves on top, making sure they do not touch. Cover gently with another 2.5 cm (1 in) layer of gel. Seal the container, and set it aside for two to four weeks. To speed up the process, microwave the container (using the defrost or half-power setting) for one minute at a time. Let the contents cool completely after each heating, then check to see whether the herbs are dry. This technique may take several minutes of microwaving. Handle the heated gel carefully, and do not remove the herbs until they are firm.

The flowers of Mentha rotundifolia *are edible; when steeped in hot water, its leaves combine well with sugar in tea.*

Preserving Herbs and Spices: Freezing Herbs

One of the simplest and quickest ways to retain the flavours of herbs and spices for culinary use is to freeze them. The herbs best suited for freezing are tender-leaved plants with fleeting flavours: basil, chervil, chives, coriander, comfrey, dill, lemon balm, lovage, marjoram, most mint, parsley, savory, sorrel, sweet cicely, sweet fennel, tarragon and some thymes.

Freezing Herb Cubes

Frozen herb ice cubes are easy to make, and useful to have on hand in the kitchen. They work well as flavouring in soups, stews, sauces and braised dishes. To make herb cubes, chop about 43 g (1¼ oz) of fresh herb leaves to the desired fineness, and then divide the herbs among the sections of an ice-cube tray. Add just enough water to cover the chopped leaves, then place the tray into the freezer.

When the cubes are frozen solid, remove them from the tray and store them in the freezer in resealable bags labelled with the herb type and date. Use within three months for freshest flavour.

It is also possible to freeze edible herb flowers from such plants as borage, scented geraniums and violets, in ice cubes that make spectacular additions to drinks. Consult the the list of edible herb flowers to the right for more options.

Freezing Herbs in Oil Herbs and spices are commonly used in dishes that also contain oils: dressings, marinades, dips and spreads. An excellent way to retain the powerful flavours of fresh herbs is to mix them with oil and freeze them, creating a sort of frozen pesto. In a blender or food processor, purée 60 g (1½ oz) loosely packed cleaned herb leaves (basil, dill, lovage, marjoram, oregano, or tarragon, for example) with 60 ml (4 oz) olive oil or a mild oil such as rapeseed. Freeze the purée in labelled containers or resealable bags.

Preserving Herbs and Spices: Herb Salts and Herb Sugars

Both salt and sugar are age-old herbal preservatives, as they inhibit the growth of bacteria. A traditional method of preserving herbs for cooking is to salt-cure them. In a container, place alternating layers of chopped or whole herbs and noniodized coarse-grade or regular table salt. Make sure each herb layer is completely covered with salt. Seal the mixture for a week or so in an airtight container such as a glass jar or plastic tub. The salt will draw the moisture from the leaves and absorb some of their essential oils, creating both a seasoning salt and crisp, dried herb leaves for cooking. Thin-leaved herbs such as dill, marjoram, rosemary, savory, tarragon and thyme dry well with salt.

Herb-flavoured sugars make a perfect addition to teas, icings or other sweet foods that will showcase but not overwhelm their subtle fragrance and flavour. Herbs that combine well with sugar include lavender, lemon or bee balm, lemon verbena, mint, orange or lemon zest, and rose- or lemon-scented geraniums. Tightly wrap 3 tablespoons (8 g/¼ oz) of chopped fresh herbs in a piece of cheesecloth. Embed this bundle in a jar filled with 450 g (¾ lb) of granulated sugar. Or, simply layer herb leaves in a jar of sugar, covering each layer completely with sugar. Leave the mixture for two weeks to let the flavour permeate the sugar, stirring occasionally to prevent clumping. Remove the cheesecloth bundle or sift out the loose herbs. Seal the jar tightly to retain the herbs' fragrance and flavour.

EDIBLE HERBS FLOWERS

BOTANICAL NAME	COMMON NAME
Agastache foeniculum	anise hyssop
Allium schoenoprasum	garden chives
Aloysia triphylla	lemon verbena
Angelica archangelica	angelica
Anthum graveolens	dill
Borago officinalis	borage
Brassica spp.	mustard
Calendula officinalis	calendula
Centaurea cynaus	cornflower, bachelor's buttons
Chamaemelum nobile	chamomile
Cichorium intybus	chicory
Coriander sativum	coriander
Dianthus caryophyllus	carnation
Foeniculum vulgare	fennel
Hyssopus officinalis	hyssop
Lavendula spp.	lavender
Lonicera japonica	Japanese honeysuckle
Mentha spp.	mint
Monarda spp.	bee balm
Ocimum basilicum	basil
Origanum majorana	marjoram
Pelargonium spp.	scented geranium
Rosa rugosa rose	rose
Rosmarinus officinalis	rosemary
Salvia officinalis	sage
Sanguisorba minor	burnet
Satureja hortensis	summer savory
Tagetes tenuifolia	'Lemon Gem' marigold
Taraxacum officinalis	dandelion
Thymus vulgaris	thyme
Tropaeolum majus	nasturtium
Viola spp.	violet
Viola tricolour	Johnny-jump-up
Viola X wittrockiana	pansy

Preserving Herbs and Spices: Candied Herbs

The process that captures the beauty and flavour of fresh herb flowers and leaves, creating ethereal additions to cakes and other sweets is referred to as candying. Be sure to candy only edible flowers and leaves that have not been treated with pesticides. Good choices for candying include: borage, dianthus, 'Lemon Gem' marigold, lemon verbena, mint, pansy, violets and rose. Consult the list of edible herb flowers on page 125 for more options.

To make these garnishes, select and then set aside several unblemished blossoms or leaves. Lightly whisk an egg white and strain it through a sieve. Hold one blossom or leaf with a pair of tweezers, and use a fine-bristled watercolour paintbrush to apply a coat of egg white. Next, dip the blossom or leaf into caster sugar. Lightly sprinkle more sugar on top. Gently shake off excess sugar and let the herb dry for four to eight hours on a tray lined with parchment paper. Stored in an air-tight container at room temperature, candied herbs will last around three months.

USING HERBS IN COOKING

From pastes to infusions, herbs contribute a fresh flavour and aroma to a wide variety of dishes, including grilled meats and seafood, soups, salads and baked goods.

Cooking with Fresh Herbs

Herbs can be used fresh or dried, chopped, whole, pureed or ground. Using whole herbs is perhaps the easiest way to put them to work. By simply adding a sprig or whole leaf to a sauce, soup or pan of meat or vegetables, a delicate flavour is imparted into the dish. This method of using fresh herbs is called an infusion. Whole herbs are generally removed prior to serving.

If more intensity is needed from herbs, they can be torn, chopped, minced or ground into a paste. Of these forms, a paste contributes the most powerful flavour to a dish. Torn, leafy, tender herbs, such as fresh basil or coriander, will supply a soft, nuanced flavour that is more intense than an infusion (since the herbs are being consumed), yet less concentrated than chopped herbs. Torn herbs can be tossed in salads or sprinkled on vegetables and meats as an edible garnish. Chopping and mincing herbs completely integrates them into a dish, imparting a fuller, richer flavour with each bite. Chopped herbs can also add colour and texture to food.

To store fresh herbs such as sage (left) and thyme (right) that will be used within a day or two, stand them up in a glass or pitcher of cold water on a windowsill, kitchen counter or in the refrigerator.

To chiffonade fresh basil or other fresh leafy herbs, wash the leaves and pat them dry. Stack six to eight of the leaves neatly, placing larger ones at the bottom.

Starting at the short end of the stack, gently roll the leaves into a tight cylinder.

When the leaves are rolled, hold them firmly and, using a sharp knife, cut the cylinder into thin strips, about 1 cm (½-in) wide.

Once the leaves are sliced and separated, you can keep them fresh for 30 minutes by placing them in a bowl of ice water until ready to use.

When using fresh herbs as an ingredient, be sure to add hardy, slower-cooking herbs, such as ginger, thyme, rosemary and bay leaves, at the beginning of the cooking process. This allows time for their flavour to be released. To preserve their tenderness, it is best to add delicate herbs, such as basil, tarragon and parsley, at the end of cooking. For tender herbs, pluck the leaves from the stems and chop them (basil leaves may be stacked and rolled lengthwise, and then sliced into thin ribbons). The easiest way to remove hardy herbs, such as lavender or rosemary, from their woody stems is to pull the needles or buds in the opposite direction of their growth.

❧ CREATING SPICE BLENDS ❧

Many types of cuisine use traditional spice blends, which generally prepare ahead of time and store for future use. There are more than twenty spices in curry powder, for example, which is used in many of India's stews and braises. A common Mediterranean blend, *herbes de Provence* contains basil, fennel seed and marjoram, among other spices, and is used to flavour roasted meats, soups and sauces. Italian food so frequently uses a combination of basil, marjoram, oregano and thyme that creating a ready-to-use custom blend of these spices can be a real time saver.

To create a ready-to-use spice blend, simply mix together the selected crushed spices. Store them in a labelled, dated spice jar or resealable plastic bag.

Herbes de Provence is a herb blend comprised of (anti-clockwise from top): basil, fennel seed, marjoram, thyme, summer savory, sage, lavender and rosemary.

To smash spices, place whole spices in a heavy-duty plastic bag. Use a heavy-bottomed pan or rolling pin to crush the spices inside the bag. Work with force, but carefully, to avoid tearing the bag.

Cooking with Dried Herbs and Spices

Dried herbs and spices are often more convenient than fresh herbs for adding flavour. While fresh herbs have a limited life span, dried herbs can be stored for up to six months in a cool, dark, dry place.

When dried, fresh herbs lose water (this loss can constitute as much as 90 percent of their weight), which evaporates in the process. The herb's essential oils become more concentrated, which means that a more intense (but not as fresh) flavour is imparted. When substituting dried herbs for fresh, use about half as much. If the dried ones are finely ground or pulverized, further reduce the substitution to one-third as much as fresh.

Hardy herbs such as rosemary, lavender, thyme and oregano are fine to use in their dried state. It is best to add them to a dish in the first stages or during initial preparation; for example, sprinkle lamb with dried oregano prior to roasting, or add dried thyme to onions as they cook in a pan. With the exception of dried sage, most leafy tender herbs are best used in their fresh state rather than dried. Tender herbs, such as basil, tarragon and parsley, lose their distinction when dried.

Dried herbs and spices can be used whole or ground. As with whole fresh herbs, whole spices infuse flavour into a dish. They can be placed in a tea ball, wrapped in a cheesecloth packet (see instructions on page 132), or added whole to a dish. Saltwater brines (salt dissolved in a large quantity of water), used to tenderize pork or poultry prior to cooking, can benefit from the addition

Use a mortar and pestle or an electric or manual coffee grinder to pulverize dried herbs (such as corriander shown here) into powder. Herbs must be completely dried before grinding; or they will not grind completely.

Glass is the best container for infused vinegars because it does not react with the acid in vinegar. Left to right: Fresh sage-infused balsamic vinegar; thyme-infused champagne vinegar; chervil-infused red wine vinegar.

of whole spices such as clove and peppercorn. Whole spices may be sautéed with butter or oil to add flavour and crunch to puddings, pilafs and stir-fried vegetables.

Ground spices are used to add an extra layer of intensity to the flavour of foods. To grind spices, a coffee mill comes in handy – many cooks have one mill specifically for grinding spices in addition to one for grinding coffee. A mortar and pestle is another option, as is a microplane grater the best option for grinding large, whole spices, such as nutmeg and cinnamon.

To coax more flavour, toast spices prior to grinding them. Dry toast herbs and spices such as cumin seeds, mustard seeds, chillies, peppercorns, poppy seeds and sesame seeds. To dry toast spices, place them in a pan (do not add fat) over medium heat. Shake the pan occasionally until the spices become fragrant. In some instances, they may even crackle and pop. Immediately remove spices from the pan once they are toasted. Toasted spices may be used whole, or, after being cooled for five to ten minutes, ground and used as a powder.

When it is desirable to have more flavour than whole spices can provide but less intensity than ground spices, crushed spices are an option. They can be used in infusions or to coat food prior to cooking, as in the classic French dish steak *au poivre*. To smash spices, place whole spices in a heavy-duty plastic bag. Use a heavy-bottomed pan or rolling pin to crush the spices inside the bag.

Cooking with Herb-Infused Oils

One of the best ways to make use of herbs in cooking is by infusing them first in oil. The aromatic compounds (essential oils) of herbs are fat soluble, so oil is an excellent medium for holding their intense essences. Herb flavoured oils have many uses in cooking: in salad dressings, as a marinade, as a dip for bread, to stir-fry or sauté meats and vegetables, to drizzle on fresh tomatoes or on meat, seafood and vegetables that are headed for the grill.

There are three basic methods for infusing oils with herbs. In the traditional method, whole herbs are submerged in oil and flavour the oil over time. In warm infusion, herbs are heated with oil so they rapidly release their essential oils. In cold infusion, herbs are puréed with oil and later strained out.

Making herb-infused oils is not an exact science, and the quality of the infusion depends on the strength and freshness of the herbs that are used. Start by making small

❧ PESTO'S ORIGINS ❧

Pesto alla Genovese, or pesto sauce, is commonly believed to have originated in Genoa in northern Italy. However pesto, which has been known in various forms since ancient Roman times, most likely originated in North Africa. A German variety uses wild garlic leaves instead of basil.

Ocimum minature, *or miniature purple basil, makes a delicious infused oil for salads and dipping.*

Wash jars or bottles with hot soapy water. Dry well, and pack with one part dried chilli peppers or other herbs. Pour in an equal amount of oil, stirring well to blend.

batches. When making oils for cooking, experiment to see which method and which combination of oil and herbs results in the best flavour.

If not stored properly, herb-flavoured oils can become dangerous to consume because of the growth of food-poisoning bacteria. Be sure to store these infusions in the refrigerator immediately after making them, and use them within two weeks.

Herbs commonly used in oil infusions that will be used for cooking – as opposed to used cold – include basil (sweet, lemon and dark opal, which all give the oil an amethyst hue), bay leaf, chives, chervil, coriander, dill, fennel, garlic, lemon balm, marjoram, mint, oregano, parsley, rosemary, savory, thyme and tarragon. Infuse tarragon early in the season, when its flavour is particularly sweet. Oil can also be infused with herbs such as lemongrass and lavender, or with other flavourful ingredients such as whole chillies or hot pepper flakes, ginger, lemon or orange zest, kumquats, peppercorns, and seeds of anise, cumin, dill and fennel. Some common herb combinations include basil with garlic; bay, peppercorn, rosemary and thyme; bay, dill, garlic and peppercorn; and tarragon with chillies.

Cover the top of the jar with plastic wrap; seal with a rubber band if the wrap does not cling well. Store the oil in the refrigerator. Taste the oil each day until the desired strength of flavour is reached.

When making herb-flavoured oil, use either a high-quality olive oil that does not have an assertive, fruity taste, which can overwhelm the flavour of the herbs, or a more mild-flavoured oil such as rapeseed, grape seed, safflower or sunflower. Herbs can also be paired with more flavourful oils, such as nut oils.

To use the traditional method of herb infusion to make a cooking oil, combine the desired herbs and oil in a one-to-one proportion: 60 g (1½ oz) fresh herbs to 237 ml (8 fl.oz) oil. If the flavour is too weak or too strong, it can be adjusted later with the addition of oil to dilute the infusion, or more herbs to strengthen the flavour of the final product.

Strain the oil into a decorative bottle, if desired. Store infused oil in the refrigerator and use within two weeks of preparation.

To begin, wash a glass jar with hot, soapy water, then fill it with boiling water and set aside for 10 minutes. Discard the water, and thoroughly dry the jar, then loosely fill it with the herb and oil mixture. Cover the jar with plastic wrap, seal it tightly, and place it in the refrigerator. Let it stand for two weeks, then strain out and discard the herbs. The resulting oil will be flavourful, but it will lack the more vibrant colour achieved through warm infusion.

The warm-infusion method works particularly well with strong flavoured, resinous herbs such as thyme, sage, marjoram, rosemary and savory. Prepare a jar as directed above, and then heat a one-to-one mixture of herbs and oils in a heavy-bottomed saucepan set over medium heat. Stir constantly until the oil starts to bubble. Lower the heat and cook for another minute or until the oil is very aromatic. Remove the pan from the heat and let the oil and flavourings cool. Taste the oil to make sure the herb flavour has reached the right strength. If it is too weak, add more herbs and reheat the mixture. If the flavour is too strong, dilute the mixture with additional oil. Strain the infused oil through cooking cheesecloth, pour into a prepared jar, and tightly seal. Oil created by this method can be used immediately or stored in the refrigerator for up to one week.

The cold-infusion method results in intensely coloured and flavoured oils. Quickly blanch leafy herbs by dunking them in boiling water for five seconds. Or, pour boiling water over herbs in a sieve, then immediately submerge them in icy water to halt the cooking process. Blanching helps preserve the colour of the herbs, and gives the finished oil a lovely hue.

Thoroughly dry the herbs with a paper towel, then combine them with oil in a one-to-one proportion. Blend in a food processor until smooth. Pour the mixture into a widemouthed container with a tight lid. Store this mixture in the refrigerator. It will become solid but will liquefy again at room temperature (more quickly if the jar is run under hot water).

Taste the oil after a week or so, and if the flavour is to your liking, strain it through a very fine sieve or a funnel lined with a double layer of cheesecloth or a paper coffee filter that has been wetted and squeezed dry. After straining, the oil will be ready to use.

Cooking with Herb Pastes

Chopped fresh herbs and ground spices are often blended with oil to create a paste that can be served as a condiment, sauce, spread or dip. Italian pesto (basil pulverized with olive oil, Parmesan or pecorino cheese, garlic and pine nuts) and Argentinean chimichurri (parsley, oregano, onion and garlic blended with olive oil, vinegar and cayenne pepper) are two examples. Herb pastes also act as intermediary agents: try rubbing a ham roast or lamb chops with a mixture of sage, garlic, salt and pepper prior to cooking. Other simple blends such as minced garlic with basil and hot pepper flakes will have a profound effect on the flavour of shrimp or kebab-sized pieces of chicken or fish.

Cooking with Herb Butter

Like oil and herbs, butter and herbs pair well. Float disks of herb butter on soups just before serving, or use herb butter as a spread for bread, melted on fish or vegetables, or

Sage, cinnamon and peppercorns, wrapped tightly in cheesecloth and fastened with kitchen twine, makes a spicy bouquet garni.

Herb butters, such as this one made with minced parsley, are easy to prepare and make an elegant addition to any table.

whisked into sauces. Butter marries well with herbs including basil, chervil, chives, dill, fennel and thyme. Brightly coloured flecks of chopped nasturtium or calendula leaves will add a splash of colour to a herbal butter, while the nasturtium adds peppery flavour.

To make herb butter, finely chop dry, clean herbs. Depending on how intensely flavoured and coloured you want the butter to be, use anywhere from 30–240 g (1–8½ oz) of herbs per 454 g (1 lb) of unsalted butter, softened to room temperature. Thoroughly mix the herbs and butter by hand or in a food processor. If desired, add 1 teaspoon of citrus zest or juice for each 114 g (¼ lb) of butter. Minced shallots and garlic can also be added to a herb butter. Store herb butter in the refrigerator, sealed in an airtight container or wrapped into a log and covered in plastic wrap. Use within two weeks for best flavour.

Cooking with Herb-Flavoured Vinegars

Preserving herbs in vinegar creates a versatile, flavour-packed addition to a condiment shelf. Flavoured vinegars bring piquancy and nuance to any recipe that calls for plain vinegar. Add them to marinades for meats and fish, or to dressings for salads and pastas. Drizzle on raw tomatoes or cucumbers, or on cooked greens or beans.

When preparing herbal vinegars, do not use kitchen tools made of metal, such as aluminum, stainless steel or copper, all of which will react with the vinegar's acids and impart an unpleasant flavour. Use glass or enamel pots for heating, wooden spoons, plastic funnels, and glass or plastic containers for storage.

HERB/BUTTER COMBINATION	PAIR WITH
Chives and garlic	Eggs, seafood, vegetables
Coriander, garlic and lime zest	Beef, seafood
Sage and orange zest	Pork
Mint and lemon zest	Lamb, seafood, vegetables
Tarragon and shallot	Beef, eggs, seafood, vegetables

To make a herb-flavoured vinegar, first wash the storage bottles or jars with hot, soapy water and rinse well. Fill them with boiling water, let stand for about ten minutes, then discard the water. Clean and dry the herbs, and then place them in a wide-mouthed glass jar or plastic container.

Heat the vinegar to just below boiling. Pour it over the herbs in the warmed jars, and stir. To prevent the vinegar from reacting with metal lids, cover the mouth of the jar with wax paper or plastic wrap before sealing.

Place the mixture in a cool, dark place for a week, then taste. When the vinegar is ready, strain the solids through a cheesecloth-lined funnel, coffee filter, or jelly bag into a decorative bottle or jar with a tight-fitting (non-reactive) lid. Add a herb sprig if desired. Store the flavoured vinegar in a cool, dark place, where it will keep for about six months.

A wide variety of culinary herbs can be used to flavour vinegars: for example you could try basil, bay, chervil, chives, dill (seeds and leaves), fennel, garlic, ginger, lavender, marjoram, mint, rosemary, savory, tarragon and thyme. For variety add herb flowers, including borage (which will impart a blue tint to vinegar), chives and nasturtium (include a little of the stem and leaves as well as the flowers for a more intense flavour). Combine herb flavours, or pair them with fruits such as raspberries, and orange, lemon or lime zest, or with spicy or hot elements such as chillies, onions and peppercorns.

Almost any variety of cooking vinegar will work as a base. However, for reasons of safety, only commercially produced vinegars – which are free of sediment and contain at least five percent acetic acid which retards spoilage almost indefinitely – should be used. Distilled white vinegar is sometimes recommended for making herb vinegars, but keep in mind that its flavour is sharp and acidic, and can overpower the flavour of some herbs. Wine and champagne vinegars, on the other hand, have a more delicate flavour that works well with lemony herbs such as lemon thyme, lemon verbena and lemongrass. Red wine vinegars pair well with stronger herbs such as rosemary. Pair hearty herbs such as garlic and chives with robust vinegars, such as those made from apple cider and malt. Experiment with flavours, too: combine herbs with sherry, rice and fruit vinegars, for instance.

Other classic vinegar and herb combinations include tarragon and white wine vinegar, with or without garlic; bay, garlic, rosemary and thyme in red wine vinegar; raspberry and thyme in white wine vinegar; chive flowers with lemon balm in white wine vinegar; basil, chillies and garlic in red or white wine vinegar.

Clean and pat dry the herbs, and then place them in a clean widemouthed glass jar or plastic container. Most recipes call for 3 or 4 sprigs (30 g/¾ oz) coarsely chopped fresh herbs for every 475 ml (16 fl.oz) of vinegar. More or less vinegar can be used according to taste. In a saucepan set over medium heat, warm the vinegar until it is just below boiling. Pour it over the herbs, and then stir.

To prevent the vinegar from reacting with metal lids, cover the mouth of the jar with waxed paper or plastic wrap before sealing. Place the mixture in a cool, dark place for a week, then taste. If the flavour is too weak, allow it to infuse for another week or so. When the vinegar tastes right, prepare the storage jars: wash with hot, soapy water and rinse well; fill with boiling water, and let stand for ten minutes, before discarding the water.

Next, strain out the solids from the vinegar through a cheesecloth-lined funnel, coffee filter or jelly bag into a decorative bottle or jar that has a tight-fitting (non-reactive) lid. Add a decorative sprig of the herb to the mixture, if desired.

Remember to store the flavoured vinegar in a cool, dark place, where it will keep for about six months.

Do not store flavoured vinegars in sunny or very hot area; sunlight leaches flavour and makes the infusions more prone to spoiling. Bacterial growth is less of a concern with herb-infused vinegars than infused oils because vinegar's high acidity can retard or eliminate it. However, homemade flavoured vinegars can develop mould or yeast, so immediately discard any flavoured vinegars that show signs of fermentation, such as bubbling, cloudiness or sliminess.

PAIRING FOOD WITH HERBS AND SPICES

There is a seemingly infinite number of combinations of foods with herbs. Regional cuisines tend to feature their own unique pairings: in Greece, for example, lamb is often roasted with rosemary; in India, it may be coated with a spice blend – or a masala – that includes chillies and cinnamon; in England the lamb is roasted and served with mint sauce. Following are some of the most common matches of herbs and spices with foods. Use these pairings as a guideline, or experiment to discover favourite new combinations.

PAIRING MEAT AND POULTRY WITH HERBS

MEAT AND POULTRY	FRESH OR DRIED HERBS	SPICES
Beef	basil, ginger, oregano, parsley, thyme	caraway, cumin, fenugreek, juniper, paprika
Lamb	bay, garlic, ginger, spearmint, tarragon	allspice, cayenne, cumin, cinnamon, saffron
Pork	coriander, garlic, rosemary, sage, thyme	allspice, cinnamon, cloves, paprika, chillies, turmeric
Poultry	coriander, garlic, ginger, lovage, rosemary, tea	allspice, cumin, fenugreek, paprika

Herbs are a natural accompaniment to poultry of all kinds. Tea-smoked duck is a popular dish in China and the use of tea and tea-based oils, marinades and dressings is common in Asian countries, including China, Japan and Vietnam.

A sage-rubbed pork loin roast may be elegantly cushioned on a platter full of fresh sprigs of sage, which will impart its flavour to the meat.

Meat and Poultry

When meats and poultry are roasted or grilled with whole herbs, the heat of cooking causes a transfer of flavour from the herbs to the meat.

There are many ways to pair meat and poultry with herbs. Whole herbs and spices can be inserted into a chicken's cavity, placed into slices made in meat or fish before roasting, or added to saltwater brines (salt dissolved in a large quantity of water that the meat or poultry is soaked in to add flavour and tenderize) prior to cooking pork and poultry. Herbs and spices may be blended to form a dry or wet rub (in which oil is added to herbs to make a paste) before roasting, grilling or broiling meat or poultry.

PAIRING SEAFOOD WITH HERBS		
FISH	**FRESH OR DRIED HERBS**	**SPICES**
Flaky freshwater fish (catfish, perch, trout)	chervil, fennel, ginger, lemongrass, thyme	cloves, cumin, chillies, tamarind, saffron
Shellfish (lobster, mussels, prawns)	basil, chervil, garlic, ginger, tarragon	chillies, coconut, mustard seed, saffron, turmeric
Firm deep-sea fish (halibut, swordfish, tuna)	ginger, garlic, lemongrass, rosemary, thyme	cinnamon, cloves, cumin, juniper, paprika
Oily saltwater fish (anchovies, bluefish, mullet)	basil, garlic, ginger, rosemary, thyme	cayenne, chillies, horseradish

PAIRING VEGETABLES WITH HERBS

VEGETABLE	FRESH OR DRIED HERBS	SPICES
Asparagus	chives, sage, savory, tarragon, thyme	chillies, saffron, sesame seeds
Artichokes	basil, chives, garlic, oregano, rosemary, thyme	chillies, cardamom
Aubergine	basil, ginger, mint, oregano, parsley	chillies, cinnamon, coriander, paprika
Broccoli	basil, curry leaves, garlic, marjoram, oregano, tarragon	cayenne pepper, chillies, fenugreek, mustard seed, tamarind
Brussels sprouts	dill, garlic, parsley, rosemary, tarragon	anise, caraway, chilies, mustard seed, turmeric
Cabbage	curry leaves, dill, marjoram, savory, tarragon	caraway, cayenne pepper, cumin, paprika, turmeric
Carrots	basil, chervil, chives, ginger, parsley	anise, cardamom, cinnamon, clove, coriander, cumin
Cauliflower	basil, chives, coriander, dill, rosemary	caraway, chillies, coriander, cumin, turmeric
Corn	basil, chervil, chives, coriander, thyme	chillies, paprika, saffron, turmeric
Couscous	bay, garlic, parsley, spearmint	anise, chillies, cinnamon, saffron, turmeric
Dried legumes	bay, garlic, mint, oregano, parsley, sage, thyme	chillies, cinnamon, coriander, cumin, mustard seed, turmeric
Green beans	basil, dill, garlic, marjoram, spearmint, thyme	caraway, cloves, coconut, cumin, tamarind
Peas	basil, chervil, chives, garlic, spearmint	caraway, chillies, coconut, fenugreek, turmeric
Potatoes	basil, chives, lovage, tarragon, thyme	caraway, chillies, cumin, mustard seed, turmeric
Rice	basil, dill, garlic, oregano, thyme	cardamom, cinnamon, clove, nutmeg, saffron
Spinach	basil, chervil, dill, garlic, parsley	anise, caraway, cinnamon, nutmeg, sesame seeds
Squash	basil, ginger, marjoram, rosemary, sage	caraway, cardamom, cinnamon, nutmeg, star anise
Tomatoes	basil, coriander, lemongrass, spearmint, thyme	chillies, coriander, mustard seeds, saffron, turmeric

To stuff a whole fish with herbs, first butterfly the fish (leave skeleton connected at one side) and remove its frame. Insert fresh herbs such as chervil, lemongrass, or thyme, salt and lemon or lime slices. Wrap in aluminum foil or tie with butcher's twine before grilling or roasting.

Garnishes

Fresh herbs may also be used for decorative purposes. Reinforce the sage element of a sage-rubbed pork loin roast by cushioning it on a platter covered by fresh sprigs of sage. Serve a cocktail garnished with a slender stalk of lemongrass or sprigs of mint rather than a swizzle stick. Make a beautiful centrepiece with lavender, mint and fresh bay leaves.

Seafood

Though seafood is often perceived as having a delicate flavour that needs to be paired with other delicate tastes, many varieties can actually take on the boldest flavoured herbs and spices. Whole herbs may be stuffed into a deboned fish, and hardy whole herbs – such as vanilla beans, rosemary and lemongrass – can act as skewers when grilling prawns or other fish.

Another excellent use of whole hardy herbs is for "smoking" fish and shellfish on a grill. To do this, loosely wrap herbs, such as rosemary, vanilla beans, black tea or basil stems, in a sheet of heavy-duty aluminum foil, and then poke ventilation holes in the top layer of foil to allow steam to escape. Place the herb packet on the grill rack, along with the food that is being prepared, and cover during cooking.

Minced herbs and ground spices can be transformed into wet or dry rubs for fish that has a steaklike consistency, such as salmon, swordfish and tuna.

Vegetables and Grains

Herb and spice flavours – from subtle and delicate to bold and spicy – are very well complemented by vegetables, from aubergine to turnip, and grains, including amaranth, quinoa,

and rice. Vegetables may be drizzled with olive oil and roasted with whole herbs, or sautéed with dried herbs in the beginning of the cooking process; fresh herbs should be added at the end of cooking because their flavour is more delicate and can become bitter if overcooked.

Rosemary stems, lemongrass and other sturdy herbs can act as skewers when grilling vegetables. When choosing herbs for this purpose, make sure to select woody sections of the plant that are stiff enough to pierce the vegetables. Although wooden skewers need to be soaked for around 20 minutes before using on a grill, it is not necessary to soak herb stems.

Spices such as basil, dill, garlic, oregano and thyme blend well with rice and other grains to make a flavourful pilaf. Or toss couscous or cooked chickpeas with chopped fresh herbs such as bay, garlic, parsley or spearmint just before serving.

Soups and Sauces

Herbs and spices are great natural additives to soups and sauces. A liquid can be infused with herbal flavour from either fresh whole herbs or dry herbs in a tea ball, or wrapped in a square of cheesecloth and fastened with twine, also known as a bouquet garni. Leave one end of the twine long and tie it to the soup pot or saucepan handle for easy removal. Let the herbs steep for a few minutes at the end of the cooking process, and remove before serving. Sprinkle fresh herbs over a finished soup or sauce as an accent.

The flavours of soups and sauces can be enhanced with an easy herbal oil. Gently sauté herbs and spices such as basil, garlic, ginger and dried chillies in hot olive or vegetable oil. Drizzle the oil onto a bowl of soup before serving, or add it to a sauce for an extra hit of flavour. This method works especially well with paprika and saffron, since they add colour as well as extra taste to the oil.

Baked Goods

Both sweet and savoury baked goods can benefit from the addition of herbs and spices. Rye bread with caraway seed, gingerbread, anise biscotti and semolina pudding with saffron and cardamom are but a few examples. Fresh and dried herbs – lavender, grated ginger, thyme – and spices – cinnamon nutmeg, poppy seeds, allspice – may be added to the dry ingredients in recipes of biscuits and

To grill vegetables on a rosemary skewer, hold a rosemary sprig upside down and use its pointy stem to pierce pieces of squash, bell pepper, mushrooms and tomatoes. Move each piece down towards the tip of the rosemary and repeat with three or four more pieces per sprig.

breads before mixing with wet ingredients (oil, water, eggs, milk). Spices – cinnamon, nutmeg, ground cloves – may also be tossed with sliced fresh fruit, such as apples or peaches, before baking, roasting or grilling.

Beverages

Teas, cocktails, fruit and vegetable juices – almost any beverage – can be made even more flavourful with the addition of herbs and spices. In Spain and Mexico, cinnamon is added to rice milk to make a popular drink called *horchata*. Fresh mint- or sage-steeped tea is a trademark drink throughout the Middle East. Ground cinnamon, clove and nutmeg are used in North America to spice apple cider. In Central America, cinnamon gives a spicy kick to hot chocolate.

Herb-Flavoured Cocktails

From Kentucky mint juleps, made with fresh mint, sugar, and bourbon, to Cuban *mojitos* made with rum, mint and sugar, herb-flavoured cocktails are becoming increasingly popular in restaurants and bars around the world. A Bloody Mary can be made with fresh wasabi, horseradish or with hot pepper flakes and cumin. Martinis can be flavoured with herbs such as basil or lemongrass. A spice mixture around the rim of a glass adds a kick to a cocktail. Run a damp napkin around the rim of a drink glass, and then dip the rim in a savoury (such as celery salt) or sweet (ground anise mixed with granulated sugar) mixture.

Herb-Infused Vodkas

When herb leaves, flowers, roots or bark are immersed in alcohol, their aromatic elements are drawn out and held in the liquid. Vodka – a pure alcohol-water blend that has usually been filtered through charcoal to remove flavours and impurities – is the base for medicinal and homeopathic remedies called tinctures, as well as traditional beverages enjoyed throughout the Slavic and Nordic regions of Europe and Asia. Slavs combine flavourings such as cayenne pepper, ginger, various fruits, vanilla, unsweetened chocolate and cinnamon with vodka. Ukrainians produce a commercial vodka using St John's wort. In the Nordic region, vodka is seasoned with herbs, fruits and spices to make drinks for traditional midsummer festivities. Sweden alone makes forty common varieties of herb-flavoured vodka, which are called *kryddat brännvin*. Russia produces vodkas that have been flavoured with herbs such as aralia, which is related to ginseng, and magnolia vine, which is more commonly known as *schisandra*.

Chesnochnaya, a classic eastern European vodka, is flavoured with dill, garlic and peppercorns. Combine 1 clove of garlic, 1 sprig of dill and 3 white peppercorns in a pint of vodka. Infuse at room temperature for 24 hours then serve.

To make a simple aperitif at home, combine neutral-tasting vodka with a selection of herbs and edible flowers. Flavoured vodkas are usually blends of two or more herbal infusions. To prepare them, it is best to start by steeping each herb separately, then blend the resulting infusions to create tasty herbal drinks. Dill blends well with coriander; rosemary with basil, peppermint, sweet cicely or thyme; and lemon balm with peppermint and tarragon.

Start with a good quality vodka that has no added colour or flavour. An alcohol content of 35 to 45 percent (70 or 90 proof) is optimal (higher level of alcohol will extract bitter as well as aromatic constituents of herbs). Wash and chop the selected herbs, and place them in a jar. Pour the vodka over the chopped herbs, and store the jar in a dark place at room temperature. If the infusion is exposed to excessive heat or light, the colour and aroma may not be optimal. Steep the herbs for one to seven days, tasting the mixture every day or so to determine whether the flavour has reached its peak. If the infusion is too strong, it can be diluted with additional vodka. If it is too weak, infuse the mixture again or enhance the flavour by adding a bit of sweetness in the form of a sugar syrup or honey.

Separate the solids from the infusion by filtering them through a steel strainer, fine-mesh sieve, or steel funnel lined with gauze or cheesecloth. Store the

A herb garnish in iced tea adds style and serves as a visual reminder of the natural quality of the beverage's main ingredient.

Gunpowder green teas (far left and far right) are so-named because their leaves are rolled into small pellets; the broad-leaved green tea leaves in the centre are more common.

resulting liquid in a clean glass bottle or jar. To prevent oxidation, seal with a tight-fitting lid or screw cap. Store in the freezer to preserve flavour.

Iced Herbal Teas and Lemonades

In the summertime, iced herbal teas (tisanes) make a refreshing drink. To make iced herbal tea, brew water for the tea and add herbs such as mint, chamomile or lemon verbena to the pot. Steep until the mixture is heady and intense. Add a favourite herbal tea in a bag or a tea ball to hot water, and complement the tea with a few sprigs of fresh herbs such as mint or lavender. Pour the cooled tea over ice to serve. Lemonades can also be made more complex and interesting with the addition of finely chopped ginger or mint. Sweeten both iced tea and lemonade with a herbal simple syrup. To make simple syrup, bring to a boil 475 ml (16 fl. oz) of water with 200 g (7 oz) of sugar. Stir to dissolve the sugar. Reduce heat to a gentle simmer and add herbs, such as basil. Turn off the heat and allow the mixture to steep for five to ten minutes, then strain before use.

Cooking with Tea

After water, tea is the most-consumed beverage in the world. There are also many culinary uses for this versatile herb. In the Asian countries of China, Japan and Vietnam, tea leaves traditionally are used to flavour, tenderize, and colour food. In the West, many chefs have begun to experiment with tea, adding it to everything from ice cream to poaching liquids for fish and fruit.

Loose-leaf tea may be simmered with rice or stuffed into fish or chicken before roasting. Tea leaves can be finely ground in a coffee or spice mill, and combined with other herbs as a dry rub on meat and poultry, or added to the dry ingredients for sweet shortbread or tea cakes. Tea oil, which is made from cold-pressed tea

TEAS USED IN COOKING

BLACK TEA	FLAVOUR	USE
Assam	medium-bodied	dessert infusions and sauces
Darjeeling	full-bodied	dessert and savory infusions; dry rubs; marinades; smoking poultry
Earl Grey	astringent, fruity	dessert infusions; chocolate desserts; marinades
Keemum	smooth, spicy	dessert bases, poaching liquids and sauces; savoury infusions for poultry and shellfish
Lapsang	smoky, strong	chocolate desserts; dry rubs; smoking poultry souchong
Yunnan	astringent, peppery	savoury infusions; poultry sauces
GREEN TEA	FLAVOUR	USE
Genmaicha	smoky	fish and rice infusions; smoking poultry, fish and shellfish
Gunpowder	fresh, grassy	dessert bases and infusions; shellfish sauces, infusions and broths
Macha	light, sweet	dessert bases; vegetable infusions and sauces
Sencha	astringent, sweet	dessert bases; vegetable infusions and sauces

SPICE BLENDS

BLEND	ORIGIN	HERB OR SPICE
Aliño	Chile	lemon balm, marjoram, oregano, rosemary, sage, spearmint, tarragon, thyme
Berbere	Ethiopia	ajowan, allspice, black peppercorn, cardamom, cinnamon, clove, coriander, cumin, dried chillies, fenugreek, ginger, nutmeg
Chilli powder	North and Central America	clove, coriander, cumin, dried chillies, garlic, oregano, paprika
Five spice	China	cinnamon, clove, fennel seed, star anise, Sichuan peppercorn
Garam masala	India	black pepper, caraway, cardamom, cinnamon, clove, coriander, cumin, chillies, fennel seed, mace, nutmeg
Herbes de Provence	France	basil, fennel seed, lavender, marjoram, rosemary, sage, summer savory, thyme
Italian herb blend	Italy	basil, marjoram, oregano, thyme
Za'atar	Middle East	sesame seed, sumac, thyme

Chai masala, Indian spiced tea, adds warmth and intensity to ice cream and custard-based dishes, such as crème brûlée.

seeds, is a sweet, herbaceous addition to vinaigrettes that can be drizzled over salads, steamed vegetables or delicate seafood.

Black and green teas are the commonly used varieties in cooking. Unfermented green tea contributes a grassy, herbal, astringent flavour; fermented black tea (like red wine) adds full-bodied dimension to soups and spice rubs. To make tea for cooking, brew two teaspoons of loose-leaf tea per 215 ml (8 fl.oz) of liquid (water, stock, milk). Steep the tea in below-boiling water for 20 to 30 minutes. Strain the mixture before using in any recipe.

CHAPTER 8

Growing Herbs

Gardeners grow herbs for various reasons: to enjoy the beauty of a formal or informal garden, to harvest medicinal plants as needed, to have easy access to fresh culinary ingredients, to admire the birds and butterflies that are attracted to herbs. Whatever the intention, growing herbs at home can be both an enjoyable hobby and an excellent way to ensure a ready supply of fresh, sometimes hard-to-obtain plants.

Growing herbs can be a pleasure for both experienced and amateur gardeners. Herbs blend well with other garden plants and may be grown directly in the ground or in containers. Many species will thrive in all kinds of difficult growing conditions – too wet, too dry, poor soil or shade. Compared with other plants, herbs also tend to be free of pest and disease problems.

Transplanting seedlings such as chamomile (Chamaemelum nobile) *requires a delicate touch.*

Choosing Herbs to Grow

When deciding which herbs to plant in the garden, both practical and aesthetic factors come into play. Aside from choosing plants for their individual and specific purposes, such as use in medicine, for cooking or for craft work, herbs can be selected for their beautiful and colourful flowers, or their fascinating variegated foliage. In addition to the function and appearance of the plants, it is important to consider the life cycle of herbs when selecting plants for a garden. Plants have one of three life cycles: they are either annual, perennial or biennial.

Annual plants die away at the end of the growing season, and new plants sprout from seeds that are borne during a preceding season. These annual plants vary in how well they are able to tolerate cold temperatures. The seeds of some annuals must be sown before the end of one growing season and then be exposed to a chill before they will germinate at the beginning of the next year's growing season. The seeds of other annuals must be sown after the year's last frost. Popular annual herbs include basil (*Ocimum basilicum*), chamomile (*Chamaemelum nobile*), coriander (*Coriandrum sativum*), dill (*Anethum graveolens*) and borage (*Borago officinalis*).

Perennials are plants whose upper portions die in the dormant season while the portions of the herbs below ground remain alive. These plants make new stems and foliage at the beginning of the growing season. The root systems of perennial plants usually grow larger year after year. Among common perennial herbs are bee balm (*Monarda* spp.), catnip (*Nepeta cataria*), chives (*Allium schoenoprasum*), echinacea (*Echinacea* spp.) and lovage (*Levisticum officianale*). Some woody herbs, such as chamomile (*Chamaemelum nobile*) and rosemary (*Rosmarinus officinalis*),

retain a woody, above ground portion throughout the dormant months of the year. At the beginning of the growing season, new foliage forms on these older woody stems.

Biennials have a two-year life cycle. They grow from seed their first season; in their second season they die, after sending up flowers and making seeds. Angelica (*Angelica Archangelica*), caraway (*Carum carvi*), evening primrose (*Oenothera biennis*) and parsley (*Petroselinum crispum*), are all biennial herbs.

Herb gardens often contain a variety of annuals, perennials and biennials. When planting a home herb garden, there are various ways to combine the different types of herbs in a single space. The life cycle of annuals is relatively brief, and so many plants of this type require a more fertile soil than perennials. Because they die at the end of each season, annuals leave behind barren and potentially unattractive spaces in the garden as they disappear. So gardeners sometimes make use of successive sowings throughout the season to ensure a steady supply of the herb. This approach to planting annuals could be difficult in the middle of a perennial bed, so it is often sensible to segregate herbs with different life cycles.

The resilience of flowering chives makes them ideal for home gardens.

Matching herbs to a garden's microclimate will help ensure healthy plants.

WHERE TO GROW HERBS OUTDOORS

Many gardeners choose to grow herbs by themselves in a dedicated garden space. But herbs may also be mixed with other plants in vegetable beds, in borders and edgings, or grown in indoor and outdoor containers. The ideal location for planting herbs depends to some extent on their purpose. Culinary herbs, for example, are most convenient when they are grown near the cook's kitchen so they will be close at hand as meals are prepared. If a garden is intended to serve as a contemplative retreat, the best site would be a tranquil distance away from the human activity immediately surrounding a home.

In addition to the purpose of the garden, a key concern when deciding where to grow plants is matching them to their appropriate environment. Herbs have specific light, heat and soil requirements. They may not grow well, or grow at all, in climates that are too hot, cold, damp, dry or shady for them. Some herbs are more forgiving of climatic extremes, while others are fussy about their growing conditions.

Most outdoor spaces are made up of several microclimates, which are small areas with unique environmental characteristics such as levels of sunlight and soil moisture. Some areas of a garden may receive direct, intense sunlight all day, while others are in dappled or full shade, or receive indirect, reflected light. The amount of sunlight often varies tremendously from season to season. The same site may be sunny during one season but shady during another. Conversely, a site under a densely leaved deciduous tree may be sunny during the dormant months of the year but shady during the growing season.

Water is essential to a plant's growth, but it is as important to avoid over-watering them.

Some microclimates may receive more moisture than others. In elevated spots, soil moisture will be less than in low-lying areas. Gardens that have been sited beneath overhanging foliage or a manufactured structure will receive significantly less precipitation than those in open spots. Soil that is exposed to wind and sun will rapidly lose moisture. Finally, the quality of soil may vary among microclimates. Soil composition is influenced by local sources, such as the foliage of many evergreen plants or naturally occurring alkaline limestone.

Before planting a garden, it is important to first assess the growing conditions of the intended garden space. Herbs should then be selected to match the growing conditions. For example, many herbs do best when they receive a full six hours of sunlight each day, so if a garden site offers only partial shade, only shade-tolerant herbs should be planted. In sunny garden spots, herbs such as shade-loving sweet woodruff, which will not survive sunny conditions, should not be planted.

Altering Growing Conditions

In addition to selecting herbs to match garden microclimates, the growing conditions of these microclimates may be altered to suit the selected plants. To grow warm-climate perennials (scented geranium, lemon verbena, rosemary) in a cold-climate area, for example, structures such as fences and windbreaks can protect herbs in exposed spots, where the wind would stunt their growth and rapidly dry out the soil. Mulch, row covers and cold frames can help herbs that are at the limit of their cold-temperature tolerance survive the dormant months of the year.

The easiest way to alter growing conditions is by changing the composition of the soil in the area. Soil is a plant's sole source of nutrients, water and physical anchorage. All plants have a preferred soil pH value range, meaning the composition of soil on a scale of 0 to 14, from acidic to alkaline. Soil with a pH value of 7 is neutral, above 7 is alkaline and below is acidic. Soil pH affects the availability of nutrients within the soil. The nutrient nitrogen, for example, is readily available in soil with a pH value above 5.5. Similarly, the nutrient phosphorous is available when a pH value is between 6 and 7. If a plant is grown in the wrong kind of soil for its particular nutritional needs, it will lack nutrients that it needs to flourish. Although most herbs prefer a pH of about 6.5, some herbs have specific requirements. Lavender, marjoram, rosemary, sage, thyme and dormant season savory, for example, grow best in alkaline soil. Blueberries grow best in soil that is acidic.

The pH of acidic or neutral soil can be raised by adding lime, a compound of calcium and magnesium. It is usually applied in the form of ground agricultural limestone, burnt lime or hydrated (slaked) lime, available from most garden supply stores. The pH of alkaline or neutral soil can be lowered by adding aluminum sulphate or sulphur, which converts to sulphuric acid with the help of bacteria in the soil.

Herbs generally prefer loose soil that contains some organic matter, is moderately fertile and is well-drained. But the composition and drainage of soil can vary from area to area within a garden. And while some herbs grow well in sandy soil, others may prefer soil that is dense and compacted. Sandy soil is composed of large, round rock particles with spaces between particles, creating lots of room for air and water. This type of soil drains well and warms quickly, but it is usually low in nutrients, because water rapidly leaches them out as it runs through the spaces. Heavy clay soils are composed of tiny soil particles that cling tightly together, leaving little space for air. This leads to waterlogged soil, causing plant roots to have shallow growth and leaving them susceptible to disease. They also may not get enough oxygen, which can cause rot.

There are several ways to change and improve soil quality. Gardeners whose soil is too wet can get a fresh start by planting in raised beds. A raised bed is a bottomless box with sides that are about 20 cm (8 in) high. The raised box sits on the ground and can be filled with any type of soil. Because plants in a raised bed are elevated, air circulation is improved around them, which deters diseases and allows the soil to drain more freely. The soil in raised beds thaws and warms more quickly at the beginning of the growing season than later, so planting can be done earlier. Because the soil will never be walked on, it will not become compacted.

Raised beds can be constructed from wooden boards, stones, concrete blocks or bricks. Avoid using pressure-treated lumber, which may contain heavy

❧ SHADE-TOLERANT HERBS ❧

Angelica	*Angelica archangelica*
Chervil	*Anthriscus cerefolium*
Chives	*Allium schoenoprasum*
Coltsfoot	*Tussilago farfara*
Costmary	*Chrysanthemum balsamita*
Foxglove	*Digitalis purpurea*
Horseradish	*Armoracia rusticana*
Lady's mantle	*Alchemilla vulgaris*
Lemon balm	*Melissa officinalis*
Lovage	*Levisticum officinale*
Marsh mallow	*Althaea officinalis*
Mint	*Mentha* spp.
Parsley	*Petroselinum crispum*
Sweet cicely	*Myrrhis odorata*
Sweet flag	*Acorus calamus*
Sweet woodruff	*Galium odoratum*
Tarragon	*Artemisia dracunculus*

When buying herbs for part or full shade, read labels carefully; some plants, such as mint (Mentha spp.), tolerate shade, but will grow better when exposed to at least a few hours of sunlight each day.

Even a garden area that receives only partial sun can be beautiful; many plants and herbs will thrive in part or full shade. Angelica (Angelica archangelica), foxglove (Digitalis purpurea) and sweet woodruff (Galium odoratum) are some of those that flourish.

metals that can leach from the lumber and damage plants. Over time, the soil may push apart the sides of wooden beds if the corners are not securely put together. Building with pre-fabricated metal corners, available from many garden supply companies, can solve this problem. For large plants with deep roots, it may be necessary to loosen the soil before planting. This will encourage the root systems of the plants to develop vertically rather than horizontally, which in turn reduces the need for watering.

Both heavy clay soil and coarse sandy soil can be improved with the addition of organic matter such as well-rotted manure, compost, peat moss or leaf mould. Any of these can improve the texture and aeration quality of soil, and also slowly release plant nutrients.

Purchasing Plants

Plants and seeds can be bought at local plant nurseries or greenhouses. When buying plants, make sure they are robust and healthy. Always choose the bushiest plants

Scent, colour and bushiness are three elements that can provide clues to a herb plant's overall health.

with the most intensely coloured foliage. Avoid those with pot-bound roots or pest-infested leaves. Plants can also be ordered from a catalogue by mail or on the Internet.

Most plant nurseries will ship seeds, young plants, shrubs and trees to even distant locales. Trees and shrubs that are purchased in this way will arrive in dormant, bare-root form. These plants should have full, slightly moist, well-coloured roots. Plants with dry brown or soggy black roots, and those with any indication of insects or disease, have been poorly stored and are unlikely to grow well. Do not hesitate to return these unhealthy plants to the retailer for a refund.

PROPAGATING HERBS

In addition to purchasing herbs from a nursery or other retailer, herbs may be grown at home for future plantings. Some herbs can be started from seeds, either indoors or directly in the garden. Some herbs will grow from cuttings taken from plant stems or roots. Large, healthy specimens of many herb varieties can be divided to make several smaller plants.

Growing Herbs from Seeds

Many herbs, such as angelica, borage, caraway, chervil, dill, fennel, feverfew and parsley, will seed themselves freely throughout a garden. Other herbs will need help to ensure their seeds germinate at the proper time and in the right location.

Sowing Seeds Outdoors Some herbs, such as basil, borage, caraway and chamomile, will grow easily from seeds sown in the ground outdoors. Members of the parsley family, such as chervil, coriander and dill, can be sown in the ground outdoors, or in peat pots, and then transplanted outdoors into the ground. These plants have sensitive roots, which prompt the plant to bolt or go to seed, if disturbed. Perennials are generally more difficult to start from seed, but there are some exceptions: angelica, anise hyssop, chives, fennel, lemon balm, lovage, sage, sorrel and summer savory are worth sowing outdoors.

To prepare a garden bed for seeds, first remove stones and clumps of soil, and then add and dig in several handfuls of compost. For optimal germination, the soil should be finely textured and lightweight. Because certain seeds require light to germinate, planting depth is an important consideration. If planted too deep, small seeds may run out of energy before sprouts can reach the soil surface. Other seeds will germinate only in the absence of light, and so they must be planted deeper in the soil. For those, a general rule of thumb is that seeds should be planted

To sow seeds in trays, press holes into planting medium with fingertips.

Next, sprinkle seeds evenly over the soil. Read package directions carefully for complete sowing directions, as they vary by herb.

Finally, cover seeds sparingly with more planting medium. A general rule is that seeds should be planted no more than three to four times as deep as each seed is wide. Finish by watering the seeds until the medium is thoroughly moistened, but not soaked.

❧ HERBS TO START FROM SEED ❧

Anise	*Pimpinella anisum*
Anise hyssop	*Agastache foeniculum*
Basil	*Ocimum basilicum*
Bee balm	*Monarda didyima*
Borage	*Borago officinali*
Catnip	*Nepeta cataria*
Chamomile, German	*Matricaria recutita*
Chilli peppers	*Capsicum annuum*
Chiso	*Perilla frutescens*
Chives	*Allium schoenoprasum*
Chives, garlic	*Allium tuberosum*
Cress	*Nasturtium officinale*
Dill	*Anethum graveolen*
Fennel	*Foeniculum vulgare*
Hyssop	*Hyssopus officinalis*
Lavender	*Lavandula angustifolia*
Lemon balm	*Melissa officinalis*
Lovage	*Levisticum officinale*
Marjoram	*Origanum majorana*
Onion	*Allium cepa*
Oregano	*Origanum vulgare*
Parsley	*Petroselinum crispum*
Pennyroyal	*Hedeoma pulegioides*
Rosemary	*Rosmarinus officinalis*
Sage	*Salvia officinalis*
Salad burnet	*Sanguisorba minor*
Sorrel	*Rumex acestosa*
Summer savory	*Satureja hortensis*
Thyme	*Thymus vulgaris*
Valerian	*Valeriana officinalis*

Fennel, a perennial that grows well from seed, will thrive if planted in spring in full sun. Space rows 1 m (3 ft) apart.

about as deep as three or four times their height. Lightly water the seeded bed and keep the soil moist (but not saturated) until the seeds sprout.

Starting Seeds Indoors To give plants a headstart on the growing season, their seeds can be germinated indoors before the weather warms and they be transferred outdoors. Seeds can be started in a variety of container types, as long as water will easily drain through them so the seedlings will not become waterlogged. Some commercially available "seedling trays" are designed to draw up water from the bottom. Others, called plug trays, have thimble-sized indentations in which seedlings rest.

Seeds should be germinated in a special growing mixture. Commercial growing mixes are lightweight, allowing delicate seedling roots to move easily, and sterile, or free of pathogens, pests and weeds. A growing mix may be purchased at a garden supply centre or prepared at home by combining 2 litre (4 pints) peat moss with 2 litre (4 pints) perlite and 1 tablespoon crushed limestone. Be sure to follow the instructions on the seeds' packaging. Some seeds need to be covered with a damp starter mix, while others should simply be pressed into it. Growing mix should be kept consistently moist – not wet or dry. Seedling trays may be covered with clear plastic wrap to prevent water from evaporating too rapidly.

Seeds will germinate most readily in soil that is kept at a constant, warm temperature. Seed trays may be placed on top of a heat-generating appliance, such as a clothes dryer, refrigerator or radiator, or a commercially available seedling heat mat, which supplies heat to the bottom of the seed container. Once seeds sprout, the trays should be moved to a spot where they may receive 14 to 16 hours of light each day. An optimal location is 8 cm (3 in) below a fluorescent light fixture that has both a warm and a cool tube.

When the first true leaves appear above or between the seed halves, seedlings should be transplanted into pressed peat pots, peat pellets or cell packs so they have enough space to grow properly. To transplant, make holes in the moistened growing mix filling the pots of cell packs. Gently lift seedlings by their leaves, rather than by their stems. Place the seedlings' roots in the holes, gently press down the soil around them and add water. The sprouts will need to be fed weekly with an organic fertilizer, such as fish emulsion, diluted to half-strength.

Indoor seedlings must be made ready for outdoor wind, sun and varying temperatures through a process called "hardening off", which allows the plants' cell

Bee balm	*Monarda didyma*
Catmint	*Nepeta cataria*
Catnip	*Nepeta cataria*
Chives	*Allium schoenoprasum*
Germander	*Teucrium chamaedrys*
Hyssop	*Hyssopus officinalis*
Lady's mantle	*Alchemilla vulgaris*
Lemon balm	*Melissa officinalis*
Lemongrass	*Cymbopogon citratus*
Mint	*Mentha x piperita*
Oregano, Italian	*Origanum majorana*
Rue	*Ruta graveolens*
Sorrel	*Rumex acestosa*
Sweet woodruff	*Galium odoratum*
Tarragon	*Artemisia dracunculus*

Chives are produced from very tiny bulbs, which makes them easy to propagate by division.

walls to thicken and their new growth to change from soft and tender to firm. Seedlings should first be placed in a shady outdoor location with an ideal temperature of 7 to 10°C (45 to 50°F). Over the next few days, they should be moved into sunlight for increasing periods of time. After ten days, the seedlings should spend both days and nights outdoors.

Growing Herbs from Divisions

Three types of herbs may be propagated by division: herbs that form bulbs, cloves or corms (such as garlic, onions and saffron), herbs that creep by way of rhizones (mint, oregano, sweet woodruff), and herbs that form clumps (lemon balm, catmint, germander). At the

beginning of the growing season (for peak- or end-of-growing-season bloomers) or at the end of the growing season (for early growing season bloomers), use a garden fork to carefully dig up an entire plant. Gently separate the roots into smaller sections. Each new, small plant should contain a good set of roots and some strong healthy shoots. Replant these immediately, or store bulbs, corms or tubers in a cool dry spot for planting later.

Growing Herbs from Cuttings

When the stems of some plants touch the ground, the plant may sprout roots at the point of contact. When this occurs naturally in the garden, the new plantlets can be separated from the main plant, dug up and relocated. Gardeners can use this same process, called layering, to create offspring of favourite plants. Woody herbs such as chamomile, creeping and English thymes, lavender, prostrate rosemary, santolina, Vietnamese coriander and winter savory can be propagated like this. Layering may be done in soil, water or growing mix.

Layering in Soil Take a long, flexible stem that is low to the ground and remove the leaves from a section a few centimetres long, and 8 to 10 cm (3 to 4 in) from the tip. Gently scrape the bark from that section. This will encourage the stem to make roots at that point. Carefully bend the stem to the ground and cover the scraped section with soil. Anchor it in place with a small rock or piece of brick.

Over the next few months, check periodically to see whether roots have developed. When the stem is well rooted, clip it so that the new plant includes roots and

Basil	*Ocimum basilicum*
Chamomile	*Chamaemelum nobile*
Creeping thyme	*Thymus serpyllum coccineus*
Lavender	*Lavandula angustifolia*
Lemon verbena	*Aloysia triphylla*
Mint	*Mentha* spp.
Pineapple sage	*Salvia elegans*
Rosemary	*Rosmarinus officinalis*
Rosemary, prostrate	*Rosmarinus officinalis* 'Prostratus'
Santolina	*Santolina chamaecyparissus*
Scented geranium	*Pelargonium* spp.
Thyme, English	*Thymus vulgaris*
Vietnamese coriander	*Polygonum odoratum*
Winter savory	*Satureja montana*

STEP 1
To layer a low, creeping herb such
as winter savory (right), first dig a
hole next to the plant using a
spade; be careful to avoid damaging
the roots of the existing plant.

STEP 2
Next, use a pair of sharp scissors to
clip off one of the stems just below
one of the nodes to form a cutting that
is 7.5 to 13 cm (3 to 5 in) long.

the foliage-covered tip. Make sure that the newly
developed roots are well covered with soil; keep the
soil constantly moist and loosely packed enough for air
to circulate to the stem and roots.

Layering in Water or Growing Mix The stems of
many varieties of herbs will readily put out new roots
from cuttings; this method of propagation is called layering. The best time to take cuttings is early in the growing
season, when plants have just put out some new growth.
Use a sharp tool such as a scissors or pruning shears to
clip a piece of stem about 15 cm (6 in) long that has
several leaf nodes on it. Clip just below one of these
nodes. Cuttings of basil, lavender, lemon verbena, mint,

pineapple sage, rosemary and scented geranium will
root quite quickly in water. Place a stem of one of these
herbs in a clean, water-filled glass container and set in a
sunny window, remembering to change the water daily.
Roots should soon form along the lower portion of the
cutting. When the roots are about 1 cm (¼ in) long, the
cutting may be planted in potting soil.

Cuttings can also be rooted in a growing medium
such as a combination of peat moss and sand or a shop-
bought mixture. Dip a cutting into a rooting hormone
solution, then plant it in the growing medium. The
cutting will require a moist environment, so cover its
container with a plastic bag. Lift an edge periodically to
mist the plant with a spray bottle filled with water.

STEP 3
Plant the clipped stem in the hole and cover with more soil. Press down gently to pack the soil and also to eliminate any air pockets.

STEP 4
Place a small rock or pebble over the compacted soil to hold the new stem in place. Water thoroughly. How quickly new roots grow from the stem depends on the plant, but they should grow within 4 to 6 weeks.

PLANTING HERBS

Whether herbs are propagated at home from seeds or cuttings or plants that have been purchased from a garden supply, nursery or mail-order company, they will not thrive in the garden unless they are properly planted and adequately spaced. This is especially important for shrubs and trees, which are usually a larger financial investment than small annuals and perennials.

Seedlings

Annuals should be planted early in the growing season after the last expected frost date. Perennials can be planted one or two weeks earlier. Planting on an overcast day or during the late afternoon or evening will place less stress on the plants. Water annuals and perennials several hours before transplanting, and soak seedling trays and the roots of bare-root plants for an hour or two.

To plant seedling of annuals and perennials, first dig a hole that is deeper and wider than the spread roots. Perennials grow best when a dose of compost is placed in the bottom of the hole. Next, gently remove the plants by inverting their containers and pushing the bottoms until the plants fall out. Avoid holding seedlings by their tender stems or leaves, which can put unnecessary stress on this fragile part of the plant.

Set the plants into the holes so the tops of the roots are level with the ground. Cover the roots with soil, pressing down firmly to eliminate any air pockets that

STEP 1
To transplant herbs such as dwarf winter savory (above), dig a hole deeper and wider than the roots when spread out.

STEP 2
After removing the plant from its container, place it in the hole so that the tops of the roots are level with the ground.

STEP 3
Cover the roots with soil, pressing down firmly to eliminate any air pockets that may have formed around the roots.

STEP 4
Water the transplanted herb well, enough so that the soil is soaked; that will ensure the roots have received enough water.

may have formed around the roots. Water the plants immediately. When working with plants that were grown in peat pots or peat pellets, place the entire container directly into the ground – the plant's roots will grow right through the walls of the pot, which will disintegrate. Cover the tops of pots completely or tear off their top lips. An edge sticking out of the soil can act as a wick, drawing water away from the plant's roots.

To help plants recover from the shock of being transplanted, shelter them from wind and sun for a few days by covering them with a flowerpot, basket or small tree branch with leaves. If there is little or no rain during the first week after transplanting, water the plants daily. During the second week after transplanting, water the plants every other day, and then every third day the third week. Constant watering is especially important for seedlings because their roots are not long enough to reach deep soil moisture.

Planting Shrubs and Trees

Shrubs and trees are sold in one of four forms: balled-and-burlapped (also called B&B), container-grown, containerized or bare-root. Most mail-order nurseries ship deciduous trees, bushes and roses in bare-root form and wrapped in sphagnum moss to reduce shipping charges. When bare-root plants arrive by mail, unpack them as soon as possible and soak the roots in water for several hours. It is a good idea to plant shrubs and trees as soon as possible, but if immediate planting is not possible, store the plants in a shady spot. Moisten the soil of B&B or containerized plants, and cover bare roots with moist soil, sand or peat moss.

Plant B&B shrubs and trees at the end of the growing season, during the dormant months, or at the very beginning of the growing season, when they are most likely to generate new roots and least likely to lose moisture through their leaves. Shrubs and trees that are container-grown and containerized may be planted at any time. Deciduous shrubs and trees are the only type always sold bare-root. These should be planted at the very end or the very beginning of the growing season, when they are dormant. Do not purchase or plant a bare-root shrub or tree that has new growth – that new growth has been nourished at the expense of the plant's overall health. Shrubs and trees that are smaller when planted will adapt more quickly to their new surroundings and will be less likely than larger plants to suffer transplant shock.

Before planting, be sure to site shrubs and trees far enough from foundations and paths so that, when fully grown, these plants will not block windows, crowd or damage buildings or interfere with foot traffic. Then dig a hole twice as wide but only as deep as the plant's roots. Ease the plants out of their pots, then use clean, sharp pruning shears to remove any damaged or diseased roots. Place the root-ball in the hole. When planted, the top of the roots or root-ball should be level or slightly above the surface of the surrounding ground. In soil that is heavy clay or compacted, up to a third of the root-ball may be left above the soil surface.

For B&B plants, pull the burlap off the root-ball, leaving it in the hole. If the root-ball is enclosed in a wire basket, cut the wires so that they are below the soil surface and will not interfere with raking or cultivation.

Fill the hole three-quarters full with the soil. Make sure the plant is level, and then gently press down the soil around it. Add water to eliminate any air pockets, and then fill the hole to ground level. Use soil to build a ring, or berm, about 16 cm (6 in) from the outside edge of the hole. Water heavily again.

Finally, add a 5 to 8 cm (2 to 3 in) layer of mulch, such as pine needles, straw, bark chips or slightly decomposed or shredded leaves around the base of the plant to reduce moisture loss and discourage weed growth. However, keep in mind that a mulch layer that is too thick will promote shallow roots, disease and pests.

During the first growing season, it is important to water shrubs and trees once a week if there is no rain, slowly soaking the soil. The water should reach the top of the berm so it will penetrate deeply and encourage root development. Watering is particularly crucial for B&B and container-grown shrubs and trees. In the nursery, the roots of these plants become concentrated in a small cluster. Until the roots are able to spread into surrounding soil, the plants draw water mostly from their root-ball, which will dry out more quickly than the soil around them.

GARDEN MAINTENANCE

Three elements to keep in mind when maintaining a garden are water, soil and fertilizer. With the wrong amount or type of any of the above, a garden can go from being a herbs haven to an over- or under-grown mess.

Deep watering is much better than lightly watering everyday. Irrigate about 2.5 cm (1 in) deep every week. This should be increased during very dry and hot periods, to about 2.5 cm (1 in) of water every 3 days. Early mornings or any time after sunset are usually the best time to water, to avoid evaporation.

Watering needs will vary depending on the type of soil. Apart from having soil analysed there are some steps that can be taken to ensure proper care. Before watering,

Water newly planted herbs well so that roots receive enough moisture – that means watering so that 7.5 to 10 cm (3 to 4 in) of the soil below the surface is well soaked. Early morning and evening are best times to water.

loosen the soil that surrounds the plants for easier absorption. Using mulch around the root area on the soil's surface will lessen soil erosion.

Fertilizers can add nutrients such as nitrogen, phos-phorus and potassium, which are essential to plant growth, root development and disease resistance. Fertilizer should be applied in small amounts when the soil is moist and followed up with a light watering. Avoid applying fertilizer before a heavy rainstorm, because it can run off and pollute water supplies.

Watering

In most areas, rainfall provides adequate moisture for herbs. In arid regions, or during very dry weather, it may be necessary to supply herbs with additional mois-ture. Watering options include hoses, watering cans and sprinklers. Drip irrigation systems and soaker hoses are the most efficient irrigators. They release water close to the soil, at the root zone of plants, fostering deep root

growth and minimizing runoff and evaporation. This method of watering also keeps foliage dry, protecting plants from diseases that are spread by water droplets or are promoted by dampness.

Watering is best done in the morning so the sun can evaporate any water droplets that splash foliage. Watering to about 8 to 10 cm (3 to 4 in) below the surface will ensure healthier root development. Be sure to watch plants closely during periods of sparse rainfall, especially if they are in containers. If the plants look wilted or distressed, water them occasionally but deeply.

Composting

For most herbs, a yearly application of compost is enough to keep their soil nutrient-rich. Compost is made from plant matter that decomposes into a porous, spongy substance called humus. Humus helps soil retain air and moisture around a plant's roots while allowing water to circulate freely through the pores surrounding

Composting creates fertile growing material for herbs and other plants, and allows a gardener to recycle both garden and kitchen waste.

the root. It protects plants from disease and insect pests, releases a slow, steady supply of nutrients, and darkens the soil so it warms up earlier in the growing season, thereby extending the length of the season.

Compost can be made from garden waste such as grass clippings, pine needles, wood chips and sawdust from wood that has not been chemically treated, fresh and dried leaves and straw, combined with vegetable waste from the kitchen, such as melon rinds, tea leaves and coffee grounds, and fruit and vegetable peelings. Fatty foods and waste from meat, dairy products and eggs take much longer to decompose and can attract insects and animals and so are usually avoided. Eggshells, however, are an excellent source of nutrients for the compost pile.

Combine the waste in a 1 m by 1m (3-ft by 3-ft) pile. Be sure to include equal amounts of green ingredients (grass clippings, vegetable scraps, etc.) and brown ingredients (dry leaves and plants, wood chips, etc.), and turn the mixture periodically with a shovel or pitchfork. Compost is considered "finished' when it breaks down into a crumbly, deep brown substance.

Fertilizing

Some herbs, especially fast-growing annuals such as basil, chives, coriander and dill, benefit from the enrichment of the soil with organic fertilizers such as fish emulsion or liquid seaweed. Avoid using inorganic fertilizers, because most herbs do not heavily consume nitrogen, a leading ingredient in inorganic fertilizers. Soil with excessive amounts of nitrogen will produce weak plants that have disease and will suffer from the ravages of cold weather.

A "tea" made from compost can be an effective liquid fertilizer and a preventive for some forms of mildew that attack plants. Compost tea is made by placing a litre

(1 quart) of finished compost in a 19 litre (5 gallon) bucket, and then half-fill the bucket with water. Let the mixture sit for five to fifteen days, then strain. Reserve the liquid and dilute it until it is the colour of a cup of black tea. Spray on plant leaves early in the morning or apply to the soil around fast-growing herbs.

Mulching

A layer of organic or inorganic matter called mulch, laid on top of the soil, helps keep soil cool during the growing season and provides insulation during the dormant months. Mulch releases nutrients slowly into the soil and suppresses the growth of weeds around plantings. A woody mulch is useful on paths and other places where it is desirable to stop weed growth. In this method, the decomposing wood takes up nitrogen from the soil, making it unavailable to plants.

Commonly available garden mulches include compost, hay, straw, pine needles, shredded leaves, finely chipped tree bark, and even hulls from cocoa, buckwheat and

Regular routine garden maintenance – weeding, pruning, and watering – keeps a herb garden healthy and beautiful.

❧ CONTAINING INVASIVE HERBS ❧

Certain herbs are notorious for growing so enthusiastically that they can take over a garden if they are not monitored. Mint, for example, which spreads by sending out rhizomes below the soil, can sneak through a garden and choke out other plants. Horseradish, sweet woodruff, and tarragon may spread in a similar fashion. Herbs such as lemon balm, perilla, catnip, mugwort and fennel are prolific seeders, and generously spread their offspring all around a garden.

To keep creeping herbs such as mint under control, plant them in containers. For the sake of appearance, bury the containers in the garden, but keep the top of the rims above ground. Be sure to pull up a pot periodically and check to make sure that the roots of the plant in the container have not escaped through a drainage hole. To curtail the spread of seeding herbs, remove their flowerheads before they go to seed.

If the plant has already invaded an area, use a tool called a weed wrench to remove the plant by the roots. Continue to treat the area because new plants may sprout from seeds that have been produced.

To keep invasive herbs, such as catnip (above), in check, it is necessary to plant them in their pots in the ground.

cottonseed. Gardeners and commercial growers sometimes use inorganic mulches such as gravel and plastic to cover the soil, which dramatically increase its temperature, providing a beneficial environment for the plants.

Avoid mulching damp areas, as the material can harbour slugs and snails and retain moisture that encourages disease. In dry, stony areas, however, a layer of mulch mixed with pea gravel or oyster shells mixed with coarse sand can reflect light towards plants and help prevent fungal diseases.

Apply mulch at the end of the growing season and once the top of the soil has frozen to discourage small rodents from taking shelter. Remove the mulch from garden beds at the beginning of the growing season to let the soil "breathe". After a month or so, spread a new layer of mulch to suppress weeds, cool the soil and retain moisture.

Pruning

Proper pruning encourages plants to produce healthier, bushier growth. Woody, aromatic herbs, such as curry, lavender, sage, santolina, southernwood and wormwood should be pruned at the beginning of the growing season. Use clean, sharp gardening shears to remove older, leggy growth. This will prompt the plant to generate young, healthy stems.

A bit later in the growing season, perennials such as artemesia, chamomile, chervil, costmary, lemon verbena, oregano and sorrel will form flower stems that divert the plants' energy from the formation of fragrant or flavourful foliage. To prevent or delay flowering, use gardening shears to cut the flower stems at their bases. For tender herbs such as basil, pinch off flowers as they form to prolong the production of aromatic foliage. In the middle of the growing season, after they have flowered, perennials including comfrey, lemon balm, marjoram, mint, sweet cicely, and salad burnet will produce less-flavourful and tougher foliage. Cut these plants back by one-third to one-half to encourage a burst of tender new foliage.

Extending the Growing Season

For annuals and tender-leaved perennials in temperate regions, the first and last frost of the year generally signal the beginning and the end of the growing season. Neither annuals nor tender perennials tolerate temperatures below freezing: a night of frost may turn a healthy plant into a cluster of blackened, shrivelled sticks. On the other end of the spectrum, plants that are accustomed to cool weather may fail to germinate under a blistering sun.

In all climates, sheltering structures can be used to modulate soil and air temperature below and around plants, protecting individual plants or whole beds.

STEP 1
To prune the roots of herbs such as white elphin (above), first gently remove the plant from its container.

STEP 2
Using a serrated knife, cut each corner from the root base. Do not cut too close to the herb's main stem.

STEP 3
Use a pair of sharp scissors or garden shears to neaten any straggling roots. Do not cut too deeply into the root ball.

STEP 4
Return the herb to the pot and then use scissors to snip off older, leggy stems to encourage the growth of new, healthy stems.

In hot areas, a shade net of woven polypropylene fabric stretched over wire hoops or a moveable wooden frame can help keep the soil cool and moist. Shade netting can be placed over newly sown seedbeds and transplanted seedlings to shield them from drying winds and buffer the intense heat and light of the sun.

In cool weather regions, a cold frame can be used to trap the sun's heat, encouraging plant growth and extending the harvest of cold-weather crops into the dormant season. A cold frame is a bottomless boxlike structure that acts like a greenhouse. It usually has a high south-facing back wall, a white interior to deflect light throughout the box, a glass or clear plastic cover that allows the sun's rays to penetrate, and a thermometer to monitor the interior temperature. A cloche or a bell-shaped cover made from such materials as a plastic milk jug, can be used to protect individual plants.

In all climates, strong winds can prevent herbs from developing sturdy root systems, thereby preventing healthy growth. A wooden fence or row of planted shrubs can act as an effective windbreak.

GARDEN PROBLEMS AND SOLUTIONS

If all goes well in a garden, home-grown herbs should provide a bountiful harvest with limitless potential for use. However, even though herbs are among the plants least susceptible to disease, insect infestation and predation by four-legged pests such as rabbits and deer, they sometimes suffer from problems that keep them from producing healthy leaves, seeds or roots. The very qualities that make herbs appealing to humans – the intense fragrance and flavour of their essential oils – are also what keep away most bothersome creatures. But herbs can be susceptible to disease and insect infestation if they are stressed by too little water or light, insufficient nutrients or poor air circulation.

Plant trouble in a garden can be signalled by a variety of symptoms that show up on leaves, stems, or fruit: yellowing, browning or wilting; black or whitish powdery coatings; holes, bumps or depressions. The symptoms of some conditions overlap those of others, so it is important to observe a plant carefully to correctly identify and address any underlying problem that may be affecting it. The charts on pages 185–186 detail the most common environmental conditions, pests and diseases that can afflict herb gardens, along with treatments for each. Solutions for most garden problems include simple, non-toxic physical barriers and traps, and chemical controls, which include insecticidal soap, horticultural oil, diatomaceous earth, silica aerogel and botanical pesticides.

❧ BENEFICIAL INSECTS ❧

The pollen- and nectar-rich herbs listed below will lure insects – parasitic wasps, ladybirds, lacewings, hoverflies, tachinid flies, and soldier beetles – that attack many common garden pests, including scale, aphids and whitefly.

COMMON NAME	BOTANICAL NAME
Angelica	*Angelica archangelica*
Anise	*Pimpinella anisum*
Bee balm	*Monarda* didyma.
Black-eyed Susan	*Rudbeckia* spp.
Borage	*Borago officinalis*
Butterfly weed	*Asclepias tuberosa*
Caraway	*Carum carvi*
Catnip	*Nepeta cataria*
Coneflower	*Echinacea* and *Rudbeckia* spp.
Dill	*Anethum graveolens*
Fennel	*Foeniculum vulgare*
Goldenrod	*Solidago* spp.
Lemon balm	*Melissa officinalis*
Lavender	*Lavandula* spp.
Marigold	*Tagetes* spp.
Marjoram	*Origanum majorana*
Onions, garlic chives	*Allium* spp.
Parsley	*Petroselinium* spp.
Peppermint	*Mentha piperata*
Rosemary	*Rosemarinus* spp.
Sage	*Salvia* spp.
Spearmint	*Mentha spicata*
Tansy	*Tanacetum vulgare*
Thyme	*Thymus* spp.
Yarrow	*Achilles* spp.

Beneficial insects are a boon to herb gardens. Attracting them – including this hoverfly – can be as simple as planting suitable herbs, such as calendula (above) or sweet alyssum.

ENVIRONMENTAL PROBLEMS: SYMPTOMS AND CONTROLS

SYMPTOM	POSSIBLE CULPRIT	SUSCEPTIBLE HERBS	CONTROL
Brown leaf tips.	Excessive fertilizer, over- or underwatering, high levels of fluoride, boron or copper in the water.	All plants	Correct by changing watering and fertilizing habits. If symptoms remain, have water-quality test performed.
Poor growth, yellowing leaves, new growth that shrivels and dies.	pH imbalance, lack of nutrients, poor drainage. Rule these out before suspecting nematodes.	All plants	Check drainage around plant; perform a soil test. Correct by amending soil with appropriate additives, or move plant to an area with better drainage.

PESTS: SYMPTOMS AND CONTROLS

SYMPTOM	POSSIBLE CULPRIT	SUSCEPTIBLE HERBS	CONTROL
Stunted and deformed leaves and stems; plant parts covered with a sticky, dark substance.	Aphids: tiny pear-shaped insects suck sap from plants, producing a sugary "honeydew" that attracts other pests.	Calendula, mint, oregano, rosemary	Spray plants with water, wipe with rubbing alcohol on a cotton swab or with a mild solution of dish detergent and water.
Wilted leaves, may be coated with sooty mold; lose vitality and may eventually die.	Whitefly: pests of greenhouses, houseplants, and outdoor gardens; feed on undersides of leaves and can cause extensive damage.	Calendula, lemon verbena, rosemary	Spray plants with water. If indoors, lower growing temperature to decrease whitefly activity. *Encarsia formosa*, a species of tiny wasps, prey on whiteflies and are often effective in controlling them.
Yellowish or silvery leaves; severe yellowing and rusty spots; fine webbing on leaves and stems.	Spider mites: puncture plant leaves and stems and feed on sap.	Lemon verbena, mint, oregano, parsley, rosemary, sage, thyme	Apply horticultural oil or insecticidal soap. Wash plants with a mild solution of dish detergent and water solution. Prune heavily infested branches and isolate infested plants
Holes at edges of leaves; plants are eventually defoliated.	Japanese beetles: metallic green insect with copper-coloured wings; feeds on foliage of plants.	More than 200 plant species including borage, comfrey, foxglove and sweet basil	Remove from leaves by hand. Control larvae with parasitic nematodes and the bacteria milky spore.
Yellow foliage; plants lose leaves, may weaken and die.	Scales: sap-feeding insects.	Wide range of plants, including bay and rosemary	Remove with a soft-bristled toothbrush dipped in rubbing alcohol or mild solution of dish detergent and water. Attract beneficial beetles and wasps; (see chart on page 184 for list of herbs). Horticultural oils may be effective.
Irregular holes in the middle or at the edges of leaves; plants may be defoliated; shiny slime trails on and around plants.	Snails and slugs: eat seedlings and soft-tissued parts of plants; feed at night and on cloudy, damp days.	Bee balm, calendula, sage, sorrel	Remove by hand daily, then weekly when numbers drop. Set copper strips around tree trunks, or raised beds or other home made traps. Pests will gather in dark, moist spaces under a board raised on low edges; then they can be easily removed from the garden. Slugs may also be lured to a shallow container filled with beer. Set the container into the ground with rim at soil level. Diatomaceous earth is effective against slugs.

DISEASE: SYMPTOMS AND CONTROLS

SYMPTOM	POSSIBLE CULPRIT	SUSCEPTIBLE HERBS	CONTROL
Yellow, drooping foliage. Plants turn brown and die; symptoms first appear on lower and outer leaves.	Verticillium wilt: a fungal disease.	Woody and herbaceous plants, including mint	Plant disease-resistant varieties.
Weakened stems with flowers develop a fluffy grey or white growth, which spreads to fruits.	Botrytis blight: a fungal disease.	Woody and herbaceous plants, including rosemary and scented geranium	Destroy infected plant parts. Promote air circulation around plants by cutting back or removing any that crowd each other.
Yellow or white spots on surface of leaves; crusty orange or yellow bumps on undersides. Plants weaken and become stunted.	Rust: a disease caused by 4,000 or so related fungi.	Germander, mint, yarrow	Destroy infected plant parts. Promote air circulation around plants by cutting back or removing any that crowd each other.
Grey or white powdery growth on leaves; new leaves are distorted in shape. Plants may exhibit poor growth and low yield.	Powdery mildew: a fungal disease that thrives in hot weather.	Woody and herbaceous plants, including bee balm, catmint, germander and lemon	Promote air circulation around plants by cutting back or removing plants that crowd each other. Spray affected plants with sulphur, lime-sulphur, horticultural oil, or a weak solution of baking soda and water.
Yellow foliage; brown colouration along leaf edges; plants may wilt and become stunted; roots may be soft and waterlogged.	Root rot: a fungal disease.	Oregano, rosemary, sage, tarragon, thyme	Use sterile potting soil when propagating plants. Avoid overwatering, but do not let plants dry out between waterings. Remove and destroy affected plants.
Yellow stunted leaves. Plants may wilt.	Nematodes: microscopic wormlike creatures feed on roots, leaves, and stems; spread readily in water and on garden tools.	Calendula, parsley	Remove and destroy infested plants. Amend soil with organic fertilizers and products containing seaweed and humic acids.

There is a wide variety of ways to control most garden problems, and it is always best to use the least-toxic approach before trying any others.

Preventing Garden Problems

Of course, prevention is the best way to maintain a healthy, problem-free garden. Regular additions of compost will keep soil nutrient rich. Herbs should be planted only if they have consistent, deep foliage colour and show no signs of disease or infestation. Herbs should be planted in well-drained soil in a site that receives appropriate light: shade-loving plants in shade; water-loving in moist areas; sun-loving in sun.

Diseases and insect infestations spread rapidly through related plants. As a deterrent, mix different herb species together in beds and other plantings. Lure natural predators of garden pests by planting herbs known to attract those beneficial organisms.

HARVESTING HERBS

Herbs can be harvested throughout the growing season – and even throughout the dormant season if they are grown indoors. The following tools are useful to have on hand at harvest time: pruning shears (remember that sharp shears are less likely to injure plants or even slip and injure the gardener); rubber bands or twine for tying bunches of stems together; and, on very hot days, a bucket of cool water in which to immerse the herb stems. This prevents them from wilting from being in heat and sunlight for too long.

When to Harvest

Small amounts of herbs can be harvested for immediate use throughout the growing season. Major harvests, however, should occur a few days before each plant flowers, when the concentration of essential oils in the leaves is highest. The timing of flowering varies among

Tent caterpillars build gauzy nests in the forks of tree branches. They feed on the tree's leaves during the day.

The damage caused by snails and slugs is obvious – holes that cause significant harm to the leaves and impeding overall plant growth.

One way to control snails and slugs is to remove their habitat from the garden area. That can include bricks, garden clippings and boards.

herbs, so plant life cycles must be observed carefully. Perennials should not be pruned heavily after 45 days or before the first seasonal frost is expected; this will ensure that the plants are strong enough to survive the dormant season. It is possible to harvest annuals right up until the end of the growing season, after which the entire plant will be removed and discarded.

When planning a large herb harvest for drying, making vinegars and potpourris, or other purposes, it is best to work during the cooler times of the day, when the herbs' essential oils are unlikely to evaporate and their foliage is less likely to wilt. It is also important to hold off harvesting until the morning dew has dried, because this moisture can cause the herbs to mould, which renders them useless for any kind of preparation.

Harvesting Leaves

It is important to prune the leaves and stems of herbs in a way that will help promote new growth, rather than harming the plant. The method for doing that varies from herb to herb. Fortunately for the home gardener, most common herbs fall into just two of the more than 300 identified plant families, so it is relatively simple to learn the pruning preferences of these two families.

To harvest the leaves of herbs including bee balm (below), cut the plant in the middle of its stem, just above a set of leaves.

BEST PROPAGATION METHODS FOR DIFFERENT HERBS

DURING THE LAST FROST OF THE YEAR

Pruning	Prune woody herbs by removing the leggy old growth to promote new stems and a better shape.
Weeding	At the beginning of the growing season, weeds are small and have shallow roots. This is the easiest time to pull them out.
Starting seeds	Six to eight weeks before the last expected frost, start herb seeds indoors. Take cuttings from an indoor herb garden to propagate new outdoor garden plants. Herbs can be started outdoors when nighttime temperatures exceed 13°C (55°F).
Improving the soil	Add a layer of compost or other organic material to garden beds.
Dividing and moving	To create new contrasts or complements of flowers or foliage, move herbs around so they can become established before the active-growth season. This is also a good time to divide and transplant herbs that have outgrown their original sites.

DURING THE GROWING SEASON

Planting	Herbs that quickly go to seed, such as dill, borage, coriander, fennel, and German chamomile, can be sowed every few weeks to ensure a continuous supply throughout the growing season.
Watering	In arid climates and during dry periods, water herbs occasionally and deeply.
Dead-heading	Remove the spent flowers and seed heads of perennial herbs such as geraniums, marigolds and roses to encourage the plants to direct their energy into new flower production.
Harvesting	Harvest and pinch back rapidly growing perennials. Cut back annual herbs by one-third to one-half.
Preserving	Dry foliage and flowers of herbs for later use. Prepare herbal vinegars, oils, infusions and tinctures.

END OF THE GROWING SEASON

Planting bulbs and seeds	Plant bulbs of herbs such as garlic and saffron, and seeds of dill, caraway, mustard, parsley and sweet cicely. In warm areas, plant seeds of cool-season herbs such as chervil, coriander and parsley, which will put forth a second season of growth.
Dividing	Hardy perennials reach the end of their period of active growth as the weather cools. Divide them and replant, or take note of what should be divided and moved when the weather warms again.
Cleaning up	Rake leaves and pull weeds. Remove spent annuals, saving their seeds for the next growing season. Leave some stalks and seeds of herbs such as chervil, fennel, lavender, marjoram and sweet cicely to feed hungry birds during the dormant season.
Preparing for the dormant season	Some perennial herbs survive cold weather well, while others will do so only with protection provided by the gardener. Shelter herbs that are at the edge of their hardiness-zone range. Only herbs that are perennials in warm climates should be moved indoors. These include bay, lemon verbena, pineapple sage, rosemary, scented geranium.

DURING THE DORMANT SEASON

Caring for indoor herbs	To keep the plants alive, gardeners must supply the three essentials: light, water and nutrients.
Propagating cuttings	Take cuttings from indoor herbs to get new plants started for the next growing season.
Planning for the new growing season	Plan small or large projects for the next year: planting or moving a tree; rerouting paths; adding new plant beds.
Making herb crafts	Use previously harvested herbs to make herbal crafts such as potpourris, wreaths and sachets.

Herbs in the mint (*Labiatae*) family – basil, bee balm hyssop, lavender, lemon balm, marjoram, mint, oregano, rosemary – should be cut in the middle of their stems, just above a set of leaves. Otherwise, the growing tips should be pinched off from the ends of stems. Two new stems will form at these junctures, promoting abundant, bushy growth. Members of the mint family will put forth vigorous new growth when they are cut back by one-third between the time they flower and set seeds, increasing their yield substantially.

Plants in the parsley (*Umbelliferae*) family – angelica, caraway, coriander, cumin, dill, fennel, parsley, sweet cicely – sprout stems from a central point at ground level. Parsley family members should be harvested by cutting stems at their bases from around the outside of the plant. Employing this pruning method will encourage new shoots to grow from the centre. Annuals in the parsley group produce leaves for a short period of time before they flower. Leaves can be harvested three to six times during the period before flowering.

Other types of herbs can be harvested and pruned using methods suggested by their growth habits. Chives (*Allium schoenoprasum*), for example, sprout a dense cluster of blades from their bulbs. Individual chive blades should be cut close to the ground; otherwise, the entire plant can be cut to 2.5 cm (1 in) above the soil's level. New blades will generate from the bulbs.

Bay (*Laurus nobilis*) and scented geranium (*Pelargonium* spp.) both sprout leaves in a series along their stems. These leaves should be harvested individually. Tarragon and lemon verbena have growth habits similar to mint, and should be harvested using the same methods.

Harvesting Seeds

Seeds should be gathered when they are ripe. On most plants, ripening is signalled by a change in seed colour from green to tan to light brown.

To harvest seeds, pull up the whole plant from the soil when the seeds are barely ripe. Hang the plant upside-down with a paper bag tied over the seed heads; as they become ready, the seeds will drop into the bag.

Alternatively, muslin bags tied over the seed heads of plants as they grow will catch seeds as they drop naturally. Store harvested seeds in a cool, dry place, in cardboard boxes or in twists of aluminum foil.

Harvesting Flowers

Herb flowers should be picked just before they are fully open. They will continue to open slightly after they have been cut; however, the flowers are more likely to lose their petals if harvested after they are completely open. Harvest flowers early in the day and transfer the stems to a vase or glass of water until ready to use.

Harvesting Roots

Most roots should be dug up and harvested as they reach maturity, at the end of the growing season, after a plant's leaves have yellowed and begin to die back. The roots of horseradish are best dug when they are younger, before they develop too strong a taste or too coarse a texture. Roots are harvested using a garden fork: carefully lift the root, then cut it away from the rest of the plant. Roots should be rinsed with water, patted dry and stored in a dry, well-ventilated area.

Cleaning Herbs

Plants that grow on long stems – basil (*Ocimum basilicum*), coriander (*Coriandrum sativum*), and chives (*Allium schoenoprasum*), for instance, are usually fairly free of soil or sand, and so are relatively easy to clean before using; however, those that creep along the ground, such as thyme (*Thymus* spp.) and oregano (*Origanum vulgare*), can easily collect sand or mud on their leaves and stems, making them trickier to clean. In addition, herbs with crinkled leaves, or those showing from pest problems should be rinsed in water and carefully patted dry before using.

To remove grit, dust or other residue, rinse the leaves under cold running water for a minute or two. Or, fill the sink with cold water and immerse the herbs in the water. Swish them around, which will cause the debris to to drop to the bottom of the sink. Repeat if necessary.

Harvest horseradish root when it is young; otherwise, the flavour will be strong and unpleasant, and the texture coarse.

Pick herb flowers, such as marigold (right), just before they have fully bloomed; they will continue to open after they have been cut. Cut flowers early in the day and immediately place in a vase or glass of water.

PART

II

Gallery
of
HERBS

Sage
Salvia microphylla

Gallery of Herbs

Herbs have been used for both medicinal and culinary purposes for centuries. This Gallery of Herbs highlights more than 250 herbs from all over the world, with special two- and four-page features of the ten most important herbs or herb families.

Throughout the Gallery, details about each herb's origins and significant properties are discussed, along with descriptions of popular varieties, and optimum growing conditions in both its natural environment and for gardening in non-native places.

Each herb's culinary application is also detailed, where applicable, as well as its employment in medicine, including specific instructions for use and dosages, and contra-indications for the general population as well as more specific groups, such as pregnant women.

All of the herbs, which are arranged alphabetically by Latin botanical name, are identified with descriptive text and full-colour images. Up to five common names are included, as well. Where relevant, the derivation of an herb's name also offers a mini history lesson for the curious reader. For instance, hawthorn's Latin name, *Crataegus laevigata,* comes from the Greek *kratus*, which means "strength", referring to the characteristic hardness of the tree's wood; and bay's genus name, *Laurus*, comes from the Latin "laus" meaning "praise". Wreaths made of bay leaves were used in ancient Greece and Rose to crown scholars, poets and Olympic victors – and are still presented today to signify athletic achievement.

The special feature pages offer a more in-depth examination of families, such as the onion, which possesses the largest number of species of all herbs, including chives, garlic and spring onions – not to mention the wide variety of onions themselves. These different species are described, displayed and compared and contrasted – offering up a information for both the layperson and expert gardener.

Chinese desert-thorn
Lycium chinense

Milfoil
Achillea Millefolium

*A*CHILLEA MILLEFOLIUM

MILFOIL, YARROW

A member of the Compositea family, this upright, aromatic perennial is native to Europe and Asia and naturalized in North America, Australia and New Zealand. One of the plant's common names, milfoil (from the French *mille feuille*, meaning "one thousand leaves"), refers to yarrow's feathery leaves, which are divided into thousands of tiny leaflets. The genus name *Achillea* is derived from the Greek hero Achilles, who reportedly used yarrow to heal the wounds of his troops during the Trojan War. Yarrow bears greyish-white, flat-topped, umbrella-shaped flowers. Some cultivars, such as *Achillea mille-folium* 'Cerise Queen', produce brilliant pink flowers.

GROWING CONDITIONS Yarrow flourishes in rich, well-drained soil under full sun. The plant's long-blooming flowers attract beneficial insects such as ladybirds, and it is a favourite inclusion in gardens as a border plant. Yarrow can be invasive, so it is often best grown in a container. Seeds or root divisions can be planted in the spring, and the plant may be harvested when in flower in the summer.

CULINARY USE Once used as a substitute for hops in brewing beer, yarrow is occasionally used in small amounts to flavour salads, soups and egg dishes.

MEDICINAL USE Yarrow leaf is composed of a complex mixture of constituents. Two of them, achilletin and achilleine, increase blood coagulation, which encourages the healing of wounds. Flavonoids in the plant stimulate gastric secretions to improve digestion. Yarrow may also have anti-inflammatory and antispasmodic properties, and has been used to treat menstrual and stomach cramps. **Note:** Yarrow should not be taken during pregnancy. People who are prone to allergies from Asteraceae family members, such as ragweed, may experience skin inflammation and itching when exposed to yarrow.

DOSAGE Tea: Use 0.25 litre (8 oz) three times daily. Tincture: Use 1 to 3 ml (0.03 to 0.1 oz) two or three times daily.

*A*ESCULUS HIPPOCASTANUM

BUCKEYE, HORSE CHESTNUT

Native to central Asia, horse chestnut was introduced into Europe in the 17th century.

It is commonly grown as a shade tree in North America. This member of the *Hippocastanaceae* (horse chestnut) family bears palmate leaves, erect spikes of fragrant white flowers and round, green, spiny fruits that contain shiny reddish-brown seeds, known as conkers. These seeds were thought to resemble the eyes of a deer, hence the tree's common name, "buckeye". The seeds are poisonous if not properly processed. Native American tribes once crushed the fresh seeds and scattered them in the water when fishing; compounds in the seeds slowed the fish and made them easier to catch. Horse chestnut wood was long used to make furniture. Its bark yields a yellow dye used in crafts. Horse chestnut extract is an ingredient in some cosmetics and hair-care products.

GROWING CONDITIONS Fast-growing horse chestnut trees prefer well-drained, fertile soil in sun or partial shade. Seeds may be planted in the spring or autumn.

CULINARY USE None.

MEDICINAL USE Horse chestnut contains a substance called aescin, which helps strengthen and increase vein elasticity. These effects are beneficial in the treatment of varicose veins, haemorrhoids, chronic venous insufficiency (a condition in which the veins do not efficiently return blood from the lower limbs back to the heart), and oedema (fluid retention). Extract of the herb prevents blood from pooling and helps tighten tissues. Aescin diminishes

A

the number of openings in capillary walls, helping prevent fluids from leaking into surrounding tissue, making horse chestnut a good topical treatment for bruises and sports injuries. The herb also has anti-inflammatory properties, and has traditionally been used to relieve arthritis pain. **Note:** Raw, unprocessed horse chestnut bark, seeds and leaves may be toxic and should not be ingested. Horse chestnut should not be used internally by pregnant women. External preparations should not be applied to broken skin.

✎ DOSAGE Tincture: Use 5 to 20 drops, three times daily. **Capsule:** Take one 300 mg capsule twice daily. **Standardized extract:** Take one 300 mg capsule standardized to 16 to 20 percent triterpene saponins twice daily. **Creams, ointments, external preparations:** Follow label directions.

AGASTACHE FOENICULUM

ANISE HYSSOP, BLUE GIANT HYSSOP, FENNEL GIANT HYSSOP

A member of the mint family (Lamiaceae), anise hyssop takes its botanical name from the Greek *agan* ("very much") and *stachys* ("an ear of corn or wheat"), referring to the plant's spiky blue-purple flowers. Native to the midwest United States, and naturalized in North and Central America, the plant has been grown commercially for more than 100 years as a source of delicious, slightly anise-flavoured honey. Its flowers produce copious bee- and butterfly-attracting nectar.

✎ GROWING CONDITIONS An excellent garden border plant, anise hyssop prefers well-drained sandy loam and full sun. It will tolerate somewhat poor soil and dry conditions. Seeds, root divisions or cuttings may be planted in the spring. Leaves may be harvested in the spring and summer; flowers are harvested in the summer.

✎ CULINARY USE Anise hyssop's leaves and flowers have a liquorice-mint flavor. They may be added to salads, brewed into hot and iced teas, and used to flavour fruit (particularly cranberries), soups, stews and meats.

✎ MEDICINAL USE Traditionally used by Native Americans to treat colds and coughs, the leaves of anise hyssop contain ingredients that increase perspiration (thus helping "break" a fever) and help clear bronchial congestion. The plant may also contain antiviral compounds useful in treating herpes. A related species, *Agastache rugosa*, has been used in Traditional Chinese Medicine to treat heartburn and symptoms of gastric reflux.

✎ DOSAGE Tea: Use 0.25 litre (8 oz) two or three times daily.

AGRIMONIA EUPATORIA

AGRIMONY, CHURCH STEEPLES

Native to Europe, northern Africa, and Asia, this perennial is a member of the Rosaceae (rose) family. It produces small yellow flowers at the top of tall, slender spikes, evocative of church spires. The flowers become prickly seed burrs with hooked bristles that commonly attach themselves to passersby. Agrimony's botanical name may come from the Greek *arghemon*, translating to "albugo", an eye disease once treated with the plant. Alternatively, *Agrimonia* may come from the Latin *agri moenia*, or "defender of the fields", because of the plant's tendency to grow in clumps near fields.

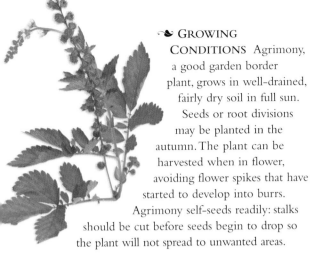

⚜ GROWING CONDITIONS Agrimony, a good garden border plant, grows in well-drained, fairly dry soil in full sun. Seeds or root divisions may be planted in the autumn. The plant can be harvested when in flower, avoiding flower spikes that have started to develop into burrs. Agrimony self-seeds readily: stalks should be cut before seeds begin to drop so the plant will not spread to unwanted areas.

⚜ CULINARY USE None.

⚜ MEDICINAL USE Agrimony's leaves, stems and flowers contain astringent and antibacterial tannins. It has been used to treat diarrhoea, to staunch bleeding wounds, and soothe inflammation of the skin, mouth and pharynx. Agrimony may also have antioxidant and liver-protective effects. A related species, *Agrimonia pilosa,* is used in traditional Chinese medicine to treat nosebleeds, bleeding gums, blood in the urine and uterine bleeding.

⚜ DOSAGE Tea: Use 0.25 litre (8 oz) two or three times daily. **Tincture:** Use 1 ml (0.03 oz) twice daily.

*A*LOE VERA
SYN A. BARBADENSIS

ALOE, ALOE VERA, BARBADOS ALOE

Native to East Africa, aloe is naturalized in other regions, including the Caribbean, where it is cultivated for commercial use. A member of the Liliaceae (lily) family, aloe is a clumping perennial that may grow to 1 m (3 ft) tall. It bears yellow, orange or red flowers and long, spiky, succulent green leaves that may have red spots when the plant is young. Aloe was used by ancient Egyptians as an embalming ingredient, and to treat skin conditions such as burns. Queen Cleopatra is said to have considered skin lotions made with aloe to be the source of her renowned beauty. Legend has it that in the 4th century B.C.E., the Greek philosopher Aristotle told Alexander the Great to conquer the East African island of Socotra, the only place where aloe was cultivated, so that a reliable supply of aloe would be available to Greece. "Aloe" comes from the Arabic word *alloeh*, meaning "bitter and shiny", which accurately describes the gel found inside aloe leaves. Aloe is widely used in cosmetics today.

⚜ GROWING CONDITIONS Aloe grows in well-drained soil in full sun. It requires little care, but is intolerant of cold. The plant may be potted and brought indoors when outside temperatures fall below 4°C (40°F) . Aloe produces offshoots, which may be uprooted and individually replanted when they are 5 to 8 cm (2 to 3 in) tall.

⚜ CULINARY USE None.

⚜ MEDICINAL USE Aloe contains polysaccharides thought to accelerate healing of skin tissue and reduce inflammation. The juice and gel (a clear, thin, jellylike substance) of aloe leaves may be used to soothe burns, superficial skin wounds, sunburn, eczema and rashes caused by exposure to poison oak or poison ivy. Aloe gel has been applied to the fingernails to prevent nail biting. When taken internally, the gel may be soothing to the digestive tract. It has been taken to treat conditions including colitis, Crohn's disease and peptic ulcers. Studies have shown that it may be useful in reducing blood sugar levels of people with diabetes. Aloe latex, or aloin, a brownish-yellow gel found along the sides of aloe's leaf blades, is dried and used in commercial laxative products. It is extremely strong, and can cause diarrhoea and intestinal cramps. Commercial aloe gel and juice do not contain this substance. **Note:** Aloe latex should not be used by pregnant women, because the herb may stimulate uterine contractions, or by breastfeeding mothers, because it may cause painful stomach cramps in babies. The latex should be avoided by those who suffer from irritable bowel syndrome, kidney disease or haemorrhoids.

⚜ DOSAGE Fresh aloe gel for external use: Apply liberally to burns and wounds as needed. **Aloe gel or capsule for internal use:** Take up to 1 tbsp, three times daily.

ALLIACEAE
Onions

One of the largest and most diverse plant families, Alliaceae contains well over 500 species, including garlic, onions, chives and spring onions. Bulbs of these plants have been used for medicinal and culinary purposes for many centuries. In recent years, studies have shown that both garlic and onions have a multitude of health benefits.

ALLIUM CEPA
ONION

A member of the Liliaceae (lily) family, the onion is thought to be native to western Asia. (*Cepa* is Latin for onion.) Onions are grown all over the world; hundreds of cultivars of different colours, flavours and sizes are adapted to different climates. This perennial or biennial bears star-shaped, greenish-white flowers at the end of a single long, cylindrical, hollow stem, which emanates from a pungent, edible, underground bulb. The world's largest onion producers are the United States, Spain, Italy, Turkey and Egypt. Some of the more interesting varieties include onion (*A. cepa* 'Ailsa Craig'), which produces a large, yellow-skinned, mild-flavoured bulb; North Holland blood-red onion (*A. cepa*. 'Noordhollandse Bloedrode'), which produces a bulb with a mild flavour, red skin and pink flesh; and Sweet sandwich onion (*A. cepa*. 'Sweet Sandwich'), which produces large, brown-skinned bulbs that have a mild, sweet flavour.

GROWING CONDITIONS
Onions thrive in rich, well-drained soil in full sun. Seeds may be planted in the spring or autumn; small bulbs (sets) may be planted in the spring.

CULINARY USE Onion bulbs are widely used to flavor meat and vegetable dishes, as a condiment for soups and casseroles, and in many snack foods and gravies. They can be eaten raw or cooked, boiled or pickled. Onions may be preserved by being dried and stored as flakes and salts for later use.

A. cepa. var. proliferum
Tree onion is a popular garden plant that produces small bulbs among its flowers.

A. cepa
Sweet Sandwich, like many onions, has important culinary and medicinal uses.

A. cepa Linné
Often added to sandwiches
and salads, red onions offer a
mild sweet flavour along with
colour to any dish.

MEDICINAL USE Onion bulbs contain sulphur
compounds, which cause the eyes to water when the
flesh of an onion is cut or broken. Medicinally, these
compounds may help prevent atherosclerosis and
reduce the risk of stomach cancer. They may also
help lower blood sugar and blood pressure levels,
prevent the formation of clots in the blood, and
stimulate the appetite in the elderly. During the late
1800s and early 1900s, doctors recommended a syrup
made of onion juice and sugar to treat coughs and
bronchitis. Onion extract has been taken to treat kidney stones and oedema. Fresh onion juice, considered
antibacterial and antifungal, may be applied to minor
cuts, athlete's foot, acne and boils.

DOSAGE Fresh: Eat 57 to 227 g (2 to 8 oz) chopped
onions daily for cardiovascular benefits. **Cough syrup:**
Dissolve 43 g (1½ oz) sugar in 30 ml (1 oz) raw onion
juice. Take ½ tsp two or three times each day.

ALLIUM SATIVUM
GARLIC

A Liliaceae (lily) family member, garlic is
generally believed to have originated in Asia.
It is commercially cultivated on a large scale
in many countries, including the United
States, Argentina, Spain, France, Germany,
Hungary, Egypt, China, India and South
Korea. This perennial bears long, flat leaves,
an umbel of greenish-white to pink flowers, and an edible underground bulb made
up of five to fifteen "cloves" enclosed in a
papery white, or pale purple skin. Garlic's name is
thought to have originated from the Anglo-Saxon
words *gar* (spear) and *lac* (plant), referring to the
spearlike shape of the plant's leaves. *Sativum*, the
species name, means "cultivated". *A. ampeloprasum* var.
ampeloprasum (elephant garlic), a perennial, produces
bulbs that lack the plant's characterisitc papery skin.

GROWING CONDITIONS Garlic prefers rich, moist,
sandy soil and sunny locations. Individual cloves may
be planted in the spring or autumn; seeds may be
planted in the autumn. Harvest is in early autumn.

A. fistulosum
Spring onion is the most popular Allium
variety in Asia. Its bulbs are smaller than
many onion varieties, and its stems are
often used in cooking.

A. sativum
Garlic, usually known for its pungent
fragrance, makes a great insect repellent.

CULINARY USE One of the world's most
popular herbs, garlic is used worldwide to flavour
an enormous variety of foods, including salad
dressings, pasta sauces, soups, vegetables, meat
and fish dishes, vinegars, and herb butters and
salts. The entire bulb can be baked or roasted,
softening the cloves into a paste that may be used
as a seasoning or eaten as a spread.

MEDICINAL USE Garlic has been used in various
cultures for more than 5,000 years as a pungent
medicinal herb. In ancient Egypt, the builders of
the Great Pyramids ate garlic to prevent colds,
bronchitis, and other upper-respiratory conditions. During the Middle Ages, French
priests used garlic to protect themselves
from the bubonic plague. During World
War I, soldiers in Europe applied garlic
externally to wounds as a disinfectant.
During World War II, Russians made so
much use of garlic for this purpose that the
herb became known as "Russian penicillin".
The chemistry of garlic is so complex that
researchers are still trying to understand exactly
how it works. Garlic bulbs contain the sulphur
compound allicin, which is activated when garlic is

A. sativum
German white is a strong, flavourful
garlic that has little aftertaste.

crushed but is rendered inactive when
cooked. Sometimes called the "pungent
panacea", garlic is still taken as a treatment
for upper-respiratory conditions. It also
lowers cholesterol and blood pressure
levels, improves circulation, and rids
the body of intestinal parasites.

DOSAGE Fresh: Eat two or three
cloves (cooked or raw) daily with
meals. **Tincture:** Take 1 ml (0.03 oz)
two or three times daily. **Standardized
extract:** Take up to three 500 mg
capsules daily, or follow directions.

ALLIUM SCHOENOPRASUM
CHIVES

Chives is thought to be native to
Siberia. This perennial member of
the Liliaceae (lily) family produces
light purple or pink bell-shaped
flowers, and clumps of tender,
hollow, dark green spears that grow
out of small, edible, underground
bulbs. The name "chives" derives
from the French word *cive*, which
in turn comes from the Latin
name for onion, *cepa*. Chives
has similar properties to
onions and garlic but a
milder effect, and is
primarily used for
culinary purposes.

GROWING
CONDITIONS

Chives grow well in
wetter, heavier soil than
that preferred by onions and
garlic. The plant also requires
less sun than onions. Seeds
may be planted in the spring;
divisions may be planted in
the spring or autumn.

A. senescens glaucum
Corkscrew chives is a tufted variety with round pink
flowers and an unusual, twisted growing habit.

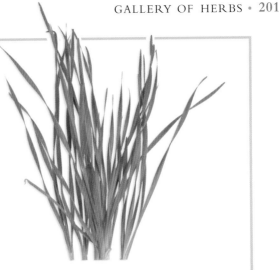

A. carinatum pulchellum
Keeled garlic is a clump forming perrennial
known for its white and pink flowers.

A. schoenoprasum 'Schnittlauch'
Schoenoprasum chives is a dwarf cultivar that grows to
about half the height of the common chive plant.

A. schoenoprasum 'Forescate'
Forescate chives, which bears pink flowers, are
larger than the common chive plant.

CULINARY USE Chives are used in cooking to impart
a mild onionlike flavour to cheese, egg and potato dishes.
The herb is also used as a garnish and flavouring in
soups, salads, spreads and dips. Chive flowers may be
added to salads and incorporated in vinegars. Chives are
an ingredient in the popular French spice mixture *fines
herbes* which also includes tarragon, chervil and parsley.

MEDICINAL USE Historically, chives has often been
used to treat colds, flu and lung congestion because of
its high vitamin C content. It is not commonly used in
modern herbal medicine.

DOSAGE Fresh: Consume 1 tbsp, as desired.
Dried: Use 1 tsp, as desired.

A. tuberosum
Chinese or garlic chives, a perennial, bears white flowers.

A

*A*LOYSIA TRIPHYLLA SYN. A. CITRIODORA

LEMON VERBENA, VERBENA

Lemon verbena is a member of the Verbenaceae (verbena) family, native to South America. This tall, deciduous shrub bears small white to pale purple flowers and long, finely toothed yellow-green leaves that have a sweet, lemony odour and taste.

GROWING CONDITIONS

Because of its attractive leaves and pleasant scent, lemon verbena has been a favourite garden plant since Victorian times, when it was known as the "lemon plant". It is cultivated in temperate climates as an aromatic ornamental. The herb grows well in light, well-drained soil in full sun. It can survive cold winters in areas where the ground does not freeze, but is hardiest in warm climates. The leaves of lemon verbena should be harvested in the late summer.

CULINARY USE
Lemon verbena is a favourite culinary herb, used as an ingredient in a variety of foods ranging from preserves and stuffings to fruit salad, baked goods and wine. Lemon verbena makes a delicious hot or cold tea, and has been used to flavour liqueurs in its native South America. The herb has a strong flavour, so a light touch is best when adding it to recipes.

MEDICINAL USE
Traditionally used as a treatment for settling the stomach, lemon verbena contains a volatile oil (mainly consisting of citral, cineole, lemonene and geraniol) that benefits digestion. A tea of lemon verbena leaves or flowering tops can be drunk to relieve digestive upsets and reduce fever. The plant contains flavonoids and iridoids, which give it antispasmodic, sedative, and fever-reducing effects.

DOSAGE
Tea: Use 0.5 litre (8 oz) two or three times daily.

*A*NANAS COMOSUS

ANANAS, PINEAPPLE

Pineapple, an exotic member of the Bromeliaceae (bromeliad) family, is native to Central and South America. This herbaceous perennial is cultivated throughout the tropics, particularly in Hawaii (the world's leading pineapple producer), for its succulent yellow fruit. The plant has a short, sturdy stem and bears spiny, green leaves. Pineapple's common name alludes to the appearance of the fruit, which looks like a very large pinecone. It is also called *ananas*, from the Paraguayan word *nana*, which means "exquisite fruit".

GROWING CONDITIONS
Pineapple grows in well drained, rich, sandy soil in hot and humid climates.

CULINARY USE
Pineapple fruit has a tangy, citrusy flavor. It is eaten fresh, in fruit desserts, and salads. It is also used as a garnish for meat and vegetable dishes. The fruit can be sautéed, grilled, or added to baked goods, such as pineapple upside-down cake. Canned pineapple – in chunks, rings, tidbits or crushed pieces – is widely available packaged in its own juice or in sugar syrup.

MEDICINAL USE
Pineapple fruit is a good source of vitamins A and C. It contains bromelain, an enzyme that may aid the digestion of starches and relieve some stomach upset. Bromelain also has anti-inflammatory properties, making it useful as a dietary supplement to help the body heal more quickly after surgery, and for those suffering from arthritis.

When taken regularly, bromelain may help reduce inflammation and scarring of the arteries that can lead to cardiovascular disease. Fresh pineapple is a good source of fibre, which helps relieve constipation. Its juice has mild diuretic properties.

❧ **DOSAGE** **Standardized extract:** Take two 500 mg capsules per day, as needed.

ANETHUM GRAVEOLENS

DILL

Native to the Mediterranean region and Asia, dill is extensively naturalized throughout North America and Europe. This member of the Apiaceae (parsley) family is an annual or biennial herb that resembles the fennel plant. It bears umbels of yellow flowers that appear in the summer, followed by aromatic seeds. Dill leaves have a strong aroma. Romans in the 1st century C.E. considered the plant a good luck symbol. In the Middle Ages, dill was used by magicians in spells and for charms against witchcraft.

❧ **GROWING CONDITIONS** Dill grows best in well-drained, slightly acidic soil in full sun. It is a good garden or border plant, because its flowers attract beneficial insects that feed on aphids. Dill seeds should be planted in the spring or summer; leaves and seeds may be harvested in the summer. After sowing, seedlings should be thinned to 203 mm (8 in) apart, as dill will bolt (go to seed prematurely) if it is overcrowded.

❧ **CULINARY USE** Dill has a distinctive, tangy taste. It is best known as a pickling spice, especially for flavouring cucumber pickles. The seeds and leaves are used fresh or dried in cooking. Dill pairs well with eggs, seafood and potatoes. Cucumbers are also partnered with dill in salads, chilled soups and sandwiches.

❧ **MEDICINAL USE** Both dill seed and dill seed oil have a long history of use in Western and traditional Chinese medicine in the treatment of flatulence, particularly in children. The seeds and leaves contain a volatile oil that acts as a digestive aid, relieving trapped wind and calming the digestive tract. Dill also retards the growth of *E. coli*, a bacteria that may cause gastrointestinal and urinary tract infections. Chewing dill seeds is believed to alleviate bad breath. Seed and leaf teas have been given to breastfeeding mothers to increase milk production, and babies have been given the tea, called "gripe water", to relieve colic.

❧ **DOSAGE** **Tea:** Use 0.5 litre (8 oz) two or three times daily.

ANGELICA ARCHANGELICA

ANGELICA, ARCHANGEL, EUROPEAN ANGELICA

Thought to be native to Syria and then naturalized in Europe, this member of the Apiaceae (parsley) family grows abundantly in northern and eastern Europe, and central Asia. Angelica is a tall, robust, aromatic biennial or short-lived perennial. The plant, which is often described as "celery-like", has thick stems and long-stalked leaves, and bears small greenish-white flowers.

Angelica has been used medicinally for more than 1,000 years. The herb's name comes from the Latin *herba angelica*, or "angelic herb", because of the belief that it would cure all conditions. In England, it was believed to ward off the plague. European peasants placed necklaces of angelica leaves around the necks of

A

their children to protect against illness and witchcraft. The fragrance of angelica root is attractive to deer and fish. It was often used as fish bait by early European and North American hunters.

❧ **GROWING CONDITIONS** Angelica grows in rich, moist, well-drained, slightly acidic soil in sun or partial shade. Seeds or root divisions may be planted in the spring or autumn. Angelica is an attractive garden plant, but it also attracts blackflies and fruit flies. For this reason, the herb is best planted away from the home. The centre of a herb bed is a good location for the plant, which can grow to 2 m (7 ft) tall.

❧ **CULINARY USE** Angelica's foliage, which has a tart flavour, is eaten as a vegetable in Scandinavian countries. The plant's roots and fruit (commonly called "seeds") are used to flavour liqueurs: angelica is found in vermouth, gin, Benedictine and Chartreuse. The root has a sour taste, but cooking it with rhubarb has a sweetening effect. The young stalks can be added to orange marmalade to impart a bittersweet flavour. The stems can be steamed and eaten with butter as a vegetable. Angelica stems are also candied and eaten on their own or made into a colourful jelly. They were originally used in fruitcake, before being replaced by dried fruit.

❧ **MEDICINAL USE** One of the most popular herbs in Europe during the 15th century, angelica contains digestion-enhancing volatile oils that support the herb's historical use as a remedy for indigestion. The plant's roots and fruit (seeds) are used to treat appetite loss, flatulence and abdominal discomfort. The herb is sometimes used to treat colds, bronchitis and asthma. **Note:** Angelica can cause a skin rash if someone has ingested the herb and then been exposed to sunlight, a reaction called photosensitivity. Angelica should not be taken by women who are pregnant, breastfeeding, or trying to conceive, nor should it be consumed by children younger than age two. The roots of angelica should be thoroughly dried before use; they are poisonous when fresh.

❧ **DOSAGE Tea:** Use up to 0.5 litre (16 oz) daily, before meals. The tea will have a bitter flavour. **Tincture:** Use 1 or 2 ml (0.03 or 0.07 oz) once or twice daily.

*A*NTHRISCUS CEREFOLIUM

CHERVIL, GARDEN CHERVIL

Native to northern and eastern Europe and Asia, this annual grows freely along roadsides. It is cultivated as a popular garden plant in North America and Europe. A member of the Apiaceae (parsley) family, chervil resembles parsley in appearance.

❧ **GROWING CONDITIONS** Chervil grows well in partial shade, in rich, light soil that retains moisture. The plant will bolt in high temperatures or if it receives too much sun. Chervil is a good choice for inclusion in pots indoors, because it does not require a lot of sun. Seeds may be planted in the early spring to early autumn, and the seedlings should be thinned to 20 cm (8 in) apart. Leaves should be harvested before the plant flowers.

❧ **CULINARY USE** Chervil has been used in cooking since ancient Egyptian and Roman times. A basket of chervil seeds was found in the tomb of the Egyptian pharaoh Tutankhamen. The herb has a mild, anise-like flavour, and tastes best when eaten fresh. The flavour does not hold up to prolonged heat, so it is best to add chervil to a dish just before serving, or use it finely chopped or in sprigs as a garnish. Chervil is one of the ingredients in the popular French herb mix *fines herbes*, which is often added (fresh or dried) to tomato, chicken, and egg salads, savoury egg dishes, potato soup, and rice and pasta dishes.

❧ **MEDICINAL USE** Regarded primarily as a culinary herb, chervil also contains a volatile oil, coumarins and flavonoids that make it useful for calming the digestion. It has diuretic effects, and its juice has been applied externally to treat superficial wounds and skin irritations such as eczema.

❧ **DOSAGE Tea:** Use 0.5 litre (8 oz) two or three times daily.

ARCTIUM LAPPA

BURDOCK, GOBO, GREAT BURDOCK

Native to Europe and Asia, this weedy biennial grows freely in temperate regions all over the world. It is cultivated in Europe, China, and Japan. A member of the Asteraceae (daisy) family, burdock bears long leaves and crimson-purple, thistlelike flowers. It produces spiny seed heads covered with stiff hooks that cling stubbornly to clothes and animals. These burrs are said to have inspired the Swiss inventor George de Mestral (1907–1990) to develop Velcro™, which was patented in 1955. The plant's common name comes from *bur*, for its tenacious burrs, and *dock*, an Old English word for plant.

❧ GROWING CONDITIONS Burdock prefers dry, medium-rich, well-drained soil in full sun, but will tolerate poorer soils. Seeds should be planted in the spring and seedlings thinned to 15 cm (6 in) apart. Roots are harvested in the autumn. Some gardeners mix wood chips and sawdust into burdock beds to make the roots easier to harvest.

❧ CULINARY USE In Japan, burdock root is commonly eaten as a vegetable called *gobo*. The roots are slivered, soaked in water to remove their bitter flavour, and stir-fried with sesame oil and soy sauce. Found in sushi bars worldwide, burdock roots are also eaten raw in salads or cooked like carrots. In Scandinavian countries, the young spring leaves are eaten in salads.

❧ MEDICINAL USE Burdock roots and seeds contain bitter glycosides, flavonoids and tannins. In Traditional Chinese Medicine, burdock has long been considered an important blood purifier and is included in formulas designed to detoxify the liver and improve digestion.

Modern research indicates that burdock may have a liver-protective effect, as well as anti-inflammatory and antioxidant properties. Burdock is a mild antibacterial agent, making it useful in the topical and internal treatment of skin conditions including acne and boils. It also contains a substance called arctigenin, which has demonstrated anti-tumour effects in animal studies. Burdock is usually taken in combination with other herbs, such as dandelion.

❧ DOSAGE Tea: Use 0.5 litre (8 oz) three times daily. **Tincture:** Use 1 ml (0.03 oz) two or three times daily.

ARMORACIA RUSTICANA

HORSERADISH

Horseradish, a large-rooted perennial native to Europe and Asia, is naturalized in many parts of the world. A member of the Brassicaceae (mustard) family – which includes kale and cauliflower – horseradish bears broad, lance-shaped leaves and tiny, white, four-petalled flowers.

❧ GROWING CONDITIONS Horseradish prefers loose, rich, well-drained soil in full sun or partial shade. Root divisions may be planted in the early spring or autumn. Seeds may be planted in the spring. Seedlings should be thinned to 31 cm (12 in) apart. Horseradish leaves should be harvested in the spring; the roots should be harvested in the autumn.

❧ CULINARY USE Horseradish is one of the five bitter herbs included in the traditional Jewish Passover ceremony. The leaves are sometimes included as an ingredient in salads, but the plant is mainly used for its pungent, spicy roots, which are grated and included in sauces and condiments.

❧ MEDICINAL USE Horseradish root contains isothiocyanates (sulphur compounds also found in garlic and onions), as well as sulforaphane, an

A

antioxidant in broccoli. Both agents clear sinus congestion, open nasal passages, and promote epidermal blood flow. Horseradish has antibiotic properties, making it useful for treating respiratory and urinary-tract infections. **Note:** Those suffering from gastrointestinal or kidney disorders should not take horseradish in therapeutic doses.

DOSAGE Tea: Use 1 ml (0.03 oz) three times daily. **Fresh:** Eat 1 to 2 tbsp daily or in a dressing, as desired. **Poultice:** Grate fresh horseradish root and spread onto a linen cloth. Apply the cloth to the skin until a burning sensation is experienced.

Arnica Montana

ARNICA, EUROPEAN ARNICA, LEOPARD'S BANE, MOUNTAIN TOBACCO

Arnica, a member of the Asteraceae (daisy) family, is an aromatic perennial native to Europe. Other *Arnica* species, such as American arnica and North American meadow arnica, are native to mountainous areas of western North America. Arnica bears ovate, hairy leaves and yellow, daisylike flowers. Its name may be derived from *arnakis*, the ancient Greek word for "lambskin", in reference to the plant's soft leaves.

GROWING CONDITIONS Arnica grows in well-drained, acidic, humus-rich soil in full sun. Seeds may be planted in the autumn; root divisions may be planted in the spring. The plant makes a good addition to a rock garden. It is advisable to plant arnica in raised beds, as the plant dislikes too much moisture during the winter. Flowers may be harvested when fully open.

CULINARY USE None.

MEDICINAL USE Arnica has anti-inflammatory and antiseptic properties. It is toxic, and so is traditionally used externally to treat sprains, bruises, swelling and rheumatic pain. It is a key ingredient in first-aid creams and gels. Arnica is a popular remedy around the world, but particularly in Europe; there are 300 arnica products available on

the German market alone. **Note:** Arnica ointments or creams should not be applied to broken skin; it may cause contact dermatitis. Arnica should not be taken internally except homeopathically under the guidance of a healthcare professional. Because the herb has been over-harvested in the wild, it is best to purchase preparations made from cultivated arnica or those made from plants such as calendula (*Calendula officinalis*) and yarrow (*Achillea millefolium*).

DOSAGE Creams, salves, gels, and ointments: Follow label directions. **Homeopathic remedies:** Follow label directions.

Artemisia Dracunculus

ESTRAGON, FRENCH TARRAGON, TARRAGON

Native to southern Europe and Asia, French tarragon is cultivated in North America and northern Europe. This aromatic perennial, a member of the Asteraceae (daisy) family, has upright stems, bears tiny green flowers, and has smooth leaves with a mint-anise flavour. "Tarragon" is a corruption of the French *esdragon*, derived from the Latin *dracunculus* ("little dragon"), which may allude to the herb's sharp taste, its reputation as a treatment for poisonous insect bites and stings, or its purported ability to kill intestinal parasites.

GROWING CONDITIONS French tarragon grows in well-drained, slightly alkaline or neutral soil in full sun. Seeds should be planted in the spring; cuttings should be planted in the summer. Leaves may be harvested before the plant flowers in the summer.

CULINARY USE Tarragon leaves, widely used in French cooking, are added to egg and chicken dishes, sauces, and salad dressings. The herb is a key ingredient in béarnaise sauce and is one of the ingredients in the popular French herb mix *fines herbes*.

MEDICINAL USE Tarragon, like other culinary herbs, has been shown to have antibacterial properties. The crushed leaves are used widely in the kitchen and garden to treat minor wounds, and are applied directly to the skin. Tarragon oil contains eugenol, a compound that has anaesthetic properties, making it an effective temporary treatment for oral pain. The oil also contains rutin, a compound known to strengthen blood vessel walls. The herb has been used as a treatment for varicose veins and haemorrhoids and also contains estragole, which is carcinogenic when given in large amounts to animals. The plant also contains anti-carcinogenic compounds. The significance of this is unclear, but tarragon appears to have been safely consumed by humans for centuries. **Note:** Tarragon should not be taken by pregnant women in therapeutic doses, although it is safe to consume in small doses as a spice in food. The herb should not be taken therapeutically for periods exceeding four weeks.

DOSAGE Tea: Use up to 0.75 litre (24 oz) daily.

AVENA SATIVA

OATS

Native to the Mediterranean region, this grain-producing grass has been cultivated throughout Europe since around 2000 B.C.E. It is now grown in northern temperate areas across the globe, wherever water and humidity are plentiful. An annual member of the Poaceae (grass) family, oats has flat leaves, smooth, thin stems, and pendulous, seed-containing spikes in the summer. Oats are grown as animal feed and as a cereal grain for humans.

GROWING CONDITIONS Oats grow in well-drained, fertile soil in full sun. Seeds are planted in the spring, and the plants are harvested in the summer, before the seeds are fully ripe, and then threshed to separate the grain from the stems. The grain's husks are removed during processing.

CULINARY USE Oats are the most nutritious cereal grass available. They are consumed as fibre-rich oat groats (oats that have been cleaned, toasted, and hulled), rolled oats (oat groats that have been steamed and flattened), or oat bran (the outer casing of the oats). Rolled oats are usually eaten in breakfast cereals such as muesli and oatmeal.

MEDICINAL USE Oat bran contains soluble fibre, which increases the elimination of cholesterol and has been shown to lower the body's cholesterol, triglyceride and blood pressure. When oats are consumed, soluble fibre traps cholesterol in the intestines and eliminates it through the stools. Fibre also helps prevent constipation. It attracts water, creating soft, bulky stools that stimulate bowel movements. Oat are used externally in products that help relieve the pain and itching of skin conditions such as dryness and eczema.

DOSAGE Tea: Steep 1 tbsp dried oat tops in 0.5 litre (8 oz) water for 15 minutes; strain and drink 0.5 litre (8 oz) three or four times daily. **Tincture:** Use 2 to 3 ml (0.07 to 0.1 oz) three to four times daily. **Cooked:** Eat 227 g (8 oz) oatmeal daily.

AZADIRACHTA INDICA

BEAD TREE, NEEM, NIMBA, MARGOSA

Native to India, Pakistan and Sri Lanka, this large, fast-growing evergreen tree can be found in tropical areas of western Africa, Indonesia and Australia. A member of the Meliaceae (mahogany) family, the neem tree can reach heights of 15 m (50 ft) tall. It bears bright green, oval leaves and small, yellowish-white, fragrant flowers.

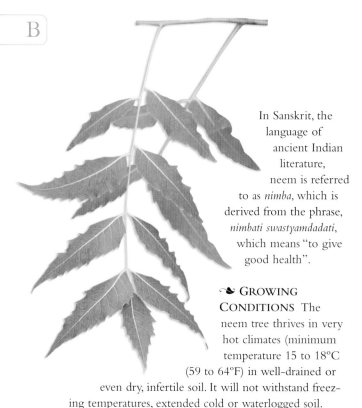

In Sanskrit, the language of ancient Indian literature, neem is referred to as *nimba*, which is derived from the phrase, *nimbati swastyamdadati*, which means "to give good health".

🌿 GROWING CONDITIONS The neem tree thrives in very hot climates (minimum temperature 15 to 18°C (59 to 64°F) in well-drained or even dry, infertile soil. It will not withstand freezing temperatures, extended cold or waterlogged soil.

🌿 CULINARY USE The flowers produce a nectar that is commonly used as a sweetener. Neem leaf and bark have a bitter flavour and are commercially available as a tea, often combined with herbs such as spearmint and cinnamon.

🌿 MEDICINAL USE The compounds in neem include triterpenes, tannins and volatile oil, which have anti-inflammatory, fever-reducing and vermifuge properties. Internally, the herb has been used to treat malaria, inflammation, tuberculosis, scabies, jaundice, intestinal worms, ulcers, diabetes and skin conditions. Externally, neem oil has been used to treat lice, ringworm, eczema, fungal infections and painful joints. It is a popular ingredient in hair- and skincare products. Small sticks of neem wood have long been used as toothbrushes.

🌿 DOSAGE Tea: Use 0.5 litre (8 oz) two or three times daily. **Tincture:** Use 40 drops three times daily. **Standardized extract:** Take two 500 mg capsules three times daily. **Ointment:** Follow label directions.

*B*AROSMA CRENULATA SYN. AGATHOSMA CRENULATA

BUCHU, OVATE BUCHU

Native to South Africa, buchu is a low-growing, tender shrub in the Rutaceae (rue) family. It bears white, five-petalled flowers and pale green, finely toothed leaves with a strongly aromatic taste and scent reminiscent of blackcurrant. The leaves are dotted with oil glands, which are visible when the leaves are held up to the light.

🌿 GROWING CONDITIONS Buchu is a popular ornamental plant in warm regions and a common potted patio plant in temperate areas. It thrives in well-drained, acidic soil under full sun, at a minimum temperature of 5°C (41°F). Cuttings can be planted in the late summer, and leaves should be harvested when the plant flowers in the spring.

🌿 CULINARY USE Buchu leaves are a key ingredient in the liqueur cassis. In parts of Africa, the herb is used to flavour brandy and wine. Buchu oil is added to ice cream, sweets, baked goods, condiments and relishes, and is used in artificial fruit flavourings, especially blackcurrant products. It is also an ingredient in perfumes.

🌿 MEDICINAL USE Buchu contains constituents with antiseptic, diuretic and antispasmodic properties. The herb has been used to stimulate and cleanse the

urinary tract, making it useful (in combination with other herbs such as cornsilk and juniper) as a treatment for acute cystitis. It has also been used to treat chest congestion, digestive ailments and gout. **Note:** Buchu should not be taken by women during pregnancy, while breastfeeding, or by those who suffer from kidney inflammation.

DOSAGE Tea: Use 0.5 litre (8 oz) two or three times daily. **Tincture:** Use 40 drops three times daily. **Standardized extract:** Take one 500 mg capsule twice daily.

*B*ERBERIS VULGARIS

BARBERRY, EUROPEAN BARBERRY

Barberry is native to Europe, naturalized in eastern North America and widely cultivated in India. A member of the Berberidaceae (barberry) family, this erect deciduous shrub has long, flexible branches, bristly leaves and bears yellow flowers and red, oval berries.

GROWING CONDITIONS Barberry shrubs thrive in moist, well-drained soil under full sun or partial shade. The shrub grows densely and is often planted in hedges. Seeds are planted in the spring or summer. The berries are gathered in the autumn; the bark is gathered in the spring or autumn.

CULINARY USE Barberry's juicy, tart berries have a high vitamin C content. They are a common ingredient in jams, and can be candied and used in baked goods such as muffins and quick breads.

MEDICINAL USE Barberry contains berberine, a powerfully antimicrobial alkaloid that has been used to treat gastrointestinal conditions such as diarrhoea and constipation. Barberry acts as a cholagogue, stimulating the flow of bile from the liver. It has been used to treat liver congestion, as well as inflammation of the gallbladder. The herb may have anti-cancer, and immune-supporting properties, and may be effective in combating antibiotic-resistant bacteria. **Note:** Barberry should not be taken during pregnancy. Because of its antimicrobial effects, barberry can deplete intestinal bacteria (similar to the effect of antibiotics) and its use should be followed by a course of acidophilus.

DOSAGE Tea: Use 0.5 litre (8 oz) three times daily as needed. **Tincture:** Use 1 or 2 ml (0.03 or 0.07 oz) two times daily. **Standardized extract:** Take one or two 450 mg capsules twice daily.

*B*ETULA PENDULA

BIRCH, EUROPEAN WHITE BIRCH, SILVER BIRCH, WEEPING BIRCH

Widely cultivated for its ornamental silver-white bark in northern regions of the globe, this deciduous tree is native to Europe and Asia. A member of the Betulaceae (birch) family, it is fast-growing and has a limited life span. The tree's leaves turn yellow in the autumn, and its bark develops dark spots with age. Birch wood was once used to make writing materials.

B

🌿 **GROWING CONDITIONS** Birch trees are hardy and tolerant of a wide range of habitats, though they thrive in dry, sandy soil in sunny or partially shady locations. Leaf buds and young leaves are harvested in the spring.

🌿 **CULINARY USE** The tree's sap has been used as an ingredient in wine and vinegar. Birch bark, which has a crisp, wintergreenlike taste, is a key ingredient in the soft drinks birch beer and root beer.

🌿 **MEDICINAL USE** Birch oil, distilled from the tree's leaves, is rich in methyl salicylate, a pain-reliever (also found in wintergreen) that does not irritate the stomach. Salicylate staves off the body's production of prostaglandins associated with fever and inflammation of muscles, bones, and connective tissues caused by injuries or arthritis. Birch oil is also used topically in creams and ointments to treat eczema and psoriasis. Birch bark contains phytochemicals that may have astringent, diuretic, antiviral and anti-tumour properties. The leaves, bark and oil have been used to treat bladder stones, kidney stones and urinary tract infections.

🌿 **DOSAGE Tea:** Use 0.5 litre (8 oz) two or three times daily. **Oil:** Follow label directions.

*B*ORAGO OFFICINALIS
BORAGE

Borage, a member of the Boraginaceae (borage) family, is a hairy or prickly annual native to the Mediterranean and naturalized in parts of North America, throughout Europe and in parts of Australia. The plant's name is thought to derive from the Latin *borra*, meaning "a hairy garment", in reference to its bristly leaves. Borage bears edible, bee-attracting, bright blue star-shaped flowers, which bloom for most of the summer.

🌿 **GROWING CONDITIONS** Borage grows best in well-drained, moist soil in full sun. The plant will tolerate poor soil but grows larger and healthier in better conditions. A prolific plant, borage will self-seed rapidly in the garden. Seeds are planted in the spring, and seedlings should be thinned to 46 cm (18 in) apart. The leaves may be harvested in the spring or summer as the plant begins flowering. Flowers may be picked as they open.

🌿 **CULINARY USE** Borage flowers have a cucumber-like flavour, and are a tasty and attractive addition to salads. They can be used as a garnish, floating on a cold soup or punch, or decorating a cake. The flowers have prickly backs that should be removed before serving.

🌿 **MEDICINAL USE** Although modern science has found little evidence that borage flowers or leaves have any therapeutic effects, borage leaf tea has been used traditionally to treat fevers and bronchial infections. Borage seed oil is a rich source of gamma-linolenic acid (GLA), a compound that helps balance abnormalities of essential fatty acids. It can be taken to relieve premenstrual discomfort, thrombosis and chronic inflammation, as in multiple sclerosis. The oil is also used to treat fevers, bronchial infections, oral infections, dry skin conditions and chronic nephritis. According to one clinical study, borage seed oil may reduce the effects of stress on the body by lowering heart rate and systolic blood pressure.

🌿 **DOSAGE Standardized extract:** Take 1,000 to 1,300 mg of borage oil daily, which provides 240 to 300 mg of GLA.

*B*OSWELLIA SERRATA
BOSWELLIA, INDIAN FRANKINCENSE, INDIAN OLIBANUM

A member of the Burseraceae (frankincense) family, boswellia is native to tropical Asia and Africa. It is often found in hilly areas of India. Plants in the Burseraceae family, which grow as evergreen bushes or small trees with small, white, fragrant flowers, are characterized by resin ducts in their thick, aromatic bark. When cuts are made in the bark, a milky fluid emerges and hardens

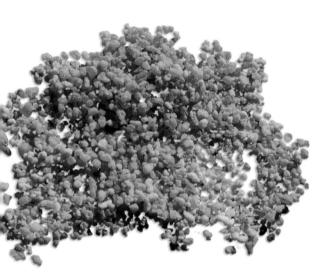

upon contact with the air. The *Boswellia* genus includes twenty-five species, including *B. sacra* or frankincense. Creams containing boswellia extract are used to relieve the aches and pains of arthritis, and to moisturize dry skin and minimize wrinkles. Boswellia has a soft, balsamic scent, and is commonly used in perfume-making.

🌿 GROWING CONDITIONS Boswellia trees grow in dry, hilly areas in warm climates. They prefer well-drained to dry soil in full sun.

🌿 CULINARY USE None.

🌿 MEDICINAL USE The solidified resin of the boswellia is made into capsules and tablets for internal use and creams, perfume, and cosmetics for external use. Boswellia resin contains anti-inflammatory compounds, including boswellic acids, which may be helpful in the treatment of rheumatoid arthritis and bowel disorders such as ulcerative colitis and Crohn's disease. Studies have shown that boswellia may be as effective as synthetic drugs in treating these conditions, without the side effects of pharmaceuticals. In Indian Ayurvedic medicine, boswellia (called *shallak*) is used as an astringent to treat diarrhoea and included in ointments used to treat sores and boils. Boswellia seeds are taken to encourage hair growth.

🌿 DOSAGE Standardized extract: Take one 195 mg capsule three times daily. **Standardized extract:** Use three 400 mg capsules standardized to 65 percent boswellic acids three times daily. **Note:** As a resin, frankincense is not soluble in water, so it is not useful in tea form.

*B*RASSICA JUNCEA

BROWN MUSTARD, CHINESE MUSTARD, INDIAN MUSTARD, LARGE-LEAF MUSTARD, MUSTARD

There are about thirty species of mustard. Brown mustard, an annual with pale yellow flowers, is native to Eurasia, but now grows throughout temperate regions of the world. The word "mustard" comes from the Roman words *mustum* and *ardens*, meaning "burning wine". In ancient Roman times, the seeds of the plant were ground and mixed with must, unfermented grape juice. Today, mustard seeds are ground and mixed with vinegar, water and salt to make the familiar condiment, mustard. In addition to brown mustard, other species include *B. alba*, white mustard, and *B. nigra*, black mustard.

🌿 GROWING CONDITIONS Mustard grows in rich, well-drained soil in full sun. Seeds are planted in the spring. Leaves and flowers may be harvested when they are young; seedpods are harvested when they begin to change colour from green to brown. They are then dried to finish ripening so that valuable seeds will not fall out of the pods while still in the field.

🌿 CULINARY USE The condiment mustard is available in three basic varieties. American mustard uses the less pungent white mustard seeds (*B. alba*), and is coloured with turmeric to make the finished paste appear yellow. English mustard uses white and black seeds (*B. alba* and *B. nigra*). French, or Dijon, mustard is made with brown seeds (*B. juncea*). Mustard seeds are used as a spice to flavour curries, relishes and pickles. The leaves can be added to salads or cooked as a vegetable.

C

❧ **MEDICINAL USE** Mustard seeds contain a volatile oil with antibacterial and antifungal properties, brought out when cold water is added to dried, ground, ripe seeds. Native Americans once made a tea of the seeds to treat coughs and improve digestion. Mustard seed oil is absorbed through the skin and eliminated by the lungs. It has long been used externally in liniments, plasters and poultices, which are applied directly to the chest to relieve lung congestion and the symptoms of the common cold. Mustard seed can also be used to relieve muscle, joint and back pain. **Note:** Prolonged external contact with mustard seed oil, as in a plaster left on the skin for too long, may cause blistering. Topical preparations should not be used on children younger than six years of age.

❧ **DOSAGE** **Tea:** Use 0.5 litre (8 oz) two or three times daily. **Liniment:** Follow label directions. **Poultice or plaster:** Combine 3 tbsp of flour and 1 tbsp dried, ground mustard seed with enough hot water to make a paste. Smooth the paste onto a linen cloth or clean sheet, and apply to skin.

CALENDULA OFFICINALIS

CALENDULA, COMMON MARIGOLD, POT MARIGOLD

A member of the Asteraceae (daisy) family, calendula is native to the Mediterranean region and northern Africa, and is naturalized all over the world. This bushy, long-lived annual has been grown since the Middle Ages and bears bright yellow to orange flowers that are so brilliantly coloured they were once said to be reflections of the sun. Dried calendula flowers were traditionally included as ingredients in soups and stews, eaten to help ward off illness. The herb was also used as a dye for food, fabrics and cosmetics. Used in hair rinses, calendula brings out gold highlights in the hair. Calendula should not be confused with the French or African marigold (*Tagetes* spp.), which is a strongly scented, orange-flowering ornamental, commonly planted in gardens or in flower beds to deter pests.

❧ **GROWING CONDITIONS** Calendula's long flowering season was first noted by the ancient Greeks and Romans; in fact, the name Calendula comes from

the Latin word *calends*, which means "calendar". Calendula grows in well-drained soil in full sun. The herb self-seeds readily, so dead flower heads should be removed immediately during blooming periods to prevent excessive self-seeding and also to prolong duration of flowering. Flowers may be harvested when the plant is dry. *Calendula officinalis* 'Prolifera', also known as hen-and-chickens calendula, has long been a popular garden plant. Its main flower head produces several smaller flowers from its base.

❧ **CULINARY USE** Calendula petals make a colourful addition to green salads, and have been used as an economical, though less vividly coloured, substitute for saffron in cheese, rice dishes and soups. Calendula leaves can be eaten raw, but some people find their flavour unpleasant. When using petals in food, be sure to use those from flowers that have not been treated with pesticides. The dried, powdered herb is sometimes used as a natural colouring agent.

❧ **MEDICINAL USE** In ancient Greece and Rome, calendula was taken internally as a tea to treat stomach ailments and applied externally as a poultice to treat superficial skin wounds. Today, calendula leaves and flowers, which contain triterpenes and flavonoids, are common ingredients in topical salves and creams used to decrease the inflammation of skin irritations such as rashes, insect bites and burns. It has traditionally been used to treat nappy rash and cradle cap. A mild tea may help soothe sore nipples. The herb is also used to treat inflammatory eye conditions, such as conjunctivitis. It has mild cleansing properties; calendula tea can be used as a gargle to treat sore throat or mouth inflammation. A mild infusion may be used as a douche to treat yeast infections. Calendula tea or tincture is taken to ease inflammatory digestive conditions such as gastritis, colitis and peptic ulcers. **Note:** Those allergic to other members of the aster family, such as ragweed, may also be sensitive to calendula.

❧ **DOSAGE** **Tea:** Use 0.5 litre (8 oz) two or three times daily. **Tincture:** Take 1 ml (0.03 oz) three times daily. **Gargle or mouthwash:** Mix 1 tsp calendula tincture per 0.5 litre (8 oz) of water. **Salves and creams:** Follow label directions.

Calendula officinalis, *which is derived from the Latin word* calendae, *meaning "first day of the month", is an annual flower that prefers cooler temperatures. With its insect-repellent properties,* Calendula, *often called pot marigold, is a popular addition to gardens. Easy to care for and fast-growing, it is often cut and used in floral arrangements.*

CAMELLIA SINENSIS

BLACK TEA, CHINESE TEA, GREEN TEA, TEA

Native to Asia, the tea plant is extensively cultivated in tropical and subtropical countries, including China, India, Sri Lanka, Indonesia and Japan. This evergreen shrub or small tree, a member of the Theaceae (tea) family, can grow to 9 m (30 ft) tall in the wild. In cultivation, the plant is grown as a bushy shrub to facilitate the harvesting of its dark green leaves. Tea has a remarkably long history of use as a beverage in China, Japan and India, the largest tea-producing nation in the world. These cultures believe that drinking tea optimize their health and ensured longevity. Tea leaves contain caffeine, a mild stimulant; Eastern religious practitioners once drank tea to stay awake during long meditations. When tea was first introduced in North America, early settlers applied cooled tea bags as a poultice to puffy eyes. Cooled tea was also used as a wash to treat sunburn.

GROWING CONDITIONS The tea plant grows best in regions that enjoy a warm, humid climate with ample rainfall. Tea will grow in shade or direct sunlight in areas from sea level up to altitudes as high as 2,500 m (8,200) ft. The flavour of tea leaves can be affected by the type of soil, altitude and climate of the area in which the plant is grown.

CULINARY USE Tea is widely enjoyed as a beverage, both hot and cold around the world. There are many tea varieties, including bancha, black tea, genmaicha, green tea, hojicha, kukicha, matcha, oolong, sencha and white. Black tea leaves are fermented; green tea leaves are not. Oolong tea leaves are semi-fermented. Tea extract is used as a flavouring agent in many food products, including ice cream, sweets, baked goods and puddings.

MEDICINAL USE Both black and green teas are rich in free radical-fighting antioxidants, and both have similar heart health and anticancer benefits. Since the mid 1980s, an impressive number of scientific studies have suggested green tea's ability to protect the body against cancer as well as heart disease and ulcers. Tea is second only to water as the world's most popular beverage. It is estimated that 88 percent of the Chinese population drinks it every day. Green tea has been used as a mouthwash to prevent plaque formation on the teeth, and may be taken internally to treat diarrhoea and to invigorate the mind and central nervous system. Black tea acts as an astringent, which makes it useful for treating diarrhoea. Black tea has a stimulating effect on the central nervous system, generally evinced by a feeling of comfort and exhilaration, although it can also cause insomnia when taken in large quantities. **Note:** Tea contains caffeine, which can cause nervousness, heart palpitations, anxiety, insomnia and digestive disturbances. It should be avoided by pregnant women and by people who suffer from hypertension, anxiety, eating disorders, diabetes and ulcers.

DOSAGE Tea: Drink 0.5 to 1 litre (16 to 40 oz) daily, using 1 tsp of tea leaves to 0.25 litre (8 oz) of water. **Standardized extract:** Take one 250 to 400 mg capsule daily standardized to 90 percent polyphenols.

CANANGA ODORATA

YLANG YLANG

A member of the Annonaceae (cherimoya) family, this exotic evergreen tree is native to tropical lowland forests in areas ranging from India to northern Australia, and is cultivated in tropical areas of Africa and Asia. The tree's drooping branches bear oblong leaves and strongly scented flowers that have six narrow, yellow petals that bloom all year. The name "ylang ylang" means "flower of flowers", and, indeed, the flowers are highly prized for their essential oil, which is clear with a yellow tinge. The scent of ylang ylang oil can vary substantially, depending upon the climate where the tree is grown. As a result, commercially available ylang ylang oils may have distinctly different aromas, from fresh and floral to sweet and slightly fruity.

$\mathcal{C}$APSICUM ANNUUM

CAYENNE PEPPER, CHILI PEPPER, RED PEPPER, TABASCO PEPPER

A member of the Solanaceae (nightshade) family, cayenne pepper is a tender annual or short-lived perennial, native to South America and cultivated in warm regions throughout the world. The plant was taken by the Portuguese to Europe, India, and Africa in the 16th century. Cayenne pepper bears white, bell-shaped flowers, followed by fruits that are generally green but turn red as they ripen. The genus name, *Capsicum*, is thought to refer to these hollow fruits; the Latin capsa means "box". Used by ancient Mayan Indians to treat mouth sores, cayenne pepper was first described in 1493 by a physician travelling with the explorer Christopher Columbus (1451–1506). Cayenne pepper's primary compound, capsaicin, is the main ingredient in many self-defence pepper sprays.

GROWING CONDITIONS Cayenne peppers grow in rich, well-drained soil in full sun, in areas with a minimum temperature of 18 to 21°C (64 to 70°F). Seeds may be planted in the early spring. Unripe peppers may be picked at any time; ripe peppers are harvested in the summer. Many popular cultivars are available.

CULINARY USE After black pepper, cayenne pepper is the second most popular spice in the world. It is used in the spicy dishes of many tropical and subtropical countries, including Mexico, Spain and India. Ranging from pungent to sweet, different varieties of cayenne are dried, ground and used to make the spices cayenne, chilli powder and paprika. Cayenne is the main flavouring in many hot sauces, including Tabasco®. Cayenne is used in curries, chutneys, bean dishes and savoury egg and cheese dishes.

GROWING CONDITIONS Ylang ylang grows in well-drained, moist soil in full sun, in areas of extreme humidity and minimum temperatures of 10 to 18°C (50 to 64°F). Ylang ylang flowers are harvested at night, and dried for tea or distilled for essential oil.

CULINARY USE Ylang ylang oil is used to enhance peach and apricot flavourings.

MEDICINAL USE Ylang ylang's flowers and essential oil have sedative and antimicrobial properties. The oil also has a long-standing reputation as an aphrodisiac. Aromatherapists consider ylang ylang to be one of the most relaxing fragrances for both the mind and the body. It is often combined with other oils – particularly bergamot, lemon and sandalwood – and made into massage oils or added to baths to enhance relaxation. **Note:** Essential oil of ylang ylang is only for external use. It should be used lightly, as the intensity of its scent may cause headache or nausea.

DOSAGE **Aromatherapy bath:** Add 5 drops of essential oil to a bath of warm water. **Aromatherapy massage oil:** Add 10 to 20 drops of essential oil to 30 ml (1 oz) almond or jojoba oil, and shake to mix.

C

MEDICINAL USE Cayenne pepper contains antioxidant carotenoids, and is rich in vitamin C. The herb's pungency is due to the well-known and studied constituent called capsaicin. In external products, such as ointments and creams available over-the-counter and by prescription, minute amounts of capsaicin irritate the body tissue, which increases blood supply to painful areas and blocks the transmission of pain impulses throughout the body. Capsaicin is used in this manner to treat conditions such as arthritis, minor sprains, shingles and carpal tunnel syndrome. Commercially available capsaicin creams, not homemade cayenne pepper preparations, should be used for these purposes. Cayenne also has antiseptic properties, and has been shown to inhibit the growth of *Helicobacter pylori,* the bacterium shown to cause ulcers. Cayenne pepper is believed to help warm the body. It has been used to treat fevers, and to stimulate the digestive and circulatory systems. **Note:** Cayenne pepper should not be taken by those who have peptic ulcers or acid indigestion, or in medicinal doses by pregnant or nursing women. The herb is very irritating to the eyes and mucous membranes. It should not be applied to wounds or broken skin. When cutting cayenne peppers, it is important to wear rubber gloves and not to touch the eyes, because the capsaicin can burn the skin and delicate membranes such as those of the eye.

DOSAGE **Tea:** Use ½ tsp cayenne powder in 0.25 litre (8 oz) of hot water daily. **Tincture:** Add 5 to 10 drops to 118 to 237 ml (4 to 8 oz) of water once daily. **Standardized extract:** Take one to three 500 mg capsules twice daily. **Ointments and creams:** Use those containing 0.025 to 0.075 percent capsaicin: Follow label directions carefully.

$\mathcal{C}$ARICA
PAPAYA
⤬
PAPAYA

Papaya, of the Caricaceae (papaya) family, belongs to a genus of twenty-two species of trees and shrubs. The best known variety is *Carica papaya*, native to lowland rainforests of South America and cultivated in tropical areas all over the world. Papaya is a fast-growing evergreen tree that bears seven-lobed, palmate leaves and pear-shaped yellow to orange fruits with black seeds. The fruits can weigh up to 5 kg (11 lb). Both male and female trees are needed for fruiting, but a cultivar called *Carica papaya* 'Solo' produces male and female flowers on one plant.

GROWING CONDITIONS Papaya trees grow in rich, moist soil in sun, in areas of high humidity and minimum temperatures of 13 to 15°C (55 to 59°F). The trees reach their full height of about 6 m (20 feet) in 18 months. Seeds are planted in the spring, when temperatures range from 24 to 30°C (75 to 86°F). The leaves may be harvested at any time; the fruit is harvested when ripe.

CULINARY USE Ripe papayas are an excellent source of vitamins A and C. They can be eaten as fruit or added to desserts. Unripe, green papayas may be steamed, boiled or roasted like a vegetable. Papaya's black peppery-tasting seeds are edible and are used in salad dressings. Hundreds of years ago, native Caribbean Indians noticed that, when they wrapped meat in papaya leaves, the meat became more tender. This is due to the plant's protein-digesting properties. Today, papaya extract is the primary ingredient in many commercially available meat tenderizers.

MEDICINAL USE Unripe papaya contains papain, an enzyme similar to the human digestive enzyme pepsin. Papain helps digest protein. It is available in supplement form, and can be taken to treat poor digestion and stomach inflammation. A tea made from papaya leaves may also be taken as a mild digestive aid. Ripe papaya has gentle laxative effects. Papaya may help protect the stomach from ulcers caused by aspirin and steroid medications. **Note:** Papaya's seeds, leaves and unripe fruit should be avoided during pregnancy. In addition, papaya leaf should not be ingested by children younger than two years of age.

DOSAGE **Tea (leaf):** Drink 0.25 litre (8 oz) daily, during or after meals. **Standardized extract:** Take 100 mg of papain daily.

CARUM CARVI
CARAWAY

A member of the Apiaceae (parsley) family, this biennial is native to Asia Minor. It also grows in northern and central Europe and Asia, and is cultivated in North America and North Africa. The plant bears fernlike leaves and umbels of tiny white to pink flowers, which are followed by aromatic, narrow seeds. Caraway seed has been used medicinally and in cooking since at least 3500 B.C.E. It is one of the only herbs whose primary medicinal use (as a digestive aid) has remained the same throughout history.

❧ GROWING CONDITIONS Caraway grows in well-drained soil in full sun. Seeds are planted in the spring or early autumn. The plant will self-seed in favourable conditions but does not transplant well. The seeds may be gathered when ripe and then dried for use.

❧ CULINARY USE Caraway is perhaps best known as the flavouring in rye bread. The seeds are also popular in the cuisines of Germany, Austria and Hungary, where they are used to flavour cheese, bread, meat, stew, vegetables, sauerkraut and pickling brines. Caraway is also used to flavour the German liqueur Kümmel. Caraway leaves have a mild flavour similar to caraway seeds. The plant's roots may be cooked as a vegetable.

❧ MEDICINAL USE The volatile oil in caraway contains the constituents carvol and carvene, compounds that help soothe the digestive tract and expel intestinal gas. The herb has long been used to treat flatulence and colic in babies. Caraway also has antispasmodic properties, and may be useful in the treatment of menstrual

cramps and diarrhoea. **Note:** Pregnant or breastfeeding women should avoid medicinal doses of caraway; small doses used in cooking are not harmful. If giving the herb to colicky infants, a low-strength infusion should be used.

❧ DOSAGE Tea: Take up to 0.75 litre (24 oz) daily. **Tincture:** Use 0.5 to 1 ml (0.015 to 0.03 oz) up to three times daily. **Fresh or dried seeds:** Chew 1 tsp as needed.

CASSIA SENNA
SYN. SENNA ALEXANDRINA

ALEXANDRIAN SENNA, INDIAN SENNA, SENNA, TINNEVELLY SENNA, TRUE SENNA

A member of the Fabaceae (pea) family, senna is native to Egypt and Sudan and is cultivated throughout the warm regions of the world. The genus *Cassia* contains more than 400 species. The species of senna used medicinally is grown in the Tinnevelly region of India, hence one of the herb's common names. A shrubby, woody perennial herb with a tea-like aroma, senna bears slender, hairy leaves and small yellow flowers followed by seedpods up to 8 cm (3 in) long.

❧ GROWING CONDITIONS Senna grows in well-drained soil in full sun. The plant cannot tolerate temperatures lower than 5°C (41°F). Seeds may be planted in the spring; semi-ripe cuttings may be planted in the summer.

❧ **CULINARY USE** None.

❧ **MEDICINAL USE** Senna has a long history of use as a laxative in both Eastern and Western herbalism. Arab physicians first wrote of the herb's bowel-stimulating effects in the 9th century, but senna was probably used for centuries before that. The herb contains compounds called anthraquinones, which stimulate the colon. When senna is digested, the herb provokes intestinal contractions, thereby speeding the body's elimination of waste. Senna is one of the most potent natural laxatives available, often taken with carminative (digestion-improving) herbs, such as ginger (*Zingiber officinale*), both to reduce intestinal cramping and to mask senna's bitter and unpleasant (even nauseating) taste. Senna is an ingredient in many commercial laxatives. **Note:** Senna may cause intestinal discomfort and cramping. To reduce the risk of laxative dependency, the herb should not be used for more than one week unless directed by a healthcare provider. It should not be taken by women who are pregnant or breastfeeding, by children younger than ten years of age, or by anyone suffering from chronic gastro-intestinal conditions, such as colitis or ulcers.

❧ **DOSAGE** **Over-the-counter laxatives:** Follow label directions. **Tincture:** Take ½ to 1 tsp in the morning.

lengthen life; in folklore, the long memories of elephants has been attributed to their consumption of gotu kola leaves.

❧ **GROWING CONDITIONS** Gotu kola grows abundantly in marshy and wet areas. Seeds are planted in the spring in moist to wet soil in sun or partial shade. The herb's leaves can be harvested year-round.

❧ **CULINARY USE** In Thailand, India and Sri Lanka, gotu kola leaves are eaten raw as a vegetable in salads or cooked in curries. It is also consumed as a beverage.

❧ **MEDICINAL USE** Gotu kola leaves contain phyto-chemicals that are believed to accelerate the formation of collagen and reduce the formation of scar tissue, making the herb useful in the healing of superficial wounds. It may also be helpful in the treatment of conditions involving the veins and connective tissues, such as varicose veins and oedema. The herb has adaptogenic properties for the skin, making it a common ingredient in topical preparations that help skin recover from burns, sunburn and wounds. **Note:** Gotu kola may cause sensitivity to sunlight. The herb should not be taken by children younger than two years of age.

❧ **DOSAGE** **Tea:** Drink 0.5 to 0.75 litre (16 to 24 oz) two or three times daily. **Tincture:** Take 2 to 4 ml (0.07 to 0.14 oz) two or three times daily. Products made from fresh gotu kola plants are preferable, as the herb rapidly loses its medicinal properties when dried.

*C*ENTELLA ASIATICA

ASIAN PENNYWORT, GOTU KOLA, INDIAN PENNYWORT

More than 20 species belong to the genus *Centella*. Gotu kola (*C. asiatica*), a member of Apiaceae (parsley) family, is native to southern North America and India, and is also found in tropical and subtropical areas of Africa, Asia and Australia. A smaller version of the plant is grown in temperate regions of North America, often as an annual in colder regions. A low-growing perennial, gotu kola produces clusters of scalloped leaves and tiny pink flowers. The herb has been used traditionally to

*C*HAMAEMELUM NOBILE SYN. ANTHEMIS NOBILIS

DOG FENNEL, ENGLISH CHAMOMILE, ROMAN CHAMOMILE

Native to the Mediterranean region, Roman chamomile is cultivated throughout Europe and other temperate areas of the world. A member of the Asteraceae (daisy)

Chammoile (Chamaemelum nobile) *has long been known for its ability to calm upset stomachs; its flowers make a popular tea.*

family, chamomile makes a pleasantly aromatic evergreen ground cover. With downy stems and feathery leaves, this perennial bears long-stalked flowers with white petals and yellow centres. The word "chamomile" comes from the Greek *chamaimelon*, meaning "apple on the ground", because of the strong applelike scent that emerges when the plant's foliage is stepped on or crushed. Although also known as Roman chamomile, the plant did not arrive in Rome until the 16th century. The Spanish name for chamomile is *manzanilla*, or "little apple". In Germany, chamomile is called *alles zutraut*, which means "capable of anything". For culinary and medicinal use, Roman chamomile is used interchangeably with German chamomile (*Matricaria recutita*). *Chamaemelum nobile* 'Flore Pleno', also known as double chamomile, is a popular cultivar that has shaggy white double flowers. *C. n.* 'Treneague', a non-flowering cultivar, is also known as lawn chamomile. Essential oil of chamomile is found in commercial products including perfumes, shampoos, lotions, bath oils and salves.

ᕗ GROWING CONDITIONS

Roman chamomile grows in almost any type of soil but prefers a moist, well-fertilized loam in full sun. Seeds may be planted in the spring or autumn; root divisions may be planted in the early spring. Chamomile flowers may be harvested as they open.

ᕗ CULINARY USE

Chamomile tea is a widely enjoyed beverage. Worldwide, about one million cups of chamomile tea are consumed daily.

ᕗ MEDICINAL USE

Chamomile contains a volatile oil that supports the herb's long-standing use to relieve indigestion and as an appetite stimulant. The herb also has anti-inflammatory properties, and has been used to relieve headache and treat insomnia, nausea, colic, superficial wounds and skin irritations such as eczema and puffy eyes. In aromatherapy, the essential oil of chamomile is used to treat inflamed, irritated skin and nervous conditions such as anxiety. **Note:** Although chamomile is a very safe, time-tested herb, it may provoke an allergic reaction in people who are sensitive to ragweed or other members of the aster family. Chamomile may also cause contact dermatitis in sensitive individuals. The essential oil of chamomile is for external use only.

ᕗ DOSAGE

Tea: Drink up to 1 litre (32 oz) per day. **Tincture:** Use 10 to 40 drops three times daily. **Aromatherapy bath:** Add 5 drops of essential oil to a bath of warm water. **Aromatherapy massage oil:** Add 10 to 20 drops of essential oil to 30 ml (1 oz) of almond or jojoba oil, and shake to mix.

$\mathcal{C}$IMICIFUGA RACEMOSA SYN. ACTAEA RACEMOSA

BLACK BUGBANE, BLACK COHOSH, BLACK SNAKEROOT, RHEUMATISM WEED, SQUAW ROOT

Black cohosh, a member of the Ranunculaceae (buttercup) family, is a tall perennial with small, creamy flowers, supported on tall spikes, and broad, ovate leaves that are divided into three-lobed leaflets with toothed margins. Native to eastern North America, black cohosh is one of six species of *Cimicifuga* that grow there. Thirteen additional species grow in Asia. Commercial cultivation of black cohosh has begun in Europe. *Cimicifuga* comes from the Latin *cimex*, or bug, and *fugare* " to drive away", referring to the herb's strong scent. Native Americans called the plant black cohosh, because of the dark colour of its roots, and the name squaw root describes its use as an aid in childbirth and a treatment for women's menopausal and premenstrual symptoms.

ᕗ GROWING CONDITIONS

Black cohosh grows in moist, humus-rich soil in partial shade. Root divisions may be planted at any time. Seeds may be sown under cover in the autumn. Roots may be harvested in the autumn.

ᕗ CULINARY USE

None.

ᕗ MEDICINAL USE

The roots and rhizomes of black cohosh have mild sedative and anti-inflammatory properties. The herb may be useful in the treatment of rheumatoid conditions such as arthritis. One variety, *C. foetida*, is used in China in the treatment of headache, the measles, and prolapse of the uterus, stomach, intestines, and bladder. Black cohosh is most well known as a treatment for menopausal symptoms, including hot flushes, night sweats, heart palpitations and vaginal atrophy. It is also used to treat psychological symptoms associated with menopause, such as insomnia, nervousness, tension and depression. Although oestrogenic activity in black cohosh has not been confirmed, its usefulness is supported by a long history of traditional application and by the results of recent scientific studies. **Note:** This herb should not be taken by pregnant women. Because of its increasing popularity as a treatment for symptoms associated with menopause, black cohosh has been overharvested in the wild; conservationists recommend growing the plant at home or using only products that are made from cultivated sources.

❧ **DOSAGE** **Tea:** Use 0.25 litre (8 oz) twice daily. **Tincture:** Take 1 ml (0.03 oz) one or two times daily. **Capsules:** Take one 500 mg capsule three times daily. **Standardized extract:** Take one 40 mg capsule standardized to 2.5 percent triterpene glycosides twice daily.

CINNAMOMUM SPP.

CASSIA, CINNAMON, TRUE CINNAMON

There are approximately 250 species in the *Cinnamomum* genus. Cultivated in the West Indies, Asia, southern India and Sri Lanka, this evergreen tree in the Lauraceae (laurel) family is native to southern Asia. Cinnamon trees have aromatic, light brown, paperlike bark, and bear small yellow flowers and purple berries. The bark is harvested from young branches during the rainy season, when it is most pliable. When dry, the bark curls into long quills, which are used, powdered or whole, as a spice. In addition to being used in the embalming process by the ancient Egyptians, cinnamon was used as an aphrodisiac and a perfume by ancient Romans. In fact, it was so valued as a spice that in the 16th century, the Portuguese invaded the Indian island of Ceylon to obtain a monopoly on cinnamon production. In the late 1700s, the Dutch began to cultivate cinnamon, and the Dutch East Indian Company became a leading supplier of the spice.

❧ **GROWING CONDITIONS** Cinnamon trees grow in moist, well-drained soil in full sun or partial shade. The tree will not tolerate temperatures below 15°C (59°F). Seeds may be planted under cover when ripe; semiripe cuttings may be planted in the summer.

❧ **CULINARY USE** A beloved spice, cinnamon is used around the world to flavour sweet dishes, such as biscuits, breads, cakes and pies, as well as savoury curries, soups and stews. Cinnamon, along with fennel seed, star anise, clove and Szechuan peppercorn, is an ingredient in the famous Chinese five-spice blend. Cinnamon bark oil is used to flavour cola, ice cream, liqueurs and sweets.

❧ **MEDICINAL USE** A reference to cinnamon's use in treating diarrhoea was recorded in China in 2700 B.C.E. Hebrews, Greeks and Romans all used cinnamon to treat indigestion. Cinnamon bark contains volatile oil and tannins, which may explain its effectiveness as a treatment for gastrointestinal disorders, as well as bloating, flatulence and vomiting. The herb contains eugenol, the same natural anaesthetic compound found in cloves which may help kill bacteria and viruses, prevent infection, and to help ease pain. Diluted essential oil of cinnamon is included as an ingredient in some dental products, such as toothpastes and mouthwashes. Research has shown that cinnamon powder may help lower blood sugar and may be useful in the treatment of type 2 diabetes. Cinnamon is used to warm the body and clear mucus congestion during colds and flu. It also improves circulation, especially to cold fingers and toes. **Note:** Pregnant women should not use cinnamon medicinally, but the herb is safe to use in small quantities as a spice. Because undiluted essential oil of cinnamon is highly irritating to sensitive skin, label directions should be followed when using products, such as liniments, that contain it.

❧ **DOSAGE** **Tea:** Use up to 0.75 litre (24 oz) daily. **Tincture:** Drink 20 drops in water, up to three times daily. **Supplements:** Follow label directions. **Powder:** For scrapes and cuts sprinkle one pinch on the affected area.

RUTACEAE
Citrus Fruits

The citrus family is made up of about 1,700 species, including lemon, lime, orange, grapefruit and kumquat, all of which are economically important crops. Known for their colour, fragrance and nectar, members of the Rutaceae family are also used for wood. Most citrus fruits have been cultivated for so long that their exact origins are uncertain.

CITRUS SINENSIS
ORANGE, SWEET ORANGE

The evergreen sweet orange tree, a member of the Rutaceae (rue) family, produces a thick-skinned, orange-fleshed fruit that is eaten throughout the world. Originally taken to the Mediterranean from Asia during the 15th century, orange trees now grow in the United States, Portugal, Spain, Sicily, North Africa and Israel. The United States is the world's largest producer of oranges. The word "orange" comes from the Sanskrit *naranga*, which means "fragrant". The orange blossom is traditionally associated with good fortune, and is often included in bridal bouquets. Orange oil, produced by pressing the peel of the fruit, is used to remove grease and to condition wooden furniture. Orange spray, extracted from orange peels and sold commercially, is an extremely efficient, nontoxic, environmentally friendly cleaning agent. Important varieties include: Washington navel orange (*C. s.* 'Washington'), which produces easy-to-peel, seedless fruits known for their superb flavour; clementine or clementine mandarin (*C. reticulata*

C. reticulata
Mandarin orange or tangerine is a small tree that produces yellow to red-orange sweet fruits.

'Clementine'), which produces small, sweet, tangy, fruit; and satsuma mandarin (*C. r.* 'Satsuma'), which produces small easy-to-peel fruit with few seeds.

GROWING CONDITIONS The orange tree is unusual in that it can produce fruit, flowers and leaves all at once. Citrus trees grown in tubs and wintered under cover were once popular in Renaissance gardens. Sweet orange trees grow in fertile, well-drained soil in full sun. The trees must be protected from frost.

CULINARY USE Orange fruits, which vary in flavour from sweet to sour, are commonly peeled and eaten fresh, or squeezed for juice. The fruit has a thick, bitter rind that is usually discarded, but is some-times used as a garnish and can be processed into animal feed. The outermost layer of the rind is grated to produce "zest", popularly used in cooking because its flavour is similar to the fleshy inner part of the

C. sinensis 'Valencia'
Valencia orange, thought to originate in
Portugal, produces fruit that has excellent
flavour and colour. Valencia oranges are the
most popular orange variety worldwide.

orange. The white part of the rind, called the pith,
is almost always discarded. Orange juice is drunk
as a beverage by itself and is used to flavour sauces,
marinades and baked goods. It is also also an ingredient in several popular cocktails, including the screw-
driver (vodka and orange juice) and the mimosa
(champagne and orange juice). Orange blossom petals
can be made into a delicately citrus-scented version of
rosewater. Orange blossom honey, which is produced
by placing beehives in citrus groves during bloom, has
an pleasant orange flavour and is highly prized.

MEDICINAL USE Oranges are an excellent dietary
source of vitamin C and fibre. In aromatherapy, sweet
orange oil is used to ease indigestion and reduce
anxiety. **Note:** Essential oil of sweet orange can irritate
the skin. It should be used only in small amounts, and
avoided by pregnant women and young children.

DOSAGE Aromatherapy bath: Add 2 drops of
essential oil to a bath of warm water. **Aromatherapy
massage oil:** Add 5 to 10 drops of essential oil to
30 ml (1 oz) of almond or jojoba oil; shake to mix.

CITRUS X AURANTIUM
BITTER ORANGE, SEVILLE ORANGE,
SOUR ORANGE

The evergreen bitter orange tree or shrub, a member
of the Rutaceae (rue) family, is native to tropical areas
of Asia. Bitter orange is cultivated in tropical and
subtropical regions throughout the world. The tree
produces a fruit that is considered by most people
to be too sour to eat raw. Most of the world's bitter
orange supply comes from Spain.

GROWING CONDITIONS Bitter orange trees grow
in rich, well-drained soil in full sun, in areas with a
minimum temperature of 7°C (45°F). The plant
requires plenty of moisture during the growing season.
Ripe seeds may be planted when temperatures reach
16°C (61°F); semiripe cuttings may be planted in the
summer. Fruits may be harvested at any time.

CULINARY USE Bitter orange fruit is used in
marmalade and to flavour liqueurs such as curaçao and
triple sec. The fruit's peel is often candied and eaten as
sweets. Orange-flower water, made from the tree's blossoms, is used to flavour desserts, baked goods, sweets and
some cocktails, such as the Ramos gin fizz.

MEDICINAL USE Bitter oranges are rich in vitamins
C and A. The fruit has been used medicinally as an
expectorant, a digestive stimulant, a remedy for constipation and flatulence, and also as a agent for calming
nerves. The peel of the fruit contains essential oil that is
used externally to treat loss of appetite and indigestion.
In aromatherapy, bitter orange flower oil, known as
neroli, is a popular remedy used
externally as an antidepressant
and mild sedative. Petitgrain,
another essential oil, is
derived from bitter

Citrus. x aurantium
Chinotto (myrtle leaf
orange) is a dwarf cultivar.

Citrus limon
Citrus limon bears small yellow
fruit with a thick skin covering
the acidic pulp.

orange's leaves and twigs and is used externally for similar purposes. Its scent is less elegant than neroli's and so is not as popular.

DOSAGE Tea (fruit or peel:) Drink up to 0.5 litre (16 oz) daily. **Aromatherapy bath:** Add 5 drops of essential oil to a bath of warm water. **Aromatherapy massage oil:** Add 10 to 20 drops of essential oil to 30 ml (1 oz) of almond or jojoba oil, and shake to mix.

CITRUS X LIMON
LEMON

The lemon tree, a member of the Rutaceae (rue) family, is thought to be native to India. The first description of the lemon fruit is found in Arabic writings from the 12th century. This is a small, shrubby evergreen with thorny branches, oval, yellow green leaves, and sweet-smelling flowers that are violet-streaked on the underside and white on the outside. Lemon trees are now cultivated in the Mediterranean region and in subtropical climates around the world. The small, oval-shaped, thick-skinned, vitamin C-rich yellow fruits of the lemon tree were commonly used to treat and prevent the deficiency disease scurvy. Lemons were used by sailors in the Royal Navy, who mistook the fruits for overripe limes and became known as limeys. One important variety is variegated lemon (*Citrus x limon* 'Variegata'), which is grown as an attractive potted plant. It bears immature, yellow and green striped fruits.

GROWING CONDITIONS Lemon trees grow in rich, well-drained soil in full sun, in areas with a minimum temperature of 5°C (41°F). They require plenty of moisture during the growing season. Ripe seeds may be planted when temperatures reach 16°C (61°F); semiripe cuttings may be planted in the summer. It is best to harvest lemon fruits in the winter, when their vitamin C content is highest.

CULINARY USE Lemons are considered by most people to be too sour to eat out of hand. Lemon juice, however, is used to flavour many sweet and savoury foods, from baked goods to sauces, marinades, yogurt, dressings, and chicken and vegetable dishes. Lemon juice is commonly used to dress fish, as the acidic juice neutralizes the flavour of amines in fish. Lemon juice is used in beverages, including lemonade and tea, and is added to jams and jellies to help them "gel", or solidify.

MEDICINAL USE Lemons contain about twice as much vitamin C as oranges. The pith and peel of the fruit contain bioflavonoids, which may help strengthen veins and capillaries and are given as

C. x medica 'Buddha's hand'
Buddha's hand lemon bears a
very unusual-looking fruit that
resembles a human hand.

a treatment for varicose veins and to reduce susceptibility to bruising. Lemons contain compounds known as limonoids, which are thought to help prevent cancer. Lemon juice is considered cleansing to the body and believed to help maintain general health. The juice is also used to treat colds, flu, gout and rheumatism. Lemon juice may be applied to skin conditions including warts, acne and ringworm. Essential oil of lemon has antiviral and antibacterial properties, and can be diluted and applied externally to cold sores. In aromatherapy, the oil is believed to have energizing and anti-depressant abilities and to improve concentration.

DOSAGE Tea (peel): Drink up to 0.75 litre (24 oz) daily. **Cold sore remedy:** Dilute 5 drops of essential oil in 1 tsp almond or jojoba oil; shake to mix. **Aromatherapy bath:** Add 2 drops of essential oil to a bath of warm water. **Aromatherapy massage oil:** Add 5 to 10 drops of essential oil to 30 ml (1 oz) of almond or jojoba oil; shake to mix.

CITRUS X AURANTIFOLIA
LIME

The lime tree, a member of the Rutaceae (rue) family, is native to the East Indies. The tree now grows in subtropical and tropical areas all over the world. A small, shrubby evergreen, the lime tree produces, on spiny branches, light green leaves and clusters of white flowers. Like lemons, the small, oval, thick-skinned, vitamin C-rich green fruits of the lime tree were once given to sailors to prevent scurvy. Limes are biologically almost identical to lemons. They are mutations of lemon trees.

GROWING CONDITIONS Lime trees grow in rich, well-drained soil in full sun in areas with a minimum temperature of 13 °C (55°F). They require plenty of moisture during the growing season. Ripe seeds may

Citrus hystrix
Wild lime bears bumpy-skinned green or yellow fruit. Its leaves are commonly used as a flavouring in Asian cuisines.

Citrus x aurantifolia 'Key'
Key lime bears fruit that is smaller, rounder and more yellow than regular limes. Key lime trees may be grown indoors as potted plants.

be planted when temperatures reach 16 °C (61°F); semiripe cuttings may be planted in the summer. Fruits may be picked when ripe.

CULINARY USE Like lemons, lime fruits are considered too sour to eat. Lime juice is a popular marinade for fish and is used to "cure" the raw fish in the Central and South American dish *seviche*. Lime juice is an ingredient in limeade and in cocktails, including the margarita, the *mojito* and the Moscow mule. In Central and South America, particularly Mexico, slices of lime are used to accent the taste of beer. Lime provides the flavouring for key lime pie, a speciality of the southern United States and the Caribbean islands. Pickled limes are used as a condiment in Indian cuisine.

MEDICINAL USE Limes are very rich in vitamin C. They contain flavonoid compounds, called limonoids, which have antioxidant properties and may help prevent cancers of the mouth, skin, lung, breast, stomach and colon. In southeastern Asia, lime juice is a popular remedy for diarrhoea.

DOSAGE Fresh lime juice: Add 1 tsp to 0.25 litre (8 oz) water.

C

*C*OFFEA ARABICA

ARABIAN COFFEE, COFFEE

Coffee, a member of the Rubiaceae (madder) family, is native to northeastern Africa and is cultivated in tropical areas around the world. Brazil and Colombia are leading exporters. The *Coffea* genus contains about forty species of small trees and evergreen shrubs, the most widely grown of which is *C. arabica*. This shrub bears glossy leaves, dense clusters of fragrant white flowers and red fruits. The fruits contain two seeds, known as beans, which are the main ingredient of one of the world's most widely consumed beverages.

❧ **GROWING CONDITIONS** Coffee grows in well-drained, moisture-retentive soil in partial shade in areas with a minimum temperature of 10°C (50°F). In warm, humid climates, coffee can be grown in containers as an ornamental plant. Ripe seeds are planted in the spring, when temperatures reach 30°C (86°F). Fruits are harvested when ripe. Coffee beans are then dried, fermented and roasted for use.

❧ **CULINARY USE** In addition to the widespread use of the beans to make a beverage, coffee has an extract that is used to flavour liqueurs and foods such as Italy's classic espresso-soaked tiramisu dessert. Coffee is famously paired with chocolate to make a flavour combination called mocha.

❧ **MEDICINAL USE** Most of coffee's health effects are owed to its high caffeine content. Caffeine has antioxidant properties and acts as a stimulant for the heart and digestive system, a laxative, a diuretic and an appetite suppressant. Caffeine is found in many over-the-counter headache remedies, in combination with conventional analgesic medications. Drinking one to two cups of coffee daily may help prevent kidney stones. **Note:** Coffee can cause insomnia, jitteriness and irritability. Coffee is not advised for people with high blood pressure, gastric ulcers, glaucoma or heart disease. It should be avoided during pregnancy and when trying to conceive.

❧ **DOSAGE Drink:** Up to 0.5 litre (16 oz) daily.

In addition to its use as a source of coffee beans,
Coffea Arabica is sometimes grown as an
ornamental container plant in cooler climates.

*C*OLEUS FORSKOHLII SYN. PLECTRANTHUS BARBATUS

COLEUS, FORSKOHLII, HAUSA POTATO

This member of the Lamiaceae (mint) family grows wild in India on the dry plains and in the foothills of the Himalayan mountains. Other members of this genus of about 300 species are found growing in tropical and subtropical regions of the Indian subcontinent. An aromatic evergreen, it is a semi-succulent perennial that bears downy, dramatically coloured ovate leaves with scalloped margins. The undersides of the leaves are dotted with red glands.

❧ **GROWING CONDITIONS** *C. forskohlii* grows best in light, rich, well-drained soil in sun or partial shade. It is commonly grown in gardens and in pots for its attractive foliage. Stem cuttings or root divisions may be planted in the spring or summer. The plant needs plenty of water during the growing season, but should be kept dry in winter. Roots may be collected in the autumn when the herb's active constituents are at their highest levels.

❧ **CULINARY USE** *C. forskolhlii* is cultivated on a large scale in India, where its roots are pickled and eaten.

C

❧ MEDICINAL USE The leaves and roots of *C. forskohlii* are the source of a compound called forskolin, which was first isolated in the 1970s. This herb may be beneficial in the treatment of heart failure, bronchial asthma and glaucoma. Research has shown that it may have the ability to lower high blood pressure levels, relax smooth muscle (for example, in the bronchial airways), increase hormone release from the thyroid gland and stimulate digestion. Forskolin shows some potential for reducing intraocular pressure when suspension eye drops are applied topically to the cornea. In Indian Ayurvedic medicine, another species, *C. amboinicus*, also called Indian borage, has been used traditionally to treat bronchitis and asthma as well as digestive difficulties such as flatulence, bloating and abdominal pain. *C. forskohlii* leaves have a strong, camphorlike scent, and have been used as a body rub to cleanse and deodorize the skin. **Note:** Scientific research on this herb is preliminary. What is known relates primarily to its compound forskolin, rather than the entire herb.

❧ DOSAGE Standardized extract: Take one capsule twice daily standardized to contain 18 percent forskolin (9 mg per capsule).

*C*OMMIPHORA MUKUL SYN. C. WIGHTII

BDELLIUM TREE, FALSE MYRRH, GUGGUL

Guggul is a member of the Burseraceae (torchwood) family, which is comprised of 180 deciduous, thorny shrubs or small trees. The guggul tree, native to India, can be found in desert environments of the Middle East and India. It grows to about 2 m (6½ ft) tall. A close relative of myrrh, guggul's bark produces a gum resin that is used medicinally.

❧ GROWING CONDITIONS Guggul trees grow in well-drained soil in full sun in areas with minimum temperatures of 10 to 16°C (50 to 60°F). Seeds may be planted in the spring; hardwood cuttings may be planted at the end of the growing season. The plant's gum resin is collected from cut branches and then dried for use.

❧ CULINARY USE None.

❧ MEDICINAL USE Guggul's resin contains fat soluble steroids known as guggulsterones, which have anti-inflammatory properties and may help ease the pain of arthritis. The resin has long been used in Ayurvedic medicine as a blood thinner and to lower cholesterol levels. In clinical studies, participants had an average drop in cholesterol levels of about 12 percent. Early Ayurvedic writings also describe guggul's use as treatment for obesity. Because of its diuretic ability to relieve water retention, the herb is still used today to promote weight loss. **Note:** Guggul should not be taken during pregnancy or while breastfeeding.

❧ DOSAGE Standardized extract: Take 1 to 1.5 g of guggul daily, equivalent to 50 to 75 mg of guggulsterones.

*C*ORIANDRUM SATIVUM

CORIANDER, CHINESE PARSLEY

Coriander, a member of the Apiaceae (parsley) family, is one of the world's oldest-known herbs. Native to southern Europe and western Asia, coriander has been cultivated there for more than 3,000

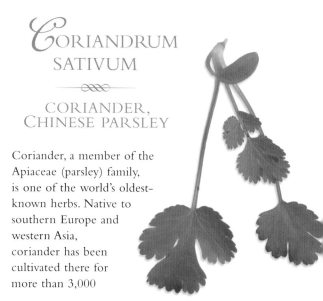

years, and is now grown throughout the world. This erect annual has pungent leaves and white flowers, followed by pale brown fruits. The plant's finely cut upper leaves and rounded seeds are both used in cooking and to flavour many foods, while the seeds also have medicinal uses. The genus name *Coriandrum* comes from the Greek *koriannon*, which was a type of bedbug thought to have an odour similar to that of coriander leaves.

GROWING CONDITIONS
Coriander grows in well-drained soil in full sun. The plant prefers a cool, damp spring and a hot, dry summer. When grown as a culinary herb, it grows best in a partially shady location. Seeds are planted in the spring for summer harvest or in the summer for autumn harvest. This fast-growing herb usually produces edible leaves in a month and seeds after a month and a half. Fresh leaves may be gathered when young; seeds are harvested when ripe.

CULINARY USE
The seeds and leaves of coriander have completely different tastes, but both are commonly used in cooking. Whole coriander seeds taste like a mixture of lemon and sage and are used as an ingredient in pickling brine and in some beverages, such as mulled wine. Ground coriander seed is a popular ingredient in curry blends, soups and baked goods, especially in Scandinavia and Thailand. The leaves are a fragrant mix of parsley and citrus and are often found in the cuisines of Mexico, the Caribbean, India and Asia. They have a pungent odour and are used in highly seasoned dishes.

MEDICINAL USE
Coriander seeds have carminative properties, and have been used as a mild digestive tonic to improve the appetite and relieve flatulence, intestinal spasms, bloating, and cramps. In ancient Egypt, coriander was considered an aphrodisiac – and still is in Europe. Coriander seeds can be chewed after meals to sweeten the breath, particularly after eating garlic.

DOSAGE
Tea: Use up to 0.75 litre (24 oz) daily. **Fresh or dried seeds:** Take one small handful of seeds daily.

CRATAEGUS LAEVIGATA SYN. C. OXYACANTHA

ENGLISH HAWTHORN, HAWTHORN, MAY TREE, WHITE THORN

Native to northern Europe, *C. laevigata* is one of 280 hawthorn species found in northern temperate regions, including North America, Europe and northern Asia. A member of the Rosaceae (rose) family, hawthorn is a deciduous shrub or small tree with dark brown bark; it bears clusters of aromatic white flowers followed by dark-red, egg-shaped fruits. These fruits, called haws, resemble rose hips or tiny apples. *Crataegus* is derived from the Greek *kratus*, meaning "strength", referring to the characteristic hardness of hawthorn's wood.

GROWING CONDITIONS
Hawthorn grows in most soils in sun or partial shade, although it may flower and fruit better in open, sunny locations. Propagation is by seed gathered when ripe and layered for eighteen months before a spring planting.

CULINARY USE
Hawthorn fruits have been eaten as a food and made into wines and jellies.

MEDICINAL USE
Hawthorn's leaves, flowers and fruits contain compounds that have the ability to dilate coronary vessels and lower blood pressure levels. The herb has been shown to be effective in the treatment of

C

hypertension related to a weak heart, angina, arteriosclerosis, early stage congestive heart failure, age-related heart disorders and arrhythmia. Practitioners often encourage use of hawthorn products for several months, and even years, to reap its optimum benefits. In Traditional Chinese Medicine, hawthorn fruits, known as *shan zha rou*, are a well-known remedy often prescribed to stimulate digestion. Both Native American and Chinese medical practitioners have used hawthorn to treat diarrhoea and strengthen the heart. **Note:** Unlike some medicinal plants that act on the heart, hawthorn is relatively nontoxic. However, people who are taking digitalis should consult their healthcare provider before taking hawthorn products because they necessitate a reduction in the dosage of digitalis.

🍃 **DOSAGE** **Tea:** Drink 0.25 litre (8 oz) two or three times daily. **Tincture:** Use 1 or 2 ml (0.03 or 0.07 oz) three times daily. **Capsule (powder):** Take up to nine 500 mg capsules daily. **Standardized extract:** Take one 120 to 240 mg capsule three times daily.

🍃 **CULINARY USE** Pungent and aromatic, saffron is the world's most expensive spice. Each saffron flower contains three stigmas, which are the part of the plant that is used for the spice. Saffron flowers must be hand-picked, and it takes more than 14,000 stigmas to make 28 g (1 oz) of saffron. Off-setting its high cost is the fact that a very little saffron goes a long way in cooking. Saffron adds flavour and colour to baked goods and to such Mediterranean savoury dishes as bouillabaisse, risotto and paella. The spice is also used as a flavouring and colourant in liqueurs.

🍃 **MEDICINAL USE** Saffron has long been associated with healing. In ancient Rome, the wealthy slept on pillows filled with saffron in the belief that it would cure hangovers. In the Middle Ages, saffron was used to treat fever in children and chronic uterine bleeding in women. Today, saffron may still be used to relieve indigestion and colic, to encourage perspiration and to ease menstrual pain, but equally effective, and much less expensive, herbs are available. **Note:** Saffron should not be used in large doses during pregnancy. The small amounts used in cooking do not present a problem.

🍃 **DOSAGE** **Tea:** Drink up to 0.5 litre (16 oz) daily.

*C*ROCUS SATIVUS

SAFFRON, SPANISH SAFFRON, TRUE SAFFRON

There are about eighty species in the *Crocus* genus, which is native to the eastern Mediterranean region, the Balkans and India. *C. sativus* is cultivated in Europe, the Middle East and India. A member of the Iridaceae (iris) family, saffron is a hardy, low-growing perennial with linear leaves and lilac-coloured flowers.

🍃 **GROWING CONDITIONS** Saffron grows in well-drained, warm soil in full sun. Offshoots removed from the parent plant can be planted in the late spring. The plant will grow, but will not flower, in areas with cool, wet summers. The flowers are picked when open; the stigmas are removed and dried as a spice.

*C*URCUMA LONGA

COMMON TURMERIC, INDIAN SAFFRON, TURMERIC, YELLOW GINGER

There are approximately forty species in the *Curcuma* genus, including *C. aromatica* (wild turmeric). Native to southern Asia, common turmeric is widely grown in India, Jamaica, China, Malaysia and Indonesia. Common turmeric, a member of the Zingiberaceae (ginger) family, is an aromatic, yellow-flowering perennial with a bitter, pungent flavour, large leaves and a tuberlike rhizome. Turmeric yields an orange and yellow dye that has been used in India and Asia to colour the robes of Buddhist monks.

🍃 **GROWING CONDITIONS** Turmeric prefers well-drained soil in sunny, humid locations, with a minimum temperature of 15°C (59°F). The seeds are sown in the autumn and the rhizomes divided during their dormant period. Turmeric rhizomes are harvested while dormant and then boiled, dried, and polished.

❧ **CULINARY USE** A vital ingredient in East Indian cooking, turmeric is the source of the distinctive yellow colour of widely used curry spice blends – which can contain up to twenty different spices. Turmeric is also mixed with white mustard seeds to colour yellow mustard.

❧ **MEDICINAL USE** Curcumin, a yellow pigment found in turmeric rhizomes, is the source of the herb's potent health benefits. Long revered in Asian healing practices, turmeric is considered an excellent anti-inflammatory and antioxidant. Researchers are currently exploring the herb's potential in treating cancer, AIDS, high cholesterol, ulcers, and gallbladder and liver disease. **Note:** Turmeric should not be used medicinally by pregnant women or by those who suffer from bile duct obstruction, gallstones, stomach ulcers or stomach hyperacidity. Consumption of the herb as a spice, in small amounts, does not pose a problem.

❧ **DOSAGE Tea:** Use 0.25 litre (8 oz) two or three times daily. **Tincture:** Take 1 to 3 ml (0.04 to 0.12 oz) two to three times daily. **Standardized extract:** Take one 450 mg capsule standardized to 95 percent curcuminoids three times daily.

𝒞YMBOPOGON CITRATUS

FEVER GRASS, LEMONGRASS, WEST INDIAN LEMONGRASS

A member of the Poaceae (grass) family, lemongrass is commercially grown in large quantities in Mexico, Guatemala, China, India and Thailand. This dense perennial generally does not flower. Its sharply tapered, grasslike leaves emit a strong lemon scent when broken. The genus name *Cymbopogon* derives from the Greek words *kymbe* (boat) and *pogon* (beard) in reference to the appearance of the plant's leaves.

❧ **GROWING CONDITIONS** Lemongrass thrives in temperate climates, in well-drained, dry, even poor, soil in full sun. The plant is propagated from root divisions of clumps in the spring. In cold climates, the roots can be dug up and brought inside for the winter.

❧ **CULINARY USE** Lemongrass is an integral part of Thai, Vietnamese and Sri Lankan cuisines. A tea made from the plant's leaves is a popular drink in tropical countries. Lemongrass is a major source of lemon flavouring and fragrance, and is used commercially in ice cream, sweets and baked goods. Because of its popularity in cooking – as well as its therapeutic uses – lemongrass oil is said to be one of the best-selling essential oils in the world. Two related species, *C. nardus* (citronella) and *C. martini* (palma rosa), are also popular essential oils.

❧ **MEDICINAL USE** Lemongrass tea is believed to relax the stomach and intestines and help relieve flatulence, making it a useful digestive aid. Lemongrass oil has antifungal and antiseptic properties. A compress of the oil can be applied topically to skin conditions such as ringworm and infected sores. Lemongrass leaves can be applied directly to the skin to repel insects, and are an ingredient in a formula known as "fever tea" in East India and Sri Lanka, which is traditionally taken to lower body temperature. Modern herbalists also advise the use of lemongrass as a cooling agent in the treatment of fever and a stomach soother for diarrhoea.

❧ **DOSAGE USE Tea:** Drink 0.25 litre (8 oz) two or three times daily. **Oil:** Follow label directions.

C

CYNARA SCOLYMUS

∞

ARTICHOKE, CYNARA, GLOBE ARTICHOKE

Native to southern Europe and northern Africa, this perennial is widely cultivated as a perennial vegetable and as an ornamental. Artichoke, a member of the Asteraceae (daisy) family, bears large, deeply divided leaves and massive, thistlelike flower heads. In midsummer, artichoke's blue flowers are highly attractive to bees. These flowers are seldom seen in full bloom, because they are picked when immature and eaten as a vegetable. Artichoke may come from the Arabic *al-khursuf*, which translates to thistle. The plant is thought to have been brought to Spain by Muslims during the Middle Ages, when the name became *alcarchofa*, later modified to the Italian *articiocco*.

GROWING CONDITIONS Artichoke grows in deep, rich, well-drained soil in full sun. Seeds are planted in the spring; side shoots are planted in the spring or autumn.

CULINARY USE Artichokes have been eaten as vegetables since ancient Greek and Roman times. The plant's young, unopened flowers are boiled or steamed. The vegetable's tough outer leaves are removed, leaving behind a soft "heart" covered by an inedible, prickly "choke" that must be removed and discarded.

MEDICINAL USE The bitter leaves and flower buds of artichoke have diuretic properties. They also stimulate the liver's secretion of bile helping the digestion of fats and the uptake of fat-soluble vitamins. Because bile acts as a vehicle for the elimination of toxins and cholesterol, artichokes may have the ability to reduce serum or blood cholesterol levels and lower LDL (bad) cholesterol. The herb may also be useful in treating sluggish liver and gallbladder functions, gallstones, jaundice, poor digestion and lack of appetite, dyspepsia, flatulence, nausea and the symptoms of irritable bowel syndrome. **Note:** Artichokes should be avoided in cases of complete blockage of the gallbladder or bile duct.

DOSAGE **Tincture:** Take 2 or 3 ml (0.07 or 0.1 oz) two or three times daily, preferably before meals. **Standardized extract:** Take one 160 to 320 mg capsule standardized to caffeoylquinic acids, three times daily.

DIGITALIS PURPUREA

∞

DIGITALIS, FOXGLOVE, PURPLE FOXGLOVE

Native to western Europe and Morocco, this member of the Scrophulariaceae (figwort) family is naturalized in both North and South America. The common name "foxglove" and the genus name *Digitalis* both refer to the shape of the plant's flowers, which can fit over the fingers like a glove. "Foxglove" derives from the Anglo-Saxon *foxes glola* (fox glove), referring to a fairy's glove. *Digitalis* derives from the Latin *digitus*, meaning finger. Foxglove's flowers produce a yellow green dye and normally grow to approximately 2 m (6 ft) in height.

❧ GROWING CONDITIONS

Foxglove is poisonous, but it is a popular garden plant because of its showy, elegant flowers. Foxglove grows in well-drained, neutral-to-acidic soil in partial shade. Seeds are planted under cover in the fall. Full development takes two years.

❧ CULINARY USE None.

❧ MEDICINAL USE

Foxglove, a diuretic, contains cardiac glycosides that have been used in traditional and modern medicine to increase the force of the heart's contractions. The herb has been taken to treat irregular heartbeat and heart failure. It is still the source of widely used contemporary cardiac drugs. **Note:** Foxglove is toxic and should not be used unless under a physician's supervision. Ironically, the early-warning nausea that could occur as a result of a foxglove overdose once made the herb a safer cardiac drug than the more powerful synthetic drugs used today.

❧ DOSAGE Prescription only.

𝒟IOSCOREA VILLOSA

—◦◦◦—

CHINA ROOT, COLIC ROOT, NORTH AMERICAN WILD YAM, RHEUMATISM ROOT, WILD YAM

Wild yam, a member of the Dioscoreaceae (yam) family, is native to North America and naturalized throughout the world in warmer regions. Approximately 600 species make up the *Dioscorea* genus of tropical and subtropical climbing plants. Some of the edible yams in the genus produce tubers that can reach a weight of up to 50 kg (110 lb). The genus is named for Dioscorides (40–90 C.E.), famed Roman physician and naturalist.

❧ GROWING CONDITIONS Wild yam grows in rich soil in full sun or partial shade. Seeds are planted in spring; root divisions are planted in early spring or autumn.

❧ CULINARY USE Wild yam, a relative of *D. batatus*, is a dietary staple like the common sweet potato. The tubelike roots of the plant are often boiled and then mashed, but can also be fried, roasted or baked. The finished product varies in taste from sweet to bitter, and sometimes tasteless. *D. villosa*, however, is used solely for medicinal purposes.

❧ MEDICINAL USE With strong anti-inflammatory properties, wild yam root has a history of medicinal use as a treatment for cramping or contractions in the pelvic area, including false labour pains, menstrual cramps, uterine spasms, gallbladder pain, and intestinal spasms and cramps. Wild yam relaxes spasms, dilates blood vessels and stimulates blood flow. It contains a steroidlike compound called diosgenin that was once used in contraceptive hormones such as birth control pills. Though widely promoted for menopausal symptoms, scientists have found it no more effective than a placebo. Many wild yam creams (mostly marketed to ease menopausal symptoms) contain human progesterone created in the laboratory, often synthetically derived from diosgenin.

❧ DOSAGE **Tea:** Drink 0.25 litre (8 oz) two or three times each day. **Tincture:** Use 2 to 4 ml (0.07 to 0.14 oz) two or three times daily. **Standardized extract:** Take up to two 400 mg capsules daily.

ECHINACEA SPP.

ECHINACEA, KANSAS SNAKEROOT, NARROW-LEAF ECHINACEA, NARROW-LEAF PURPLE CONEFLOWER

There are nine species of *Echinacea*. This member of the Asteraceae (daisy) family is native to the eastern United States and is widely cultivated in North America and Germany. A large perennial, echinacea bears spectacular purplish flowers with orange-brown inner cones. The common name "purple coneflower" refers to the distinctive appearance of the plant's flowers. *Echinacea* derives from the Greek *echinos*, meaning "sea urchin or hedgehog", another reference to the plant's urchinlike cone. In traditional medicine, echinacea was used by North American Plains tribes more than any other plant. Samples of echinacea have been found in archaeological digs of Native American sites dating back to the 17th century. The herb served as a treatment for toothache, sore throat, coughs, infection, cold, flu, snakebite and superficial sores and wounds.

❧ GROWING CONDITIONS Echinacea thrives in well-drained, fairly poor soil in full sun or in light shade in very hot climates. Propagation is by seeds or by crown division. *Echinacea angustifolia* is much more difficult to grow than *E. purpurea*.

❧ CULINARY USE None.

❧ MEDICINAL USE Of the *Echinacea* species, *E. purpurea* is most widely used, followed by *E. angustifolia* and *E. pallida*. Echinacea roots, flowers, leaves and seeds contain polysaccharides and cichoric acid, which stimulate the immune system; they also have antimicrobial, antibacterial, and antiviral properties. Studies have shown that echinacea stimulates phagocytosis in the blood stream, encouraging white blood cells to attack invading organisms. Echinacea activates macrophagesm that destroy both cancerous cells and pathogens, and has an effect on properidin levels, helping the body control and prevent infections. This herb is most widely known for its effectiveness in preventing upper respiratory infections, such as colds, flu, laryngitis and tonsillitis. Echinacea is used externally in salves and tinctures to treat superficial cuts, canker sores, leg ulcers and burns.

Note: Echinacea may cause allergic reactions in those sensitive to other plants in the aster family. Because some wild populations are becoming endangered, purchasing products made with organically grown echinaceais recommended.

❧ DOSAGE Tea: Drink 0.25 litre (8 oz) several times daily. **Tincture:** Use 2 ml (0.07 oz) two to four times daily. **Capsule:** Take six to nine 300 to 400 mg capsules daily. **Standardized extract:** Take two 125 mg capsules standardized to 3.2 to 4.8 percent echinacoside two or three times daily.

ELETTARIA CARDAMOMUM

CARDAMOM, CEYLON CARDAMOM

Cardamom, one of the oldest spices in the world, is the seed of a rhizomatous, tropical perennial in the Zingiberaceae (ginger) family. Native to Indian rainforests, cardamom grows in tropical areas of Asia, South America and the Pacific Islands. The plant bears long, lance-shaped leaves and white flowers with purple-striped lips. Its fruits, or seedpods are pale green and

contain up to twenty aromatic seeds. The fragrance of the seeds is similar to that of eucalyptus, which dissipates when the seeds are ground. In ancient Egypt, cardamom was used to make perfume.

❧ GROWING CONDITIONS Cardamom grows in rich, moist, well-drained soil in partial shade in areas with a minimum temperature of 16°C (61°F). Cardamom can be grown under cover in temperate regions but will rarely flower or fruit. Seeds may be planted in the autumn; root divisions may be planted in the spring or summer. The plant is handpicked just before seedpods begin to open in the autumn.

❧ CULINARY USE Cardamom is widely used in both Scandinavian and East Indian cooking. It is one of the primary flavourings of the popular herbal beverage called *chai*. In northern Europe, cardamom seeds are used to flavour baked goods. In the Middle East, the spice is used to add a warm, spicy flavour to coffee. Cardamom is also generally used – albeit with a light hand – to flavour stews, curries, bean dishes, sausage, cream sauces and fruit dishes.

❧ MEDICINAL USE Cardamom contains a volatile oil that supports the herb's traditional use as a digestive tonic. The herb "warms" and stimulates digestion, and may relieve intestinal spasms and wind, and ease stomach pain. Cardamom has a pleasant flavour and is often used in digestive herb blends, because it masks the taste

of less pleasant herbs, such as the bitter gentian (*Gentiana lutea*). The herb is believed to treat for bad breath, especially when caused by eating garlic. It may also have aphrodisiac properties. Cardamom has been used in Indian Ayurvedic medicine for thousands of years.

❧ DOSAGE Tea: Drink 0.25 litre (8 oz) after meals, up to 1.2 litre (40 oz) daily. **Tincture:** Take 5 drops three times daily. **Oil rub:** Mix 10 drops cardamom essential oil in two tbsp sweet almond or jojoba oil, shake to mix; gently rub on the stomach to relieve digestive discomfort.

EPHEDRA SINICA

CHINESE EPHEDRA, CHINESE JOINTFIR, EPHEDRA, MA HUANG

A member of the Ephedraceae (ephedra) family, ephedra is native to central Asia and is found throughout northern China. About forty species are included in this genus. This low shrub has greenish stems and bears very small leaves. *Ephedra* is Greek for climbing, referring to the

plant's tendency to climb across dry rocky soil. Traces of the herb were found in a Middle Eastern grave dating back 60,000 years, indicating ephedra's possible use as a medicine as long ago as the Stone Age.

GROWING CONDITIONS Ephedra thrives in full sun and dry, sandy soil. The plant is mostly cultivated, and is harvested before the first frost of the winter. Stems may be collected throughout the year.

CULINARY USE None.

MEDICINAL USE Ephedra was first mentioned in a classic Chinese herbal text from the first century C.E. It is one of the first Chinese herbs to be widely used in Western medicine. Ephedra derivatives are the main ingredients in many over-the-counter decongestant pharmaceuticals. The herb is also an ingredient of herbal preparations that stimulate weight loss, athletic performance, and physical and mental energy. Ephedra contains ephedrine and pseudoephedrine, alkaloids that stimulate the central nervous system, elevate blood pressure, dilate the bronchi, decrease intestinal tone and motility, and cause cardiac stimulation and tachycardia. Ephedra is an effective nasal decongestant, used to treat the common cold, sinusitis and hay fever, and to relieve the congestion of bronchial asthma and the symptoms of allergies. Side effects, including insomnia and high blood pressure, may occur when the recommended dosage of over-the-counter ephedra products is exceeded. Several North American species, including *Ephedra nevadensis* (known as Mormon tea), contain little if any ephedrine, so they can be made into teas and safely taken to treat cold and allergy symptoms. Practitioners of Traditional Chinese Medicine consider a person's constitutional type before prescribing ephedra, and usually combine it in formulas with other herbs that have the potential to counteract any side effects. **Note:** Ephedra is not recommended for excessive or long-term use. It should not be used by pregnant or breastfeeding women, or by those who have anorexia, bulimia, or glaucoma. Ephedra acts as a thyroid stimulant and may increase the effects of pharmaceutical MAO-inhibitors.

DOSAGE **Tea:** Drink 0.25 litre (8 oz) two or three times daily. **Tincture:** Use 0.5 to 1 ml (0.017 to 0.03 oz) four times daily. **Capsule:** Take one 500 to 1,000 mg capsule two to three times daily. **Standardized extract:** Take one 12 to 25 mg capsule (standardized to total alkaloids calculated as ephedrine) two or three times daily.

EUCALYPTUS GLOBULUS

BLUE GUM, EUCALYPTUS, SOUTHERN BLUE GUM, TASMANIAN BLUE GUM

There are more than 600 species and varieties of this Myrtaceae (guava) family member. A tall evergreen tree, with large bands of shedding bark and bluish green, highly aromatic leaves, *E. globulus* is native to Australia, where it is a favourite food of koala bears. The tree has also been established in North America, South America, southern Europe, Africa and India. It is commercially cultivated in Portugal, Spain and India.

GROWING CONDITIONS Eucalyptus trees are often planted in dry swampy areas, particularly in Italy and on the western coast of North America. They are fast-growing, commonly reaching heights of 15 to 24 m (50 to 80 ft). The trees grow in fertile, neutral-to-acidic, well-drained soil in full sun in areas with an average temperature of 16°C (60°F). The tree can withstand a minimum temperature of -15°C (5°F). Seeds are planted under cover in the spring or autumn.

CULINARY USE None.

MEDICINAL USE Before being carried to the West during the 19th century, eucalyptus was valued in traditional Australian Aboriginal medicine for hundreds of years. The tree's leaves contain eucalyptol, an active ingredient in over-the-counter chest rubs used for colds. Eucalyptol helps loosen phlegm in the chest to ease coughs. Inhaling the vapour of a few drops of eucalyptus essential oil placed in boiling water can help clear sinus and bronchial infections. With a sharp medicinal taste and antiseptic properties, eucalyptus is used as a flavouring agent in some pharmaceutical products, and gives some branded mouthwashes their intense, camphorlike taste. In addition, eucalyptus can help reduce blood sugar levels and rid the body of intestinal worms. Essential oil of eucalyptus can be used to treat diseases such as flu, measles and typhoid, and as an analgesic, anti-inflammatory rub for muscles and joints. Eucalyptus oil has been found to contain a compound as effective as 20-percent DEET (N,N-diethyl-meta-toluamide, an active ingredient in many commercial insect repellants) against mosquitoes that carry and transmit malaria. Cooling on the skin, eucalyptus can also be used to treat insect bites, stings, wounds and blisters. **Note:** Eucalyptus should not be used by those suffering from severe liver disease, inflammatory disease of the bile ducts or gastrointestinal tract or by children younger than two years of age. Additionally, eucalyptus preparations should not be used on certain areas of the face, particularly the nose and eyes, as it can irritate delicate skin.

❧ **DOSAGE** Tea: 0.25 litre (8 oz) two times daily. **Oil:** Follow label directions.

*E*UPATORIUM PURPUREUM

GRAVEL ROOT, JOE-PYE WEED

Gravel root, a member of the Asteraceae (daisy) family, is native to eastern North America and Eurasia. This hardy perennial can grow to a height of 3 m (10 ft). It bears finely toothed leaves, which have an aroma similar to vanilla when crushed, and pink flowers. Its fruits are used to produce a pink or red dye. The name *Eupatorium* refers to the 1st-century Greek king Mithridates Eupator (120–63 B.C.E.), who is said to have used a local species of this genus as medicine. The genus includes 40 species. Gravel root's imposing height and attractive appearance have given it the common name "queen-of-the-meadow". The name

"joe-pye weed" refers to the name of a Native American, said to have used the plant to cure American colonists of typhus. Some Native Americans were also believed to have carried a piece of gravel root to bring good luck when they were gambling.

❧ **GROWING CONDITIONS** Gravel root grows in sun or partial shade in well-drained, moist soil. Seeds may be planted in the spring; root divisions may be planted when the plant is dormant. The roots grow to a substantial size in 2 to 3 years. Once established, the plant requires little care or maintenance to thrive.

❧ **CULINARY USE** None.

❧ **MEDICINAL USE** Gravel root takes one of its common names from its traditional use in the prevention and treatment of kidney and urinary stones. The plant's roots and rhizomes have been found to be of particular benefit to the genital and urinary organs. Other traditional uses include the treatment of pelvic inflammatory disease, menstrual cramps, prostate and urinary tract infections, as well as rheumatism and gout. The herb has, however, been found to contain a toxic alkaloid, and its use is discouraged by many medicinal-plant experts.

❧ **DOSAGE** *Eupatorium purpureum* is toxic and should not be taken except under the direction of a qualified medical practitioner.

FOENICULUM VULGARE
Fennel Family

A member of the Apiaceae (parsley) family, fennel is the only plant in the *Foeniculum* genus. Native to the Mediterranean region, fennel is widely naturalized throughout temperate areas of the world. This tall, aromatic, yellow-flowering perennial or biennial grows well along ocean coasts and is common on the western coast of the United States and in Australia.

Foeniculum
Stems are often eaten like celery and can be added to salads for a crunchy texture.

The common name "liquorice plant" refers to the plant's delicate anise or liquorice-like scent and flavour. Its oil is used as an ingredient in commercial food flavourings, toothpastes, soaps and air fresheners. *Foeniculum* is Latin for "little hay", a reference to fennel's feathery leaves or to its use as goat fodder. Fennel has thick, celerylike, edible roots or bulbs, and bears fragrant seeds. It was cultivated by the ancient Greeks and Romans; the Greek battle of Marathon, in 490 B.C.E., took place in a fennel field. In the early Middle Ages, fennel was considered a herbal antidote to witchcraft. The seeds were eaten during Lent and other religious fasting days to alleviate hunger, and used especially to keep the stomach from rumbling during religious services. Fennel was grown on the farms of Charlemagne (742–814), the legendary medieval king of France.

Important varieties of this important herb include: sweet fennel (*F. v.* var. dulce), which has large stalks that may be eaten like celery; and bronze fennel (*F. v.* 'Purpureum'), a slightly hardier variety, which has bronze-coloured leaves.

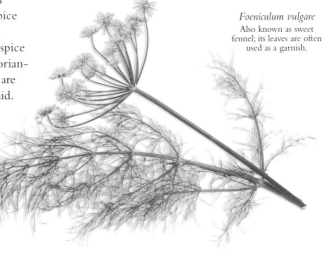

Foeniculum vulgare seeds
These are usually used as a flavour-ing agent in baked goods, sweets, liqueurs and many fish dishes.

GROWING

CONDITIONS Because of its height and attractive yellow flowers, fennel makes a good focal point in the garden. The plant prefers well-drained soil in full sun. Fennel should not be planted near bush beans, caraway or tomatoes, as it may stunt the growth of those plants. If planted near dill, the plants will hybridize and produce seedlings with an undesirable taste. Fennel will not set seed if it is planted near coriander. Seeds may be planted in the spring or autumn; root divisions may be planted in the spring. Leaves and stems may be harvested at any time. Ripe seeds may be harvested before they drop.

CULINARY USE Fennel has a mild, liquorice flavour that becomes milder when cooked. Fennel stalks and bulbs may be eaten raw or cooked as a vegetable. Sliced fennel may be combined with bitter greens, shaved Parmesan cheese, sliced apple or pear and toasted nuts, to make a delicious salad. Fennel is often sautéed or braised, and included in stir-fries, sauces and soups. The leaves can be snipped and used as a garnish. Fennel seeds, which come from the *Foeniculum vulgare* plant, are dried and used (either whole or ground) to flavour baked goods, liqueurs (notably the French *fenouillette*) and savoury dishes. The seeds are popular in fish dishes and in sausages, particularly the Italian salami *finocchiona*. Ground fennel seeds are an ingredient in Chinese five-spice powder (along with cinnamon, cloves, anise and Sichuan peppercorns) and the Ethiopian *berbere* spice blend (with garlic, red pepper, cardamom and corian-der). In Indian cuisine, whole, dried fennel seeds are commonly consumed as an after-meal digestive aid.

MEDICINAL USE Fennel is a good source of vitamin A, calcium, phosphorus and potassium. The herb has anti-microbial, anti-inflammatory, antispasmodic and mild diuretic properties. It is believed to help relax the smooth muscle of the digestive tract, and is commonly used to treat diges-tive ailments, such as bloating, stomachache,

flatulence, colic in babies and diarrhoea in children. Fennel has been used to increase breast milk production in breastfeeding mothers. A syrup made from the herb has been used to treat upper-respiratory tract inflammation. Fennel tea gargle may be used to relieve sore throat pain. Fennel seed tea can be used as an external compress to soothe inflamed, irritated eyes and conjunctivitis. In aromatherapy, essential oil of fen-nel is used externally to treat bruises and to rejuvenate dry, mature skin. The scent may aid weight loss by reducing appetite (the Greek name for fennel, *maraino*, means to grow thin), although some aromatherapists think fennel actually stimulates the appetite. **Note:** Fennel should not be used medicinally during pregnancy.

DOSAGE Tea: Drink up to 0.5 litre (16 oz) daily. **Tincture:** Use 1 or 2 ml (0.03 or 0.07 oz) in water, up to three times daily. **Standardized extract:** Take up to three 500 mg capsules daily. **Eye compress:** Steep 1 tsp fennel seeds in 0.25 litre (8 oz) water for 10 minutes; strain and apply to a clean cloth. **Bath:** Add 5 drops of essential oil to a bath of warm water. **Massage oil:** Add 10 to 20 drops of essential oil to 30 ml (1 oz) of almond or jojoba oil, and shake to mix.

Foeniculum vulgare
Also known as sweet fennel; its leaves are often used as a garnish.

F

ℱILIPENDULA ULMARIA

MEADOWSWEET, QUEEN-OF-THE-MEADOW

A member of the Rosaceae (rose) family, this hardy perennial is native to Europe and Asia and naturalized throughout North America. Meadowsweet is grown commercially in northern and eastern Europe. The herb was once called "meadwort", in reference to its use as a flavouring for the honey wine called mead. Its feathery foliage and creamy white, almond-scented flowers are the source of this attractive plant's alternative common name, queen-of-the-meadow, which describes the way it dominates a meadow. Meadowsweet flowers are made into an essential oil with a wintergreen scent and used in pot-pourris. The roots of the plant yield a black dye.

GROWING CONDITIONS Meadowsweet thrives in rich, moist-to-wet soil in sun or partial shade. Propagation is by seeds sown in the early spring or by division in the spring or autumn.

CULINARY USE Meadowsweet flowers were once added to herbal beers and wines. The leaves were placed in glasses before serving.

MEDICINAL USE Meadowsweet was revered as a sacred herb by ancient Celtic Druid priests as early as 600 B.C.E., and was mentioned in English herbal books written in the 16th and 17th centuries. Like willow bark, a herb commonly referred to as "herbal aspirin", meadowsweet contains salicylic acid. In the 19th century, salicylic acid was first isolated from meadowsweet and was later synthesized as aspirin, a word derived from the plant's former name, *Spiraea ulmaria*. The flowers and leaves of meadowsweet have been used to treat feverish colds and to alleviate rheumatic pain in muscles and joints. Meadowsweet also acts as a carminative and antacid, soothing the digestive tract, reducing acidity and relieving nausea. It has been used to treat gastritis and peptic ulcers. The herb has a gentle astringent effect that makes it useful in the treatment of diarrhoea in children. **Note:** People with sensitivity to aspirin (salicylates) should avoid the use of meadowsweet.

DOSAGE Tea: Drink 0.25 litre (8 oz) three times daily or as needed. **Tincture:** Use 30 to 40 drops three times daily. **Capsule:** Take two 500 mg capsules two or three times daily.

ℱRAGARIA VESCA AND CULTIVARS

ALPINE STRAWBERRY, STRAWBERRY, WILD STRAWBERRY

Wild strawberry is a Rosaceae (rose) family member native to Europe and Asia, now widely naturalized in northern temperate areas. This hardy, low-growing evergreen bears five-petalled white flowers with yellow centres and bright red fruits with seeds embedded in the skin. Alpine strawberries are cultivars of *F. vesca* and bear smaller, more aromatic fruits on bushier plants than ordinary strawberries.

GROWING CONDITIONS Strawberries thrive in well-drained, humus-rich soil in partial shade. Wild strawberry lack runners and therefore make neat, attractive (and edible) ground cover. Seeds are planted in the autumn, when the temperatures are approximately 18 to 24°C (64 to 75°F).

Fragaria vesca, or strawberry, is cultivated for its small, sweet fruits, which can be eaten raw, cooked or in jellies, jams and preserves. Strawberries have also been traditionally used as a home remedy for skin complaints.

🍃 **CULINARY USE** Wild strawberry leaves are frequently used in herbal tea blends. The fruits are small and delicious and are eaten raw or cooked in desserts, preserves, and in sweet and savoury dishes. Wild strawberries may also be made into wine.

🍃 **MEDICINAL USE** An infusion of strawberry leaf tea can be taken internally to treat diarrhoea and infections of the gastrointestinal and urinary tracts. Strawberry fruits contain vitamins B, C and E, and have been found to have mild diuretic properties. The fruits may be eaten to cleanse the teeth, or applied externally as a poultice to lighten the skin and soothe sunburn.

🍃 **DOSAGE** **Tea:** Drink 0.25 litre (8 oz) two or three times daily. **Poultice:** Apply crushed berries topically as necessary for burns or boils.

𝒢ENTIANA LUTEA

GENTIAN, YELLOW GENTIAN

A Gentianaceae (gentian) family member, gentian is a bright ornamental that bears large golden flowers. Native to mountainous regions of central and southern Europe and western Asia, it is commercially cultivated in North America and Europe. *Gentiana*, the genus name, derives from Gentius (180–167 B.C.E.), a king of ancient Illyria, who is said to have discovered the herb's medicinal values.

🍃 **GROWING CONDITIONS** Gentian grows in cool, moist, shady locations. The plant prefers rich soil with good drainage and a lot of water. Gentian roots take from seven to ten years to reach maturity, and wild gentian, which is becoming depleted, has protected status in several countries. Seeds can be planted in the autumn, and offshoots can be planted in the spring. Division is possible from established plants.

🍃 **CULINARY USE** Gentian is one of the most bitter-tasting herbs. It is the primary flavouring in vermouth and a key ingredient in Angostura bitters.

🍃 **MEDICINAL USE** Gentian's bitter flavour is so strong that it is detectable even at dilutions of 1 ml (0.03 oz) of the tincture in 10.5 litres (11 quarts) of water.

The herb's rhizomes and roots contain components that stimulate the production of saliva, bile and gastric juices, improving appetite and digestion. Gentian is the major ingredient in dozens of digestive bitters and tonics. It is also prescribed as a treatment for anaemia and to encourage eating during periods of convalescence. **Note:** Gentian should not be used by those with gastric and duodenal ulcers and when gastric irritation and inflammation are present. The herb may not be tolerated by pregnant women or those with high blood pressure.

🍃 **DOSAGE** **Tea:** Drink 118 ml (4 oz) two or three times daily. **Tincture:** Use 0.5 to 1 ml (0.017 to 0.03 oz) two or three times daily.

𝒢INKGO BILOBA

GINKGO, MAIDENHAIR TREE

The sole member of the Ginkgoaceae (ginkgo) family, ginkgo is the world's most ancient tree and the only surviving member of its genus. A deciduous tree not usually found in the wild, ginkgo can live for as long as 1,000 years. Native to China and Japan, where it has long been considered a sacred plant, ginkgo was first brought to

Europe in the 18th century by German physician Engelbert Kaempfer (1651–1716). It is now under commercial production in the southern United States, France, and China. Both male and female versions of the tree exist; females bear an inedible, foetid-smelling apricot-like fruit. "Ginkgo" comes from the Japanese *gin* (silver) and *kyo* (apricot). *Biloba* (bi-lobed) refers to the tree's fan-shaped two-lobed leaves. Because ginkgo is believed to have positive effects on memory, brain function and circulation, it has been called the "anti-ageing" herb and is an ingredient in herbal medicines in Europe. Ginkgo leaf extract is also found in cosmetics, shampoo and skin cream.

❧ **GROWING CONDITIONS** Ginkgos are attractive, hardy trees, commonly grown for their beauty and their ability to withstand cold temperatures, pollution, insect pests and disease. Ginkgo trees thrive in almost every soil type, except very wet, and can adapt to part shade, part sun or full sun. Male trees are planted more often than female, as the latter produce messy, foul-smelling fruits. Male and female flowers grow on separate plants, so ginkgo trees are able to fruit only when male and female trees are grown together.

❧ **CULINARY USE** Ginkgo nuts (the seeds of ginkgo fruits) are very nutritious and contain very little fat. Slightly toxic when raw, the nuts turn green when they are cooked, and taste somewhat like pine nuts. Ginkgo nuts are considered a delicacy in China, where they are served at weddings and special feasts, and are added to casseroles and to vegetable and rice dishes. In Japan, the nuts are eaten after meals to aid digestion.

❧ **MEDICINAL USE** Ginkgo seeds have been used as food and medicine in Asia for thousands of years. The Chinese eat cooked ginkgo nuts for their appealing taste, and strengthening properties, and to increase sexual energy and restore

hearing loss. Boiled as a tea, the nuts are used to treat coughs, asthma, allergies and wheezing. Today, the tree's leaves are the part that is primarily used for medicinal purposes. The leaves have antioxidant properties and contain flavonoids, called ginkgo flavone glycosides, and terpenoids, called ginkgolides and bilobalides, which appear to be responsible for the herb's ability to improve blood flow to the extremities and to the brain, eyes and ears, particularly in the elderly. Ginkgo supplements have shown promising results in treating tinnitus, dimming vision, and concentration and memory problems, as well as slowing the progression of Alzheimer's disease. Because of the plant's ability to dilate blood vessels, the herb is also used to treat intermittent claudication (intense cramping in the calf muscles).

❧ **DOSAGE Tincture:** Use 1 ml (0.03 oz) two or three times daily. **Standardized extract:** Take one 40 mg capsule standardized to 24 percent ginkgo flavone glycosides and 6 percent terpene lactones three times daily.

𝒢LYCINE MAX

SOYA, SOYBEAN

Soybeans are one of some 20,000 legume species, the majority of which are poisonous. The soybean plant, a native of southwestern Asia, was first cultivated in China around 1200 B.C.E. The plant was introduced to Europe in the 18th century and is now cultivated in warm, temperate regions throughout the world. In the late 19th century, Chinese immigrants carried the plant to North America, where approximately 50 percent of the world's soybean supply is now grown. A member of the Fabaceae (pea) family, the soybean is an annual. Fine hairs cover its stems, leaves and bean pods, giving the plant a fuzzy appearance. There are more than 1,000 soybean varieties, which bear beans in colours including red, yellow, black, brown and green. The beans are a nutritious and inexpensive source of vegetable protein. They are an ingredient in food products throughout the world. Soybean by-products are used in the production of plastic products and soap. In China, soybeans are considered to be one of the "five sacred grains", grains essential to Chinese civilization (the others are rice, barley, wheat and millet).

casseroles. (Heat deactivates the digestion-blocking toxin found in many legumes.) Soybean sprouts can be eaten in salads.

Green summer soybeans, known as *edamame*, may be steamed, lightly salted and eaten as a vegetable.

Soy milk, which is made by pressing cooked soybeans, is a high-protein, iron-rich milk substitute for those who are lactose-intolerant. It can also be used to make desserts and puddings.

Soybeans may be processed into several solid forms, including tofu and tempeh, which can be sliced and used to replace meat in sauces, stir-fries, casseroles and pasta dishes. Tofu is available in a variety of consistencies and textures, and can even be added to desserts and puddings. Tofu has a blander flavour than tempeh. It was developed by the Chinese around 200 B.C.E., and called *dofu* (*do* means curdled; *fu* means bean). To make tofu, soy milk is curdled with an acid or salt and pressed in a manner similar to the way in which cheese is produced. Nutritionally, tofu is considered to be an almost perfect food. It is low in calories, high in protein, rich in minerals, cholesterol-free, and it contains all the amino acids necessary to the human diet.

GROWING CONDITIONS Usually grown as a crop in fields, soybeans may be planted in the garden, similarly to bush beans. They prefer a well-limed, well-drained soil in full sun with plenty of room between rows. Seeds may be planted in the late spring, when soil temperatures reach 18 to 24°C (65 to 75°F). The bean pods may be harvested when ripe, and eaten fresh or dried for later use.

CULINARY USE Soybeans are used in cooking in several different forms. The dried beans can be pre-soaked and then cooked, like any dried bean, in soups and

Tempeh is a fermented soybean product, made by mixing the beans with a grain, such as rice or millet, and allowing the mixture to ferment. A substance called texturized vegetable protein (TVP), made by processing defatted soy flour into granules or chunks, is used to make vegetarian versions of almost any non-vegetarian food, from hot dogs and hamburgers to cheese and ice cream. Soybeans can be pressed to produce an oil that is a common ingredient in Chinese cuisine, and is also in margarine and vegetable shortening. Soy flour, made from dried, processed soybeans, has twice the protein of wheat flour and can be used in baking. Miso, a salty paste made from fermented soybeans, and soy sauce and tamari, which are both used to ferment boiling soybeans with roasted wheat or barley, are used to flavour soups, sauces, and many Japanese and Chinese dishes.

MEDICINAL USE Soybeans are higher in protein and lower in carbohydrates than most other legumes. They contain a group of compounds called isoflavones, including genistein and daidzein, which are believed to help lower cholesterol levels, prevent heart disease, cancer and osteoporosis, and ease the symptoms of menopause. In Asian countries, where a much lower rate of cancer and osteoporosis exists than in Western cultures, people commonly consume 150 to 200 milligrams of soy each day.

DOSAGE Capsule: Follow label directions.

GLYCYRRHIZA GLABRA

LIQUORICE, RUSSIAN LIQUORICE, SPANISH LIQUORICE, TURKISH LIQUORICE

The genus *Glycyrrhiza* includes about twenty species native to North and South America, Europe, Asia and Australia. A member of the Fabaceae (pea) family, liquorice is a perennial with downy stems and pale blue to violet flowers that appear in loose spikes, followed by oblong pods. The plant's deep, yellowish-brown taproot sends out thin, horizontal rhizomes. The Greek name for liquorice is "sweet root", and, in fact the root is about fifty times sweeter than sugar. In the 14th century, the English King Edward I (1239–1307) levied a tax on liquorice imports to finance the repair of London Bridge. The French emperor Napoleon Bonaparte (1769–1821). enjoyed chewing liquorice sticks, a habit which is said to have discoloured his teeth.

GROWING CONDITIONS Liquorice grows in sunny locations in deep, rich, sandy soil that is slightly alkaline and moisture-retentive. Roots should only be harvested only after a plant is three to four years old.

CULINARY USE Liquorice extracts are used to flavour many products, including beers and soft drinks. The herb was once used to flavour sweets, but anise is now used for this purpose. Liquorice is also used to make herbal tea.

MEDICINAL USE The primary component of liquorice root is glycyrrhizin, a compound that acts much like cortisone, stimulating the excretion of hormones by the adrenal cortex. For this reason liquorice is thought to benefit people suffering from adrenal weakness. Liquorice has long been used to treat arthritis and allergies, and as a cough suppressant. The root was once used to treat toothache and fever in children. The herb is currently used as an expectorant and demulcent because it stimulates mucous secretions of the trachea. It has also recently been used to treat gastric and duodenal ulcers. To reduce water retention, a side effect of consuming liquorice, researchers have developed a form of the herb called deglycyrrhizinated liquorice, or DGL. In this incarnation of the herb, 97 percent of the glycyrrhizin has been removed. In Traditional Chinese Medicine, another species of liquorice root (*G. uralensis*) is used as an antacid, and to control coughs and strengthen digestion. **Note:** The herb should not be taken during pregnancy or by those with heart disease, liver disease or hypertension.

DOSAGE Tincture: Use 1 ml (0.03 oz) three times daily. **Standardized extract:** Take two 500 mg capsules three times daily. **DGL (deglycyrrhizinated liquorice) tablets:** Chew two 250 mg tablets three times daily.

H

ℋAMAMELIS VIRGINIANA

WITCH HAZEL

A member of the Hamamelideaceae (witch hazel) family, this small, golden-flowered shrub or small tree is native to eastern North America. It is cultivated in the eastern United States and Canada, and, on a smaller scale, in Europe. In colonial America, the shrub's pliable forked branches were a favourite "witching stick" used by dowsers to search for hidden water supplies or precious metals.

GROWING CONDITIONS Witch hazel flourishes on shaded north-facing slopes, along fences, country roads and the stony banks of brooks. Seeds may be planted in the fall in moist, humus-rich, neutral to acid soil in sun to partial shade. Softwood cuttings are planted in the summer.

CULINARY USE None.

MEDICINAL USE For nearly 200 years, witch hazel has been valued for its astringent, tonic and mild pain-relieving properties. It is a common ingredient in a wide range of personal-care products, including deodorant, aftershave lotion, disposable wipes, soap and body cream. A distilled extract of witch hazel twigs can be taken internally to treat haemorrhoids, varicose veins and diarrhoea. The herb may have antiviral activity against *Herpes simplex* virus type 1. Witch hazel can be applied topically to treat superficial cuts, haemorrhoids and insect bites. **Note:** Used internally, witch hazel may irritate the stomach.

DOSAGE Tea: Drink 118 to 237 ml (4 to 8 oz) two to three times daily. **Tincture:** Dilute 2 ml (0.07 oz) in 118 ml (4 oz) water and apply to varicose veins. **Lotion or ointment:** Apply externally as needed. **Distilled:** Dab onto broken veins and sore skin.

ℋARPAGOPHYTUM PROCUMBENS

DEVIL'S CLAW

A member of the Pedaliaceae (sesame) family, devil's claw is a trailing perennial that bears bright red flowers and barbed, woody fruit. Native to southwestern Africa, most of the commercial devil's claw supply is wild-harvested from Namibia and the Kalahari desert. The common name, "devil's claw" and the genus name *Harpagophytum* (*harpagos* is Greek for hook) both refer to the hooks on devil claw's fruit, which tend to stick to the coats of animals passing by. In Madagascar, the fruits are said to be used as natural mouse traps.

GROWING CONDITIONS Devil's claw grows in red, sandy soil in full sun. The plant prefers roadsides and waste areas cleared of underbrush. Seeds may be planted in the spring.

CULINARY USE None.

MEDICINAL USE Commonly used in traditional African medicine, devil's claw contains a chemical constituent called harpagoside, which reduces inflammation in the joints, making the herb a popular arthritis remedy. Devil's claw has analgesic effects and may be particularly helpful in the treatment of joint and lower-back pain. The herb has

Hamamelis Virginiana
Witch hazel

Devil's claw root has been used in remedies to treat pain, and in topical ointments to heal sores, boils and other skin problems.

also been used to treat poor digestion and lack of appetite. **Note:** Devil's claw should not be used by individuals with gastric or duodenal ulcers, or those who are pregnant or nursing.

🌿 **DOSAGE** **Tea:** Drink 0.25 litre (8 oz) daily. **Tincture:** Use 1 ml (0.03 oz) three times daily. **Standardized extract:** Take up to six 500 mg capsules daily. Because the herb may be deactivated by the body's digestive juices, buying coated capsules may be advisable.

HELIANTHUS ANNUUS

SUNFLOWER

An Asteraceae (daisy) family member, the sunflower is native to North America. The plant was introduced in Europe and Russia, and is now grown extensively worldwide. This fast-growing annual bears large flowers that range in colour from gold to reddish-brown to yellow. The flower heads, which yield a yellow dye, rotate during the day to face the sun. *Helianthus* is derived from *helios* (sun) and *anthos* (a flower). Sunflowers were highly revered by ancient Peru Inca peoples. Priestesses of the Inca temples of the sun were crowned with sunflowers and carried them in their hands.

🌿 **GROWING CONDITIONS** Sunflowers thrive in well-drained and well-tilled soil in full sun. a fast bloomer, sunflowers can grow as tall as 3.5 m (12 ft). They have highly efficient root systems, and are fairly drought resistant except during their flowering stage. The blossoms attract beneficial insects that prey on garden pests such as aphids. Seeds may be planted in the spring.

🌿 **CULINARY USE** Sunflower seeds can be eaten raw, or roasted and salted, and added to breads or ground to make flour. The seeds are pressed to extract a citron-yellow vegetable oil that is used in cooking, salad dressings and margarine. Sunflower oil has a sweet taste and is considered as good as olive oil or almond oil for table use. The residue left after the oil is extracted provides a high-protein food source for livestock. Young sunflower sprouts, harvested about a week after growing, are a delicious addition to salads.

🌿 **MEDICINAL USE** On the border between food and herb, sunflowers are a source of dietary protein, fat, carbohydrates, fibre and vitamin E. The seeds have long been thought to have diuretic and expectorant properties, and have been used in the treatment of bronchial, laryngeal, and pulmonary afflictions, coughs and colds and whooping cough. The whole plant has been used to treat malaria. For external use, sunflower oil forms the base of massage oils and liniments used to treat muscle aches and rheumatic complaints.

🌿 **DOSAGE** **Massage oils and liniment:** Follow label directions.

HUMULUS LUPULUS

HOPS

Hops are a member of the Cannabaceae (hemp) family. Native to North America, Europe and Asia, the plant grows as a tall, spindly, clinging vine (the name "hops" comes from the Anglo-Saxon *hoppan,* meaning "to climb"). It bears bright green leaves with heart-shaped lobes and cone-shaped fruit, used to give beer its distinctive flavour. Hops are cultivated in nearly every country of the world, especially in the northwest of the United States and in Germany, two areas renowned for their beers. After the observation that hop-pickers often became unusually tired and were sometimes found napping on the job sleep pillows, or "dream pillows", containing hops were created to help induce restful sleep. These pillows are still popular today, and often contain lavender or rose petals.

GROWING CONDITIONS
Hops favour a deeply dug, rich, well-drained soil. The plants are drought tolerant but prefer regular watering. They can grow in sun or partial shade and thrive in the heat. Hops may be propagated from young shoots or from cuttings or underground stems in the late summer.

CULINARY USE
Hops are cultivated primarily to obtain the bitter principles used in the brewing of beer. The young shoots can be boiled, steamed or eaten raw and served like asparagus.

MEDICINAL USE
The fruit of the hop plant contains resinous bitter principles, essential oil, and flavonoids, which give it sedative and spasmolytic properties. Hops have been used therapeutically to relieve anxiety, insomnia, restlessness, and lack of appetite. **Note:** It is advisable to avoid the use of hops in cases of depression.

DOSAGE
Tea: Drink 0.25 litre (8 oz) three or four times daily. **Tincture:** Use 3 or 4 ml (0.10 or 0.14 oz) two or three times daily. **Standardized extract:** Take one 500 mg capsule three times daily.

HYDRASTIS CANADENSIS

GOLDENSEAL, ORANGE ROOT, YELLOW ROOT

A member of the Ranunculaceae (buttercup) family, goldenseal is native to the forests of eastern North America. This perennial has bright yellow roots and bears deeply toothed leaves and red, raspberry-like berries. Golden marks on the plant's roots were believed to resemble the wax seals once used to hold envelopes closed. Native Americans used goldenseal's roots as a source of natural dye for clothing.

GROWING CONDITIONS
Goldenseal thrives in rich, moist, well-drained soil in shade. The genus name *Hydrastis* is Latin for "water", referring to goldenseal's affinity for a damp growing environment. Seeds are planted in the autumn or by root division when dormant.

CULINARY USE
None.

MEDICINAL USE
Traditionally used by Native Americans to treat gastric complaints, such as indigestion and poor appetite, the root of goldenseal contains the alkaloids berberine and hydrastine, which have the ability to stimulate digestion, increase bile flow, and lower blood

H

pressure levels. Goldenseal is thought to have an astringent effect on mucous membranes. It may alleviate inflammation and act as a broad-spectrum antimicrobial and antiseptic useful in the treatment of infections caused by bacteria, including *E. coli, Giardia lamblia, Staphylococcus* and *Streptococcus*. Goldenseal has also been taken to treat menorrhagia (long, heavy menstrual periods). Used externally as an eyewash and mouthwash, it reduces inflammation and acts as an astringent and antiseptic, killing or preventing the growth of bacteria in the eyes and the mouth. According to recent studies, goldenseal may improve cardiovascular action, making it useful in the treatment of heart failure, and fast or irregular heartbeat. **Note:** Goldenseal should not be used during pregnancy. The popularity of goldenseal has led to its being overharvested in the wild. Some herb companies have begun growing their own goldenseal. Alternative herbs include Oregon grape root (*Mahonia aquifolium*) and American goldthread (*Coptis trifolia*).

❧ **DOSAGE** **Tincture:** Use 1 or 2 ml (0.03 or 0.07 oz) twice daily. **Standardized extract:** Take up to four 500 or 600 mg capsules a day.

*H*YPERICUM PERFORATUM

ST JOHN'S WORT

The *Hypericum* genus includes about 370 species of annuals, perennials and evergreen shrubs. A member of the Clusiaceae family, St John's wort is native to Europe, North Africa and western Asia, and is naturalized in parts of North and South America, Africa, Asia and Australia. *H. perforatum* is a perennial that bears blunt leaves; bright yellow, five-petalled flowers; and red, pink, orange, green or brown berries. The flowers are perforated with tiny dots that give the plant its species name, *perforatum*. The common name "St John's wort" is thought to refer either to the date the plants bloom, around the time of St John's Day (June 24) or to the reddish colour produced when the buds and flowers are crushed – a symbol of the Biblical figure John the

St John's wort has gained much fame for its antidepressant properties, but is also used around the world to treat pain associated with ailments as benign as toothache and as serious as spinal injury.

Baptist, who is often depicted wearing a red robe, a symbol of his martyrdom. An extract from the plant produces a violet-red dye that has been used to colour silks and wool. Because it is thought that the plant can heal the skin, it is a common ingredient in topical skin cleansers and face, body and hand creams.

❧ **GROWING CONDITIONS** St John's wort prefers full sun and soil that is well drained and fairly dry. It is commonly found growing wild in fields, pastures, rangelands and along roadsides. Given the right growing conditions, St John's wort can become invasive. Cattle ranchers consider it a pest, as it can be toxic to cattle if consumed in extremely large quantities. Propagation may be done in the spring or autumn by seed or root division.

❧ **CULINARY USE** None.

❧ **MEDICINAL USE** Used traditionally for more than 2,000 years to treat insomnia, anxiety and mild depression, the flowers and unopened buds of St John's wort contain hyperforin, a compound that has antibiotic properties; hypericin, a substance that gives oils and tinctures a characteristic deep red colour; and pseudohypericin, which is thought to be responsible for the plant's antidepressant action. Scientific studies and research have confirmed the safety and effectiveness of St John's wort in treating mild to moderate depression, along with accompanying fatigue, anxiety and insomnia. In Germany, the plant outsells the pharmaceutical antidepressant Prozac by 20 to 1. This remarkable herb has proven valuable in the treatment of such varied conditions as traumatic shock, spinal injuries, haemorrhoids, weakened nerves, facial pain from toothaches and dental extractions, and irritability and anxiety associated with menopause. St John's wort may have antibacterial, antifungal and anti-inflammatory properties. An oil extracted from the plant may be applied externally to accelerate the healing of injuries (especially in the case of nerve damage), sciatica, superficial wounds, bruises, varicose veins and mild burns, including sunburn. **Note:** St John's wort may increase sun sensitivity. Fair-skinned people should avoid excessive exposure to sunlight when using the herb.

❧ **DOSAGE** **Tea:** Drink 0.25 litre (8 oz) two or three times daily. **Tincture:** Use 1 or 2 ml (0.03 oz or 0.07 oz) two or three times daily. **Standardized extract:** Take one 300 mg capsule standardized to 0.3 percent hypericin three times daily.

Hyssopus officinalis

HYSSOP

A Lamiaceae (mint) family member, hyssop grows freely in the Mediterranean region, especially in the Balkans and in Turkey. The plant is commercially cultivated in Europe, Russia and India. This small perennial bears soft, hairy grey leaves and double-lipped blue flowers that are attractive to bees and butterflies. Hyssop was given its name by the ancient Greek physician Hippocrates, who called it *Hyssopus*, from the Hebrew *ezob*, meaning holy herb. The plant has long been considered a medicinal panacea. According to an old saying, "Whoever rivals hyssop's virtues, knows too much."

GROWING CONDITIONS A common garden herb, hyssop prefers sunny, dry locations. Hyssop is propagated by seed, root division, or cuttings. The flowers may be harvested in the summer.

CULINARY USE Traditionally used to flavour soups and meat dishes, some people find hyssop's bitter flavour, said to be similar to a combination of sage and mint, too strong for modern tastes. The herb can be added (with a light hand) to legumes, salads and fruit dishes. Hyssop is an ingredient in Chartreuse liqueur and a renowned flavouring for honey in France.

MEDICINAL USE Hyssop has flavonoids, tannins, resins, and terpenes, including marubin, which is a strong expectorant. The herb also contains a volatile oil (consisting mainly of camphor), which has an antispasmodic action useful in the treatment of indigestion, wind, bloating and colic. The herb's flowering tops have been used in the treatment of bronchitis and respiratory infections to clear away phlegm. Hyssop has also been used to reduce the congestion and fevers of colds and flu. The herb has a sedative effect and is thought to be useful in the treatment of asthma in both children and adults. **Note:** Hyssop should not be used during pregnancy.

DOSAGE Tea: Drink 0.25 litre (8 oz) two or three times daily. **Tincture:** Use 1 or 2 ml (0.03 or 0.07 oz) two or three times daily.

Ilex paraguariensis

MATÉ, PARAGUAY TEA, YERBA MATÉ

The genus *Ilex* includes approximately 400 species. Maté, an evergreen shrub or small tree, is a member of the Aquifoliaceae (holly) family. Native to South America, it is cultivated in Argentina, Portugal and Spain. The most common use of maté is in the production of a popular slightly bitter South American tea of the same name. The tree bears leathery, oval leaves and small red berries; the leaves are harvested when the berries are ripe. They are then heated, ground and stored in sacks for approximately one year before being used to make the beverage. More than 300 years ago, Jesuit missionaries introduced maté tea to European colonists. The Jesuits named the herb from the Spanish word for "gourd", in reference to the gourds from which South American tribal people drank their tea. Maté is still drunk from a small gourd.

GROWING CONDITIONS Maté grows wild near streams throughout South America. It thrives in moist, well-drained soil in full sun or partial shade and takes

*I*NDIGOFERA TINCTORIA

INDIGO, TRUE INDIGO

Indigo, a member of the Fabaceae (pea) family, is a perennial deciduous shrub that bears small reddish-orange flowers. The plant is native to India and is widely cultivated there. It is naturalized in Hawaii and the southern United States. Although the leaflets and branches of many *Indigofera* species yield a natural blue dye, *I. tinctoria* is believed to contain the highest number of dye-producing components. Approximately 300 kg (660 lb) of *I. tinctoria* are required to produce about 1 kg (2.2 lb) of the dye. The ancient Greek word for the dye, *indicon*, means "blue dye from

approximately 25 years to grow to its average height of about 15m (50 ft). The plant will not tolerate temperatures colder than 7°C (45°F). Seeds may be planted in the spring; semi-ripe cuttings may be planted in the late summer or autumn.

◟ CULINARY USE Maté tea is such a popular beverage in South America that more than 200 brands of the tea are sold in Argentina alone. In Uruguay, people drink an average of 10 kg (22 lb) of maté annually; in Argentina, the average is 5 kg (11 lb). A cup of maté contains about half as much caffeine as a cup of brewed coffee and is usually drunk plain, although milk, lemon or sugar are sometimes added for extra flavour. Maté also contains vitamin C and minerals, including iron, calcium, potassium and zinc. In South America, the herb is used to flavour foods ranging from bread to soft drinks.

◟ MEDICINAL USE In addition to caffeine, maté contains astringent and antiseptic tannins, similar to those in green tea (*Camellia sinensis*). In addition, the herb has diuretic properties and has been found to stimulate the nervous system, and relieve mental and physical fatigue. In South America, the herb is taken as an appetite suppressant and used to relieve mild depression, and nervous tension and migraine headaches, in addition to rheumatic pain.

◟ DOSAGE Tea: Drink up to 0.75 litre (24 oz) as needed. **Standardized extract:** Take three 500 mg capsules as needed.

J

India". Ancient Romans used the word *indicum*, which later became "indigo" in English. The worldwide cultivation of indigo declined sharply with the advent of modern synthetic dyes.

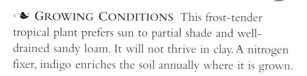

❧ **GROWING CONDITIONS** This frost-tender tropical plant prefers sun to partial shade and well-drained sandy loam. It will not thrive in clay. A nitrogen fixer, indigo enriches the soil annually where it is grown.

❧ **CULINARY USE** None.

❧ **MEDICINAL USE** Although not generally used in current medicine, indigo root and stem are thought to cleanse the liver and blood, relieve pain, reduce inflammation and fight fever. In one animal study with rats, indigo was shown to have liver-protecting properties. The herb has been used to treat hepatitis. An ointment made from indigo leaf may be applied externally to treat sores, ulcers and haemorrhoids. In Indian Ayurvedic medicine, indigo root is used to treat difficult urination, dental cavities and consumption. False indigo (*Baptisia tinctoria*) is used medicinally as an astringent, anti-inflammatory and antiseptic, as well as a fever reducer.

❧ **DOSAGE** No standard dosage has been established.

*J*ASMINUM OFFICINALE SYN. GRANDIFLORUM

JASMINE, POET'S JASMINE

Native to India, this member of the Oleaceae (olive) is part of a genus of about 350 species of evergreen shrubs and climbing plants. With its clusters of fragrant white flowers, jasmine is cultivated as a popular ornamental garden plant and a source of prized essential oil. The plant's name comes from the Persian *yasmin*, meaning "white flower". Introduced to Europe in the 16th century, jasmine's (very expensive) essential oil is used to make high-quality floral perfumes.

❧ **GROWING CONDITIONS** Jasmine grows in warm climates in rich, well-drained soil in full sun. The plant can withstand a minimum temperature of 7°C (45°F). Seeds may be planted in the spring; semi-ripe cuttings may be planted in the summer. The fragrant jasmine flowers, which are approximately 2 cm (¾ in) across, are harvested soon after they open each morning year round.

❧ **CULINARY USE** Jasmine teas are among the oldest of scented teas and are still quite popular today. They are prepared by combining the flowers of the night-blooming jasmine with tea each evening. At nightfall, the blossoms open and infuse the tea with their aroma. Each morning, the flowers are removed and replaced with fresh blossoms that evening. This process is repeated several times, depending on the grade of tea being prepared. To manufacture the highest-grade jasmine teas, this nightly infusion may continue for up to two weeks.

❧ **MEDICINAL USE** Although they are rarely used in Western medicine today, jasmine flowers were once used as an ingredient in cough syrup. In Indian Ayurvedic medicine, jasmine has been used to treat such conditions as fever, sunstroke, headache, and skin conditions including boils and abscesses. In addition, the essential oil of jasmine may have antidepressant and relaxing effects. It is used in aromatherapy to relieve tension, and may be applied externally to soothe dry, irritated or sensitive skin.

❧ **DOSAGE** **Bath:** Add 5 ml (0.25 oz) of essential oil to a bath of warm water. **Aromatherapy massage oil:** Add 10 to 20 ml (0.30 to 0.60 oz) of essential oil to 30 ml (1 oz) of almond or jojoba oil, and shake to mix.

JUGLANS REGIA

ENGLISH WALNUT, PERSIAN WALNUT

This member of the Juglandaceae (walnut) family belongs to a genus of twenty-one deciduous trees. English walnut grows wild from southern Europe to southern China and is naturalized in temperate areas throughout the world. The tree has silver-grey bark and bears dark green fruit, each containing an edible nut inside a hard shell. The genus name *Juglans* comes from the Latin *Iupiter* (Jupiter) and *glans* (acorn), in reference to a legend that when gods walked the Earth they lived on a diet of walnuts. The wood of English walnut trees is used in furniture-making.

GROWING CONDITIONS English walnut grows in deep, rich, well-drained soil in full sun. Seeds are planted in the autumn; ripe fruits are harvested in the summer and fall.

CULINARY USE Walnuts are a key ingredient in baked goods and in savoury recipes such as Middle Eastern chicken dishes. Walnut oil is used as a tasty salad dressing. Walnuts have also been substituted for pine nuts in the traditional Italian basil-based pesto sauce.

MEDICINAL USE Walnuts are a good dietary source of essential fatty acids, especially alpha-linolenic acid, which makes them useful in the treatment of dry skin, eczema and pre-menstrual syndrome. Studies have shown that walnuts

contain compounds that help lower cholesterol levels and reduce the risk of heart disease. English walnut leaves have astringent properties; a tea of the leaves has been used to expel intestinal worms. They also have antispasmodic effects that benefit digestion. A solution made from the leaves may be used to treat eczema and superficial skin wounds.

DOSAGE Tea: Drink up to 0.5 litre (16 oz) daily. **Oil:** Use 2 tsp daily as a dietary supplement. **Wash:** Steep 2 tsp crushed leaves in 0.25 litre (8 oz) of boiling water. Cool, strain and apply to affected areas.

JUNIPERUS COMMUNIS

COMMON JUNIPER, JUNIPER

A member of the Cupressaceae (cedar) family, juniper is a popular ornamental, native to North America and Europe. The plant can be an upright, spreading or prostrate shrub. Juniper has reddish brown, papery bark, and bears green fruits that turn black when ripe. Juniper sprigs were burned to ward off the plague, and thrown into fires to protect against evil spirits. The wood of eastern red cedar (*J. virginiana*) is often made into cabinets, fences and pencils.

GROWING CONDITIONS Juniper grows in moist soil in sun or partial shade, in both acid and alkaline soils. Seeds may be planted under cover in the spring or autumn; lateral-shoot cuttings may be planted, and fruits gathered when ripe, in the autumn.

CULINARY USE Juniper berries give gin its characteristic flavour. The berries are also used to flavour other foods including pork, fowl, game such as

L

boar, sauces and stuffings. The berries are too bitter to be eaten raw and so are generally crushed and used in marinades. Juniper berries are sold dried.

🍂 MEDICINAL USE Juniper's volatile oil contains more than sixty compounds that give the herb its anti-microbial, analgesic and anti-inflammatory properties. Juniper is a strong antiseptic for the urinary tract, making it a useful remedy for cystitis, when combined with soothing herbs such as marsh mallow and corn silk. It also has powerful diuretic properties, and may help settle indigestion. A massage oil whose ingredients include juniper's essential oil may help ease joint pain. **Note:** Juniper should not be used by those who suffer from kidney disease or kidney infections, or by women during pregnancy. Juniper should not be taken internally for more than six weeks at a time. The essential oil is for external use only.

🍂 DOSAGE **Tea:** Drink up to 0.25 litre (16 oz) each day. **Tincture:** Use 20 to 30 drops, three times daily. **Standardized extract:** Take one or two 400 mg capsules per day. **Massage oil:** Dilute 10 drops of essential oil of juniper in 30 ml (1 oz) of almond or jojoba oil, and shake to mix.

*L*ARREA TRIDENTATA

CHAPARRAL, CREOSOTE BUSH

A member of the Zygophyllaceae (creosote bush) family, chaparral is a thorny, woody, olive-green or yellow shrub with a strong odour of tar, or creosote. The plant dominates the landscape of the desert regions of North America.

GROWING CONDITIONS The chaparral bush can grow to 3 m (10 ft) tall. Its roots radiate beyond its above-ground parts, and contain chemicals that kill other plants.

CULINARY USE None.

MEDICINAL USE Chaparral contains nordihydroguaiauretic acid (NDGA), a strong antiseptic compound that is extracted from the leaves. The compound was formerly used by the food industry as an antioxidant that preserved cooking oils. Chaparral has traditionally been used to treat wounds and as an ingredient in mouthwash. A recent study has shown that it may reduce cavity forma-tion by up to 75 percent. Chaparral has antimicrobial, antiviral, antioxidant and hyperglycaemic properties. Native Americans used teas made of the leaves, flowers and twigs to treat respiratory, digestive tract and skin disorders. A tea made from just the leaves was used to treat colds, coughs, asthma and diarrhoea. Modern herbalists use chaparral to treat the same conditions in addition to as HIV and cancer, although Western medicine has yet to embrace chaparral as a bonafide treatment. **Note:** Chaparral should not be used during pregnancy, or while breastfeeding, or by those with liver or kidney disease. It should not be taken internally for periods of longer than two weeks at a time.

DOSAGE Tea: Drink up to 0.75 litre (24 oz) per day for 2 weeks. **Mouthwash:** Rinse or gargle with chaparral tea as desired.

ℒAURUS NOBILIS

BAY, BAY LAUREL, GRECIAN LAUREL, SWEET BAY, TRUE BAY

A dense pyramid-shaped evergreen shrub or small tree with leathery, pointed leaves, bay is native to the Mediterranean region. It is widely cultivated in Europe and northern Africa. The genus name *Laurus*, which comes from the Latin *laus*, means "praise". Wreaths of bay leaves were woven into crowns in ancient Greece and Rome and presented to scholars, poets and Olympic victors. These crowns are still presented today to signify athletic achievement. In addition, bay is a popular fragrance ingredient in aftershave lotions.

GROWING CONDITIONS Bay is an ideal con-tainer plant. It grows in well-drained soil in full sun or partial shade, but must be sheltered from cold and frost. Semi-ripe cuttings are planted in the autumn. Bay leaves may be collected year-round and dried for future use.

CULINARY USE Dried bay leaves are very popu-lar in French, Spanish and Creole cuisine and often used to flavour poultry, stews, vegetables and meat dishes. Bay is an ingredient of *bouquet garni*, a group of herbs (usually parsley, thyme and bay) that are tied together, or placed in a cheesecloth bag and used to flavour soups.

MEDICINAL USE Though bay is primarily a culinary herb, it is used as a digestive tonic to settle the stomach, stimulate the appetite and increase the secre-tion of digestive juices. When used in cooking, bay leaves help break down foods, especially meat, making digestion easier. Liniments containing essential oil of bay can be used externally to ease the pain of arthritis. **Note:** Essential oil of bay may irritate the skin of sensi-tive individuals, and should be applied only in dilute (approximately 2 percent) concentrations.

DOSAGE Bath: Add 0.25 litre (8 oz) bay leaf tea to bath water. **Liniment:** Follow label directions.

LAVANDULA ANGUSTIFOLIA
Lavender

There are twenty-one species in the *Lavandula* genus, and hundreds of cultivars. Native to France and the western Mediterranean region, lavender is naturalized in Europe, the Middle East and India. It is cultivated throughout the temperate areas of the world. This member of the Lamiaceae (mint) family bears grey-green foliage and aromatic purple or white flowers.

Referred to as *spikenard* in the Bible, the common name lavender comes from the Roman *lavare* (to wash), a reference to the herb's use as a scent for bathing and washing clothes. During the Middle Ages, lavender was believed to be an aphrodisiac. Sprinkling lavender water on a lover's head was thought to keep him faithful. In the 19th century, women who were prone to fainting would revive themselves with lavender-scented handkerchiefs. A poultice of heated lavender flowers was traditionally placed on a woman's back to relieve tension during labour. English farmers once tucked lavender under their hats to prevent sunstroke and headache. Today, lavender is used to scent skin lotions, shampoos, soaps, perfume, potpourri and herbal sachets. Lavender stalks are woven into lavender "wands" and hung in closets or placed in drawers to deter moths.

GROWING CONDITIONS Lavender, a beloved garden plant, often appears in borders and hedges. The herb releases its scent when touched, so lavender is often planted in areas where passers-by will brush against it. Lavender's grey-green foliage and purple or white flowers may be attractively paired with roses, yarrow or echinacea. The herb prefers well-drained, neutral to alkaline soil in full sun. Seeds may be planted in the autumn and semi-ripe cuttings may be planted in the summer. Flowers are cut when they begin to open, and may be dried in small bunches inside paper bags. As they age, lavender plants become woody. Some experts recommend replacing them approximately every four years.

CULINARY USE Lavender flowers and leaves add colour and a pungent, slightly bitter flavour to salads. The plant is sometimes used to flavour herbal oils and vinegars, cheese, jam, jelly, honey, and delicate baked goods such as shortbread biscuits and scones. The flowers can be candied and used to decorate cakes. Lavender sorbets and ice creams are eaten in France and in other parts of the world. On its own or in tea blends, lavender makes a delicious hot or cold drink.

Lavandula angustifolia officinalis
Also known as English lavender, *Lavandula angustifolia officinalis* is often used to soothe headaches.

MEDICINAL USE Lavender is well known for its soothing, calming properties. Lavender flowers are added to sleep pillows – small sachets tucked under pillows to help ensure restful sleep – along with hops and, sometimes, chamomile flowers or rose petals. Lavender flower tea can be used to treat ailments including anxiety, depression, insomnia, restlessness, headache and indigestion. The herb may help relax spasms, relieve nausea and settle the stomach. It stimulates the liver to secrete bile, which aids in the digestion of fats. Lavender tea may be used as a mouthwash to treat halitosis. A lavender flower infusion may be used as a douche to treat vaginal yeast infections. Essential oil of lavender is a widely used external remedy that contains more than 150 chemical compounds and may have antiseptic, antibacterial and antidepressant properties. Applied undiluted, lavender oil may relieve the itching of insect bites, alleviate the pain of minor burns, and speed healing and prevent scarring. Diluted oil can be rubbed on the temples to relieve headache. Because of its pleasant scent and relaxing effects, lavender is a popular addition to aromatherapy massage oils used to relieve sore muscles. The oil may be used in a relaxing bath to ease nervous tension and debility. **Note:** Contact dermatitis is a possible side effect in individuals with sensitive skin.

DOSAGE Tea: Drink up to 0.75 litre (24 oz) daily. **Tincture:** Use 1 or 2 ml (0.03 or 0.07 oz) daily. **Ointment:** Use 1 or 2 drops, applied undiluted. **Bath:** Add 3 to 5 drops of essential oil to a bath of warm water. **Massage oil:** Add 10 to 20 drops of essential oil to 30 ml (1 oz) of almond or jojoba oil, and shake to mix.

L. a. 'Premier'
Premier lavender is a long-stemmed cultivar that bears wonderfully scented, violet flowers.

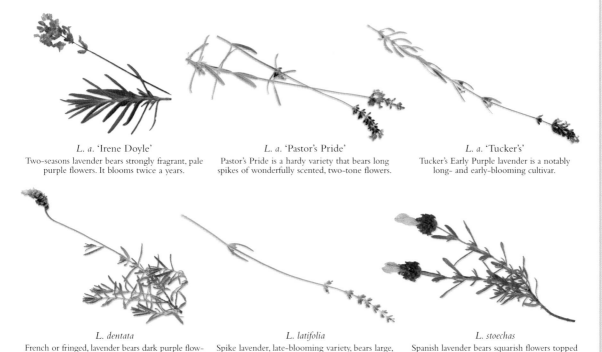

L. a. 'Irene Doyle'
Two-seasons lavender bears strongly fragrant, pale purple flowers. It blooms twice a years.

L. a. 'Pastor's Pride'
Pastor's Pride is a hardy variety that bears long spikes of wonderfully scented, two-tone flowers.

L. a. 'Tucker's'
Tucker's Early Purple lavender is a notably long- and early-blooming cultivar.

L. dentata
French or fringed, lavender bears dark purple flowers and lance-shaped leaves with downy undersides.

L. latifolia
Spike lavender, late-blooming variety, bears large, grey-green leaves and violet-green flowerheads.

L. stoechas
Spanish lavender bears squarish flowers topped by a distinctive tuft of petals.

L

*L*ENTINULA EDODES

JAPANESE FOREST MUSHROOM, SHIITAKE

Shiitake, a gilled mushroom with a tan- to cinnamon-coloured cap and solid stalk, is native to Asian countries with temperate climates, including China and Japan. It is a member of the Polyporaceae (meaning many pores) family. Shiitake's common name is derived from the mushroom's tendency to grow on the trunk of the Japanese shiia tree. Second only to the common button mushroom (*Agaricus bisporus*) in the world's mushroom production, shiitake are Japan's main agricultural export. The mushroom has long been believed to promote health and longevity.

❧ **GROWING CONDITIONS** Shiitake grows on the trunks of trees, including beech, chestnut, chinquapin, Japanese alder, maple, mulberry, oak, sweet gum and walnut. The mushroom is widely cultivated both indoors and outdoors, on logs or in sawdust.

❧ **CULINARY USE** Shiitake mushrooms are an excellent immune system-boosting addition to winter soups and stews, vegetable stir-fries and egg dishes. In most recipes, they can be substituted for more common mushrooms.

❧ **MEDICINAL USE** Lentinan, a large sugar molecule found in the cell walls of shiitake, may enhance the body's immune system response and resistance to bacteria and viruses. Shiitake's stems, caps, and its underground mass (called mycelia) have been used to treat a weakened immune system, hepatitis and environmental allergies. Shiitake also contains a compound that facilitates the excretion of blood cholesterol, making it a useful dietary supplement for people with high cholesterol levels. In recent years, shiitake has been used to help support the immune system of cancer patients who are undergoing chemotherapy and radiation.

❧ **DOSAGE Tincture:** Use 1 ml (0.03 oz) two or three times daily. **Standardized extract** Take one to five 400 mg tablets or capsules daily. **Fresh:** Eat three or four daily.

*L*EVISTICUM OFFICINALE

AMERICAN LOVAGE, LOVAGE

Native to southern Europe and southwestern Asia, lovage thrives on sunny mountain slopes. The plant is naturalized in North America. A member of the Apiaceae (parsley) family, lovage is a bittersweet, pungent perennial herb with a celery scent and flavour. It bears tiny yellow flowers, followed by aromatic seeds. Lovage is the only plant in the *Levisticum* genus and is valued because it produces new growth in the early spring, often before other fresh herbs are available. Both the plant name (lovage) and the genus name come from the Latin word *ligusticum*, or Ligurian, because lovage once grew abundantly in the Italian province of Liguria.

❧ **GROWING CONDITIONS** Lovage bears attractive, ornamental foliage and grows up to 2 m (6 ft) tall, which makes it a good choice for planting in the back of herb beds. It grows well in deep, rich, moist soil in full sun or partial shade. Seeds may be planted in the spring or autumn; root divisions may be planted in the spring. Leaves are picked before the plant flowers. Young stems are cut in the spring.

❧ **CULINARY USE** Lovage leaves have a potent flavour. They may be steamed or blanched and eaten as a vegetable, or used in small amounts to give soups and stews a celery-like flavour. The fresh, hollow stalks can be used as straws in cocktails including the tomato juice-and-vodka beverage Bloody Mary. The young stems may be candied, like angelica or citron.

Wild lovage, which is indigenous to the mountainous districts of southern France, Italy and Greece, is used to season meat stews, stocks, soups and broth. The tender leaves are chopped and added to omelettes and salads. In the Lombardy region of Italy, lovage is made into a traditional stuffing for capons, with sautéed giblets, walnuts, Parmesan cheese, fresh breadcrumbs, eggs, cream and nutmeg.

MEDICINAL USE Lovage was probably first used as a herb for scenting bath waters in the early 17th century. The herb contains a volatile oil that has properties as a sedative and anticonvulsant. It has been used as a tonic for the digestive system to treat conditions such as indigestion, wind, colic and poor appetite. Lovage may also be helpful in the treatment of upper-respiratory conditions such as bronchitis. **Note:** Lovage should not be used during pregnancy or by those with kidney disease or weak kidneys.

DOSAGE **Tea:** Drink up to 0.5 litre (16 oz) daily. **Fresh:** As desired.

*L*INUM USITATISSIMUM

FLAX, FLAXSEED, LINSEED

A member of the Linaceae (flax) family, flax is one of the world's oldest cultivated plants. Although its origins are not fully known, flax is presumed to be native to Egypt, where it has been used for thousands of years. The fibres of the plant were cooked, dried and then spun into thread which was woven into linen. Flax is a slender, branching annual; it bears delicate, five-petalled blue flowers, which turn into fruits that can hold as many as ten glossy brown seeds. Crude flaxseed oil, known as linseed oil, is a common component of paint, varnishes and linoleum tiles.

GROWING CONDITIONS Flax thrives in fertile, finely textured, clay soils, with adequate moisture. It prefers relatively cool temperatures, particularly during the period in which the plant's flowers mature into fruit.

CULINARY USE Flax seeds can be added to salads, baked goods, cereals or mixed with honey as a tasty breakfast spread. Flaxseed oil makes a good salad dressing, but it is not recommended for use in cooking.

MEDICINAL USE Flaxseed oil is a rich source of the essential fatty acid alpha-linolenic acid, which is required for the formation of cell membranes in the body. Fatty acids are converted into prostaglandins that may help reduce inflammation and allergies. Flaxseed oil has been shown to be effective in lowering blood cholesterol levels. It may offer a protective effect against cancer, particularly of the breast. The seeds have a long history of use in treating chronic constipation. Applied externally, flaxseed may help draw out toxins from the blood, reduce inflammation and speed the healing of superficial wounds. **Note:** The seed should be taken with at least 150 ml (6 oz) of liquid. Flax should not be taken in the case of bowel obstruction.

DOSAGE **Oil:** Take 1 or 2 tbsp daily. **Seed (ground):** Take 1 tbsp two or three times daily.

L

LONICERA SPP.

DUTCH HONEYSUCKLE, PERFOLIATE HONEYSUCKLE, HONEYSUCKLE, JAPANESE HONEYSUCKLE, WOODBINE

There are more than 150 species of *Lonicera*, which belongs to the Caprifoliaceae (honeysuckle) family. Honeysuckle is a delightfully aromatic climbing shrub native to southern Europe and western Asia, which has been naturalized in North America. The shrub bears pale yellow flowers that are highly attractive to bees, followed by clusters of toxic orange berries. The flowers produce a sweet, honey-flavoured nectar that children since medieval times have delighted in sucking from the blossoms. The family name Caprifoliaceae is derived from the Roman *capri* (goat) and *folium* (leaves) for the animal's habit of eating the leaves of Caprifoliaceae plants.

GROWING CONDITIONS Honeysuckle grows in moist, porous soil in partial shade. Propagation is done in the autumn by woody cuttings that are rooted in sand or peat. The plant grows well on fences, trellises and supporting walls.

CULINARY USE Honeysuckle leaves and flowers are used to make tea in Japan.

MEDICINAL USE Once a popular medicinal herb with cooling, laxative, and expectorant properties, some honeysuckle species

(*L. caprifolium* and *L. periclymenum*) are not widely used today. Honeysuckle stems and flowers contain salicylic acid, an analgesic used in the treatment of headache and fever. The flowers and leaves of one particular species, *L. japonica*, may have antiviral, antibacterial and cholesterol-lowering properties. In Traditional Chinese medicine, the flowers of *L. japonica* are used to cool the body during summer heat or fever from illness. The flowers of *L. japonica* are also included in Chinese patent medicines and prescriptions to treat colds and flu. The fruit of all the species of *Lonicera* have purgative properties, but are considered toxic.

DOSAGE **Tea:** Drink 0.25 litre (8 oz) two or three times daily.

LYCOPERSICON ESCULENTUM

TOMATO

Native to South America, the tomato plant belongs to the Solanaceae (nightshade) family, which also includes peppers, potatoes and aubergine. The fruit of the plant, which comes in a variety of shapes, sizes, colours and tastes, is an essential ingredient of many regional cuisines. The French called tomatoes *pommes d'amour*, meaning "love apples", as they considered them to be an aphrodisiac. In Italy, tomatoes were called *pomo d'oro*, or "golden apple". In northern Europe, however, they were called "stinking golden apple" and considered poisonous.

GROWING CONDITIONS Tomatoes are easy to grow and a favourite of home gardeners. They require a sunny, well-drained location with porous, fairly light soil, and a good amount of humus. The plants thrive in open locations where there is plenty of air circulation.

CULINARY USE Both raw and cooked, tomatoes are an ingredient in soups, sauces, salads and sandwiches. The popular condiment ketchup originally started out as *ketsiap*, a 7th-century Chinese sauce made of fish entrails, vinegar and spices. Tomatoes were added as an ingredient in the late 18th century.

MEDICINAL USE Tomatoes are rich in the carotenoid lycopene, an important antioxidant that gives the fruit its characteristic deep red colour. Ripe tomatoes (and especially processed tomato products) may protect the body against degenerative diseases such as lung and prostate cancer. Scientists are also studying a possible link between lycopene and the prevention of cardiovascular disease and skin, breast, colon and digestive-tract cancer, but tomatoes were not always considered helpful. In fact, doctors once warned patients against eating them, fearing they cause appendicitis and stomach cancer. **Note:** People with arthritis or those who are allergic to plants in the nightshade family should consult their physician before taking lycopene.

DOSAGE **Standardized extract:** Take one or two 5 mg capsules daily.

MELALEUCA ALTERNIFOLIA

TEA TREE, TI TREE

A Myrtaceae (myrtle) family member, there are at least 300 species and sub-species of this native Australian tree. The tea tree has papery bark and bears narrow, pointed leaves and small white flowers on dense spikes. Australian researchers first became interested in tea tree in the 1920s, when the herb's antiseptic properties were discovered. During World War II, Australian soldiers were issued tea tree oil for use as a disinfectant. In addition, the oil was applied to machine-cutting tools in ammunition factories in an effort to reduce the risk of accident-related infections. Today, tree oil is one of Australia's most popular herbal exports. The oil has a sharp, medicinal scent which many find similar to eucalyptus.

GROWING CONDITIONS Tea tree grows wild in swampy, wet locations in New South Wales and southern Queensland, Australia. It prefers well-drained and

M

neutral-to-acidic soil in sunny locations. Fast-growing and resilient, tee trees usually reach the height of 6 m (20 ft), and can be harvested each year.

❧ CULINARY USE Australian settlers once used tea tree leaves to make a beverage (thus the name tea tree) and to flavour beer. Tea tree is not currently in culinary use, but can be used as a disinfectant for cooking surfaces.

❧ MEDICINAL USE Extracted from the plant's crushed leaves, tea tree oil has antiseptic, expectorant and immune-stimulating activity. It is used externally, primarily to treat mouth, urinary tract and vaginal infections. Tea tree oil is also used in compresses, salves and massage oil to treat insect stings, burns, superficial wounds, scabies, head lice, cold sores and skin infections. Additionally, tea tree oil can be used as an insect repellent. In clinical trials, the herb has been effective in treating acne and toenail fungus. Tea tree oil may also be added to baths or vaporizers for use in the treatment of respiratory infections. It has been made into lozenges for sore throats and suppositories for vaginal infections. Because it acts like an immuno-stimulant, it has proven very helpful to people with HIV. **Note:** Tea tree oil may irritate the skin.

❧ DOSAGE **Massage oil:** Add 10 drops 30 ml (1 oz) of vegetable oil. **Bath:** Add 3 to 10 drops of essential oil to a bath of warm water. **Compress:** Use 5 drops per 0.25 litre (8 oz) of water. **Inhalant:** Put 3 to 5 drops in a bowl of hot water. **Gargle or mouthwash:** Add 1 drop per 0.25 litre (8 oz) of water. **Douche:** Use 3 to 5 drops per litre (1 quart) of warm water.

ℳELISSA OFFICINALIS

BALM, LEMON BALM, MELISSA, MELISSA BALM

Belonging to a genus of only three species, lemon balm is native to southern Europe, northern Africa, western Asia and southwestern Siberia. The plant is naturalized in North America and Europe. This citrus-scented perennial in the Lamiaceae (mint) family bears toothed, aromatic, ovate leaves and pale yellow flowers. Originally grown to attract honeybees, *melissa* is the Greek word

for honeybee. Beehives were once rubbed with lemon balm to encourage the bees' productiveness. The leaves are usually collected before bloom and has been used for over 2,000 years in traditional medicine: a "balm" is a soothing or healing ointment. The herb's pleasant smell makes it a common and popular ingredient in potpourris and perfumes.

❧ GROWING CONDITIONS Lemon balm thrives in fertile, moist, well-drained soil in full sun or partial shade. The plant may be propagated by cuttings or seeds. Lemon balm is a prolific self-sower, which blooms between June and October. Bee balm can be propagated by seed, cuttings and root division. In cool climates, bee balm requires a good mulching before the first frost of the year.

❧ CULINARY USE This herb's fresh leaves are commonly used to impart a lemony flavour to salads, soups, sauces, herb vinegars and fish dishes, and are often used in hot and cold teas. It is one of the ingredients in Benedictine and Chartreuse, healing liqueurs developed by monks hundreds of years ago, and is used to flavour alcoholic beverages including bitters and vermouth.

❧ MEDICINAL USE Lemon balm has been used since the Middle Ages to reduce stress and anxiety, promote restful sleep, improve appetite, lower fever, and ease the pain and discomfort of indigestion (particularly when associated with anxiety or depression), flatulence, bloating, wind and colic. In aromatherapy, the essential oil of lemon balm is used to promote relaxation and rejuvenation, particularly in cases of conditions such as depression and nervous tension. The herb is believed to have carminative, nervine, anti-depressant, sedative and diaphoretic properties. It contains caffeic and rosmarinic acids, which offer anti-viral effects against herpes simplex I and II. A lemon balm ointment is widely used in Europe to treat herpes blisters. Due to its pleasant taste and soothing nature, this herb is especially suitable for treatment of children.

❧ DOSAGE **Tea:** Drink 0.25 litre (8 oz) two or three times daily. **Tincture:** Use 1 ml (0.03 oz) two or three times daily. **Standardized extract:** Take three 300 mg capsules three times daily. **Creams:** Follow label directions.

Melissa officinalis, *commonly called bee balm because the plant attracts honeybees, is now used as a culinary ingredient for its lemony flavour and a medicine for its antidepressant properties.*

LAMIACEAE
Mints

The mint family is comprised of more than 3,000 species, with the largest being genus the *Mentha* which has 25 species. Mints are primarily used for flavour, fragrance and medicinal purposes.

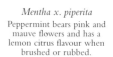

Mentha x. piperita
Peppermint bears pink and mauve flowers and has a lemon citrus flavour when brushed or rubbed.

MENTHA X PIPERITA
PEPPERMINT

A Lamiaceae (mint) family member, peppermint is native to Europe. It is often found growing wild near streams and in other wet areas in North America and Europe. This fragrant creeping perennial bears smooth, purple-tinged leaves and spikes of lilac-pink flowers. In ancient Palestine, peppermint was so highly valued that it was accepted as payment for taxes. Ancient Greeks and Romans were said to have decorated their dining tables and crowned themselves with peppermint at feasts, in addition to using the herb to flavour sauces and wine. Today, about three-quarters of the world's peppermint supply comes from the United States. It takes approximately 36 kg (80 lbs) of fresh peppermint to make 0.5 kg (1 lb) of peppermint oil, which is added to sweets and chewing gum, cough drops and breath mints, digestive aids, and cold and flu remedies. Widely used in dental products, peppermint is also added to some tobacco products. Peppermint oil is used to flavour perfumes; the leaves are often added to potpourris. Some important varieties not pictured include: eau-de-cologne mint, also known as lemon mint or orange mint (*Mentha x p.* var. 'Citrata'), which bears oval, bronze-coloured leaves and has a citrus-mint

Mentha rotundifolia
Apple mint bears round leaves, an apple scent, and a fruity taste.

flavour and aroma; lime mint (*Mentha x. p.* 'Lime'), which bears round, dark green leaves tinged with purple and has a citrus-mint aroma; and Hart's pennyroyal, or Holt's mint (*Mentha cervina*), a low-growing perennial that has a strong spearmint fragrance.

GROWING CONDITIONS Popular in kitchen herb gardens, peppermint grows best in moist to very moist soil in full sun or partial shade. Peppermint is propagated by cuttings. Most mints have a tendency to spread readily, so growing them in a confined area is often recommended. The herb may be harvested several times a year, shortly before the plant flowers.

CULINARY USE Peppermint is added to desserts, sweets, ice cream, and chewing gum. Peppermint leaves are used in hot and cold teas and in cocktails such as mint juleps. Essential oil of peppermint is the basis of the liqueur *crème de menthe*.

MEDICINAL USE Peppermint's main constituent is a volatile oil, which is generally about 50 percent menthol. Both the fresh and dried leaves of the plant, as well as its essential oil, generate an anti-spasmodic effect on the smooth muscles of the gastrointestinal tract. By stimulating digestive flow and the production of bile, peppermint may help relieve gastrointestinal conditions such as flatulence,

Mentha x pipernita 'Grapefruit'
Grapefruit mint bears light
blue flowers and has a spicy,
citrus-mint aroma.

Mentha arvensis piperescens
Japanese field mint bears
smooth, dark green, leaves and
a strong menthol flavour.

Mentha australis
Australian mint is a straggly
bush with a flavour and aroma
similar to spearmint.

Mentha haplocalyx
Bo he, Chinese mint, or field
mint is an annual or perennial mint
with a sharp menthol flavour.

Mentha 'Hillary's Sweet Lemon'
Hillary's sweet lemon mint is a
hardy, purple-flowered variety
with a very pleasant aroma.

Mentha niliaca
Egyptian mint is distinctive for
its fuzzy leaves and long spikes
of lavender flowers.

Mentha pulegium
English pennyroyal is a pungent,
creeping perennial with toothed
leaves and light purple flowers.

M. sauvelens 'Variegata'
Pineapple mint is an attractive plant
with variegated leaves and a sweet,
fruity fragrance.

painful digestion, intestinal cramping, irritable bowel
syndrome, and nausea due to stomach upset, motion
sickness and pregnancy. In aromatherapy, peppermint oil
is used as a stimulant to increase concentration and
reduce sleepiness. Placing a drop of the essential oil
in a pan of hot water and inhaling the steam may
help relieve lung and sinus congestion.

DOSAGE Tea: Drink 0.25 litre (8 oz) two or three
times daily. **Tincture:** Use 1 ml (0.03 oz) two or three
times daily. **Standardized extract:** Take two 400 mg
capsules up to three times daily. **Coated peppermint
oil capsule:** Follow label directions.

MENTHA SPICATA
SPEARMINT

Thought to be the oldest of all the mints, spearmint is
native to the Mediterranean region and is widely naturalized in North America, Europe and Australia. This
member of the (mint) family is a creeping perennial
that bears short stalks, wrinkly bright green leaves, and
pale, pink violet flowers that grow on elongated spikes.
The common name "spearmint" is a reference to the
spearlike appearance of these flowers.

GROWING CONDITIONS Spearmint thrives in
moist soil in full sun or partial shade. Propagation is
accomplished most successfully by root division or cuttings. Most mints have a tendency to spread readily, and
growing them in a confined area is often recommended.

CULINARY USE
Spearmint leaves are added
to green salads, sauces and
jellies, used as a garnish, and
to flavour hot and cold teas.
Spearmint is a flavouring for
sweets, chewing gum, cough
drops and breath mints.

MEDICINAL USE
Spearmint leaves are
often used to treat
gastrointestinal
disorders such as stom-
achache and nausea.

DOSAGE Tea: Drink 0.25
litre (8 oz) 2 or 3 times daily.

M. spicata 'Kentucky Colonel'
Kentucky Colonel spearmint,
a strongly scented
variety, is popular in cooking.

M

Monarda spp.

BEE BALM, BERGAMOT, HORSE BALM, OSWEGO TEA

Monarda is a genus of several native North American aromatic perennials in the Lamiaceae (mint) family. Named for Nicholas Monardes, a 16th-century Spanish physician who documented many New World plants, herbs in this genus are known as bergamots because of their similar aroma to bergamot orange (*Citrus bergamia*). The leaves of one variety, *M. didyma*, were dried and used as a substitute for British-imported tea during the American Revolutionary War. The common name "Oswego tea" was coined by the renowned 18th-century American botanist John Bartram (1699–1777), who first encountered the herb at Fort Oswego, New York, in the United States, where it grew abundantly.

GROWING CONDITIONS *M. didyma*, which has bright red flowers, grows in rich, moist woodland areas in full sun. *M. fistulosa*, which has lavender-coloured flowers, and *M. punctata*, which has yellow flowers, prefer dry, light, alkaline soil in full sun. *Monarda* species attract bees and butterflies, and are excellent garden plants. *M. fistulosa* is a popular border plant. Once established, these plants spread easily by runners and seed. The tops may be pinched back to encourage bushier growth. For all varieties, seeds or root divisions are planted in the spring. Leaves may be cut before the plant flowers, and used fresh or dried.

CULINARY USE The leaves of *M. didyma* have a similar flavour to that of Earl Grey tea and are used to flavour teas and iced drinks. A blend of *M. didyma* leaves, mint and orange peel makes a delicious iced tea. *Monarda* flowers are edible and can be added to salads or used to decorate cakes. *M. fistulosa* leaves add flavour to bean and meat dishes and are also used to make tea. *M. citriodora*, known as lemon bergamot, makes a tasty tea and is used to flavour meat dishes.

MEDICINAL USE Plants in this genus contain a compound with antiseptic and expectorant properties. *M. punctata* has been used to treat digestive ailments such as indigestion, nausea and vomiting and upper-respiratory conditions such as colds and flu. This variety also helps reduce fever by increasing sweating and encourages the onset of menstruation. Combined with other herbs, *M. didyma* is helpful in the treatment of urinary tract infections and indigestion, and may inhibit the herpes simplex virus and the related chicken pox virus. **Note:** *Monarda* species should not be taken during pregnancy.

DOSAGE Tea: Drink up to 0.75 litre (24 oz) daily.

Myristica fragrans

NUTMEG

A member of the Myristicaceae (nutmeg) family, the nutmeg tree is native to tropical rainforests on the Molucca Islands of Indonesia, but is now widely cultivated in tropical areas throughout Sri Lanka and Indonesia. The trees bear aromatic leaves and clusters of small, yellow flowers, followed by yellow round to pear-shaped fruits that contain a single hard, egg-shaped nutmeg seed. Nutmeg trees do not yield fruit until they have been growing for about eight years, but each tree can continue to fruit for more than 60 years. Nutmeg was once thought to ward off the plague, and was worn around the neck for protection. It was therefore highly valued. A German pricing chart from the 14th century sets the value of 0.5 kg (1 lb) of nutmeg at seven fat oxen. When Columbus

sailed from Spain in search of the East Indies, nutmeg was one of the spices he hoped to find. The Dutch traded the island of Manhattan to the British in exchange for the nutmeg-producing island of Run.

❧ **GROWING CONDITIONS** Nutmeg trees grow in well-drained, humus-rich, sandy soil in areas with minimum temperatures of 15 to 18°C (59 to 64°F). The trees may be propagated from seeds planted when ripe, or from hardwood cuttings planted at the end of the growing season.

❧ **CULINARY USE** Nutmeg, ground or grated, is widely used to flavour baked goods, custards, puddings and eggnog. It is added to savoury sauces and to meat, cheese and vegetable dishes. It particularly complements potatoes, spinach and mushrooms.

❧ **MEDICINAL USE** Nutmeg has a stimulating effect on the digestive system. It has been taken as a tea to increase appetite and alleviate nausea, vomiting and diarrhoea. Nutmeg powder can be mixed with water to form a paste, which is applied externally to treat eczema and ringworm. **Note:** Used as a culinary spice, nutmeg is a safe herb at a dose of up to 3 g (0.01 oz) per day. When taken in excess, however, nutmeg can be toxic and cause hallucinations. The consumption of two whole nutmeg seeds can cause death. Pregnant women should avoid using nutmeg as a spice, except in small quantities.

❧ **DOSAGE Tea:** Add one pinch of nutmeg powder to 0.25 litre (8 oz) peppermint tea; drink up to 0.75 litre (24 oz) daily. **Ointment:** Mix 2 tsp in water to form a paste; apply to affected areas.

NEPETA CATARIA

CATMINT, CATNIP

There are approximately 250 species in the genus *Nepeta*. A member of the Lamiaceae (mint) family, catnip is native to Europe and naturalized in North America. This aromatic perennial grows in rocky, mountainous areas and dry roadsides. In the summer and early autumn, the tops of the plants are covered with small, white to blue flowers. Catmint is a unique herb, stimulating and intoxicating to cats but relaxing to humans.

❧ **GROWING CONDITIONS** Catnip flourishes in well-drained soil in full sun or partial shade. The herb is drought tolerant, but grows more lushly with consistent watering. The plant may be grown from seed or root division. Seedlings should be thinned to 0.5 m (18 in) apart. Once established, catnip self-seeds freely. Leaves and flowers are harvested in the late summer, when the plant is in bloom.

❧ **CULINARY USE** Catnip leaves make tea with a mintlike flavour and and may be used to flavour sauces and stews.

❧ **MEDICINAL USE** Catnip has been used medicinally for at least 2,000 years. It is a gentle herb that has sedative properties and is used in various forms to settle the stomach and relieve flatulence and colic. When taken after meals, catnip tea can help relieve indigestion and heartburn. Catnip contains nepetalactone isomers, which cats find intoxicating. This component is similar to the sedative compounds found in the herb valerian, and indeed catnip has traditionally been used as a mild tranquilizer and sedative in humans. Catnip tea may be taken before bedtime as a mild sleep aid or taken to encourage relaxation during times of tension. Catnip stimulates perspiration, so it is also used to treat fevers. **Note:** Catnip should not be ingested during pregnancy because its volatile oils may irritate the uterus.

continued on page 273

OCIMUM BASILICUM
Basil, Sweet Basil

A favourite in the garden and the kitchen, basil is thought to be native to India. There are approximately 150 species of aromatic plants in the *Ocimum* genus, and there are also many cultivars available. The herb is widely grown in warm, tropical regions of the globe, including Africa. It has been cultivated in the Mediterranean region for thousands of years.

A member of the Lamiaceae (mint) family, basil has a slightly peppery flavor that has been described by some as a cross between liquorice and cloves. Ocimum comes from the Greek *okimon*, which was what the ancient Greek philosopher Theophrastus called basil. Ancient Egyptians used basil in embalming preparations and burned the herb (with myrrh) in ceremonies to appease the gods. Although ancient Romans associated basil with love, the Greeks considered it to be a symbol of mourning. The herb was once used to perfume water used for washing the hands and face. Its fragrance is still used in the manufacture of soaps, perfumes and cosmetics.

In Italy and Greece, basil is commonly grown in pots on porches or windowsills, where its scent is believed to help repel flies and mosquitoes. Sweet Basil (*O. basilicum*) is a generic term for many unnamed varieties of basil. With its strong fragrance and is excellent for most culinary uses. Important varieties include: Anise basil (*O. basilicum* 'Anise'), from Persia, which bears purplish leaves and has a sweet, liquorice scent; Cinnamon basil (*O. basilicum* 'Cinnamon'), a Mexican variety, which bears pink flowers and has a strong, cinnamon scent; Genovese basil (*O. basilicum* 'Genovese'),

from Italy, which is considered by many cooks to be the best-flavoured basil variety; Purple ruffles basil (*O. basilicum* 'Purple Ruffles'), a popular garden plant, which bears dark purple, fringed leaves; lemon basil (*O. b.* var. *citriodorum*), which produces citrus-scented leaves and seeds and white flowers, and holy basil, sacred basil or tulsi (*O. sanctum*), a perennial from India, which has soft, hairy stems and bears spicy, pungent leaves. Holy basil is sacred in India; it is

O. basilicum
Basil, or sweet basil, has dark green or purple leaves. It is a popular addition to cheese, egg and tomato dishes.

O. basilicum 'Dark Opal'
Dark opal basil is strongly scented and bears crinkled purple-black leaves and pink or light purple flowers.

O. basilicum 'Thai'
Thai basil is a sweet-smelling variety that bears purple leaves and pink flowers.

O. basilicum var. minimum
Bush basil is a dwarf variety with small leaves; it reaches a height of only 15–30 cm (6–12 in).

O. basilicum 'Siam Queen'
Siam Queen bears purple stems and flowers and makes a a great flavouring for Asian cuisine.

Ocimum americanum 'Lime'
This variety has a lime aroma and is usually paired with salads and used as an ingredient in fish dishes.

O. basilicum 'Spice'
The 'Spice' variety has a strong spicy fragrance and flavour and is often used in potpourri.

O. lesbos
Also known as Aussie sweet and Greek Column; this variety does not flower.

O. tenuiflorum
Native to India, O. tenuiflorum, is also called Tulsi, and has a long history of medicinal use.

often used in Hindu religious ceremonies and planted near temples. Pieces of the plant's stem are cut and shaped to make prayer beads.

GROWING CONDITIONS Fast-growing basil is a good choice for filling empty spots in a garden. With adequate light, basil grows well indoors. The plant's flowering tips and upper leaves should be pinched off to delay flowering. Basil prefers light, rich, well-drained to slightly dry soil in full sun in areas with minimum temperatures of 10 to 15°C (50 to 59°F). Seeds may be planted in the spring when temperatures do not fall below 13°C (55°F). In areas with cool winters, basil is commonly planted as an annual. Leaves may be picked as needed during the growing season.

CULINARY USE Basil is a primary ingredient in the Italian *pesto* sauce; it is also used in *pistou*, the French version of pesto. The herb pairs well with tomatoes and tomato-based dishes. Basil is the key flavouring in *soupe au pistou*, a signature dish from the Provence region of France. It also includes leeks, tomatoes, potatoes, garlic and green beans. Basil leaves can be eaten on sandwiches in place of lettuce. Italians often place fresh basil, on the table in a small vase of water to be used as a seasoning during their meal, as with salt or pepper.

MEDICINAL USE Basil is a good source of the vitamins A and C. The leaves, rich in volatile oils, are used to improve digestion. The herb may help relax intestinal spasms and relieve wind, bloating and nausea. Basil also has antiseptic and antibacterial properties that make it useful as a treatment for intestinal parasites. Extract of basil may be found in commercially available topical healing preparations. A poultice of crushed basil leaves may be used to treat acne or dabbed on insect bites to relieve itching. Basil has mild sedative properties and has been used to treat anxiety, depression and insomnia. The herb is also used to help lower fevers and relieve colds, coughs and flu symptoms. In aromatherapy, essential oil of basil may be added to massage oil and used externally to relax muscles. Holy basil (*Ocimum sanctum*) is a rich source of disease-fighting antioxidants, and helps the body adapt to stress. It may be useful to type 2 diabetics in reducing blood sugar levels. **Note:** Basil essential oil should not be used internally, or during pregnancy.

DOSAGE Tea: Drink up to 0.75 litre (24 oz) daily. **Syrup:** Combine equal parts basil juice and honey; take tbsp to relieve coughs. **Wash:** Combine equal parts basil juice and honey; apply to the skin to relieve itching. **Oil for external use:** Add 5 to 10 drops of essential oil to 30 ml (1 oz) almond or jojoba oil, shake to mix. **Holy basil tea:** Drink 0.25 litre (8 oz) daily. **Holy basil tincture:** Use 1 ml (0.03 oz) two or three times daily. **Holy basil supplements:** Follow label directions.

🌿 **DOSAGE Tea:** Drink up to 0.75 litre (24 oz) daily. **Tincture:** Use 1 or 2 ml (0.03 or 0.07 oz) up to three times daily.

OENOTHERA BIENNIS

EVENING PRIMROSE

The *Oenothera* genus contains eighty species. Native to eastern North America, evening primrose, a member of the Onagraceae (evening primrose) family, is widely naturalized throughout the world. It is not related to the primrose genus (*Primula*). This tall plant bears beautiful, fragrant yellow flowers that open each day at dusk. Native Americans used the seeds as food and as a poultice for skin conditions including bruises, boils and sores. Early American settlers used the herb to treat gastrointestinal upset, sore throat and rashes. Evening primrose oil is also used as an ingredient in cosmetics.

🌿 **GROWING CONDITIONS** Evening primrose grows well in dry soil, including coastal sandy areas, in full sun. Seeds may be planted in spring or autumn. The plant self-seeds freely; the seeds are collected when ripe.

🌿 **CULINARY USE** None.

🌿 **MEDICINAL USE** The oil pressed from ripe evening primrose seeds is a good source of gamma linoleic acid (GLA), an unsaturated fatty acid that reduces inflammation and ensures the health of cell membranes. The seed is grown in more than thirty countries; the United States and Canada produce more than 400,000 tonnes annually. As many as 5,000 evening primrose seeds are needed to produce one capsule of oil. Evening primrose oil may be alleviate rheumatoid arthritis, premenstrual syndrome, multiple sclerosis, hyperactivity, and skin conditions such as eczema and acne. The herb is also thought to be beneficial in the treatment of nerve damage in diabetics, high blood pressure and blood cholesterol levels, hangover, and breast pain or tenderness.

🌿 **DOSAGE Standardized extract:** Take one 1,000 mg capsule three times daily. **Oil:** Use ½ tsp daily.

Oenothera biennis, *also known as evening primrose, is frequently used in the treatment of nerve damage and to calm hyperactivity.*

OLEA EUROPAEA

OLIVE

A member of the Oleaceae (olive) family, the olive tree was first cultivated in Crete. The trees bears dark green, leathery leaves and fragrant white flowers, followed by stoned fruit. The branches are used as a symbol of peace. In the Biblical story of Noah and the Ark, a dove sent to find land returns to the ark with an olive branch in its beak – a sign that God had stopped the flood, making peace with man.

🌿 **GROWING CONDITIONS** The trees grows in well-drained soil in full sun. Seeds may be planted in the fall; semi-ripe cuttings may be planted in the summer. Leaves are gathered throughout the year. Fruits are harvested in the autumn and winter.

🌿 **CULINARY USE** The fruit called olives are eaten individually or used as an ingredient in many salads and spreads. Olives are pressed into oil, widely used in cooking, and as a dip or salad dressing.

🌿 **MEDICINAL USE** Olive leaves have a mild diuretic effect, and have been used to help lower blood pressure and improve circulatory function. The leaves have strong antibacterial and antifungal properties, and may help fight ageing and cardiovascular disease. Olive oil contains about 75 percent oleic acid that has a protective effect on the digestive tract and can be taken with lemon juice to treat gallstones. **Note:** Olive leaf may irritate the digestive tract. Skin rashes are possible in sensitive individuals.

🌿 **DOSAGE Tea:** Drink 0.25 litre (8 oz) daily. **Standardized extract:** standardized to 6 to 15 percent oleuropein. Follow label directions.

ORIGANUM VULGARE
Oregano

Oregano's botanical name, *origanum vulgareomes*, taken from the Greek *oros,* which means mountains, and *ganos,* which means joy. Composed of more than 20 species, the oregano family was once primarily used as a medicine before becoming a popular herb.

ORIGANUM MAJORANA
MARJORAM, SWEET MARJORAM

A member of the Lamiaceae (mint) family, marjoram is native to Asia and naturalized in southern Europe. It is commercially cultivated in the United States, central Europe, the Mediterranean and Asia. A small, bushy perennial, marjoram has wiry red brown stems with tiny, white to pink flowers and oval, grey-green leaves that are highly aromatic when crushed. The ancient Greeks used the herb as both a spice and a tea. They coated their hair and eyebrows with a pomade made from the plant. In ancient Crete, a sprig of marjoram was worn by distinguished leaders as a badge of honour. Greeks and Romans made marjoram wreaths to place on the heads of wedding couples as a symbol of love, honour and happiness. Today, oil of marjoram is used as a fragrance in soaps, creams, lotions and perfume.

GROWING CONDITIONS Marjoram prefers well-drained dry soil in full sun. Propagation can be done as cuttings or by root division.

CULINARY USE Dried or fresh marjoram leaves and flowering sprigs are often added to Italian and Greek meat dishes, soups, tomato sauces and pasta. Marjoram is also used to make herbal oil and vinegar. Oil of marjoram is a common flavouring for beverages, ice cream, baked goods, soup and condiments. The herb is also used as a food preservative.

O. majorana
In addition to its use as a popular herb in cooking, sweet marjoram is sometimes used as an aphrodisiac.

O. x *majoricum* 'culinary'
'Culinary' is similar to 'Italian', but
with a sweeter flavour that has floral overtones.
The herb bears white flowers.

O. dictamnus
Dittany of Crete or hop marjoram is a
prostrate shrub that bears arching stems of
woolly, greyish leaves and tiny pink flowers.

O. x *majoricum* 'Italian'
Italian oregano's flavor and scent has been
described as a cross between oregano and marjoram.
The plant bears oval leaves and white flowers.

MEDICINAL USE The leaves and flowers of marjoram are commonly used to treat the common cold. Taken through steam inhalation, in which the herb's volatile oil is vaporized by boiling water, allowing the herb to enter the respiratory passages, marjoram may help unblock sinuses and relieve laryngitis. In laboratory tests, liquid extracts of the herb have been shown to have effects against the herpes simplex virus. In aromatherapy, essential oil of marjoram is believed to help induce sleep. It may be added to a bath to encourage relaxation, and alleviate the symptoms of colds or flu. Marjoram oil is included in massage oils to help relieve muscle cramps, including menstrual and rheumatic pain.

DOSAGE **Tea:** 0.25 litre (8 oz) one to two times daily. **Aromatherapy bath:** Three to five drops essential oil added to a bathtub of warm water. **Oil for external use:** Ten drops essential oil added to 30 ml (1 oz) almond or jojoba oil, and shaken to mix.

ORIGANUM VULGARE
OREGANO, WILD MARJORAM

Oregano, a member of the Lamiaceae (mint) family, is native to Europe and central Asia. This fragrant, bushy perennial, with ascending purple-brown stems, bears hairy oval leaves and branched clusters of pink flowers. The Greek word *ganos* (joy), which comes from the second part of *Origanum*, refers to the cheerful appearance these plants give to the hillsides where they grow. The Greeks considered it a sign of happiness when oregano was found growing on the grave of a loved one. Oregano's flowering tops were once added to English beer as a preservative and to enhance its flavour. In medieval times, the plant was strewn, along with rushes, on stone floors. When they were walked on, they gave off a sweet aroma. Today, in addition to the herb's culinary use, oregano leaves and flowers are added to potpourris; the dried flowers are incorporated in wreaths. Essential oil of oregano is used as a food flavouring, and is added to men's cologne.

GROWING CONDITIONS Oregano thrives in well-drained to dry soil in full sun. Propagation is by seed, cuttings or root division. Leaves and blossoms may be harvested throughout the flowering season.

CULINARY USE Oregano is popular in Italian, Greek and Mexican cuisines. It is added to cheese, tomato, bean and egg dishes, and to pasta and pizza. Some alcoholic beverages, baked goods, meat products, condiments and relishes are flavoured with the herb.

MEDICINAL USE A volatile oil in oregano leaves contains thymol and the highly antiseptic carvacrol, which has antifungal and anthelmintic properties. The herb is used to improve digestion, kill intestinal worms, as an expectorant and a treatment for inflammation of the bronchial membranes. To relieve coughs, it may be taken as a tea or a steam inhalation, in which the herb's volatile oil is vaporized by boiling water. Diluted oregano oil may be applied externally to treat insect bites and athlete's foot. In Traditional Chinese Medicine, oregano is used to treat gastrointestinal and respiratory conditions including vomiting, dysentery, childhood malnutrition, colds and fever.

DOSAGE **Tea:** Drink 0.25 litre (8 oz) two or three times daily. **Bath:** Add 3 to 5 drops of essential oil to warm water. **Massage oil:** Add 10 drops of essential oil to 30 ml (1 oz) almond or jojoba oil; shake to mix.

P

$\mathcal{P}$AEONIA LACTIFLORA

CHINESE PEONY

A member of the Paeoniaceae (peony) family, Chinese peony is native to eastern Asia. It has been grown in the East, particularly in northeastern China and Inner Mongolia, since 900 B.C.E. This beautiful, showy perennial bears fragrant white flowers, and is considered a symbol of spring and new life. There are also many garden cuttings with flowers in shades of pink through to dark crimson.

GROWING CONDITIONS Chinese peony grows in rich, well-drained soil, protected from frost, in full sun or partial shade. Seeds may be planted in the spring; root cuttings may be planted in the winter. Seeds may take up to three years to germinate. Roots are harvested from four- to five-year-old plants in the late summer.

CULINARY USE Chinese peony is an ingredient in "four things soup", a popular female tonic in China that is also thought to alleviate menstrual cramps.

MEDICINAL USE Chinese peony has been used in traditional Chinese medicine for at least 1,500 years. It has analgesic properties and is an antispasmodic that helps relax intestinal tissue and uterine muscles. The herb may have hypotensive effects, lowering blood pressure and increasing blood flow to the heart, as well as antiviral effects against herpes simplex cold sores. Containing a unique glycoside called paeoniflorin, which has anti-oxidant properties, Chinese peony may help to stimulate immune cells. It has been used to treat menstrual problems, including cramps and breakthrough bleeding (between periods). It is believed to nourish the skin, and is found in many Asian skin care products. **Note:** Chinese peony should not be used during pregnancy.

DOSAGE Tea: Drink 118 ml (4 oz) three times daily.

PANAX QUINQUEFOLIUS; PANAX GINSENG

AMERICAN GINSENG, ASIAN GINSENG, GINSENG

American ginseng (*P. quinquefolius*) is native to eastern North America, where it is mainly wild-harvested. The plant is also cultivated in North America, Canada and China. Asian ginseng (*P. ginseng*) is native to China. It is widely cultivated in Russia, China, Korea and Japan. Both American and Asian ginseng are members of the Araliaceae (spikenard) family. Ginseng, a perennial, bears single stems with three to six leaves and a flowering stalk that produces bright red berries. Long used as a healing herb, ginseng's genus name, *Panax*, comes from the Greek word for panacea, or cure-all. It is a very important herb in Traditional Chinese Medicine.

GROWING CONDITIONS
Ginseng prefers cool and shady hardwood forests. The plant flourishes in areas with ample summer moisture and freezing temperatures in the winter. It is susceptible to fungal disease and rodent predation, and is therefore a difficult herb to cultivate. Ginseng is propagated by seed in the spring. Roots are harvested in the autumn, from plants as young as five years old. Ginseng plants are not considered fully grown until aged 20.

CULINARY USE
Ginseng has a sweet, slightly bitter flavour. It is sometimes added to soups, and sometimes used to flavour tea, soft drinks and chewing-gum.

MEDICINAL USE
Ginseng has an impressive history of medicinal use dating back 2,000 years. The root is the part of the plant most often used. It contains a stimulating compound known as ginsenoside, which may, over time, improve the body's response to stress, minimize the effects of depressants such as alcohol and barbiturates, and lower blood sugar levels. In Traditional Chinese Medicine, Asian ginseng is considered to have warming properties, which means it has a beneficial effect on the blood and circulatory systems. In addition, it is used to revitalize the body and to treat exhaustion, impotence, lack of appetite and diseases that sap the strength, such as cancer. American ginseng, which is considered to be less potent than Asian ginseng, is believed to have cooling properties that benefit the respiratory and digestive systems. The herb is used to treat nervous indigestion, weak stomach, loss of appetite and mental exhaustion caused by overwork. American ginseng is thought by some herbalists to be an especially beneficial treatment for the many people in modern society who are overstressed and overworked.

Note: Ginseng is not usually recommended for use by those under age 40. It is best suited for use by those who are weak or elderly. Because of the demands on American ginseng, herbalists recommend purchasing only cultivated root, not harvesting ginseng in the wild, and using *Panax ginseng* if American ginseng is not available.

DOSAGE
Tea: Drink 0.25 litre (8 oz) two or three times daily. **Tincture:** Use 0.03 to 1 to 2 ml (0.07 oz) two to three times daily. **Standardized extract:** Take one or two 500 mg capsules two or three times daily. **Standardized extract:** Take one 100 mg capsule standardized to 10 percent ginsenosides once or twice daily.

P

$\mathcal{P}$AUSINYSTALIA JOHIMBE

JOHIMBE, YOHIMBE

Yohimbe, a member of the Rubiaceae (madder) family, is an evergreen tree native to the forests of western Africa (Cameroon, Gabon and Zaire). The trees, with red to yellow wood and glossy, dark green leaves, can reach up to 30.5 m (100 ft) in height. They bear clusters of tubular white or pink flowers and seeds that look like small winged, paper-thin slivers.

GROWING CONDITIONS Yohimbe grows in moist soil in areas of high humidity, with minimum temperatures of 15 to 18°C (59 to 64°F). The bark is collected from trees in the wild throughout the year and dried in strips.

CULINARY USE None.

MEDICINAL USE A bitter, warming herb, the bark of the yohimbe tree has a reputation as an aphrodisiac in Africa (particularly among the Bantu people). The bark contains an alkaloid, yohimbine, which has been made into a pharmaceutical drug known as yohimbine hydrochloride, used to treat impotence and erectile dysfunction. An extract has been used to increase saliva flow in patients taking antidepressants who experienced the side effect of dry mouth. In herbal medicine, however, yohimbe is not widely used because of its potentially

toxic effects, which include increased heart rate and elevated blood pressure. **Note:** Yohimbe should not be used by individuals with high blood pressure or kidney or liver disease. Excess use can cause depression.

DOSAGE Tincture: Use 5 to 30 drops daily. **Standardized extract:** Take one to two 400 mg capsules daily. **Extract:** Take 5 to 10 mg daily.

$\mathcal{P}$ELARGONIUM SPP.

SCENTED GERANIUM

There are about 250 species of annual, perennial and subshrubs in the *P.* genus, which belongs to the Geraniaceae (geranium) family. Native to South Africa, scented geranium have been cultivated in Europe (particularly in the Mediterranean) since the 17th century. There are numerous cultivars, many with strongly aromatic leaves. Popular varieties include *Pelargonium* 'Fragrans', which has a nutmeg scent, *P. graveolens* (rose geranium), and *P. crispum* (lemon geranium). The genus name comes from the Greek word *pelargos*, meaning "stork". The shape of the fruit of scented geraniums were thought to resemble a stork's beak.

GROWING CONDITIONS Scented geraniums are commonly grown aromatic garden plant that thrives in well-drained neutral to alkaline soil in full sun in areas with minimum temperatures of 7 to 10°C (45 to 50°F). Some varieties will tolerate partial shade. Scented geraniums can be grown throughout the year in containers. Softwood cuttings may be planted from the spring to early autumn. Leaves may be harvested year-round.

CULINARY USE Scented geranium is used as a tea and to flavour vinegars and desserts. Rose geranium is made into jelly. To add subtle flavour to a cake, scented geranium leaves are placed flat on a buttered and floured pan just before pouring in cake mix. The leaves are discarded once the cake is baked and cooled.

MEDICINAL USE Scented geraniums contain complex volatile oils with more than 2,000 components. Geraniol, an antiseptic compound found in geranium oil, is commercially used in the manufacture of many high quality perfumes. In aromatherapy, essential oil of scented

geranium, especially rose geranium, is used as an ingredient in facial creams, in bath and massage oil, as an antidepressant and to help ensure restful sleep. The oil is also a natural mosquito repellent. In the plant's native South Africa, scented geranium leaves have been used to treat diarrhoea.

✍ DOSAGE Tea: Drink 0.25 to 0.5 litre (8 to 16 oz) daily. **Bath:** Add 5 drops of essential oil to a bath of warm water. **Massage oil:** Add 10 to 20 drops of essential oil to 30 ml (1 oz) of almond or jojoba oil, and shake to mix.

𝒫ETROSELINUM CRISPUM

CURLY LEAF PARSLEY, FLAT-LEAF PARSLEY, ITALIAN PARSLEY, PARSLEY

Parsley is an aromatic biennial herb in the Apiaceae (parsley) family. Native to Europe, it is now the region's most widely cultivated herb. Parsley also grows in western Asia and is cultivated throughout the world. The plant bears triangular, pinnate, curled leaves that have a fresh, slightly peppery flavour, and tiny yellow flowers followed by small fruits. There are approximately thirty varieties of parsley, but flat and curly leaf are the most popular. One of the first herbs to appear in the early spring, parsley is used in the traditional Jewish Passover meal (known as the Seder) to represent new beginnings. Ancient Greeks planted parsley on graves and fed

the herb to chariot horses. Ancient Romans ate parsley with soft cheese on bread. The ancients also used wreaths of parsley to ward off drunkenness.

✍ GROWING CONDITIONS Parsley grows in rich, well-drained, neutral soil in full sun or partial shade. Although parsley is a biennial, it is often planted as an annual because develops a bitter in flavour during its second year of growth. Flat-leaf parsley is a particularly hardy, weather-resistant variety. Parsley seeds may be planted in the spring or summer; leaves may be harvested throughout the growing season.

✍ CULINARY USE The Roman poet Pliny the Elder (23 to 79 C.E.) stated that every sauce should contain parsley. The herb is still among the world's most popular culinary flavourings and garnishes. Parsley is used as a seasoning in sauces, stuffings and savoury dishes. It pairs especially well with egg and chicken salads, tomatoes, cheese, egg dishes and peas. Parsley makes a tasty addition to pasta dishes and is a crucial component of the Middle Eastern bulgur wheat salad called *tabbouleh*. It is also one of the herbs in bouquet garni, a bundle of herbs (traditionally fresh parsley, fresh or dried thyme and bay leaf) tied together and used to flavour soups and stews.

✍ MEDICINAL USE Parsley is a good dietary source of iron, calcium and vitamins A and C. The herb has been used since ancient Roman times to freshen the breath, particularly to eliminate garlic odour. Parsley contains high levels of chlorophyll, an ingredient in many commercially available breath fresheners. It is soothing to the digestion and may be taken to relieve trapped wind and bloating. The herb has a diuretic effect, and has been used to treat urinary tract infections, oedema and kidney stones. Parsley has also traditionally been used to relieve menstrual pain. **Note:** Parsley leaf should not be used in medicinal amounts during pregnancy or by individuals with kidney disease.

✍ DOSAGE Tea: Drink one 0.25 litre (8 oz) cup two or three cups each day. **Tincture:** Use 1 or 2 droppersful two or three times daily. **Capsules:** Take one 500 mg capsule two or three times daily.

P

PHYTOLACCA AMERICANA

POKE, POKEROOT, POKEWEED

Pokeweed, a member of the Phytolaccaceae (pokeweed) family, is a toxic perennial native to North America and naturalized around the Mediterranean and in northern Africa. It bears spikes of greenish-white flowers, followed by juicy, deep purple berries.

GROWING CONDITIONS Pokeweed thrives in damp woodland areas and open spaces. It grows in rich, moist, well-drained soil in full sun or partial shade. Seeds or root divisions may be planted in the spring or autumn.

CULINARY USE Young pokeweed leaves and shoots are commonly eaten as a spring vegetable dish in parts of the eastern southern United States. The leaves and shoots are cooked twice, and the water is changed to minimize the possibility of toxicity.

MEDICINAL USE Pokeweed has stimulant, purgative, emetic and antirheumatic properties. The herb has been used to treat rheumatic and arthritic conditions, and is used as a cleanser for the lymphatic system to treat swollen glands and mumps. A poultice of the herb can be applied externally to treat acne, fungal infection, scabies, folliculitis and sore or infected nipples. **Note:** Pokeweed is highly toxic. All parts of the plant can cause digestive irritation, vomiting,

diarrhoea and decreased blood pressure. Overdoses can be fatal. Pokeweed should be taken only under the guidance of a qualified health practitioner.

DOSAGE Tincture: Use a maximum dose of 20 drops, under the guidance of a qualified health professional. **Poultice:** Mix 2 tsp powdered pokeweed with enough water to make a paste.

PIPER METHYSTICUM

AWA, KAVA KAVA, KAVA PEPPER, KAVA, YANGONA

There are more than 1,000 species in the *Piper* genus and around 120 different kava cultivars. A member of the Piperaceae (pepper) family, kava has been cultivated for so many centuries that its original birthplace is unclear. Today, the plant grows on the Pacific islands from Hawaii to New Guinea. This tender, sprawling herb has stout rhizomes and bears large, heart-shaped leaves and flowers that resemble small ears of corn. *Kava* derives from a Greek word meaning "intoxicating". Chewed fermented kava roots are the basis of a ritual Polynesian drink that is believed to heighten mental awareness and simultaneously promote calmness. In native South Pacific tribes, kava is ceremonially drunk by those seeking to resolve conflicts. Kava brew was traditionally prepared by a tribe's young people, who had strong teeth to chew the plant's fibrous roots into a pulp that would later be soaked in cold water or coconut milk.

GROWING CONDITIONS Kava thrives in well-drained, stony soil. It can be found growing in moist, sunny highlands or wet forests at elevations of 300 to 1,000 ft (100 to 305 m) above sea level.

CULINARY USE In the South Pacific, fresh or dried kava roots are ground into a thick beverage that is served during ceremonies and special events.

MEDICINAL USE Kava roots are most commonly used to treat nervousness, anxiety, stress and restlessness. The plant is believed to bind to receptors in the brain that are responsible for increasing relaxation. One study has shown that kava may help prevent the body's uptake

of noradrenaline, a hormone that initiates a stress response. Kava contains constituents called kavalactones, which relieve pain and relax muscles. In traditional use, the herb is chewed as an analgesic by those suffering from sore throat or toothache. Studies of kavalactones have shown that they may be less effective than morphine but more effective than aspirin in reducing pain, and they may also enhance aspirin's pain-relieving effects. Combined with pumpkin seed oil, kava has been used to treat irritable bladder and bowel syndrome. **Note:** Kava should not be taken by pregnant or breastfeeding women.

DOSAGE Tincture: Use 1 or 2 ml (0.03 or 0.07 oz) three times daily. **Standardized extract:** Take two 400 to 500 mg capsules two times daily. **Standardized extract:** Take one 70 mg capsule standardized to 30 percent kavalactones two or three times daily.

PIPER NIGRUM

BLACK PEPPER

There are more than 1,000 species of climbing plants, shrubs and small trees in the *Piper* genus. A member of the Piperaceae (pepper) family, black pepper is native to India and is cultivated in tropical areas throughout the world. This woody-stemmed, pungent-smelling, climbing plant bears large, oval leaves, white flowers on spikes, and small red berries, called peppercorns, that grow in clusters, similar to grapes. Male flowers and female flowers usually grow on separate plants. Black peppercorns are harvested from plants that are at least three years old. They are picked when not quite ripe and then dried. Although black pepper is now a relatively inexpensive herb, it was once so highly valued and so difficult to obtain that it was used as currency. In 408 C.E., the Mongol warrior Attila the Hun is said to have requested

1½ tonnes of black pepper as a ransom during his siege of Rome. In the 15th century, the voyages of European explorers were often undertaken in search of trade routes to the Far East, where peppercorns were grown. The wealth of some European ports, such as Venice in Italy, was as a result of the quest for pepper.

GROWING CONDITIONS Black pepper, which makes an attractive potted plant, grows in rich, well-drained soil in light shade and requires high humidity. The plant will not tolerate temperatures below 15 to 18°C (59 to 64°F). Cuttings that are semi-ripe may be planted in the summer.

CULINARY USE Black pepper, one of the world's oldest-known spices, is used in some form in nearly every regional cuisine. Before the invention of refrigeration, black pepper was used to preserve meat and to mask the taste of meat that was not fresh. Today, the spice is often used to flavour savoury dishes, meats, dressings and pickles. It is an ingredient in many commercially available food products, such as baked goods, condiments and nonalcoholic beverages. Whole black peppercorns, ground immediately before use, provide more flavour than preground pepper.

MEDICINAL USE High in antioxidants, black pepper contains volatile oil and alkaloids that cause the herb to have a stimulating, warming effect on the digestive and circulatory systems. Used to relieve stomachache, nausea, constipation, bloating and flatulence, black pepper is also taken to stimulate the appetite by increasing gastric secretions. In China, where black pepper is known as *hu jiao*, the herb is a popular remedy for "stomach chills" and food poisoning. Essential oil of black pepper, which has antiseptic and antibacterial properties, may be applied externally as a

chest rub to warm the body and alleviate the congestion of cold and flu. The oil is also added to liniments and creams to ease sore joints and relax tight muscles. **Note:** Essential oil of black pepper is for external use only.

DOSAGE **Tea:** Simmer ten black peppercorns in 0.25 litre (8 oz) water; drink up to 0.25 litre (8 oz) daily. **Chest rub:** Add 10 drops of essential oil of black pepper to 30 ml (1 oz) of sweet almond or jojoba oil. Apply to chest up to three times daily. **Liniment or cream:** Add 10 drops of essential oil of black pepper to 30 ml (1 oz) commercial liniment or cream; follow label directions.

PLANTAGO MAJOR

BROAD-LEAF PLANTAIN, GREATER PLANTAIN, RAT-TAIL PLANTAIN

The plantain family (Plantaginaceae) contains more than 250 species. *P. major* is native to Eurasia, but is naturalized throughout North America. This small perennial is commonly thought of as a weed, and is rarely cultivated because it grows so readily in the wild. Plantain bears wide green leaves and yellow-green flowers on cylindrical spikes. *Plantain* is the French version of the Latin word *plantago*, which means plant. Some Native American tribes called plantain "Englishman's foot", because it seemed to flourish in areas visited by British colonists.

GROWING CONDITIONS Plantain grows in moist soil in full sun or partial shade. It thrives in sandy or gravelly soil. Seeds or root divisions may be planted in the spring. The plant self-seeds freely and may grow where it is not wanted. Leaves are harvested before the plant flowers.

CULINARY USE Young plantain leaves can be steamed or boiled and eaten as a vegetable.

MEDICINAL USE Plantain leaves have long been used as a folk medicine. In Shakespeare's 16th-century play, *Romeo and Juliet,* Romeo tells Juliet that plantain leaf is excellent as a treatment for broken skin. Indeed, plantain leaves contain soothing, anti-inflammatory, antibiotic and vulnerary (blood coagulant) constituents. The leaves, bruised or crushed, are a common remedy for insect bites and stings, superficial wounds and skin conditions such as eczema. Plantain is also soothing to the respiratory system and the urinary tract. It has been used as a diuretic and to relieve dry cough. **Note:** Plantain may cause contact dermatitis in sensitive individuals.

DOSAGE **Tea:** Drink up to 1 litre (32 oz) daily. **Standardized extract:** Follow label directions. **Poultice:** Apply crushed leaves to wounds and stings.

PRIMULA VERIS

COWSLIP

Cowslip, a member of the Primulaceae (primrose) family, is native to Europe and western Asia, and is naturalized in temperate areas of the world. This perennial bears slightly rough, oblong leaves and clusters of sweet-smelling, yellow, bell-shaped flowers on long, thin stems. Cowslip is strongly associated with springtime. In Spain and Italy, the herb is known as *primavera*, meaning spring. The name "Cowslip" is derived from the Anglo-Saxon *cu-sloppe*, in reference to the herb's tendency to bloom in meadows among herds of dairy cattle.

GROWING CONDITIONS Cowslip, a popular garden border plant, grows wild in fields and pastures with chalky soils. It prefers dry, neutral to alkaline soil in full sun or partial shade. Seeds may be planted in the summer; root divisions may be planted in late spring or early autumn. Flowers and roots are harvested in the spring.

CULINARY USE Cowslip flowers have a very distinctive fresh fragrance and a slightly narcotic juice. In the United

Kingdom, they have been made into a fermented liquor called cowslip wine. Fresh cowslip flowers may be added to salads, used to make tea or wine, or candied.

MEDICINAL USE Shakespeare's play *A Midsummer Night's Dream* includes a reference to a traditional belief that cowslip flowers held a magic value for the complexion. The validity of this belief is unproven, but cowslip flowers do contain flavonoids that have antioxidant, anti-inflammatory and antispasmodic properties, making them useful in the treatment of asthma and allergies. The flowers also have diuretic properties. They have been used to relieve insomnia and restlessness. Cowslip roots contain triterpenoid saponins, which have powerful expectorant properties and help to thin mucus, making it easier to bring up and eliminate it from the body. Externally, cowslip is used to treat arthritis, skin blemishes and sunburn. **Note:** Cowslip should be not be used by pregnant women or by individuals taking aspirin or prescription anticoagulant drugs, such as warfarin. Overdose can cause nausea, vomiting and diarrhoea.

DOSAGE **Flower tea:** Drink up to 0.75 litre (24 oz) daily. **Root tea:** Drink up to 0.5 litre (16 oz) daily. **Tincture:** Use 1 ml (0.03 oz) three times daily. **Compress:** Apply cool tea to affected areas.

PRUNUS AFRICANA SYN. PYGEUM AFRICANUM

AFRICAN PLUM, PYGEUM

Pygeum is a member of the Rosaceae (rose) family. Other trees in this large genus of approximately 430 species include *Prunus dulcis* (sweet almond) and *P. persica* (peach). Native to Africa, the pygeum plant grows only on that continent. It is closely related to cherry. Pygeum bears small, bitter fruits and has a cherry- or almond-like fragrance.

GROWING CONDITIONS Pygeum thrives in higher elevations in temperate climates in infertile soil. The trees are often established by transplanting very small specimens from the wild.

CULINARY USE None.

MEDICINAL USE Traditionally used in Africa as a tea to relieve difficult urination, pygeum is most often used in Western medicine to treat prostate-gland enlargement (BPH, or benign prostatic hypertrophy). BPH is a common condition in men older than age 50; it is estimated to affect 50 to 60 percent of men older than age 50 and 90 percent of men older than age 80. An extract of the bark of the tree benefits the prostate by increasing glandular secretions and reducing cholesterol levels within the organ. This helps decrease local swelling and inflammation.

P

Pygeum extract also helps improve the flow of urine, which is often blocked in men with an enlarged prostate. The herb decreases nighttime urination, which is a considerable concern for men with BPH because it creates a restless sleep cycle. Pygeum is an attractive alternative to surgery, the common treatment for BPH. The herb is often used in combination with nettle (*Urtica dioica*) or saw palmetto (*Serenoa repens*).

Note: Pygeum should be taken under the guidance of a qualified healthcare professional. The herb has been overharvested in the wild, and much of its habitat has been lost to clear-cutting. The tree is considered endangered. Pygeum plantations are being established to help increase the herb's supply without sacrificing the remaining wild populations.

❧ DOSAGE Treatment: One 50 to 100 mg capsule standardized to 14 percent triterpenes and 0.5 percent n-docosanol twice daily.

*P*RUNUS ARMENIACA

APRICOT, CHINESE BITTER ALMOND

The apricot, a member of the Rosaceae (rose) family, belongs to a genus of about 430 trees and shrubs. The sturdy, deciduous apricot tree is believed to be native to China. It was taken to Italy in ancient Roman times, and

cuttings made their way throughout the Mediterranean region. The tree was then carried by Spanish explorers to the New World, specifically the western coast of the United States, in what is now California, where it was planted in the gardens of Spanish missions. The apricot now grows in South America and in northern temperate regions of the world, including North America and Europe. The tree bears rounded leaves and white or pink flowers, followed by small orange or yellow fruit.

❧ GROWING CONDITIONS Apricot trees grow in well-drained neutral to alkaline soil in full sun. Seeds may be planted in the autumn. Fruits may be harvested when they ripen, in early summer.

❧ CULINARY USE Apricots are eaten fresh or dried, and made into jams, preserves, jellies and juices. In Moroccan cuisine, apricots are commonly cooked with meat. Apricots are also used to make brandy and liqueurs.

❧ MEDICINAL USE Apricots were first mentioned in medical literature around 500 C.E. The fruit is a nutritious source of vitamins and minerals, including vitamin A, calcium and iron. Apricots also have a mild laxative effect. The kernels of the fruits contain an extract called laetrile, a controversial remedy for treating cancer. Laetrile consists of 6 percent toxic cyanide. Advocates claim that small amounts of laetrile, taken over an extended period, will selectively starve cancerous tissue of oxygen. This theory has not been proven effective. Additionally, the kernels yield an oil (similar to almond oil) that is used in cosmetics, massage oil and skin-care products.

❧ DOSAGE Fruit: Enjoy fruits in season, or eat them dried year-round. **Massage oil and skin-care products:** Follow label directions.

*P*RUNUS DULCIS

ALMOND, BITTER ALMOND, SWEET ALMOND

The almond, a member of the Rosaceae (rose) family, is the most widely grown nut tree in the world. Native to western Asia, almond trees are cultivated extensively in Australia, the Mediterranean, South Africa and the western United States. The shrub or small bushy deciduous tree

KUDZU

bears toothed leaves and pink or white flowers followed by pale green, velvety fruits containing two seeds. In folklore, the nut was believed to prevent intoxication; almonds were commonly eaten during meals when wine was consumed in quantity. Today, almonds are sometimes used to cleanse the palate during the tasting of a variety of wines.

☙ GROWING CONDITIONS The almond tree grows in well-drained neutral to alkaline soil in full sun. Seeds may be planted in the autumn; softwood cuttings may be planted in the summer.

☙ CULINARY USE The ripe fruit, or nut, of the almond tree is eaten raw, toasted, salted, candied or smoked. Almonds are a common ingredient in baked goods and breakfast cereals. They are used to flavour extracts, in cooking and liqueurs. Made into a purée, almonds make a delicious alternative spread to peanut butter. Almond milk (almonds blended with water) is a good substitute for lactose-intolerant individuals. Almonds are also ground and substituted for flour in the making of cakes and biscuits.

☙ MEDICINAL USE Almonds are a nutritious source of protein. They are rich in calcium, fibre, folic acid, potassium and vitamin E. They contain healthy fats, including omega-6 and omega-9 oils, which may improve cardiovascular health and lower cholesterol levels. Almond oil, also known as sweet almond oil, has skin-soothing and softening properties. It is used in massage oil, skin ointments and lotions.

☙ DOSAGE Nuts: Eat a handful daily, or as needed in recipes. **Massage oil and skin-care products:** Follow label directions.

Kudzu is a hardy, hairy, fast-growing vine in the Fabaceae (pea) family, native to southeastern Asia and Japan. There are about twenty species in the genus. In the late 19th century, kudzu was carried to North America where it became an invasive weed, particularly in the southern United States. According to folklore, one must close the windows at night to keep kudzu out of the house. The plant bears fragrant purple flowers mostly hidden beneath abundant foliage.

☙ GROWING CONDITIONS Popular as ground cover, in warm areas kudzu can grow 60 ft (18 m) in one season. Kudzu prefers well-drained soil in sunny locations. Regular pruning is essential to control the vine's growth. Propagation is by seed or division in the spring.

☙ CULINARY USE In Asia, kudzu roots were once a dietary staple. The roots, which contain up to 27 percent starch, are made into noodles and used to add texture to processed food products. Kudzu root powder is used in macrobiotic cooking as a thickening agent.

MEDICINAL USE Kudzu root extract has approximately 100 times the antioxidant activity of vitamin E. It contains isoflavones that may relieve chest pain and lower blood pressure, alleviating symptoms such as headache, vertigo, stiff neck and ringing in the ears. Kudzu root also contains the chemicals daidzin and daidzein, which may be useful in the treatment of alcoholism and related alcohol toxicity such as hangovers. Researchers have confirmed the herb's ability to stimulate liver regeneration and lessen the liver's vulnerability to damage from toxins.

DOSAGE **Tea:** Drink 0.25 litre (8 oz) two or three times daily. **Tincture:** Use 1 ml (0.03 oz) up to five times daily. **Standardized extract:** Take up to six 150 mg capsules daily.

RAPHANUS SATIVUS

RADISH

Native to southern Asia, cultivated varieties of radish, a Brassicaceae (mustard) family member, are grown around the world as a vegetable and for medicinal purposes. This

bristly annual is notable for its swollen taproot, which varies in colour from white and red to purple and black. *Radish* comes from the Latin *radix*, which means "root". The plant bears pale purple or white flowers and cylindrical seedpods. In ancient Egypt, the workers who built the Great Pyramids were paid with radishes as well as with onions and garlic. Radishes have also been eaten as a digestive aid since the 7th century C.E.

GROWING CONDITIONS Radish grows in rich, moist, well-drained soil in full sun. Seeds may be planted in the spring. Radish roots may be harvested in the autumn.

CULINARY USE Radish roots have a peppery flavour that can range from mild to very spicy, depending upon variety and age. They are eaten raw as a vegetable, added to salads, or shredded and grated as an accompaniment to fish. Young radish leaves can be eaten in salads. Young radish sprouts add flavour to salads and can be used as a garnish for hot and cold dishes.

MEDICINAL USE Radish contains antibiotic and antioxidant compounds. The root is eaten as a vegetable to stimulate the appetite and aid digestion. It may ease abdominal bloating, flatulence and acid reflux. It also has an expectorant effect and antifungal properties. **Note:** Radishes should not be consumed by those who suffer from gastritis, peptic ulcers or thyroid conditions.

DOSAGE **Fresh:** Eat radishes as desired, especially when an appetite stimulant is needed.

RHEUM PALMATUM

CHINESE RHUBARB, DA HUANG, TURKEY RHUBARB

There are about fifty species in the *Rheum* genus, some of which have been cultivated in China for medicinal use for more than 2,000 years. A member of the Polygonaceae (buckwheat) family, Chinese rhubarb is native to Asia and naturalized in Europe. This tall, sturdy perennial bears palm-shaped leaves, purple to white flowers and winged fruits.

Rheum palmatum, *also known as Chinese Rhubarb, is often used as a flavouring in beverages and foods.*

R

GROWING CONDITIONS Chinese rhubarb prefers well-drained, moist, humus-rich soil and full sun and can reach the height of 10 ft (3m). Propagation is accomplished by seed or division in the spring or autumn.

CULINARY USE Chinese rhubarb has an extremely bitter flavour. An extract of the herb that has had the bitter flavour removed is used as a commercial food flavouring in products ranging from alcoholic and nonalcoholic beverages to ice cream, sweets, baked goods and puddings.

MEDICINAL USE The rhizomes of Chinese rhubarb contain astringent and antiseptic tannins and laxative anthraquinones. In high doses, the herb is believed to ease constipation. At lower doses, it may relieve diarrhoea. The herb thoroughly cleanses the intestinal tract, as it first removes waste and then acts on the system with antiseptic properties. Tannins have styptic, analgesic and anti-inflammatory properties, which explains Chinese rhubarb's long history of use in healing superficial wounds. Rhubarb's extremely bitter flavour makes it useful for improving the appetite and soothing stomach upsets. It is an ingredient in the digestive tonic called Swedish Bitters, and in Essiac, a controversial cancer treatment formula. **Note:** Chinese rhubarb should not be used during pregnancy or by those suffering from intestinal obstruction or inflammation, kidney stones, abdominal pain of unknown origin or by children younger than age 12. The herb should not be used for more than ten days consecutively.

DOSAGE Tea: Drink 0.25 litre (8 oz) in the morning and evening. **Tincture:** Use 1 ml (0.03 oz) in the morning and evening.

ROSA SPP.

ROSE

Native to Iran, the rose has been cultivated for at least 3,000 years in more than 10,000 varieties. A member of the Rosaceae (rose) family, this perennial bush is grown in gardens throughout the world. Rose bushes bear smooth stems with sharp thorns, serrated leaves and fragrant flowers that range in colour from pink and red to lavender, yellow and white. Once the flowers die, scarlet berries called rose hips appear.

GROWING CONDITIONS The rose is one of the most popular garden plants in the world. It was described by Sappho, a 6th-century B.C.E. Greek poet, as the "queen of flowers". Roses grow in well-drained, moist, fertile, neutral to slightly acidic soil in full sun. Seeds and hardwood cuttings are planted in the autumn. Rose hips may be harvested in the autumn.

CULINARY USE Rose hips and petals can be made into tea, jelly, jams, sweets (such as Turkish delight) and syrups. Rose petals can be added to salads and sprinkled on buttered bread as a snack. Rosewater, a distillation of rose petals in water, is a popular flavouring in Indian and Middle Eastern cuisines. *Lassi*, a popular East Indian yogurt drink, is traditionally flavoured with a few drops of rosewater.

MEDICINAL USE Rose is not often used in herbal medicine, but some varieties may at one time have been taken to stimulate digestion and to alleviate the symptoms of the common cold. Pure rose essential oil, known as

rose attar or attar of rose, is widely used in aroma-therapy and in perfumes. Rose oil has mild sedative, anti-depressant and anti-inflammatory effects. Rosewater is mildly astringent, and is sometimes included as an ingredient in skin-care products. Rose hips, which usually come from the species *Rosa canina* (dog rose), are a good source of vitamin C and are made into teas, syrups and fruit drinks.

❧ DOSAGE **Rose hip tea:** Drink up to 0.75 litre (24 oz) daily. **Bath:** Add 5 drops of essential oil to a bath of warm water. **Massage oil:** Add 10 to 20 drops of essential oil to 1 oz (30 ml) of almond or jojoba oil, and shake to mix.

*R*UTA GRAVEOLENS

COMMON RUE, HERB-OF-GRACE, RUE

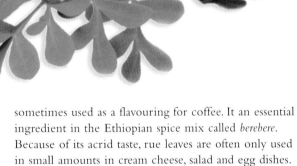

A member of the Rutaceae (rue) family and kin to citrus, rue is native to Europe and is cultivated worldwide. This evergreen shrub bears greyish blue, spade-shaped leaves and bright yellow flowers, and has a repellent odour. The generic name *Ruta* is thought to come from the Greek word *reuo*, meaning "to set free", referring to the plant's reputed ability to free people from disease. The herb was once used as an antidote to poisons and a protection against witches and The Plague. In ancient Rome, artists ate rue to preserve their eyesight. The common name "herb-of-grace" comes from the Catholic tradition of using a brush made of rue to sprinkle holy water during mass. Rue's essential oil is extracted from a steam distillation of the fresh flowering plant and is used to scent soaps, detergents, creams, lotions and perfumes.

❧ GROWING CONDITIONS Rue thrives in well-drained, neutral to alkaline soil in full sun. The plant is propagated by seed sown in the spring or by semi-ripe cuttings planted in the summer. Rue plants grow larger and more full in warm climates. This semiwoody perennial grows to 2 to 3 ft (0.5 to 1 m) tall.

❧ CULINARY USE Rue leaves are used to flavour some varieties of the Italian grape liqueur *grappa*. Rue is very popular in Ethiopia, where fresh leaves are sometimes used as a flavouring for coffee. It an essential ingredient in the Ethiopian spice mix called *berebere*. Because of its acrid taste, rue leaves are often only used in small amounts in cream cheese, salad and egg dishes.

❧ MEDICINAL USE Once considered an important herb for treating hypertension, diabetes, and allergic reactions, rue is no longer widely used medicinally. Active constituents in the leaves include volatile oil, bitters, astringent and antiseptic tannins, and the flavonoid rutin, which helps strengthen capillaries, explaining the herb's traditional use as a treatment for failing eyesight. Rue may have antibacterial, antifungal and anthelmintic properties. It contains alkaloids that have antispasmodic effects, making it useful as a treatment for a variety of ailments, including menstrual cramps, digestive upset, bowel tension and spasmodic cough. Today, the herb is primarily used to regulate the menstrual cycle. **Note:** Rue should not be used during pregnancy.

❧ DOSAGE **Tea:** Drink 0.25 litre (8 oz) two or three times daily. **Tincture:** Use 1 ml (0.03 oz) three times daily.

ROSMARINUS OFFICINALIS
Rosemary

Rosemary is the only plant in the *Rosmarinus* genus, though many cultivars are available. This member of the Lamiaceae (mint) family, native to the Mediterranean region, is a bushy evergreen shrub that bears pale blue flowers and needle-shaped, aromatic leaves that are dark green on top and grey underneath.

The genus name *Rosmarinus* comes from the Latin *ros* (dew or spray) and *marinus* (sea), a reference to the plant's tendency to grow on ocean cliffs. Said to be carried by brides in folklore, rosemary has long been revered as an emblem of fidelity in love and a strengthener of memory, and appears in Shakespeare's play *Hamlet*, when Hamlet's doomed lover, Ophelia, says, "There's rosemary, that's for remembrance." An old French name for rosemary was *incensier*, in reference to its use in religious ceremonies as a less expensive substitute for incense. Before the invention of refrigeration, rosemary was wrapped around meat to prevent spoilage. In Europe, rosemary was believed to fight illness and infection, and so was placed in sickrooms. Nurses in World War II are believed to have burned a mixture of rosemary leaves and juniper berries as an antiseptic in hospitals. Today, rosemary is used to scent cosmetics, soap, detergent, shampoo, creams, lotions and perfume.

GROWING CONDITIONS A drought-tolerant plant, rosemary prefers well-drained, fairly dry, rocky to sandy soil in full sun. Upright varieties of the herb can be planted in gardens or containers; low-growing varieties have a trailing or creeping tendency that makes an appropriate choice for planting in pots or along walls or steep banks. Rosemary does not tolerate cold temperatures well. The area around the plant must be

R. officinalis
Rosemary is grown as a culinary herb and also as a fragrant ornamental.

mulched in the winter in areas where the temperature dips below freezing. Propagation is by seed, cuttings or layering. Rosemary's flowering tops and leaves may be collected in the spring and early summer.

CULINARY USE
The fresh or dried leaves of rosemary are commonly added as a seasoning to a variety of dishes, including soups, baked goods, vegetables, meats, eggs, tofu, stuffings and dressings. Rosemary is a well-known seasoning for lamb and potatoes. Fresh sprigs of rosemary may be steeped in vinegar, wine or olive oil to infuse the liquids with the herb's characteristic flavour. Rosemary branches may be used as skewers for grilling meat and vegetable kebabs. The leaves have a rough

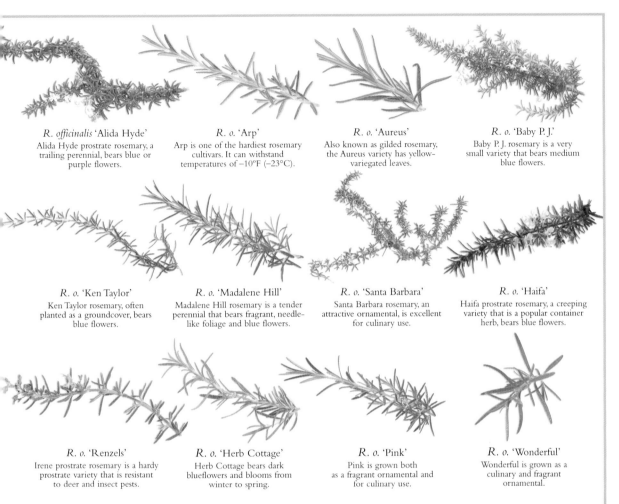

R. officinalis 'Alida Hyde'
Alida Hyde prostrate rosemary, a trailing perennial, bears blue or purple flowers.

R. o. 'Arp'
Arp is one of the hardiest rosemary cultivars. It can withstand temperatures of −10°F (−23°C).

R. o. 'Aureus'
Also known as gilded rosemary, the Aureus variety has yellow-variegated leaves.

R. o. 'Baby P. J.'
Baby P. J. rosemary is a very small variety that bears medium blue flowers.

R. o. 'Ken Taylor'
Ken Taylor rosemary, often planted as a groundcover, bears blue flowers.

R. o. 'Madalene Hill'
Madalene Hill rosemary is a tender perennial that bears fragrant, needle-like foliage and blue flowers.

R. o. 'Santa Barbara'
Santa Barbara rosemary, an attractive ornamental, is excellent for culinary use.

R. o. 'Haifa'
Haifa prostrate rosemary, a creeping variety that is a popular container herb, bears blue flowers.

R. o. 'Renzels'
Irene prostrate rosemary is a hardy prostrate variety that is resistant to deer and insect pests.

R. o. 'Herb Cottage'
Herb Cottage bears dark blueflowers and blooms from winter to spring.

R. o. 'Pink'
Pink is grown both as a fragrant ornamental and for culinary use.

R. o. 'Wonderful'
Wonderful is grown as a culinary and fragrant ornamental.

texture and should be finely chopped before use. If whole sprigs are used, they may be removed prior to a dish being served.

MEDICINAL USE Containing volatile oil, flavonoids and rosmarinic acid, rosemary leaves have anti-spasmodic, carminative, antioxidant and anti-inflammatory properties. The herb is used primarily to treat poor digestion and appetite, rheumatism and sluggish circulation. It may help increase the flow of blood to the heart, and has been prescribed for elderly individuals with impaired circulation and for young adults with weak constitutions who lack physical stamina. The herb has also shown some liver-protective and anti-tumour properties. Rosemary's antioxidant properties make it a beneficial addition to cosmetics, skin creams and lotions. Oil of rosemary, made by steam distillation of the herb's fresh flowering tops, is used to ease irritation by increasing the blood supply to the skin. It takes approximately 100 lb (45 kg) of flowering

tops to produce 8 oz (0.25 litre) of rosemary essential oil. The oil has been shown to protect the skin from cellular damage and to minimize free radical damage. Diluted rosemary oil can be rubbed into the scalp or added to shampoo to stimulate hair growth and prevent dandruff. The oil is also useful as a steam inhalant, helping relieve nasal and chest congestion from cold, flu and allergies. Rosemary oil contains natural camphor, which has an affinity for the nervous system. Applied externally, the oil has been used to relieve muscle and nerve pain, such as sciatica. In aromatherapy, rosemary oil is believed to have stimulating properties.

DOSAGE Tea: Drink 0.25 litre (8 oz) two or three times daily. **Tincture:** Use 1 ml (0.03 oz) three or four times daily. **Standardized extract:** Take two 400 mg capsules three or four times daily. **Bath:** Add 2 to 5 drops of essential oil to a bath of warm water. **Massage oil:** Add 10 to 15 drops of essential oil to 30 ml (1 oz) of almond or jojoba oil, and shake to mix.

$\mathcal{S}$ALIX ALBA

WHITE WILLOW, WILLOW

The genus *Salix* includes about 300 species of deciduous trees and shrubs. White willow, a member of the Salicaceae (willow) family, is a large tree with greyish-brown bark and can grow to 80 ft (24 m) tall. Native to temperate and cold regions of the Northern Hemisphere, white willow grows in North America, Europe, northern Africa and Asia. It is often found near waterways, such as on riverbanks. The tree once grew along the banks of the Nile River. For Hebrews living in ancient Egypt, willow trees were symbols of joy. After the destruction of the first temple of Jerusalem in 586 B.C.E., which began the Jews' exile from Babylon, the trees became symbols of sorrow, from which the term weeping willow is derived. Willow stems have been used for hundreds of years to make woven baskets.

GROWING CONDITIONS Willow trees, often planted as fast-growing shade providers, grow in heavy, moist to wet soil in full sun. Semi-ripe cuttings may be

planted in the summer; hardwood cuttings may be planted in the winter. Bark can be harvested in the spring or summer from two- to five-year-old trees.

CULINARY USE None.

MEDICINAL USE Commonly called "herbal aspirin", the bark of the willow tree has been used for more than 1,000 years to reduce fever and relieve the pain of headache, arthritis and menstrual cramps. In the 1st century C.E., the Greek physician Dioscorides wrote that willow "mashed with a little pepper and drunk with wine" could relieve lower back pain. Willow contains salicylic acid, which was synthesized by the Bayer Company from the herb meadowsweet (page 240) as the basis of pharmaceutical aspirin. Bayer was looking for a substitute for its popular pain formula, which included as ingredients toxic wintergreen and black birch oil. Willow has a weaker action than aspirin, but it also provokes fewer side effects. The tree does not share aspirin's blood-thinning effects, nor does it irritate the lining of the stomach. **Note:** Willow should not be used by pregnant or breastfeeding women, by people who are sensitive to aspirin or have stomach ulcers, or by children younger than age 16 who have a fever related to cold, flu or chickenpox.

DOSAGE **Tea:** Drink up to 0.75 litre (24 oz) daily. **Tincture:** Use 20 drops three times daily. **Standardized extract:** Take up to six 400 mg capsules daily, or follow label directions.

$\mathcal{S}$AMBUCUS NIGRA

BLACK ELDER, ELDERBERRY, EUROPEAN ELDER

A member of the Caprifoliaceae (honeysuckle) family, black elder is native to Europe, North Africa and western and central Asia, and is naturalized in North America. Growing as a shrub or small tree, elder bears flat-topped masses of sweetly scented, cream-coloured flowers, followed by purplish-blue edible berries that produce a deep blue dye. The plant's stems were once used as wind instruments and blowpipes. Because black elder is believed to have a mildly astringent effect, the herb is a common ingredient in commercial skin lotion, oil and ointment.

❧ **GROWING CONDITIONS** Black elder is a very fragile tree that favours rich soil and somewhat damp soil in sun or partial shade. It may often be found growing in hedges in Europe. Propagation of this tree is by softwood cuttings in the summer, by seeds in the autumn, and by hardwood cuttings in the winter. The flowers may be harvested in the spring and early summer; the berries may be harvested in the late summer.

❧ **CULINARY USE** Black elder flowers and berries have a long history in rural England of use in home-made jam, vinegar, chutney and drinks, including wine and a winter cordial. The flowers can be eaten raw or coated with milk and eggs and cooked as fritters. They may also be used decoratively as a garnish, to float in a punch bowl, or to flavour teas and alcoholic beverages, including bitters and vermouth.

❧ **MEDICINAL USE** Black elder has been called "the medicine chest of the people" because of the various medicinal uses of the plant's flowers and berries. There are nine species of *Sambucus*; the two most commonly used for medicine are *S. nigra* and *S. canadensis*. Black elder is believed to have diuretic and diaphoretic (sweat-promoting) activity. It has long been used to relieve the symptoms of sinusitis, cold, fever and flu. Commercial black elder syrups may be taken to prevent and heal viral infections, including cold and flu.

❧ **DOSAGE** **Tea:** Drink 0.25 litre (8 oz) two or three times daily. **Tincture:** Use 1 or 2 ml (0.03 or 0.07) three or four times daily. **Standardized extract:** Take two 500 mg capsules two or three times daily. **Standardized extract:** Take two 400 mg capsules standardized to 5 percent total flavonoids. **Syrup:** Follow label directions.

SALVIA

Sage

Sage, a member of the Lamiaceae (mint) family, is native to the Mediterranean region and cultivated in North America and Europe, particularly in Italy, Albania, Greece and Turkey. This evergreen perennial shrub has been grown in northern Europe since medieval times and was introduced to North America in the 17th century.

S. officinalis bears oval-shaped silvery-green leaves with a velvety texture, and white, pink or violet flowers. The botanical name *Salvia* derives from the Latin *salvere*, meaning to save, a reference to the herb's reputed curative powers. In medieval England, sage was added to ale and drunk as a toast to good health. Sage was held in high esteem by the Chinese, who traded it for black tea (*Camellia sinensis*). In colonial North America, sage was baked into breads and made into herb butter; the leaves and flowers were candied. Traditionally used medicinally to control excess perspiration, sage is an ingredient in present-day antiperspirant formulas. Sage leaf tea has long been used to darken the hair and is sometimes added to shampoo. There are more than 500 *Salvia* varieties. Some important varieties that are not pictured include: Holt's mammoth sage (*S. o.* 'Holt's Mammoth'), which bears blue flowers and larger leaves than most other varieties; blue sage (*S. clevelandii*), an evergreen shrub that bears wrinkled aromatic leaves and spikes of blue-violet flowers; diviner's sage (*S. divinorum*), which has square hollow stems, large green leaves and white flowers, and psychoactive properties; Greek sage (*S. fruticosa*), which bears lavender-scented leaves with downy undersides and mauve to pink flowers; narrow-leaved sage or Spanish sage (*S. lavandulifolia*), an evergreen perennial with hairy stems bearing wrinkled, grey, lavender-scented leaves;

Salvia officinalis
Sage tea was once more popular in China than black tea.

Chinese sage, or red sage (*S. miltorrhiza*), a popular medicinal herb in China, that has red roots and bears purple flowers; Purple Majesty sage (*S.* 'Purple Majesty'), a robust, fast-growing variety that bears dark purple flowers; and Bluebeard, or painted, sage (*S. viridis*) has erect stems and bears soft leaves and small pink or purple flowers.

GROWING CONDITIONS Sage is well suited to warm, dry regions. It grows best in a fairly rich, well-drained clay loam soil in full sun. Propagation is by seed, cuttings or layering. Sage plants require mulching

S. officinalis 'Berggarten'
Berggarten sage is a German
cultivar that bears rounded leaves
and lilac-purple flowers.

S. o. 'Purpurascens'
Purple sage is a colourful evergreen
shrub with purple-grey foliage
and a strong flavour.

S. o. 'Tricolour'
Tricolour sage bears grey-green
leaves with white, pink and purple
edges. It is a good container herb.

S. apiana
The leaves of white sage have
been burned as incense by Native
American peoples.

S. argentea
Silver sage, a biennial, bears
fuzzy, velvety grey leaves
and white flowers.

S. azurea 'Grandiflora'
Azure sage, or pitcher sage, has lacy
foliage and bears sky-blue flowers
that bloom on spikes.

S. elegans
Pineapple sage bears red flowers
and bright green, pointed,
pineapple-scented leaves.

S. elegans 'Freida Dixon'
Pink pineapple sage bears salmon-
pink flowers and bright green,
pointed, pineapple-scented leaves.

S. leucantha
Mexican bush sage or velvet sage,
a fast-growing perennial, bears
velvety, blue-purple flower spikes.

S. sclarea
Clary sage bears strongly
scented leaves and white or
lilac-purple flowers.

S. microphylla
Baby sage or blackcurrant sage, a
perennial, bears light coral-red flowers and blackcurrant-scented leaves.

when the temperature drops below 0°F (-18°C).
The plant is sensitive to extended dry periods and
excessively high temperatures.

CULINARY USE Sage has strong antioxidant and
antibacterial properties, and has traditionally been
added to meat as a preservative and flavouring. The herb
is commonly used in sausage and other meat products,
stuffings, condiments and relish, and processed vegetables, soup and gravy. It is often used to flavour herb
vinegar. Sage oil is added to both nonalcoholic and
alcoholic beverages, including vermouth and bitters.

MEDICINAL USE Sage leaf contains volatile oils that
exert a soothing action on mucous membranes. It is
a classic remedy for inflammation of the nose and
throat, and was traditionally used by Native Americans

to treat cold, cough and diarrhoea. The herb contains
antimicrobial phenolic acids, and has been taken internally to treat *staphylococcus* infections and used as a gargle
to treat laryngitis, pharyngitis, tonsillitis, gingivitis and
mouth sores. It may also be useful in reducing the body's
emission of fluids: it has been used to relieve menopausal
night sweats, excessive perspiration and the breast milk
flow. Sage is considered to have a relaxing effect on the
stomach and is used to treat indigestion and flatulence. In
aromatherapy, sage essential oil can be applied topically to
insect bites, boils and burns. **Note:** Sage should not be
used therapeutically by pregnant or breastfeeding women.
This caution does not apply to its culinary use.

DOSAGE **Tea:** Drink 0.25 litre (8 oz) two or three
times daily. **Tincture:** Use 1 ml (0.03 oz) two or three
times daily. **Standardized extract:** Follow label directions.

SANGUINARIA CANADENSIS

BLOODROOT, RED PUCCOON, RED ROOT

Bloodroot, native to the eastern United States, is a member of the Papaveraceae (poppy) family. This low-growing perennial bears white flowers and a single, kidney-shaped grey-green leaf that wraps around the flower. The genus name *Sanguinaria* comes from the Latin *sanguis*, or blood, which refers to the red juice found in the plant's rhizomes. The plant's rhizome and roots are the source of an orange-red dye, which was once used by Native Americans as a face paint. Bloodroot juice was also squeezed onto maple sugar to make instant throat lozenges.

✤ GROWING CONDITIONS Bloodroot thrives in sandy, well-drained and slightly rich soil that is moist but not wet. The herb prefers a shady location. Propagation is carried out by seed or root division.

✤ CULINARY USE None.

✤ MEDICINAL USE The dried rhizomes of bloodroot contain alkaloids such as sanguinarine, which have expectorant, antispasmodic, cathartic and cardiovascular

actions. The herb has a relaxing effect on the bronchial muscles and has proven useful in the treatment of bronchitis. It may also be effective in treating chronic lung congestion, such as emphysema, and has been used to treat asthma, croup and laryngitis. Bloodroot is also sometimes used externally to treat conditions such as warts, nasal polyps and benign skin tumours. Recent studies have examined the use of bloodroot's alkaloids in dental hygiene products, such as mouthwash, to fight plaque formation and gum disease. **Note:** Bloodroot should not be used during pregnancy. It should be used only in small amounts; taking too much of the herb may cause nausea and vomiting. Bloodroot has been overharvested in the wild and is at risk of becoming an endangered plant. The herb should be purchased only from cultivated (not wild-harvested) sources.

✤ DOSAGE Tea: Drink 0.25 litre (8 oz) three times daily. **Tincture:** Use 0.50 ml (0.016 oz) three times daily.

SANGUISORBA MINOR

SALAD BURNET

A member of the Rosaceae (rose) family, salad burnet is one of fifteen to twenty species in the *Sanguisorba* genus. This perennial bears rounded, toothed, parsley-like leaves and small thimble-shaped, pinkish-white to greenish flowers. Both the flower stalks and the leaf-stalks are a deep crimson colour. Native to Europe and western Asia, salad burnet has become naturalized in parts of North America. It was once extensively cultivated as fodder for sheep and cattle. *Sanguisorba* comes from the Latin *sanguis*, meaning "blood", and *sorere*, meaning "to soak up". The herb has long been used to staunch wounds. Its close relative, *S. officinalis*, was consumed as a tea before battle by soldiers in the American Revolutionary War to lessen bleeding in the event that they were wounded. Salad burnet's attractive leaves are popular for drying to make pressed flower picture arrangements.

✤ GROWING CONDITIONS Salad burnet prefers full sun and fairly well-drained soil. It is not drought tolerant. Although easily grown from seed, propagation may be done by root division in the spring or autumn.

CULINARY USE As the plant's common name suggests, the young leaves of salad burnet are often added to salads. When bruised, the leaves smell and taste somewhat like cucumber. Salad burnet is also used to flavour salad dressing, herb vinegar, cream cheese and herb butter.

MEDICINAL USE Used throughout history to staunch the bleeding of wounds, salad burnet contains astringent and antiseptic tannins. A tea from the root and leaf of the herb has an astringent effect and is used to treat diarrhoea and to stop internal and external bleeding. A leaf poultice can be applied externally to stop bleeding.

DOSAGE Tea: Drink 0.25 litre (8 oz) two or three times daily.

SANTALUM ALBUM

EAST INDIAN SANDALWOOD, SANDALWOOD, WHITE SAUNDERS, YELLOW SANDALWOOD, YELLOW SAUNDERS

A member of the Santalaceae (sandalwood) family, this small, parasitic evergreen tree is native to and cultivated in tropical Asia (specifically India, Sri Lanka, Malaysia, Indonesia and Taiwan). The tree has smooth, greyish-brown bark, and bears feathery leaves and numerous small pink flowers. Sandalwood has been used for more than 4,000 years as a medicine, incense and fragrance. It is also used as an ingredient in soap, creams and lotions, and as an aromatic carving wood. The wood is tradition-ally burned at Buddhist funerals. Sandalwood's essential oil acts as a fixative to retain the scent in perfume and potpourris. The oil is distilled from the tree's roots and heartwood, and can only be produced from trees that are between 20 and 40 years old.

GROWING CONDITIONS The sandalwood tree receives some of its nutrients from photosynthesis but primarily uses sucker roots to draw water and minerals from a host plant. The tree prefers well-drained, moist, fertile soil in partial shade. Propagation is by seed. Seedlings are planted alongside a host when the roots are 2.5 to 4 cm (1 to 1.5 in) long.

CULINARY USE In India, sandalwood is made into a tea served with honey. In Nepal, it is cooked with rice. It is a frequent ingredient in Ayurvedic recipes.

MEDICINAL USE Essential oil of sandalwood contains constituents that have antiseptic and diuretic effects on the urinary tract. The oil is often combined with other disinfectant or diuretic herbs only for external use. Commonly used in aromatherapy, sandal-wood acts as a nervous system sedative, reducing anxiety, insomnia and nerve pain. The medicinal properties of sandalwood oil are absorbed through the skin, and it is often added to massage oils. It has been used topically to treat scabies. In Indian Ayurvedic medicine, sandalwood powder is added to coconut water and given to people who are overheated or dehydrated. Mixed with water to form a paste, sandalwood powder is applied to the skin to treat heat rash, and placed on the temples to reduce a fever. **Note:** Sandalwood should not be used by those who suffer from kidney disease.

DOSAGE Bath: Add 5 drops of essential oil to a bath of warm water. **Massage oil:** Add 10 to 20 drops essential oil to 30 ml (1 oz) of almond or jojoba oil, and shake to mix.

S

SATUREJA HORTENSIS

ANNUAL SAVORY, SUMMER SAVORY

Native to the Mediterranean region, summer savory is naturalized in southwest Africa and Asia, and is a popular garden plant in temperate and warm areas throughout the world. A member of the Lamiaceae (mint) family, this small annual has widely branched stems and bears whorls of white or pale lavender flowers. Summer savory, used as a food flavouring for more than 2,000 years, tastes like a cross between thyme and mint. The genus *Satureja*, which includes thirty species of annuals, perennials and subshrubs, is so often included in pea and bean dishes that Germans call the herb *bohnenkraut*, which means "bean herb".

GROWING CONDITIONS Summer savory grows in neutral-to-alkaline soil, in full sun. Seeds may be planted in the spring; root divisions may be planted in the spring or autumn. Leaves may be harvested throughout the growing season. Flowering tops are harvested in the summer.

CULINARY USE Summer savory is milder in flavour than its perennial relative, winter savory (*Satureja montana*). In recipes, summer savory is a heavier substitute for mint, and a lighter substitute for sage. It adds a piquant flavour to soups, meat and fish dishes, beans, and patés. A small amount adds a great deal of flavour, however, and the herb should be used with a light hand. Summer savory is an ingredient in the classic French herb blend *French fines herb*, which also includes basil, fennel seed, lavender, marjoram, sage and thyme.

MEDICINAL USE Like many culinary herbs, summer savory helps improve digestion and relieve trapped wind. This is one reason it is so often added to bean dishes, which can cause this problem. Summer savory contains astringent and antibacterial properties, making it a useful remedy for

diarrhoea. It has been used to ease muscle spasms and alleviate lung congestion. **Note:** In medicinal doses, summer savory should not be used during pregnancy. Small amounts used in cooking do not pose a problem.

DOSAGE Tea: Drink up to 0.75 litre (24 oz) daily.

SCHISANDRA CHINENSIS

MAGNOLIA VINE, NORTHERN SCHISANDRA, SCHISANDRA, SCHIZANDRA

The genus *Schisandra* includes about two dozen species of climbing plants that grow in eastern North America and eastern Asia. The herb is native to China and adjacent regions of Russia and Korea. A member of the Schisandraceae (star-vine) family, schisandra is a deciduous climbing, woody vine that bears pointed leaves, fragrant pink flowers and bright red berries. In Chinese medicine, the herb is called *wu wei zi*, meaning "five-flavour seed", as the berries are said to taste of all five flavours (sweet, sour, bitter, acrid and salty). The herb was first mentioned in Chinese medical texts during the later Han dynasty (25 to 220 C.E.).

GROWING CONDITIONS Schisandra prefers rich, well-drained, moist soil in sun or partial shade. For successful fruiting, both male and female plants are needed. Propagation is by seeds sown in the autumn or in the spring after being soaked in water overnight, and by cuttings planted in the summer.

CULINARY USE Dried schisandra berries have a mild flavour. In traditional Chinese medicine, they are commonly added to soups, stews, and wine.

MEDICINAL USE Schisandra has been used to treat chronic cough from lung weakness, incontinence from a bladder weakness, and excessive sweating from menopause or chronic infections. It is also used during convalescence and to nourish the adrenal glands. Contemporary herbalists use schisandra as an

adaptogen to counteract fatigue, improve stamina and increase the body's resistance to stress. Most research on the herb has been conducted in China, where double-blind studies suggest that schisandra has liver-protectant properties and benefits for those who have viral hepatitis. **Note:** In rare cases, schisandra may cause suppressed appetite, upset stomach and skin rash.

✿ **DOSAGE Tea:** Drink 0.25 litre (8 oz) two or three times daily. **Tincture:** Use 1 ml (0.03 oz) two or three times daily. **Standardized extract:** Take up to six 500 mg capsules daily.

SCROPHULARIA NODOSA

COMMON FIGWORT

A member of the Scrophulariaceae (figwort) family, figwort is indigenous to North America, Europe, and central Asia. It is an upright, strongly scented perennial with square stems, oval toothed leaves, and small round greenish-brown flowers. The genus *Scrophularia* contains about 200 species of annuals, perennials and shrubs. The botanical name Scrophulariaceae refers to figwort's history of use as a treatment for scrofula, a disease that causes the lymph nodes in the neck to protrude beneath the skin.

✿ **GROWING CONDITIONS** This plant thrives in wet or damp locations in open woodlands and alongside riverbanks and ditches. Figwort may be planted in moist to wet soil in sun or in partial shade. Seeds may be planted in the spring or autumn; root divisions may be planted in the spring; semi-ripe cuttings may be planted in the summer. Figwort may be harvested in the summer while the plant is in flower.

✿ **CULINARY USE** None.

✿ **MEDICINAL USE** The leaves and flowers of figwort are primarily used externally, to treat skin conditions such as eczema and psoriasis. The herb has diuretic properties and a slightly laxative effect. It is considered an alterative, meaning that it may be taken to improve general body function. A poultice, ointment or wash of figwort has traditionally been used to treat abscesses, superficial wounds, ringworm, scabies, rashes, sprains, burns and skin inflammation. **Note:** Figwort should not be used by people suffering from heart conditions such as ventricular tachycardia (abnormally rapid heartbeat).

✿ **DOSAGE Tea:** Drink 0.25 litre (8 oz) three times daily. **Tincture:** Use 1 or 2 ml (0.03 or 0.07 oz) three times daily. **Poultice and ointment:** As necessary.

S

SERENOA REPENS

SABAL PALM, SAW PALMETTO

This evergreen palm, which grows to a height of 2 to 3.5 m (6 to 12 ft), is the only species in its genus. Saw palmetto is a woody rhizomatous member of the Arecaceae (palm) family. Native to the southeastern United States, its natural habitat is pinelands, coastal dunelands and sand hills. The plant bears blue-green to yellow-green leaves and small fragrant flowers, followed by distinctive blue-black, olive-shaped fruits. Saw palmetto is named for Sereno Watson, an American botanist who identified it, and several other new plants, in the 19th century. Native Americans ate saw palmetto seeds and used the leaves for making medicine baskets.

GROWING CONDITIONS Saw palmetto grows in well-drained, moist soil in full sun. The herb needs a minimum temperature of 50 to 55°F (10 to 13°C). Seeds may be planted in the spring.

CULINARY USE None.

MEDICINAL USE Once called "the old man's friend", saw palmetto has long been recommended as a treatment for enlarged prostate (a condition that generally affects older men). Saw palmetto berries contain fatty acids and steroids, which help strengthen the male reproductive system, supporting healthy prostate and urinary function. The herb appears to inhibit the production of

dihydrotestosterone (DHT), the compound that causes the multiplication of prostate cells, resulting in prostate enlargement. Saw palmetto may also relieve symptoms related to enlarged prostate, including difficulties urinating. It has also been used as a sleep aid and to treat cystitis, chronic bronchial coughs and laryngitis.

DOSAGE Tincture: Use 1 ml (0.03 oz) three or four times daily. **Standardized extract:** Take one 585 mg capsule two or three times daily. **Standardized extract:** Take one 160 mg capsule twice daily.

SESAMUM INDICUM

SESAME

This member of the Pedaliaceae (sesame) family is native to southern Africa. A strong-smelling annual or short-lived perennial, sesame is widely cultivated in tropical and subtropical climates. Nigeria, the Sudan, India and China are leading producers of the herb. Sesame plants have sticky-haired stems that bear white, bell-shaped flowers followed by capsules containing the plant's white seeds. Sesame seed is the world's first recorded seasoning, dating back to Assyria in 3,000 B.C.E.

GROWING CONDITIONS Sesame grows in well-drained, sandy soil in full sun. The plant may be easily grown from untoasted seeds purchased for culinary use. Seeds may be planted in the spring or autumn. Seed capsules are harvested when the seeds are ripe.

CULINARY USE Sesame seed has a nutty, slightly sweet flavour and is often used in breads, pastries, sweets and biscuits. It is the main ingredient in two classic Middle Eastern foods: the dessert *halvah* and *tahini,* a butter made of ground seed. Tahini may be found in such dishes as *hummus* and *baba ghanoush*. Sesame seed was brought by African slaves to North America, and it became a popular ingredient in the foods of the southern states of the USA. Sesame seed and oil are both used in Asian cuisine. Sesame oil, expressed from sesame seeds, is light in flavour and colour and used for cooking, frying and in salads. Asian sesame oil, usually known as "dark" or "toasted" sesame oil, is made from toasted sesame seeds. It is darker in colour and has a stronger flavour than regular sesame oil.

GROWING CONDITIONS Milk thistle grows in well-drained soil in full sun. Grown as an annual, seeds can be planted in the spring. As a biennial, seeds can be planted in the summer or early autumn.

CULINARY USE Young thistle leaves can be eaten as a spring vegetable, lightly steamed. It is advisable to remove the prickly outside edge of the leaves. The seeds, which are high in antioxidants, protein and "healthy" fat, can be soaked overnight, drained, ground into a powder, and then lightly toasted and sprinkled on cereal.

MEDICINAL USE Sesame seeds are a nutritious source of essential fatty acids, protein, calcium, vitamin E and folic acid. In traditional Chinese medicine, they are used to strengthen the liver and kidneys. The seeds have a lubricating action in the digestive tract and may be used to treat constipation. Sesame seeds may also stimulate the production of breast milk. The oil has a softening effect on the skin, and can be found as an ingredient in cosmetics and skin-care products.

DOSAGE Use 2 or 3 tsp of seeds daily.

$\mathcal{S}$ILYBUM MARIANUM

MARY'S THISTLE, MILK THISTLE

Native to Europe, this spiky Asteraceae (daisy) family member was carried to North America by colonists. An annual or biennial, milk thistle bears oblong, spiny, variegated leaves and purple flowers, followed by black seeds. The plant earns its common name, milk thistle, from the milky sap that exudes from its leaves. The herb was also traditionally taken to encourage the flow of milk in breastfeeding mothers. The name Mary's thistle derives from a Biblical story. According to legend, Mary, mother of Jesus, was resting beneath a thistle plant while breastfeeding the baby Jesus when a drop of her milk fell on the plant's green leaves, thus leading to the leaves' characteristic white markings.

MEDICINAL USE For more than 2,000 years, milk thistle has been used to treat liver conditions such as hepatitis, cirrhosis and drug-induced damage. The seeds contain silymarin, a flavonoid complex that acts to neutralize free radicals. Standardized milk thistle products may prevent toxic chemicals from entering the liver. If liver damage has occurred, milk thistle is believed to help the organ repair damaged cells and generate new ones. Milk thistle has also been used to treat poor digestion,

female hormone imbalance, constipation, mood disorders, haemorrhoids, varicose veins, atherosclerosis and skin conditions including psoriasis and acne. Milk thistle seeds are high in protein and linoleic acid, a healthy fat that may help balance the menstrual cycle and improve cardiovascular health.

DOSAGE Tincture: Use 2 ml (0.07 oz) two or three times daily. **Standardized extract:** Take one 140 mg capsule (standardized to 70 to 80 percent silymarin) three times daily.

STACHYS OFFICINALIS

BETONY, WOOD BETONY

A member of the Lamiaceae (mint) family, betony is native to Europe and naturalized in many parts of the world. This soft-textured plant bears stiff, slightly hairy pointed leaves, and lavender-pink flowers arranged in whorls on top of spikes. *Stachys* is Greek for "spike". Once known as woundwort, betony was traditionally applied to stop the bleeding of wounds and draw out splinters and boils. The herb's healing powers were esteemed by ancient Greek, Roman and Anglo-Saxon peoples. Antonius Musa, the physician to the Roman emperor Augustus (63 B.C.E. to 14 C.E.), listed forty-seven diseases treatable with betony. An old Italian proverb celebrated betony's value: "Sell your coat and buy betony." *Betony* means "head herb", a reference to the herb's use as a treatment for headache, dizziness and hearing problems. The dried leaves have been used to make herbal tobacco and snuff.

GROWING CONDITIONS Found in meadows and open woodlands, betony prefers a well-drained, dry, neutral to acidic soil in full sun or partial shade. Seeds may be planted in the spring or autumn; root divisions may be planted when the plant is dormant. Flowering plants may be harvested in the summer.

CULINARY USE Betony has a refreshing, astringent flavour, and is a pleasant-tasting substitute for black tea (*Camellia sinensis*).

MEDICINAL USE Betony leaves contain the alkaloid betonicine, which has the ability to reduce inflammation and is used to strengthen the nervous system and treat neuralgia. Betony also contains sedative properties and has long been used to treat headaches, particularly those due to tension and anxiety. Betony's astringent and antiseptic tannins account for its early use to staunch wounds. Once considered a cure-all, the herb is not widely used today.

DOSAGE **Tea:** Drink 0.25 litre (8 oz) two or three times daily. **Tincture:** Use 1 ml (0.03 oz) two or three times daily.

The pink-flowered Stachys officinalis *was once traded by the ancient Romans, Greeks, and Anglo-Saxons.*

STELLARIA MEDIA

CHICKWEED

Native to southern Europe, this member of the Caryophyllaceae (pink) family now grows throughout the world as a common weed. A hardy, low-growing, spreading annual, chickweed often overwinters, meaning that it does not completely die back during the winter months. It bears oval leaves and small white, star-shaped flowers. The genus *Stellaria*, which includes approximately 120 species, takes its name from the Latin word *stella*, meaning "star", in reference to the shape of the flowers of the species. Chickweed has been a popular healing herb for centuries. In many countries, it was used as a food for birds and domestic fowl.

GROWING CONDITIONS Chickweed grows in moist soil in sun or shade. Seeds may be planted at any time of the year. The plant may be harvested at any time.

CULINARY USE Fresh chickweed leaves, harvested in the early spring, are a nutritious addition to salads. Chickweed can also be cooked as a vegetable.

MEDICINAL USE Although chickweed has been used medicinally in the past, there has been very little research conducted on the herb. Chickweed leaves have been applied externally as a juice, ointment or poultice to treat irritated skin. The leaves contain steroid saponins, which may help soothe rashes and relieve the itching of

eczema. Chickweed has also been used as a digestive aid. In homeopathy, it is used in minute amounts to treat psoriasis and rheumatic pain. **Note:** Chickweed should not be used during pregnancy. Excessive amounts of the herb may cause vomiting and diarrhoea.

🌿 **DOSAGE** **Tea:** Drink 0.25 litre (8 oz) daily. **Tincture:** Use 0.50 to 1 ml (0.016 to 0.3 oz) three times daily. **Standardized extract:** Take up to eight 500 mg capsules per day. **Creams and ointments:** Follow label directions. **Poultice:** Apply fresh leaves to affected areas.

STEVIA REBAUDIANA

CANDYLEAF, PARAGUAYAN SWEET HERB, STEVIA, SWEETLEAF

Native to highland areas of Paraguay and Brazil, stevia is cultivated in those countries as well as in China, Thailand, Korea, and Japan. This perennial Asteraceae (daisy) family member has grown in popularity in recent years because of its use as a healthful sugar substitute. Stevia is said to be 300 times as sweet as granulated sugar, but it has no calories and appears to have none of sugar's negative side effects, such as causing tooth cavities. Stevia leaves are sold in leaf, liquid and powdered forms. In Paraguay, stevia leaf has been used for centuries to sweeten the herbal beverage maté. Stevia is popular in Japan, where it is used to sweeten many products, including soft drinks, chewing gum and pickles.

🌿 **GROWING CONDITIONS** Stevia grows in infertile, sandy, relatively dry soil. It prefers semihumid, subtropical environments.

🌿 **CULINARY USE** With its intensely sweet taste, stevia can be used as a healthful substitute for sugar and artificial sweeteners. It has a mild aftertaste. Powdered varieties are available for use in baking and for sweetening beverages.

🌿 **MEDICINAL USE** Stevia contains a glycoside called stevioside that is responsible for the plant's sweet taste. It has been used traditionally to lower blood sugar, but this use is unproven and the herb's principal value is likely to be as a noncalorific natural sweetener. Stevia has also been used in Paraguay as a contraceptive. **Note:** Because of limited data showing that stevia may prevent conception, the herb should not be used by pregnant women or by those trying to conceive.

🌿 **DOSAGE** **Leaves:** Add a small amount to taste as a sweetener. **Powder:** Follow label directions.

SYMPHYTUM OFFICINALE

COMFREY, HEALING-HERB, KNITBONE

The *Symphytum* genus contains approximately thirty-five species, some of which are grown as fodder crops. Comfrey, a perennial in the Boraginaceae (borage) family, is native to Europe and Asia, and is naturalized in all temperate regions of the world. This stout, vigorous plant bears large, tapered, prickly leaves and purple, blue or white bell-like flowers. Its botanical name refers to the plant's traditional use to repair broken bones: *Symphytum* is from the Greek *symphytos*, which means "to unite". "Comfrey" comes from the Latin *con firma*, meaning "with strength". Women whose virginity was in doubt were once encouraged to bathe before marriage in water infused with comfrey. The herb was believed to repair a woman's hymen.

Comfrey has been used to treat a variety of medical ailments ranging from ankle sprain to broken bones, but can be toxic if consumed.

S

GROWING CONDITIONS Comfrey grows wild in marshy areas, meadows, and ditches. The plant, which can be invasive, prefers moist to wet soil in sun or partial shade. To keep comfrey contained, many gardeners plant it in a submerged pot with drainage holes. Seeds or root divisions may be planted in the spring or autumn. Leaves and flowering tops may be harvested in the early summer.

CULINARY USE Fresh young leaves are sometimes eaten as a vegetable. Cooking removes the plant's prickly texture. Due to reports of toxicity, this use is no longer recommended.

MEDICINAL USE Comfrey root and leaves contain allantoin, a chemical that promotes the growth of new skin cells. The herb has been used to heal burns and insect stings, as well as broken bones, strains and sprains. A paste of the root, spread on cloth, will stiffen into a cast. A compress of comfrey tea, applied to an ankle immediately after a sprain, may help reduce the sprain's severity. Comfrey is a common ingredient in herbal ointments and salves. A synthesized form of comfrey is used in pharmaceutical hemorrhoid preparations. **Note:** Comfrey contains pyrrolizidine alkaloids, which may cause liver damage. Comfrey leaves should not be used internally except under the advice of a qualified medical professional. Comfrey root preparations should not be used internally under any circumstances or applied to broken skin. The herb should not be used in any form by pregnant or breastfeeding women.

DOSAGE Paste: Blend leaves or roots with enough water to make a paste, and apply to external injuries. **Creams, ointments and salves:** Follow label directions.

SYZYGIUM AROMATICUM

CLOVE

A member of the Myrtaceae (myrtle) family, clove is native to southeastern Asia and is cultivated worldwide in tropical areas (mostly Zanzibar, Africa and Indonesia). The dried, flower buds of this short, highly aromatic evergreen tree are commonly used in cooking. Clove buds yield a pale yellow essential oil used as a flavouring agent in dental products, soap, creams, lotion and insect repellent. The leaves and stems of the clove tree also yield essential oils. It is said that, in China during the Han Dynasty, subjects who addressed the emperor were made to hold cloves in their mouths as a breath sweetener.

GROWING CONDITIONS Clove trees thrive in well-drained, fertile soil in full sun. Seeds may be planted in the spring; semiripe cuttings may be planted in the summer.

CULINARY USE Clove buds are a distinctive spice, commonly used whole or in powdered form as an ingredient in curries, pies (particularly apple pie), pickles, tea blends, and mulled wine and cider.

MEDICINAL USE Clove oil contains eugenol, which has pain-relieving and mildly antiseptic properties. Eugenol is believed to depress sensory receptors that perceive pain. Essential oil of clove is an ingredient in liniments that are used to relieve muscle and arthritic pain. Applied with cotton wool, clove oil has been used to alleviate toothache. The dental industry uses the oil in preparations for treating dry tooth sockets, and includes it as an ingredient in dental cements and fillings. Because of eugenol's antiseptic properties, clove has the potential to fight bacteria, viruses and fungi such as *Staphylococcus aureus* and *Candida albicans*. The herb has been used as protection against intestinal parasites. Clove oil is also thought to have carminative activity and is used to treat stomachache and flatulent colic. In aromatherapy, the essential oil of cloves is used to reduce drowsiness and alleviate the pain of headaches.

DOSAGE Tea: Drink 0.25 litre (8 oz) daily; add 1 tsp ground cloves to 0.25 litre (8 oz) of boiling water.

TABEBUIA IMPETIGINOSA

IPE ROXO, LAPACHO, PAU D'ARCO, PINK TRUMPET TREE, TAHEEBO

Native to South America, this large tree is a member of the Bignoniaceae (bignonia) family. With smooth grey bark and dark brown vanilla-scented wood, pau d'arco bears large, showy, magenta flowers. The tree can reach 46 m (150 ft) tall, with a base trunk diameter of 1 to 2 m (4 to 6 ft). Because of its beauty, the pau d'arco is a common landscaping element in South American cities. The tree's wood has been used for hundreds of years by indigenous rainforest tribes to make hunting bows. Pau d'arco means "bow stick". Lumber from the tree is still valued for cabinetmaking.

GROWING CONDITIONS Pau d'arco trees prefer well-drained fertile soil in full sun. They may be propagated by seeds and air layering in the spring, or by cuttings in the summer.

CULINARY USE None.

MEDICINAL USE Traditionally used by South Americans to treat cancer, ulcers, syphilis, gastrointestinal problems, candidiasis, diabetes, prostatitis, constipation and allergies, the wood and inner bark of pau d'arco trees contain lapachol, a naphthoquinone that has antimicrobial properties. The herb has been widely studied for its potential as an anti-tumour, anti-inflammatory, antibacterial, antifungal and immune system stimulant. Although research results have been inconclusive, the tree is believed to be a useful treatment for chronic degenerative diseases such as cancer, fungal infections such as athlete's foot, and skin diseases such as eczema and psoriasis. Modern herbalists also use the herb to treat low blood sugar, poor digestion, as well as to promote general health.

DOSAGE Tea: Drink 0.25 litre (8 oz) two or three times daily. **Tincture:** Use 1 or 2 ml (0.03 or 0.07 oz) two or three times daily. **Standardized extract:** Take up to four 500 to 600 mg capsules daily.

TAMARINDUS INDICA

TAMARIND

Tamarind, a member of the Fabaceae (pea) family, is the only plant in its genus. Thought to be native to Africa, this tall evergreen tree is widely naturalized throughout the tropical regions of the world. It has been cultivated in India for centuries and was brought to Mexico and the West Indies by Spanish explorers in the 17th century. Tamarind, which bears orange-yellow flowers and brown seedpods (fruits), is often

T

There are about seventy species in the *Tanacetum* genus. *Tanacetum* comes from the Greek word *athanasia*, meaning "immortality", a reference to the plants' long-lasting flowers. Native to the Balkan Peninsula, feverfew is naturalized in North America, South America, Europe and Australia. The herb is cultivated in central Europe, Kenya, South Africa and Japan. A small, fragrant, bushy perennial in the Asteraceae (daisy) family, feverfew bears feathery leaves and daisylike flowers with white petals and raised yellow centres. During the Middle Ages, feverfew was called featherfoil in reference to its delicate leaves and petals. Due to its strong scent, feverfew was also used as a moth repellent.

planted as an ornamental shade tree. The genus name *Tamarindus* comes from the Arabic *tamar-Hindi*, meaning "date of India". This name refers to the sour, datelike pulp found in tamarind seedpods.

❧ **GROWING CONDITIONS** Tamarind trees grow in light, well-drained soil in full sun, in regions with a minimum temperature of 15 to 18°C (59 to 64°F). Seeds may be planted in the spring when temperatures reach 21°C (70°F) or higher. Fruits are harvested when ripe, and used fresh or dried.

❧ **CULINARY USE** The distinctive sour flavour of tamarind seedpods makes the herb a widely used flavouring in Mexican, Middle Eastern, and East Indian cuisines, incorporated into dishes in a similar way to lemon juice. The fresh or dried fruits add flavour to curries, chutneys, fish dishes and sauces. Tamarind fruit can be made into a refreshing beverage. The herb is one of the main ingredients in Worcestershire sauce, a popular seasoning sauce for meat.

❧ **MEDICINAL USE** Containing plant acids, volatile oil, pectin, potassium and fats, tamarind pulp is used to improve digestion, increase appetite, and relieve trapped wind and constipation. It is also used to soothe sore throats. Mixed with cumin and sugar, tamarind is used in Indian Ayurvedic medicine as a treatment for dysentery.

❧ **GROWING CONDITIONS** Feverfew, a common garden plant, grows in well-drained, dry soil in full sun or partial shade. The herb has many outstanding cultivars. *T. parthenium* 'Golden Ball' bears round yellow flowers, *T. p.* 'Golden Moss' is a dwarf cultivar used in garden edgings and borders, *T. p.* 'Tom Thumb White Stars' bears a profusion of double white flowers. Bees, like moths, dislike the scent of feverfew and tend to stay away from the plant. Feverfew should not be grown near plants that require bee pollination. A spray or dust is sometimes made from the pulverized feverfew flowers and used as an insect repellent. Seeds or root divisions may be planted in the spring or autumn. The plants

❧ **DOSAGE Pulp:** Take 70 to 150 g (2.5 to 5.4 oz) with salt, as desired.

should be deadheaded in the summer and autumn to prevent self-seeding. Leaves may be harvested at any time; flowers may be harvested in the summer, when the plant is flowering.

❧ CULINARY USE Feverfew has an extremely bitter taste. In Italy, it is sometimes used as a seasoning in small amounts to stimulate the appetite.

❧ MEDICINAL USE Feverfew has long been used to treat migraine headaches. The herb contains the compound parthenolide, a sesquiterpene lactone, which inhibits the release of prostaglandins and histamine, preventing blood vessel spasms in the head that cause migraine attacks. For best effect, the herb is taken regularly and at the onset of a migraine. Feverfew also has antispasmodic activity, making it useful in the treatment of indigestion and menstrual problems such as cramps and amenorrhoea. Feverfew leaves can be applied externally to soothe the pain and itching of insect bites. **Note:** Feverfew should not be used during pregnancy. Those who take blood-thinning medications should consult their healthcare provider before using this herb.

❧ DOSAGE Tincture: Use 15 to 30 drops daily. **Standardized extract:** Take up to three 300 to 400 mg capsules daily. **Fresh:** Two fresh leaves daily.

*T*ARAXACUM OFFICINALE

DANDELION, LION'S TOOTH

Native to northern temperate regions of the world, dandelion, a member of the Asteraceae (daisy) family, is grown commercially in North America and Europe, especially in France. This perennial, with its characteristic thick taproot, is both a stubbornly pervasive weed and a useful cultivated plant. Dandelion bears toothed leaves, a single bright yellow flower, which opens with the morning sun and closes in the evening, and ribbed fruits with fine white hairs. "Dandelion" comes from the Latin *dens leonis*, which means "lion's teeth", in reference to the plant's toothed leaves. The French call dandelion *pis en lit*, which translates to "wet the bed", referring to the plant's potent diuretic effects.

❧ GROWING CONDITIONS Dandelion, a very easy-to-grow plant, prefers moist to dry, neutral to alkaline soil in full sun. Seeds may be planted in the spring. Plants should be deadheaded to prevent excessive spreading.

❧ CULINARY USE Dandelion leaves are a tasty green vegetable, rich in antioxidant carotenoids, potassium and the vitamins A, B, C and D. The slightly bitter-tasting young leaves can be added to salads or cooked like spinach. Dandelion flowers are often used to produce a home-made wine. The roots of the plant may be roasted, ground and used as a coffee substitute.

T

❧ **MEDICINAL USE** Dandelion has powerful diuretic effects. Unlike conventional diuretics, which deplete the body of potassium, the herb is a good source of potassium, leaving the body with a net gain of the mineral after the herb is taken. Dandelion root is believed to increase the body's flow of bile, which helps digest fats and may help prevent gallstones. The herb has been used to detoxify the liver, gallbladder and kidneys, and is often taken to treat skin conditions such as acne, eczema and psoriasis. Dandelion root has mild laxative effects and moderate anti-inflammatory properties. It has traditionally been used to treat the joint pain and stiffness of rheumatism. **Note:** Dandelion should not be taken by individuals with gallstones or bile duct obstruction.

❧ **DOSAGE Tea:** Drink up to 0.5 litre (16 oz) daily. **Tincture:** Use 1 or 2 ml (0.03 or 0.07 oz) three times daily. **Fresh:** Eat young leaves, raw or lightly cooked, as desired. **Fresh leaf juice:** Take 1 tsp in water morning and evening.

𝒯HEOBROMA CACAO

CACAO, COCOA, CHOCOLATE

The *Theobroma* genus contains about twenty varieties. Native to lowland tropical forests in Central and South America, cocoa has been cultivated in Africa since the 19th century, and today more than half of the world's cocoa bean supply comes from that country. A member of the Sterculiaceae (cacao) family, cocoa is a small evergreen tree that bears long, thin leaves and small yellow flowers, followed by seedpods. In Central and South America, cocoa beans formed the basis of the traditional Aztec drink *chocólatl* (also known as *xocoatl*, meaning "bitter water"), which was enjoyed by the ancient Inca, Maya and Aztec peoples. Because the drink was made of pounded cocoa beans and spices, without sweeteners, it probably had an extremely bitter taste. Most people could afford the expensive drink only on special occasions, but members of royalty drank as much as they could as a sign of their elevated position. The ancient Aztec king Montezuma believed the plant had powerful aphrodisiac effects. He was said to have drunk fifty golden goblets of *chocólatl* every day. Cocoa became popular in Europe in the mid-17th century after the Spanish conquistador Hernando Cortés sent cocoa beans to the king of Spain. Today the tree's seeds are dried, and roasted to produce cocoa powder and cocoa butter, chocolate for eating and cooking (*Theobroma* translates as "food of the gods"), and a skin-softening ingredient in cosmetics.

❧ **GROWING CONDITIONS** Cocoa trees grow in fertile, moist, well-drained soil in shade. Cocoa trees grow from 12 to 15 m (40 to 50 ft) in the wild; 7 m (23 ft) in plantations. The trees thrive in areas with high humidity and must be sheltered from the wind. They require a minimum temperature of 16°C (61°F). Seeds may be planted when ripe; semiripe cuttings may be planted in the summer. A minimum temperature of 27°C (79°F) is required for planting. Seedpods may be harvested all year, usually from early summer to early winter.

❧ **CULINARY USE** Cocoa is best known as the base ingredient of chocolate. There are several types of chocolate: dark chocolate, which has the lowest sugar content, milk chocolate, which contains dried or condensed milk, and white chocolate, which is made from cocoa butter, with added milk and sugar. Chocolate is made into sweets, baked goods, and beverages. It is also used to flavour liqueurs and even meat dishes and sauces, including Mexican *mole* sauce.

❧ **MEDICINAL USE** Chocolate is a rich source of the antioxidant compounds flavonoids and catechins. Studies show that chocolate may have an effect similar to that of red wine; daily consumption of dark chocolate – the variety highest in flavonoids and lowest in sugar – may help prevent heart attacks. Chocolate does contain saturated fat, but it does not raise cholesterol levels when enjoyed in moderation. Chocolate consumption can be connected with raised cholesterol levels and obesity, however, when it is eaten as an ingredient in high-fat desserts that contain butter and cream such as brownies, puddings and ice cream. Because chocolate contains a small amount of caffeine (about 10 percent of the amount found in coffee), it provides a mildly stimulating effect without the jitteriness coffee can cause. Chocolate also contains small amounts of endorphins, the body's powerful natural painkillers.

❧ **DOSAGE Powder (unsweetened):** Take 1 to 2 tsp daily. **Dark chocolate (70 percent cocoa content)**: 30 to 59 ml (1 to 2 oz) daily.

Theobroma cacao, *more commonly known as chocolate, is an ingredient in many desserts, cakes and sweets. Although known for its sweet taste, theobromine and caffeine make the flavour of the actual plant bitter.*

THYMUS SPP.
Thyme

Thyme, a member of the Lamiaceae (mint) family, is another popular garden plant. A bush with grey-green leaves, thyme has a pungent, slightly lemony and minty aroma. Native to the Mediterranean and southern Italy, thyme is naturalized in temperate regions throughout the world. It is cultivated for commercial use of its leaves and branches in Europe, especially in Germany and Hungary.

There are about 350 species of aromatic woody perennials in the *Thymus* genus. They vary in flavour and aroma, but most varieties can be used in cooking. The ancient Greek philosopher Theophrastus called both thyme and savory by the name *Thymus*. The plant's name is thought to be derived from the Greek word *thumus*, meaning "courage" – in ancient times, thyme was thought to promote courage, and medieval knights carried thyme sprigs as a symbol of bravery. The plant also once symbolized death – the souls of the dead were believed to rest in thyme's flowers. The emperor Charlemagne ordered thyme to be planted in all of his gardens for its culinary and medicinal attributes. Ancient Romans burned the herb in the hope that the scented smoke would repel scorpions; they also strewed the sweet-smelling herb on floors, and used it to flavour cheese. The herb's antibacterial properties helped preserve meats before refrigeration was available. Dried thyme leaves are added to potpourris and used to repel moths.

GROWING CONDITIONS Thyme grows in well-drained soil in full sun. Several varieties, including *Thymus vulgaris* (common thyme) can withstand temperatures as low as -15°C (5°F). Most other varieties

T. vulgaris 'Tall German' Grows best in full sun and dry, well-drained soil.

are hardy to -10°C (14°F). Seeds may be planted in spring; softwood or semiripe cuttings may be planted in summer; and root divisions may be planted in spring or summer. Sprigs for culinary use may be picked throughout the growing season; whole plants and flowering tops may be harvested in summer. When planted near membranes of the cabbage family, such as broccoli or kohlrabi, thyme helps discourage the presence of pests, such as flea beetles (this practice is known as

Thymus 'Broadleaf English'
Broadleaf English thyme is an excellent culinary variety with dark green leaves and pale pink to purple flowers.

Thymus x citriodorus
Lemon thyme is a hybrid with lemon-scented leaves and pale purple flowers.

T. 'Lemon Mist'
Lemon mist thyme is a less-hardy variety with lemon-flavored leaves.

T. praecox 'Albus'
Albus provides a lush ground cover with white flowers.

T. praecox 'Pseudolanuginosus'
Woolly thyme has very soft, grey-green leaves and pink flowers. It is used as a ground cover.

T. praecox 'Halls'
Halls is a small low-growing herb that bears purple flowers and green leaves.

Thymus 'Passion Pink'
The roundish leaves are dark green and the bright pink flowers are very showy.

T. praecox 'Mother-of-Thyme'
A favourite of bees, this fast-growing ground cover has a sweet scent and pink or purple flowers.

companion planting). The plant will cascade over the side of a pot or the side of a raised terrace and is often planted in these locations.

CULINARY USE Common in French cooking, thyme is one of the herbs in the flavouring *bouquet garni*, along with bay and parsley. Thyme is a popular and widely used flavouring in soup, meat and seafood dishes, cream sauce and vegetable dishes. The herb pairs particularly well with courgettes and mushrooms. In slow-cooked dishes, thyme retains its flavour nicely. For hundreds of years, bees on Mount Hymettus near Athens, Greece, have produced a beloved wild thyme honey. Benedictine monks added thyme to their famous liqueur.

MEDICINAL USE Thyme was used by the ancient Romans for coughs, intestinal worms and to improve digestion – the same ailments the herb is used to treat today. Thyme contains a volatile oil that has powerful antiseptic and antifungal properties. The herb is best known for its expectorant effects, making it useful for coughs, and particularly for clearing thick phlegm deep in the chest. It is also used to ease bronchial spasms in coughs and bronchitis. A tea made from the herb helps clear congestion and mucus during colds as well. Like most culinary herbs, thyme also benefits digestion by relaxing the smooth muscle tissue of the gastrointestinal tract. It is also used to expel worms. If an injury occurs while outdoors, the

crushed leaves of thyme can be placed on minor cuts, scrapes or other wounds to prevent bacteria from entering. Extracts of the herb may be used as an antibacterial against *Helicobacter pylori*, the bacterium thought to cause stomach ulcers. Thyme is also rich in disease-fighting antioxidants. When thyme essential oil is used as an ingredient in massage oil, it helps warm and relax tired and sore muscles. An extract of the herb's volatile oil, known as thymol, is found in many commercially available products, such as cough drops, mouthwash, dental-care products, chest rubs and cosmetics. **Note:** Thyme should not be consumed in large amounts by pregnant women; however, small amounts used as a spice do not pose a problem. Thyme essential oil is for external use only, and it should not be given to children. The oil should not be used externally during pregnancy. The oil may irritate the skin and mucous membranes.

DOSAGE **Tea:** Drink up to 0.75 litre (24 oz) daily. **Tincture:** Use 0.5 ml (0.016 oz) twice daily. **Gargle:** Thyme tea or diluted tincture may be gargled as needed to soothe a sore throat. **Cough syrup:** Take 1 tbsp three times daily, or follow label directions. **Chest rub:** Mix 10 drops thyme essential oil into 30 ml (1 oz) of sweet almond or jojoba oil, and then shake to mix; rub on the chest to ease a cough. **Massage oil:** Add 5 to 10 drops of essential oil to 30 ml (1 oz) of almond or jojoba oil, and shake to mix.

T

TRIFOLIUM PRATENSE

RED CLOVER

A member of the Fabaceae (pea) family, red clover is native to Europe, but grows widely throughout North America. It is cultivated as silage and forage for animals and as a cover crop. The herb bears pink flower heads on upright hairy stems; the flowers are highly attractive to bees and an important source of wildflower honey. Clover's leaves grow in groups of three oval leaflets with pale crescent markings: the genus name *Trifolium* means "three leaves".

GROWING CONDITIONS Red clover grows in moist, well-drained, neutral soil in sunny areas. Propagation is by seeds or division in the spring. Like other pea family members, red clover helps to build healthier soil by fixing nitrogen, breaking up compacted soil, and bringing trace minerals to the soil for absorption by other plants.

CULINARY USE Red clover is abundant in vitamins and minerals, including calcium, phosphorus and vitamins A, D, E and K. Red clover sprouts, flowers and leaves can be added to salads. The flowers of red clover are added to soup stocks and can be made into tea.

MEDICINAL USE The round, flowering tops of red clover contain oestrogen-like compounds known as isoflavones, making the herb useful in the treatment of menopausal symptoms such as hot flushes and night sweats. Red clover contains the compounds daidzein and genistein (also found in soy), which may help prevent cancer. Considered an expectorant, the herb has long been used to treat coughs, bronchitis and chest congestion. Red clover is also believed to purify the blood. Externally, the herb has traditionally been applied as a poultice to cancerous growths, and used to tread skin conditions such as eczema and psoriasis, especially in children.

DOSAGE Tea: Drink 0.25 litre (8 oz) two or three times daily. **Tincture:** Use 1 ml (0.03 oz) two to three times daily. **Standardized extract:** Take four or five 30 mg capsules daily.

TURNERA DIFFUSA

DAMIANA

Native to the warm regions of western Mexico, damiana is naturalized in southern North America, Central America, northern South America, and Namibia in Africa. This small aromatic, shrubby perennial, a member of the Turneraceae (damiana) family, bears yellow-orange flowers. When young, the plant's reddish brown branches are covered with white, cottony hairs. Damiana leaves have a fragrant odour, similar to lemon balm, and a pleasant, slightly minty taste.

GROWING CONDITIONS Damiana grows wild in dry, sandy or rocky areas. It prefers dry soil in full sun. Seeds may be planted in the spring; cuttings may be planted in the summer; root divisions may be planted in the autumn. Damiana is harvested during its flowering stage.

CULINARY USE None.

MEDICINAL USE Damiana leaves contain constituents with antispasmodic and nervine properties. The herb may be taken as a mild stimulant to combat fatigue and depression and to promote

energy, especially in cases of overwork and mental stress. Damiana has antibacterial properties, making the herb a useful treatment for urinary infections such as cystitis and urethritis. It has also been used to lower blood sugar and treat constipation and menstrual disorders. Damiana was marketed as an aphrodisiac in the late 19th century.

❧ **DOSAGE** **Tea:** Drink up to 0.75 litre (24 oz) daily. **Tincture:** Use 1 or 2 ml (0.03 or 0.07 oz) in water three times daily. **Standardized extract:** Take up to six 400 mg capsules per day.

*U*LMUS RUBRA

SLIPPERY ELM

A member of the Ulmacea (elm) family, slippery elm is native to eastern North America. This medium to large deciduous tree bears large, hairy, deeply veined leaves and inconspicuous flowers followed by red-brown winged fruits with a single seed. Native Americans used the tree to make canoes and baskets, as well as for medicinal purposes.

❧ **GROWING CONDITIONS** Slippery elm grows in moist, deep soil in full sun. It is propagated in the autumn by seeds, suckers, or by layering.

❧ **CULINARY USE** The bark of slippery elm can be made into a porridge which makes a good meal during convalescence. The porridge is made by mixing 1 tsp of slippery elm powder with cold water into a thin, smooth paste; 0.5 litre (16 fl.oz) of boiling water are then added. The mixture is cooked for 10 to 15 minutes, stirring constantly. It can be flavoured with cinnamon, nutmeg or lemon rind.

❧ **MEDICINAL USE** The inner bark of slippery elm contains soothing mucilage, making the herb a gentle treatment for heartburn, diarrhoea, whooping cough, gastritis, and gastric and duodenal ulcers. Slippery elm has been made into throat lozenges, and applied topically to treat superficial skin wounds, inflammatory skin conditions, boils, abscesses and burns. Because the slippery elm tree population has been severely depleted by over-harvesting and Dutch elm disease, some modern herbalists suggest replacing slippery elm with marshmallow root, a herb with similar effects.

❧ **DOSAGE** **Tea: Drink** 0.25 litre (8 oz) two or three times daily. **Tincture:** Use 1 ml (0.03 oz) two or three times daily. **Standardized extract:** Take one 200 mg capsule two or three times daily.

*U*NCARIA TOMENTOSA

CAT'S CLAW, UÑA-DE-GATO

A member of the Rubiaceae (madder) family, cat's claw is native to Peru and grows throughout the tropical areas of South America and Asia. Supplies of the herb used for commercial purposes are wild-harvested in Peru and Brazil. Cat's claw is a twining woody vine that can grow as high as 30 m (100 ft). The vine bears large, glossy leaves and has thorny spines curved like cats' claws. Sometimes called the "life-giving vine of Peru", cat's claw has been traditionally used by native tribes as a contraceptive and to treat myriad health conditions.

❧ **GROWING CONDITIONS** Cat's claw prefers rich, moist soil and ample rain and heat, typical conditions of a tropical rainforest.

❧ **CULINARY USE** None.

❧ **MEDICINAL USE** Cat's claw is a known anti-inflammatory agent. It has been used to treat osteoarthritis of the knee and rheumatoid arthritis (in conjunction with conventional therapy), as well as Crohn's disease, chronic prostatitis, canker sore, sinus infection and flu. The plant's roots and stem bark contain constituents that

may stimulate the immune system. Cat's claw may have the potential to treat viral infections, and lower cholesterol and blood pressure levels. **Note:** This herb should not be used during pregnancy by people taking ulcer medications or by transplant patients. The plant has been overharvested in the wild, and so harvesting only the stem bark from sustainable sources is advised.

❧ **DOSAGE** **Tea:** Drink 0.25 litre (8 oz) two or three times daily. **Tincture:** Use 1 ml (0.03 oz) two or three times daily. **Standardized extract:** Take one to two 500 mg capsules three times daily. **Standardized extract:** Take 20 to 60 mg daily.

URTICA DIOICA
NETTLE, STINGING NETTLE

Native to North America and Europe, nettle is widely naturalized in temperate areas. In some places, it is considered an invasive weed. Like other plants in the Urticaceae (nettle) family, nettle is perhaps best known for its sting. The plant is a coarse perennial with toothed oval leaves that are covered with stinging hairs. Skin contact with these leaves causes a burning sensation that usually lasts for at least an hour. The genus *Urtica* contains approximately fifty species, and the name comes from the Latin word *urere*, which means "to burn". If nettles touch the skin, yellow dock (*Rumex crispus*) leaves, which often grow nearby, can be used to relieve the stinging sensation. An old English rhyme refers to this effect: "Nettle in, dock out, dock rub nettle out." Ancient Greeks once used the juice of nettle to treat everything from snakebite to coughs. Roman soldiers rubbed nettles on their skin to improve their ability to tolerate the cold winters of foreign countries, a practice known as urtication. Nettle's stems are made of strong fibres, which were used in the manufacture of cloth and paper from the Bronze Age through to the early 20th century.

❧ **GROWING CONDITIONS** Nettles grow in moist, nitrogen-rich soil in full sun or partial shade. Nettles can be invasive, but are easy to eradicate. Seeds or root divisions may be planted in the spring. Whole plants may be

Cat's Claw (Uncaria Tomentosa) *has been a staple of Peruvian herbal medicine for centuries.*

harvested for medicinal use in the summer, when the plant flowers. For culinary use, young leaf tips should be picked from plants that are less than 10 cm (4 in) tall.

❧ **CULINARY USE** Nettle leaves are a favourite spring green. Cooking (and drying, for use in the winter) destroys the plant's sting. Nettle leaves may be steamed, sautéed or stir-fried, puréed and added to soups, or used in place of spinach in recipes. In Scotland, a popular pudding is made with nettles, leeks, broccoli and rice. Nettle is also used in traditional Russian and Italian dishes, such as Russian nettle soup and risotto with wild greens.

❧ **MEDICINAL USE** Nettle contains vitamins A and C, as well as the mineral iron. The nutrients account for the herb's use as a general tonic and "blood builder", given as a treatment for anaemia, arthritis and poor circulation. Nettle has antihistamine properties, and a freeze-dried extract has been used to relieve the symptoms of seasonal allergies. The herb has a diuretic action and is considered a cleansing or detoxifying herb. It may be useful in preventing urinary tract infections and kidney stones. Nettle has astringent effects, which make it useful for reducing the flow of nosebleeds and heavy menstrual bleeding. The plant contains a high level of chlorophyll, which is extracted for commercial use as a colouring agent. Nettle root is used to treat urinary difficulties (such as frequent and nighttime urination) associated with benign prostatic hyperplasia, a condition that affects many men older than 50. Because it is thought to darken the hair and make it shiny, nettle is a common ingredient in hair-care products, such as shampoo.

❧ **DOSAGE** **Tea:** Drink 0.25 litre (8 oz) two or three times daily. **Tincture:** Use 1 or 2 ml (0.03 or 0.07 oz) two or three times daily. **Standardized extract:** Two 400 mg capsules two or three times daily. **Fresh:** Eat as desired.

VACINIACEAE
Vaccinium

The vaccinium family – more commonly known as berries – consists of approximately 450 species. The family is widely harvested for its delicious members that include blueberry, cranberry and bilberry, ingredients found in many baked goods and drinks.

VACCINIUM CORYMBOSUM
HIGHBUSH BLUEBERRY

A member of the Ericaceae (heath) family, the blueberry is native to North America. This low-growing bush or shrub bears green leaves, white or pink flowers, and small, sweet fruits that range in colour from light blue to black. Native Americans often smoked blueberry leaves mixed with tobacco and other herbs. The principal blueberry species is the North American highbush *V. corymbosum*. Important lowbush species include *V. angustifolium* and *V. lamarkii*. The southern highbush, grown in the southern United States, is a hybrid of the common highbush blueberry (*V. corymbosum*) and a native southern variety (*V. darrowi*).

GROWING CONDITIONS Blueberry bushes need full sun for optimum fruit yield and quality. They grow best in very acidic soil that has ample moisture. The bushes require cold temperatures during the winter, but generally cannot survive temperatures lower than -29°C (-20°F).

CULINARY USE Blueberry fruits may be eaten fresh or dried. They can be added to sweet baked goods, such as muffins, and cakes, and made into pies, jellies, jams and syrups. Blueberries are added to foods ranging from sweets to yogurt to tea.

V. angustifolium
The fruit of low sweet blueberry has a very sweet flavour with a slight hint of honey.

V. corymbosum
Blueberries produce sweet fruit that are high in vitamim C, fibre, and iron.

MEDICINAL USE

Blueberry fruits are rich in antioxidants. There is some evidence that blueberries may help prevent urinary tract infection. They also contain flavonoids, which may inhibit the production of LDL (bad) cholesterol, and reduce the risk of a heart attack.

DOSAGE Fresh or frozen berries: 4 oz (113 g) daily.

VACCINIUM MACROCARPON CRANBERRY

An Ericaceae (heath) family member, the cranberry is as an evergreen bush, native to North America. Cranberry bushes are cultivated for their fruit in parts of the United States. European

V. Macrocarpon
Compounds in cranberry may prevent urinary tract infections.

V. vitis idaea ssp. *minor*
Lingonberries produce short-stemmed round foliage and small red fruits.

settlers in eastern North America named the plant "craneberry" because its flower stamens were thought to resemble the bill of a crane.

GROWING CONDITIONS Cranberry flourishes in conditions that provide plenty of water, acidic soil and cool temperatures. Commercial cultivators grow the bushes in bogs and marshes.

CULINARY USE Because of their tartness, cranberries are generally cooked with sugar into sauces, jellies, jams and baked goods. The fruits are also dried and eaten like raisins. Cranberry juice is a popular beverage.

MEDICINAL USE Cranberry fruits are high in vitamin C and were once eaten to prevent scurvy, a disease caused by vitamin C deficiency. The berries contain anythocyanins and flavonol glycosides, which have antibacterial properties. Drinking cranberry juice may prevent symptoms of urinary tract infections such as increased urinary frequency and burning during urination. Active compounds in cranberry juice may inhibit microorganisms from adhering to the cells lining the urinary tract, making a less hospitable environment for the infection-causing bacteria such as *E. coli*. These same compounds are said to be responsible for preventing various types of bacteria from forming dental plaque.

DOSAGE Standardized extract: Take nine to fifteen 400 mg capsules daily. **Juice:** Drink 118 to 177 ml (4 to 6 oz) daily. Drink up to 1 litre (32 oz) when symptoms occur.

VACCINIUM MYRTILLUS HUCKLEBERRY

Native to Europe, the bilberry bush is a member of the Ericaceae (heath) family. Bilberry shrubs, which grow naturally in North America and Europe on moors and in

woods, bear round, bluish fruits about the size of black-currants. During WWII, British pilots ate bilberry jam before night missions, claiming it helped prevent night blindness. It is estimated that more than 1,600 metric tonnes of bilberries are eaten each year. The best-known species is the European *V. myrtillus*, which is rarely cultivated but is harvested from the wild in Europe. Similar species in North America include the black huckleberry (*Gaylussacia baccata*), the blue huckleberry (*G. frondosa*) and the evergreen huckleberry (*V. ovatum*).

V. myrillus
Bilberry is grown in the hilly regions of northern Europe and Asia.

GROWING CONDITIONS
Bilberries thrive in moist, acidic soil in sun or partial shade. Propagation is by seed sown in the autumn or by semiripe cuttings in summer.

CULINARY USE Bilberries are used as ingredients in pies, muffins and breads, syrups, jams, compotes and wine.

MEDICINAL USE Bilberry fruits are high in vitamin C and were once eaten to prevent scurvy, a disease of vitamin C deficiency. In England, during the 17th century, bilberries were mixed with honey to form a mixture called "rob", which was used to treat diarrhoea. Bilberry fruits contain pigments called anthocyanosides, which help strengthen capillaries by protecting them from free radical damage. The berries help improve blood flow within the body by maintaining the strength and flexibility of cell walls. The berries may also stimulate the formation of healthy connective tissue. Bilberries have a particularly beneficial effect on vision, increasing blood flow and enzyme levels responsible for energy production in the eyes.

DOSAGE Tincture: Use 1 or 2 ml (0.03 to 0.07 oz) three times daily. **Standardized extract:** Take one 160 mg capsule, standardized to 25 percent anthocyanosides, one to two times daily.

V

$\mathcal{V}$ALERIANA OFFICINALIS

GARDEN HELIOTROPE, GARDEN VALERIAN, VALERIAN

Valerian, a member of the Valerianaceae (valerian) family, is a perennial native to Europe and western Asia and naturalized in North America. Valerian is cultivated commercially in the United States and Europe. The plant has tall stalks that bear small white or pink flowers. It has a unique scent that most people consider highly unpleasant and compare to the odour of dirty socks. Valerian is added, in very minute amounts, to soaps and men's aftershave and cologne to add an earthy, forestlike or "mossy" fragrance. The herb contains compounds similar to catnip (*Nepeta cataria*), and cats – and rats – tend to find the scent of valerian appealing. It is believed that the folklore hero Pied Piper, who led the rats out of the city of Hamelin, Germany, did so not with music, but because he carried valerian in his pockets. Valerian is believed to derive from the Latin *valere*, which means "to be well".

GROWING CONDITIONS Valerian grows in moist soil in full sun or partial shade. It is often found in low meadows and damp, wooded areas. Seeds may be planted

in the spring; root divisions may be planted in the spring or autumn. Roots may be harvested during the plant's second year, after the leaves have died.

CULINARY USE Despite its strong scent and taste, valerian was once eaten in salads and as a pot herb. Today, extracts of valerian are used commercially as an apple flavouring in baked goods, soft drinks, beer and tobacco.

MEDICINAL USE Valerian, which has been used as a mild sedative since ancient Roman times, is best known as a nonaddictive natural sleep aid that has no side effects, such as the hungover feeling commonly associated with prescription sleep aids. The herb may help lower blood pressure levels, and is used to relieve insomnia, excitability and exhaustion, and anxiety-related symptoms such as heart palpitations, sweating and feelings of panic. After World War I, it was used to treat symptoms of shell shock, including loss of memory. Valerian has antispasmodic properties, and may depress the central nervous system and help relieve muscle spasms, making it useful in the treatment of menstrual cramps (in combination with cramp bark, *Viburnum opulus*), stomach cramps and irritable bowel syndrome. **Note:** Valerian may cause stomach upset in sensitive individuals, and it may cause stimulating, rather than calming, effects, in a small percentage of people. The herb should not be used by those taking prescription- or over-the-counter sleep aids. Pregnant women may want to avoid this herb.

DOSAGE **Tea:** Drink 0.25 litre (8 oz) two or three times daily. **Tincture:** Use 2 or 3 ml (0.07 or 1 oz) daily. **Standardized extract:** Take one 300 to 400 mg capsule daily. **Standardized extract:** Take one 300 to 400 mg capsule daily (standardized to valerenic acid, valtrate, or essential oil).

$\mathcal{V}$ANILLA PLANIFOLIA

BOURBON VANILLA, MEXICAN VANILLA, MADAGASCAR VANILLA, VANILLA

There are approximately 100 species in the *Vanilla* genus of orchids. *Vanilla* is the only member of the entire (approximately 20,000 species) Orchidaceae (orchid) family that is cultivated for commercial use, rather than

as an ornamental plant. It is the only orchid that bears an edible fruit. *V. planifolia* is a climbing evergreen perennial vine, native to the southeastern United States, South America and the West Indies. The plant is cultivated in Tahiti, Madagascar, the Seychelles and Java. Vanilla has a thick, succulent stem and bears bright green, pointed leaves, and pale yellow to celadon flowers. Its fruit, commonly called the vanilla bean, is a pendent pod that contains hundreds of tiny seeds. Vanilla beans have been highly prized for hundreds of years for use in confectionery and perfumery. With its reputation as an aphrodisiac, vanilla is often included as a fragrance in hand and body lotions, soap, makeup, and deodorants, as well as scented candles.

✿ **GROWING CONDITIONS** Vanilla is a difficult plant to grow in most climates. It is planted in epiphytic soil mix with plenty of moisture, shade and humidity, at a temperature of 27°C (81°F). Cuttings are planted at the end of the dry season for best results. Vanilla plants must be pollinated by hand in order to produce fruit (beans), which take 5 to 7 months to ripen. The fruits are harvested when fully ripe, but before they split open. Vanilla beans are then cured, which takes 3 to 6 months.

✿ **CULINARY USE** Vanilla is a much-loved food flavouring, used around the world. Its enchanting taste and scent are due to a substance called *vanillin*, which is developed during the curing process. Vanilla extract is used to flavour ice cream, baked goods, syrup, soft drinks and liqueurs, such as Kahlua. A vanilla bean can be stored in a jar of sugar to add a delicate flavour to desserts and tea sweetened

with the sugar. Pure vanilla extract is expensive, and there is a large market for synthetic vanillas, many of which are made of artificial flavourings including paper-industry byproducts treated with chemicals.

✿ **MEDICINAL USE** Although vanilla is primarily used as a scent and culinary flavouring, in folk medicine it is believed to exhilarate the brain, prevent sleep, increase muscular energy, and stimulate sexual appetite. It has also been taken medicinally to improve digestion.

✿ **DOSAGE** As desired.

*V*IOLA ODORATA

ENGLISH VIOLET, GARDEN VIOLET, SWEET BLUE VIOLET, SWEET VIOLET, VIOLET

A member of the Violaceae (violet) family, sweet violet belongs to a genus of approximately 500 species. Native to Europe and Asia, violet is naturalized throughout the temperate regions of the world. This creeping perennial bears oval to heart-shaped leaves and sweet-scented, dark purple or white, five-petalled flowers. Violet flowers have a wonderful fragrance when they first blossom, but the scent fades quickly when inhaled due to the chemical composition of the plant. After a few sniffs, the aroma can no longer be detected. Ancient Romans were known to have drunk violet-flavoured wine. Violets were the favourite flower of the French emperor

V

Napoleon Bonaparte (1769–1821): when Napoleon died, he was wearing a locket of violets taken from the grave of his first wife, Josephine.

❧ GROWING CONDITIONS

Violets grow in well-drained, moist soil in full sun or partial shade. They are often found growing wild along roadsides and in woodland areas. Seeds may be sown in the spring or autumn; cuttings may be planted in the summer. Violet leaves and flowers may be harvested during the plant's flowering season. Although violet flowers are full of nectar and are well constructed to attract bees, they generally bloom before bee season.

❧ CULINARY USE

Violet flowers add colour to salads and can be used fresh or candied, as a dessert garnish. The fresh flowers can also be floated on cold soups.

❧ MEDICINAL USE

Violet leaves and flowers have a mild expectorant action and may be used to treat coughs, cold and congestion. Violet can also be taken to induce sweating to help lower a fever. A tea made from the flowers is drunk to alleviate headache. One species, *V. adunca*, may be taken as a tea to treat stomach pain and asthma in children. Externally, the tea is used as a wash to treat sore and swollen joints. **Note:** Large amounts of violet leaves can cause diarrhoea and vomiting.

❧ DOSAGE

Tea: Drink up to 0.75 litre (24 oz) daily. **Syrup:** Follow as directed.

*V*ITEX AGNUS-CASTUS

AGNUS-CASTUS, CHASTEBERRY, CHASTE TREE, MONK'S PEPPER, VITEX

Vitex is a genus of about 250 species of mainly evergreen trees and shrubs. A member of the Verbenaceae (verbena) family, *Vitex agnus-castus* is native to the Mediterranean and western Asia. This deciduous, aromatic shrub bears long, slender, pointed leaves and tubular lilac flowers followed by dark, fleshy, peppercorn-like fruits. The herb takes two of its common names from its connection in folk medicine to the promotion of the virtue of chastity. Vitex was strewn on the ground as women and men entered convents and monasteries to prepare for their vows of chastity. Another of the plant's common names, monk's pepper, refers to the consumption of vitex fruit by monks in an effort to suppress their sexual urges.

❧ GROWING CONDITIONS

A water-loving plant, vitex thrives along streams and riverbanks. It prefers average, well-drained soil in full sun or partial shade. Propagation occurs in the spring by seeds, cuttings, or layering from young woody cuttings.

❧ CULINARY USE

None.

❧ MEDICINAL USE

Vitex has been used for over 2,500 years to treat female reproductive system ailments. It was recommended by the ancient Greek physician Hippocrates (ca. 460 B.C.E.–ca. 377 B.C.E.) as an aid to women's reproductive health. Scientific studies have confirmed the positive effects of this plant in treating symptoms of premenstrual syndrome (PMS), including breast tenderness, oedema, tension and constipation. Vitex has been used to regulate the menstrual cycle when there is excessive or too-frequent bleeding. Its long history of use to stimulate the production of breast milk in breastfeeding mothers has also been confirmed by clinical studies. The herb is commonly used in Europe to treat symptoms before, during and after menopause. It has also been used to treat uterine fibroids and infertility from low progesterone levels. While vitex does not contain hormones, it does affect the pituitary gland, which has a regulating effect on hormone levels. It may be helpful in reducing hormone-related teenage acne. **Note:** Vitex should not be used by pregnant women or by those taking birth control pills or receiving hormone replacement therapy (HRT).

❧ DOSAGE

Tea: Drink 0.25 litre (8 oz) two times daily. **Tincture:** Use 1 or 2 ml (0.03 or 0.07 oz) daily. **Standardized extract:** Take one 650 mg capsule two to three times daily. **Standardized extract:** One 580 mg capsule standardized to 0.5 percent acubin one or two times daily.

VITIS VINIFERA

EUROPEAN GRAPE, GRAPE, WINE GRAPE

Native to southern Europe and northwestern Asia, the grape is cultivated in warm, temperate regions throughout the world. There are hundreds of grape cultivars. A member of the Vitaceae (grape) family, this deciduous climbing vine has a twisted trunk and bears clusters of oval to round, green to black fruits. The fruit of its vine, the grape, has long been a nutritious source of food and drink. The use of grapes to make wine dates to ancient Egyptian times, at least 4,500 years ago.

GROWING CONDITIONS Grapevines thrive in deep, moist, neutral to alkaline soil in full sun. Hardwood cuttings and seeds may be planted in the late autumn.

CULINARY USE Grapes, rich in flavonoids that appear to lower the risk of heart disease, are eaten as a fresh fruit or made into wine, vinegar, juice and jelly. Dried grapes, called raisins, are eaten as a snack or used in baked goods, fruit salad and in some ethnic dishes such as Moroccan tagines or couscous. The spice cream of tartar is extracted from the residue of pressed grapes, found in the sediment of wine barrels. The leaves of the grape plant are used to make *dolmades*, savoury rice-filled appetizers found in Greek and Middle Eastern cuisine. The seeds of grapes are pressed to yield a polyunsaturated oil that is used to make mayonnaise and for frying foods.

MEDICINAL USE Grapes are mildly laxative fruits. Raisins have mild expectorant properties. The skin of red grapes contains resveratrol, a strong antioxidant, and so red wine and red grape juice are believed to offer antioxidant and heart-protective benefits. Grape leaves have astringent properties and may be used to treat diarrhoea and varicose veins. Grape seeds contain oligomeric procyanidins (also known as procyanidolic oligomers, or PCOs), which are strong antioxidants. Extract of grape seed has been used to treat circulatory problems such as capillary fragility and varicose veins, and to reduce inflammation. Grape seed may also help slow the aging process of the skin.

DOSAGE Red wine: Drink one to two glasses daily. **Grape seed extract:** Take 150 mg of procyanidins daily; follow label directions.

WITHANIA SOMNIFERA

ASHWAGANDHA, INDIAN GINSENG, WINTER CHERRY

Ashwagandha is a Solanaceae (nightshade) family member, native to India and found in the countries of the Mediterranean and the Middle East. This small, upright evergreen shrub has a long, tuberous root, and bears ovate leaves and inconspicuous green to yellow flowers. *Ashwagandha* is Sanskrit for "winter cherry", a reference to the plant's tiny red berries, which contain yellow seeds enclosed in a paper-thin calyx. The species name *somnifera* refers to the herb's traditional use as a sedative.

GROWING CONDITIONS Ashwagandha grows as a subshrub in dry, stony soil at altitudes of between 1,524 and 1,829 m (5,000 and 6,000 ft).

CULINARY USE Ashwagandha roots have a bitter, sharp taste. They have been made into a tonic wine. In India, the powdered roots are used to thicken milk, and also mixed with milk and given to the elderly as a restorative.

MEDICINAL USE A very popular herb in India, ashwagandha is mentioned in 3,000-year-old Ayurvedic texts. The herb is widely used in Ayurvedic medicine to prevent premature ageing and to treat age-related physical debility and impotence. Bittersweet and astringent, ashwangandha acts primarily on the reproductive and nervous systems. The roots are believed to have sedative, rejuvenative and anti-inflammatory properties.

Z

Ashwagandha is thought to act as an adaptogen, a substance that increases immune function and helps the body cope with stress. Externally, ashwagandha tea has been used as a wash to treat superficial skin wounds, sores and inflammation. **Note:** This herb should not be used during pregnancy or by those taking pharmaceutical sedatives.

❧ DOSAGE **Tea:** Drink 0.25 to 0.75 litre (8 to 24 oz) daily. **Tincture:** Use 1 ml (0.03 oz) three times daily. **Standardized extract:** Take one 500 mg capsule two or three times daily. **Standardized extract:** Take one capsule (standardized to 2.5 percent withanolides) two or three times daily.

ZINGIBER OFFICINALE

GINGER, GINGERROOT

Native to tropical Asia, ginger is cultivated in tropical regions of the world, including Jamaica, Africa, China, India, Indonesia and Australia. Ginger is a member of the Zingiberaceae (ginger) family, which includes the equally spicy herbs turmeric, cardamom and galanga. The deciduous perennial has thick, pungent rhizomes and bears long, pointed, lanceolate leaves and yellowish-green flowers with deep purple lips. Ginger is important in Traditional Chinese and Indian Ayurvedic medicine. Oil extracted from the freshly ground, dried rhizome is used to flavour ice cream, sweets and soft drinks. Ginger oil is also used as an antiseptic and fragrance in soap, cream and perfume.

❧ GROWING CONDITIONS Ginger grows in well-drained, humus-rich soil in sun or partial shade. It will not tolerate freezing temperatures. Propagation is by planting rhizomes in the early spring. Ginger may also be grown indoors, in a greenhouse environment.

❧ CULINARY USE Especially popular in Asian cooking, ginger is added as a spice to curry, chutney, pickles, meat and fish dishes, soup and marinade. Powdered ginger is used to flavour baked

goods such as cakes and muffins. In Japan, ginger is pickled and used as a condiment with sushi. In India and China, ginger and cinnamon are made into a warming tea.

❧ MEDICINAL USES Ginger has been used in Asia for at least 5,000 years. It is a common ingredient in traditional Chinese medicine formulas used to treat ulcers, stomachache, diarrhoea and nausea. Ginger's thick rhizomes contain gingerol and shogaol, which explains the plant's usefulness in the treatment of gastrointestinal conditions such as stomach upset, indigestion and motion sickness. Also useful in treating fevers, ginger acts as a diaphoretic, increasing perspiration. Hot compresses of ginger tea may be applied externally to treat arthritis, painful joints, strains, sprains and sore backs. Cool ginger tea compresses are used to ease the pain of minor burns and rashes. As a gargle, ginger tea can ease sore throats. In traditional medicine, ginger was also used in tea and soup to treat cold and bronchitis. **Note:** Although safe when used as a spice, ginger should not be taken medicinally during pregnancy or by people with gallstones.

❧ DOSAGE **Tea:** Drink 0.25 litre (8 oz) two or three times daily. **Tincture:** Use 2 or 3 dropperful two to three times daily. **Capsule:** Take two to three 500 mg capsules two to three times daily. **Standardized extract:** One 100 to 200 mg capsule standardized to 5 percent gingerols two or three times daily. **Tincture:** Use 2 or 3 dropperful two to three times daily. **Capsule:** Take two to three 500 mg capsules two to three times daily. **Standardized extract:** One 100 to 200 mg capsule standardized to 5 percent gingerols two or three times daily.

The root of ginger (right) is used in its fresh and dried forms in foods ranging from tea to desserts. It also has a long history of use in Asian medicine and cuisines. The plant (left) grows in tropical climates.

Medical Reference Charts

In this section of *Herbs: The Essential Guide for a Modern World*, three types of charts provide essential information about the medicinal uses of major herbs.

The three types of charts in the Reference Guide are designed to (1) help readers understand the types of evidence-based support major herbs have for the treatment of common conditions; (2) provide a listing of herbs accompanied by the ailments for which they have been found effective; (3) present a list of common ailments, along with the herbs that can effectively treat each.

The *Rating the Herbs* chart (opposite) summarizes each herb's critical status and safety record. It can be used to check a herb's efficacy before beginning therapy, or to study herbs by selected characteristics, such as level of international acceptance. Herbs are rated on a five-star system, from "excellent" (five stars) to "poor" (one star). Stars are assigned across the following categories:

Clinical Research This criteria indicates evidence resulting from direct clinical trials, which many consider the strongest evidence of a herb's efficacy.

Milk thistle (Silybum marianum).

Laboratory Research This category evaluates laboratory experiments conducted in glassware *(in vitro)* pharmacological research. *In vitro* research can be especially useful in determining the mechanisms of a herb's action. Although there are serious ethical considerations pertaining to *in vitro* research, there are some cases in which clinical research would be impossible. For example, studies investigating the ability of milk thistle to protect the liver from dangerous toxins could not be conducted in humans.

Traditional Use In many cases, there would be no scientific research on a herb if it was not known to have a traditional use in folk or indigenous medicine. Popular reputation is often what brings a herb to the attention of medical researchers.

Safety Record This rating is based on a subjective interpretation of chemical composition, pharmacology, clinical research, clinical use and traditional knowledge.

International Acceptance Many countries across the globe have developed ways to assess the safety and effectiveness of herbs used by their citizens. This category reflects a thoughtful synthesis of a herb's acceptance worldwide, based on whether it appears in pharmacopoeias, is widely used or has a strong reputation among scientists and medical practitioners.

Other Charts The *Ailment-to-Herb* charts, which begin on page 358, are organized by health condition, and provide a list of herbs commonly used to treat each one. The herbs are listed in order of efficacy, beginning with the herb generally considered most effective. For example, the condition of ageing is followed by the list: cayenne *(Capsicum annuum)*, p. 254, frankincense *(Boswellia serrata)*, p. 250, guggul *(Commiphora mukul)*, p. 250, sesame *(Sesamum indicum)*, p.333

Organized alphabetically by botanical name, the *Herb-to-Ailment* chart, which begins on page 364, lists health conditions each herb may be used to treat. The ailments included have been chosen for their common occurrence (colds and flu) or for their relevance to modern life. Not included in this chart are chronic diseases, such as cancer, which require ongoing medical care.

This example illustrates how herbs are listed in the chart: the botanical name *Agrimonia eupatoria* is followed by the plant's common name, agrimony, which is followed by a list of ailments that the plant may be used to treat: eyeache, indigestion, throat irritation, sore throat.

Rating the Herbs

When making decisions about if and when to use herbs and herbal remedies for health care, it is important to have reliable information at one's disposal. But what constitutes "reliable information" can vary widely from individual to individual. For instance, one person may feel that a herb is safe to use because it has long history of traditional use. Another person may feel a herb is safe to use only if it has been proven so in clinical research. The chart below provides ratings for herbs based on several of these different criteria. Each herb is given a rating of between one (poor) and five (excellent) stars based on different standards. This allows each individual to use the criteria most important to him or her in making decisions about using herbs and herbal remedies for health.

Common Name	Botanical Name	Clinical Research	Laboratory Research	History	Safety	International Acceptance
Agrimony	Agrimonia eupatoria	★	★ ★	★ ★ ★ ★ ★	★ ★ ★ ★	★ ★ ★
Almond	Prunus dulcis	★ ★	★ ★ ★ ★	★ ★ ★ ★ ★	★ ★ ★ ★ ★	★ ★ ★ ★ ★
Aloe vera (gel)	Aloe vera	★ ★	★ ★ ★ ★	★ ★ ★ ★ ★	★ ★ ★	★ ★ ★ ★
Angelica	Angelica archangelica	★	★ ★ ★	★ ★ ★ ★	★ ★ ★	★ ★ ★ ★
Anise hyssop	Agastache foeniculum	★	★ ★	★ ★ ★ ★	★ ★ ★ ★	★ ★ ★
Arnica (homeopathic)	Arnica montana	★ ★	★ ★ ★	★ ★ ★ ★	★ ★ ★	★ ★ ★ ★ ★
Artichoke	Cynara scolymus	★ ★	★ ★ ★	★ ★ ★ ★	★ ★ ★ ★	★ ★ ★ ★
Ashwagandha	Withania somnifera	★ ★	★ ★ ★ ★	★ ★ ★ ★ ★	★ ★ ★ ★	★ ★ ★
Barberry	Berberis vulgaris	★	★ ★ ★ ★	★ ★ ★ ★	★ ★ ★	★ ★ ★ ★
Bee balm	Monarda spp.	★	★	★ ★ ★ ★	★ ★ ★ ★	★ ★ ★
Benzoin extract	Styrax benzoin	★	★ ★ ★ ★	★ ★ ★	★ ★ ★	★ ★ ★
Bilberry	Vaccinium myrtillus	★ ★	★ ★ ★	★ ★ ★	★ ★ ★ ★ ★	★ ★
Birch	Betula spp.	★	★ ★ ★	★ ★ ★ ★	★ ★ ★ ★	★ ★ ★ ★
Black cohosh	Actaea racemosa	★ ★ ★ ★	★ ★ ★ ★	★ ★ ★ ★	★ ★ ★	★ ★ ★ ★ ★
Bloodroot	Sanguinaria canadensis	★	★ ★ ★ ★	★ ★ ★	★	★ ★
Blueberry	Vaccinium corymbosum	★ ★	★ ★ ★ ★	★ ★	★ ★ ★ ★ ★	★ ★ ★
Borage	Borago officinalis	★ ★	★ ★ ★	★ ★	★ ★ ★ ★ ★	★ ★ ★
Buchu	Agathosma betulina	★	★ ★	★ ★ ★ ★	★ ★ ★	★ ★ ★
Burdock	Arctium lappa	★	★ ★	★ ★ ★ ★	★ ★ ★ ★ ★	★ ★ ★
Calendula	Calendula officinalis	★ ★	★ ★ ★ ★	★ ★ ★ ★	★ ★ ★ ★	★ ★ ★ ★
Catnip	Nepeta cataria	★ ★	★ ★	★ ★ ★ ★	★ ★ ★	★ ★ ★
Cat's claw	Uncaria tomentosa	★	★ ★	★ ★ ★	★ ★	★ ★
Cayenne	Capsicum annuum	★ ★ ★	★ ★ ★ ★	★ ★ ★	★ ★ ★	★ ★ ★
Chamomile, Roman	Chamemelum nobile	★	★ ★	★ ★ ★ ★	★ ★ ★	★ ★ ★ ★

Common Name	Botanical Name	Clinical Research	Laboratory Research	History	Safety	International Acceptance
Chaparral	Larrea divaricata	★	★★★	★★	★★	★★
Chickweed	Stellaria media	★	★	★★★	★★★★★	★★★
Cinnamon	Cinnamomum verum	★★	★★★	★★★	★★★★	★★★
Citronella	Cymbopogon citratus	★	★★★	★★★★	★★★★	★★★★
Clove	Syzygium aromaticum	★★	★★★	★★★★	★★★★	★★★★
Cocoa	Theobroma cacao	★★	★★★★	★★★★	★★★★	★★★★★
Coffee	Coffea arabica	★★	★★★★	★★★★	★★★★	★★★★★
Comfrey[1]	Symphytum officinale	★	★★★	★★★★	★★	★★
Cranberry	Vaccinium macrocarpon	★★★	★★★	★★★	★★★★★	★★★★★
Damiana	Turnera diffusa	★	★	★★★	★★★★	★★
Dandelion	Taraxacum officinale	★★	★★★	★★★★	★★★★	★★★
Devil's claw	Harpagophytum procumbens	★★★	★★★	★★★	★★★	★★★
Echinacea	Echinacea spp.	★★★	★★★★	★★★★	★★★★	★★★★★
Elderberry	Sambucus nigra	★★★	★★★	★★★★	★★★★	★★★★
Eleuthero	Eleutherococcus senticosus	★★	★★★	★★★★	★★★	★★
Ephedra	Ephedra spp.	★★★	★★★★	★★★★★★	★★★	★★
Eucalyptus[2]	Eucalyptus globulus	★★	★★★	★★★	★★★	★★★★
Evening primrose	Oenothera biennis	★★	★★	★★	★★★	★★★
Fennel	Foeniculum vulgare	★	★★	★★★★	★★★★	★★★
Feverfew	Tanacetum parthenium	★★★	★★★	★★★	★★★★	★★★★
Flax	Linum usitatissimum	★★	★★★	★★★★	★★★★	★★★
Foxglove[3]	Digitalis purpurea	★★	★★★★	★★★★		★
Garlic	Allium sativum	★★★	★★★★	★★★★★	★★★★	★★★★
Gentian	Gentiana lutea	★	★★★	★★★★	★★★★	★★★★
Ginger	Zingiber officinale	★★★	★★★★	★★★★★	★★★★★	★★★★
Ginkgo	Ginkgo biloba	★★★★	★★★★	★★	★★★★	★★★★
Ginseng	Panax ginseng	★★	★★★★	★★★★★	★★★	★★★
Goldenseal	Hydrastis canadensis	★	★★★	★★★	★★★	★★
Gotu kola	Centella asiatica	★	★★★	★★★	★★★★	★★★
Grapeseed	Vitis vinifera	★★	★★★	★★	★★★★	★★★

Common Name	Botanical Name	Clinical Research	Laboratory Research	History	Safety	International Acceptance
Guggul	Commiphora mukul	★ ★	★ ★	★ ★ ★ ★	★ ★	★ ★
Hausa potato[4]	Coleus forskohlii	★ ★	★ ★ ★	★ ★ ★	★ ★ ★ ★	★ ★
Hawthorn	Crataegus laevigata	★ ★ ★	★ ★ ★	★ ★ ★ ★	★ ★ ★ ★	★ ★ ★ ★
Hops	Humulus lupulus	★ ★	★ ★ ★	★ ★ ★ ★	★ ★ ★ ★	★ ★ ★
Horse chestnut	Aesculus hippocastanum	★ ★ ★	★ ★ ★	★ ★ ★	★ ★ ★	★ ★ ★ ★
Horseradish	Armoracia rusticana	★	★ ★	★ ★ ★ ★	★ ★ ★	★ ★
Hyssop	Hyssopus officinalis	★	★ ★	★ ★ ★ ★	★ ★ ★ ★	★ ★ ★
Indian frankincense	Boswellia serrata	★ ★	★ ★ ★	★ ★ ★ ★	★ ★ ★ ★	★ ★ ★
Juniper	Juniperus communis	★	★ ★	★ ★ ★	★ ★ ★	★ ★
Kava	Piper methysticum	★ ★ ★	★ ★ ★	★ ★ ★ ★	★ ★ ★	★ ★ ★
Kudzu	Pueraria lobata	★	★ ★ ★	★ ★ ★	★ ★ ★ ★	★ ★
Lavender	Lavandula angustifolia	★ ★	★ ★	★ ★ ★ ★	★ ★ ★ ★	★ ★ ★ ★
Lemon balm	Melissa officinalis	★ ★	★ ★ ★	★ ★ ★ ★	★ ★ ★ ★	★ ★ ★
Liquorice	Glycyrrhiza glabra	★ ★ ★	★ ★ ★	★ ★ ★ ★	★ ★	★ ★ ★ ★
Lovage	Levisticum officinale	★	★ ★	★ ★ ★ ★	★ ★ ★	★ ★
Maté	Ilex paraguariensis	★	★ ★ ★	★ ★ ★	★ ★ ★ ★	★ ★ ★
Meadowsweet	Filipendula ulmaria	★	★ ★	★ ★ ★ ★	★ ★ ★ ★	★ ★ ★
Milk thistle	Silybum marianum	★ ★ ★	★ ★ ★ ★	★ ★ ★ ★	★ ★ ★ ★	★ ★ ★
Neem	Azadirachta indica	★ ★	★ ★ ★	★ ★ ★ ★	★ ★ ★ ★	★ ★ ★
Nettle	Urtica dioica	★ ★	★ ★ ★	★ ★ ★ ★	★ ★ ★ ★	★ ★ ★
Olive	Olea europaea	★	★ ★ ★	★ ★ ★	★ ★ ★	★ ★
Onion	Allium cepa	★ ★	★ ★	★ ★ ★ ★	★ ★ ★ ★	★ ★
Oregano	Origanum vulgare	★	★ ★	★ ★ ★ ★	★ ★ ★	★ ★
Papaya	Carica papaya	★ ★	★ ★	★ ★ ★ ★	★ ★ ★ ★ ★	★ ★ ★
Parsley	Petroselinum crispum	★	★ ★	★ ★ ★ ★	★ ★ ★ ★	★ ★ ★
Pau d'arco	Tabebuia impetiginosa	★	★ ★ ★	★ ★ ★	★ ★ ★	★ ★
Pennyroyal	Mentha pulegium	★	★ ★	★ ★ ★	★ ★	★ ★
Peony, Chinese	Paeonia spp.	★	★ ★	★ ★ ★	★ ★ ★ ★	★ ★ ★
Peppermint	Mentha x piperita	★ ★	★ ★ ★ ★	★ ★ ★ ★	★ ★ ★ ★	★ ★ ★ ★
Plantain	Plantago major	★ ★	★ ★ ★	★ ★ ★ ★ ★	★ ★ ★ ★ ★	★ ★ ★ ★

Common Name	Botanical Name	Clinical Research	Laboratory Research	History	Safety	Inernational Acceptance
Poke	Phytolacca americana	★	★★	★★★	★★	★
Primrose	Primula veris	★	★	★★★	★★★★	★★
Pygeum[5]	Prunus africana	★★	★★★	★★	★★★★	★★★
Queen-of-the-meadow	Eupatorium purpureum	★	★	★★★	★★★	★★★
Red clover	Trifolium pratense	★★	★★	★★★★	★★★	★★★
Rhubarb, Indian	Rheum palmatum	★	★★	★★★★	★★	★★★
Rose	Rosa spp.	★	★★	★★★★	★★★★	★★★
Rosemary	Rosmarinus officinalis	★	★★	★★★★	★★★★	★★★
Rue	Ruta graveolens	★	★★	★★★	★★	★★
Saffron	Crocus sativus	★★	★★★	★★★	★★★★	★★
Sage	Salvia officinalis	★	★★	★★★★	★★★★	★★★★
Saw palmetto	Serenoa repens	★★★★	★★★★	★★★★	★★★★	★★★★
Schisandra	Schisandra chinensis	★★	★★★	★★★★★	★★★★	★★★★
Senna	Cassia senna	★★	★★★	★★★★	★★	★★★★
Shiitake	Lentinus edodes	★★	★★★	★★★★	★★★★	★★★
Slippery elm	Ulmus rubra	★	★★	★★★★	★★★★	★★★★
Soy	Glycine max	★★★	★★★★	★★★★	★★★	★★★
Spearmint	Mentha spicata	★	★★★	★★★★	★★★★	★★★
St John's wort	Hypericum perforatum	★★★★	★★★★	★★★★	★★★	★★★★
Tea	Camellia sinensis	★★	★★★★	★★★★	★★★★	★★★★
Tea tree	Melaleuca alternifolia	★★	★★★	★★★	★★★	★★★
Thyme	Thymus vulgaris	★	★★	★★★★	★★★★	★★★
Turmeric	Curcuma longa	★★	★★★★	★★★★	★★★★	★★★
Valerian	Valeriana officinalis	★★	★★★	★★★	★★★	★★★
Vitex	Vitex agnus-castus	★★★	★★★	★★★	★★★★	★★★★
Wild oat	Avena fatua	★	★★	★★★★	★★★★★	★★★
Wild yam	Dioscorea villosa	★	★★	★★★	★★★★	★★
Wood betony	(Stachys officinalis)	★	★	★★★★	★★★★	★★★
Yarrow	Achillea millefolium	★	★★	★★★★	★★★	★★★
Yohimbe	Pausinystalia johimbe	★★	★★★	★★	★★★	★★★

Notes: [1] Ratings are for internal use; comfrey is safe for external use; [2] Essential oil; [3] Not for self-care use; [4] syn. *Plectranthus barbatus*; [5] syn. *Pygeum africanum*

Using Herb Remedies Safely

Individuals choose a doctor and dentist with care. When it comes to searching for and selecting a herbal practitioner to consult, that very same diligence should be exercised.

It is common knowledge that a doctor or pharmacist requires a different level of training from a health-food shop employee, just as receiving emergency medical care is vastly different to self-medicating at home with an over-the-counter remedy for an upset stomach.

In a pharmacy the standards for prescription drugs are different for those for packaged, over-the-counter ones that are commonly available for colds and headache, for example. Just as there are no over-the-counter drugs that treat life-threatening conditions, there are no herbal remedies or dietary supplements for this category. Herbs should not be viewed as miracle cures. Instead they help maintain and enhance health and protect the body.

Working with a Practitioner Many people enjoy the feelings of self-empowerment they experience when they have enough knowledge to take the appropriate herb or combination of herbs to treat health conditions that arise. If treating the disease becomes beyond an individual's area of expertise, then it may be necessary to seek the advice of a healthcare practitioner who has been trained in the use of herbal medicine. It can be difficult to find qualified practitioners who have a thorough understanding of herbs. The kinds of practitioners who are often herb-friendly include naturopathic physicians, homeopathic physicians, doctors of Oriental medicine (OMD), licenced acupuncturists, chiropractors, certain physicians, lay herbalists and medical herbalists.

In the United States, becoming a professional member of the American Herbalists Guild lends some credibility to a herbal practice. In the United Kingdom, the British Homeopathic Association distributes a free list of medically qualified homeopaths working in that country. Practitioners worldwide who work with Bach flower remedies and who qualify, can register and be certified by The Dr. Edward Bach Foundation, which is based in the United Kingdom. Registered Bach practitioners – who work in countries all over the world, from China and Australia to Kenya and Mexico – work to the Foundation's professional code of practice, which also includes a full complaints procedure.

However, because certification standards vary from place to place, it is the consumer's responsibility to make educated decisions when choosing a herbal practitioner. This is done by ascertaining their level of training, experience and proficiency. Some questions to pose to potential practitioners could include any or all of the following:

- What is your stance on incorporating herbs and dietary guidelines into a treatment programme?
- Do you consider yourself well-trained in natural remedies?
- Where did you receive your education in herbal medicine, and how many hours of training did you receive?
- How much experience do you have incorporating herbs in your treatment protocols?

Herb Safety The primary types of safety evidence fall under the following categories:
- Human use throughout history
- Toxicity testing in laboratories
- Side effects recorded in clinical trials
- Reported illnesses or fatalities in people using the herb

The primary supporting evidence of herb safety is the long history of human use without major problems. The World Health Organization (WHO), in its 1998 publication, "Guidelines for the Appropriate Use of Herbal Medicines," recommends that herbal medicines be deemed safe if they have been used widely over a long period of time with no reports of toxicity – and that their health benefits are assumed to be correct unless proven otherwise.

Although there is much work to be done, significant herbal research has been conducted in laboratories and clinics around the world. In Europe, expert panels such as the German Commission, a regulatory agency composed of scientists, toxicologists, doctors and

Chaparral (Larrea tridentata) *was once a popular Native American remedy for colds.*

pharmacists who evaluate herbs, have considered existing research evidence and used their own expertise when approving herbal remedies.

It should be reassuring that many of the most common herbs have been in widespread use by millions of people for years, and serious problems (death, liver failure, heart attacks, seizures and the like) have been very rare. This is because botanicals have a much wider safety margin, or "therapeutic index" than most drugs.

Controversial Herbs Although most herbs are safe, some need to be used with caution, as do certain pharmaceuticals. Stimulants, sedatives and diet aids are three categories for which caution is strongly advised. Powerful drugs, when they are first discovered, seem so miraculous that they are almost always used to excess. Stimulants, sedatives and diet aids have proven far more troublesome than so-called "wonder drugs" in other categories, such as antibiotics or stomach remedies.

For instance, in the 1800s, opiates such as morphine, heroin and codeine, were overprescribed by healthcare providers. This was followed in the twentieth century first by the over-promotion of cocaine and marijuana, and then the weight loss craze, with amphetamines and phen-fen (two drugs, phentermine and fenfluramine, used in combination as slimming pills) and sedatives such as Valium that caused unpleasant side effects. In the mid-1990s as herbs began to be used more widely, a few similar problems emerged. The following herbs, and in some cases category of herbs, are those that have caused varying levels of controversy.

Chaparral (*Larrea tridentata*) This shrub from the deserts of the southwestern United States and northern Mexico was widely used by Native Americans to treat colds and flu. In the 1970s and 1980s the herb was used to treat cancer. Although chaparral has been rumoured to cause liver toxicity in susceptible individuals, it was deemed safe in a 1994 report of an independent review panel of medical records provided by the United States Food and Drug Administration (FDA). "In summary," the report said, "this review did not reveal evidence that Chaparral is inherently hepatotoxic."

Comfrey (*Symphytum officinale*) Although this garden herb has been used for centuries to treat wounds, burns and broken bones, modern scientists now know that it contains toxic pyrrolizidine alkaloids that stress the liver. It is not recommended for internal use, particularly for children, pregnant women and people with pre-existing liver conditions. However, it can be applied externally in creams, salves and poultices.

Ephedra (*Ephedra sinica*) In the mid-1990s, reports about the abuse of ephedra surfaced: Many people, including some athletes, were buying and using this ancient Chinese herb as a stimulant. Many experienced severe reactions; some died. When these stories came to light, ephedra came under close scrutiny. The herb has a long history of use for the relief of sinus congestion, allergy and asthma attacks and can also be useful to raise the metabolic rate and aid weight loss. Ephedra contains a potent plant constituent called ephedrine that affects the nervous system, giving users an extra boost of energy. Ephedrine has the added action of potentially causing weight loss. Products containing ephedra are ubiquitously found in convenience stores, petrol stations, supermarkets and natural food shops. Side effects include disrupted sleep, nervousness, anxiety, irritability, heart palpitations, high blood pressure, nausea and vomiting, and overall weakness.

Kava (*Piper methysticum*) Kava is used to treat anxiety disorders, stress, and restlessness and has long been considered to have a high degree of safety. However, because of reports concerning kava-associated liver toxicity, kava has been banned in several countries, including Austria, Canada, France, Ireland, Singapore, Switzerland and the United Kingdom. At this time, there are few clear answers about kava's safety: some clinical researchers have concluded that kava-induced hepatotoxicity is very rare, others say that something other than the kava caused the hepatotoxicity.

Kava
(Piper methysticum)

Pennyroyal essential oil (*Mentha pulegium*) Pennyroyal oil, known for its use as a repellent for fleas and mosquitoes, has become notorious as a herb that causes a foetus to be aborted. There is evidence to confirm its toxicity but little proof that it can cause spontaneous abortion. However, use of the herb, both as an essential oil and a tea, is strongly discouraged.

Sassafras (*Sassafras albidum*) Once widely known as the true flavour of root beer and as a springtime blood purifier, sassafras volatile oil contains a compound known as safrole that has been found to be carcinogenic in animals. Use of the herb in food products is now banned in both the United States and Canada, unless it is safrole-free.

Yohimbe (*Pausinystalia johimbe*) Yohimbe bark has a long history of safe use as a sexual aphrodisiac, especially in male erectile disorders. Although it has been found to have no side effects in some studies, its use in higher dosages has been linked to an increase in blood pressure, particularly when taken in conjunction with tricyclic antidepressants. Yohimbe has been approved by the United States Food and Drug Administration (FDA) for the treatment of male erectile disorder.

Stimulant laxatives This category of herbs, which includes aloe latex (Aloe spp.), buckthorn (*Rhamnus cathartica*), cascara sagrada (*Frangula purshiana*), Chinese rhubarb root (Rheum spp.), and senna leaf and pod (*Senna alexandrina*), is also controversial, because this type of laxative is considered a last resort option for treating constipation. These herbs can lead to laxative dependency, which causes the intestines to lose muscle tonality and weakens the digestive system. Many people use these laxative herbs when attempting to lose weight with the mistaken belief that the laxitives will aid weight loss.

Highly toxic plants Some plants contain extremely potent compounds and are not found in shops except in highly dilute homeopathic preparations. Among these extremely toxic herbs are aconite (Aconitum spp.), belladonna (*Atropa belladonna*), foxglove (Digitalis spp.), mandrake (*Mandragora officinarum*) and mayapple (Podophyllum spp.).

Herb Use During Pregnancy and Breastfeeding
Although many herbal remedies have time-honoured reputations as being beneficial when taken during pregnancy, some are controversial, and others are completely contraindicated during this time. In general, it is recommended that women who are pregnant and/or breastfeeding should use caution and consult a qualified healthcare practitioner before using any active substances – including herbs, vitamins or drugs.

Herbs for Children Herbs have long been used to treat children's common complaints in a gentle, effective way. Catnip (*Nepeta cataria*), chamomile (*Matricaria recutita*) and fennel (*Foeniculum vulgare*), for example, have traditionally been used for calming small children and easing their stomach upsets. Some herbs, such as echinacea (Echinacea spp.), have been included in clinical trials involving children. To err on the side of safety, it is advisable to consult a qualified healthcare practitioner before giving herbs to children.

Drug/Herb Interactions Herbal and conventional medicines can often work hand-in-hand with no ill effects; however, there is always the possibility that a herb constituent could either increase or decrease the amount of a pharmaceutical drug in the bloodstream; it might aid absorption of a drug or inhibit its breakdown. It might also increase the effect of the drug or create an unexpected and/or unwanted effect.

Currently, very little information has been published about drug/herb interactions and there are many discoveries yet to be made. Generally speaking, it is advisable to seek guidance from qualified healthcare practitioners before combining substances that have similar effects. For instance, St John's wort (*Hypericum perforatum*) is known to have an affect on the way certain drugs are metabolized in the liver, and combining it with prescription antidepressants, chemotherapy drugs, certain cardio-vascular drugs, HIV medications, antidepressants and contraceptive pills is not recommended. (Some psychiatrists have reported, however, that their patients who had been combining the herb with their antidepressant medications were experiencing no side effects.)

Healthcare practitioners have an important responsibility to continue educating themselves and their patients about drug/herb interactions. This will help them prevent their patients from taking inappropriate herbal medicines for their individual health conditions, and avoid problems of mixing with prescription medications.

Dosage In this book, the dosage recommendations are those supported by clinical evidence and research whenever possible. In cases where clinical research on the herb is limited, the dosage information is taken from traditional or historical use.

Most herbs – especially those that are used commonly in foods – are safe enough that the dosage can be slightly adjusted if necessary. For example, research published in medical journals ranging from *Healthnotes Review of Complementary and Integrative Medicine* (1999) to *The Lancet* (1982) and *Pharmacology* (1991) have suggested that a 400 mg dose of powdered ginger (*Zingiber officinale*) is effective in preventing motion sickness. That dose amounts to less than ½ teaspoon of ginger – and taking two or three times that amount would be safe.

It is important to take into account that if a herb is not producing the desired effect, taking more of it is not necessarily the solution. That herb may not be the right one to treat your individual constitution or health condition. It is always advisable to seek the advice of a qualified healthcare practitioner for any serious health condition or if the condition is long-term.

Sage (Salvia officinalis) has a long history of traditional use and international acceptance as a treatment for sore throat.

PART III

Reference Guide

Phyla scaberrima
(Aztec sweet herb)

Gazetteer of Herbs

Of the thousands of kinds of plants that can be defined as herbs (see page 18), the focus in this book is on the nearly 500 herbs that are most important worldwide for their medicinal and/or culinary uses. More than 250 of these receive special attention in the Gallery of Herbs (pages 193 to 325).

This gazetteer is a quick reference guide for another 200 species. Alphabetized by Latin botanical name from *Acacia* to *Zea mays*, the entries here give the most frequently used common names for each herb, as well as a range of other information about the plant. This usually includes a physical description of the herb, facts regarding its native habitat as well as its current range, and (when relevant) brief discussion of the plant's medical use throughout history in both conventional and alternative therapies. For example, it is said that British mariner and explorer Captain James Cook gave his crew sea celery (*Apium prostratum*), which has high levels of vitaman C, because eating it could prevent and treat scurvy. And self-heal (*Prunella vulgaris*), a member of

the mint family that grows in temperate regions all over the world, has been found to have positive effects in the treatment of both HIV/AIDS and herpes.

Herbs are often associated with fascinating and colourful myths, and when that information is either particularly interesting or pertinent, it is included here as well. For instance, wolfsbane (*Aconitum napellus*) takes its name from the fact that according to medieval folklore, European hunters tipped their arrows with the juice of the herb to kill wolves. In legend, calamint (*Calamintha nepeta*) was a tall fruit tree until it offended Mother Earth; its punishment was to be reduced to its present size, small and bushy. During the American Revolutionary War, colonists used goldenrod (*Solidago*) as a substitute for British-taxed black tea, calling it "liberty tea".

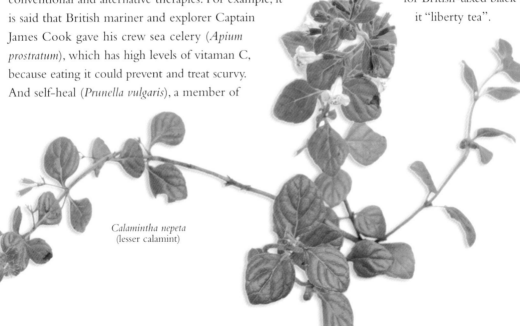

Calamintha nepeta
(lesser calamint)

A

Acacia species (acacia, wattle) There are more than 1,000 species of the acacia tree and shrub, found primarily in Australia, but also in Africa, Asia and the Americas. The West African *Acacia senegal* is the source of gum arabic, one of the most widely used thickeners and emulsifiers in food products. Acacia bark is used mostly to treat gastrointestinal problems such as diarrhoea. An astringent called *catechu*, or cutch, is extracted from the wood of the Asian *Acacia catechu*. The bark and roots of western Australian species such as *A. holoserica* are used to treat coughs and colds. The twigs and leaves of desert species such as *A. trachycarpa* and *A. ancistrocarpa* have been used by Australian Aborigines to treat headaches.

Aconitum napellus (aconite, monkshood, wolfsbane) A native of the Far East, this perennial produces a purple-hooded flower that accounts for one of its common names, monkshood. According to Greek legend, when Hercules fought Cerberus, the canine gatekeeper of Hades, the dog's saliva fell onto the plant and made it poisonous. (Wolfsbane is derived from hunters' folkloric use of arrows tipped with the plant's toxic juice to kill wolves.) The plant has long been associated with death and magic: in the Middle Ages, witches were said to put aconite in "flying ointments", which they rubbed on their skin to create the sensation of flight. Aconite's root contains aconitine, an extremely potent alkaloid that stimulates and then paralyzes the nerves and the heart. It is used in traditional Chinese medicine as a remedy for inflammation and pain, but prepared in a way that reduces its toxicity. **Note:** Aconite is poisonous even in small amounts, and importation and sales of aconite preparations are banned in some countries.

Aconitum napellus
(monkshood)

Alchemilla vulgaris
(lady's mantle)

Acorus calamus (calamus, cinnamon sedge, sweet flag, sweet myrtle) This irislike perennial, native to India and North America, now grows worldwide. In the Middle Ages, the plant was strewn on the floors of churches and houses in place of rushes. The powdered root has been used in cooking as a substitute for cinnamon, nutmeg and ginger, and as an insecticide, to ward off fleas. The rhizome can be chewed or taken as a tea or tincture to stimulate appetite and relieve gas and indigestion. **Note:** In animal studies, malignant tumours occurred in rats exposed to high doses of calamus – and in the United States, the Food and Drug Administration (FDA) has banned its use in food.

Aframomum melegueta (grains of paradise, Guinea pepper, Melegueta pepper) This reedlike plant, native to western Africa and a member of the ginger family, bears seeds that have been used as a culinary substitute for pepper. With a flavour described as a cross between pepper, cardamom and ginger, the seeds are used to spice traditional dishes. They are also chewed to sweeten the breath, and, on cold days, to warm the body. The seeds have stimulant, carminative and diuretic properties. *Aframomum* is reputed to have benefits for sexual function in both men and women.

Alchemilla vulgaris (bear's foot, lady's mantle, lion's foot, stellaria) Found throughout the Northern hemisphere, this perennial takes one of its common names from the shape of its leaves, which resembles a lady's cloak. *Alchemilla* comes from medieval alchemists, who believed that dewdrops gathered on the plant could help them in their quest to turn metals into gold. In folk medicine, lady's mantle has been used to relieve menstrual pain and some complaints of menopause. The herb is also said to promote quiet sleep if kept under one's pillow.

Alpinia galanga (galangal, greater galangal, Thai ginger) A close relative of ginger, this spice is in wide use in Southeast Asian countries. Like ginger, galangal is a rhizome; the roots are sliced up and added to curries, soups and many seafood dishes, imparting a spicy, pungent flavour. The plant resembles ginger in its medicinal propertie sas well; it is a stimulant and carminitive used to treat nausea and digestive problems. During the Middle Ages, galangal root was believed to have aphrodisiac properties.

Althaea officinalis (marsh mallow) Marsh mallow, a perennial, is native to marshy areas of Europe and Asia. Its botanical name, *Althaea*, comes from the Greek word for "heal". Marsh mallow roots and leaves contain mucilage, a substance that soothes inflamed mucous membranes. Marsh mallow root has been used to treat sore throat, coughs and gastrointestinal irritations such as ulcers and diarrhoea. A compress or poultice made from the root can be applied to skin irritations to soothe them. Marsh mallow roots were once used to make marshmallows (now made from gelatin).

Amaranthus species (amaranth) There are more than sixty *Amaranthus* varieties, including grain amaranths, leaf amaranths and dual-purpose amaranths. Amaranth leaves, which can be eaten as is or juiced, contain calcium, antioxidants and fibre. A nutty, sweet grain made from amaranth seeds is used as a high-protein wheat substitute in cereals, breads and other baked goods.

Ammi majus (bishop's weed) This Mediterranean annual, a member of the parsley family, is cultivated as an ornamental. The plant contains medicinal psoralens, which are helpful in the treatment of skin disorders such as psoriasis and vitiligo.

Ammi visnaga (khella, toothpick weed) A relative of Queen Anne's lace, this Mediterranean annual has white flowers with stiff stalks once used as dental hygiene tools. The seeds of the plant's small fruits contain khellin, a substance that expands the arteries supplying blood to the heart, thus providing relief to those who suffer the stabbing pain of angina pectoris. Khellin is also a bronchodilator, which means that it expands airways that have become constricted from ailments such as asthma, bronchitis and emphysema.

Anchusa officinalis
(alkanet)

Anchusa officinalis (**common alkanet, dyer's bugloss**) The root of this boragelike European biennial contains the dye alkannin, which was used in ancient Rome as a facial rouge, and later as a red or pink fabric dye and mahogany-toned wood stain. "Alkanet" comes from the Arabic *alhinna*, or henna. Alkanet's leaves and roots have expectorant, diuretic and astringent properties. The herb has been used to ease coughing, to break a fever and to "purify the blood" (remove toxins from the body).

Angelica sinensis (**Chinese angelica, dong quai**) A perennial member of the parsley family, dong quai grows in China, Korea and Japan. In traditional Chinese medicine, the herb is used to treat menstrual problems such as cramps, and to relieve menopausal symptoms such as hot flushes. Dong quai's root contains coumarin, which dilates blood vessels, stimulating the central nervous system and increasing blood flow throughout the body. It has been used to treat high blood pressure, poor circulation and anaemia. Researchers have also found that dong quai stimulates production of the red blood cells that carry oxygen throughout the body, thus increasing energy and combating fatigue.

Annona muricata (**Brazilian pawpaw, graviola, guanabana, soursop**) This small evergreen tree is native to tropical regions of North and South America, particularly the Amazon region. The genus *Annona* includes several very popular tropical fruits, and its food use far surpasses any medical application. All parts of the tree are used medicinally, including the bark, leaves, roots, fruit and fruit seeds. Soursop has been found to have antimicrobial and antiviral properties, making it useful in the treatment of bacterial and fungal infections and parasitic illnesses and worms. The herb has sedative and hypotensive properties, and may lower blood pressure and alleviate depression. In addition, studies have shown that it may have the ability to destroy cancer cells and slow tumour growth.

Anthoxanthum odoratum (**sweet vernal grass**) A perennial native to Europe and Asia, sweet vernal grass has a pleasant scent of freshly mown hay and can often be found in potpourris. The flowers can be made into a topical solution that increases blood circulation and relieves joint pain. A tincture can be taken internally to alleviate the symptoms of hay fever.

Apium graveolens (**celery**) A Eurasian annual or biennial, this mild vegetable has been cultivated for at least 3,000 years. Ancient Greeks crowned their winning athletes with celery stems and leaves. This herb has been used to treat high blood pressure and water retention. The seeds contain phytochemicals that act as natural calcium channel blockers and diuretics. People suffering from gout, a joint condition caused by high uric acid levels in the blood, may find relief with celery extract, which contains components that may keep uric acids below critical levels. Arthritis and other rheumatic pains have been treated with celery extract or juice to lessen inflammation. **Note:** A few people have allergic reactions to celery seed. It has provoked uterine contractions in fewer still.

Apium prostratum (**sea celery**) This perennial, native to eastern Australian coastal areas, belongs to a genus of twenty species. Its botanical name, *Apium,* comes from the Latin word *apon,* meaning water, the plant's natural habitat. The explorer Captain Cook is said to have given sea celery to his crew as a preventive for scurvy. Today, the salty-tasting leaves are used like parsley as a garnish or to flavour soup; the stems are blanched and eaten like celery.

Arachis hypogaea (**groundnut, goober pea, peanut**) The peanut plant is an annual legume, native to South America and cultivated in Asia, Africa and northern Central America. The pod, or nut, may stabilize blood sugar levels, so it is suggested for diabetics. The red skins on Spanish peanuts contains compounds that are thought to help prevent heart attacks. Recent research shows that peanuts satisfy hunger longer than carbohydrates, produce better weight-loss effects, and offer cardiovascular benefits including lower overall cholesterol and triglycerides, reduced cardiovascular risk, and elevated levels of HDL (the so-called "good") cholesterol.

Artemisia abrotanum
(southernwood)

Arctostaphylos uva-ursi (**bearberry, kinnikinnik, uva-ursi**) Originally native to Spain, this shrub now grows throughout Europe, Asia and North America. It is often called bearberry, perhaps because its bad-tasting berries are suitable to be eaten only by bears or because bears are especially fond of them. Bearberry has long been used to treat urinary tract infections. It contains an antibacterial substance called arbutin. **Note:** Pregnant or breastfeeding women should not take bearberry.

Artemisia abrotanum (**garderobe, lad's love, lover's plant, southernwood**) A native of Italy and Spain and a close relative of wormwood, this hardy perennial has been given to children in powdered-leaf form as a worming medicine. The scent of the plant is said to repel insects; it is sometimes used as a moth-repellent in clothing. In Italy, southernwood is used as a culinary herb. The leaves contain absinthol, which has a pungent lemony scent used for home and personal fragrances. In folklore, southernwood is a male aphrodisiac. Women once carried bundles of the herb to church, as the strong scent could ward off drowsiness.

Artemisia absinthium (**green ginger, wormwood**) This bitter-tasting – and smelling – perennial is native to Europe; however it now grows in Africa, Asia and the eastern United States. Wormwood is used in the production of absinthe, a green liqueur with a bitter liquorice or anise flavour. *Artemisia* is no longer legal as an ingredient of the liqueur absinthe because it contains the toxic compound thujone, which has been shown to cause brain damage. In folk medicine, wormwood has been used as an antiseptic, local anaesthetic, topical insect repellent, digestive aid and worming treatment.

Artemisia vulgaris (**mugwort**) Found throughout most of Europe, Asia and North America, this shrubby perennial was once thought to confer protection from evil spirits, wild animals, sunstroke and fatigue. Milder in action than other *Artemisia* species, mugwort has been taken to treat indigestion, intestinal worms and anxiety. It is a very important herb in the traditional Chinese medicinal practice of moxibustion, in which heat from burning dried mugwort leaves is applied to acupuncture points.

Asclepias tuberosa (**butterfly weed, orange milkweed, pleurisy root**) A fleshy-rooted North American perennial and a member of the milkweed family, pleurisy root gained one of its common names as a treatment by Native Americans for respiratory problems such as pleurisy (lung inflammation), cough, colds, bronchitis and pneumonia. It is also called butterfly weed because butterflies are attracted to its orange flowers. The herb is said to be an effective treatment for respiratory disorders because of its ability to reduce inflammation and relieve spasms and congestion in the airways. **Note:** This herb should not be taken by pregnant or breastfeeding women. Large amounts of pleurisy root can be toxic when taken internally.

Aspalathus linearis (**red bush tea, rooibos**) This South African shrub is brewed into a tea that has been used traditionally to soothe digestion and relieve stomach cramps, colic and diarrhoea. The herb is high in antioxidants, minerals, and vitamin C, and has antiviral properties. Rooibos is caffeine-free and becoming increasingly popular as a tea substitute. Like tea, it undergoes an oxidization process, turning the green leaves into a red colour, producing a brilliant red infusion.

Aspidosperma quebracho-blanco (**quebracho**) The bark of this South African evergreen tree has been used as a male aphrodisiac. Its active ingredient is yohimbine, which brings on an erection in men but also raises blood pressure. Women who take quebracho may experience increased desire stemming from a blood-engorged clitoris. The wood of the tree is prized for its hardness; quebracho means "the axe break". **Note:** The herb is not recommended for those of either sex who have high blood pressure.

Astragalus membranaceus (**astragalus, huang qi, yellow leader milk vetch**) Native to Mongolia and northern and eastern China, this member of the bean family is an important herb in traditional Chinese medicine. Its yellow root contains compounds that stimulate the immune system, promoting the formation of antibodies, increasing the production of T cells, and boosting the supply of infection-fighting white blood cells. Astragalus has long been used to increase energy and improve health by helping the body fight viral and bacterial infections responsible for causing colds, flu, bronchitis and sinus infection. An antioxidant, the herb may counteract cell damage caused by unstable oxygen molecules called free radicals. It may also boost heart function and improve cardiac output. **Note:** Other plants in the *Astragalus* genus, including North American "locoweed", can be toxic.

Atropa belladonna (**belladonna, deadly nightshade**) This perennial, native to Europe, Asia and Africa and cultivated worldwide, takes its common name of belladonna (Italian for "beautiful lady") from its use in the Middle Ages as an eyedrop that dilated the pupils and made the eyes appear more brilliant. The plant's scientifc name comes

from the Greek Atropos, one of the Fates who held the shears to cut the thread of human life. Every part of this herb contains the toxic alkaloid atropine, which relaxes and relieves spasms in the heart muscle and the smooth muscle in the digestive tract, and is still used by doctors to dilate the pupils. Today, several prescription medicines use the active ingredients in deadly nightshade to treat intestinal disorders such as diarrhoea, irritable colon and peptic ulcer. **Note:** Use of deadly nightshade is not recommended.

B

Backhousia citriodora (**lemon ironwood, lemon myrtle, sweet verbena myrtle**) This evergreen shrub or tree is native to New South Wales and Queensland, Australia. Its leaves, flowers and seeds are used to treat the symptoms of the common cold. A popular culinary flavouring and perfume scent, lemon myrtle is grown on plantations for commercial use.

Ballota nigra (**black horehound**) Native to Europe, this perennial is naturalized in North and South America. Its leaves contain compounds that are believed to relieve spasms of the stomach, and it is also a mild sedative. The herb is used to treat nausea and vomiting caused by nervousness and anxiety, as well as motion sickness and insomnia. Black horehound is a mild expectorant, and has been made into a lozenge taken to relieve sore throats and dry coughs. It has astringent properties, and can be applied topically to soothe skin irritated by insect bites and sunburn. (An astringent shrinks and tightens the top layers of skin or mucous membranes, thereby reducing secretions, relieving irritation and firming tissue.)

Belamcanda chinensis (**blackberry lily, leopard flower**) The rhizome of this east Asian perennial, a member of the iris family, has been used medicinally by the Chinese since the 1st century B.C.E. Administered internally, blackberry lily acts on the lungs and liver to fight infection and relieve cough and fever. **Note:** This herb is not recommended for use by pregnant women.

Ballota nigra
(black horehound)

Belamcanda chinensis
(blackberry lily, leopard flower)

Boehmeria nivea
(ramie)

Bertholettia excelsa (**Brazil nut**) Native to the Amazon rainforest, this enormous tree can reach ages of 500 to 800 years. When ripe, its large fruit pods make a loud crashing noise as they fall to the forest floor. The fruit, or nuts, contain 70 percent fat and burn like candles when lit. In Brazilian folk medicine, the husks of the seedpods have been brewed into tea to treat stomachaches, and the tree bark is brewed into tea to treat liver ailments. Brazil nuts are high in nutrients, including protein, fibre, vitamin E, vitamin B6, calcium, iron, and the antioxidants selenium and flavonoids. Brazil nut oil is often used as an ingredient in soaps and hydrating, antioxidant skin creams.

Bixa orellana (**annatto, achiote, lipstick tree**) Native to the Caribbean region, Mexico, and Central and South America, the annatto shrub (or small tree) is prized primarily for its seeds, which are the source of an orange-yellow dye long used by indigenous tribes. Today, annatto seed paste is used as a colouring for margarine, cheese, microwave popcorn and other yellow or orange foodstuffs. The herb may have anti-inflammatory, diuretic, laxative and expectorant properties. Annatto seeds and leaves have been used to treat indigestion and fevers and, topically, to treat burns.

Boehmeria nivea (**Chinese silk plant, ramie, white ramie**) The stalk of this flaxlike tropical Asian perennial is used commercially to make cord and fabric. The tops of the plants are high in proteins, minerals and vitamins such as beta carotene, and are used as livestock feed. Ramie has been transferred successfully to regions in the West, such as the United States.

C

Calamintha grandiflora "Rockwell" (**mint savory, showy savory, showy calamint**) This perennial, the leaves of which produce a pleasant tangerine-mint fragrance, is an aromatic addition to gardens from Asia to Europe. This herb contains pulegone, which hundreds of years ago made it useful for bringing on abortion. It is now taken to relieve indigestion. **Note:** This herb is not recommended during pregnancy.

Calamintha nepeta (**basil thyme, lesser calamint, mountain mint**) This peppermint-scented perennial is native to Europe, Africa and the Middle Eastern countries. "Calamint" comes from the plant's ancient Greek name, *kalaminthe*, which means "beautiful mint". In legend, this herb was a tall fruit tree until it offended Mother Earth and was reduced to its present bushy size as punishment. Calamint's medicinal use is limited: the leaves are used in preparations to treat indigestion, anxiety and painful periods. The herb has expectorant properties, and may help break a fever by promoting sweating. **Note:** This herb contains pulegone, which may cause abortion. It is not recommended for use during pregnancy.

Cannabis sativa (**marijuana**) Native to the Caucasus region – China, Iran, and northern India – this hardy annual is cultivated worldwide: legally, for its fibre (hemp), and illegally, for use as a recreational drug. Marijuana has a long medicinal history as an analgesic. The herb relieves pain and nausea and stimulates the appetite. It is useful for those experiencing the side effects of chemotherapy or severe weight loss due to illness. For those suffering from muscular illnesses such as multiple sclerosis, marijuana can reduce neurological and muscular hyperactivity. It reduces intraocular pressure, making it a useful treatment for glaucoma. **Note:** This herb is illegal or falls under government control in many countries, though approved in some for specific medicinal purposes.

Calamintha grandiflora 'Rockwell'
(showy savory, mint savory)

Calamintha nepeta
(lesser calamint)

Capparis canescens (**native caper**) Native capers have antiseptic, diuretic and tonic properties. The flower buds and roots can be used to treat conditions as diverse as the common cold, eye infections and arteriosclerosis.

Capparis spinosa (**caper, caper berry, caper bush**) There are 250 species of the evergreen caper bush. "Caper" comes from the Latin *capra*, or goat, so named because of the plant's strong smell. The bush is a native Mediterranean plant. Its ancient habitat is thought to have been the dry areas of western or central Asia, and the Near or Middle East. The herb has been used medicinally and in cooking for thousands of years. Capers are rich in aldose-reductose inhibitors, which may stem the development of cataracts. Capers also act as astringents, diuretics and stimulating tonics; to those ends, the herb is used to treat skin and gastrointestinal problems. The immature flower buds are pickled in vinegar or preserved in salt, then used in salads, pastas, sauces and garnishes.

Capsella bursa-pastoris (**shepherd's purse**) A member of the mustard family, this white-flowered, weedy annual is native to Europe and Asia and is now prevalent in the world's temperate regions. Its seedpods look like tiny triangular purses. Medicinally, the herb has been used to staunch the flow of blood inside and outside the body. It works by constricting blood vessels and speeding coagulation, and it is an astringent. A cold tea can be applied topically to bloody noses and skin lacerations, or ingested to treat excessive menstrual bleeding or haemorrhage after childbirth. **Note:** This herb should not be taken during pregnancy.

Carthamus tinctorius (**false saffron, safflower**) Thought to be native to parts of the Middle East, Asia and Africa, this annual is also found throughout North America and Europe. In the Middle Ages, the safflower's distinctive orange-yellow flowers were used to treat constipation and fevers. In addition, the flowers are also used in the manufacture of yellow and red dye for use in cosmetics and silk. Today, safflower's primary health benefit is as a cooking oil, which is derived from the plant's seeds and which may lower harmful cholesterol levels.

Carya species (**hickory**) There are several species of the deciduous hickory tree, a North American native. Archaeologists have traced its first human use to 6100 B.C.E., in what is now southwestern United States. Seventeenth-century histories describe hickory oil, extracted from nuts, as used by Native Americans for cooking and to soothe the stomach. In the United States today, the wood and bark of the tree are used to fuel fires to smoke or barbecue foods.

Catharanthus roseus (**Madagascar periwinkle, rosy periwinkle, tropical periwinkle**) This Madagascar native, a perennial shrub, has been naturalized worldwide. Medieval Europeans believed it had the power to exorcise evil spirits, and so included the herb in protective garlands. The French called it "sorcerer's violet", in reference to its use in charms and love potions. Medicinally, this plant is useful as an astringent and reducer of blood sugar levels. In the Bahamas, it is used as an asthma treatment. In the West Indies, it is used to treat diabetes. The herb's alkaloid and synthetic derivatives have been developed into therapies for cancers including childhood leukaemia, lung and breast cancer, and Hodgkin's disease.

Caulophyllum thalictroides (**blue cohosh, squaw root**) This perennial grows wild in much of eastern North America. Scientific research has not proven its usefulness, but it is taken widely by women (and, to a lesser extent, men) for bronchial and muscle ailments. Women ingest the rhizome and root, which contain components that stimulate uterine contractions during childbirth, encourage the onset of delayed menstruation, and alleviate heavy menstrual bleeding and cramps.

Ceanothus americanus (**New Jersey tea, prairie redroot, redroot**) Historically, this deciduous shrub, native to the United States, was used by Native Americans to treat fevers, dysentery and sore throat. During the American Revolutionary War, colonists used it as a substitute for British-taxed black tea. The roots and root bark contain antiseptic and astringent tannins. The herb is taken orally as a tea or gargle to treat asthma and throat irritation, including coughs, sore throats and bronchitis.

Cephaelis ipecacuana (**ipecac**) This shrub grows wild in the Amazon rain forest and is grown commercially in other tropical regions. The roots and rhizome have long been used to treat parasitic diseases, including amoebic dysentery and bilharziasis. Ipecac also acts as an expectorant in the treatment of dry coughs. An extremely effective emetic, ipecac syrup is a common inclusion in first-aid kits to induce vomiting in case of poison ingestion.

Ceratonia siliqua (**carob, locust bean, St John's bread**) This tall evergreen tree, native to southeastern Europe, western Asia, and North Africa, produces seedpods that can be made into a substitute for chocolate. One of the herb's common names comes from the belief that the biblical John the Baptist was believed to have eaten carob. Used to treat bacterial infection and stomach upset, carob is a mild laxative, but it also absorbs water in the intestines, combating diarrhoea by binding together watery stools.

Cetraria islandica (**Iceland moss**) This lichen, native to northern and alpine areas of Europe, has been used as a medicine as well as a dyeing and perfuming agent for thousands of years. It is an expectorant and antibiotic, and it also soothes irritated tissue, making it a treatment for gastrointestinal and respiratory tract irritations, such as ulcers, sore throats, bronchitis and dry coughs. Preliminary research shows that compounds in Iceland moss inhibit a certain enzyme that may make it useful in preventing HIV replication and AIDS.

Chelidonium majus (**greater celandine, swallowwort**) When any part of this North American perennial is broken, the plant exudes a sticky, unpleasant-smelling orange juice. The name "celandine" comes from *chelidon*, the Greek word for swallow: the plant was thought to flourish with the arrival of these birds in springtime and wither with their autumn departure for warmer climates. In folk medicine, the sap and entire plant are made into topical preparations used to treat skin problems including warts, pimples and calluses. The herb has mild pain-killing and sedative effects, and it may inhibit the growth of cancers, combat infection and boost immune-system resistance.

Chenopodium ambrosioides (**epazote, wormseed, Mexican tea**) An annual herb native to Mexico and the tropical regions of Central and South America, epazote has a history of medicinal use as a remedy for intestinal parasites. Epazote is commonly used as a culinary herb: its leaves are used to season corn, black beans, mushrooms and fish. Epazote is reputed to inhibit gas formation caused by eating beans.

Chimaphila umbellata (**ground holly, pipsissewa, prince's pine**) This evergreen is a native to North America, Europe and Asia. Native Americans believed it had the ability to dissolve kidney stones: the Cree tribe called the plant pipsisikweu, which means "it breaks into small pieces". The leaves have astringent and diuretic properties, and are taken in an infusion to treat inflammatory kidney and urinary tract conditions such as nephritis and urethritis. Until the early 20th century, pipsissewa

was used as a home remedy in rural North America. The herb is still included as one of the traditional ingredients of root beer.

Chlorella pyrenoidosa, Chlorella vulgaris (**chlorella**) These single-cell green algae are a rich source of chlorophyll (the substance responsible for the green colour in plants), offering ten times as much as is found in alfalfa sprouts. Chlorella is grown in Japan and Taiwan, where it is a popular food supplement. It is also marketed as a nutritional supplement in the United States, and it is sometimes combined with other "green foods", such as wheatgrass, barley grass and spirulina. Chlorella protects the liver from toxins, improves the body's resistance to infection, and stimulates the production of virus-fighting interferon. It also helps promote overall health by lowering blood-cholesterol and triglyceride levels.

Chondrus crispus (**carragheen, Irish moss**) In hard times, such as during the Irish potato famine of the mid-19th century, this bushy, long-stemmed seaweed was eaten to ward off starvation. The name "carragheen" refers to a village in southeastern Ireland where the seaweed is plentiful. Irish moss can be found off the Atlantic coasts of Europe and North America, attached to rocks just below the waterline. The seaweed has a high mucilage content, making it a useful internal treatment for coughs, sore throats, bronchitis, peptic ulcers and a topical treatment for skin irritations. Irish moss is also used commercially as a stabilizing agent and thickener in baked goods and dairy products, and is incorporated as an emulsifier into cosmetics and skin lotions.

Chrysanthemum balsamita (**costmary**) A native of Europe and Asia, and naturalized in North America, this perennial was once known as Bible-leaf because early American settlers used its long, balsam-scented leaves as bookmarks. In 18th-century Europe, it was widely used as a diuretic and laxative. The leaves are used externally to treat wounds, burns and bee stings.

Chrysanthemum coronarium (**garland chrysanthemum, crown daisy**) This Mediterranean annual, an edible variety of the chrysanthemum, is most widely used in Asia. Chrysanthemum flower tea is immensely popular in China. The strongly flavoured leaves, which are known as "shungikee" in Japan and as "kortongho" in China, are sometimes colloquially called "chop suey greens". Garland chrysanthemum can be used as an ingredient in salads, soups and stir-fries, or steamed and sautéed. Chrysanthemum may also have antibacterial properties.

Cichorium intybus
(chicory)

Cichorium intybus (**chicory, succory**) An ancient plant native to Europe and now found growing wild in North America, North Africa and western Asia, chicory is a perennial member of the daisy family. In folk medicine, chicory root is believed to have mild diuretic and laxative effects, similar to dandelion. The bruised leaves may be applied topically to treat skin lacerations, swelling and inflammation. Today, chicory is used principally as a strong-flavoured salad leaf. The plant's caffeine-free roots are dried, roasted, ground and blended with coffee to add a pleasantly bitter flavour while reducing the beverage's stimulating effect. Chicory is one of the major sources of insulin, and a popular ingredient for encouraging the growth of beneficial microorganisms in the intestines.

Cinchona species (**cinchona, fever tree, Peruvian bark, quinine tree**) There are forty species of this evergreen tree, native to mountainous regions of South America, especially Peru. Cinchona is now also grown in Africa and Indonesia. It was reputedly named for the Spanish Countess of Chinchon, who recovered from a fever by chewing the bark. When Jesuits visited Peru in the 17th century, they discovered that the native people chewed cinchona bark to relieve shaking and chills. In 1820, scientists identified a substance in the bark that cures malaria: the alkaloid quinine. Cinchona bark also contains the alkaloid quinidine, which is used today to treat abnormal rhythms of the heart.

Cnicus benedictus (**blessed thistle, holy thistle, St. Benedict's thistle**) This hairy-stemmed plant, once considered a cure-all, originated in southern Europe. It is now primarily used to treat digestive problems: by stimulating the body's production of saliva and

Cnicus benedictus
(blessed thistle)

digestive juices, the herb improves appetite and soothes indigestion. Women have also taken it to increase the flow of breast milk after birth. Blessed thistle has also been shown in animal studies to hinder the formation of abnormal cancer cells.

Cola nitida (**cola, kola**) There are about 100 species of the tropical cola tree, which is native to Africa. The nut, or seedpod, of this evergreen contains caffeine, which stimulates the production of digestive system acids, speeds up the heart rate and has diuretic properties. Cola nut is chewed to counter fatigue and appetite loss, and to treat diarrhoea.

Colchicum autumnale (**autumn crocus**) This native European plant, with its pink or lavender leaves, has been used since the 5th century B.C.E. to treat gout, rheumatism and arthritis. Col-chicum takes its name from Colchis, the area in which the mythical Medea practised witchcraft. The herb's bulb and seeds contain a powerful toxic alkaloid called colchicine, which is one of the ingredients of a contemporary prescription gout medication. In the 1930s, scientists discovered that this alkaloid inhibits cell division, giving the herb undeveloped potential as a cancer treatment. **Note:** This toxic herb should not be taken by pregnant or breastfeeding women.

Commiphora myrrha (**myrrh**) One of the Biblical wise men's gifts to the infant Jesus, myrrh is associated in mythology with the goddess Myrrha, daughter of Thesis. The resin of this shrub or small tree, native to Africa and the Arabian peninsula, has been used since pre-Biblical times in incense and perfumes. Ancient Egyptians used it in the process of embalming their dead. The resin has disinfectant properties and acts as an astringent, tightening and drying the body's tissues. This herb can be taken to relieve mild oral inflammations, such as sore throat. In Asian medicine, it is used to treat stomach pain and amenorrhoea.

Conium maculatum (**hemlock, poison parsley**) Famed as a favourite ingredient in medieval witches' potions and the source of the poison that

Convallaria majalis
(lily of the valley)

brought death to the Greek philosopher Socrates, hemlock is a native-European biennial in the parsley family, now naturalized in North America. The plant's botanical name is derived from a Greek verb that means "to whirl around", a reference to the vertigo that is one of the characteristic symptoms of hemlock poisoning. The entire plant contains the toxic alkaloid coniine, which, when ingested, causes paralysis, convulsions, and death. Today, hemlock is a regulated drug, and is regularly used externally to treat tumours and haemorrhoids.

Convallaria majalis (**lily of the valley, May lily**) Native to Europe and now found in temperate regions of North America and northern Asia, this widely cultivated ornamental perennial has fragrant, bell-shaped white flowers. According to Greek mythology, the plant was first discovered by the sun god Apollo, who gave it to Aesculapius, the god of medicine. Lily of the valley has been used in the treatment of heart failure: it contains phytochemicals that encourage the heart to beat more regularly and efficiently. It is also a strong diuretic, and acts to reduce blood volume and blood pressure. **Note:** Lily of the valley is toxic and should be used only under medical supervision.

Coptis chinensis (**cankerroot, goldthread**) This low-growing relative of the peony, is native to the mountains of China. In traditional Chinese medicine, the root is used to treat diarrhoea, hypertension, and bacterial and viral infections. This herb contains an alkloid, berberine, that has been found in laboratory studies to reduce blood-cholesterol levels and hinder the development of atherosclerosis. Other studies have found that berberine may lower blood sugar levels in diabetic animals, and stop the replication of human colorectal and liver cancer cells.

Corchorus olitorius (**jute**) This tropical annual, native to India, produces a coarse fibre that is used worldwide to make hessian, rope and insulation. It is rich in folate, the naturally occurring form of the B vitamin folic acid, which has been found to be critical in reducing spinal birth defects in developing foetuses.

Corylus avellana (**filbert, hazelnut**) There are several hazelnut species native to Europe and Asia Minor, all of which produce edible nuts that are harvested from the wild by humans and are important sources of food for wildlife. Filbert may be derived from "full beard", a reference to the long, leafy husk surrounding the nuts. Filberts are grown commercially in Turkey, Italy and the Pacific northwest United States. The word "hazel" comes from

Crithmum maritimum
(rock samphire)

the Anglo-Saxon word for bonnet, *haesel*; this probably derives from the Greek *korys* (as in *corylus*), for helmet or hood. The nuts, which are high in protein, calcium, iron and phosphorus, are thought to be part of a heart-healthy diet. They are eaten roasted or used in cooking and baking.

Crithmum maritimum (**rock samphire**) Native to coastal Europe and the Black Sea and Mediterranean regions, this perennial's common name comes from its French name, which refers to the biblical fisherman: *herbe de Saint Pierre*. Rock samphire has been used as a diuretic, internal cleanser and digestive aid. Rich in vitamin C and strongly aromatic, its leaves and flowers can be added to salads and eaten as a vegetable.

Cryptotaenia japonica (**Japanese parsley, Japanese wild chervil, mitsuba**) Native to temperate Asian countries, the leaves and leaf stalks of this long-stemmed annual are commonly included in soups, stews, salads and fried dishes. The herb, a good source of vitamins, is generally considered more nutritive than medicinal.

Cucurbita pepo (**pumpkin**) This long, trailing vine originated in North America, but is now grown worldwide. It shares its family tree with melons and cucumbers. The fruit is a traditional ingredient in autumn holiday pies in the United States. Research has found that the seeds exhibit antioxidant and anti-inflammatory properties. The seeds are dense in several nutrients, providing protein, fibre, iron, calcium, linolenic acid (believed to help prevent hardening of the arteries) and the minerals zinc and selenium (important nutrients for prostate health).

Cuminum cyminum (**cumin**) A common culinary spice in Indian and Mexican cuisines, this annual is cultivated throughout the Mediterranean region and in some countries in the Middle East, Asia and North and South America. In Greece, cumin was once kept at the dining table in its own container, much as pepper and salt are today. Cumin's name is taken from the Persian city Kerman, where most of ancient Persia's cumin was produced. The herb is thought to have pain-relieving and anti-inflammatory properties, and has been used to treat joint inflamation and gastrointestinal problems such as indigestion and diarrhoea.

Cytisus scoparius (broom, Scotch broom) This native European perennial, a stiff-branched shrub, takes its name from the Latin word for besom (a broom made of twigs). It is considered an invasive weed in some countries, such as the United States and New Zealand, where it has been naturalized. In the Middle Ages, the plant's twigs and branches were bundled into a broom for sweeping the floor. It was thought to ward off witches, but when used in full bloom the branches could bring bad luck. Broom is used mainly to treat an irregular heartbeat. The herb contains a phytochemical that constricts blood vessels and raises blood pressure. Another of its components is a cardiac depressant that can, in large amounts, dangerously lower the heartbeat. **Note:** This herb should be used only under the care of a qualified health practitioner.

D

Datura stramonium (Jamestown weed, jimsonweed, mad apple, stinkweed, thorn apple) For thousands of years, humans have used the fifteen *Datura* species as medicine and as mind-altering drugs. Although *Datura* is rumoured to have been carried by Gypsies from western Asia into Europe, it is not known whether the plant is native to the New World or the Old World. *Datura* now grows in most temperate and subtropical parts of the globe. Every part of this weedy annual, a member of the nightshade family, is poisonous. *Datura* contains atropine, a potent chemical that combats spasms and diminishes muscular activity in the digestive system, lungs and other internal organs. The herb has been used, in low doses, to treat asthma, muscle spasm and the symptoms of Parkinson's.

Datura stramonium
(jimsonweed)

Daucus carota, Daucus carota subsp. *sativus* (carrot, Queen Anne's lace, wild carrot) Wild carrot (Queen Anne's lace), a biennial, is native to Europe. Its cultivated annual relative, the familiar garden carrot (subsp. *sativus*), is grown around the world. Carrots have been made into wine, liquor, and a coffee substitute. In 17th-century England, feathery carrot leaves adorned the hats and coifs of fashionable ladies. Taken as food, carrots can be beneficial to the heart. They are a major source of antioxidant carotenoids in the modern diet and contain compounds that help lower blood pressure and cholesterol. Eaten cooked, the plant's fleshy orange root can soothe an upset stomach and replace vitamins lost through diarrhoea.

Desmodium styracifolium (beggar lice) This Asian vine takes its name from a Greek word meaning "chain", in reference to the plant's jointed seed-pods. The pods contain small, loose fruits that stick to clothing. The whole plant is used in traditional Chinese medicine to treat kidney stones. It is increasingly becoming an accepted herbal supplement in the medical treatment of this condition. During recent studies, Japanese researchers have found a compound in the plant that decreases the likelihood of kidney stone formation.

Drosera rotundifola (sundew) Like its relative, the Venus flytrap, this bog-dwelling plant is an insect predator. It grows in areas of wet, spongy ground in Europe, northern Asia and North America. The leaves of the plant contain decongestant and anti-inflammatory agents, and can be used to treat respiratory conditions such as bronchitis and asthma. Sundew juice has been applied topically to reduce growths such as warts and corns.

E

Elymus repens (couch grass, dog's grass, twitch) This perennial is an invasive weed found in Europe, the Americas, northern Asia and Australia. In folk-lore, dogs were said to seek out the plant's leaves when they were ill, and would then chew them to induce vomiting. Couch grass is a gentle diuretic that has been used to treat urinary tract infections and kidney stones.

Epimedium species (epimedium, horny goatweed, yin yang huo) This low-growing herb, which is native to China, has been used to treat kidney, liver, and joint disorders. Legend has it that long ago, a herder noticed his goats becoming more sexually active

Eryngium foetidum
(culantro)

after eating this plant. The herb is said to increase and intensify sexual desire and stimulate the sensory nerves in both men and women.

Equisetum arvense (bottle brush, horsetail, scouring rush) This 200-million-year-old plant has hollow, bamboolike stems that end in distinctive brownish cones. The dried stems are made into tea or liquid extract that acts as a mild diuretic, taken to treat bladder infections and kidney stones. Horsetail has anti-inflammatory qualities, and has been used to treat the gastrointestinal inflammation of Crohn's disease. The stems contain silica. The belief that it can strengthen nails, hair, teeth and connective tissue is unsupported, as the body cannot use the form of silica in plants. Applied directly to a wound, the herb can help stop bleeding. **Note:** Horsetail is toxic in large doses.

Eryngium foetidum (culantro, false coriander, fitweed) This biennial is indigenous to tropical regions of the Americas and the West Indies. Culantro is often used as a flavouring in South American, Caribbean and Asian cuisines. One of its common names, fitweed, is derived from the herb's supposed anti-convulsant properties. Its leaves and roots have been used to treat fevers, constipation, diarrhoea, diabetes and the flu.

Erythroxylum coca (coca) This shrubby tree, native to the Andes region of South America, has been cultivated since the time of the Inca Empire. For centuries, indigenous people have chewed the leaves, mixed with lime, to suppress hunger and combat fatigue and the symptoms of altitude sickness.

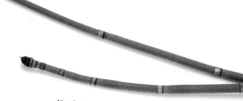

Equisetum arvense
(horsetail)

In the 19th century, it was discovered that the drug could act as a topical anaesthetic. Later, an American pharmacist combined coca leaves with the juice of the cola nut in a beverage he called Coca-Cola™. Coca's principal alkaloid is cocaine, and though it is no longer an ingredient in Coca-Cola™, cocaine is still used as a topical anaesthetic in eye, nose and throat surgery. It is also taken illegally as a narcotic, stimulant drug. **Note:** In concentrated form, coca is addictive and dangerous.

Euphrasia officinalis (**eyebright**) Eyebright is a small annual found in the meadows of Europe and North America. Long used as an eye medication, its name means "gladness". Eyebright contains astringent and antibacterial tannins and other components that make it useful as a treatment for stinging or watering eyes, eye fatigue and eye inflammation, such as conjunctivitis. It has also been used to treat infectious and allergic conditions affecting the middle ear, sinuses and nasal passages.

F

Fagus grandifolia (**American beech, beech**) This deciduous North American tree yields seeds, or beechnuts, that were once a popular substitute for coffee beans and the source of a cooking oil. Native Americans used the tree's astringent and antiseptic bark and leaves externally to treat poison ivy rash and burns, and internally to treat tuberculosis, fevers and intestinal worms. Today, beech is valued chiefly for its wood, which is used to make flooring, furniture, crates and tool handles. Tar from the wood is distilled to make creosote, a medicinal antiseptic.

Ferula asafoetida (**asafoetida, devil's dung, food-of-the-gods**) This unpleasant-smelling perennial, native to Afghanistan, Iran and the Kashmir region, takes its name from the Persian *aza*, for resin, and the Latin *foetidus*, for stinking. The sap of the roots produces

Ficus carica
(fig)

a gum, or resin, that has been used as a spice since ancient Roman times. It is still used as an ingredient in Worcestershire sauce, and is a common flavouring in Indian cooking. Believing that the plant's bad smell would deter germs, in some European countries a piece of the resin was tied on a string around children's necks to protect from disease. Asafoetida is known as an antidote for indigestion and flatulence, and is also prescribed for respiratory conditions such as asthma, bronchitis and whooping cough. **Note:** Asafoetida is not recommended for use during pregnancy.

Ficus carica (**fig**) The deciduous fig tree is native to Asia Minor, Syria, and Iran. Today it is grown in subtropical regions around the world. The fig is mentioned frequently in the Bible, and was held sacred by ancient Romans, who believed that Romulus and Remus, the twin founders of Rome, were suckled beneath the limbs of a fig tree. The fruit of the tree can be eaten as a gentle laxative. When made into a topical preparation, figs contain an enzyme that may break down the proteins in common skin conditions such as corns and warts.

Forsythia suspensa (**weeping forsythia**) This delicate, yellow-flowering deciduous bush originated in China, but can now be found all over the world. The seeds are thought to have antibacterial and antifungal properties, and have been used to treat cough, nasal congestion and earache. Forsythia's effects are enhanced when administered with honeysuckle.

Fucus vesiculosus (**bladderwrack**) This seaweed, found in the Atlantic and Pacific oceans, and in the North Sea and the western Baltic, is supported by air bladders on the body of the plant. *Fucus* is the Latin name for brown seaweed; *vesiculosus* means "little blisters". Rich in iodine, bladderwrack has been used to treat goitre, a swelling of the thyroid gland related to iodine insufficiency. Bladder wrack may be used to treat the symptoms of an underactive thyroid, including weight gain. It contains mucilage, useful for soothing inflamed and irritated tissues. It has been taken in tablet form or infusion to relieve the symptoms of arthritis and rheumatism, and applied topically to relieve joint ache.

Fumaria officinalis (**fumitory**) This weak-limbed annual, native to Europe and North Africa, also grows in Asia, North America and Australia. Fumitory takes its name from the plant's blue-green colour, which is reminiscent of smoke rising from the earth. In folk medicine, fumitory has been used to treat skin problems, such as psoriasis, eczema and acne.

G

Galium aparine (**cleavers, goosegrass**) Common throughout Europe and North America, cleavers is found in other temperate regions, including in Australia. True to its name, the bristly fruit of this annual cleaves to those who pass by. A diuretic, the herb can be used to stimulate the elimination of wastes from the body via the urinary system. Cleavers is also thought to promote lymphatic drainage of toxins and wastes. It has been used to treat kidney stones and urinary tract disorders, such as cystitis. In addition, the herb's eliminative nature makes it helpful for treating skin conditions such as eczema and psoriasis.

Galium odoratum (**sweet woodruff**) Native to Europe, this perennial ground cover is also found in Asia and North Africa. Sweet woodruff smells pleasantly of freshly mown grass, and its fragrance, unlike that of most herbs, can persist for years. This can be explained by the presence of the chemical substance coumarin, which is sometimes used as a fixative for perfumes. Sweet woodruff was once used as a scenting herb for homes and churches, and as a stuffing for mattresses. The dried leaves are commonly used in herb wreaths and in potpourris. Medicinally, sweet woodruff has diuretic properties and can stimulate perspiration, helping the body eliminate waste through the skin. Coumarin dilates blood vessels, which increases blood flow.

Galium verum (**cheese rennet, lady's bedstraw, yellow bedstraw**) This yellow-flowered perennial is found throughout Europe and western Asia, and is naturalized in North America. The plant has a calming, sedative scent, and its dried foliage was traditionally used as mattress stuffing. According to Biblical legend, it was included in the hay in the manger at Bethlehem. A strong extract of the leaves and stems acts as a curdling agent and was once used to make cheese. Lady's bedstraw has been taken internally to treat epilepsy, and applied topically to relieve skin problems such as psoriasis. It can be added to a warm bath to soothe aching muscles. Its roots produce a deep red dye; the stems and flowers produce a yellow dye.

Ganoderma lucidum (**ling zhi, reishi**) In Asia, reishi is known as the "phantom mushroom" because of the difficulty in finding it. Although 99 percent of all wild reishi mushrooms are found growing on old plum trees, fewer than ten mushrooms will be found on 100,000 trees. Reishi is cultivated commercially in North America, China, Taiwan, Japan and Korea. It is believed to improve blood flow and increase

Galium verum
(lady's bedstraw)

the body's metabolism of oxygen. It has been used to counter fatigue and the symptoms of altitude sickness. The mushroom's active ingredients, ganoderic acids, appear to combat high blood pressure and reduce LDL ("bad") cholesterol and triglyceride levels. Reishi also has immune-stimulating effects, anti-tumour properties, and liver protective benefits, all of which seem to support its reputation as a longevity tonic.

Gaultheria procumbens (teaberry, wintergreen) This bushy evergreen perennial is native to North America and Canada. During the American Revolutionary War, it was used as a substitute for British-supplied tea. Wintergreen has been used to relieve muscle, joint and nerve pain. It stimulates temperature-sensitive nerve endings, temporarily overriding nearby pain signals. A synthetic version of its active ingredient, methyl salicylate, is found in over-the-counter topical ointments. Wintergreen's leaves and red berries were once the essence used in flavouring for sweets, cough drops, gum and toothpaste.

Genista tinctoria (dyer's broom, dyer's greenweed, woadwaxen) Native to Europe and Asia and naturalized in North America, this broomlike perennial has bright yellow flowers that were said to have been used, together with the herb woad, to make the Saxon green colour used to dye the tunic worn by Robin Hood. The flowers and seeds have diuretic, emetic and purgative properties, and have been used to treat gout and rheumatism. The herb can be applied externally to treat abscesses, sciatica and tumours.

Geranium maculatum (American cranesbill, cranesbill, wild geranium) The geranium family takes its name from the Greek *geranos*, meaning "crane", because the plants' seedpods are thought to be shaped like cranes' bills. The rhizome (an elongated, usually horitontal underground stem) of this North American and European perennial has a high tannin content, which makes it effective as an external astringent (an agent that causes the skin and mucous membranes to constrict) and a haemostatic (an agent that stops bleeding). The herb has been applied externally to staunch wounds, and taken internally to treat diarrhoea and excessive menstrual bleeding.

Geranium robertianum (geranium, herb Robert) This rank-smelling annual is native to Europe and central Asia, and is naturalized in North America. With hairy stems and small, pungent pinkish to purplish flowers, herb Robert is employed in much the same way as American cranesbill, as an astringent and wound healer.

Geum urbanum (avens, herb Benedict) Native to Europe and central Asia, this spiky perennial is a common roadside plant. The botanical name *Geum* comes from the Greek *geno*, meaning "to yield an agreeable fragrance". When freshly dug, the root has a clovelike aroma. Avens can be used as an antiseptic and astringent, and is helpful in the treatment of gastrointestinal inflammations such as ulcerative colitis, diverticulitis and diarrhoea. It may be taken internally to treat fever or applied externally to soothe haemorrhoids, reduce excess vaginal discharge, and reduce inflammation of the mouth and gums.

Grindelia species (asthma weed, grindelia, gumplant) The sixty species of grindelia, a North American perennial, are characterized by their ability to relieve topical skin irritations caused by poison ivy and poison oak. Grindelia has yellow flowers that produce a sticky resin containing an anaesthetic constituent. Taken internally, grindelia has expectorant and antispasmodic properties. The herb helps rid the lungs of excess mucus while relaxing and dilating airways. It has been used to treat bronchitis, asthma and whooping cough.

Gymnema sylvestre (gymnema) A member of the milkweed family, this climbing plant is native to the tropical regions of India. It offers a promising herbal therapy for type 2 diabetes: research has shown that this plant may enhance the action of insulin, lower blood sugar levels, and even increase the number of insulin-producing cells in the pancreas. It may also have a role in lowering levels of LDL ("bad") cholesterol. **Note:** Those with diabetes should consult a qualified health practitioner before beginning a *Gymnema* regime.

Geranium robertianum
(Herb Robert)

H

Helleborus niger (black hellebore, Christmas rose) Part of a genus of fifteen poisonous perennials, this Eurasian evergreen takes one of its common names from its pure white blossoms that appear in the depth of winter. Another common name refers to the dark colour of its rootstock. The plant's botanical name comes from the Greek *elein* (to injure) and *bora* (food). The herb contains cardiac glycosides, which increase the heart's efficiency, and diuretic steroid saponins. It also contains a toxic component that can, with external contact, cause skin irritation and blistering. Ingestion in excess amounts can induce abortion. **Note:** There is no known herb that safely induces abortion. Several herbs have this reputation; all are toxic.

I

Ilex paraguariensis (yerba maté, maté) A highly popular herb in South America, this evergreen member of the holly family is the main ingredient of an important South American beverage, the national tea of Argentina and Brazil as well as its namesake, Paraguay. Maté drinking is an important part of South American culture. The leaves are made into a stimulant tea, taken to reduce appetite, alleviate nervous tension and depression, rid the body of excess water, and increase energy and mental alertness. Maté has a pleasant, slightly bitter flavour, much like green tea. The herb contains caffeine, although less than tea or coffee.

Illicium verum (star anise) Star anise is the fruit of a small evergreen tree native to China and Vietnam. Shaped like an eight-pointed star, it has a pronounced liquorice flavour similar to that of aniseed. Star anise is a key ingredient in Chinese five-spice powder, and is used to flavour many Asian dishes. It is a major source of anise flavouring. The herb may have carminative, stimulant and diuretic properties. It has been taken as a tea to treat colic and rheumatism.

Impatiens capensis (impatiens, jewelweed, touch-me-not) This North American orange-flowered annual takes one of its common names from the way in which the ripe fruits burst open to the touch, releasing seeds in all directions. The plant is often found growing in the same area as poison ivy, which is helpful, because jewelweed can be used to treat rashes and hives caused by contact with skin irritants such as poison ivy and poison oak.

Inula helenium (**elecampane, horseheal, scabwort, wild sunflower**) Native to Europe and Asia, this perennial shrub, whose flowers resemble small sunflowers, now grows in many temperate regions, including parts of North America. The plant's botanical name is said to reflect its association with Helen of Troy: the plant either sprang from her tears, or she was holding a branch of it when Paris stole her away. Elecampane inherits two of its common names from its early use by veterinarians to treat pulmonary disorders in horses and skin diseases in sheep. Elecampane is thought to have a soothing effect on the intestinal tract, dating back to ancient Roman times when it was taken to relieve the symptoms of post-banquet indigestion.

Iris species (**blue flag, white flag, pale flag, orris**) All three of the *Iris* species are native to southern Europe. In Greek mythology, Iris was the goddess of the many-coloured rainbow and messenger of the gods. Her name was given to this family of plants to reflect the variable colours of their flowers. (The common name "orris" is a corruption of the word "Iris.") With its pleasant, violet-like scent, orris root has served as a fragrance since the days of the ancient Egyptians. A tea made from the root can be used to treat bronchitis, coughs and diarrhoea. Today, orris root has little to no medicinal application. Instead, it is used commercially, primarily to scent cosmetics, perfumes and potpourris.

Isatis tinctoria (**woad**) This southeastern European perennial was once a dominant source of blue dye. In folklore, it is said to have been one of the ingredients used to colour the green tunic of Robin Hood. Ancient warriors in the British Isles painted their bodies with woad to frighten their opponents. The plant was cultivated as a major industry and trade item until the mid-17th century, when it was largely replaced by indigo imported from the New World. Both woad and indigo have been eclipsed by synthetic aniline dyes. Although woad may have astringent properties, it is toxic and is not to be taken internally.

K

Krameria triandra (**rhatany**) Rhatany is a small shrub found mostly in the mountains of Peru with numerous branching stems. The root has a pleasant but definite astringent effect, drying and tightening human tissue. It can be made into a tea or gargle to relieve mild inflammation of the mouth, throat and gums. It is generally gentle on the stomach.

L

Laminaria **species (kelp)** There are several species of *Laminaria,* found in temperate and Arctic waters on exposed rocky shores in the low intertidal and subtidal zones. The greenish brown seaweed is farmed in China, Korea and Japan, and harvested from the wild in northeastern North America, Iceland, Greenland and western Europe. A concentrated source of minerals including iodine, potassium, magnesium, calcium and iron, kelp is eaten as a vegetable in Japan. Westerners have added powdered kelp to their diets to curtail thyroid disease; studies have shown that Japanese who eat kelp and do not follow a Western diet have a low incidence of thyroid disease. Because of natural variations in iodine content, other sources of this mineral are preferred today.

Lawsonia inermis (**henna**) Native to Africa, Asia and Australia, this perennial shrub is cultivated in North America, Egypt, India and parts of the Middle East. Since antiquity, henna leaves have been a source of dye used to colour hair, hands and nails a deep red-orange. Medicinally, the plant has astringent, antiseptic and antibacterial properties. Henna bark has been used to treat liver problems. The leaves may alleviate the symptoms of diarrhoea and amoebic dysentery.

Leontopodium alpinum (**edelweiss**) Originating in Asia, this white-flowered alpine perennial can also be found on high mountains in Europe and South America. Its name comes from the Swiss German *edel* (noble) and *weiß* (white). The national flower of Switzerland, edelweiss is a protected plant in many countries. Recent research has found that it may have powers to fight bacteria, including *Staphylococcus* and *Streptococcus.*

Leonurus cardiaca (**lion's ear, lion's tail, motherwort**) Originating in central Europe, Scandinavia, Russia and central Asia, this tall perennial is naturalized in North America. Its shaggy leaves are thought to resemble a lion's

Leonurus cardiaca
(motherwort)

Lobelia inflata
(lobelia)

tail. Motherwort primarily affects the cardiovascular system and the female reproductive system. The plant has a mildly relaxing effect on the heart, and acts as a sedative. It may have a short-term ability to lower blood pressure. By stimulating the uterine muscles, it can help bring on delayed or suppressed menstruation, especially when anxiety or tension is involved. **Note:** This herb should not be taken by pregnant or breastfeeding women.

Lepidium species (**peppergrass, sciatica cress**) There are several species of this perennial, a member of the mustard family. Sciatica cress can be applied externally to relieve musculo-skeletal discomfort, such as the pain of sciatica. One Peruvian variety, *Lepidium peruvianum* (maca), has been used to treat male impotence, erectile dysfunction, menstrual disorders, menopausal symptoms and fatigue. Research in the Middle East suggests that a local *Lepidium* may speed the healing of broken bones.

Lewisia rediviva (**bitterroot**) Named after its discoverer, the American explorer Meriwether Lewis, bitterroot is native to western North America. This perennial has a remarkable ability to bloom following periods of great dehydration. Its edible root was a staple food of some native North American tribes, who removed the root's bitter outer layer before drying or boiling it.

Ligusticum porteri (**osha**) Osha, a perennial herb native to western North America, has a camphorlike scent. It has antibacterial and anti-inflammatory properties, and may be useful in the treatment of infections of the sinuses, throat, and upper and lower respiratory systems. Osha also aids wound healing. It helps loosen respiratory secretions and relaxes smooth muscle tissue, making it beneficial for treating coughs and asthma.

Lobelia inflata (**asthma weed, Indian tobacco, lobelia, pukeweed**) This hairy-leaved annual or biennial is native to northern United States, Canada and eastern Siberia. Native American Indians smoked its leaves to relieve asthma and bronchitis (hence the common name Indian tobacco). The herb contains a muscle-relaxing alkaloid called lobeline. By relaxing the muscles of the smaller bronchial tubes, lobeline opens airways, stimulates breathing and promotes the loosening of phlegm. Applied externally, lobelia can relieve muscle tension. Lobeline mimics the effects of nicotine, and the herb has been used to combat nicotine addiction. It has also been used to induce vomiting in people who had been poisoned. **Note:** Even a minuscule amount of this herb can cause paralysis, coma and death. It is no longer used medicinally.

Lomatium dissectum (**lomatium**) Native American Indians have chewed this parsleylike herb to treat respiratory problems. There is some evidence of an antiviral effect. It may alleviate the symptoms of other respiratory problems, including asthma and hay fever. **Note:** This herb is not advised for pregnant women unless prescribed by a qualified health practitioner.

Lophophora williamsii (**mescal, peyote**) This cactus, native to northern Mexico and the southwestern United States, is known for its hallucinogenic "buttons", or greyish mushroom-shaped tops. Peyote buttons contain numerous alkaloids, principally mescaline. Aztec and Native American Indians have long taken peyote as a ritual or spiritual practice. In addition to its mind-altering effects, peyote may have the ability to lower blood sugar levels. **Note:** Possession of peyote is illegal in the United States, except by Native Americans who use it as part of their religious ritual practice.

Lycium species (**boxthorn, matrimony vine, Chinese wolfberry**) Often reaching a height of 12 ft (3.7 m), *Lycium* can be found throughout much of China and Tibet. The herb is traditionally believed to promote long life: according to legend, it helped one Chinese herbalist live to be 252 years old. The plant's bright-red berries may protect the liver from damage caused by toxins, and correct vision problems such as blurred eyesight. The root may

Lycium chinensis
(wolfberry)

relax artery muscles, thereby lowering blood pressure. The root may also have the ability to reduce fever and relieve coughing and wheezing.

Lycopus species (**bugleweed, gypsywort**) Both the North American bugleweed and gypsywort, its European cousin, are creeping perennials with a mintlike scent. Historically, bugleweed and related species were used as sedatives and cough treatments. Today, the herb helps relieve common symptoms of mild hyperthyroidism, including nervousness and insomnia.

M

Macadamia integrifolia; Macadamia tetra-phylla (**Australian nut, macadamia, Queensland nut**) Macadamias are large, spreading evergreen trees, native to Australia but also found in South Africa and North and Central America. The tree's fruit, or nut, is a creamy white kernel surrounded by a green husk that splits open as the nut matures. Macadamia nuts are comprised of nearly 60 percent monounsaturated fatty acids, making them a useful addition to a medically mandated low protein, high complex-carbohydrate diet. Macadamia nuts may help type 2 diabetics maintain their correct blood sugar levels without increasing their cholesterol levels.

Mahonia aquifolium (**Oregon grape**) The American Northwest produces this evergreen shrub with hollylike leaves. The root contains the alkaloid berberine, which inhibits the ability of bacteria to attach to human cells, and may enhance immune-cell function. The herb can be useful in the treatment of infections, particularly in the throat, intestines and urinary tract. Topically, Oregon grape has been found to be mildly effective for reducing the irritation, inflammation and itching of skin disorders such as psoriasis.

Malus domestica (**domestic apple**) The deciduous apple tree is native to Europe and Asia. *Malus* has the dual meaning of either apple or evil, which probably stems from the fruit's association with the "forbidden fruit" of the Biblical tree of knowledge of good and evil. The average apple contains about five grams of fibre, which helps maintain normal bowel function. Apples contain flavonoids, which may reduce the risk of heart disease and stroke. Studies have found that eating apples or drinking apple juice daily may reduce the buildup of arterial plaque. The bark and roots of most *Malus* species contain phloretin, an antibiotic-like compound. Apple seeds contain toxic compounds.

Marrubium vulgare
(horehound)

Mandragora officinarum (**devil's apple, mandrake, mayapple, Satan's apple**) This toxic perennial is native to southeastern Europe and some Himalayan and Middle-Eastern areas. Its parsniplike root divides in two, resembling a pair of human legs. According to folklore, the root would shriek when dug up. Mandrake has been associated with magic since the time of the early Egyptians. The root was a favourite ingredient of witches' brews and love potions, and was reputed to exorcise demons. Although it is no longer used medicinally, mandrake root was taken to combat impotence and sterility, and employed as an anaesthetic.

Maranta arundinaceae (**arrowroot**) This creeping perennial is native to the West Indies and tropical America, from Mexico to Brazil. It has become naturalized in southeastern Asia, India and Africa. A powder made from the plant's fleshy tubers was used by the Native American Arawak tribe to withdraw poison from toxic arrow wounds. Arrowroot soothes irritated mucous membranes, and can be used in the treatment of indigestion and diarrhoea. The dried rhizomes are a natural moisture absorber, making the herb useful in cooking as a thickener for sauces. A topical application of powdered arrowroot can provide relief for the skin condition athlete's foot.

Marrubium vulgare (**horehound**) Native to Europe, this woolly leaved perennial thrives in sandy areas across Asia, North America and Africa. The genus name *Marrubium* is thought to be derived from *marrob*, the Hebrew word for "bitter juice": horehound may have been one of the original bitter herbs of the Jewish Passover tradition. The herb's common name may have come from the ancient Egyptians, who called it the Seed of Horus, or the ancient Greeks, who were said to have used it to treat the bite of mad dogs. Horehound has expectorant properties, and can be used to soothe coughs and treat respiratory problems such as colds and bronchitis.

Medicago sativa (**alfalfa, lucerne**) Native to Asia, Europe and North Africa, this grass is primarily used as animal fodder.

The plant is a good source of vitamins A, B₁, B₆, C, E and K, as well as calcium, potassium, iron and zinc. Discovery of an oestrogen-like action in animal tests has led to its use as a remedy for the symptoms of menopause. In addition, alfalfa may prevent the body's absorption of cholesterol. Alfalfa sprouts are commonly eaten in salads and sandwiches. **Note:** Alfalfa should be avoided by pregnant and lactating women, by patients with hormone-sensitive cancer, by those with gout, and by people with a history of systemic lupus erythematosus.

Mentha pulegium (**fleabane, mosquito plant, pennyroyal**) A member of the mint family, its botanical name reflects its power as an insect repellent: The species name *pulegium* derives from the Latin word for flea. Though it does repel insects, it also contains the toxic chemical pulegone, so caution is advised. Internal use is discouraged. **Note:** Pennyroyal should not be used by people with liver or kidney disease, or by pregnant or breastfeeding women. The essential oil is highly toxic.

Menyanthes trifoliata (**bogbean**) A perennial aquatic plant, bogbean is native to Europe and North America. Its leaves are thought to resemble those of bean plants. Bogbean is a digestive stimulant and pain reliever. It can be taken to alleviate the symptoms of musculoskeletal disorders such as arthritis and rheumatism, particularly when this condition is associated with weakness, weight loss and lack of vitality.

Mitchella repens (**partridgeberry, squaw vine**) Native to eastern and central North America, this evergreen vine has a long history of use among Native American women. It was taken to treat menstrual pains and cramps, to regulate menstrual cycles and relieve heavy bleeding, to induce childbirth and ease delivery. Its salve eased the pain of sore nipples in lactating women. Its common name comes from its fruits, which were said to be favoured by a North American bird similar to the European partridge.

Momordica charantia (**balsam pear, bitter gourd, bitter melon**) Bitter gourd grows in tropical areas, including parts of East Africa, Asia, the Caribbean and South

Murraya koenigii
(curry leaf)

Myrrhis odorata
(sweet cicely)

America, where the bitter-tasting fruit (which resembles a bumpy, light green cucumber) is used as a food as well as a medicine. Studies have shown that the herb may improve blood sugar control in people with adult-onset (type 2) diabetes, and may have antiviral activity against HIV and herpes. **Note:** This herb should not be used by pregnant women.

Morus alba (**white mulberry**) The name of this native Chinese tree comes from the Latin *demorari*, meaning "to delay", for mulberry's habit of forming buds after winter's first frost. Various parts of the tree have been used in traditional Chinese medicine for 1,500 years. The leaves have antibacterial, cardioprotective, liver-protective, antidiabetic and antioxidant qualities, and may be eaten. The root bark has immune-stimulating, analgesic, diuretic, antitussive, anti-inflammatory, sedative, anticonvulsant and hypotensive properties. The fruits can improve kidney function and may reduce urinary incontinence.

Mucuna pruriens (**cowage, cowitch, velvet bean**) The velvet bean is a climbing plant, indigenous to tropical regions, especially Africa, India and the West Indies. In Central America, velvet beans are roasted and ground to make a coffee substitute. The bean is rich in L-dopamine, a neurotransmitter that may be useful in the treatment of Parkinson's disease. Velvet bean is also thought to be helpful in the treatment of erectile dysfunction disorder. In Spain, it is considered an aphrodisiac.

Murraya koenigii (**curry leaf**) The curry leaf tree is native to India and Sri Lanka. Its leaves, rich in essential oils, are used to flavour curries and other dishes of southern Asia. The leaf has a pungent aroma, reminiscent of tangerine.

Myrciaria dubia (**camu-camu**) The lemon-size fruit of this native Amazon shrub contains more vitamin C than any other known fruit. It is not commonly eaten by indigenous people because of its sour, acidic taste, and is not yet available outside the Amazon.

Myrica cerifera (**bayberry, candleberry, wax myrtle**) Bayberry is a deciduous shrub native to the eastern and southern United States. A wax extracted from its berries is used to make sweet-smelling

candles that are particularly popular during winter holidays. As an astringent and tonic, the herb was thought to tighten and dry mucous membranes, making it useful for treating nasal congestion, colds, sore throat, and diarrhoea. **Note:** bayberry may have carcinogenic effects; it should not be ingested without first consulting a health care provider.

Myrrhis odorata (**sweet cicely**) An aromatic native European perennial, sweet cicely has long been used as a mild laxative. Externally, it acts as an antiseptic. Eating sweet cicely was once thought to offer protection against bubonic plague. The delicately flavoured leaves can be added to salads, soups and stews.

Myrtus communis (**myrtle**) A small, aromatic shrub native to the Middle East and the Mediterranean region, myrtle has traditionally been used to treat coughs and respiratory infections, such as bronchitis. It has a reputation for promoting good digestion, treating urinary tract disorders and preventing infections in wounds.

N

Nasturtium officinale (**cress, true nasturtium, watercress**) A member of the mustard family, this aquatic perennial is native to Europe and Asia. *Nasturtium* is Latin for "twisted nose", an allusion to the herb's pungent odour. Rich in calcium, iron and vitamins A and C, the peppery-tasting leaves and stems can be made into a tea to treat cough and bronchitis. Watercress may also stimulate the appetite, aid digestion and act as a diuretic. Non-medically, it is served raw in salads and sandwiches and cooked in soup.

O

Oenanthe javanica (**Korean watercress, Vietnamese celery, water celery**) This creeping perennial is native to wetlands in both the Northern and Southern hemispheres. Studies have found it to

Oenanthe javanica
(water celery)

Osmanthus fragrans
(sweet olive)

have antioxidant properties. It may help stabilize blood sugar levels, and protect the liver from toxins. Preparations made from the plant's leaves, shoots and fruits can be taken to treat fever and control excess bleeding, such as heavy menses. Poultices can be applied to treat insect bites and abscesses.

Orthosiphon aristatus (**Java tea**) Found throughout southeastern Asia and tropical Australia, this herb is thought to have a mild diuretic action, useful for flushing the kidneys and urinary tract in the treatment of kidney and bladder stones and urinary tract infections. It may relieve spasms of the smooth muscle in the walls of the internal organs. Researchers have found it to be mildly antiseptic as well.

Osmanthus fragrans (**sweet olive**) The flowers of this native Asian evergreen have an exquisite, apricot-like scent. Oil extracted from the plant is an expensive addition to perfumes worldwide. The flowers and leaves are made into a tea and can be used as a dye. **Note:** Sweet olive is not indicated for medicinal use.

P

Pandanus species (**pandan, pandan wangi, screw pine**) There are several *Pandanus* species, found in Africa, Asia, Australia and the Pacific Islands. These shrubs or small trees have long, narrow leaves that are used primarily for cooking, usually to flavour rice or desserts.

Papaver somniferum (**opium poppy**) The bulbous seedpod of this annual, native to southeastern Europe and western Asia, produces a milky-white latex. Opium latex is the basis of important pain-relieving pharmaceuticals (morphine, codeine) as well as addictive recreational drugs (heroin). Opium has been used medicinally for thousands of years, traditionally considered an analgesic, antidiarrhoeal, antispasmodic, aphrodisiac, astringent, diaphoretic, expectorant, narcotic and sedative. The ripe seedpods are also

the source of poppy seeds, used as a flavouring in cooking and baking. The cultivation of opium poppies is an illegal practice in many countries.

Passiflora incarnata (**maypop, passion flower**) This perennial vine grows naturally from southeastern North America to northern South America, and is cultivated in Europe. The blossoms were thought to resemble the crown of thorns Christ wore during his Biblical crucifixion, thus giving the plant one of its common names. *Passiflora* is also nicknamed maypop, mimicking the popping sound the fruit makes when mashed. Medicinally, passion flower has sedative properties, and may be used to treat insomnia, anxiety and nervousness.

Paullinia cupana (**guarana**) Guarana is a climbing perennial vine indigenous to the Amazon basin, found particularly in northern Brazil. A gum or paste is derived from the roasted, pulverized seeds, and used in beverages or herbal preparations. The seeds are high in caffeine, which speeds the heartbeat, relaxes blood vessels and opens bronchial airways. Guarana is taken to treat fatigue, headache and diarrhoea.

Perilla frutescens (**beefsteak plant, chiso**) This aromatic, weedy mint is a popular food and medicine in its native Asia. Traditionally used to alleviate symptoms of gout, it contains a compound that prevents the synthesis of uric acid.

Phyla scaberrima (**Aztec sweet herb, yerba dulce**) This creeping perennial is native to Central America, Mexico and the Caribbean. A 16th-century herbal text refers to its use by ancient Aztec people as an expectorant. Its essential oil has been found to contain more than 50 percent camphor, making the herb an effective treatment for coughs. Aztec sweet herb also stimulates the uterus, and has been used to bring on menstruation. Non-medicinally, the leaves contain a chemical that is much sweeter than refined table sugar but with a low calorific value, making the herb

Pandanus amaryllifolius
(pandan/screw pine)

Perilla frutescens
(chiso)

potentially useful as a sugar substitute. **Note:** This herb is not recommended for use by pregnant women.

Pilocarpus microphyllus (**jaborandi**) The name of this perennial shrub, native to Brazil, means "slobber weed". The surfaces of jaborandi leaves are sprinkled with translucent dots, glands that secrete an oil from which the alkaloid pilocarpine can be extracted. Pilocarpine affects the body's saliva, sweat and tear glands. The herb has been used to increase salivation in those with dry mouth. It has also been used in ophthalmology to contract the pupil to diagnose and treat early-stage glaucoma.

Pimenta dioica (**allspice, Jamaican pepper**) This evergreen tree is indigenous to South America and the West Indies, and is extensively grown in Jamaica. Its wood was once in such demand for the making of walking sticks that the tree was nearly extinct. Its dried berries are used to produce allspice, a common culinary flavouring that tastes like a mixture of cinnamon, cloves, nutmeg and pepper. The botanical name *Pimenta* is derived from the Spanish word for pepper, because the ripe fruits resemble peppercorns. Allspice has been used to treat ailments including indigestion, flatulence and muscle pain.

Pimpinella anisum (**anise, aniseed**) Anise, a member of the same family as parsley and carrots, is native to the eastern Mediterranean, western Asia and North Africa. The plant is cultivated in Europe, Asia and North America for its seeds, which are used medicinally and as a flavouring agent in cooking. Anise seeds are thought to relieve wind, bloating, nausea, bad breath and indigestion. They have antispasmodic and expectorant properties, which

Phyla scaberrima
(Aztec sweet herb)

may make them helpful in the treatment of menstrual cramps and respiratory complaints such as asthma, whooping cough and bronchitis.

Pimpinella major (**burnet-saxifrage, pimpernel**) This European perennial, a member of the carrot family, has been naturalized in North America. The plant's rancid-smelling root has astringent and cough suppressant properties. It is used to treat upper respiratory conditions such as bronchitis, laryngitis and sore throats.

Pinus sylvestris (**Scots pine**) Native to mountainous regions of Europe and northern and western Asia, this ever-green tree is now widely distributed throughout the Northern hemisphere. The leaves, branches, stems and seeds may have antiseptic, expectorant, anti-inflammatory and antioxidant properties. The herb has been used to treat upper respiratory conditions such as asthma and bronchitis, as well as arthritic and rheumatic problems, and digestive disorders such as wind.

Piper cubeba (**cubeb, Java pepper, tailed pepper**) Cubeb, a tropical southeastern Asian shrubby vine, bears berrylike fruits that can be used in cooking as a substitute for the more familiar black pepper, *Piper nigrum*. Cubeb berry is also used for its fragrance in soaps and perfumes. The herb has a stimulating effect on the mucous membranes of the urinary and respiratory tracts, and has been used in the treatment of urethritis, cystitis, prostate infections, chronic bronchitis and digestive ailments.

Pisum sativum (**pea, snap pea, snow pea**) This native Eurasian climbing annual vine is now cultivated all over the world. Its seeds, enrobed in an edible pod, are a commonly eaten vegetable. Peas contain genistein, which is thought to have cancer-fighting properties.

Podophyllum peltatum (**American mandrake, duck's foot, mayapple, ground lemon**) Mayapple is a small, unpleasant-smelling perennial native to northeastern North America. The plant takes its scientific name from the Greek words *podos* and *phyllon* (foot-shaped leaves); *peltatum* means "shieldlike." While mayapple's ripe fruit is edible, the unripe fruit, root, leaves and seeds can all be poisonous. The herb has a powerful laxative effect, so strong that it is considered unsafe for this use. It often is used as an ingredient in prescription pharmaceuticals used to treat genital warts. Research has found that mayapple may have tumour inhibiting properties. The herb has been included in prescription pharmaceuticals for treating several kinds of cancer. **Note:** Other than its ripe fruit, mayapple is extremely poisonous and should not be taken internally.

Pogostemon cablin
(patchouli)

Pogostemon cablin (**patchouli**) The essential oil of this fragrant perennial, native to India and Malaysia, has a rich, spicy scent that is said to improve with age. It is prized by perfumers, and used in aromatherapy to alleviate stress and depression, and is considered an aphrodisiac. The herb may have antibacterial and antifungal properties, and has been used topically to treat skin conditions such as dry or oily skin and scalp, acne and athlete's foot. It has been taken internally to treat digestive disorders, colds and fever.

Polygala senega (**milkwort, rattlesnake root, Seneca snakeroot, snakeroot**) A perennial indigenous to central and western North America, this plant contains a milky liquid (*Polygala* means "much milk"). Once valued by the Seneca Indians as a cure for rattlesnake bite, the dried root is more commonly used as an expectorant and decongestant, helpful in the treatment of upper respiratory conditions such as bronchitis, asthma, coughs and colds.

Polygonatum multiflorum, Polygonatum officinale (**Solomon's seal**) A relative of lily of the valley, this perennial is native to Europe and temperate regions of Asia and North America. According to legend, medieval herbalists believed that the scars on the plant's rootstock were placed there by the wise King Solomon as a testament to the plant's medicinal virtues. Each year, the rootstock produces a new stem that withers in the summer, leaving a scar resembling the wax stamps once used to seal letters. The plant's age can be estimated by counting the scars. Solomon's seal roots contain a substance called allantoin, which is used in modern medications for the external treatment of wounds, bruises and skin irritations.

Polygonum aviculare (**cow grass, knotgrass, pigweed**) Knotgrass is a sturdy annual plant, native to southeastern Asia. The Latin name *aviculare* comes from *aviculus*, meaning bird – a reference, perhaps, to the birds attracted to the plant's seeds. A member of the

buckwheat family, knotgrass has also served as food for cows, pigs and even humans. This herb is useful for treating respiratory ailments, from cough to bronchitis. It has astringent and diuretic properties, and is used to treat diarrhoea, staunch nosebleeds and bleeding wounds, and reduce heavy menstrual flow.

Polygonum odoratum (**rau ram, Vietnamese coriander, Vietnamese mint**) This European, Asian and North American perennial, a member of the buckwheat family, is a common ingredient in Vietnamese salads. Its flavour is evocative of coriander, with a strong, peppery aftertaste. It has anti-inflammatory and expectorant qualities, and has been used to treat throat and stomach irritations, heart disease and tuberculosis.

Populus species (**aspen, cottonwood, poplar**) Trees of the deciduous *Populus* genus can be found in Europe, Asia, North America and Africa. The leaves of many poplars, including cottonwoods and aspens, have laterally flattened stems, so the leaves are easily stirred by wind, giving the trees a "twinkling" appearance. The leaf buds contain salicylic acid (closely related to over-the-counter aspirin). Poplar buds have been made into tinctures, ointments and infusions, and used as anti-inflammatories and analgesics in the treatment of wounds and burns, haemorrhoids, frostbite and sunburn.

Portulaca oleracea (**purslane**) An annual native to India or the Middle East, this spinachlike leafy plant is eaten fresh or cooked throughout much of Europe and Asia. The herb is high in vitamin C and omega-3 fatty acids, the largest quantities of which are commonly found in cold-water fish, such as salmon. Omega-3s are believed to have a beneficial effect on blood pressure and circulation, cholesterol levels, and the immune system.

Potentilla anserina (**cinquefoil, potentilla, silverweed**) The *Potentilla* genus is derived from the Latin word *potens*, meaning powerful. Found in temperate and colder regions of the Northern hemisphere, silverweed is a low-growing perennial with an almondlike fragrance and a dry flavour. The plant contains

Polygonum odoratum
(Vietnamese coriander)

Prunella vulgaris
(self-heal)

Psidium guajava
(guava)

tannins, compounds that cause it to
have a tightening, astringent effect on
tissues of the body.

Prunella vulgaris (**self-heal**) Self-heal, a
member of the mint family, is native
to Europe and can be found in temperate regions worldwide. Its name
can be traced to a 16th-century
German fever, known as "the browns"
because it was characterized by a brown-
coated tongue. Self-heal was a common
treatment for the browns, and it became
known as *Bronella*, or *Pronella*, and
thus *Prunella*. Self-heal is rich in
rosmarinic acid, which regulates the
production of the thyroid hormone,
making it useful in the treatment of
overactive or underactive thyroid. It is
an immune-system stimulant, and has
anti-viral properties. It has been found
to have positive effects in the treatment of HIV/AIDS and herpes.
Self-heal soothes inflamed mucous
membranes, making it useful as a
treatment for diarrhoea. It has been
found to lower LDL ("bad") cholesterol, and may protect the liver.
Self-heal contains free radical-fighting,
anti-ageing antioxidants.

Prunus virginiana (**chokecherry**) This
North American shrub or small tree
bears a dark red, pea-sized fruit that is
edible but bitter tasting. The stones are
poisonous. Native American tribes
used chokecherry juice to treat sore
throat and diarrhoea. The bark was
used as a cold remedy. The roots were
used as a sedative and treatment
for stomach indigestion.

Psidium guajava (**guava**)
The guava tree is native
to tropical regions of Central
and South America. Its fruit
is high in vitamin C: in some
varieties, the vitamin C content
can be higher than five times that
of fresh orange juice. Guava leaves,
bark and fruit are rich in astringent
and antibiotic tannins. The leaves
and bark have been used to tan
hides and to make a black dye for
silk and cotton. The roots, leaves, bark
and fruits have been used as a treatment for gastrointestinal problems
such as diarrhoea and dysentery.

Pulmonaria officinalis (**lungwort**)
Lungwort is a perennial native to Europe
and the Caucasus region. As indicated
by both its botanical and common names,
the plant has a reputation for relieving
lung problems. The plant's white-spotted
leaves are even said to resemble a lung.
Lungwort has a high mucilage content,
and has been used to treat mild upper
respiratory problems such as bronchitis,
coughs and asthma.

Pulsatilla vulgaris syn. *Anemone pulsatilla*
(**pasqueflower, windflower, wild crocus**) This silky-haired plant grows wild
in the dry soils of northern and central
Europe. In Greek legend, the jealous
wife of the god Zephyr turned the
nymph Anenome into a flower, which
her husband abandoned to blow in the
wind. The flowers contain astringent
tannins and have antispasmodic qualities that are useful in the treatment
of menstrual cramps and tension.
Note: Pregnant women should avoid
ingesting this herb.

Punica granatum (**pomegranate**) The
pomegranate tree (or large shrub) is
native to central Asia, from Iran to
the Himalayas. It has been cultivated
since ancient times throughout the
Mediterranean regions of Asia, Africa
and Europe. The tree bears a fruit that
is technically a berry. It is filled with
crunchy seeds, each of which is encased
in red pulp. Pomegranate juice is
gaining popularity as an anti-aging,
free radical–fighting antioxidant.
Pomegranate's astringent root and stem
bark has been used to treat diarrhoea,
and as a nontoxic anthelminthic, rid-
ding the body of intestinal worms.

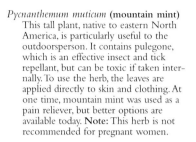

Punica granatum
(pomegranate)

Pycnanthemum muticum (**mountain mint**)
This tall plant, native to eastern North
America, is particularly useful to the
outdoorsperson. It contains pulegone,
which is an effective insect and tick
repellant, but can be toxic if taken internally. To use the herb, the leaves are
applied directly to skin and clothing. At
one time, mountain mint was used as a
pain reliever, but better options are
available today. **Note:** This herb is not
recommended for pregnant women.

Pyrus communis (**pear**) The pear tree,
native to Europe and western Asia, bears
a fruit that may contain agents that
stimulate the immune system. For this
reason, eating pears is often recommended to those suffering immune
system-related illnesses such as shingles
and AIDS. Pears can be eaten raw,
cooked or juiced.

Q

Quercus alba, Quercus robur (**white oak,
English oak**) Of the hundreds of species
found in the Northern hemisphere,
Quercus alba is most valued in North
America, while *Quercus robur* is common in Europe. The bark of this deciduous tree is a jack-of-all-trades astringent. Made into a gargle or brewed as
a tea, it may reduce the inflammation
of laryngitis and tonsillitis. A slightly
weaker tea or liquid extract can be
taken to treat diarrhoea. Oak bark can
be applied topically as a treatment for
minor wounds, inflamed haemorrhoids
and skin conditions including eczema
and shingles lesions. In Europe, a commercial oak bark preparation is used to
treat kidney stones.

R

Ranunculus ficaria (**figwort, lesser
celandine, pilewort, smallwort**)
Native to Europe and western Asia,
this perennial takes one of its common
names from its use as a remedy for
haemorrhoids, or piles. Lesser
celandine is an effective astringent
that may reduce inflammation. The
herb has been used as a bath additive
to treat wounds, warts and scratches.
Although rich in vitamin C, the plant
can be toxic when taken internally
and is therefore not a good choice as
a dietary supplement.

Rauvolfia serpentina (**Indian snakeroot,
serpentwood**) There are more than
100 species of *Rauvolfia* (named after a
16th-century German physician and
explorer, Dr. Leonhard Rauwolf)
growing in moist tropical forests of the
Pacific region, South America, Asia

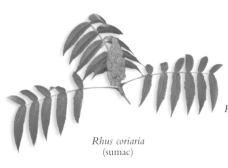

Rhus coriaria
(sumac)

and Africa. According to legend, holy men in India, including Mahatma Gandhi, chewed the root of serpent-wood to help achieve a state of philosophic detachment while meditating. In 1952, serpentwood was found to contain an alkaloid, called reserpine, which has powerful depressant and sedative properties. Reserpine was once the only drug available to calm seriously disturbed mental patients. Other tranquillizers have since taken over reserpine's role in mental health therapy, but it is still commonly prescribed to treat hypertension.

Rhamnus cathartica (buckthorn) This shrub or small tree is native to Eurasia and Africa, and naturalized to North America. It contains powerful compounds that stimulate the colon, reducing water absorption by the intestines by moving food more quickly through them. This softens stools, easing constipation.

Rhamnus purshiana (cascara sagrada, sacred bark) This deciduous tree originated in the Pacific Northwest region of the United States, but was given its common name, which translates to "sacred bark", by 17th-century Spanish explorers. The bark of the tree contains a gentle laxative that stimulates contractions of the large intestine that move food through the digestive system. This helps the body produce a softer, quicker bowel movement, because the intestine has had less chance to absorb the liquid from the stool. Today,

Rubia tinctorum
(common madder)

numerous over-the-counter laxatives include cascara sagrada as a key ingredient. Before use, the bark must be cured for at least one year or heated and dried to speed up the aging process. Aging is essential because the fresh bark is very irritating to the gastrointestinal system, causing vomiting and intestinal spasms.

Rhus coriaria (sumac, Sicilian sumac, Tanner's sumac) The name sumac is derived from the Aramaic word for "dark red", a reference to the berries of this bushy native Mediterranean shrub. While sumac (a relative of poison ivy) is used mainly as an ornamental plant in the West, in Middle Eastern countries it is grown for culinary purposes. Dried ground sumac berries are prized for their astringent, sour taste. They are one of the components of za'tar, a spice blend popular in Turkey and North Africa. Sumac berries may have diuretic properties, and have been used to treat bowel complaints and to reduce fever.

Ribes nigrum (blackcurrant) Blackcurrant is a perennial shrub native to Europe and Asia and naturalized in North America. It bears small, soft, dark purple berries that have traditionally been used for jams, pies, brandy, wine and the French liqueur cassis. The berries have astringent and antibacterial properties, and blackcurrant juice and leaf tea have been used to treat sore throats, tonsillitis and coughs. The seeds contain gamma-linolenic acid (GLA), an omega-6 fatty acid that helps the body make a hormonelike substance called prostaglandin, which may have anti-inflammatory properties.

Ricinus communis (castor oil plant) The castor oil plant, a global tropical weed, is cultivated for the oil it produces in its seeds, or beans. The beans contain the protein ricin, which is said to be one of the most toxic natural poisons. This poison is destroyed in the process of extracting oil from the beans. Castor oil has long been used as a laxative. It may also be applied topically as a moisturizer and to treat skin inflammations and warts. **Note:** Castor oil is not recommended for pregnant and breastfeeding women and young children. The beans should never be taken internally.

Rubia tinctorum (common madder) The root of this southwestern Asian perennial has been used since ancient times to make a red dye, alizarin. Madder began to fall out of use in 1869, when scientists were able to synthesize artificial alizarin. Madder root is still used in medical testing to colour bones and fluids for study.

Rubus canadensis, Rubus fruticosus (blackberry, bramble) The prickly stemmed blackberry bush, which grows wild

across parts of Europe (*R. fruticosus*) and North America (*R. canadensis*), produces a midnight-coloured fruit, which is eaten fresh or cooked in baked goods and jams. The Ancient Greeks called it "goutberry" because it was used to lessen gout-related joint pain. Today, blackberry is taken as a treatment for diarrhoea. The leaves and roots contain antibacterial and astringent tannins, which tighten mucous membrane tissue along the intestinal tract, minimizing watery stools. Cooled blackberry tea is also useful as a gargle for inflamed sore throats, and as a topical compress for soothing varicose veins and haemorrhoids. In addition, the berries contain antioxidants, which may help destroy the free-radical molecules associated with the development of heart disease and cancer.

Rubus idaeus (raspberry) Native to Europe and Asia and naturalized in North America, this bushy plant produces red berries that can be eaten fresh or used in baked goods and jams. The leaves of the plant contain antibacterial and astringent tannins, and can be made into a tea used to treat indigestion and diarrhoea, lessen menstrual cramps and alleviate morning sickness. Raspberry leaf tea has also been used as a mouthwash and gargle. It should not be used in early pregnancy.

Rudbeckia hirta (black-eyed Susan) This daisylike wildflower, with bright yellow petals surrounding a black centre, is a perennial native to the eastern United States. Studies have shown that its root extract has a beneficial ability to stimulate the immune system.

Rumex crispus (curled dock, yellow dock) The botanical name of this green-yellow native European perennial refers to the shape of the plant's leaves: *Rumex* means "lance" and *crispus* means "curly". Yellow dock root has been taken internally as a laxative, and used externally to provide relief from inflammatory skin conditions, boils, rashes and burns. The plant's roots contain iron, calcium and astringent/antibacterial tannins. Its edible leaves contain vitamins A and C.

Ruscus aculeatus (box holly, butcher's broom, pettigree) The tough stems of this evergreen bush, a relative of asparagus and native of the Mediterranean region, were once bundled and used as brooms. The plant's underground stem contains steroidlike compounds called saponins that can narrow blood vessels and help reduce inflammation. Butcher's broom has been used externally to treat haemorrhoids. It has also been used to relieve the discomforts of varicose veins and the circulatory condition chronic venous insufficiency, including cramps, pain, itching and swelling caused by pooling of blood in the veins.

Rudbeckia hirta
(black-eyed Susan)

Rumex crispus
(yellow dock)

S

Santolina chamaecyparissus (**cotton lavender, lavender cotton, santolina**)
The aromatic leaves of this native Mediterranean evergreen shrub have a sage-like scent. The herb has been taken internally to treat poor digestion and menstrual problems, such as cramps, and to kill intestinal worms in children. Topically, it has been used to ease the pain of insect stings or bites. The leaves can flavour sauces and soups, and may be dried for use in potpourris.

Saponaria officinalis (**bouncing Bet, soapwort**) Native to temperate regions of Europe, Asia and North America, this perennial has roots that produce suds when rubbed in water. Soapwort root has been used as a mild detergent, and was once added to beer to create a frothy head. The root may have anti-bacterial and expectorant properties. In folk medicine, it has been taken internally to treat upper respiratory conditions such as cough and bronchitis, and applied externally to treat skin problems such as eczema, psoriasis, acne and poison ivy.

Sassafras albidum (**sassafras**) The sassafras tree is native to eastern North America. Its root bark (once used to flavour root beer, a popular American

carbonated beverage) contains a volatile oil called safrole, which has been found to be carcinogenic in animal studies. Although the herb should not be taken internally, it has been used externally to treat skin irritations such as eczema, psoriasis, and poison oak and ivy.

Scutellaria lateriflora (**blue pimpernel, mad dog weed, skullcap**) This perennial, a member of the mint family, is native to North America. Skullcap's botanical name refers to its dislike flower: *scutella* means dish. The herb was once thought to cure rabies, earning it the name "mad dog weed". Skullcap has a mild sedative effect and has been used in the treatment of anxiety and insomnia. It may also have the ability to calm spasms and reduce inflammation, making it useful for the treatment of menstrual cramps and conditions in which nervous stress can cause muscular tension. A closely related European variety, *S. galericulata*, has similar properties. The properties of Chinese skullcap (*S. baicalensis*) are quite different: this herb contains a component that has been shown in studies to have protective actions on the liver. The herb has also been used to treat allergies and hayfever.

Sida cordifolia (**country mallow**) This small shrub is native to tropical India and Nepal. It contains ephedrine, an alkaloid that stimulates the cardiovascular and central nervous systems. Ephedrine is also a decongestant and bronchodilator, making this herb useful in the treatment of nasal congestion and upper respiratory conditions such as bronchitis and asthma.

Sida rhombifolia (**broomweed**) A relative of *S. cordifolia*, this herb may be native to the Canary Islands. It contains ephedrine, which is a stimulant and decongestant. Broomweed can be taken as a tea to revive someone who feels faint, and it helps to relieve the congestion of a cold.

Smilax species (**sarsaparilla**) A climbing vine native to Central and South America, sarsaparilla takes its name from the Spanish words for bramble (*sarza*) and vine (*parilla*). In the 19th century, sarsaparilla root was reputed to cure syphilis. Later, it became a flavouring agent in root beer, a popular American carbonated beverage. Sarsaparilla has been used to treat urinary tract infections, psoriasis and eczema, and rheumatism and rheumatoid arthritis. The herb contains steroidal saponins, which have been found in studies to produce anti-inflammatory and liver-protecting effects.

Solanum melongena (**aubergine, eggplant**) A member of the nightshade family, aubergine is native to southeastern Asia but is cultivated worldwide as a garden

vegetable. The plant produces a beautiful, dark purple (occasionally white) fruit, rich in vitamin C. Aubergine may contain components that lessen the constriction of bronchial tubes, making it a good food to be eaten by asthmatics. The fruit may also act as a topical analgesic, and has been applied externally to soothe minor skin irritations such as sunburn.

Solanum nigrum (**black nightshade**) Black nightshade is part of a genus of nearly 1,500 species, many of which are toxic. Before they ripen, the fruits of this plant contain a poisonous alkaloid. Black nightshade berries were once cultivated and marketed as medicinal "wonderberries," used to treat such ailments as dropsy, gastritis and general inflammation of mucous membranes.

Solanum tuberosum (**potato**) The common garden potato, an annual native to South America, is cultivated worldwide for its edible, starchy tuber. The blossoms, seeds, sprouts, vine and unripe (green) tubers contain solanine, an alkaloid that can be poisonous when consumed in large quantities. In folk medicine, the tuber is believed to have anti-inflammatory properties. A raw slice of potato can be applied topically to relieve the bruising and swelling of a black eye. The tuber's peel can be applied to a stye (small growth on or near the eyelid).

Solidago species (**goldenrod**) There are more than 130 species of goldenrod, a fast-growing perennial weed with yellow flowers that can be found throughout North America, Europe, northern Africa and some parts of Asia. Goldenrod is commonly thought to be an intensely allergenic plant because it blooms at the same time and often in the same locations as the truly allergenic ragweed. During the American Revolutionary War, colonists used goldenrod as a substitute for British-taxed black tea, calling it "liberty tea". Goldenrod has diuretic properties, and has been used to treat kidney and bladder stones as well as infections by increasing the body's output of urine.

Sorbus aucuparia (**mountain ash, rowan**) This deciduous tree, native to Europe and naturalized to North America, was once associated with witchcraft. It yields orange red berries (similar in taste to cranberries) and bark that can be taken as a tea to treat diarrhoea. The ripe berries have astringent properties and can be used in gargles to soothe sore throats and as topical preparations to treat haemorrhoids.

Stillingia sylvatica (**queen's delight, stillingia, yaw root**) This leathery-leaved perennial is native to North America. The root was once a popular home remedy, taken as a laxative, an emetic, an expectorant and as a treatment for syphilis. The fresh root may be taken to treat constipation and upper respiratory conditions such as bronchitis.

Strychnos nux-vomica (**nux-vomica, strychnine**) The evergreen strychnine tree is native to southeastern Asia. The seeds of its berries contain strychnine, a poison that is both a stimulant and a convulsant (agent that causes uncontrolled spasms). When the Egyptian queen Cleopatra decided to commit suicide, she reportedly used her slaves to test the effects of different poisons, including the seed of the strychnine tree. Today, doctors may give strychnine in controlled doses to increase muscular activity and as an antidote to poisoning caused by nervous system depressants, such as alcohol. **Note:** Strychnine is toxic, and should be used only under medical supervision.

T

Tanacetum vulgare (**tansy**) This perennial is native to Europe and naturalized in North America. In Greek mythology, it was said to have given immortality to Ganymede, the cup bearer of the gods. The herb's common name comes from the Greek word for immortality, *athanasia*. Because of its strong odour, tansy is a natural insect repellent. In the Middle Ages, dried tansy was strewn on the floor, hung from rafters, and packed between bed sheets and mattresses to discourage lice, flies and other vermin. The plant contains varying levels of toxic thujone. It has been used to relieve indigestion, rid the body of intestinal worms, and induce abortion. **Note:** Even in small amounts, this herb is highly poisonous. Its use is not recommended.

Tasmania lanceolata (**mountain pepper berry, Tasmanian pepper leaf**) This aromatic evergreen shrub, native to Australia, produces pungent berries that are dried and used as a spice by native Australian Aborigines. The berries have an intensely strong, pepperlike bite. The leaves, which are milder, are also used as a culinary flavouring. Medicinally, the plant has been used to relieve indigestion and colic.

Terminalia catappa (**Indian almond**) A deciduous tree native to India, the Indian almond produces nutty fruits that taste much like commercially grown almonds. Animal studies have shown that Indian almond may help shrink tumours and treat liver disease. A tea made from the leaves has been used to treat ailments including dysentery, stomach upset, indigestion and diarrhoea. The leaves,

which may have antibacterial properties, are used in tropical aquariums to help keep fish healthy.

Teucrium chamaedrys (**wall germander**) Wall germander, a native European perennial, looks like a miniature hedge and was once known as "poor man's box" because it could be substituted in gardens for the more expensive *Boxus*. The plant is a common addition to formal herb gardens. Medicinally, it has been used to treat gout. **Note:** *Teucrium* can cause liver failure and is not recommended for use.

Thymbra spicata (**zatar**) Native to the Middle East, zatar is a culinary herb with a thymelike flavour. It is used to flavour a variety of foods, including bread, meat and condiments.

Tilia species (**basswood, common lime, linden**) There are about thirty species of *Tilia*, a deciduous tree native to Europe, Asia and eastern North America. The tree is prized for its wood, which is used to make the sounding boards of pianos. Though the linden is not related to the citrus lime fruit, it produces a fragrant flower called lime blossom. Lime blossom is an important herb for beekeepers, as it produces a richly flavoured honey. Linden flowers have several medicinal properties: they loosen phlegm, flush excess water from the body, soothe irritation and promote sweating. The herb has been used to treat indigestion, anxiety, the common cold and bronchitis.

Trigonella foenum-graecum (**fenugreek**) Originally native to southeastern Europe and western Asia, fenugreek grows today in many parts of the world, including India, northern Africa and North America. The ripe, dried seeds are commonly used as a spice in Asian and African cuisines. Medicinally, fenugreek has been used to treat indigestion and upper respiratory conditions such as bronchitis. The herb has a soothing effect on the skin and has been used externally to treat conditions such as boils, ulcers, hives and eczema. Studies have shown that fenugreek

Tanacetum vulgare
(tansy)

Teucrium chamaedrys
(wall germander)

may help lower cholesterol levels; it may be useful to type 2 diabetics as an aid in regulating blood sugar levels.

Triticum aestivum (**wheat**) Thought to be native to the Middle East, this sturdy grass is cultivated worldwide for its edible seed, which is ground into flour. There are many wheat species, but *T. aestivum* is the highest-yielding and widest-ranging. Whole wheat, wheat bran and wheat germ provide dietary fibre that can help maintain gastrointestinal health. The young, green grass, or sprouted seeds, can be made into a juice that is taken as a dietary supplement. Wheat grass may have antioxidant effects and is a source of vitamins, minerals, amino acids and chlorophyll, which may prevent the absorption of carcinogens in the intestines.

Tropaeolum majus (**nasturtium**) Native to Peru, this vinelike annual produces a fragrant, vibrantly coloured flower. The plant was brought to Spain by conquistadores in the 1500s. The blossoms have a high vitamin C content, making them good for preventing colds. Nasturtium has been used to soothe respiratory tract conditions, such as bronchitis and sore throat.

Tussilago farfara (**coltsfoot, coughwort, cough plant, horse hoof**) This groundhugging native European perennial takes part of its botanical name from *tussis*, the Latin word for cough. For centuries, this plant's dried roots, yellow flowers, and hoof-shaped leaves have been used to suppress dry coughs, soothe sore throats and ease respiratory conditions such as asthma, bronchitis and laryngitis. Coltsfoot contains mucilage, which coats mucous membranes and protects them against irritants. The herb may also suppress the body's production of a blood protein that triggers the narrowing of air passages, prompting asthmatic wheezing. The mucilage in coltsfoot also makes it useful as a topical ointment applied to insect bites, burns and skin inflammations. **Note:** Coltsfoot contains alkaloids that may damage the liver. Its use is not recommended.

Typha latifolia (**cattail, great reedmace**) This tall perennial is found in shallow, standing water at the edges of ponds, rivers, and lakes in Europe, Asia, Africa and North America. At the top of each

Tussilago farfara
(coltsfoot)

cattail stem are thousands of tiny brown flowers, compressed into a compact mass. The root, stems, flowers, leaves and pollen may all have medicinal properties: Cattail improves circulation, stems bleeding and acts as a diuretic. The herb has been used to treat haemorrhoids, angina and post-birth bleeding. The pollen has been applied externally to treat tapeworms and diarrhoea. Interestingly, the pollen, which is highly inflammable, was once used to make fireworks.

V

Verbascum thapsus (**mullein, torch weed**) There are more than 360 species of this perennial roadside weed, native to Asia and Europe and naturalized in North America. Mullein is often called torch weed because its rigid, 6-foot tall (2 m) stem could be soaked in oil and used as a torch. The plant's leaves and flowers contain antibacterial and astringent tannins and soothing mucilage, making the herb a useful treatment for respiratory conditions, such as bronchitis and cough, and also skin conditions.

Verbena hastata (**blue vervain**) North American blue vervain, a biennial with deep blue flowers, has been used historically as a mild sedative and to reduce fevers and relieve congestion. **Note:** This herb is not recommended for use during pregnancy or lactation.

Verbena officinalis (**European verbena, vervain**) There are more than 250 species of vervain. *V. officinalis* is native to Europe, Asia and Africa, and naturalized to North America. Its name is derived from the ancient Celtic words *fer* (to drive away) and *faen* (stone), reflecting a belief in the herb's ability to treat kidney stones. Vervain is sometimes recommended for the treatment of coughs, bronchitis and sore throats. It may have the ability to clear bronchial passages, stimulate the digestive system, stimulate production of breast milk, flush excess water from the body, reduce inflammation and relieve anxiety.

Viburnum prunifolium (**black haw**) Native to North America, this deciduous shrub or small tree has antispasmodic and astringent properties. It has been used to alleviate the pain of menstrual cramps, low backache, and dysmenorrhoea. It may also halt early miscarriage, reduce blood pressure and calm the nerves.

Vicia faba (**broad bean, fava bean**) Native to northern Africa and southwestern Asia, the broad bean is among the most ancient cultivated plants. Along with lentils and chickpeas, broad beans became part of the eastern Mediterranean diet around 6000 B.C.E. The bean is still extensively grown for its edible seeds and young pods. In Italy, broad beans are traditionally sown on All Souls Day, and are thus known as the "beans of the dead". Some people carry a broad bean for good luck in the belief that having one means one will never lack the essentials of life. Broad beans are high in lethicin and choline, said to be useful for enhancing brain function. **Note:** Broad beans should not be eaten by people with the inherited condition glucose-6-phosphate dehydrogenase deficiency (G6PD, or "favism").

Vinca minor (**lesser periwinkle**) Originating in Europe, this ground-hugging evergreen shrub can also be found in northwestern Africa, central Asia and some parts of North America. In the Middle Ages, periwinkle was associated with magic and called "sorcerer's violet" for its purple blue flowers. This herb has probably been used in medicine for a long time; its botanical name, *Vinca,* is derived from the Latin word *vincere,* meaning "to overcome". Periwinkle contains astringent and antibiotic tannins and an alkaloid called vincamine. It has been used to staunch excessive blood flow, such as heavy menstruation and gum- and nosebleeds.

Viscum album (**mistletoe**) Mistletoe is a semiparasitic plant that lives on trees in northern Europe and Asia, tapping water and nutrients from its host. According to folklore, the wood of the cross carried by Jesus was made from mistletoe. The plant was therefore "punished" by being forced to depend

Verbena officinalis
(European verbena, vervain)

on other plants for survival. The Christmas holiday custom of kissing beneath a sprig of mistletoe may come from the plant's alleged power to increase fertility, or it may be a remnant of pagan orgies once held before mistletoe altars. The name mistletoe is said to derive from the Celtic word for "all heal", and the plant was indeed used for a variety of medicinal purposes. Mistletoe is believed to have a calming effect on the body, and has been used to lower blood pressure, improve circulation and relax tight muscles. It is being studied as a treatment for breast, colon, cervix, rectum and stomach cancer: supporters claim that mistletoe-based preparations stimulate the release of immune-system cells that kill cancer cells in the body. **Note:** Use only under the direction of a qualified health practitioner.

Z

Zanthoxylum americanum (**northern prickly ash, toothache tree**) There are between twenty and thirty prickly ash species. This North American native (and its close relative, *Z. clava-herculis* or southern prickly ash) was used by Native Americans as a remedy for toothache and rheumatism. The herb is believed to stimulate blood flow to painful and stiff joints, increasing the supply of oxygen and nutrients to an infected area and removing waste. Prickly ash may also relieve dry mouth and lower blood pressure.

Zanthoxylum piperitum (**Sichuan pepper, Szechuan pepper**) Originating in the Sichuan province of China, this tree, a relative of the North American prickly ash, produces berries that resemble black peppercorns. The berries are dry roasted to release their flavour, then used whole or ground into powder. An essential ingredient in Chinese five-spice powder, Sichuan pepper is also used in Japanese cooking and in the cuisines of Himalayan countries such as Tibet and Bhutan. The berries may have carminative and antispasmodic properties.

Zea mays (**maize, sweetcorn**) Maize, a grain-producing annual cultivated around the world, is believed to have originated in Central America 7,500 to 12,000 years ago. The genus name, *Zea,* means "cause of life"; *mays* means "mother". The plant's fruit (its cob, or ear) is eaten as a vegetable and also ground into flour or pressed for oil and sweet syrup. Beneath the husk that covers each ear of maize is a layer of "silk", a hairlike tassle that has diuretic properties. It is used to treat conditions involving the kidneys and urinary tract such as oedema (water retention) and urinary tract infection.

Ailment-to-Herb Charts

These charts present an A to Z listing of common ailments and their herbal treatments. The list of herbs that accompanies each condition is arranged in alphabetical order. Some of the herbs are generally considered most effective, for instance, in the treatment of Chronic Fatigue, lomatium (*Lomatium dissectum*) is more effective than St John's wort (*Hypericum perforatum*), which in turn is more effective than shiitake mushroom (*Lentinula edodes*). However, all three herbs are considered appropriate treatment for the condition. Specific preparation and dosage information for each herb and ailment is provided in the Gallery of Herbs, which begins on page 192. The dosage recommendations provided are those supported by clinical evidence and research whenever possible. In cases where clinical research on the herb is limited, the dosage information is taken from traditional or historical use.

No matter what the ailment or herb, it is wise to consult a healthcare provider before taking any herbal remedy, especially if it may be taken in combination with other drugs or supplements.

GENERAL AILMENTS

AGEING
ashwagandha (*Withania somnifera*) pp.323-4
ginkgo (*Ginkgo biloba*), pp.242-3
grape (*Vitis vinifera*), p.323
olive (*Olea europaea*), p.273

CHILLS
cayenne (*Capsicum annuum*), pp.215-16

CHRONIC FATIGUE
lomatium (*Lomatium dissectum*), p.345
St John's wort (*Hypericum perforatum*), p.251
shiitake mushroom (*Lentinula edodes*), p.260

COLDS AND FLU
cinnamon (*Cinnamomum spp.*), p.221
echinacea (*Echinacea spp.*), p.234
elderberry (*Sambucus nigra*), pp.292-3
ephedra (*Ephedra sinica*), pp.235-6
eucalyptus (*Eucalyptus globulus*), pp.236-7
ginger (*Zingiber officinale*), p.325
honeysuckle (*Lonicera spp.*), p.262
hyssop (*Hyssopus officinalis*), p.252

DEPRESSION
basil (*Ocimum basilicum*), pp.270-1
damiana (*Turnera diffusa*), pp.314-15
lavender (*Lavandula spp.*), pp.258-9
lemon balm (*Melissa officinalis*), p.264
maté (*Ilex paraguarensis*), pp.252-3
patchouli (*Pogostemon cablin*), p.348
rose (*Rosa spp.*), pp.288-9
St John's wort (*Hypericum perforatum*), p.251
yerba maté (*Ilex paraguarensis*), pp.252-3

FEVER
avens (*Geum urbanum*), p.348
catnip (*Nepeta cataria*), p.269
European elder (*Sambucus nigra*), pp.292-3
honeysuckle (*Lonicera spp.*), p.262
hyssop (*Hyssopus officinalis*), p.252
lemon balm (*Melissa officinalis*), p.264

lemon verbena (*Aloysia triphylla*), p.202
meadowsweet (*Filipendula ulmaria*), p.240
neem (*Azadirachta indica*), pp.207-8
sandalwood (*Santalum album*), p.297
willow (*Salix alba*), p.292

HANGOVER
evening primrose oil (*Oenothera biennis*), p.273
kudzu (*Pueraria lobata*), pp.285-6

IMMUNE SYSTEM WEAKNESS
astragalus (*Astragalus membranaceus*), p.337
blueberry (*Vaccinium corymbosum*), p.318
cat's claw (*Uncaria tomentosa*), p.315
echinacea (*Echinacea spp.*), p.234
shiitake mushroom (*Lentinus edodes*), p.260

INFECTION
cat's claw (*Uncaria tomentosa*), p.315
echinacea (*Echinacea spp.*), p.234
European elder (*Sambucus nigra*), pp.293-4
garlic (*Allium sativum*), pp.199-20
goldenseal (*Hydrastis canadensis*), pp.249-50
neem (*Azadirachta indica*), pp.207-8
tea tree (*Melaleuca alternifolia*), pp.263-4

INSOMNIA
hops (*Humulus lupulus*), pp.248-9
kava (*Piper methysticum*), pp.280-1
lavender (*Lavandula spp*), pp.258-9
passionflower (*Passiflora incarnata*), p.347
reishi (*Ganoderma lucidum*), pp.342-3
Roman chamomile (*Chamaemelum nobile*), pp.218-20
St John's wort (*Hypericum perforatum*), p.251
sandalwood oil (*Santalum album*), p.297
skullcap (*Scutellaria laterifora*), p.351
valerian (*Valeriana officinalis*), p.320

PAIN
bay oil (*Laurus nobilis*), p. 257

cayenne (*Capsicum frutescens*), pp.215-16
clove oil (*Syzygium aromaticum*), p.306
kava (*Piper methysticum*), p.280
meadowsweet (*Filipendula ulmaria*), p.240
sandalwood oil (*Santalum album*), p.297
St John's wort (*Hypericum perforatum*), p.251
willow (*Salix alba*), p.292
wintergreen (*Gaultheria procumbens*), p.343

STRESS AND ANXIETY
ashwagandha (*Withania somnifera*), pp.323-4
basil (*Ocimum basilicum*), pp.270-1
hops (*Humulus lupulus*), pp.248-9
kava (*Piper methysticum*), pp.280-1
lavender (*Lavandula spp.*), pp.258-9
lemon balm (*Melissa officinalis*), p.264
passionflower (*Passiflora incarnata*), p.347
reishi (*Ganoderma lucidum*), pp.342-3
Roman chamomile (*Chamaemelum nobile*), p.218-20
St John's wort (*Hypericum perforatum*), p.251
sandalwood oil (*Santalum album*), p.297
valerian (*Valeriana officinalis*), p.320

SUPERFICIAL WOUNDS
agrimony (*Agrimonia eupatoria*), pp.196-7
aloe vera (*Aloe vera*), p.x197
calendula (*Calendula officinalis*), p.212
cayenne (*Capsicum annuum*), pp.215-16
chaparral (*Larrea divaricata*), pp.256-7
cranesbill (*Geranium maculatum*), p.353
gotu kola (*Centella asiatica*), p.218
herb-Robert (*Geranium robertianum*), p.343
horsetail (*Equisetum arvense*), p.341
plantain (*Plantago major*), p.282
St John's wort (*Hypericum perforatum*), p.251
slippery elm (*Ulmus rubra*), p.315
tarragon (*Artemisia dracunculus*), pp.207-8
tea tree (*Melaleuca alternifolia*), pp.263-4
yarrow (*Achillea millefolium*), p.195

EARS, EYES, MOUTH, NOSE AND THROAT

ABSCESS
figwort (*Scrophularia nodosa*), p.299
slippery elm (*Ulmus rubra*), p.315

ALLERGY
ephedra (*Ephedra sinica*), pp.235-6
eyebright (*Euphrasia officinalis*), p.342
flaxseed (*Linum usitatissimum*), p.261
liquorice (*Glycyrrhiza glabra*), p.245
shiitake mushroom (*Lentinula edodes*), p.260
slippery elm (*Ulmus rubra*), p.315
stinging nettle (*Urtica dioica*), p.317

BAD BREATH
anise (*Pimpinella anisum*), pp.347-8
cardamom (*Elettaria cardamomum*), pp.234-5
dill (*Anethum graveolens*), p.203

CANKER SORE
cat's claw (*Uncaria tomentosa*), pp.315-16
echinacea (*Echinacea* spp.), p.234

CATARACT
bilberry (*Vaccinium myrtillus*), p.319
caper (*Capparis spinosa*), p.338

COLIC
caraway (*Carum carvi*), p.217
catnip (*Nepeta cataria*), p.269
dill (*Anethum graveolens*), p.203
fennel (*Foeniculum vulgare*), pp.238-9
hyssop (*Hyssopus officinalis*), p.253
lemon balm (*Melissa officinalis*), p.264
lovage (*Levisticum officinale*), pp.260-1
Roman chamomile (*Chamaemelum nobile*), pp.218-20
rooibos (*Aspalathus linearis*), p.337
wild yam (*Dioscorea villosa*), p.233

CONGESTION
anise hyssop (*Agastache foeniculum*), p.196
black pepper (*Piper nigrum*), pp.281-2
ephedra (*Ephedra sinica*), pp.235-6

horseradish (*Armoracia rusticana*), pp.205-6
mustard (*Brassica juncea*), pp.211-12
oregano oil (*Origanum vulgare*), p.275
red clover (*Trifolium pratense*), p.314
rosemary oil (*Rosmarinus officinalis*), pp.290-1
thyme (*Thymus vulgaris*), pp.312-13

CONJUNCTIVITIS
calendula (*Calendula officinalis*), p.212
eyebright (*Euphrasia officinalis*), p.342
fennel (*Foeniculum graecum*), pp.238-9

COUGHS
anise hyssop (*Agastache foeniculum*), p.197
basil (*Ocimum basilicum*), pp.270-1
bitter orange (*Citrus x aurantium*), pp.223-4
elecampane (*Inula helenium*), p.344
Iceland moss (*Cetraria islandica*), p.339
Irish moss (*Chondrus crispus*), p.245
liquorice (*Glycyrrhiza glabra*), p.245
lungwort (*Pulmonaria officinalis*), p.349
mullein (*Verbascum thapus*), p.353
onion (*Allium cepa*), pp.199-200
oregano (*Origanum vulgare*), pp.274-5
plantain (*Plantago major*), p.282
red clover (*Trifolium pratense*), p.314
slippery elm (*Ulmus rubra*), p.315
thyme (*Thymus vulgaris*), pp.312-13
violet (*Viola odorata*), pp.321-2

DRY MOUTH
jaborandi (*Pilocarpus microphyllus*) p.347
prickly ash (*Zanthoxylum americanum*), p.353
yohimbe (*Pausinystalia johimbe*), p.279

EARACHE
mullein (*Verbascum thapsus*), p.353
onion (*Allium cepa*), pp.199-200

EYEACHE
calendula (*Calendula officinalis*), p.212
fennel (*Foeniculum graecum*), pp.238-9
goldenseal (*Hydrastis canadensis*), pp.249-50

GINGIVITIS
bloodroot (*Sanguinaria canadensis*), p.298

GLAUCOMA
Hausa potato (*Coleus forskohlii*), pp.227-8
jaborandi (*Pilocarpus microphyllus*), p.347
marijuana (*Cannabis sativa*), p.338

LARYNGITIS
bloodroot (*Sanguinaria canadensis*), p.296
echinacea (*Echinacea* spp.), p.234
saw palmetto, (*Serenoa repens*), p.300
sweet marjoram (*Oregano majorana*), pp.274-5

MACULAR DEGENERATION
bilberry (*Vaccinum myrtillus*), p.319
ginkgo (*Ginkgo biloba*), pp.242-3

SINUSITIS
ephedra (*Ephedra sinica*), pp.235-6
European elder (*Sambucus nigra*), pp.292-3
goldenseal (*Hydrastis canadensis*), pp.249-50

SORE THROAT
bloodroot (*Sanguinaria canadensis*), p.298
echinacea (*Echinacea* spp.), p.234
ginger (*Zingiber officinalis*), p.325
Iceland moss (*Cetraria islandica*), p.339
marshmallow (*Althea officinalis*), p.335
myrrh (*Commiphora myrrha*), p.228
sage (*Salvia* spp), pp.294-5
slippery elm (*Ulmus rubra*), p.315
tea tree (*Melaleuca alternifolia*), pp.263-4
thyme (*Thymus vulgaris*), pp.312-13

TINNITUS
ginkgo (*Ginkgo biloba*), pp.242-3

TOOTHACHE
clove (*Syzygium aromaticum*), p.306

BRAIN AND NERVOUS SYSTEM

ALZHEIMER'S DISEASE
ginkgo biloba (*Ginkgo biloba*), pp.242-3

CARPAL TUNNEL SYNDROME
cayenne (*Capsicum annuum*), pp.215-16

DIZZINESS
wood betony (*Stachys betonica*), p.303

FAINTNESS
lavender (*Lavandula* spp), pp.358-9

HEADACHE
chamomile (*Chamaemelum nobile*), pp.218-20
feverfew (*Tanacetum parthenium*), pp.308-9
guaraná (*Paullinia cupana*), p347
lavender (*Lavandula* spp.), pp.358-9
linden (*Tilia* spp.), p.352
maté (*Ilex paraguariensis*), pp.252-3
rosemary (*Rosmarinus officinalis*), pp.290-1
skullcap (*Scutellaria lateriflora*), p.351
willow (*Salix alba*), p.292
wood betony (*Stachys betonica*), p.303

MIGRAINE
feverfew (*Tanacetum parthenium*), pp.308-9
ginger (*Zingiber officinale*), p.325

SHINGLES
cayenne (*Capsicum annuum*), pp.215-16

VERTIGO
kudzu (*Pueraria lobata*), p.285

SKIN AND HAIR

ACNE
burdock (*Arctium lappa*), p.205
dandelion (*Taraxacum officinale*), pp.309-10
evening primrose (*Oenothera biennis*), p.273
lemon (*Citrus sinensis*), pp.223-4
milk thistle (*Silybum marianum*), p.301
onion (*Allium cepa*), pp.199-200
tea tree (*Melaleuca alternifolia*), pp.263-4
vitex (*Vitex agnus-castus*), p.322

BALDNESS
rosemary oil (*Rosmarinus officinalis*), pp.290-1

BRUISES
arnica (*Arnica montana*), p.206
fennel (*Foeniculum graecum*), pp.238-9
horse chestnut (*Aesculus hippocastanum*), pp.195-6
St John's wort (*Hypericum perforatum*), p.251

BURNS
aloe vera (*Aloe vera*), p.197
calendula (*Calendula officinalis*), p.221
comfrey (*Symphytum officinale*), pp.304-6
ginger (*Zingiber officinale*), p.325
gotu kola (*Centella asiatica*), p.218
lavender (*Lavandula* spp.), pp.358-9
St John's wort (*Hypericum perforatum*), p.251

CUTS AND SCRAPES
aloe vera (*Aloe vera*), p.197
cinnamon (*Cinnamomum verum*), p.221
comfrey (*Symphytum officinale*), pp.304-6
shepherd's purse (*Capsella bursa-pastoris*), p.338
tea tree (*Melaleuca alternifolia*), pp.263-4
thyme (*Thymus vulgaris*), pp.312-13
witch hazel (*Hamamelis virginiana*), p.246

DANDRUFF
rosemary (*Rosmarinus officinalis*), pp.290-1

DRY SKIN
almond (*Prunus dulcis*), pp.284-5
borage (*Borago officinalis*), p.210
English walnut (*Juglans regia*), p.255
Indian frankincense (*Boswellia serrata*), pp.210-11

ECZEMA
chickweed (*Stellaria media*), pp.303-4
English walnut (*Juglans regia*), p.255
evening primrose (*Oenothera biennis*), p.273
figwort (*Scrophularia nodosa*), p.299
neem (*Azadirachta indica*), p.207-8
oats (*Avena sativa*), p.207

au d'arco (*Tabebuia impetiginosa*), p.307
red clover (*Trifolium pratense*), p.314
sarsaparilla (*Smilax* spp.), p.351

FUNGAL INFECTION
neem (*Azadirachta indica*), pp.207-8
pau d'arco (*Tabebuia impetiginosa*), p.307
poke (*Phytolacca americana*), p.180
tea tree (*Melaleuca alternifolia*), p.263-4

HERPES
anise hyssop (*Agastache foeniculum*), p.196
bergamot (*Monarda didyma*), p.268
bitter melon (*Momordica charantia*), p.346
Chinese peony (*Paeonia lactiflora*), p.276
lemon balm (*Melissa officinalis*), p.264
sweet marjoram (*Origanum majorana*), pp.274-5
witch hazel (*Hamamelis virginiana*), p.246

INSECT BITES AND STINGS
basil (*Ocimum basilicum*), pp.270-1
black horehound (*Ballota nigra*), p.337
costmary (*Chrysanthemum balsamita*), p.339
feverfew (*Tanacetum parathenium*), pp.308-9
French tarragon (*Artemisia dracunculus*), pp.206-7
lavender (*Lavandula* spp), pp.358-9
oregano (*Oreganum vulgare*), pp.274-5
plantain (*Plantago major*), p.282
witch hazel (*Hamamelis virginiana*), p.246

JAUNDICE
artichoke (*Cynara scolymus*), p.232
milk thistle (*Silybum marianum*), p.301
neem (*Azadirachta indica*), pp.207-8
oregano (*Oreganum vulgare*), pp.274-5

LICE
neem (*Azadirachta indica*), pp.207-8
tea tree (*Melaleuca alternifolia*), pp.263-4

LIGHTENING OF SKIN
strawberry (*Fragaria vesca*), pp.240-2

MEASLES
black cohosh, (*Cimicifuga racemosa* syn. *Actaea racemosa*), pp.220-1
eucalyptus (*Eucalyptus globulus*), pp.236-7

PLANT RASHES
aloe vera (*Aloe vera*), p.197
bitterroot (*Lewisia rediviva*), p.344

grindelia (*Grindelia species*), p.343
jewelweed (*Impatiens capensis*), p.343
sassafras (*Sassafras albidum*), p.351
soapwort (*Saponaria officinalis*), p.351

PSORIASIS
bishop's weed (*Ammi majus*), p.335
dandelion (*Taraxacum officinale*), pp.309-10
figwort (*Scrophularia nodosa*), p.299
milk thistle (*Silybum marianum*), p.301
mullein (*Verbascum thapsus*), p.353
Oregon grape (*Mahonia aquifolium*), p.345
pau d'arco (*Tabebuia impetiginosa*), p.307
red clover (*Trifolium pratense*), p.314
sarsaparilla (*Smilax* spp.), p.351

SNAKE BITE
echinacea (*Echinacea* spp.), p.234
milk thistle (*Silybum marianum*), p.301

SUNBURN
aloe vera (*Aloe vera*), p.197
black horehound (*Ballota nigra*), p.337
gotu kola (*Centella asiatica*), p.218
St John's wort (*Hypericum perforatum*), p.251
strawberry (*Fragaria vesca*), pp.240-2
tea (*Camellia sinensis*), p.214

VARICOSE VEINS
butcher's broom (*Ruscus aculeatus*), p.350
horse chestnut (*Aesculus hippocastanum*), pp.195-6
lemon (*Citrus x limon*), pp.222-5
milk thistle (*Silybum marianum*), p.301
St John's wort (*Hypericum perforatum*), p.251
witch hazel (*Hamamelis virginiana*), p.246

WARTS
bloodroot (*Sanguinaria canadensis*), p.296
celandine (*Chelidonium majus*), p.339
fig (*Ficus carica*), p.342
lemon (*Citrus limon*), pp.222-5
sundew (*Drosera rotundifola*), p.341

WRINKLES
Indian frankincense (*Boswellia serrata*), pp.210-11

BONES, JOINTS AND MUSCLES

ARTHRITIS
black cohosh (*Cimicifuga racemosa* syn.
 Actaea racemosa), pp.220-1
cat's claw (*Uncaria tomentosa*), pp.315-16
cayenne (*Capsicum annuum*), pp.215-16
celery (*Apium graveolens*), p.336
devil's claw (*Harpagophytum procumbens*),
 pp.246-8
ginger (*Zingiber officinale*), p.325
guggul (*Commiphora mukul*), p.228
horse chestnut (*Aesculus hippocastanum*),
 pp.195-6
Indian frankincense (*Boswellia serrata*),
 pp.210-11
sarsaparilla (*Smilax spp.*), p.351
stinging nettle (*Urtica dioica*), p.317
willow (*Salix alba*), p.292

BACKACHE
ginger (*Zingiber officinale*), p.325
willow (*Salix alba*), p.292

CRAMPS, INTESTINAL
coriander (*Coriandrum sativum*), pp.228-9
wild yam (*Dioscorea villosa*), p.233

CRAMPS, MUSCULAR
oregano (*Oreganum vulgare*), pp.274-5

CRAMPS, STOMACH
valerian (*Valeriana officinalis*), p.320
wild yam (*Dioscorea villosa*), p.233

GOUT
buchu (*Barosma crenulata*), pp.208-9
celery (*Apium graveolens*), p.336
lemon (*Citrus x limon*), pp.223-4
perilla (*Perilla frutescens*), p.347

INFLAMMATION
arnica (*Arnica montana*), p.206
betony (*Stachys betonica*), p.303
birch (*Betula pendula*), pp.209-10
borage seed oil (*Borago officinalis*), p.210
cat's claw (*Uncaria tomentosa*), pp.315-16
devil's claw (*Harpagophytum procumbens*),
 pp.247-8
flax (*Linum usitatissimum*), p.261
goldenseal (*Hydrastis canadensis*), pp.249-50
Indian frankincense (*Boswellia serrata*),
 pp.210-11
Hausa potato (*Coleus forskohlii*), pp.227-8
liquorice (*Glycyrrhiza glabra*), p.245
neem (*Azadiracta indica*), pp.207-8
pineapple (*Ananas comosus*), pp.202-3
rhubarb (*Rheum palmatum*), pp.286-8
Roman chamomile (*Chamaemelum*

nobile), pp.218-20
yarrow (*Achillea millefolium*), p.195

MUSCULAR TENSION
basil (*Occimum basilicum*), pp.270-1
kava (*Piper methysticum*), pp.280-1
meadowsweet (*Filipendula ulmaria*), p.240

OSTEOPOROSIS
red clover (*Trifolium pratense*), p.314
soy (*Glycine max*), pp.243-4

SCIATICA
rosemary oil (*Rosmarinus officinalis*), pp.290-1
St John's wort (*Hypericum perforatum*),
 p.251

SPASMS
lavender (*Lavandula officinalis*), pp.290-1
valerian (*Valeriana officinalis*), p.320
wild yam (*Dioscorea villosa),* p.233

SPRAINS
arnica (*Arnica montana*), p.206
cayenne (*Capsicum annuum*), pp.215-16
comfrey (*Symphytum officinale*), pp.304-6
ginger (*Zingiber officinale*), p.325

REPRODUCTIVE SYSTEM

AMENORRHOEA
feverfew (*Tanacetum parthenium*), pp.308-9
milk thistle (*Silybum marianum*), p.301
motherwort (*Leonurus cardiaca*), p.345
vitex (*Vitex agnus-castus*), p.322

ENLARGED PROSTATE
pumpkin seed (*Cucurbita pepo*), p.340
pygeum (*Pygeum africanum*), p.xxx
saw palmetto (*Serenoa repens*), p.300
tomato (*Lycopersicon esculentum*), pp.214-15

ERECTILE DYSFUNCTION
yohimbe (*Pausinystalia johimbe*), p.278

GENITAL HERPES
sweet marjoram (*Origanum majorana*),
 pp.274-5

IMPOTENCE
ashwagandha (*Withania somnifera*),
 pp.323-4
ginseng (*Panax ginseng*), p.277
maca (*Lepidium meyenii*), p.344
yohimbe (*Pausinystalia johimbe*), p.278

INFERTILITY
vitex (*Vitex agnus-castus*), p.322

LACK OF SEXUAL DESIRE
damiana (*Turnera diffusa*), pp.314-15
epimedium (*Epimedium species*), p.341
ginkgo (*Ginkgo biloba*), pp.242-3
quebracho (*Aspidosperma quebracho-blanco*),
 p.337
ylang-ylang (*Cananga odorata*), pp.214-15

MENOPAUSE
black cohosh (*Actaea racemosa*), pp.220-1
dong quai (*Angelica sinensis*), p.336
maca (*Lepidium meyenii*), p.344
red clover (*Trifolium pratense*), p.314
St John's wort (*Hypericum perforatum*), p.251
soy (*Glycine max*), pp.243-4
vitex (*Vitex agnus-castus*), p.322

MENORRHAGIA
cranesbill (*Geranium maculatum*), p.343
knotweed (*Polygonum aviculare*), p.348
lady's mantle (*Alchemilla vulgaris*), p.335
partridge berry (*Mitchella repens*), p.346

shepherd's purse (*Capsella bursa-pastoris*),
 p.338

MENSTRUAL CRAMPS
black haw (*Viburnum prunifolium*), p.353
blue cohosh (*Caulophyllum thalictroides*),
 p.338
Chinese peony (*Paeonia lactiflora*), p.277
oregano (*Oreganum vulgare*), pp.274-5
partridge berry (*Mitchella repens*), p.346
valerian (*Valeriana officinalis*), p.320
wild yam (*Dioscorea villosa*), p.233
willow (*Salix alba*), p.292
yarrow (*Achillea millefolium*), p.195

PREMENSTRUAL SYNDROME
evening primrose (*Oenothera biennis*), p.273
passionflower (*Passiflora incarnata*), p.347
skullcap (*Scutellaria lateriflora*), p.351
vitex (*Vitex agnus-castus*), p.322
walnut (*Juglans regia*), p.255

YEAST INFECTION
calendula (*Calendula officinalis*), p.212
lavender (*Lavandula officinalis*), pp.358-9
tea tree (*Melaleuca alternifolia*), pp.263-4

HEART, BLOOD AND LUNGS

ANAEMIA
ashwagandha (*Withania somnifera*), pp.323-4
dong quai (*Angelica sinensis*), p.336
gentian (*Gentiana lutea*), p.243
nettle (*Urtica dioica*), p.317

ANGINA
hawthorn (*Crataegus laevigata* syn. *C. oxyacantha*), pp.229-30

ASTHMA
angelica (*Angelica archangelica*), pp.203-4
bloodroot (*Sanguinaria canadensis*), p.296
ephedra (*Ephedra sinica*), pp.235-6
Hausa potato (*Coleus forskohlii*), pp.227-8
khella (*Ammi visnaga*), p.335
hyssop (*Hyssopus officinalis*), p.252
lobelia (*Lobelia inflata*), pp.344-5
lungwort (*Pulmonaria officinalis*), p.349
red root (*Ceanothus americanus*), p.338
Seneca snakeroot (*Polygala senega*), p.348
sundew (*Drosera rotundifola*), p.341

BRONCHITIS
angelica (*Angelica archangelica*), pp.203-4
bloodroot (*Sanguinaria canadensis*), p.296
cubeb (*Piper cubeba*), p.348
garlic (*Allium sativum*), pp.199-200
ginger (*Zingiber officinale*), p.325
grindelia (*Grindelia species*), p.343
hyssop (*Hyssopus officinalis*), p.252
Iceland moss (*Cetraria islandica*), p.339

lungwort (*Pulmonaria officinalis*), p.349
onion (*Allium cepa*), pp.199-200
oregano (*Origanum vulgare*), pp.274-5
pleurisy root (*Asclepias tuberosa*), pp.336-7
red clover (*Trifolium pratense*), p.314
red root (*Ceanothus americanus*), p.338
sundew (*Drosera rotundifola*), p.341
thyme (*Thymus vulgaris*), pp.312-13

CARDIAC ARRHYTHMIA
hawthorn (*Crataegus laevigata* syn. *C. oxyacantha*), pp.229-30
Peruvian bark (*Cinchona* spp.), p.339

EMPHYSEMA
bloodroot (*Sanguinaria canadensis*), p.296

HEART DISEASE
English walnut (*Juglans regia*), p.255
grape (*Vitis vinifera*), p.323
green tea (*Camellia sinensis*), p.214
hazelnut (*Corylus avellana*), p.340
soy (*Glycine max*), pp.243-4

HIGH BLOOD PRESSURE
evening primrose oil (*Oenothera biennis*), p.273
garlic (*Allium sativum*), pp.199-200

HIGH CHOLESTEROL
alfalfa (*Medicago sativa*), pp.345-6

almond (*Prunus dulcis*), pp.284-5
artichoke (*Cynara scolymus*), p.232
cat's claw (*Uncaria tomentosa*), pp.315-16
fenugreek (*Trigonella foenum-graecum*), p.352
flax (*Linum usitatissimum*), p.261
garlic (*Allium sativum*), pp.199-200
green tea (*Camellia sinensis*), p.214
guggul (*Commiphora mukul*), p.228
gymnema (*Gymnema sylvestre*), p.343
oats (*Avena sativa*), p.207
purslane (*Portulaca oleracea*), p. 348
reishi (*Ganoderma lucidum*), pp.342-3
shiitake mushroom (*Lentinula edodes*), p.260
turmeric (*Curcuma longa*), pp.230-1

OEDEMA
horse chestnut (*Aesculus hippocastanum*), pp.195-6
parsley (*Petroselinum crispum*), p.279

POOR CIRCULATION
bilberry (*Vaccinium myrtillus*), p.319
cayenne (*Capsicum annuum*), pp.215-16
cinnamon (*Cinnamomum* spp.), p.221
garlic (*Allium sativum*), pp.199-200
ginkgo (*Ginkgo biloba*), pp.242-3
grape (*Vitis vinifera*), p.323
hawthorn (*Crataegus laevigata*), pp.229-30
horse chestnut (*Aesculus hippocastanum*), pp.195-6
rosemary (*Rosmarinus officinalis*), pp.290-1

DIGESTIVE, ENDOCRINE AND URINARY SYSTEMS

BLADDER INFECTIONS
blueberry (*Vaccinium corymbosum*), p.318
buchu (*Agathosma crenulata*), pp.208-9
cranberry (*Vaccinium macrocarpon*), pp.318-19
horseradish (*Armoracia rusticana*), pp.205-6
nettle (*Urtica dioica*), p.317
parsley (*Petroselinum crispum*), p.279

CONSTIPATION
barberry (*Berberis vulgaris*), p.209
black pepper (*Piper nigrum*), pp.281-2
buckthorn (*Rhamnus cathartica*), p.350
cascara sagrada (*Rhamnus purshiana*), p.350
castor bean (*Ricinus communis*), p.350
Chinese rhubarb (*Rheum palmatum*), pp.286-8
damiana (*Turnera diffusa*), pp.314-15
flax (*Linum usitatissimum*), p.261
pineapple (*Ananas comosus*), p.202
senna (*Cassia senna*), pp.217-18
tamarind (*Tamarindus indica*), pp.307-8
yellow dock (*Rumex crispus*), p.350

DIABETES
aloe vera (*Aloe vera*), p.197
bitter melon (*Momordica charantia*), p.346
cinnamon (*Cinnamomum* spp.), p.221
fenugreek (*Trigonella foenum-graecum*), p.352
ginseng (*Panax* spp.), p.277
gymnema (*Gymnema sylvestre*), p.343
holy basil (*Ocimum sanctum*), pp.270-1
Madagascar periwinkle, (*Catharanthus roseus*), p.338
macadamia (*Macadamia integrifolia*), p.345
mulberry (*Morus alba*), p.346
neem (*Azadirachta indica*), pp.207-8
pau d'arco (*Tabebuia impetiginosa*), p.307

DIARRHOEA
blackberry (*Rubus fruticosus*), p.350
cinnamon (*Cinnamomum* spp.), p.221
coptis (*Coptis chinensis*), p.340
cranesbill (*Geranium maculatum*), p.343
nutmeg (*Myristica fragrans*), pp.268-9
salad burnet (*Sanguisorba minor*), pp.298-9

scented geranium (*Pelargonium* spp.), pp.278-9
slippery elm (*Ulmus rubra*), p.315
strawberry (*Fragaria vesca*), pp.240-2
summer savory (*Satureja hortensis*), p.298
witch hazel (*Hamamelis virginiana*), p.246

DYSENTERY
bilberry (*Vaccinum myrtillus*), p.319
cat's claw (*Uncaria tomentosa*), pp.315-16
ipecac (*Cephaelis ipecacuana*), p.338
oregano (*Oreganum vulgare*), pp.274-5
tamarind (*Tamarindus indica*), pp.307-8

FLATULENCE
anise (*Pimpinella anisum*), p.347
artichoke (*Cynara scolymus*), p.232
bitter orange (*Citrus x aurantium*), pp.223-4
caraway (*Carum carvi*), p.217
catnip (*Nepeta cataria*), p.269
dill (*Anethum graveolens*), p.203
fennel (*Foeniculum vulgare*), pp.238-9
peppermint (*Mentha x piperita*), pp.266-7

DIGESTIVE, ENDOCRINE AND URINARY SYSTEMS (CONT)

GALLSTONES AND KIDNEY STONES
artichoke (*Cynara scolymus*), p.232
birch (*Betula pendula*), p.209
coffee (*Coffea arabica*), p.227
coin-leaf desmodium (*Desmodium styracifolium*), p.341
couchgrass (*Elymus repens*), p.341
goldenrod (*Solidago* spp.), p.351
horsetail (*Equisetum arvense*), p.341
java tea (*Orthosiphon aristatus*), p.347
lemon (*Citrus limon*), pp.224-5
olive (*Olea europaea*), p.273
parsley (*Petroselinum crispum*), p.279
pipsissewa (*Chimaphila umbellata*), p.339

GASTRITIS
calendula (*Calendula officinalis*), p.212
meadowsweet (*Filipendula ulmaria*), p.240
slippery elm (*Ulmus rubra*), p.315

HAEMORRHOIDS
aloe vera (*Aloe vera*), p.197
avens (*Geum urbanum*), p.343
butcher's broom (*Ruscus aculeatus*), p.350
horse chestnut (*Aesculus hippocastanum*), pp.195-6
milk thistle (*Silybum marianum*), p.301
tarragon (*Artemisia dracunculus*), pp.206-7
witch hazel (*Hamamelis virginiana*), p.246

HEARTBURN
catnip (*Nepeta cataria*), p.269
slippery elm (*Ulmus rubra*), p.315

INDIGESTION
calamus (*Acorus calamus*), p.335
catnip (*Nepeta cataria*), p.269
cayenne (*Capsicum annuum*), pp.215-16
cinnamon (*Cinnamomum* spp.), p.221
elecampane (*Inula helenium*), p.344
gentian (*Gentiana lutea*), p.242
ginger (*Zingiber officinale*), p.325
goldenseal (*Hydrastis canadensis*), pp.249-50
hyssop (*Hyssopus officinalis*), p.252
lavender (*Lavandula* spp.), pp.358-9
lemon balm (*Melissa officinalis*), p.264
lovage (*Levisticum officinale*), pp.260-1
mugwort, (*Artemisia vulgaris*), pp.206-7

oregano (*Origanum vulgare*), pp.274-5
peppermint (*Mentha x piperita*), pp.266-7
Roman chamomile (*Chamaemelum nobile*), pp.218-20
saffron (*Crocus sativus*), p.230

INTESTINAL WORMS
basil (*Ocimum basilicum*), pp.270-1
eucalyptus (*Eucalyptus globulus*), pp.236-7
garlic (*Allium sativum*), pp.199-200
mugwort, (*Artemisia vulgaris*), pp.206-7
neem (*Azadirachta indica*), p.207-8
pomegranate (*Punica granatum*), p.349
tarragon (*Artemisia dracunculus*), pp.206-7
walnut (*Juglans regia*), p.255

LIVER AND GALLBLADDER DISEASE
artichoke (*Cynara scolymus*), p.232
barberry (*Berberis vulgaris*), p.209
burdock (*Arctium lappa*), p.205
cranberry (*Vaccinium macrocarpon*), pp.318-19
dandelion (*Taraxacum officinale*), pp.309-10
kudzu (*Pueraria lobata*), pp.285-6
liquorice (*Glycyrrhiza glabra*), p.245
milk thistle (*Silybum marianum*), p.301
schisandra (*Schisandra chinensis*), pp.298-9

NAUSEA AND VOMITING
artichoke (*Cynara scolymus*), p.232
basil (*Ocimum basilicum*), pp.270-1
ginger (*Zingiber officinale*), p.325
lavender (*Lavandula angustifolia*), pp.358-9
nutmeg (*Myristica fragrans*), pp.268-9
peppermint (*Mentha x piperita*), pp.266-7
Roman chamomile (*Chamaemelum nobile*), pp.218-20
spearmint (*Mentha spicata*), p.267

POOR APPETITE
bay (*Laurus nobilis*), p.257
blessed thistle (*Cnicus benedictus*), p.339
coriander (*Coriandrum sativum*), pp.228-9
devil's claw (*Harpagophytum procumbens*), pp.246-8
gentian (*Gentiana lutea*), p.243
goldenseal (*Hydrastis canadensis*) pp.249-50
lovage (*Levisticum officinale*), p.260-1
radish (*Raphanus sativum*), p.286

Roman chamomile (*Chamaemelum nobile*), pp.218-20
watercress (*Nasturtium officinale*), p.346

ULCER
aloe (*Aloe vera*), p.197
calendula (*Calendula officinalis*), p.212
cat's claw (*Uncaria tomentosa*), pp.315-16
ginger (*Zingiber officinale*), p.325
liquorice (*Glycyrrhiza glabra*), p.245
marshmallow (*Althea officinalis*), p. 335
meadowsweet (*Filipendula ulmaria*), p.240
papaya (*Carica papaya*), p.216
slippery elm (*Ulmus rubra*), p.315
turmeric (*Curcuma longa*), pp.230-1

URINARY TRACT INFECTION
bilberry (*Vaccinum myrtillus*), p.319
birch (*Betula pendula*), pp.209-10
buchu (*Agathosma betulina*), pp.208-9
cleavers (*Galium aparine*), p.342
corn silk (*Zea mays*), p.353
couchgrass (*Elymus repens*), p.341
cranberry (*Vaccinium macrocarpon*) pp.318-19
cubeb (*Piper cubeba*), p.x348
dill (*Anethum graveolens*), p.203
goldenrod (*Solidago* spp.), p.351
horseradish (*Armoracia rusticana*), pp.205-6
horsetail (*Equisetum arvense*), p.341
juniper (*Juniperus communis*), pp.255-6
Oregon grape (*Mahonia aquifolium*), p.x345
parsley (*Petroselinum crispum*), p.279
pipsissewa (*Chimaphila umbellata*), p.339
plantain (*Plantago major*), p.282
sandalwood oil (*Santalum album*), p. 297
strawberry (*Fragaria vesca*), pp.240-2
uva-ursi (*Arctostaphylos uva-ursi*), p.336

WATER RETENTION
buchu (*Agathosma betulina*), pp. 208-9
corn silk (*Zea mays*), p.353
dandelion (*Taraxacum officinale*), pp.309-10
guggul (*Commiphora mukul*), p.228
juniper (*Juniperus communis*), pp.255-6
mulberry (*Morus alba*), p.346
nettle (*Urtica dioica*), p.317
watercress (*Nasturtium officinale*), p.346

black pepper
Capsicum anuum

pineapple mint
M. sauvelens. 'Variegata'

oregano
Ocimum vulgare

walnut
Julans regia

Herb-to-Ailment Charts

These charts present an alphabetical listing (by common name) of popular medicinal herbs and the ailments they treat. For dosage information, refer to the individual herb's listing in the Gallery of Herbs, which begins on page 192.

HERB	PAGE	AILMENT
agrimony (*Agrimonia eupatoria*)	pp.196-7	superficial wounds
alfalfa (*Medicago sativa*)	pp.345-6	high blood pressure
almond (*Prunus dulcis*)	pp.284-5	dry skin, high cholesterol
aloe vera (*Aloe vera*)	p.197	burns, cuts and scrapes, diabetes, haemorrhoids, skin rashes, sunburn, superficial wounds, ulcer
angelica (*Angelica archangelica*)	pp.203-4	asthma, bronchitis
anise (*Pimpinella anisum*)	pp.347-8	bad breath, flatulence
anise hyssop (*Agastache foeniculum*)	p.196	congestion, coughs, herpes
arnica (*Arnica montana*)	p.206	bruises, inflammation, sprains
artichoke (*Cynara scolymus*)	p.232	flatulence, gallstones and kidney stones, high cholesterol, jaundice, liver and gallbladder disease, nausea and vomiting
ashwagandha (*Withania somnifera*)	pp.323-5	ageing, anaemia, impotence, stress and anxiety
astragalus (*Astragalus membranaceus*)	p.337	immune system weakness
avens (*Geum urbanum*)	p.343	fever, haemorrhoids
barberry (*Berberis vulgaris*)	p.209	constipation, liver and gallbladder disease
basil (*Ocimum basilicum*)	pp.270-1	congestion, coughs, depression, diabetes, insect bites and stings, intestinal worms, muscular tension, nausea and vomiting, stress and anxiety
bay (*Laurus nobilis*)	p.257	poor appetite
bay oil (*Laurus nobilis*)	p.257	pain
bergamot (*Monarda didyma*)	p.268	herpes
betony (*Stachys betonica*)	p.303	inflammation

HERB	PAGE	AILMENT
bilberry (*Vaccinium myrtillus*)	pp.318-19	cataract, dysentery, macular degeneration, poor circulation, urinary tract infection
birch (*Betula pendula*)	pp.209-10	gallstones and kidney stones, inflammation, urinary tract infection
bishop's weed (*Ammi majus*)	p.335	psoriasis
bitter orange (*Citrus x aurantium*)	pp.222-5	coughs, flatulence
bitter melon (*Momordica charantia*)	p.346	diabetes, herpes
bitterroot (*Lewisia rediviva*)	p.344	skin rashes
black cohosh (*Cimicifuga racemosa* syn. *Actaea racemosa*)	pp.220-1	arthritis, measles, menopause
black haw (*Viburnum prunifolium*)	p.353	menstrual cramps
black horehound (*Ballota nigra*)	p.337	insect bites and stings, sunburn
black pepper (*Piper nigrum*)	pp.281-2	congestion, constipation
blackberry (*Rubus fruticosus*)	p.350	diarrhoea
blessed thistle (*Cnicus benedictus*)	pp.339-40	poor appetite
bloodroot (*Sanguinaria canadensis*)	p.296	asthma, bronchitis, emphysema, gingivitis, laryngitis, sore throat, warts
blue cohosh (*Caulophyllum thalictroides*)	p.338	menstrual cramps
blueberry (*Vaccinium corymbosum*)	p.318	bladder infections, immune system weakness
borage (*Borago officinalis*)	p.210	dry skin
borage seed oil (*Borago officinalis*)	p.210	inflammation
buchu (*Barosma crenulata*)	pp.208-9	bladder infections, gout, urinary tract infection, water retention
buckthorn (*Rhamnus cathartica*)	p.350	*constipation*

HERB	PAGE	AILMENT
burdock (*Arctium lappa*)	p.205	acne, liver and gallbladder disease
butcher's broom (*Ruscus aculeatus*)	p.330	haemorrhoids, varicose veins
calamus (*Acorus calamus*)	p.335	indigestion
calendula (*Calendula officinalis*)	p.212	burns, conjunctivitis, eyeache, gastritis, superficial wounds, ulcer, yeast infection
caper (*Capparis spinosa*)	p.338	cataract
caraway (*Carum carvi*)	p.217	colic, flatulence
cardamon (*Elettaria cardamomum*)	p.234-5	bad breath
cascara sagrada (*Rhamnus purshiana*)	p.350	constipation
castor bean (*Ricinus communis*)	p.350	constipation
catnip (*Nepeta cataria*)	p.269	colic, fever, flatulence, heartburn, indigestion
cat's claw (*Uncaria tomentosa*)	pp.315-17	arthritis, canker sore, dysentery, high cholesterol, immune system weakness, infection, inflammation, ulcer
cayenne (*Capsicum annuum*)	pp.215-16	arthritis, carpal tunnel syndrome, chills, indigestion, pain, poor circulation, shingles, sprains, superficial wounds
celandine (*Chelidonium majus*)	p.339	warts
celery (*Apium graveolens*)	p.336	arthritis, gout
chamomile, Roman (*Chamaemelum nobile*)	pp.218-20	colic, headache, inflammation, indigestion, insomnia, nausea and vomiting, poor appetite, stress and anxiety
chaparral (*Larrea divaricata*)	pp.256-7	superficial wounds
chickweed (*Stellaria media*)	pp.303-5	eczema
Chinese peony (*Paeonia lactiflora*)	p.276	herpes, menstrual cramps
Chinese rhubarb (*Rheum palmatum*)	pp.286-8	constipation
cinnamon (*Cinnamomum spp.*)	p.221	colds and flu, cuts and scrapes, diabetes, diarrhoea, indigestion, poor circulation

HERB	PAGE	AILMENT
cleavers (*Galium aparine*)	p.342	urinary tract infection
clove oil (*Syzygium aromaticum*)	p.306	pain, toothache
coffee (*Coffea arabica*)	p.227	gallstones and kidney stones
coin-leaf desmodium (*Desmodium styracifolium*)	p.341	gallstones and kidney stones
comfrey (*Symphytum officinale*)	pp.304-6	burns, cuts and scrapes, sprains
coptis (*Coptis chinensis*)	p.340	diarrhoea
coriander (*Coriandrum sativum*)	pp.228-9	intestinal cramps, poor appetite
corn silk (*Zea mays*)	p.353	urinary tract infection, water retention
costmary (*Chrysanthemum balsamita*)	p.339	insect bites and stings
couchgrass (*Elymus repens*)	p.341	gallstones and kidney stones, urinary tract infections
cranberry (*Vaccinium macrocarpon*)	pp.318-19	bladder infections, liver and gallbladder disease, urinary tract infections
cranesbill (*Geranium maculatum*)	p.343	diarrhoea, menorrhagia, superficial wounds
cubeb (*Piper cubeba*)	p.348	bronchitis, urinary tract infections
damiana (*Turnera diffusa*)	pp.314-15	constipation, depression, lack of sexual desire
dandelion (*Taraxacum officinale*)	pp.309-10	acne, liver and gallbladder disease, psoriasis, water retention
devil's claw (*Harpagophytum procumbens*)	pp.246-8	arthritis, inflammation, poor appetite
dill (*Anethum graveolens*)	p.203	bad breath, colic, flatulence, urinary tract infections
dong quai (*Angelica sinensis*)	p.336	anaemia, menopause
echinacea (*Echinacea spp.*)	p.234	canker sore, colds and flu, immune system weakness, infection, laryngitis, snakebite, sore throat, toothache
elder, European (*Sambucus nigra*)	pp.292-3	fever, infection, sinusitis

HERB	PAGE	AILMENT
elderberry (*Sambucus nigra*)	pp.292-3	colds and flu
elecampane (*Inula helenium*)	p.344	cough, indigestion
English walnut (*Juglans regia*)	p.255	dry skin, eczema, heart disease, intestinal worms
ephedra (*Ephedra sinica*)	pp.235-6	allergies, asthma, colds and flu, congestion, sinusitis
epimedium (*Epimedium* spp.)	p.341	lack of sexual desire
eucalyptus (*Eucalyptus globulus*)	pp.236-7	colds and flu, intestinal worms, measles
evening primrose oil (*Oenothera biennis*)	p.273	acne, eczema, hangover, high blood pressure, premenstrual syndrome
eyebright (*Euphrasia officinalis*)	p.342	allergies, conjunctivitis
fennel (*Foeniculum vulgare*)	pp.238-9	bruises, colic, conjunctivitis, eyeache, flatulence
fenugreek (*Trigonella foenum-graecum*)	p.352	diabetes, high cholesterol
feverfew (*Tanacetum parathenium*)	pp.308-9	amenorrhoea, headache, insect bites and stings, migraine
fig (*Ficus carica*)	p.342	warts
figwort (*Scrophularia nodosa*)	p.299	abscess, eczema, psoriasis
flaxseed (*Linum usitatissimum*)	p.261	allergies, constipation, high cholesterol, inflammation
French tarragon (*Artemisia dracunculus*)	pp.206-7	insect bites and stings
garlic (*Allium sativum*)	pp.199-200	bronchitis, high blood pressure, high cholesterol, infection, intestinal worms, poor circulation
gentian (*Gentiana lutea*)	p.243	anaemia, indigestion, poor appetite
geranium, scented (*Pelargonium* spp.)	pp.278-9	diarrhoea
ginger (*Zingiber officinale*)	p.325	arthritis, backache, bronchitis, burns, colds and flu, headache, indigestion, migraine, nausea and vomiting, sore throat, sprains, ulcer
ginkgo (*Ginkgo biloba*)	pp.242-3	ageing, Alzheimer's, lack of sexual desire, macular degeneration, poor circulation, tinnitus

HERB	PAGE	AILMENT
ginseng (*Panax* spp.)	p.277	diabetes, impotence
goldenrod (*Solidago* spp.)	p.351	gallstones and kidney stones, urinary tract infections
goldenseal (*Hydrastis canadensis*)	p.249	eyeache, indigestion, infection, inflammation, poor appetite, sinusitis
gotu kola (*Centella asiatica*)	p.218	burns, sunburn, superficial wounds
grape (*Vitis vinifera*)	p.323	ageing, heart disease, poor circulation, psoriasis, urinary tract infection
green tea (*Camellia sinensis*)	p.214	heart disease, high cholesterol
grindelia (*Grindelia* spp.)	p.343	bronchitis, skin rashes caused by plants
guaraná (*Paullinia cupana*)	p.347	headache
guggul (*Commiphora mukul*)	p.228	arthritis, high cholesterol, water retention
gymnema (*Gymnema sylvestre*)	p.343	diabetes, high cholesterol
Hausa potato (*Coleus forskohlii*)	pp.227-8	asthma, glaucoma, high blood pressure, inflammation
hawthorn (*Crataegus laevigata* syn. *C. oxyacantha*)	pp.229-30	angina, cardiac arrhythmia, high blood pressure, poor circulation
hazelnut (*Corylus avellana*)	p.340	heart disease
herb Robert (*Geranium robertianum*)	p.343	superficial wounds
holy basil (*Ocimum sanctum*)	pp.270-1	diabetes
honeysuckle (*Lonicera* spp.)	p.262	colds and flu, fever
hops (*Humulus lupulus*)	pp.248-9	insomnia, stress and anxiety
horse chestnut (*Aesculus hippocastanum*)	pp.195-6	arthritis, bruises, haemorrhoids, oedema, poor circulation, varicose veins
horseradish (*Armoracia rusticana*)	pp.205-6	bladder infections, congestion, urinary tract infections
horsetail (*Equisetum arvense*)	p.341	gallstones and kidney stones, superficial wounds, urinary tract infections
hyssop (*Hyssopus officinalis*)	p.252	asthma, bronchitis, colds and flu, colic, fever, indigestion

HERB	PAGE	AILMENT
Iceland moss (*Cetraria islandica*)	p.339	bronchitis, cough, sore throat
Indian frankincense (*Boswellia serrata*)	pp.210-11	arthritis, dry skin, inflammation, wrinkles
ipecac (*Cephaelis ipecacuanha*)	p.338	dysentery
Irish moss (*Chondrus crispus*)	p.339	cough
jaborandi (*Pilocarpus microphyllus*)	p.347	dry mouth, glaucoma
java tea (*Orthosiphon aristatus*)	p.347	gallstones and kidney stones
jewelweed (*Impatiens capensis*)	p.343	skin rashes caused by plants
juniper (*Juniperus communis*)	pp.255-6	urinary tract infections, water retention
kava (*Piper methysticum*)	pp.280-1	insomnia, muscular tension, pain, stress and anxiety, toothache
khella (*Ammi visnaga*)	p.335	asthma
knotweed (*Polygonum aviculare*)	p.348	menorrhagia
kudzu (*Pueraria lobata*)	pp.285-6	hangover, high blood pressure, liver and gallbladder disease, vertigo
lady's mantle (*Alchemilla vulgaris*)	p.339	menorrhagia
lavender (*Lavandula* spp.)	pp.258-9	burns, depression, faintness, headache, insect bites and stings, indigestion, insomnia, nausea and vomiting, spasms, stress and anxiety, yeast infection
lemon (*Citrus sinensis*)	pp.222-5	acne, gallstones and kidney stones, gout, varicose veins, warts
lemon balm (*Melissa officinalis*)	p.264	colic, depression, fever, herpes, indigestion, stress and anxiety
lemon verbena (*Aloysia triphylla*)	p.202	fever
liquorice (*Glycyrrhiza glabra*)	p.245	allergies, cough, inflammation, liver and gallbladder disease, ulcer
linden (*Tilia* spp.)	p.352	headache
lobelia (*Lobelia inflata*)	pp.344-5	asthma
lovage (*Levisticum officinale*)	pp.260-1	colic, indigestion, poor appetite
lungwort (*Pulmonaria officinalis*)	p.349	asthma, bronchitis, cough
maca (*Lepidium meyenii*)	p.344	impotence, menopause
macadamia (*Macadamia integrifolia*)	p.345	diabetes
Madagascar periwinkle (*Catharanthus roseus*)	p.338	diabetes
marijuana (*Cannabis sativa*)	p.338	glaucoma
marjoram (*Oregano majorana*)	p.274-5	genital herpes, laryngitis
marshmallow (*Althea officinalis*)	p.335	sore throat, ulcer
maté (*Ilex paraguarensis*)	pp.252-3	depression
meadowsweet (*Filipendula ulmaria*)	p.240	fever, gastritis, muscular tension, pain, ulcer
milk thistle (*Silybum marianum*)	p.301	acne, amenorrhoea, haemorrhoids, jaundice, liver and gallbladder disease, psoriasis, snakebite, varicose veins
motherwort (*Leonurus cardiaca*)	p.344	amenorrhoea
mugwort (*Artemisia vulgaris*)	p.336	indigestion, intestinal worms
mulberry (*Morus alba*)	p.346	diabetes, water retention
mullein (*Verbascum thapsus*)	p.353	coughs, earache, psoriasis
mustard (*Brassica juncea*)	pp.211-12	congestion
myrrh (*Commiphora myrrha*)	p.228	sore throat
neem (*Azadirachta indica*)	pp.207-8	diabetes, eczema, fever, fungal infection, infection, intestinal worms, jaundice, lice
nutmeg (*Myristica fragrans*)	pp.268-9	diarrhoea, nausea and vomiting
nettle (*Urtica dioica*)	p.317	bladder infections, water retention
oats (*Avena sativa*)	p.207	eczema, high cholesterol

HERB	PAGE	AILMENT
olive (*Olea europaea*)	p.273	ageing, gallbladder and kidney stones
onion (*Allium cepa*)	pp.198-9	acne, bronchitis, cough, earache
oregano (*Origanum vulgare*)	pp.274-5	bronchitis, cough, dysentery, indigestion, insect bites and stings, jaundice, menstrual cramps, muscular cramps
oregano oil (*Origanum vulgare*)	p.275	congestion
Oregon grape (*Mahonia aquifolium*)	p.345	psoriasis, urinary tract infections
papaya (*Carica papaya*)	p.216	ulcer
parsley (*Petroselinum crispum*)	p.279	bladder infections, gallstones and kidney stones, oedema, urinary tract infections
partridge berry (*Mitchella repens*)	p.346	menorrhagia, menstrual cramps
passionflower (*Passiflora incarnata*)	p.347	insomnia, stress and anxiety, premenstrual syndrome
patchouli (*Pogostemon cablin*)	p.348	depression
pau d'arco (*Tabebuia impetiginosa*)	p.307	diabetes, eczema, fungal infection, psoriasis
peppermint (*Mentha x piperita*)	pp.267-8	flatulence, indigestion, nausea and vomiting
perilla (*Perilla frutescens*)	p.347	gout
Peruvian bark (*Cinchona* spp.)	p.339	cardiac arrhythmia
pineapple (*Ananas comosus*)	pp.202-3	constipation, inflammation
pipsissewa (*Chimaphila umbellata*)	p.339	gallstones and kidney stones, urinary tract infections
plantain (*Plantago major*)	p.282	cough, insect bites and stings, superficial wounds, urinary tract infections
pleurisy root (*Asclepias tuberosa*)	pp.336-7	bronchitis
poke (*Phytolacca americana*)	p.280	fungal infection
pomegranate (*Punica granatum*)	p.349	intestinal worms
prickly ash (*Z. americanum*)	p.353	dry mouth, toothache
pumpkin seed (*Cucurbita pepo*)	p.340	enlarged prostate

HERB	PAGE	AILMENT
purslane (*Portulaca oleracea*)	p.349	high blood pressure, high cholesterol
pygeum (*Pygeum africanum*)	p.353	enlarged prostate
quebracho (*Aspidosperma quebracho-blanco*)	p.337	lack of sexual desire
radish (*Raphanus sativum*)	p.286	poor appetite
red clover (*Trifolium pratense*)	p.314	bronchitis, congestion, cough, eczema, menopause, osteoporosis, psoriasis
red root (*Ceanothus americanus*)	p.338	asthma, bronchitis
reishi (*Ganoderma lucidum*)	pp.342-3	high cholesterol, insomnia, stress and anxiety
rhubarb (*Rheum palmatum*)	pp.286-8	inflammation
rooibos (*Aspalathus linearis*)	p.337	colic
rose (*Rosa* spp.)	pp.288-9	depression
rosemary (*Rosmarinus officinalis*)	pp.290-1	dandruff, headache, poor circulation
rosemary oil (*Rosmarinus officinalis*)	pp.290-1	baldness, congestion, sciatica
saffron (*Crocus sativus*)	p.230	indigestion
sage (*Salvia* spp)	pp.294-5	sore throat
salad burnet (*Sanguisorba minor*)	pp.296-7	diarrhoea
sandalwood (*Santalum album*)	p.297	fever
sandalwood oil (*Santalum album*)	p.297	insomnia, pain, stress and anxiety, urinary tract infections
St. John's wort (*Hypericum perforatum*)	p.251	bruises, burns, chronic fatigue, depression, insomnia, menopause, pain, sciatica, stress and anxiety, sunburn, superficial wounds, toothache, varicose veins, wounds
sarsaparilla (*Smilax* spp.)	p.351	arthritis, eczema, psoriasis
sassafras (*Sassafras albidum*)	p.355	skin rashes caused by plants

HERB	PAGE	AILMENT
saw palmetto (*Serenoa repens*)	p.300	enlarged prostate, laryngitis
schisandra (*Schisandra chinensis*)	pp.298-9	liver and gallbladder disease
Seneca snakeroot (*Polygala senega*)	p.348	asthma
senna (*Cassia senna*)	pp.217-18	constipation
shepherd's purse (*Capsella bursa-pastoris*)	p.338	cuts and scrapes, menorrhagia
shiitake mushroom (*Lentinula edodes*)	p.260	allergies, chronic fatigue, high cholesterol, immune system weakness
skullcap (*Scutellaria lateriflora*)	p.351	insomnia, premenstrual syndrome
slippery elm (*Ulmus rubra*)	p.315	abscess, allergies, coughs, diarrhoea, gastritis, heartburn, sore throat, superficial wounds, ulcer
soapwort (*Saponaria officinalis*)	p.351	skin rashes caused by plants
soy (*Glycine max*)	pp.243-4	heart disease, menopause, osteoporosis
spearmint (*Mentha spicata*)	pp.266-7	nausea and vomiting
stinging nettle (*Urtica dioica*)	p.317	allergies, anaemia, arthritis
strawberry (*Fragaria vesca*)	pp.240-2	diarrhoea, lightening of skin, sunburn, urinary tract infections
summer savory (*Satureja hortensis*)	p.298	diarrhoea
sundew (*Drosera rotundifola*)	p.341	asthma, bronchitis, warts
sweet marjoram (*Origanum majorana*)	pp.274-5	herpes
tamarind (*Tamarindus indica*)	pp.307-8	constipation, dysentery
tarragon (*Artemisia dracunculus*)	pp.206-7	haemorrhoids, intestinal worms, superficial wounds
tea (*Camellia sinensis*)	p.214	sunburn, tooth decay
tea tree (*Melaleuca alternifolia*)	pp.263-4	acne, cuts and scrapes, fungal infection, infection, lice, sore throat, superficial wounds, yeast infection

HERB	PAGE	AILMENT
thyme (*Thymus vulgaris*)	pp.312-13	bronchitis, congestion, cough, cuts and scrapes, sore throat
tomato (*Lycopersicon esculentum*)	pp.262-3	enlarged prostate
turmeric (*Curcuma longa*)	pp.230-1	high cholesterol, ulcer
uva-ursi (*Arctostaphylos uva-ursi*)	p.336	urinary tract infections
valerian (*Valeriana officinalis*)	p.320	insomnia, menstrual cramps, stomach cramps, spasms, stress and anxiety
violet (*Viola odorata*)	pp.321-2	coughs
vitex (*Vitex agnus-castus*)	p.322	acne, amenorrhoea, infertility, menopause, premenstrual syndrome
walnut, English (*Juglans regia*)	p.255	dry skin, eczema, heart disease, intestinal worms, premenstrual syndrome
watercress (*Nasturtium officinale*)	p.346	poor appetite, water retention
wild yam (*Dioscorea villosa*)	p.233	colic, intestinal cramps, menstrual cramps, spasms, stomach cramps
willow (*Salix alba*)	p.292	arthritis, backache, fever, headache, menstrual cramps, pain
wintergreen (*Gaultheria procumbens*)	p.343	pain
witch hazel (*Hamamelis virginiana*)	p.246	cuts and scrapes, diarrhoea, haemorrhoids, herpes, insect bites and stings, varicose veins
wood betony (*Stachys betonica*)	p.303	dizziness, headache
yarrow (*Achillea millefolium*)	p.195	inflammation, menstrual cramps, superficial wounds
yellow dock (*Rumex crispus*)	p.350	constipation
ylang ylang (*Cananga odorata*)	pp.214-5	lack of sexual desire
yohimbe (*Pausinystalia johimbe*)	pp.278-9	dry mouth, erectile dysfunction, impotence

Glossary

A

absinthe A green liqueur flavoured with wormwood or a substitute, anise and other herbs.

aconitine A poisonous alkaloid found in aconite, used externally as an analgesic.

aescin A chemical found in the seed of the horse chestnut (*Aesculus hippocastanum*) tree that has been found to reduce swelling.

alizarin An orange or red dye that is derived from the madder plant (*Rubia tinctorum*).

alkaloids One of a large group of nitrogen-containing substances found naturally in seed plants. Although the plant from which they come may be poisonous, they may also contain valuable compounds.

alkannin A red colouring matter used primarily to colour drinks, pharmaceuticals and cosmetics.

allantoin Any of several nitrogen-containing organic compounds that are found in some plants; allantoin is used to promote the healing of wounds.

alternate leaves Leaves that are not directly opposite to each other on the stem, but are arranged singly at different heights on the stem.

annatto seed paste A paste made from the seeds of annatto (*Bixa orellana*), which are soaked, dried and then crushed into the paste. The paste is used as a food colouring for margarine, soups, cheeses and other foods.

annual (plant) A plant that dies away at the end of the growing season, and new plants that sprout from seeds that are borne during a preceding season.

anthelmic A compound that kills parasites and intestinal worms.

anthraquinones Plant chemicals known for their ability to relieve constipation.

antioxidants Substances, such as vitamin E, vitamin C or beta carotene, that are thought to protect body cells from the damaging effects of oxidation.

arbutin A chemical found in plants such as the Ericaceae family; sometimes used to treat urinary tract infections.

arctigenin A substance found in certain plants, including burdock (*Arctium lappa*). It has been shown to have antiviral and anticancer properties.

astringents A substance or preparation that draws together or constricts body tissues and is effective in stopping the flow of blood or other secretions.

atropine A toxic chemical taken from members of the nightshade (Solanaceae) family. It is typically used to dilate the pupil of the eye and to stop muscular spasms.

B

balled-and-burlapped Also known as B&B. A plant, tree, or shrub that has been taken out of the ground and its rootball wrapped in burlap (hessian) for support. Many plants are sold this way.

bare-root A plant that has been prepared for transporting by having all the soil removed from around its roots.

beechnuts The small nut of a beech tree.

beneficials Also known as beneficial garden insects; insects that are helpful to gardeners in some way. They can include flower pollinators such as bees and butterflies, or those that are natural enemies of insects and pests, including praying mantis and ladybirds.

berbere spice blend A spice blend of fennel, garlic, red pepper, cardamom and coriander, common in Ethiopian cuisine.

berberine A poisonous chemical found in the roots of certain plants such as barberry (*Berberis vulgaris*) and goldenseal (*Hydrastis canadensis*). Berberine kills amoebas and is used as a tonic in medicine.

beta-carotene A yellow pigment and antioxidant that gives a reddish colour to plants such as carrots, tomatoes, and dark yellow vegetables and fruits.

betonicine A substance found in some plants, such as wood betony (*Stachys officinalis*) that has the ability to reduce inflammation, strengthen the nervous system and treat neuralgia.

biennial (plants) Plants that have a two-year life cycle. They grow from seed their first season; in their second season they die, after sending up flowers and making seeds.

bilobalides Substances found in the leaves of the ginkgo biloba (*Ginkgo biloba*) plant that appear to be responsible for the herb's ability to improve blood flow to the extremities and to the brain, eyes and ears, particularly in the elderly.

bitter principles Substances found in some plants, such as hops (*Humulus lupulus*) that have a strong bitter flavour, but with no sharply defined chemical characteristics

boswellia resin A gummy substance yielded when the bark of the boswellia tree (*Boswellis serrata*) is peeled away. The solidified resin is made into capsules and tablets for internal use and creams, perfumes and cosmetics. Boswellia resin contains anti-inflammatory compounds, including boswellic acids, which may be helpful in the treatment of rheumatoid arthritis and bowel disorders such as ulcerative colitis.

botanical name The system of naming plants for scientific study. Each plant name is indicated by two words, the genus (capitalized) and species (lower case) names.

bouquet garni A mixture of herbs or herbs and spices tied together, wrapped in cheesecloth or enclosed in a small cloth sack, and immersed in a soup or stew during cooking. The mixture is usually removed before serving.

C

caffeine A bitter chemical found especially in the beverages coffee and tea. Caffeine is used as a stimulant and also to increase the discharge of urine (diuretic).

capsaicin A colourless plant compound found in various members of the pepper family. Capsaicin gives hot peppers their hotness. It is used in cooking and medicine and as a main ingredient in many self-defence pepper sprays.

carotenoids Any of many usually yellow to red pigments found widely in plants.

cellulose The main component of plant cell walls and the most abundant organic compound on Earth, it is a complex carbohydrate or homopolysaccharide.

Chinese five-spice powder A mixture of cinnamon cloves, fennelseed, star anise and szechuan pepper, widely used in Chinese cuisine.

chlorophyll The pigment in plants that absorbs sunlight and uses its energy to create carbohydrates from carbon dioxide and water.

colchicine A poisonous chemical extracted from the corms or seeds of the autumn crocus (*Colchicum autumnale*), which is used to treat gout.

cold frame A structure, covered in glass or plastic, used to protect and warm plants and seedlings.

common name Name given to plants by nonscientists. A common name may reflect a plant's use, lore or appearance.

compost Decomposed organic matter (including kitchen scraps such as fruit and vegetable rinds, egg shells and coffee grounds) used to enrich soil in a garden.

compost tea A liquid made by steeping *compost* in water. It is sprayed on plant leaves and applied to the soil around some herbs.

compound leaf A leaf composed of multiple parts or leaflets.

cotyledon The first leaves developed by a plant.

coumarin A toxic compound that has an odour of new-mown hay. Found in plants and also produced synthetically, it is used in the making of perfumes.

cultivars A plant variety developed from a natural species and maintained under cultivation

cutting Plant pieces cut from a parent plant and rooted to form new plants.

cyanogenic Capable of producing cyanide, a very toxic liquid. Some plants are cyanogenic.

D

diatomaceous earth A porous, pale-coloured material made up of the skeletons of diatoms (microscopic algae with cell walls containing silica). The material, which resembles microscopic pieces of broken glass, can be sprinkled around plants to eliminate slugs. The sharp pieces in the material damages the insect's body, causing death.

dicotyledon A flowering plant with two cotyledons (the first leaves developed by a plant).

dioecious Having male reproductive organs in one individual and female in another within the same species.

diuretic Tending to increase the flow of urine.

division A technique used to propagate plants that do not have a single stem.

drip irrigation A method of watering plants in which tubes or hoses, sometimes porous, are brought close to plants and water is allowed to trickle out at a very slow, but constant, rate.

E, F

ephedrine A plant chemical extracted from Chinese ephedra (*Ephedra sinica*) that is used in remedies for hay fever, asthma and nasal congestion.

emetic An agent, such as an herbal medicine, that induces vomiting.

family Groups of related plant genera, Some plant families are quite large – the orchid, aster and pea families are three of the biggest. Other plant families, such as the ginkgo family, contain only one or two plants. In plant classification, family is the category above genus and below order.

favism Severe allergy to the fava bean or its pollen. It is a hereditary condition, especially of males who are of Mediterranean descent.

fermented (tea) Fermented teas are those that have been allowed to dry before being further processed. The drying causes natural browning enzymes present in tea leaves to oxidize them. Black teas are fermented.

fines herbes A mixture of finely chopped herbs, including parsley, chives, tarragon and thyme. A popular seasoning used in French cuisine.

flavonoids. A plant chemical called a *metabolite* that contains many important antioxidant compounds, which help eliminate harmful substances, called free radicals, from the body.

G

genistein An isoflavone (plant chemical) that is particularly abundant in soybeans, and which has been shown to have anti-tumour properties.

genus A genus consists of a group of species that are closely related to one another, determined primarily by the reproductive parts of their flowers. The taxonomic category ranking above a species and below a family. *Pl.* genera.

growing medium Any material in which a plant can grow.

gum arabic Substance from an acacia tree (*Acacia* spp.); used as a thickener in drugs and sweets.

H

herb Any plant or plant part that is valued for its medicinal, culinary or aromatic qualities.

horticultural oil A highly refined petroleum oil that is sprayed on plants to kill harmful insects and mites.

hu jiao The common name by which black pepper (*Piper nigrum*) is known in China.

humus Partially or completely decomposed vegetable matter. Humus is often used to enrich soil.

hybrids An offspring of two plants of different varieties, species or genera.

hydrastine A poisonous compound, taken from the root of goldenseal (*Hydrastis canadensis*) and once used locally to treat inflamation of mucous membranes.

I, K

imperfect flowers A flower that contains only one set of sexual organs. Technically known as dioecious plants, they bear male and female flower parts on separate plants, which means both male and female plants must be present for pollination to occur.

inflorescence The way that flowers are borne or arranged on a plant.

insecticidal soap A specifically formulated soap that kills insects that are have the potential to harm the plant; at the same time, it is safe for most plant species.

invasive Used to describe plants that grow and spread aggressively from the place where they were originally planted.

iodine A chemical element required as a trace element for most living organisms.

isoflavones Plant chemicals that are being studied for their preventative health benefits and nutritional value.

khellin A compound taken from the fruit of the khella plant (*Ammi visnaga*) of the Umbelliferae family. It is used as an antispasmodic to treat asthma. It also improves blood flow to the heart.

kingdom One of the five major groupings under which all living organisms are classified. They are: Animalia (animals), Plantae (plants), Fungi (fungal organisms, including mushrooms), Protista (simple organisms, such as protozoans and algae, whose cells have nuclei and organelles) and Monera (simple one-celled or colony-forming organisms, including bacteria, whose cells do not have nuclei or organelles).

L

laetrile A substance derived from peach pits. Laetrile was once publicized as an anticancer treatment, although there is no supporting scientific evidence of its effectiveness.

layering A way of propagating or producing new plants in which a stem is induced to send out roots by surrounding a section of it with soil while it is still attached to a parent plant.

Linnaean Classification System A system of grouping living organisms into categories based on their similarity to other organisms. The system is named for its inventor, Swedish naturalist Carolus Linnaeus (1707–1778).

Linnaeus, Carolus Swedish botanist; a father of modern systematic botany and of modern system of nomenclature.

lipids A group of organic compounds, (fats, oils, waxes, sterols and triglycerides), that are insoluble in water. Lipids are oily to the touch. With carbohydrates and proteins, lipids are the principal structural material of living cells.

lobeline A poisonous narcotic compound that is extracted from the leaves of Indian tobacco (*Lobelia inflata*). This yellow oil, which has a tobacco-like flavour and odour, is use as a respiratory stimulant and smoking deterrent.

M

metabolites Chemical compounds produced by plants as part of their normal life processes. Some of these compounds allow plants to store energy in the form of sugar; others help plants defend themselves against disease or predators.

microclimate The climate of a very small, specific place within an area, as contrasted with the climate of the entire area.

monocotyledons A flowering plant with one cotyledon (the first leaves developed by a plant).

moxibustion A technique used in Tradi-tional Chinese Medicine in which a stick or cone of mugwort (*Artemesia vulgaris*) is placed on an acupuncture point over an inflamed or affected area on the body. This is thought to stimulate and strengthen the blood and the life energy (qi) of the body.

mucilage A viscous, slimy material exuded by certain plants.

mulch An organic or inorganic soil covering that is used to discourage weed growth, and maintain soil temperature and moisture levels.

O

opposite leaves Leaves of a plant that are arranged along a stem in pairs directly opposite from each other.

organic and inorganic fertilizer Organic fertilizers are derived from living or once living material. These materials include animal wastes, crop residues, compost and numerous other by-products of living organisms. Inorganic fertilizers are derived from non-living sources and include most of our manufactured, commercial fertilizers.

overwinter The process of bringing plants that cannot tolerate cold or frost through the winter by moving them indoors or otherwise protecting them.

P

papain A plant chemical derived from papaya and certain other plants. Used to tenderize meat and other protein and as a dietary supplement to treat indigestion. It is also used as a remedy for jellyfish stings.

perennial (plant) Perennials are plants whose upper portions die in the dormant season while the portions of the herbs below ground remain alive. These plants make new stems and foliage at the beginning of the growing season. The root systems of perennial plants usually grow larger year on year.

perfect flower A type of flower that has both female (pistillate) and male (staminate) parts. It may or may not have petals or sepals. The pollen is produced in the same flower that produces the seed and the plant can pollinate itself without assistance.

petitgrain The essential oil from the orange tree (*Citrus sinensis*) leaf. Has a fresh, floral, citrus and slightly woody fragrance. Used as a deodorant and astringent as well as a treatment for fatigue and stress.

pH value A measure of a substance's level of acidity or basicity. The letters pH stand for "power of hydrogen".

phloretin A natural antibiotic found in the leaves of the apple tree (*Malus domestica*) and milk thistle (*Silybum marianum*).

photosensitivity An abnormally heightened response, especially of the skin, to sunlight or ultraviolet radiation. Photosensitivity can be caused by some chemicals including drugs, and also by certain physiological disorders.

photosynthesis The process by which plants use the energy of sunlight to convert water and carbon dioxide into carbohydrates, which they use as food.

pilocarpine A compound obtained from the leaves of certain tropical American shrubs such as the jaborandi *(Pilocarpus microphyllus)* and used in the treatment of glaucoma.

polyphenols Substances found in green tea, white tea, red wine, olive oil, dark chocolate and pomegranates. Research suggests they are a powerful type of antioxidant.

propagation To increase the number of plants, by seeds, cuttings, layering or other methods.

pruning The practice of removing diseased, overmature or otherwise unwanted portions from a woody plant. Pinching back herbaceous plants to encourage denser growth or more profuse or delayed flowering, is a form of pruning. So is the gardener's practice of "deadheading" a flowering plant, or removing spent flowers before they begin to set seed, in order to concentrate a plant's energy on continued flower production.

psoralens Compounds in Dong quai *(Angelica sinensis)* and other species of the herb angelica *(Sassafras albidum)* that can cause an allergic reaction to exposure to the sun.

pulegone A naturally occurring organic compound obtained from essential oils of catnip *(Nepeta cataria),* peppermint *(Mentha piperita)*, and pennyroyal *(Mentha pulegium)*. Pulegone has a pleasant odor similar to peppermint and camphor. It is used as a flavouring agent, in perfumery and in aromatherapy.

Q, R

quinidine A plant chemical related to quinine. Used in treating malaria and certain heart disorders. Extracted from the bark of shrubs in the *Cinchona* genus.

raised beds A bottomless box with sides that are about 20 cm (8 in) high. The raised box sits on the ground and can be filled with any type of soil. Because plants in a raised bed are elevated, air circulation is improved around them, which deters diseases and allows the soil to drain more freely. The soil in raised beds thaws and warms faster at the beginning of the growing season than later, so planting can be done earlier. Because the soil will never be walked on, it will not become compacted.

reserpine A plant chemical extracted from the root of Indian snakeroot *(Rauwolfia serpentina)*. Used for centuries in India to treat ailments ranging from cholera and hypertension to insanity, and snakebite. The purified compound was isolated in 1952 and is considered the first modern drug for the treatment of hypertension.

ricin A poisonous protein found in the castor bean.

rosmarinic acid A fragrant compound found in plants including rosemary *(Rosmarinus officinalis)*, oregano *(Origanum vulgare)*, sage *(Salvia officinalis)* and marjoram *(Origanum majorana)*. The compound has strong antioxidant properties and is used as a food preservation.

S

saccharides Molecules made of carbon, hydrogen and oxygen, also called carbohydrates. The name is derived from the Latin for sugar.

safrole A colourless or pale yellow oily liquid derived from oil of sassafras *(Sassafras albidum)* and other essential oils. Once used in making perfume and soap. Also used in the manufacture of the illegal drug MDMA (ecstasy).

saponins Various, mostly toxic plant chemicals that produce a soapy lather.

scurvy Disease caused by the lack of vitamin C; marked by spongy gums, loosening of the teeth, and bleeding into the skin and mucous membranes

selenium A trace mineral essential to good health, only required in small amounts. Selenium is incorporated into proteins to make selenoproteins, which are important antioxidant enzymes.

silica A chemical compound also known as silicon dioxide, found in nature in several forms, including quartz and opal. Used in the manufacture of glass, ceramics, portland cement, and the heat-proof tiles on the underside of the Space Shuttles.

silymarin An antioxidant from the milk thistle plant *(Silybum marianum)* that may is used to clear the liver of toxins; also used in dietary supplements and herbal remedies.

simple leaf A leaf that is composed of only one part.

solanine A bitter poisonous plant chemical from several plants of the Solanaceae (nightshade) family, which includes tomatoes, eggplants, potatoes and peppers.

species The smallest, most basic unit of organization in the Linnaean system of classification. A species is composed of individuals that resemble one another more nearly than they resemble any other organisms and can breed to produce fertile offspring.

strychnine A bitter, poisonous chemical taken from from plants of the Loganiaceae family. Used as both a poison for rodents and medicinally as a central nervous system stimulant.

subspecies The rank immediately subordinate to a species.

T

T cell A type of white blood cell (leukocyte) that belongs to the acquired immune system that learns to combat invading bacteria and viruses The abbreviation "T" stands for thymus, the organ in which their final stage of development occurs.

tannins Astringent substances found in plants that are used in tanning, dyeing and medicine.

terpenes Terpenes and terpenoids are the primary constituents of the essential oils of many types of plants and flowers. Menthol, a topical pain reliever derived from mint, and borneol, a disinfectant and deodorant derived from pine oil, are two common examples.

thujone A compound used as a flavouring agent in certain foods. Best known as a component of the drink absinthe, and of natural oil of wormwood *(Artemisia absinthium)*.

thymol A an aromatic compound derived from thyme oil and other oils; used an antiseptic, a fungicide and a preservative.

U, W, Z

unfermented (tea) Tea that has not been allowed to dry before being further processed. Green teas are unfermented varieties Any of various groups of plants ranking below a species.

wild-harvesting The practice of collecting edible, medicinal, fragrant, or ornamental plants from the wild.

World Health Organization (WHO) The United Nations specialized agency for health.

Za'atar A Middle Eastern spice blend of sesame seed, sumac and thyme.

Bibliography

Ball, Jeff. *Rodale's Garden Problem Solver: Vegetables, Fruits and Herbs.* Rodale Books, 1988.

Bown, Deni. *RHS Encyclopedia of Herbs and Their Uses.* DK, 2002

Boxer, Arabella. *Herb and Spice Handbook.* Bay Soma Publishing, 1999.

Bradley, Fern Marshall and Ellis, Barbara W. *Rodale's All-New Encyclopedia of Organic Gardening.* Rodale Books, 1993.

Brennan, Georgeanne and Leubbermann, Mimi. *Little Herb Gardens: Simple Secrets for Glorious Gardens Indoors and Out.* Chronicle Books, 2004.

Carter, George. *Gardening with Herbs.* Ryland Peters & Small, 2001.

Creasy, Rosalind. *The Edible Herb Garden.* Periplus Editions, 1999.

Duke, James. *Field Guide to Medicinal Plants and Herbs of Eastern and Central North America.* Houghton Mifflin, 2000.

Duke, James A. *Green Pharmacy Herbal Handbook.* Rodale Books, 2000.

Fillon, Mike. *Supplements Under Siege: Inside the Conspiracy to Take Away Your Vitamins, Minerals and Herbs.* Woodland Publishing, 2006.

Fisher, Kathleen. *Herbal Remedies: Dozens of Safe, Effective Treatments to Grow and Make.* Rodale Books, 1999.

Gilbertie, Sal. *Growing Herbs in Containers.* North Adams: Storey Publishing, 1998.

Graedon, Joe and Graedon, Teresa. *The People's Pharmacy Guide to Home and Herbal Remedies.* St. Martin's Press, 2001.

Green, James. *The Herbal Medicine Maker's Handbook: A Home Manual.* Crossing Press, 2000.

Hanson, Beth (ed.). *Designing an Herb Garden.* Brooklyn Botanic Garden, 2004.

Harding, Jennie. *The Herb Bible.* Barnes and Noble Books, 2005.

Hartung, Tammi. *Growing 101 Herbs that Heal: Gardening Techniques, Recipes and Remedies.* Storey Publishing, 2000.

Hemphill, Ian. *The Spice and Herb Bible: A Cook's Guide.* Robert Rose, 2002.

Hershoff, Asa. *Herbal Remedies: A Quick and Easy Guide to Common Disorders and their Herbal Remedies.* Avery, 2001.

Hill, Tony. *The Contemporary Encyclopedia of Herbs and Spices.* Wiley, John and Sons, 2004.

Hoffman, David. *The Herbal Handbook: A User's Guide to Medical Herbalism.* Healing Arts Press, 1998.

James, Tina. *Cooking with Herbs: 100 Seasonal Recipes and Herbal Mixtures to Spice Up Any Meal.* Rodale Books, 2000.

Kelville, Kathi and Korn, Peter. *Herbs for Health and Healing.* Rodale Books, 1998.

Kidd, Randy, DVM. *Dr. Kidd's Guide to Herbal Dog Care.* Storey Publishing, 2000.

Kowalchik, Claire (ed.) and William H. Hylton (ed.). *Rodale's Illustrated Encyclopedia of Herbs.* Rodale Books, 1998.

McCaleb, Robert, Leigh, Evelyn, and Morien, Krista. *The Encyclopedia of Popular Herbs.* Prima Publishing, 2000.

Michalak, Patricia S. *Rodale's Successful Organic Gardening: Herbs.* Rodale Press, 1993.

Minter, Sue. *The Healing Garden.* Random House, 2005

Moore, Arden and Doherty, Bridget. *Women's Edge: Herbs that Heal.* Rodale Books, 1999.

Norman, Jill. *Herbs and Spices: The Cook's Reference.* DK Publishing, 2002.

Ondra, Nancy J. Rodale's *Essential Herbal Handbooks: Landscaping with Herbs.* Rodale Books, 2000.

Organic Gardening Magazine (eds.). *Herbs: Organic Gardening Basics, Volume 5.* Rodale Books, 2001.

Pears, Pauline. *Rodale's Illustrated Encyclopedia of Organic Gardening.* Rodale Books, 2005.

Scoble, Gretchen and Field, Ann. *The Meaning of Herbs: Myth, Language & Lore.* San Francisco: Chronicle Books, 2001.

Segall, Barbara et al. *A Handful of Herbs.* Ryland Peters and Small, 2002.

Sombke, Laurence. *Beautiful Easy Herbs.* Rodale Books, 2000.

Smith, Miranda. *Your Backyard Herb Garden.* Rodale Books, 1999.

White, Linda B, MD. *The Herbal Drug Store.* Rodale Books, 2003.

Web Sites

American Herb Association
www.ahaherb.com

The American Herb Association promotes the understanding and ecological use of medicinal herbs and aromatherapy. Membership is open to anyone interested in herbalism and includes a 20-page quarterly newsletter written by well-known, professional herbalists.

American Herbal Pharmacopoeia
www.herbal-ahp.org

The Mission of the American Herbal Pharmacopoeia® (AHP) is to promote the responsible use of herbal medicines and ensure they are used with the highest degree of safety and efficacy as is achievable. The primary way to accomplish this is through the development of standards of identity, purity and analysis for botanicals, as well as to critically review traditional and scientific data regarding their efficacy and safety.

American Herbal Products Association
www.ahpa.org

The American Herbal Products Association (AHPA) exists to promote the responsible commerce of herbal products. Founded in 1983, AHPA is the recognized leader in representing the responsible centre of the botanical trade, and is comprised of the finest growers, processors, manufacturers and marketers of herbal products. One hundred percent of AHPA's resources are dedicated to furthering the responsible sale and use of herbs and herbal products through AHPA's expertise and experience.

Lavender (Lavandula angustifolia).

American Herbalists Guild
www.americanherbalistsguild.com

The American Herbalists Guild (AHG) was founded in 1989 as a non-profit, educational organization to represent the goals and voices of herbalists. It is the only peer-review organization in the United States for professional herbalists specializing in the medicinal use of plants.

Essential Herbal Magazine
www.essentialherbal.com

The *Essential Herbal* is a herb magazine that contains recipes and information on herbs, health food, natural food and healthy living. It provides information on where and how to shop for the best all-natural products.

Flower Essence Society
www.flowersociety.org

The Flower Essence Society (FES) is an international membership organization of health practitioners, researchers, students and others interested in deepening knowledge of flower essence therapy.

Garden Guides
www.gardenguides.com/herbs/remedy.htm

A gardening web site that offers tips on plants, vegetables, flowers and herbs. The Herbal Home Remedies page allows users to click on a condition such as coughs, cramping or hayfever and then view descriptions of how to use fresh herbs as therapy.

Heart of Scotland Herb Society
www.herbsociety.co.uk/scotheart.htm

A thriving, enthusiastic group affiliated to the Royal Horticultural Society and associated with The Herb Society, Great Britain. Wide-ranging and varied interests include cooking, gardening, herbal remedies, home crafts, beauty products and much more.

Herb Federation of New Zealand
www.herbs.org.nz

Dedicated to promoting the knowledge, use and delight of herbs through educational programmes, research, and sharing the experience of its members within the federation and throughout the community.

Herb Med
www.herbmed.org

HerbMed® is an interactive, electronic herbal database providing hyperlinked access to the scientific data underlying the use of herbs for health. It is an impartial, evidence-based resource provided by the nonprofit Alternative Medicine Foundation.

Herb Net
www.herbnet.com
A comprehensive web site on the internet that provides information on a variety of topics related to herbs. Herb products, remedies, publications and more can all be found here.

Herb Research Foundation
www.herbs.org
The Herb Research Foundation (HRF) is the world's most comprehensive source of accurate scientific information on medical plants. Since 1983, HRF has been educating the public, health practitioners, legislators and the media about the health benefits and safety of herbs, drawing on a speciality botanical library containing more than 300,000 scientific papers on thousands of herbs and multiple online sources.

Herb Society of America
www.herbsociety.org
The Herb Society of America (HSA) focuses on educating its members and the public on the cultivation of herbs and the study of their history and uses, both past and present. The Society maintains a library at its national headquarters, produces a variety of publications and educational programmes, coordinates networking and learning opportunities, and awards grants to researchers and educators.

The Herb Society, UK
www.herbsociety.co.uk
Based in Banbury, England, this is an historic and internationally renowned educational charity dedicated to encouraging the appreciation and use of herbs, and bringing together anyone interested in herbs, professional or amateur.

Herb Society of Manitoba
www.herbsocietymb.com
Founded in Canada in 1995 to promote knowledge, use and enjoyment of herbs through education, programmes, research and sharing the experience of its members with the community.

Herb Society of Western Australia
www.herbsocietywa.com
Incorporated in 1982, this society publishes a bi-monthly newsletter, *The Herbal Thymes*, and organizes regular meetings.

Herbal Gardens
www.herbalgardens.com
This site is dedicated to the education, resources and uses of garden bounty. It has gathered many herb-related links, book listings, ideas and much more.

Herbal Remedies Information
www.herbalremediesinfo.com
Simple herbal remedies information. Offers information and resources organized across sections such as Herbs for Kids, Buying and Storing Herbs, Herbal Nutrition and Homeopathy.

International Herb Association
www.iherb.org
A professional trade association providing educational service and development opportunities for those involved in herbal endeavours since 1985, the IHA encourages herbal entrepreneurs through newsletters, publications and conferences, and offers guidance as an association of peers supporting herbal businesses, as well as the latest information on growing, marketing and using herbs.

A Modern Herbal
www.botanical.com/botanical/mgmh.html
This is the electronic version of *A Modern Herbal*, by Maude Grieve, published in England in the early 1900s. A charming curiosity, the information may now be considered innaccurate, or not in accordance with modern medicine.

The National Association for Holistic Aromatherapy
www.naha.org
The National Association for Holistic Aromatherapy (NAHA) is an educational, nonprofit organization dedicated to enhancing public awareness of the benefits of true aromatherapy and its safe and effective application in everyday life. NAHA is actively involved with promoting and elevating academic standards in aromatherapy education and practice for the profession.

National Garden Association
www.garden.org
The National Gardening Association (NGA), founded in 1973, is a nonprofit leader in plant-based education. Programmes and initiatives highlight the opportunities for plant-based education in schools, communities and gardens. Serves as a bridge to connect people to gardening in five core fields: plant-based education, health and wellness, environmental stewardship, community development and responsible home gardening.

Natural Healers.com
www.naturalhealers.com
Natural Healers is dedicated to providing the best information to prospective students of natural healing techniques. The website provides resources that allow students to compare schools, contact them, read common questions and answers, and ask questions. The larger goal is to encourage the respect for and trust in the use of herbs to heal.

Night and Day Herb Society, Norway
(Natt og Dag Urtelag)
http://home.online.no/~gebby/index.cfm
Lively website includes recipes and photos.

Queensland Herb Society
www.queenslandherbsociety.com
An informative website for everyone who wants to know more about growing and using herbs. Contains meeting details, recipes, herb index, members list and lots of photos.

Herb & Botanical Gardens

NORTH AMERICA

CANADA

**Arboretum University
of Guelph**
Ontario N1G 2W1
Tel: +001 519 824 4120
www.uoguelph.ca/arboretum

Cedar Valley Botanical Gardens
Brighton,
Ontario K0K 1H0
Tel: +001 319 226 4966
www.cedarnet.org/gardens

Château Ramezay
280 Notre-Dame Street East,
Montréal,
Québec H2Y 1C5
Tel: +001 514 861 3708
www.chateauramezay.qc.ca

Columbia Valley Botanical Gardens
3300 Johnston Rd,
Invermere,
British Columbia V0A 1K4
http://www.conservancy.bc.ca/CVBG/
welcome.htm

**Devonian Botanic Garden,
University of Alberta**
University of Alberta,
Edmonton,
Alberta T6G 2E9
www.devonian.ualberta.ca/

Harriet Irving Botanical Gardens
PO Box 48
32 University Avenue,
Wolfville,
Nova Scotia B4P 2R6
Tel: +001 902 585 5242
botanicalgardens.acadiau.ca

Jardin Botanique de Montréal
C/- The Library
4101 est,
rue Sherbrooke,
Montreal
Québec H1X 2B2,
Tel: +001 514 872 1452

Jardin Roger-Van den Hende
Université Laval
Pavillon de l'Environtron, local 1227
2480, Hochelaga,
Québec
G1K 7P4
Tél.: +001 418 656 3742
http://www.jardin.ulaval.ca/accueil-
jardin0.html

**Niagara Parks Botanical Gardens
and School of Horticulture**
The Niagara Parks Commission,
P.O. Box 150, Niagara Falls,
Ontario L2E 6T2
Tel: +001 905 356 8554
www.niagaraparks.com/nature/
botanical.php

**Reford Gardens and International
Garden Festival**
200, route 132
Grand-Métis, Québec G0J 1Z0
Tel: +001 418 775 2222
http://www.jardinsmetis.com

**Royal Botanical Gardens
(Hamilton & Burlington)**
680 Plains Road West,
Burlington,
Ontario L7T 4H4
Tel: +001 905 527 1158
www.rbg.ca

Tofino Botanical Gardens
1084 Pacific Rim Highway,
PO Box 886,
Tofino, BC V0R 2Z0
Tel: +001 250 725 1220
http://tofinobotanicalgardens.com

**University of British Columbia
Botanical Garden**
6804 S.W. Marine Drive,
Vancouver,
British Columbia V6T 1Z4
Tel: +001 604 822 9666
www.ubcbotanicalgarden.org/

VanDusen Botanical Garden
5251 Oak Street,
Vancouver,
British Columbia V6M 4H1
Tel: +001 604 257 8666
www.vandusengarden.org

UNITED STATES

Alaska
Alaska Botanical Garden
PO Box 202202,
Anchorage, AK 99520
Tel: +001 907 770 3692
www.alaskabg.org

Arizona
Desert Botanical Garden
1201 N. Galvin Parkway,
Phoenix, AZ 85008
Tel: +001 480 481 8124
http://dbg.org/

Tuscon Botanical Gardens
2150 North Alvernon Way,
Tucson, Arizona 85712
Tel: +001 520 326 9686
http://www.tucsonbotanical.org/

California
San Francisco Botanical Garden
9th Avenue at Lincoln Way,
San Francisco, CA 94122
Tel: +001 415 661 1316 x312
http://www.sfbotanicalgarden.org/

Colorado
Hudson Gardens & Event Center
6115 South Santa Fe Drive,
Littleton, CO 80120
Tel: +001 303 797 8565
www.hudsongardens.org

Florida
Florida Botanical Gardens
Pinewood Cultural Park,
12175 125th Street N,
Largo, FL 33774-3695
Tel: +001 727 582 2200
www.flbg.org

Kanapaha Botanical Gardens
4700 S.W. 58th Drive
Gainesville, FL 32608
Tel: +001 352 372 4981
www.kanapaha.org

Hawaii
**Waimea Arboretum & Botanical
Gardens**
Waimea Falls Park,
59-864 Kamehameha Highway,
Haleiwa, Oahu, HI 96712
Tel: +001 808 638 8655

Illinois
Chicago Botanical Garden
1000 Lake Cook Road,
Glencoe, IL 60022
Tel: +001 847 835 5440
www.chicagobotanic.org

Iowa
**Dubuque Arboretum & Botanical
Gardens at Marshall Park**
3800 Arboretum Drive,
Dubuque, IA 52001
Tel: +001 563 556 2100
www.dubuquearboretum.com

Kansas
**Overland Park Arboretum &
Botanical Gardens**
179th & Antioch,
8500 Santa Fe Drive,
Overland Park, KS 66212
Tel: +001 913 685 3604
www.360kc.com/Attractions/Overland
ParkArboretum.html

Maine
Coastal Maine Botanical Gardens
Barters Island Road (physical address),
PO Box 234,
Boothbay, ME 04537
Tel: +001 207 633 4333
www.mainegardens.org

Massachusetts

The Arnold Arboretum of Harvard University
125 Arborway,
Jamaica Plain, MA 02130-3500
Tel: +001 617 524 1718
http://www.arboretum.harvard.edu/index.html

Michigan

Matthaei Botanical Gardens
Univerity of Michigan,
1800 North Dixboro Rd,
Ann Arbor, MI 48105
Tel: +001 734 647 7600
http://www.sitemaker.umich.edu/mbgna

Minnesota

Normandale Japanese Garden
9700 France Avenue South,
Bloomington, MN 55431
Tel: +001 952 487 8145
www.normandale.edu/japanesegarden

Montana

ZooMontana and Botanical Gardens
2100 South Shiloh Road,
Billings, MT 59106
Tel: +001 406 652 8100
www.zoomontana.org

New Mexico

Rio Garden Botanic Garden
Albuquerque Biological Park,
2601 Central Ave. NW
Albuquerque, NM 87104
Tel: +001 505 764 6200
www.cabq.gov/biopark/garden/index.html

New York

Brooklyn Botanic Garden
1000 Washington Avenue,
Brooklyn, NY 11225
Tel: +001 718 623 7200
www.bbg.org

New York Botanical Garden
200th Street and Kazimiroff Boulevard,
Bronx, NY 10458-5126
Tel: +001 718 817 8700
http://www.nybg.org/footer/contact_the_garden.php

Cornell Plantations
1 Plantations Road,
Ithaca, NY 14850
Tel: +001 607 255 3020/255 2400
www.plantations.cornell.edu

North Carolina

Botanical Gardens at Asheville
University of North Carolina,
151 W.T. Weaver Blvd.
Asheville, NC 28804-3414
Tel: +001 828 252 5190
http://www.ashevillebotanicalgardens.org/

Ohio

Cleveland Botanical Garden
11030 East Boulevard,
Cleveland, OH 44106-1786
Tel: +001 216 721 1600
www.cbgarden.org

Oklahoma

Oklahoma Botanical Garden & Arboretum
Oklahoma State University,
360 Agriculture Hall,
Stillwater, OK
Tel: +001 405 744 5404
http://home.okstate.edu/Okstate/dasnr/hort/hortlahome.nsf/toc/obga

Pennsylvania

Longwood Gardens
Route 1, PO Box 501,
Kennett Square,
PA 19348-0501
Tel: +001 610 388 1000
http://longwoodgardens.org/

Rhode Island

Blithewold Mansion, Gardens & Arboretum
101 Ferry Road, Rte. 114
Bristol, RI 02809
Tel: +001 401 253 2707
www.blithewold.org

Texas

Dallas Arboretum & Botanical Garden
8625 Garland Road,
Dallas, TX 75218-3914
Tel: +001 214 327 8263
www.dallasarboretum.org

Vermont

Vermont Wildflower Farm
3488 Ethan Allen Highway, Route 7
PO Box 96,
Charlotte, VT 05445
Tel: +001 802 425 3641
www.vermontwildflowerfarm.com

Washington

University of Washington Medicinal Herb Garden
Botany Department,
University of Washington,
Box 355325,
Seattle, WA 98195-5325
Tel: +001 206 543 1126
http://nnlm.gov/pnr/uwmhg/

Washington, D.C.

United States National Arboretum
3501 New York Avenue, NE
Washington D.C. 20002
Tel: +001 202 245 2726
http://www.usna.usda.gov/index.html

Wisconsin

Olbrich Botanical Gardens
3330 Atwood Avenue,
Madison, WI 53704
Tel: +001 608 246 4550
www.olbrich.org

Wyoming

Cheyenne Botanic Gardens
710 S Lions Park Drive,
Cheyenne, WY 82001
Tel: +001 307 637 6458
www.botanic.org

CENTRAL AMERICA

BELIZE

Belize Botanic Gardens
P.O. Box 180,
San Ignacio, Cayo
Tel: +00501 824 3101
http://www.belizebotanic.org/about_us.html

COSTA RICA

INBioparque
National Biodiversity Institute (InBio)
of Costa Rica
Santo Domingo de Heredia
Tel: +00506 507 8274
http://www.inbio.ac.cr/es/default2.html

MEXICO

Jardin Botanico
Instituto Tecnologico de Oaxaca,
Calz W. Massieu s/n Esq. Av. Tecnologico,
A.P. 1416, Oaxaca,
C.P. Oaxaca

Jardin Botánico del Instituto de Biologia (UNAM)
Universidad Autonoma de Mexico,
A.P. 70-614, C.P. 04510,
Coyoacan
Tel: +0052 (01) 5616 1297
http://www.ibiologia.unam.mx/

Jardín Botánico Francisco Javier Clavijero
Instituto de Ecologia,
A.C. Km 2.5 Carretera antigua a
Coatepec No 351,
Congregación El Haya,
PO Box. 63, 91000
Xalapa, Veracruz 91070
Tel: +0052 (01) 2842 1827
www.ecologia.edu.mx

Jardin Etnobotánico y Museo de Medicina Tradicional y Herbolaria
Matamoros No. 14 Col.,
Acapatzingo,
Cuernavaca,
Morelos C.P. 62440
Tel: +0052 (01) 777 312 5955
www.inah.gob.mx/jardin_etnobotanico/

SOUTH AMERICA

ARGENTINA

Jardín Botánico 'Arturo E. Ragonese'
Instituto de Recursos Biologicos,
Las Cabanas y Los Reseros s/n, Castelar,
Buenos Aires 1712
Tel: +0054 (0)11 4621 1819/0840

Jardín Botánico 'Dr Miguel J. Culaciati'
San Martin 668,
Huerta Grande,
Córdoba 5174
Tel: +0054 (0)35 4842 5496
www.argentinapeopleandnature.org

BRAZIL

Jardim Botánico do Rio de Janeiro
Rua Pacheco Leao 915,
Rio de Janeiro 22460-030
Tel: +0055 (21) 2511 0511
www.jbrj.gov.br/ingles/arboreto/
sens_gd.htm

CHILE

Jardin Botánico Nacional
P. O. Box 488,
Vina Del Mar,
V Región de Valparaiso
Tel: +0056 (32) 672 566
www.jardin-botanico.cl

COLOMBIA

Jardin Botánico de Plantas Medicinales
Corpoamazonia, Edificio Marillac,
Mocoa,
Putumayo
http://corpoamazonia.gov.co/ce_
jarbot.htm

VENEZUELA

Jardin Botánico de Caracas
Fundacion Instituto Botanico de Venzuela
Av. Salvador Allende,
Plaza Venezuela,
Entrada U.C.V. Caracas
Tel: +0058 (212) 605 3979/605 3994
www.ucv.ve/Fundacion2001/Jardin

EUROPE

AUSTRIA

Botanic Garden of University of Vienna
Department of Plant Systematics and
Evolution,
Rennweg 14, Wien,
Vienna A-1030
Tel: +0043 (0)1 4277 54124/54100
http://www.botanik.univie.ac.at/hbv/
english/hbv.htm

Botanischer Garten und Alpengarten Patscherkofel
Universitat Innsbruck,
Sternwartestrasse 15,
Innsbruck, 6020
Tel: +0043 (0) 512 507 5910
bot-garden.uibk.ac.at

Höhere Bundeslehr- und Versuchsanstalt für Gartenbau Wien - Schönbrunn
Schlob Schonbrunn,
Vienna, A-1130
Tel: +0043 (0)1 813 59500
http://www.hblagart.bmlf.gv.at/

BELGIUM

Ghent University Botanic Garden
Plantentuin Universiteit Gent,
K.L. Ledeganckstraat 35,
Ghent B-9000
Tel: +0032 (0)9 264 5056
www.plantentuin.ugent.be

Kalmthout Arboretum
Arboretum Kalmthout,
Heuvel 2,
Kalmthout B-2920
Tel: +0032 (0)3 666 6741
www.arboretumkalmthout.be

Leuven Botanic Garden
Kruidtuin Stad Leuven,
Kapucijnenvoer 30,
B-3000 Leuven
Tel: +0032 (0)1 623 2400
http://www.leuven.be/showpage.asp
?iPageID=1722

National Botanic Garden of Belgium
Domein van Bouchout
Meise B-1860
Tel: +0032 (0)2 260 0920
www.botanicgarden.be

DENMARK

Botanisk Have Københavns Universitet
Øster Farimagsgade 2B,
1353 København K
Tel: +0045 3532 2222/3532 224
http://www.botanic-garden.ku.dk

FRANCE

La Chatonnière
37 190 Azay-le-Rideau,
Loire
Tel: +0033 (0)2 47 45 40 29
http://www.lachatonniere.com

Château de Villandry
37510 Villandry
Tél : +0033 (0)2 47 50 02 09
www.chateauvillandry.com

Conservatoire Botanique National du Brest
Vallon du Stang-alar,
52 Allee du Bot,
F-29200 Brest
Tel: +0033 (0)2 98 41 88 95
www.cbnbrest.fr

Fondation Claude Monet
84, rue Claude Monet,
27620 - Giverny
Tel: +0033 (0)2 32 51 28 21
www.fondation-monet.com

Jardin Botanique de la Ville de Bordeaux
Terrasse du Jardin Public,
Place Bardineau,
F-33000 Bordeaux,
Tel: +0033 (0)5 56 52 18 77
www.mairie-bordeaux.fr

Jardin Botanique de la Ville de Lyon
Parc de la Tete d'Or,
Cedex 06,
Lyon F-69459
Tel: +0033 (0)4 72 82 35 04
http://www.jardin-botanique-lyon.com/

Jardin Botanique de la Ville de Nice
78 Corniche Fleurie,
F-06200 Nice
Tel: +0033 (0)4 93 83 92 59

Jardin Botanique du Montet
100, Rue du Jardin Botanique,
F-54600 Villiers-les-Nancy
Tel: +0033 (0) 3 83 41 47 47
www.cjbn.uhp-nancy.fr/accueil.html

Jardin des Plantes et Musée National d'Histoire Naturelle
Service des Cultures MNHN,
43 rue Buffon,
F-75005 Paris
Tel: +0033 (0)1 43 36 12 33
http://www.mnhn.fr/museum/foffice/
transverse/transverse/accueil.xsp

Le Potager du Roi, Versailles
10, rue du Maréchal Joffre,
78000 Versailles
Tel: +0033 (0)1 39 24 62 62
http://www.potager-du-roi.fr

Le Prieuré d'Orsan
18170 Maisonnais
Tel : +0033 (0)2 48 56 27 50
www.prieuredorsan.com

GERMANY

Botanischer Gärten und Botanisches Museum Berlin-Dahlem
Konigin-Luise-Strasse 6-8,
Berlin D-14191
Tel: +0049 (0) 308 385 0100
http://www.bgbm.org/

Botanische Gärten der Universitat Bonn
Meckenheimer-Allee 171,
D-53115 Bonn,
Northrhine Westfalia
Tel: +0049 (0) 228 73 5523
www.botgart.uni-bonn.de

Botanischer Gärten München-Nymphenburg
Menzinger Straße 61-65,
D-80638 München
Tel: +0049 (0) 89 1786 1310
http://www.botanik.biologie.uni-muenchen.de/botgart/e/default.html

Botanischer Gärten der Technischen Universitaet
Stuebelallee 2,
D - 01307 Dresden
Tel: +0049 (0) 351 459 3185
http://www.tu-dresden.de/bot-garten

Palmengärten der Stadt Frankfurt am Main
Siesmayerstrasse 61,
Frankfurt am Main,
D-60323
Tel: +0049 (0) 692 123 3383
www.Palmengarten-Frankfurt.de

Schloss Wackerbarth
Sächsisches Staatsweingut GmbH
Wackerbarth Str. 1,
01445 Radebeul,
Saxony
Tel. +0049 (0)351 89550
www.schloss-wackerbarth.de

GREECE

Balkan Botanic Garden at Kroussia Mountains
Agricultural Research Center of Macedonia and Thrace,
Laboratory of Conservation and Evaluation of the Native and Floricultural Species,
PO Box 60 125,
Thessaloniki 570 01
Tel: +0030 231 047 1613
www.bbgk.gr

Julia & Alexander N. Diomides Botanic Garden
University of Athens,
405 Iera Street,
Chaidari,
Athens 124 61
Tel: +0030 210 581 1557

IRELAND

Ardgillan Demesne Regional Park
Fingal, Dublin
Parks Division Tel:
+00353 (0) 1890 2324
http://www.fingalcoco.ie/Leisureand Tourism/ParksHeritageProperties/ ArdgillanDemesneRegionalPark/

Ballymaloe Cookery School Herb Garden
Shanagarry,
Midleton, Co Cork
Tel: +00353 (0)21 464 6785
http://www.cookingisfun.ie/gardens/ herbgarden.htm

ITALY

Giardini Botanici Hanbury
Università degli Studi di Genova,
43, C.so Montecarlo,
La Mortola,
18039 Ventimiglia
Tel: +0039 (0)1 84 22 98 52
http://www.mediterraneangardensoci-ety.org/gardens/Hanbury.Botanic.html

Istituto ed Orto Botanico della Università
Via Luca Ghini 5,
I-56100 Pisa
Tel: +0039 (0)50 56 0045

Orto Botanico dell'Università
Viale Caduti in Guerra 127,
I-41100 Modena
Tel: +0039 (0)59 205 60 04
http://www.ortobot.unimo.it/

Orto Botanico dell'Università di Palermo
Via Lincoln 2,
I-90133 Palermo, Sicilia
Tel: +0039 (0)91 616 1493
http://ortobotanico.palermo.it/index.php

Orto Botanico 'Giardino dei Semplici'
Museo di Storia Naturale,
Universita degli Studi di Firenze,
Via P.A. Micheli 3,
50121 Firenze
Tel: +0039 (0)55 275 7402
http://www.horti.unimore.it/CD/ Firenze/obfi_home.html

Orto Botanico Università degli Studi di Padova
Via Orto Botanico 15,
I-35123 Padova
Tel: +0039 (0)49 827 2119
www.ortobotanico.unipd.it

Orto dei Semplici Elbano
Hermitage S. Caterina,
Mount Serra, nr Rio nell'Elba,
Catania, Sicilia
Tel: +0039 (0)56 594 326

LITHUANIA

Vilniaus universiteto (VU) Botanikos sodas
Kairòn˘ 43, 10239,
Vilnius-40
Tel: +0370 5231 7933
http://www.botanikos-sodas.vu.lt/lt/ index.php

THE NETHERLANDS

Botanic Garden Delft University of Technology
Julianalaan 67,
NL- 2628 BC Delft,
Gate: Poortlandplein 6
Tel: +0031 (0)15 278 2356/278 9396
www.botanischetuin.tudelft.nl

Hortus Botanicus Amsterdam
Plantage Middenlaan 2a,
1018 DD Amsterdam
Tel: +0031 (0)20 625 90 21
http://www.hortus-botanicus.nl/

Leiden University Botanic Garden
P.O. Box 9516,
2300 RA Leiden
Tel: +0031 (0)71 275144/273188

Stekkenplek Zingelspaan
Zwingelspaansedijk 4
4793 SH Zwingelspaan
Tel: +0031 (0)64 142 0880
http://members.home.nl/ruudenien/ Tuin%20(Stekkenplek%20Zwingelspaan)/

Utrecht University Botanic Garden
P.O. Box 80.162,
Budapestlaan 17 (main garden),
Harvardlaan 2 (office),
Utrecht NL-3508
Tel: +0031 (0)30 253 1826
www.botanischetuinen.uu.nl

POLAND

Warsaw University Botanic Garden
Al. Ujazdowskie 4,
00-478 Warszawa
Tel. +0048 22 628 75 14
http://www.garden.uw.edu.pl/

PORTUGAL

Jardim Botânico do Faial
c/o Secretaria Regional do Ambiente,
9900 - Horta,
FAIAL, Acores
Tel: +00351 292 391 119
www.sra.azores.gov.pt

Jardim Botânico da Madeira
Caminho do Meio - Bom Sucesso,
Funchal,
Madeira 9064-512
Tel: +00351 291 211 200
http://www.sra.pt/jarbot/

Parque Botânico da Tapada da Ajuda
Instituto Superior de Agronomia,
Tapada da Ajuda,
Lisboa 1349-017
Tel: +00351 21 365 3168
www.isa.utl.pt

Jardim Botânico da Universidade de Coimbra
Departamento de Botanica,
Faculdate de Ciencias e Tecnologia,
Cacada Martim de Freitas (Arcos do Jardim),
3049 Coimbra
Tel: +00351 239 855233/10
http://www.uc.pt/botanica/jardim.htm

SPAIN

Jardi Botanic de Barcelona
C/- Dr Font Quer s/n
Parc de Montjuic,
08038 Barcelona
Tel: +0034 93 426 4935

Jardin Botanico de Cordoba
Avda de Linneo s/nApdo. 3048,
14080 Corboba
Tel: +0034 957 200 355
www.uco.es/jardin-botanico/

Jardin Botanico-Historico 'La Concepcion' de Malaga
Patronato Botanico Municipal 'Ciudad de Malaga',
C.N. 331 Km166,
29014 Malaga
Tel: +0034 52 250 787

Jardin Botanico 'Viera y Clavijo'
Apartado de Correos 14 de Tafira Alta,
35017 Las Palmas de Gran Canaria,
Islas Canarias
Tel: +0034 928 21 9582/9583/9580
http://www.step.es/jardcan/

Jardi Botanic Marimurtra
Fundacion Carlos Faust No9,
Box 112,
17300 Blanes,
Provincia Girona
Tel: +0034 972 330 826
www.jbotanicmarimurtra.org/eng/jardi.htm

Jardí Botànic de la Universitat de València
Quart, 80,
46008 Valencia
Tel: +0034 963 15 68 00
http://www.jardibotanic.org/

Real Jardin Botanico
Plaza de Murillo 2,
28014 Madrid
Tel: +0034 914 203 017
www.rjb.csic.es

UNITED KINGDOM

Bede's Herb Garden
Church Bank,
Jarrow,
Tyne & Wear, NE32 3DY
Tel: +0044 (0)191 489 2106
http://www.bedesworld.co.uk/bedesworld-herbgarden.php

Belfast Botanic Garden
Botanic Gardens Park,
Botanic Avenue,
Belfast BT7 1JP,
Northern Ireland
Tel: +0044 (0)232 324902

Birmingham Botanical Gardens and Glasshouses
Westbourne Road,
Edgbaston,
Birmingham B15 3TR
Tel: +0044 (0)121 454 1860
www.birminghambotanicalgardens.org.uk

Cambridge University Botanic Garden
Cory Lodge,
Bateman Street,
Cambridge, CB2 1JF
Tel: +0044 (0)1223 336265
www.botanic.cam.ac.uk/

Chelsea Physic Garden
66 Royal Hospital Road,
London SW3 4HS,
Tel: +0044 (0)20 7352 5646
http://www.chelseaphysicgarden.co.uk

Eden Project
Bodelva
St. Austell,
Cornwall PL24 2SG
Tel: +0044 (0)1726 811900
www.edenproject.com

Glasgow Botanic Gardens
730 Great Western Road,
Glasgow G12 0UE,
Tel: +0044 (0)141 334 2422

Herb Garden
Hardstoft,
Pilsley,
Chesterfield,
Derbyshire
Tel: +0044 (0)1246 854268
http://www.peakdistrictonline.co.uk/content.php?categoryId=1785

National Botanic Garden of Wales
Middleton Hall, Llanarthne,
Carmarthenshire, SA32 8HG,
Wales
Tel: +0044 (0)1558 668768
www.gardenofwales.org.uk

National Herb Centre
Banbury Road,
Warmington,
Warks OX17 1DF
Tel: +0044 (0)1295 690999
http://www.herbcentre.co.uk/index.html

Oxford University Botanic Garden
Rose Lane,
Oxford, OX1 4AZ
Tel: +0044 (0)1865 286690
www.botanic-garden.ox.ac.uk

Royal Botanic Garden Edinburgh
20A Inverleith Row,
Edinburgh EH3 5LR
Tel: +0044 (0)131 248 2866/552 7171
www.rbge.org.uk

Royal Botanic Gardens, Kew
Kew,
Richmond,
Surrey TW9 3AB
Tel: +0044 (0)208 332 5000
http://www.kew.org

Sheffield Botanical Gardens
Sheffield City Council Recreation Department,
P.O. Box 151,
Meersbrook Park,
Brook Road,
Sheffield
Tel: +0044 (0)114 250 0500/273 4599
www.sbg.org.uk

University of Bristol Botanic Garden
Bracken Hill,
Leigh Woods,
Bristol BS8 3PF
Tel: +0044 (0)117 973 3682

ASIA

CHINA

Guangxi Medicinal Herb Garden
No.189, Changgang Lu,
Nanning,
Guangxi Province 530023

Lavender Garden Hong Kong
DD76 Lot 655 Hok Tau Road,
Fanling N.T.
Tel: +00852 2674 7822
http://www.lavendergarden.com.hk/Introduction.asp

Nanjing Botanic Garden Mem. Sun Yat-Sen
Zhongshanmen Wai,
Nanjing,
Jiangsu, 210014
Tel: +0086 (0)25 8434 7110
http://www.cnbg.net/

BHUTAN

Royal Botanic Garden (Bhutan)
National Biodiversity Program, Ministry of Agriculture,
Thimphu
http://www.geocities.com/royalbotanicgarden_bhutan/Welcome.html

INDIA

Mughal Garden
Rashtrapati Bhawan (President's House),
New Delhi
http://presidentofindia.nic.in/mughalGarden.html

ISRAEL

The Jerusalem Botanical Gardens
Hebrew University,
Givat Ram Campus,
Jerusalem 91904
Tel: +00972 (0)2 679 4012
http://www.botanic.co.il/

Tel Aviv University Botanic Gardens
Department of Botany,
George S. Wise Faculty of Life Sciences,
Tel Aviv University,
69978 Tel Aviv
Tel: +00972 (0)3 640 9910
http://www.tau.ac.il/lifesci/botany/
Gardens/

JAPAN

Koishikawa Botanical Gardens
3-7-1 Hakusan,
Bunkyo-ku, Tokyo, 112-0001
Tel: +0081 (0)3 3814 2625
http://www.bg.s.u–tokyo.ac.jp/
koishikawa/eigo/e.html

Nunobiki Gardens,
Kobe
Tel: +0081 (0)78 271 1131
http://www.kobe–park.or.jp/

SOUTH KOREA

Korea National Arboretum
51-7 Jikdong-ri,
Soheul-eup,
Pocheon-si,
Gyeonggi-do, 487821
Tel: +0082 (0)31 540 1030
http://www.koreaplants.go.kr:9300/eng/

RUSSIA

Botanic Garden of the Irkutsk State University
Koltsova Street, bldg. 93,
PO Box 1457,
Irkutsk
Tel: +007 395 238 7476
http://bogard.isu.ru/indexe.htm

Komarov Botanical Institute
Russian Academy of Sciences,
2 Prof. Popova Str.,
St. Petersburg 197376
Tel. +007 812 234 1237.
http://spbrc.nw.ru/!english/org/bin.htm

SRI LANKA

Royal Botanic Gardens,
Peradeniya
Tel: +0094 81 238 8238
http://www.agridept.gov.lk/NBG/RBG.htm

VIETNAM

Tam Dao Botanic Garden
Tam Dao National Park Headquarters
Ho Son Com,
Tam Duong District,
Tam Dao,
Vinh Phuc Province
Tel: +0084 (0)21 867 399

AFRICA

ALGERIA

Jardin Botanique du Hamma
Cite said Hamdine Bt K1,
No 3 Bir Mourad Rais,
Hamma
Tel: +00213 267 4750

GHANA

Aburi Botanic Gardens
PO Box 23,
ABURI,
Akwiapim
Tel: +00233 2176 4337
http://www.unep–wcmc.org/species/
plants/ghana/aburi.htm

University of Ghana Botanical Garden
PMB 49 Legon,
Accra
Tel: +00233 2140 1143
www.ubglegon.org

KENYA

Nairobi Arboretum
Friends of Nairobi Arboretum
Nature Kenya
PO Box 44486
GPO 00100
Nairobi
Tel: +00254 20 374 9957
http://www.naturekenya.org/FON
Arboretum.htm

MAURITIUS

Sir Seewoosagur Ramgoolam Botanic Garden
Pamplemousses
Tel: +00230 243 9401
http://www.gov.mu/portal/site/ssrbg

MOROCCO

Jardin Botanique, Institut Agronomique et Vétérinaire, Hassan II
BP 6202 Madinat Al Irfane,
10101 Rabat
Tel: +00212 (0)37 77 17 58/59
http://www.iav.ac.ma/

SOUTH AFRICA

Bloemfontein National Botanical Garden
Rayton Road, off Dan Pienaar Drive,
R702 PO Box
29036, Danhof, 9310
Tel : +0027 (0)51 436 3612/3530
http://www.nbi.ac.za/freestate/
mainpage.htm

Durban Botanic Garden
70 St Thomas Rd,
Durban 4001,
Tel: +0027 (0)31 2011 303
http://www.durban.gov.za/eThekwini/
Services/parks/dbn_botanic_gardens

The Garden Route Botanical Garden
c/o Southern Cape Herbarium,
49 Caledon Street,
George 6529
Tel: +0027 (0)44 874 1558
www.botanicalgarden.org.za

Johannesburg Botanical Garden
PO Box 2824,
Johannesburg 2000
Tel: +0027 (0)11 782 7064
http://www.jobot.co.za/

Karoo Desert National Botanical Garden
Roux Road,
Van Riebeeck Park (off National Road),
PO Box 152, Worcester, 6850
Tel: +0027 (0)23 347 0785
http://www.sanbi.org/frames/
karfram.htm

Kirstenbosch National Botanical Garden
Rhodes Drive, Newlands,
Private Bag X7,
Claremont 7735,
Cape Town
Tel: +0027 (0)21 799 8899
http://www.nbi.ac.za/frames/
kirstfram.htm

KwaZulu-Natal National Botanical Garden
P.O. Box 21667,
Mayors Walk,
Pietermaritzburg,
KwaZulu-Natal Province
Tel: +0027 (0)33 344 3585
http://www.sanbi.org/frames/
natalfram.htm

Pretoria National Botanical Garden
2 Cussonia Avenue,
Brummeria,
Private Bag X101,
Pretoria, 0001
Tel: +0027 (0)12 843 5194
http://www.sanbi.org/frames/
pretoriafram.htm

AUSTRALASIA

AUSTRALIA

Alice Springs Desert Park
Dept. of Infrastructure, Planning
and Environment,
PO Box 2130,
Alice Springs,
NT 0871
Tel: +0061 (0)8 8951 8788
www.alicespringsdesertpark.com.au

**Australian Arid Lands Botanic
Garden**
PO Box 2083,
Port Augusta,
SA 5700
Tel: +0061 (0)8 8641 1049
www.australian-aridlands-botanic-
garden.org/

Australian Inland Botanic Garden
PO Box 2809,
Mildura,
VIC 3502
Tel: +0061 (0)3 5023 3612

Australian National Botanic Gardens
GPO Box 1777,
Clunies-Ross St., Black Mtn.
Canberra City,
ACT 2601
Tel: +0061 (0)2 6250 9450
www.anbg.gov.au/anbg

Botanic Gardens of Adelaide
North Terrace,
Adelaide,
South Australia 5000
Tel: +0061 (0)8 8222 9311
http://www.environment.sa.gov.au/
botanicgardens/

**Brisbane Botanic Gardens and
Queensland Herbarium**
Mt Coot-tha Rd,
Toowong QLD 4066
Tel: +0061 (0)7 3896 9326
http://www.epa.qld.gov.au/nature_
conservation/plants/queensland_
herbarium/

Darwin Botanic Gardens
Parks and Wildlife Commission of the
Northern Territory,
PO Box 496, Palmerston,
NT 0831,
Darwin
Tel: +0061 (0)8 8981 1958
http:/www.nt.gov.au/paw

Flecker Botanic Gardens
Cairns City Council,
PO Box 359,
Cairns,
Queensland 4870
Tel: +0061 (0)7 4044 3398

Illawarra Grevillea Park
Illawarra Grevillea Park Society Inc,
Princes Highway,
Bulli,
NSW 2516
Tel: +0061 (0)2 4284 9216

Kings Park and Botanic Garden
Botanic Gardens and Parks Authority
Fraser Avenue,
West Perth,
Western Australia 6005
Tel: +0061 (0)8 9480 3600
www.bgpa.wa.gov.au

Mount Annan Botanic Garden
Mount Annan Drive,
Mount Annan,
NSW 2567
Tel: +0061 (0)2 4648 2477
www.rbgsyd.gov.au

Mount Lofty Botanic Garden
Summit Road or Piccadilly Road,
Crafers SA 5152
Tel: +0061 (0)8 8370 8370
http://www.environment.sa.gov.au/
botanicgardens/mtlofty.html

Myall Park
24 Victoria Terrace,
Annerley,
Brisbane,
Queensland 4103
Tel: +0061 (0)7 3391 4287
www.users.bigpond.com/myall_park_
b_garden/

**North Coast Regional Botanic
Garden**
C/- Parks Branch, Coffs Harbour
City Council,
Coffs Harbour,
NSW 2450
Tel: +0061 (0)2 6652 0779
http://www.holidaycoast.net.au/42.html

Royal Tasmanian Botanical Gardens
Queens Domain,
Hobart,
Tasmania 7000
Tel: +0061 (0)3 6236 3050
www.rtbg.tas.gov.au

Royal Botanic Gardens,
Melbourne,
Private Bag 2000,
Birdwood Avenue,
South Yarra,
VIC 3141
Tel: +0061 (0)3 9252 2300
http:/www.rbgmelb.org.au

Royal Botanic Gardens Sydney
Mrs Macquaries Road,
Sydney,
NSW 2000,
Tel: +0061 (0)2 9231 8111
http:/www.rbgsyd.gov.au

Stony Range Flora Reserve
Pittwater Road,
Dee Why,
NSW 2099
Tel: +0064 (0)2 9981 3026

Tasmanian Arboretum Inc
PO Box 370,
46 Old Tramway Road
Devonport,
TAS 7310
Tel: +0064 (0)3 6424 5954/6427 1690

Wittunga Botanic Garden
Shepherd's Hill Road,
Blackwood SA 5051
Tel: +0061 (0)8 8370 8370
http://www.environment.sa.gov.au/
botanicgardens/wittunga.html

Wollongong Botanic Gardens
Locked Bag 8821,
South Coast Mail Centre,
Wollongong,
NSW 2521
Tel: +0061 (0)2 4225 2636/2637
http://botanicgarden.wollongong.
nsw.gov.au/

NEW ZEALAND

Auckland Botanic Gardens,
102 Hill Road,
Manurewa, 1702
Tel: +0064 (0)9 267 1457
www.aucklandbotanicgardens.co.nz

Christchurch Botanic Gardens
City Council,
Greenspace Unit,
P.O. Box 237,
Christchurch
Tel: +0064 (0)3 941 6840
www.ccc.govt.nz/parks/BotanicGardens/

Dunedin Botanic Garden
Dunedin City Council,
Corner of Great King Street
and Opoho Road,
Dunedin
Tel: +0064 (0)3 477 4000
www.cityofdunedin.com/city/

Otari Native Botanic Garden
Wilton,
P.O. Box 2199,
Wellington N 5
Tel: +0064 (0)4 475 3245

Timaru Botanic Garden
Parks and Recreation Department,
City Council,
P.O. Box 522,
2 George St,
Timaru
Tel: +0064 (0)3 688 6163

Wellington Botanic Garden
Wellington City Council,
P.O. Box 2199, Wellington
Tel: +0064 (0)4 499 1400
www.wellington.govt.nz

Common Name Key

A plant's common name is the identifying term bestowed upon it by non-scientists. Common names can reflect a plant's (1) appearance – devil's claw (*Harpagophytum procumbens*) is so named because its leaves look like claws; (2) legend – Mary's thistle (*Silybum marianum*) takes its name from a story in which Mary, mother of Jesus, was resting beneath a thistle plant while breastfeeding the baby Jesus – a drop of her milk fell on the plant's green leaves, leading to the leaves' characteristic white markings; or (3) use – native Americans use colic root (*Dioscorea villosa*) to treat colic. Common names can vary widely by region and so one plant can have many different common names. This chart connects each common name referred to in this book to the herb's botanical name for easy reference.

COMMON NAME	BOTANICAL NAME
acacia	*Acacia* spp.
achiote	*Bixa orellana*
aconite	*Aconitum napellus*
African plum	*Prunus africana; Pygeum africanum*
agnus-castus	*Vitex agnus-castus*
agrimony	*Agrimonia eupatoria*
Alexandrian sennasenna	*Cassia senna; senna Alexandrina*
alfalfa	*Medicago sativa*
allspice	*Pimenta dioica*
almond	*Prunus dulcis*
aloe	*Aloe vera; a. barbadensis*
aloe vera	*Aloe vera; a. barbadensis*
alpine strawberry	*Fragaria vesca* 'Alexandria'
amaranth	*Amaranthus* spp.
American beech	*Fagus grandifolia*
American cranberry	*Vaccinium macrocarpon*
American cranesbill	*Geranium maculatum*
American ginseng	*Panax quinquefolius; Panax ginseng*
American lovage	*Levisticum officinale*
American mandrake	*Podophyllum peltatum*
ananas	*Ananas comosus*
anenome	*Pulsatilla vulgaris*
angelica	*Angelica Archangelica*
anise	*Pimpinella anisum*
anise hyssop	*Agastache foeniculum*
aniseed	*Pimpinella anisum*
annatto	*Bixa orellana*
annual savory	*Satureja hortensis*
apricot	*Prunus armeniaca*
Arabian coffee	*Coffea Arabica*
archangel	*Angelica Archangelica*
arnica	*Arnica montana*
arrowroot	*Maranta arundinaceae*
artichoke	*Cynara scolymus*
asafetida	*Ferula asafoetida*
ashwagandha	*Withania somnifera*
Asian ginseng	*Panax quinquefolius; Panax ginseng*
Asian pennywort	*Centella asiatica*
aspen	*Populus* spp.
asthma weed	*Grindelia* spp.
astragalus	*Astragalus membranaceus*

COMMON NAME	BOTANICAL NAME
aubergine	*Solanum melongena*
Australian nut	*Macadamia integrifolia; Macadamia tetraphylla*
autumn crocus	*Colchicum autumnale*
avens	*Geum urbanum*
awa	*Piper methysticum*
Aztec sweet herb	*Phyla scaberrima*
balm	*Melissa officinalis*
balsam pear	*Momordica charantia*
Barbados aloe	*Aloe vera; a. barbadensis*
barberry	*Berberis vulgaris*
basil	*Ocimum basilicum*
basil thyme	*Calamintha nepeta*
basswood	*Tilia* spp.
bay	*Laurus nobilis*
bay laurel	*Laurus nobilis*
bayberry	*Myrica cerifera*
bdellium tree	*Commiphora mukul; c. wightii*
bead tree	*Azadirachta indica*
bear's foot	*Alchemilla vulgaris*
bearberry	*Arctostaphylos uva-ursi*
bee balm	*Melissa officinalis*
beech	*Fagus grandifolia*
beggar lice	*Desmodium styracifolium*
belladonna	*Atropa belladonna*
bergamot	*Monarda* spp.
betony	*Stachys officinalis*
bilberry	*Vaccinium myrtillus*
birch	*Betula pendula*
bishop's weed	*Ammi majus*
bitter almond	*Prunus dulcis*
bitter melon	*Momordica charantia*
bitter orange	*Citrus x aurantium*
bitterroot	*Lewisia rediviva*
black bugbane	*Cimicifuga racemosa; actaea racemosa*
black cohosh	*Cimicifuga racemosa; actaea racemosa*
black elder	*Sambucus nigra*
black haw	*Viburnum prunifolium*
black hellebore	*Helleborus niger*
black horehound	*Ballota nigra*
black nightshade	*Solanum nigrum*
black pepper	*Piper nigrum*

COMMON NAME	BOTANICAL NAME
black snakeroot	Cimicifuga racemosa; actaea racemosa
black tea	Camellia sinensis
blackberry	Rubus canadensis; Rubus fruticosus
blackberry lily	Belamcanda chinensis
blackcurrant	Ribes nigrum
black-eyed Susan	Rudbeckia hirta
bladder wrack	Fucus vesiculosus
blessed thistle	Cnicus benedictus
bloodroot	Sanguinaria canadensis
blue cohosh	Caulophyllum thalictroides
blue flag	Iris spp.
blue giant hyssop	Agastache foeniculum
blue gum	Eucalyptus globulus
blue pimpernel	Scutellaria lateriflora
blue vervain	Verbena hastata
blueberry	Vaccinium corymbosum
bogbean	Menyanthes trifoliata
borage	Borago officinalis
boswellia	Boswellia serrata
bottle brush	Equisetum arvense
bouncing Bet	Saponaria officinalis
bourbon vanilla	Vanilla planifolia
box holly	Ruscus aculeatus
bramble	Rubus canadensis; Rubus fruticosus
Brazil nut	Bertholettia excelsa
Brazilian pawpaw	Annona muricata
broad bean	Vicia faba
broad-leaf plantain	Plantago major
broom	Cytisus scoparius
broomweed	Sida rhombifolia
brown mustard	Brassica juncea
buchu	Barosma crenulata; Agathosma crenulata
buckeye	Aesculus hippocastanum
buckthorn	Rhamnus cathartica
bugleweed	Lycopus spp.
burdock	Arctium lappa
burnet-saxifrage	Pimpinella major
butcher's broom	Ruscus aculeatus
butterfly weed	Asclepias tuberosa
cacao	Theobroma cacao
calamus	Acorus calamus
calendula	Calendula officinalis
camu-camu	Myrciaria dubia
candleberry	Myrica cerifera
candyleaf	Stevia rebaudiana
cankerroot	Coptis chinensis
caper	Capparis spinosa
caper berry	Capparis spinosa
caper bush	Capparis spinosa

COMMON NAME	BOTANICAL NAME
caraway	Carum carvi
cardamom	Elettaria cardamomum
carob	Ceratonia siliqua
carrageen	Chondrus crispus
carrot	Daucus carota; Daucus carota sativus
cascara sagrada	Rhamnus purshiana
cassia	Cinnamomum spp.
castor bean	Ricinus communis
cat's claw	Uncaria tomentosa
catmint	Nepeta cataria
catnip	Nepeta cataria
cattail	Typha latifolia
cayenne pepper	Capsicum annuum
celandine	Chelidonium majus
celery	Apium graveolens
Ceylon cardamom	Elettaria cardamomum
chaparral	Larrea tridentata
chaste tree	Vitex agnus-castus
chasteberry	Vitex agnus-castus
cheese rennet	Galium verum
chervil	Anthriscus cerefolium
chickweed	Stellaria media
chicory	Cichorium intybus
chilli pepper	Capsicum annuum
China root	Dioscorea villosa
Chinese angelica	Angelica sinensis
Chinese bitter almond	Prunus armeniaca
Chinese ephedra	Ephedra sinica
Chinese jointfir	Ephedra sinica
Chinese mustard	Brassica juncea
Chinese parsley	Coriandrum sativum
Chinese peony	aeonia lactiflora
Chinese rhubarb	Rheum palmatum
Chinese silk plant	Boehmeria nivea
Chinese tea	Camellia sinensis
Chinese wolfberry	Lycium spp.
chiso	Perilla frutescens
chives	Allium schoenoprasum
chlorella	Chlorella pyrenoidosa; Chlorella vulgaris
chocolate	Theobroma cacao
chokecherry	Prunus virginiana
Christmas rose	Helleborus niger
church steeples	Agrimonia eupatoria
cilantro	Coriandrum sativum
cinchona	Cinchona spp.
cinnamon	Acorus calamus; Cinnamomum spp.
cinquefoil	Potentilla anserina
cleavers	Galium aparine
clove	Syzygium aromaticum

COMMON NAME	BOTANICAL NAME
coca	*Erythroxylum coca*
cocoa	*Theobroma cacao*
coffee	*Coffea Arabica*
coleus	*Coleus forskohlii; plectranthus barbatus*
colic root	*Dioscorea villosa*
coltsfoot	*Tussilago farfara*
comfrey	*Symphytum officinale*
common alkanet	*Anchusa officinalis*
common juniper	*Juniperus communis*
common lime	*Tilia* spp.
common madder	*Rubia tinctorum*
common marigold	*Calendula officinalis*
common rue	*Ruta graveolens*
common sage	*Salvia officinalis*
common turmeric	*Curcuma longa*
coriander	*Coriandrum sativum*
corn	*Zea mays*
costmary	*Chrysanthemum balsamita*
cotton lavender	*Santolina chamaecyparissus*
cottonwood	*Populus* spp.
couch grass	*Elymus repens*
cough plant	*Tussilago farfara*
coughwort	*Tussilago farfara*
country mallow	*Sida cordifolia*
cow grass	*Polygonum aviculare*
cowslip	*Primula veris*
cranberry	*Vaccinium macrocarpon*
cranesbill	*Geranium maculatum*
creosote bush	*Larrea tridentata*
cress	*Nasturtium officinale*
crown daisy	*Chrysanthemum coronarium*
cubeb	*Piper cubeba*
culantro	*Eryngium foetidum*
cumin	*Cuminum cyminum*
curly-leaf parsley	*Petroselinum crispum*
curry leaf	*Murraya koenigii*
cynara	*Cynara scolymus*
da huang	*Rheum palmatum*
damiana	*Turnera diffusa*
dandelion	*Taraxacum officinale*
deadly nightshade	*Atropa belladonna*
devil's claw	*Harpagophytum procumbens*
devil's dung	*Ferula asafoetida*
digitalis, foxglove	*Digitalis purpurea*
dill	*Anethum graveolens*
dog fennel	*Chamaemelum nobile; Anthemis nobilis*
dog's grass	*Elymus repens*
domestic apple	*Malus domestica*
dong quai	*Angelica sinensis*

COMMON NAME	BOTANICAL NAME
duck's foot	*Podophyllum peltatum*
Dutch honeysuckle	*Lonicera* spp.
dyer's bugloss	*Anchusa officinalis*
dyer's green weed	*Genista tinctoria*
East Indian sandalwood	*Santalum album*
echinacea	*Echinacea* spp.
edelweiss	*Leontopodium alpinum*
eggplant	*Solanum melongena*
elderberry	*Sambucus nigra*
elecampane	*Inula helenium*
English chamomile	*Chamaemelum nobile; Anthemis nobilis*
English hawthorn	*Crataegus laevigata; c. oxyacantha*
English violet	*Viola odorata*
English walnut	*Juglans regia*
epazote	*Chenopodium ambrosioides*
ephedra	*Ephedra sinica*
epimediue	*Epimedium* spp.
estragon	*Artemisia dracunculus*
eucalyptus	*Eucalyptus globulus*
European angelica	*Angelica Archangelica*
European arnica	*Arnica montana*
European barberry	*Berberis vulgaris*
European blueberry	*Vaccinium myrtillus*
European elder	*Sambucus nigra*
European grape	*Vitis vinifera*
European verbena	*Verbena officinalis*
European white birch	*Betula pendula*
evening primrose	*Oenothera biennis*
eyebright	*Euphrasia officinalis*
false myrrh	*Commiphora mukul; c. wightii*
false saffron	*Carthamus tinctorius*
fava bean	*Vicia faba*
fennel	*Foeniculum vulgare*
fennel giant hyssop	*Agastache foeniculum*
fenugreek	*Trigonella foenum-graecum*
fever grass	*Cymbopogon citratus*
fever tree	*Cinchona* spp.
feverfew	*Tanacetum parthenium*
fig	*Ficus carica*
figwort	*Ranunculus ficaria; Scrophularia nodosa*
filbert	*Corylus avellana*
fit weed	*Eryngium foetidum*
flat-leaf parsley	*Petroselinum crispum*
flax	*Linum usitatissimum*
flaxseed	*Linum usitatissimum*
fleabane	*Mentha pulegium*
flowery knotweed	*Polygonum multiflorum; polygonum officinale*
food-of-the-gods	*Ferula asafoetida*
forskohlii	*Coleus forskohlii; plectranthus barbatus*

COMMON NAME	BOTANICAL NAME
French tarragon	*Artemisia dracunculus*
fumitory	*Fumaria officinalis*
gag root	*Lobelia inflata*
galangal	*Alpinia galanga*
garden chervil	*Armoracia rusticana*
garden heliotrope	*Valeriana officinalis*
garden valerian	*Valeriana officinalis*
garden violet	*Viola odorata*
garderobe	*Artemisia abrotanum*
garland chrysanthemum	*Chrysanthemum coronarium*
garlic	*Allium sativum*
gentian	*Gentiana lutea*
geranium	*Geranium robertianum*
germander	*Teucrium chamaedrys*
giant whortleberry	*Vaccinium corymbosum*
ginger	*Zingiber officinale*
gingerroot	*Zingiber officinale*
ginkgo	*Ginkgo biloba*
ginseng	*Panax quinquefolius; Panax ginseng*
globe artichoke	*Cynara scolymus*
gobo	*Arctium lappa*
goldenrod	*Solidago* spp.
goldenseal	*Hydrastis canadensis*
goldthread	*Coptis chinensis*
goober pea	*Arachis hypogaea*
goosegrass	*Galium aparine*
gotu kola	*Centella asiatica*
grains of paradise	*Aframomum melegueta*
grape	*Vitis vinifera*
gravel root	*Eupatorium purpureum*
graviola	*Annona muricata*
great burdock	*Arctium lappa*
great reedmace	*Typha latifolia*
greater galangal	*Alpinia galanga*
greater plantain	*Plantago major*
Grecian laurel	*Laurus nobilis*
green ginger	*Artemisia absinthium*
green tea	*Camellia sinensis*
grindelia	*Grindelia* spp.
ground holly	*Chimaphila umbellata*
ground lemon	*Podophyllum peltatum*
groundnut	*Arachis hypogaea*
guanabana	*Annona muricata*
guarana	*Paullinia cupana*
guava	*Psidium guajava*
guggul	*Commiphora mukul; c. wightii*
guinea pepper	*Aframomum melegueta*
gymnema	*Gymnema sylvestre*
gypsywort	*Lycopus* spp.

COMMON NAME	BOTANICAL NAME
hawthorn	*Crataegus laevigata; c. oxyacantha*
hazelnut	*Corylus avellana*
healing-herb	*Symphytum officinale*
hemlock	*Conium maculatum*
henna	*Lawsonia inermis*
herb Benedict	*Geum urbanum*
herb Robert	*Geranium robertianum*
herb-of-grace	*Ruta graveolens*
hickory	*Carya* spp.
high bush blueberry	*Vaccinium corymbosum*
holy thistle	*Cnicus benedictus*
honeysuckle	*Lonicera* spp.
hops	*Humulus lupulus*
horehound	*Marrubium vulgare*
horny goatweed	*Epimedium* spp.
horse chestnut	*Aesculus hippocastanum*
horse hoof	*Tussilago farfara*
horsebalm	*Monarda* spp.
horseheal	*Inula helenium*
horseradish	*Armoracia rusticana*
horsetail	*Equisetum arvense*
huang qi	*Astragalus membranaceus*
huckleberry	*Vaccinium myrtillus*
hyssop	*Hyssopus officinalis*
Iceland moss	*Cetraria islandica*
impatiens	*Impatiens capensis*
Indian almond	*Terminalia catappa*
Indian frankincense	*Boswellia serrata*
Indian ginseng	*Withania somnifera*
Indian mustard	*Brassica juncea*
Indian olibanum	*Boswellia serrata*
Indian pennywort	*Centella asiatica*
Indian saffron	*Curcuma longa*
Indian senna	*Cassia senna; senna alexandrina*
Indian snakeroot	*Rauwolfia serpentina*
Indian tobacco	*Lobelia inflata*
indigo	*Indigofera tinctoria*
ipe roxo	*Tabebuia impetiginosa*
ipecac	*Cephaelis ipecacuana*
Irish moss	*Chondrus crispus*
Italian parsley	*Petroselinum crispum*
jaborandi	*Pilocarpus microphyllus*
Jamaican pepper	*Pimenta dioica*
Jamestown weed	*Datura stramonium*
Japanese forest mushroom	*Lentinula edodes*
Japanese honeysuckle	*Lonicera* spp.
Japanese parsley	*Cryptotaenia japonica*
Japanese wild chervil	*Cryptotaenia japonica*
jasmine	*Jasminum officinale; grandiflorum*

COMMON NAME	BOTANICAL NAME
java pepper	*Piper cubeba*
java tea	*Orthosiphon aristatus*
jewelweed	*Impatiens capensis*
jimsonweed	*Datura stramonium*
joe-pye weed	*Eupatorium purpureum*
johimbe	*Pausinystalia johimbe*
juniper	*Juniperus communis*
jute	*Corchorus olitorius*
kaffir potato	*Coleus forskohlii; plectranthus barbatus*
Kansas snakeroot	*Echinacea spp.*
kava	*Piper methysticum*
kava kava	*Piper methysticum*
kava pepper	*Piper methysticum*
kelp	*Laminaria spp.*
khella	*Ammi visnaga*
kinnikinnik	*Arctostaphylos uva-ursi*
knitbone	*Symphytum officinale*
knotgrass	*Polygonum aviculare*
Korean watercress	*Oenanthe javanica*
kudzu	*Pueraria lobata*
lad's love	*Artemisia abrotanum*
lady's bedstraw	*Galium verum*
lady's mantle	*Alchemilla vulgaris*
lapacho	*Tabebuia impetiginosa*
large cranberry	*Vaccinium macrocarpon*
large-leaf mustard	*Brassica juncea*
lavender	*Lavandula angustifolia*
lavender cotton	*Santolina chamaecyparissus*
lemon	*Citrus x limon*
lemon balm	*Melissa officinalis*
lemon ironwood	*Backhousia citriodora*
lemon myrtle	*Backhousia citriodora*
lemon verbena	*Aloysia triphylla; Aloysia citriodora*
lemongrass	*Cymbopogon citratus*
leopard flower	*Belamcanda chinensis*
leopard's bane	*Arnica montana*
lesser calamint	*Calamintha nepeta*
lesser celandine	*Ranunculus ficaria*
lesser periwinkle	*Vinca minor*
liquorice	*Glycyrrhiza glabra*
lily of the valley	*Convallaria majalis*
lime	*Citrus x aurantifolia*
linden	*Tilia spp.*
ling zhi	*Ganoderma lucidum*
linseed	*Linum usitatissimum*
lion's ear	*Leonurus cardiaca*
lion's foot	*Alchemilla vulgaris*
lion's tail	*Leonurus cardiaca*
lion's tooth	*Taraxacum officinale*

COMMON NAME	BOTANICAL NAME
lipstick tree	*Bixa orellana*
lobelia	*Lobelia inflata*
locust bean	*Ceratonia siliqua*
lomatium	*Lomatium dissectum*
lovage	*Levisticum officinale*
lover's plant	*Artemisia abrotanum*
lucerne	*Medicago sativa*
lungwort	*Pulmonaria officinalis*
ma huang	*Ephedra sinica*
macadamia	*Macadamia integrifolia; Macadamia tetraphylla*
mad apple	*Datura stramonium*
mad dog weed	*Scutellaria lateriflora*
Madagascar vanilla	*Vanilla planifolia*
magnolia vine	*Schisandra chinensis*
maidenhair tree	*Ginkgo biloba*
maize	*Zea mays*
mandrake	*Mandragora officinarum*
margosa	*Azadirachta indica*
marijuana	*Cannabis sativa*
marjoram	*Origanum majorana*
marsh mallow	*Althaea officinalis*
Mary's thistle	*Silybum marianum*
maté	*Ilex paraguariensis*
matrimony vine	*Lycium spp.*
May lily	*Convallaria majalis*
may tree	*Crataegus laevigata; c. oxyacantha*
mayapple	*Podophyllum peltatum*
maypop	*Passiflora incarnata*
meadowsweet	*Filipendula ulmaria*
melegueta pepper	*Aframomum melegueta*
Melissa	*Melissa officinalis*
Melissa balm	*Melissa officinalis*
mescal	*Lophophora williamsii*
Mexican cilantro	*Eryngium foetidum*
Mexican coriander	*Eryngium foetidum*
Mexican tea	*Chenopodium ambrosioides*
Mexican vanilla	*Vanilla planifolia*
milfoil	*Achillea millefolium*
milk thistle	*Silybum marianum*
milkwort	*Polygala senega*
mint savory	*Calamintha grandiflora "Rockwell"*
mistletoe	*Viscum album*
mitsuba	*Cryptotaenia japonica*
monk's pepper	*Vitex agnus-castus*
monkshood	*Aconitum napellus*
mosquito plant	*Mentha pulegium*
motherwort	*Leonurus cardiaca*
mountain ash	*Sorbus aucuparia*
mountain mint	*Calamintha nepeta*

COMMON NAME	BOTANICAL NAME
mountain pepper berry	*Tasmania lanceolata*
mountain tobacco	*Arnica montana*
mugwort	*Artemisia vulgaris*
mulberry	*Morus alba*
mullein	*Verbascum thapus*
mustard	*Brassica juncea*
myrrh	*Commiphora myrrha*
myrtle	*Myrtus communis*
narrow-leaf echinacea	*Echinacea* spp.
nasturtium	*Tropaeolum majus*
native caper	*Capparis canescens*
neem	*Azadirachta indica*
nettle	*Urtica dioica*
New Jersey tea	*Ceanothus americanus*
nimba	*Azadirachta indica*
North American wild yam	*Dioscorea villosa*
northern prickly ash	*Zanthoxylum americanum*
northern schisandra	*Schisandra chinensis*
nutmeg	*Myristica fragrans*
nux-vomica	*Strychnos nux-vomica*
oak	*Quercus alba; Quercus robur*
oats	*Avena sativa*
ojo de buey	*Mucuna pruriens*
ojo de llama	*Mucuna pruriens*
olive	*Olea europaea*
onion	*Allium cepa*
opium poppy	*Papaver somniferum*
orange	*Citrus sinensis*
orange milkweed	*Asclepias tuberosa*
orange root	*Hydrastis canadensis*
oregano	*Origanum vulgare*
Oregon grape	*Mahonia aquifolium*
orris	*Iris* spp.
osha	*Ligusticum porteri*
Oswego tea	*Monarda* spp.
ovate buchu	*Barosma crenulata; Agathosma crenulata*
pale flag	*Iris* spp.
pandan	*Pandanus* spp.
pandan wangi	*Pandanus* spp.
papaya	*Carica papaya*
Paraguay tea	*Ilex paraguariensis*
Paraguayan sweet herb	*Stevia rebaudiana*
parsley	*Petroselinum crispum*
partridgeberry	*Mitchella repens*
pasqueflower	*Pulsatilla vulgaris*
passion flower	*Passiflora incarnata*
patchouli	*Pogostemon cablin*
pau d'arco	*Tabebuia impetiginosa*
pea	*Pisum sativum*

COMMON NAME	BOTANICAL NAME
peanut	*Arachis hypogaea*
pear	*Pyrus communis*
pennyroyal	*Mentha pulegium*
peppergrass	*Lepidium* spp.
peppermint	*Mentha x piperita*
perfoliate honeysuckle	*Lonicera* spp.
Persian walnut	*Juglans regia*
Peruvian bark	*Cinchona* spp.
pettigree	*Ruscus aculeatus*
peyotep	*Lophophora williamsii*
pigweed	*Polygonum aviculare*
pilewort	*Ranunculus ficaria*
pimpernel	*Pimpinella major*
pineapple	*Ananas comosus*
pink trumpet tree	*Tabebuia impetiginosa*
pipsissewa	*Chimaphila umbellata*
plantain	*Plantago major*
pleurisy root	*Asclepias tuberosa*
poet's jasmine	*Jasminum officinale; grandiflorum*
poison parsley	*Conium maculatum*
poke	*Phytolacca americana*
pokeroot	*Phytolacca americana*
pokeweed	*Phytolacca americana*
pomegranate	*Punica granatum*
poplar	*Populus* spp.
pot marigold	*Calendula officinaliss*
potato	*Solanum tuberosum*
potentilla	*Potentilla anserina*
prairie redroot	*Ceanothus americanus*
prince's pine	*Chimaphila umbellata*
puke weed	*Lobelia inflata*
pumpkin	*Cucurbita pepo*
purple foxglove	*Digitalis purpurea*
purslane	*Portulaca oleracea*
pygeum	*Prunus africana; Pygeum africanum*
quebracho	*Aspidosperma quebracho-blanco*
Queen Anne's lace	*Daucus carota; Daucus carota sativus*
queen's delight	*Stillingia sylvatica*
queen-of-the-meadow	*Eupatorium purpureum*
Queensland nut	*Macadamia integrifolia; Macadamia tetraphylla*
quinine tree	*Cinchona* spp.
radish	*Raphanus sativus*
ramie	*Boehmeria nivea*
raspberry	*Rubus idaeus*
rau ram	*Polygonum odoratum*
red bush tea	*Aspalathus linearis*
red clover	*Trifolium pratense*
red pepper	*Capsicum annuum*
red puccoon	*Sanguinaria canadensis*

COMMON NAME	BOTANICAL NAME
red root	*Sanguinaria canadensis*
redroot	*Ceanothus americanus*
reishi	*Ganoderma lucidum*
rhatany	*Krameria triandra*
rheumatism root	*Dioscorea villosa*
rheumatism weed	*Cimicifuga racemosa; actaea racemosa*
rock samphire	*Crithmum maritimum*
Roman chamomile	*Chamaemelum nobile; Anthemis nobilis*
rooibus	*Aspalathus linearis*
rose	*Rose* spp.
rosemary	*Rosmarinus officinalis*
rosy periwinkle	*Catharanthus roseus*
rowan	*Sorbus aucuparia*
rue	*Ruta graveolens*
Russian liquorice	*Glycyrrhiza glabra*
sabal palm	*Serenoa repens*
sacred bark	*Rhamnus purshiana*
safflower	*Carthamus tinctorius*
saffron	*Crocus sativus*
salad burnet	*Sanguisorba minor*
sandalwood	*Santalum album*
santolina	*Santolina chamaecyparissus*
sarsaparilla	*Smilax* spp.
sassafras	*Sassafras albidum*
Satan's apple	*Mandragora officinarum*
saw palmetto	*Serenoa repens*
scabwort	*Inula helenium*
scented geranium	*Pelargonium* spp.
schisandra	*Schisandra chinensis*
schizandra	*Schisandra chinensis*
sciatica cress	*Lepidium* spp.
Scotch broom	*Cytisus scoparius*
Scots pine	*Pinus sylvestris*
scouring rush	*Equisetum arvense*
screw pine	*Pandanus* spp.
sea celery	*Apium prostratum*
self-heal	*Prunella vulgaris*
seneca snakeroot	*Polygala senega*
serpentwood	*Rauwolfia serpentina*
sesame	*Sesamum indicum*
Seville orange	*Citrus x aurantium*
shepherd's purse	*Capsella bursa-pastoris*
shiitake	*Lentinula edodes*
showy calamint	*Calamintha grandiflora* "Rockwell"
showy savory	*Calamintha grandiflora* "Rockwell"
Sichuan pepper	*Zanthoxylum piperitum*
Sicilian sumac	*Rhus coriaria*
silver birch	*Betula pendula*
silverweed	*Potentilla anserina*

COMMON NAME	BOTANICAL NAME
skullcap	*Scutellaria lateriflora*
slippery elm	*Ulmus rubra*
smallwort	*Ranunculus ficaria*
snakeroot	*Polygala senega*
snap pea	*Pisum sativum*
snow pea	*Pisum sativum*
soapwort	*Saponaria officinalis*
Solomon's seal	*Polygonum multiflorum; polygonum officinale*
sour orange	*Citrus x aurantium*
soursop	*Annona muricata*
southern blue gum	*Eucalyptus globulus*
southernwood	*Artemisia abrotanum*
soya	*Glycine max*
soybean	*Glycine max*
Spanish liquorice	*Glycyrrhiza glabra*
Spanish saffron	*Crocus sativus*
Spearmint	*Mentha spicata*
squaw root	*Cimicifuga racemosa; actaea racemosa*
squaw vine	*Mitchella repens*
St Benedict's thistle	*Cnicus benedictus*
St John's bread	*Ceratonia siliqua*
St John's wort	*Hypericum perforatum*
star anise	*Illicium verum*
stellaria	*Alchemilla vulgaris*
stevia	*Stevia rebaudiana*
stillingia	*Stillingia sylvatica*
stinging nettle	*Urtica dioica*
stinkweed	*Datura stramonium*
strawberry	*Fragaria vesca* 'Alexandria'
strychnine	*Strychnos nux-vomica*
succory	*Cichorium intybus*
sumac	*Rhus coriaria*
summer savory	*Satureja hortensis*
sundew	*Drosera rotundifola*
sunflower	*Helianthus annuus*
swallowwort	*Chelidonium majus*
sweet almond	*Prunus dulcis*
sweet basil	*Ocimum basilicum*
sweet bay	*Laurus nobilis*
sweet blue violet	*Viola odorata*
sweet cicely	*Myrrhis odorata*
sweet flag	*Acorus calamus*
sweet marjoram	*Origanum majorana*
sweet myrtle	*Acorus calamus*
sweet olive	*Osmanthus fragrans*
sweet orange	*Citrus sinensis*
sweet verbena myrtle	*Backhousia citriodora*
sweet vernal grass	*Anthoxanthum odoratum*
sweet violet	*Viola odorata*

COMMON NAME	BOTANICAL NAME
sweet woodruff	*Galium odoratum*
sweetleaf	*Stevia rebaudiana*
Szechuan pepper	*Zanthoxylum piperitum*
tabasco pepper	*Capsicum annuum*
taheebo	*Tabebuia impetiginosa*
tamarind	*Tamarindus indica*
tanner's sumac	*Rhus coriaria*
tansy	*Tanacetum vulgare*
tarragon	*Artemisia dracunculus*
Tasmanian blue gum	*Eucalyptus globulus*
Tasmanian pepper leaf	*Tasmania lanceolata*
tea	*Camellia sinensis*
tea tree	*Melaleuca alternifolia*
teaberry	*Gaultheria procumbens*
Thai ginger	*Alpinia galanga*
thorn apple	*Datura stramonium*
thyme	*Thymus* spp.
ti tree	*Melaleuca alternifolia*
tinnevelly senna	*Cassia senna; senna alexandrina*
tomato	*Lycopersicon esculentum*
toothache tree	*Zanthoxylum americanum*
toothpick weed	*Ammi visnaga*
torch weed	*Verbascum thapus*
touch-me-not	*Impatiens capensis*
tropical periwinkle	*Catharanthus roseus*
true bay	*Laurus nobilis*
true cinnamon	*Cinnamomum* spp.
true indigo	*Indigofera tinctoria*
true nasturtium	*Nasturtium officinale*
true saffron	*Crocus sativus*
true senna	*Cassia senna; senna alexandrina*
turkey rhubarb	*Rheum palmatum*
Turkish liquorice	*Glycyrrhiza glabra*
turmeric	*Curcuma longa*
uña-de-gato	*Uncaria tomentosa*
uva-ursi	*Arctostaphylos uva-ursi*
valerian	*Valeriana officinalis*
vanilla	*Vanilla planifolia*
velvet bean	*Mucuna pruriens*
verbena	*Aloysia triphylla; Aloysia citriodora*
vervain	*Verbena officinalis*
Vietnamese celery	*Oenanthe javanica*
Vietnamese coriander	*Polygonum odoratum*
Vietnamese mint	*Polygonum odoratum*
violet	*Viola odorata*
vitex	*Vitex agnus-castus*
vomit root	*Lobelia inflata*
water celery	*Oenanthe javanica*
watercress	*Nasturtium officinale*

COMMON NAME	BOTANICAL NAME
wattle	*Acacia* spp.
wax myrtle	*Myrica cerifera*
weeping birch	*Betula pendula*
weeping forsythia	*Forsythia suspense*
West Indian lemongrass	*Cymbopogon citratus*
wheat	*Triticum aestivum*
white flag	*Iris* spp.
white ramie	*Boehmeria nivea*
white saunders	*Santalum album*
white thorn	*Crataegus laevigata; c. oxyacantha*
white willow	*Salix alba*
whortleberry	*Vaccinium myrtillus*
wild carrot	*Daucus carota; Daucus carota sativus*
wild crocus	*Pulsatilla vulgaris*
wild geranium	*Geranium maculatum*
wild marjoram	*Origanum vulgare*
wild strawberry	*Fragaria vesca* 'Alexandria'
wild sunflower	*Inula helenium*
wild yam	*Dioscorea villosa*
willow	*Salix alba*
windflower	*Pulsatilla vulgaris*
wine grape	*Vitis vinifera*
winter cherry	*Withania somnifera*
wintergreen	*Gaultheria procumbens*
witch hazel	*Hamamelis virginiana*
woad	*Isatis tinctoria*
woadwaxen	*Genista tinctoria*
wolfsbane	*Aconitum napellus*
wood betony	*Stachys officinalis*
woodbine	*Lonicera* spp.
wormseed	*Chenopodium ambrosioides*
wormwood	*Artemisia absinthium*
yangona	*Piper methysticum*
yarrow	*Achillea millefolium*
yaw root	*Stillingia sylvatica*
yellow bedstraw	*Galium verum*
yellow dock	*Rumex crispus*
yellow gentian	*Gentiana lutea*
yellow ginger	*Curcuma longa*
yellow leader	*Astragalus membranaceus*
yellow root	*Hydrastis canadensis*
yellow sandalwood	*Santalum album*
yellow saunders	*Santalum album*
yerba dulce	*Phyla scaberrima*
yerba maté	*Ilex paraguariensis*
yin yang huo	*Epimedium* spp.
ylang ylang	*Cananga odorata*
yohimbe	*Pausinystalia johimbe*
zatar	*Thymbra spicata*

Index

Acknowledgements

The publisher offers grateful thanks to: Well-Sweep Herb Farm of Port Murray, New Jersey and models Nick Simonds and LaTricia Watford.

Picture Credits

Chapter 1: **16–17** Marian Purcell **19–24** Dan Lipow **26–30** Scan from *How to Grow Plants: A Simple Introduction to Structural Botany* by Asa Gray, MD **31** Shamona Stokes

Chapter 2: **33** Allan Kohl **35** iStockphoto/Dan Cooper **36** NLM **37** Scan from: *The Complete Book of Illustration*, by J.G.Heck, published by Crown Publishers Inc. **39** Photos.com/Jupiter Images **40** Shutterstock / Vera Bogaerts **42** google (Morse Library, Beloit College) **43** *Burton's Anatomy of Melancholy*(1) published in 1621 **44** Great Meteoron Monastery **45** Dan Lipow **47** Photos.com/Jupiter Images **49** NLM **50** Shutterstock/Arnold John Labrentz **50** iStockphoto/Paul Cowan **53** Shutterstock/Doxa **55** NLM **55** iStockphoto/Paul Senyszyn **56** iStockphoto/Sang Nguyen **58** Dan Lipow **59** iStockphoto/Judy Watt **60** National Library of Medicine/ Science Photo Library **61** Dan Lipow **63** Dan McGarry

Chapter 3: **64** Courtesy of Chelsea Physic Garden **67** Photo: © Karen Landis; From The Maumee Valley Herb Society at Toledo Botanial Garden. **67** iStockphoto/Anne Clark **68** Courtesy of Kew Royal Botanical Gardens **69** Dan Lipow **70** Photos.com/Jupiter Images **72** Courtesy of Ballymaloe Cookey School **75** Dan Lipow **77** Dr Michael Hickman **78** Romi Ige **79** Dan Lipow **80** Courtesy of The National Botanic Garden of Belgium **82** Botanic Garden and Botanical Museum Berlin-Dahlem, Fotos: I. Haas **82** Courtesy of Kew Royal Botanical Gardens **83** Dan Lipow **85** Shutterstock/Joanne and Daniel

Chapter 4: **87** photos.com/Jupiter Images **89** Dan Lipow **89** photos.com/Jupiter Images **90–101** Dan Lipow

Chapter 5: **103** Photos.com/Jupiter Images **105** IndexOpen/Photolibrary.com pty. ltd. **105** Dan Lipow **106** Marian Purcell **107** IndexOpen/Photolibrary.com pty. ltd. **108** Photos.com/Jupiter Images **108** IndexOpen/LLC, VStock **109** photos.com/Jupiter Images **110** Marian Purcell **110** Shamona Stokes

Chapter 6: **112** Photos.com/Jupiter images **115** Fitness and Well Being Stock CD **115** Photos.com/Jupiter images **116–117** Photos.com/Jupiter images **118** Fitness and Well Being Stock CD **118** Photos.com/Jupiter images **119** Photos.com/Jupiter images **119** Fitness and Well Being Stock CD **120–124** Photos.com/Jupiter images **127** Fit for Life Stock CD **129** Marian Purcell **130** Fitness and Well Being Stock CD **131** IndexOpen/Photolibrary.com pty. ltd. **132** Photos.com/Jupiter images **134** Marian Purcell **136** Photos.com/Jupiter images

Chapter 7: **139–165** Dan Lipow

Chapter 8: **167** Dan Lipow **168** Photos.com/Jupiter Images **168** Dan Lipow **168** IndexOpen/Photos.com Select **170–180** Dan Lipow **181** Shutterstock/ Jeff Gynane **181–183** Dan Lipow **184** Shutterstock/ Vasil Z. Ishmatov **187–188** Dan Lipow **190** IndexOpen / Photolibrary.com pty. ltd. **191** Shutterstock/Fotosav (Victor & Katya)

Front Matter: **2–3** Shutterstock/Steve Lovegrove **5** Martin Wall **5** Dan Lipow **6** Beth Baugh **6** Martin Wall **7** Dan Lipow **7** Martin Wall **7** Dan Lipow **8–9** Shutterstock/Irene Pearcey **10–13** Dan Lipow **14–15** Dan Lipow

Gallery: **192/193** Marian Purcell **194-195** Dan Lipow **196** Martin Wall **196–197** Dan Lipow **198** Martin Wall **198** Dan Lipow **199** iStockphoto/Pierre Janssen **199–200** Photos.com/Jupiter Images **200–206** Dan Lipow **207–208** Martin Wall **209** Cathi Keville **209–210** Dan Lipow **211** Cathi Keville **211** Dan Lipow **213** Martin Wall **214** Dan Lipow **215** Martin Wall **215** Dan Lipow **216** Photos.com/Jupiter Images **217–221** Dan Lipow **222** Martin Wall **223** Dan Lipow **223** Martin Wall **224** Martin Wall **224** Dan Lipow **225** Martin Wall **225** Dan Lipow **226** Dan Lipow **227** Martin Wall **228** Dan Lipow **228** Martin Wall **229–231** Dan Lipow **232** Photos.com/Jupiter Images **233** Martin Wall **234** Dan Lipow **235** Dan Lipow **235** Martin Wall **236–237** Dan Lipow **238** Marian Purcell **239** Martin Wall **239** Dan Lipow **240** Martin Wall **241** Cathi Keville **242** Inmagine/Goodshoot **243** Dan Lipow **244** Martin Wall **245–246** Dan Lipow **247** Martin Wall **248** IndexOpen/Ablestock **249** Beth Baugh **249–255** Dan Lipow **255** Photos.com/Jupiter Images **256** Martin Wall **257–259** Dan Lipow **260** Martin Wall **261** Dan Lipow **261** Martin Wall **262** Dan Lipow **263** Photos.com/Jupiter Images **263** IndexOpen/Photolibrary.com pty. ltd. **265–268** Dan Lipow **269** IndexOpen/Photolibrary.com pty. ltd. **269–271** Dan Lipow **272** Martin Wall **273–275** Dan Lipow **276** Shutterstock/Gabrielle Chan **277** Martin Wall **278** Inmagine/Photodisc **279–280** Dan Lipow **281** Martin Wall **281** Dan Lipow **282** Dan Lipow **283** Martin Wall **284** IndexOpen/Photolibrary.com pty. ltd. **285** IndexOpen/photolibrary.com pty. ltd. **285** Martin Wall **286** IndexOpen/Photos.com Select **287** Dan Lipow **288** Photos.com/Jupiter Images **289–291** Dan Lipow **292** Martin Wall **293–297** Dan Lipow **297** Kathi Keville **298** Dan Lipow **299** Martin Wall **299** Dan Lipow **300** Martin Wall **301** Marian Purcell **301–302** Dan Lipow **303** Martin Wall **304–305** Dan Lipow **306** IndexOpen/Photolibrary.com pty. ltd. **307** Martin Wall **308** Dan Lipow **309** Photos.com/Jupiter Images **311–312** Martin Wall **313** Dan Lipow **314** Martin Wall **314** Dan Lipow **315** Martin Wall **316** Nature's Images/Photo Researchers, Inc **317** Dan Lipow **318–319** Martin Wall **320** Dan Lipow **321** Martin Wall **321** Dan Lipow **322** Dan Lipow **323** Photos.com/Jupiter Images **324** Martin Wall **325** Photos.com/Jupiter Images

Gazetteer: **336–337** Marian Purcell **338–357** Dan Lipow

Cross referencing section: **363** Dan Lipow **326** Dan Lipow **332** Dan Lipow **333** Dan Lipow **335** Shutterstock/Steve Lovegrove

Backmatter: **375** Shutterstock/Irene Pearcey